Health Law and the European Union

How does the law of the European Union affect health law and policy? At first sight, the impact of EU law in this area seems limited. However, despite its restricted formal competence, over recent years, the EU has become increasingly involved in the health field. Litigation based on EU law has resulted in a 'right to receive health care services' across national boundaries within the EU, which may have huge practical implications for national health systems.The EU has promulgated legislation regulating clinical research, and the marketing of pharmaceuticals; patients' rights are affected by EU legislation on data protection and product liability; the qualifications of health care professionals are legally recognised across the EU; and the EU has acted to promote public health. The authors of this book (expert in EU law and health law respectively) seek to explain and explore the various impacts of measures of EU law on national health law and policy. Through elaboration of selected examples, the authors show that, within the EU, health law cannot be regarded as a purely national affair.

Tamara K. Hervey is Professor of Law at the University of Nottingham, UK. She teaches and researches in European Union law. She is author of a number of books and journal articles on EU law, especially its social and constitutional dimensions, including *European Social Law and Policy* (1998). Her current research is on the EU's regulation of stem cell research, new modes of EU governance in the field of health, the 'right to health' in European law, and EU equality law.

Jean V. McHale is Professor of Law at the University of Leicester, UK. Her research is in the area of health law, and she has written a number of books and articles in the area, including *Health Care Law: text and materials* (with M. Fox, 1997) and *Framing the Clinical Body* (with M. Fox, forthcoming 2005). Recent research includes the legal regulation of clinical and scientific research, health law and human rights, and mental health.

The Law in Context Series

Editors: William Twining (University College, London) and
Christopher McCrudden (Lincoln College, Oxford)

Since 1970 the Law in Context series has been in the forefront of the movement to broaden the study of law. It has been a vehicle for the publication of innovative scholarly books that treat law and legal phenomena critically in their social, political and economic contexts from a variety of perspectives. The series particularly aims to publish scholarly legal writing that brings fresh perspectives to bear on new and existing areas of law taught in universities. A contextual approach involves treating legal subjects broadly, using materials from other social sciences, and from any other discipline that helps to explain the operation in practice of the subject under discussion. It is hoped that this orientation is at once more stimulating and more realistic than the bare exposition of legal rules. The series includes original books that have a different emphasis from traditional legal textbooks, while maintaining the same high standards of scholarship. They are written primarily for undergraduate and graduate students of law and of other disciplines, but most also appeal to a wider readership. In the past, most books in the series have focused on English law, but recent publications include books on European law, globalization, transnational legal processes, and comparative law.

Books in the Series

Ashworth: *Sentencing and Criminal Justice*
Barton & Douglas: *Law and Parenthood*
Bell: *French Legal Cultures*
Bercusson: *European Labour Law*
Birkinshaw: *European Public Law*
Birkinshaw: *Freedom of Information: The Law, the Practice and the Ideal*
Cane: *Atiyah's Accidents, Compensation and the Law*
Collins: *The Law of Contract*
Cranston: *Consumers and the Law*
Cranston: *Legal Foundations of the Welfare State*
Davies: *Perspectives on Labour Law*
Davies & Freedland: *Labour Law: Text and Materials*
de Sousa Santos: *Toward a New Legal Common Sense*
Detmold: *Courts and Administrators: A study in Jurisprudence*
Diduck: *Law's Families*
Doggett: *Marriage, Wife-Beating and the Law in Victorian England*
Dummett & Nicol: *Subjects, Citizens, Aliens and Others: Nationality and Immigration Law*
Elworthy & Holder: *Environmental Protection: Text and Materials*
Fortin: *Children's Rights and the Developing Law*
Glover-Thomas: *Reconstructing Mental Health Law and Policy*
Gobert & Punch: *Rethinking Corporate Crime*
Goodrich: *Languages of Law*
Hadden: *Company Law and Capitalism*
Harlow & Rawlings: *Law and Administration: Text and Materials*

Harris: *An Introduction to Law*
Harris: *Remedies, Contract and Tort*
Harvey: *Seeking Asylum in the UK: Problems and Prospects*
Hervey & McHale: *Health Law and the European Union*
Lacey & Wells: *Reconstructing Criminal Law*
Lewis: *Choice and the Legal Order: Rising above Politics*
Likosky: *Transnational Legal Process*
Maughan & Webb: *Lawyering Skills*
Moffat: *Trusts Law: Text and Materials*
Norrie: *Crime, Reason and History*
O'Dair: *Legal Ethics*
Oliver: *Common Values and the Public–Private Divide*
Oliver & Drewry: *The Law and Parliament*
Page & Ferguson: *Investor Protection*
Palmer & Roberts: *Dispute Processes – ADR and the Primary Forms of Decision Making*
Picciotto: *International Business Taxation*
Ramsay: *Consumer Protection: Text and Materials*
Reed: *Internet Law: Text and Materials*
Richardson: *Law, Process and Custody*
Seneviratne: *Ombudsmen: Public Services and Administrative Justice*
Snyder: *New Directions in European Community Law*
Stapleton: *Product Liability*
Turpin: *British Government and the Constitution: Text, Cases and Materials*
Twining: *Globalisation and Legal Theory*
Twining & Anderson: *Analysis of Evidence*
Twining & Miers: *How to Do Things with Rules*
Ward: *A Critical Introduction to European Law*
Ward: *Shakespeare and the Legal Imagination*
Zander: *Cases and Materials on the English Legal System*
Zander: *The Law-Making Process*

For Rosalind, Geneviève and James,
without whom this book would probably
have been written years ago . . .

Health Law and the European Union

Tamara K. Hervey
and
Jean V. McHale

PUBLISHED BY THE PRESS SYNDICATE OF THE UNIVERSITY OF CAMBRIDGE
The Pitt Building, Trumpington Street, Cambridge, United Kingdom

CAMBRIDGE UNIVERSITY PRESS
The Edinburgh Building, Cambridge CB2 2RU, UK
40 West 20th Street, New York, NY 10011-4211, USA
477 Williamstown Road, Port Melbourne, VIC 3207, Australia
Ruiz de Alarcón 13, 28014 Madrid, Spain
Dock House, The Waterfront, Cape Town 8001, South Africa

http://www.cambridge.org

First published 2004

Printed in the United Kingdom at the University Press, Cambridge

Typefaces Minion 9.75/12.5 pt, and Frutiger *System* LaTeX 2ε [TB]

A catalogue record for this book is available from the British Library

ISBN 0 521 60524 5 paperback

Contents

Acknowledgements — *page* xi
Table of abbreviations — xiii
Table of conventions and treaties — xv
Table of EU legislation — xxii
Table of national provisions — l
Table of cases — lv

Part One

1 Introduction — 3

I **Health law and the European Union** — 3
II **What is health law?** — 6
What is health? — 7
The evolution of law's engagement with health — 10
Definitions: delineating the boundaries of a discipline — 13
The elements of "health law" — 16
III **Conclusion** — 27

2 Historical, legal and institutional contexts — 31

I **Introduction: what is the European Union?** — 31
II **What does the European Union do?** — 37
III **What methods of governance does the European Union employ?** — 43
Deregulation — 44
"Old style" harmonisation — 48
"New approach" harmonisation — 53
Regulatory coordination — 59
"Soft" coordination — 61
Financial incentives — 62
IV **Courts and fundamental rights** — 63
V **Conclusions** — 67

3 Community competence in the field of health 69

I **Introduction** 69
II **Article 152 EC** 72
Historical context 72
The elements of Article 152 EC 76
Secondary legislation adopted on the basis of Article 152 EC 81
III **Other legal bases** 84
Common policies as legal basis: "mainstreaming" of health protection 84
Article 308 EC: health protection as a Community objective 87
The internal market 90
IV **Conclusions** 105

Part Two

4 Access to health care services 109

I **Introduction** 109
II **Access to health care services** 112
Free movement of patients 112
Impact on access to health services and wider implications 138
III **"Reproductive tourism"** 144
IV **Conclusions** 156

5 Data protection and health information privacy 159

I **Introduction** 159
Why safeguard health information privacy? 160
II **Rights to health information privacy in international and EU law** 163
III **The Data Protection Directive** 166
Introduction 166
Processing of personal data 168
Ordinary personal data 169
Special data 170
Further exceptions allowing disclosure 177
Clinical research and public health monitoring 179
Control rights for data subjects 182
Implementation and compliance with the Directive 184
Transfer of data outside the EU 185
IV **Conclusions** 185

6 Regulation of health care professionals 189

I **Introduction** 189
II **The impact of EU law on health care professional practice** 193

	EU employment law	194
	EU law on provision of services	197
III	**EU law and entry into professional practice in Member States**	199
	Freedom of establishment: Treaty provisions	199
	The sectoral (professional) directives	203
	The general directives on mutual recognition of qualifications	215
	Assessment of the sectoral and general directives	218
	Non-EU citizens and qualifications from non-EU states	230
IV	**Conclusions**	233
7	**The regulation of clinical research**	237
I	**Introduction**	237
II	**Co-ordinating and funding clinical research activities**	239
III	**The Clinical Trials Directive**	248
IV	**The regulation of medical research using genetic technology**	259
	Cloning	271
	Stem cell research	274
V	**Conclusions**	280
8	**Regulating pharmaceuticals: risk, choice and compensation**	282
I	**Introduction**	282
II	**EU-level patient (consumer) protection measures**	288
	Introduction	288
	Marketing authorisations	289
	Pharmacovigilance	300
	Labelling and packaging	302
	Advertisement	304
	Product liability	307
III	**Proposed reform and wider implications**	312
	Reform proposals	312
	Wider implications and assessment	317
IV	**Internal market law**	319
	The Transparency of Pharmaceuticals Pricing Directive	323
V	**Conclusions**	327
9	**Public health law**	330
I	**Introduction**	330
II	**Communicable diseases**	334
	Introduction	334
	HIV/AIDS	336
	BSE/nvCJD	348

III **Health promotion** 366
Cancer and tobacco 368
IV **Conclusion** 384

Part Three

10 Conclusions and future prospects 389

I **Introduction: the roles of the EU in health law** 389
Four themes of "European health law"? 390
II **The "spectrum": how does EU law affect health law and policy in the member states?** 394
Areas of health law affected most strongly 395
Areas of health law affected by general measures of EU law 396
Marginal effect 399
"Slow convergence" effect 400
No prospect of convergence or consensus? 400
III **Future directions** 404
The Draft Constitutional Treaty 404
A "health" open method of coordination? 412
Enlargement 414
Regulating the use of human material 421
"e-Health" 426
Further future developments? 433
IV **Conclusions: health law and the European Union** 436

Bibliography 437
Index 467

Acknowledgements

We gratefully acknowledge support from the following organisations:

The Arts and Humanities Research Board, Award RLS/AN4207/APN14210;
The Leverhulme Trust, Award RF&G2000/138;
The Society of Legal Scholars;
The University of Leicester, for provision of study leave first semester academic year 2003–4;
The Faculty of Law, University of Leicester;
The School of Law, University of Nottingham.

We are also indebted to the following individuals:

Miriam Aziz, Catherine Barnard, Mark Bell, Sandra Carlson, Marie Fox, John Harrington, Jeff Kenner, Graeme Laurie, Sue Millns, José Miola, Thérèse Murphy, Philip Rostant, Joanne Scott, Sally Sheldon; and, for research assistance, Tawhida Ahmed, Richard Burchill, Margaret Cunningham and Mark Flear.

The law contained in this book is, to the best of our knowledge, accurate as at 1 December 2003. Some minor amendments up to 1 May 2004 have been included in the footnotes. In particular, at the time of writing, the EU had 15 Member States: it now has 25.

TKH and JVM, Nottingham and Leicester, May 2004.

Table of abbreviations

AC	Appeal Cases
AG	Advocate General
AIDS	Acquired Immune Deficiency Syndrome
All ER	All England Reports
BMJ	British Medical Journal
BMLR	British Medical Law Reports
BSE	Bovine Spongiform Encephalopathy
CA	Court of Appeal
CAP	Common Agricultural Policy
CFLQ	Child and Family Law Quarterly
CLJ	Cambridge Law Journal
CMLR	Common Market Law Reports
CMLRev	Common Market Law Review
COM	Commission document
Court	European Court of Justice
CPMP	Committee for Proprietory Medicinal Products
DCT	Draft Treaty establishing a Constitution for Europe
DG	Directorate General
EC	Treaty establishing the European Community
ECOSOC	Economic and Social Committee
ECHR	European Convention on Human Rights and Fundamental Freedoms
ECR	European Court Reports
EEC	Treaty establishing the European Economic Community
EFSA	European Food Safety Authority
EHRLR	European Human Rights Law Review
EHRR	European Human Rights Reports
ELJ	European Law Journal
ELRev	European Law Review
EMEA	European Medicines Evaluation Agency
EPC	European Patent Convention
EST	expressed sequence tag
EU	European Union

EUCFR	Charter of Fundamental Rights of the European Union
EUI	European University Institute
EWHC	England and Wales High Court
FLR	Family Law Reports
HIV	Human Immunodeficiency Virus
HRLR	Human Rights Law Review
ICH	International Conference on Harmonisation
ICLQ	International and Comparative Law Quarterly
IGC	intergovernmental conference
ILJ	Industrial Law Journal
ILRM	Irish Law Reports Monthly
IVF	in vitro fertilisation
JCMS	Journal of Common Market Studies
JSWFL	Journal of Social Welfare and Family Law
LQR	Law Quarterly Review
MEP	Member of the European Parliament
MJ	Maastricht Journal of European and Comparative Law
MLR	Modern Law Review
NGO	non-governmental organisation
nvCJD	new variant Creutzfeldt Jacob Disease
OJ	Official Journal
OJLS	Oxford Journal of Legal Studies
OMC	open method of coordination
QB	Queen's Bench
QMV	qualified majority voting
SARS	severe acute respiratory syndrome
SI	statutory instrument
SME	small and medium-sized enterprise
SUSAR	suspected unexpected serious adverse reaction
TEU	Treaty on European Union
TRIPS	Agreement on Trade Related Aspects of Intellectual Property Rights
UK	United Kingdom
US	United States of America
WHO	World Health Organisation
WLR	Weekly Law Reports
WTO	World Trade Organisation
YEL	Yearbook of European Law

Table of conventions and treaties

Accession Treaty 2003, Athens 10, 32, 48, 401, 415
Art 1 (2) 48
Art 2 32
Art 20 221
Art 24 418
Art 34 421
Protocol No 7 147, 401, 402
Annexes V–XIV 418
Annex XII 420
Act concerning the Conditions of Accession
Art 12 48
Annex II 221
Act of Accession of Austria, Finland and Sweden, Art 151 376
Additional Protocol to the American Convention on Human Rights in the Area of Economic, Social and Cultural Rights (Protocol of San Salvador) 1988
Art 10 8
Amsterdam Protocol on Animal Protection and Welfare 247
Charter of Fundamental Rights of the European Union 2000 25, 26, 64, 66, 67, 84, 145, 160, 165, 168, 174, 247, 268, 269, 343, 344, 368, 391, 392, 402, 405, 406, 407, 408, 409, 410, 414, 422
Art 1 26, 368
Art 2 145
Art 3 26, 145, 368
Art 3 (1) 84
Art 3 (2) 84, 273, 276, 345, 422
Art 3 (2) (d) 272
Art 6 165
Art 7 145, 368
Art 8 165, 166, 175
Art 9 145
Art 11 306, 368
Art 17 378

Art 21 342
Art 35 84, 156, 414
Art 52 (3) 67, 306
Community Development Cooperation Agreement with India 88, 89
Art 19 89
Convention for the Protection of Individuals with regard to Automatic Processing of Personal Data 1981, Council of Europe 26, 168
Convention on Biological Diversity 269
Convention on the Elimination of all forms of Discrimination Against Women 1979
Art 12 8
Convention on the Grant of European Patents 1973 261, 269
Art 53 261
Convention on Human Rights and Biomedicine 1997, Council of Europe 24, 25, 80, 164, 237, 247, 248, 266, 273, 401
Art 2 26
Art 3 8
Art 4 26
Art 7 26
Art 8 26
Art 9 26
Art 10 26, 164
Art 11 26
Art 13 27
Art 18 276
Art 21 27, 277, 343, 345, 422
Art 22 267
Art 24 27
Art 25 27
Art 26 27
Art 35 27
Additional Protocol on the Prohibition of Cloning Human Beings 1998 247
Protocol on Transplantation of Organs and Tissues of Human Origin 2002 80
Additional Protocol to the Convention for the protection of Human Rights and Dignity of the Human Being with regard to the Application of Biology and Medicine, on the Prohibition of Cloning Human Beings 1998 272, 273
Convention on the Rights of the Child 1989
Art 24 8
Declaration of Helsinki 1964, World Medical Assembly 24, 237, 247, 248
para 4.1 252
EC Treaty. See Treaty of Rome 1957
EEA Agreement
Annex VI 230

EEC Treaty. See also Treaty of Rome 1957 39, 48, 49, 50, 147, 402
Art 2 73
Art 6 52
Art 8 (1) 54
Art 8 (6) 54
Art 27 88
Art 36 45
Art 48 51
Art 52 200
Art 56 51
Art 66 51
Art 100 49, 71, 72, 308
Art 100a 72, 92, 94
Art 100a (3) 92
Art 222 45
Art 235 73, 88, 95
Europe Agreements 418, 419, 421
Europe Agreement, Hungary
Art 46 419
European Atomic Energy Community Treaty 94
Art 2(b) 94
Art 31 94
European Conference on Promotion of Mental Health and Social Inclusion 1999 435
European Conference on Tobacco and Health 1988
Conclusions
point 8 376
European Convention on Human Rights and Fundamental Freedoms 1950, Council of Europe 23, 25, 64, 67, 269, 391, 402, 405, 406, 408, 409
Art 2 402, 407
Art 6 324
Art 8 26, 145, 154, 163
Art 10 306
Art 12 145
Art 13 324
protocol 1
Art 1 378
European Social Charter 1961, Council of Europe 8
Art 11 8, 410
Art 13 8
European Social Charter 1996, Council of Europe 8
Art 11 8, 410
Art 13 8

International Conference on Harmonisation of Technical Requirements of Pharmaceuticals for Human Use 1990 249, 284
International Covenant on Civil and Political Rights 1966 23
International Covenant on Economic, Social and Cultural Rights 1966 23
  Art 12 8
Laeken Declaration on the Future of the European Union 2001 33, 69, 70, 71, 74, 90, 404
Maastricht Treaty 1992 32, 33, 34, 37, 56, 70, 72, 73, 147, 244, 263, 288, 344, 361, 372, 402, 412
  Art 1 37
  Art 2 38
  Art 6 (1) 414
  Art 49 414
  Protocol No 17 152, 402
  Protocol on Enlargement of the EU 415
    Art 3 48
Single European Act 1986 32, 54, 72, 92
Treaty of Amsterdam 1997 40, 48, 72, 76, 81, 392, 412
Treaty of Nice 48, 72, 415
  Arts 2, 3, 4 415
Treaty of Rome 1957 32, 33, 37, 44, 45, 46, 48, 49, 54, 58, 64, 70, 71, 75, 90, 91, 106, 123, 137, 143, 147, 149, 150, 200, 201, 203, 286, 296, 319, 322, 325, 334, 340, 341, 356, 369, 402
  Title IV 341
  preamble 37
  Art 2 38, 75, 77, 102
  Art 3 77, 102
  Art 3 (1) (c) 98
  Art 3 (o) 75
  Art 5 73, 99, 243
  Art 5 (1) 40, 70
  Art 5 (2) 40, 70
  Art 5 (3) 41, 70
  Art 10 64, 122, 202
  Art 12 52, 119, 200
  Art 13 195
  Art 14 (2) 38, 98
  Art 16 392
  Art 17 113
  Art 18 118
  Art 19 89
  Art 23 44, 213, 320
  Art 24 44, 213, 320

Art 25 213, 320
Art 28 44, 56, 97, 213, 318, 320, 325, 377, 429
Art 29 44, 213, 320
Art 30 45, 46, 47, 53, 91, 92, 95, 99, 213, 320, 352, 429
Art 31 213, 320
Art 37 79, 85, 86, 87, 93, 362
Art 39 51, 118, 123, 124
Art 39 (1) 44
Art 39 (2) 119
Art 39 (3) 44, 122, 202
Art 43 44, 93, 199, 200, 202
Art 44 203
Art 45 201
Art 46 51, 123, 124, 201
Art 46 (1) 122
Art 47 222, 379, 382
Art 47 (1) 204
Art 47 (2) 197, 2004
Art 47 (3) 204
Art 49 44, 118, 119, 120, 121, 122, 123, 126, 127, 128, 129, 132, 133, 135, 136, 137, 138, 149, 151
Art 49 (1) 119
Art 50 119, 120, 126, 129
Art 54 119
Art 55 51, 122, 197, 379, 382
Art 56 44
Art 57 (2) 100
Art 59 3, 152
Art 60 3, 151, 152
Art 66 100
Art 71 85, 93
Art 81 322
Art 86 (2) 322
Art 94 49, 71, 72, 94, 99, 288, 290, 308, 351
Art 95 53, 54, 70, 86, 92, 93, 94, 95, 96, 99, 101, 104, 105, 166, 197, 222, 223, 237, 249, 250, 269, 278, 281, 288, 290, 323, 336, 345, 346, 362, 374, 378, 382, 395, 411
Art 95 (3) 54, 72, 92, 102, 103, 104, 105, 106, 374
Art 95 (4) 53, 55, 57, 94, 100
Art 95 (4)–(10) 57
Art 100 86, 95
Art 100a 98, 99, 100, 380
Art 100a (3) 98

Art 118a 41, 194
Art 129 74, 75, 76, 77, 78, 86, 344, 372
Art 129 (4) 98, 104
Art 133 85, 93, 101, 362
Art 137 85, 94, 194
Art 141 195
Art 149 199
Art 150 199
Art 152 4, 29, 71, 72–84, 87, 88, 89, 90, 97, 102, 104, 105, 280, 333, 336, 344, 346, 348, 356, 362, 366, 372, 385, 395, 411, 415, 420, 435
Art 152 (1) 77, 78, 84, 87, 93, 105, 288
Art 152 (1) (a) 279
Art 152 (2) 79, 411
Art 152 (4) 79, 102, 344, 346
Art 152 (4) (a) 79, 87, 88, 103, 344
Art 152 (4) (b) 79, 87, 88, 103, 362
Art 152 (4) (c) 79, 104
Art 152 (5) 80, 111, 194, 346
Art 153 85, 87, 93, 288
Art 163 268
Art 164 268
Art 171 (2) 56
Art 174 (2) 361
Art 175 85, 93, 94
Art 177 89
Art 181 85, 88, 89, 93
Art 205 (2) 344
Art 226 56, 186, 187, 211, 220, 309, 324, 352
Art 230 40, 41, 63, 268, 294, 407, 408
Art 234 63, 64, 97, 103, 122, 149, 168, 175, 202, 211, 326, 378, 398
Art 249 42, 357
Art 260 (2) 422
Art 251 76, 344
Art 254 40
Art 253 40
Art 286 26
Art 295 45, 95
Art 300 375
Art 308 41, 49, 70, 73, 87–90, 308, 96, 102, 103, 105, 106, 269, 278, 280, 290, 395
Protocol 30 on Subsidiarity and Proportionality 40
Protocol on Enlargement of the EU 415
Art 3 48

Treaty on European Union. See Maastricht Treaty 1992
UN Charter
Art 55 20
UN Convention on Psychotropic Substances 1971 362
UN Convention on the Rights of the Child 247
UN Single Convention on Narcotic Drugs 1961 362
Universal Declaration on the Human Genome and Human Rights 1997, UNESCO 164, 247, 248
Universal Declaration of Human Rights 1948 23
Art 25 8
WHO Conference of Drug Regulatory Authorities 1989 284
WHO Constitution
preamble 41
Art 19 384
WHO Europe Amsterdam Declaration (principles of patients' rights in Europe) 24
WHO Framework Convention on Tobacco Control 375, 384
Art 2.1 384
Arts 13.2, 13.3 384
WHO International Health Regulations
Forward 20
WHO and UNICEF Declaration of Alma Ata, 1978 7
Art 12 8
WTO Agreement on Trade Related Aspects of Intellectual Property Rights (TRIPS Agreement) 268, 269
Art 20 378

Table of EU legislation

Regulations

Regulation 803/68/EEC on the valuation of goods for customs purposes, OJ 1968 L 148/6 88

Regulation 1612/68/EEC on freedom of movement for workers within the Community, OJ 1968 L 257/2; OJ Sp Ed 1968 II p 475

Art 7 (2) 118

Regulation 1408/71/EEC on the application of social security schemes to employed persons and their families moving within the Community, OJ 1971 L 149/2; OJ Sp Ed 1971 II p 416 52, 61, 112, 113, 114, 115, 116, 117, 118, 119, 122, 124, 127, 142, 143, 399, 418

Title III 399

Art 1 (o) (i), (2) 114

Art 2 (1) 113

Art 3 113

Art 3 (1) 113

Art 4 113

Art 4 (1) (a), (b) 113

Art 4 (2) 113

Art 4 (2) (a) 113

Art 10 (1) 113

Art 12 (1) 113

Art 18 (1) 113

Art 19 (1) 114

Art 20 114

Art 22 118, 127, 132, 133, 134, 151

Art 22 (1) (a) 115

Art 22 (1) (c) 115

Art 22 (2) 115, 116

Arts 27–34b 114

Art 31 114, 115, 117

Art 36 117, 128, 133

Art 38 113

Art 45 113
Art 46 (3) 113
Art 64 113
Art 67 113
Art 72 113
Regulation 574/72/EEC fixing the procedure for implementing Regulation (EEC) No 1408/71 on the application of social security schemes to employed persons and their families moving within the Community, OJ 1972 L 74/1 61, 112
Regulation 1898/87/EEC on the protection of designations used in marketing of milk and milk products, OJ 1987 L 182/36 351, 352
Regulation 3954/87/EEC laying down maximum permitted levels of radioactive contamination of foodstuffs and of feedingstuffs following a nuclear accident or any other case of radiological emergency, OJ 1987 L 371/11 94
Regulation 1601/91/EEC 1991 laying down general rules on the definition, description and presentation of aromatized wines, aromatized wine- based drinks and aromatized wine-product cocktails, OJ 1991 L 149/1 351
Regulation 1768/92/EEC concerning the creation of a supplementary protection certificate for medicinal products, OJ 1992 L 182/1 95
Regulation 259/93/EEC on the supervision and control of shipments of waste within, into and out of the European Community, OJ 1993 L 30/1 94
Regulation 2309/93/EEC laying down Community procedures for the authorization and supervision of medicinal products for human and veterinary use and establishing a European Agency for the Evaluation of Medicinal Products, OJ 1993 L 214/1 60, 245, 290, 293, 313
preamble 291
Art 3 (1), (2) 293, 294
Art 6 (4) 294
Art 10 294
Art 12 295
Art 13 295
Arts 19–26 300
Art 20 301
Art 23 301
Art 55 290
Arts 56–58 290
Art 71 312
Recital 3 292
Annex
Part A 293
Part B 293
Regulation 2991/94/EC laying down standards for spreadable fats, OJ 1994 L 316/2 352

Regulation 540/95/EC laying down the arrangements for reporting suspected unexpected adverse reactions which are not serious, whether arising in the Community or in a third country, to medicinal products for human or veterinary use authorized in accordance with the provisions of Council Regulation (EEC) No 2309/93, OJ 1995 L 55/5 300

Regulation 258/97/EC concerning novel foods and novel food ingredients, OJ 1997 L 43/1 (Novel Foods Regulation) 245, 349

Regulation 577/97/EC laying down certain detailed rules for the application of Council Regulation (EC) No 2991/94 laying down standards for spreadable fats and of Council Regulation (EEC) No 1898/87 on the protection of designations used in the marketing of milk and milk products, OJ 1997 L 87/3352

Regulation 820/97/EC establishing a system for the identification and registration of bovine animals and regarding the labelling of beef and beef products, OJ 1997 L 117/01 86

Regulation 141/2000/EC on orphan medicinal products, OJ 2000 L 18/1 245, 399

Art 3 (1) 244

Art 8 245

Regulation 1326/2001/EC laying down transitional measures to permit the changeover to the Regulation of the European Parliament and of the Council (EC) No 999/2001 laying down rules for the prevention, control and eradication of certain transmissible spongiform encephalopathies, and amending Annexes VII and XI to that Regulation, OJ 2001 L 177/60 355

Regulation 178/2002/EC laying down the general principles and requirements of food law, establishing the European Food Safety Authority and laying down procedures in matters of food safety, OJ 2002 L 31/1 105, 351, 358, 359, 361, 394

Chapter II 362, 364

Chapter III 364

Chapter IV 365

Art 1 (1) 362

Art 2 362

Art 3 (1) 362

Art 4 (2), (3) 362

Art 5 362

Art 5 (1), (2) 362

Art 6 362, 363

Art 7 362, 363

Art 8 362, 363

Art 10 365

Art 14 363

Art 15 363

Art 17 363

Art 18 363
Art 19 363
Art 20 363
Art 22 (2) 364
Art 25 (1) 364
Art 26 364
Art 27 364
Art 28 364
Art 28 (2), (3) 364
Art 29 (1) 364
Art 30 365
Art 33 365
Art 34 365
Art 35 365
Art 38 365
Art 39 365
Art 50 (2) 365
Art 52 (1) 365
Arts 55–57 365
Art 62 (1) 364

Regulation 260/2003/EC amending Regulation (EC) No 999/2001 of the European Parliament and of the Council as regards the eradication of transmissible spongiform encephalopathies in ovine and caprine animals and rules for the trade in live ovine and caprine animals and bovine embryos, OJ 2003 L 37/7 355

Regulation 859/2003/EC extending the provisions of Regulation (EEC) No 1408/71 and Regulation (EEC) No 574/72 to nationals of third countries who are not already covered by those provisions solely on the ground of their nationality, OJ 2003 L 124/1

Art 1 113

Regulation 1829/2003/EC on genetically modified food and feed, OJ 2003 L 268/1 245

Regulation 1830/2003/EC concerning the traceability and labelling of genetically modified organisms and the traceability of food and feed products produced from genetically modified organisms and amending Directive 2001/18/EC, OJ 2003 L 268/24 245

Regulation 1882/2003/EC adapting to Council Decision 1999/468/EC the provisions relating to committees which assist the Commission in the exercise of its implementing powers laid down in instruments subject to the procedure referred to in Article 251 of the EC Treaty, OJ 2003 L 284/1 160, 195

Regulation 631/2004/EC amending Council Regulation (EEC) No 1408/71 on the application of social security schemes to employed persons, to self-employed persons and to members of their families moving within the Community, and Council Regulation (EEC) No 574/72 laying down the procedure for

implementing Regulation (EEC) No 1408/71, in respect of the alignment of rights and the simplification of procedures, OJ 2004 L 100/1 427
Regulation 726/2004/EC laying down Community procedures for the authorisation and supervision of medicinal products for human and veterinary use and establishing a European Medicines Agency, OJ 2004 L 136/1 313
Art 3 313
Art 3 (3) 314
Art 3 (3) (c) 314
Art 6 (3) 313
Art 11 316
Art 14 315
Art 14 (2), (3) 315
Art 14 (9) 313
Art 14 (11) 314
Art 61 (2) 314

Directives

Directive 64/221/EEC on the co-ordination of special measures concerning the movement and residence of foreign nationals which are justified on grounds of public policy, public security or public health, OJ L 1964 P 056/850; OJ Sp Ed 1963-4 p 117 51, 202
Art 1 51
Art 2 (1) 123, 202
Art 4 52
Art 4 (1) 341
Annex 52, 202, 341
Directive 64/432/EEC on animal health problems affecting intra-Community trade in bovine animals and swine, OJ 1964 P 121/1977 356
Directive 64/433/EEC on health problems affecting intra-Community trade in fresh meat, OJ 1964 P 121/2012 356
Directive 65/65/EEC on the approximation of provisions laid down by Law, Regulation or Administrative Action relating to proprietary medicinal products, OJ 1965 P 022/369; OJ Sp Ed 1965-6 I p 24 49, 214, 251, 285, 291, 302, 362
Art 1 (2) 251, 289
Art 3 289
Art 5 292
Art 6 292
Recital 1 288
Recital 2 288
Directive 70/50/EC on the abolition of measures which have an effect equivalent to quantitative restrictions on imports and are not covered by other provisions adopted in pursuance of the EEC Treaty, OJ 1970 L 13/29 46

Directive 72/461/EEC on health problems affecting intra-Community trade in fresh meat, OJ 1972 L 302/24 356
Directive 73/148/EEC on the abolition of restrictions on movement and residence within the Community for nationals of Member States with regard to establishment and the provision of services, OJ 1973 L 172/14 203
Directive 73/173/EEC on the approximation of Member States' laws, regulations and administrative provisions relating to the classification, packaging and labelling of dangerous preparations (solvents), OJ 1973 L 189/7 53
Directive 73/241/EEC on the approximation of the laws of the Member States relating to cocoa and chocolate products intended for human consumption, OJ 1973 L 228/23 351
Directive 74/409/EEC on the harmonization of the laws of the Member States relating to honey, OJ 1974 L 221/10 351
Directive 75/318/EEC on the approximation of the laws of Member States relating to analytical, pharmaco-toxicological and clinical standards and protocols in respect of the testing of proprietary medicinal products, OJ 1975 L 147/1 285
Directive 75/319/EEC on the approximation of provisions laid down by Law, Regulation or Administrative Action relating to proprietary medicinal products, OJ 1975 L 147/13 60, 285, 290, 291, 292, 302
Art 16 299
Art 16 (2) 299
Art 29a 300
Directive 75/362/EEC concerning the mutual recognition of diplomas, certificates and other evidence of formal qualifications in medicine, including measures to facilitate the effective exercise of the right of establishment and freedom to provide services, OJ 1975 L 167/1 52, 204, 206, 208, 209
Art 2 210
Art 3 210
Arts 4–8 210
Directive 75/363/EEC concerning the coordination of provisions laid down by law, regulation or administrative action in respect of activities of doctors, OJ 1975 L 167/014 52, 204, 206, 208, 211
Art 1 210
Directive 75/442/EEC on waste, OJ 1975 L 194/39 334
Directive 76/160/EEC concerning the quality of bathing water, OJ 1976 L 31/1 333
Directive 76/207/EEC on the implementation of the principle of equal treatment for men and women as regards access to employment, vocational training and promotion, and working conditions, OJ 1976 L 39/40 195
Directive 76/768/ EEC on the approximation of the laws of the Member States relating to cosmetic products, OJ 1976 L 262/169 362

Directive 77/187/EEC on the approximation of the laws of the Member States relating to the safeguarding of employees' rights in the event of transfers of undertakings, businesses or parts of businesses, OJ 1977 L 61/26 195
Directive 77/452/EEC concerning the mutual recognition of diplomas, certificates and other evidence of the formal qualifications of nurses responsible for general care, including measures to facilitate the effective exercise of this right of establishment and freedom to provide services, OJ 1977 L 176/1 52, 205
Directive 77/453/EEC concerning the coordination of provisions laid down by Law, Regulation or Administrative Action in respect of the activities of nurses responsible for general care, OJ 1977 L 176/8 52, 205
Directive 78/686/EEC concerning the mutual recognition of diplomas, certificates and other evidence of the formal qualifications of practitioners of dentistry, including measures to facilitate the effective exercise of the right of establishment and freedom to provide services, OJ 1978 L 233/1 52, 204, 231
Directive 78/687/EEC concerning the coordination of provisions laid down by Law, Regulation or Administrative Action in respect of the activities of dental practitioners, OJ 1978 L 233/10 52, 204
Directive 79/112/EEC on the approximation of the laws of the Member States relating to the labelling, presentation and advertising of foodstuffs for sale to the ultimate consumer, OJ 1979 L 33/1 351
Art 3 351
Directive 80/154/EEC concerning the mutual recognition of diplomas, certificates and other evidence of formal qualifications in midwifery and including measures to facilitate the effective exercise of the right of establishment and freedom to provide services, OJ 1980 L 33/1 52, 205
Directive 80/155/EEC concerning the coordination of provisions laid down by Law, Regulation or Administrative Action relating to the taking up and pursuit of the activities of midwives, OJ 1980 L 33/8 52, 205
Directive 80/777/EEC on the approximation of the laws of the Member States relating to the exploitation and marketing of natural mineral waters, OJ 1980 L 229/1 351
Directive 80/778/EEC relating to the quality of water intended for human consumption, OJ 1980 L 229/11 362
Directive 83/189/EEC laying down a procedure for the provision of information in the field of technical standards and regulations, OJ 1983 L 109/8 (Transparency Directive) 56, 352
Directive 84/450/EEC relating to the approximation of the laws, regulations and administrative provisions of the Member States concerning misleading advertising, OJ 1984 L 250/17 305
Directive 85/374/EEC relating to the approximation of the laws, regulations and administrative provisions of the Member States concerning liability for defective

products, OJ 1985 L 210/29 (Product Liability Directive) 308, 309, 310, 312, 364, 397
preamble
Recital 5 308
Recital 6 308
Art 1 308
Art 2 308
Art 3 (1), (2) 308
Art 6 308, 310, 311
Art 7 311
Art 7 (e) 309, 311, 312
Directive 85/432/EEC concerning the coordination of provisions laid down by Law, Regulation or Administrative Action in respect of certain activities in the field of pharmacy, OJ 1985 L 253/34 52, 205, 211, 212
Art 1 211
Art 1 (2) 212
Art 2 211
Art 6 212
Directive 85/433/EEC concerning the mutual recognition of diplomas, certificates and other evidence of formal qualifications in pharmacy, including measures to facilitate the effective exercise of the right of establishment relating to certain activities in the field of pharmacy, OJ 1985 L 253/37 52, 205, 211, 212
Art 2 (2) 212
Directive 85/649/EEC prohibiting the use in livestock farming of certain substances having a hormonal action, OJ 1985/L 382/228 93
Directive 86/457/EEC on specific training in general medical practice, OJ 1986 L 267/26 204, 210
Art 1 210
Art 2 210
Art 3 210
Directive 87/18/EEC on the harmonization of laws, regulations and administrative provisions relating to the application of the principles of good laboratory practice and the verification of their applications for tests on chemical substances, OJ 1987 L 15/29 285
Directive 87/22/EEC on the approximation of national measures relating to the placing on the market of high-technology medicinal products, particularly those derived from biotechnology, OJ 1987 L 15/38 293
Annex
Part B 294
Directive 88/320/EEC on the inspection and verification of Good Laboratory Practice (GLP), OJ 1998 L 145/35 285

Directive 88/378/EEC on the approximation of the laws of the Member States concerning the safety of toys, OJ 1999 L 187/1 (Toy Safety Directive) 58
Art 2 58
Annex II
Recital 1 58
Directive 89/48/EEC on a general system for the recognition of higher-education diplomas awarded on completion of professional education and training of at least three years' duration, OJ 1989 L 19/16 215, 217, 226, 230
Directive 89/49/EEC concerning nationals of Member States who hold a diploma conferred in a third State, OJ 1989 L 19/24 230
Directive 89/105/EEC relating to the transparency of measures regulating the prices of medicinal products for human use and their inclusion in the scope of national health insurance systems, OJ 1989 L 40/8 (Transparency of Pharmaceuticals Pricing Directive) 318, 321, 323–327
preamble
Recital 9 323
Art 2 (1) 323
Art 2 (2) 323
Art 2 (3) 323
Art 3 (3) 323
Art 4 (1) 323
Art 4 (2) 323
Art 5 323
Art 5 (a)–(d) 324
Art 6 324
Art 6 (1) 324
Art 6 (2) 324
Art 6 (4) 324
Art 6 (5) 324
Art 6 (6) 324
Art 7 324, 326
Art 7 (1), (3) 324
Art 7 (4) 324
Art 9 327
Directive 89/107/EEC on the approximation of the laws of the Member States concerning food additives authorized for use in foodstuffs intended for human consumption, OJ 1989 L 40/27 352
Directive 89/381/EEC extending the scope of Directives 65/65/EEC and 75/319/EEC on the approximation of provisions laid down by Law, Regulation or Administrative Action relating to proprietary medicinal products and laying down special provisions for medicinal products derived from human blood or human plasma, OJ 1989 L 181/44 344

Directive 89/342/EEC extending the scope of Directives 65/65/EEC and 75/319/EEC and laying down additional provisions for immunological medicinal products consisting of vaccines, toxins or serums and allergens, OJ 1989 L 142/14 285
Directive 89/343/EEC extending the scope of Directives 65/65/EEC and 75/319/EEC and laying down additional provisions for radiopharmaceuticals, OJ 1989 L 142/16 285
Directive 89/369/EEC on the prevention of air pollution from new municipal waste incineration plants, OJ 1989 L 163/32 334
Directive 89/381/EEC extending the scope of Directives 65/65/EEC and 75/319/EEC on the approximation of provisions laid down by Law, Regulation or Administrative Action relating to proprietary medicinal products and laying down special provisions for medicinal products derived from human blood or human plasma, OJ 1989 L 181/44 285
Art 3 (1) 345
Directive 89/391/EEC on the introduction of measures to encourage improvements in the safety and health of workers at work, OJ 1989 L 183/1 (Framework Health and Safety at Work Directive) 334
Art 17 195
Directive 89/397/EEC on the official control of foodstuffs, OJ 1989 L/186/23 352
Directive 89/398/EEC on the approximation of the laws of the Member States relating to foodstuffs intended for particular nutritional uses, OJ 1989 L 186/27 352
Directive 89/552/EEC on the coordination of certain provisions laid down by Law, Regulation or Administrative Action in Member States concerning the pursuit of television broadcasting activities, OJ 1989 L 298/23 (Television without Frontiers Directive) 305, 379, 380
preamble
Recital 17 380
Art 13 380
Art 14 305
Directive 89/622/EEC on the approximation of the laws, regulations and administrative provisions of the Member States concerning the labelling of tobacco products, OJ 1989 L 359/1 362, 374, 381
preamble
Recitals 4, 5 375
Directive 89/662/EEC concerning veterinary checks in intra-Community trade with a view to the completion of the internal market, OJ 1989 L 395/13 355
Directive 90/364/EEC on the right of residence, OJ 1990 L 180/26 118, 122, 202

Directive 90/365/EEC on the right of residence for employees and self-employed persons who have ceased their occupational activity, OJ 1990 L 180/28 118, 122, 202
Directive 90/366/EEC on the right of residence for students, OJ 1990 L 180/30 118
Directive 90/385/EEC 1990 on the approximation of the laws of the Member States relating to active implantable medical devices, OJ 1990 L 189/17 285, 433
Directive 91/156/EEC amending Directive 75/442/EEC on waste, OJ 1991/ L 78/32 93
Directive 91/271/EEC concerning urban waste-water treatment, OJ 1991 L 135/40 334
Directive 91/356/EEC laying down the principles and guidelines of good manufacturing practice for medicinal products for human use, OJ 1991 L 193/30
preamble
Recital 6 299
Arts 6–14 299
Directive 91/507/EEC modifying the Annex to Council Directive 75/318/EEC on the approximation of the laws of Member States relating to analytical, pharmacotoxicological and clinical standards and protocols in respect of the testing of medicinal products, OJ 1991 L 270/32
Annex
Part 4.B 248
Directive 91/689/EEC on hazardous waste, OJ 1991 L 377/20 334
Directive 92/25/EEC on the wholesale distribution of medicinal products for human use, OJ 1992 L 113/1 286
Directive 92/26/EEC concerning the classification for the supply of medicinal products for human use, OJ 1992/ L 113/5 286
Directive 92/27/EEC on the labelling of medicinal products for human use and on package leaflets, OJ 1992 L 113/8 286, 302
Directive 92/28/EEC on the advertising of medicinal products for human use, OJ 1992 L 113/13 286, 305
Directive 92/41/EEC amending Directive 89/622/EEC on the approximation of the laws, regulations and administrative provisions of the Member States concerning the labelling of tobacco products, OJ 1992 L 158/30 374, 376
Directive 92/51/EEC on a second general system for the recognition of professional education and training to supplement Directive 89/48/EEC, OJ 1992 L 209/25 215, 217, 226, 230
Directive 92/59/EEC on general product safety, OJ 1992 L 228/24 (General Product Safety Directive) 94
Art 9 94, 95
Directive 92/73/EEC widening the scope of Directives 65/65/EEC and 75/319/EEC on the approximation of provisions laid down by Law, Regulation or

Administrative Action relating to medicinal products and laying down additional provisions on homeopathic medicinal products, OJ 1992 L 297/8 362
Directive 93/16/EEC 1993 to facilitate the free movement of doctors and the mutual recognition of their diplomas, certificates and other evidence of formal qualifications, OJ 1993 L 165/1 204, 206, 208, 223, 227, 232
Art 1 206
Art 2 206
Art 3 207
Art 4 207
Art 5 207
Art 10 207
Art 11 207, 224
Art 12 207, 224
Art 13 207
Art 14 (9) 224
Art 15 207
Art 23 (1), (2) 207
Arts 24–27 207
Annex A 206
Annex B 207
Annex C 207
Directive 93/39/EEC amending Directives 65/65/EEC, 75/318/EEC and 75/319/EEC in respect of medicinal products, OJ 1993 L 214/22 49, 60, 285, 291
Directive 93/42/EEC concerning medical devices, OJ 1993 L 169/1 279, 285, 433
preamble 344
Art 1 (2) (h) 289
Art 11 344
Directive 93/43/EEC on the hygiene of foodstuffs, OJ 1993 L 175/1 352
Directive 93/96/EEC on the right of residence for students, OJ 1993 L 317/59 118, 122, 202
Directive 93/104/EC concerning certain aspects of the organization of working time, OJ 1993 L 307/18 (Working Time Directive) 41, 94, 194, 195, 196, 197, 233, 334, 397
Art 1 (3) 194
Art 6 195
Art 8 195
Art 17 (2.1) (c) (i) 196
Art 17 (2.4) (a) 196
Art 18 (1) (b) (i) 197
Directive 94/65/EC laying down the requirements for the production and placing on the market of minced meat and meat preparations, OJ 1994 L 368/10 354

Directive 95/46/EC on the protection of individuals with regard to the processing of personal data and on the free movement of such data, OJ 1995 L 281/31 (Data Protection Directive) 19, 26, 29, 160, 165, 166–185, 186, 187, 188, 252, 267, 394, 397, 409, 432

preamble

Recital 1 167

Recital 2 167

Recital 3 167

Recital 7 166

Recital 8 166, 167

Recital 9 167

Recital 10 167

Recital 26 174

Recital 31 176

Recital 70 176

Art 1 (1) 167, 170

Art 2 175

Art 2 (a) 168, 172, 182

Art 2 (b) 168, 175

Art 3 (1) 169

Art 3 (c) 168

Art 4 186

Art 5 167, 169

Art 6 180

Art 6 (1) (a)–(e) 169

Art 6 (1) (b) 177, 180

Art 6 (1) (e) 172, 180

Art 7 179, 186

Art 7 (a) 169, 176, 177

Art 7 (b)–(f) 170

Art 7 (f) 182

Art 8 175, 179

Art 8 (1) 170, 171, 175, 177, 186

Art 8 (2) 177

Art 8 (2) (a) 170, 175

Art 8 (2) (b) 170

Art 8 (2) (c) 170, 176, 179

Art 8 (2) (d) 170

Art 8 (2) (e) 170

Art 8 (2) (h) 176

Art 8 (3) 171, 177, 178, 179

Art 8 (4) 171, 178, 179, 181, 182

Art 10 182, 186

Art 10 (a)–(c) 183
Art 11 (1) 180
Art 11 (2) 181, 183
Art 12 183
Art 13 169, 186
Art 13 (1) 169
Art 13 (1) (g) 183
Art 14 170, 183
Art 14 (c) 170
Art 15 183
Art 16 183
Art 17 183
Art 18 184
Arts 22–24 184
Art 25 185
Art 25 (4) 185
Art 25 (6) 185
Art 27 184
Art 28 184
Art 31 160
Directive 96/70/EC amending Council Directive 80/777/EEC on the approximation of the laws of the Member States relating to the exploitation and marketing of natural mineral waters, OJ 1996 L 299/26 351
Directive 96/71/EC concerning the posting of workers in the framework of the provision of services, OJ 1996 L 18/1 (Posted Workers Directive) 197, 198
Directive 97/7/EC on the protection of consumers in respect of distance contracts - Statement by the Council and the Parliament re Article 6 (1) - Statement by the Commission re Article 3 (1), first indent, OJ 1997 L 144/19 429
Art 14 429, 430
Directive 97/50/EC amending Directive 93/16/EEC to facilitate the free movement of doctors and the mutual recognition of their diplomas, certificates and other evidence of formal qualifications, OJ 1997 L 291/35 226, 227
Directive 98/21/EC to facilitate the free movement of doctors and the mutual recognition of their diplomas, certificates and other evidence of formal qualifications, OJ 1998 L 119/15 227
Directive 98/43/EC on the approximation of the laws, regulations and administrative provisions of the Member States relating to the advertising and sponsorship of tobacco products, OJ 1998 L 213/9 (Tobacco Advertising Directive) 53, 96, 97, 98, 99, 100, 103, 105, 181, 367, 371, 378, 380, 381, 382, 383, 394
preamble
Recitals 1, 2 99
Art 1 382
Art 2 381

Art 3 98
Art 3 (2) 99
Art 3 (5) 99
Art 4 96, 381
Art 5 98, 381
Directive 98/44/EC on the legal protection of biotechnological inventions, OJ 1998 L 213/13 (Legal Protection of Biotechnological Inventions Directive; Biotechnology Directive) 25, 239, 246, 260, 261, 264, 266, 268, 269, 270, 272, 273, 281, 407, 408
preamble
Recital 20 266
Recital 22 264, 266
Recital 23 265
Recital 25 266
Recital 26 267, 268
Recitals 36–42 266
Recital 41 272
Art 2 264
Art 3 (2) 260
Art 5 265
Art 5 (1), (2), (3) 265
Art 6 266, 267, 269, 272
Art 6 (1) (b) 267
Art 6 (2) (a) 272
Art 6 (2) (c) 266, 275
Art 7 268
Art 16 268
Directive 98/63/EC amending Council Directive 93/16/EEC to facilitate the free movement of doctors and the mutual recognition of their diplomas, certificates and other evidence of formal qualifications, OJ 1998 L 253/24 227
Directive 98/79/EC on in vitro diagnostic medical devices, OJ 1998 L 331/1 433
Annex II 345
Directive 98/83/EC on the quality of water intended for human consumption, OJ 1998 L 330/32 333, 362
Directive 99/34/EC amending Council Directive 85/374/EEC on the approximation of the laws, regulations and administrative provisions of the Member States concerning liability for defective products, OJ 1999 L 141/20
Art 1 308
Directive 99/46/EC amending Council Directive 93/16/EEC to facilitate the free movement of doctors and the mutual recognition of their diplomas, certificates and other evidence of formal qualifications, OJ 1999 L 139/25 227

Directive 2000/13/EC on the approximation of the laws of the Member States relating to the labelling, presentation and advertising of foodstuffs, OJ 2000 L 109/29 351
Directive 2000/31/EC on certain legal aspects of information society services, in particular electronic commerce, in the Internal Market ("Directive on electronic commerce"), OJ 2000 L 178/1 (E-Commerce Directive) 19, 160, 166, 432
Art 1 (1) 166
Art 1 (2) 432
Art 8 (1) 166, 433
Art 8 (2) 166, 433
Directive 2000/34/EC amending Council Directive 93/104/EC concerning certain aspects of the organisation of working time to cover sectors and activities excluded from that Directive, OJ 2000 L 195/41 (Working Time Directive) 196, 334
Art 1 196
Directive 2000/36/EC relating to cocoa and chocolate products intended for human consumption, OJ 2000 L 197/19 351
Directive 2000/43/EC implementing the principle of equal treatment between persons irrespective of racial or ethnic origin, OJ 2000 L 180/22 195
Directive 2000/60/EC establishing a framework for Community action in the field of water policy, OJ 2000 L 327/1 334
Directive 2000/70/EC amending Council Directive 93/42/EEC as regards medical devices incorporating stable derivates of human blood or human plasma, OJ 2000 L 313/22 279
Directive 2000/76/EC on the incineration of waste, OJ 2000 L 332/91 334
Directive 2000/78/EC establishing a general framework for equal treatment in employment and occupation, OJ 2000 L 303/16 195
Directive 2001/18/EC on the deliberate release into the environment of genetically modified organisms and repealing Council Directive 90/220/EEC - Commission Declaration, OJ 2001 L 106/1 245
Directive 2001/19/EC amending Council Directives 89/48/EEC and 92/51/EEC on the general system for the recognition of professional qualifications and Council Directives 77/452/EEC, 77/453/EEC, 78/686/EEC, 78/687/EEC, 78/1026/EEC, 78/1027/EEC, 80/154/EEC, 80/155/EEC, 85/384/EEC, 85/432/EEC, 85/433/EEC and 93/16/EEC concerning the professions of nurse responsible for general care, dental practitioner, veterinary surgeon, midwife, architect, pharmacist and doctor–Statements, OJ 2001 L 206/1 52, 205, 206, 212, 215, 224, 227
preamble
Recital 6 232
Art 1 (3) 218
Art 2 (2) 218
Art 12 (5) 233
Art 14 (12), (13) 210
Art 14 (16) 233

Directive 2001/20/EC on the approximation of the laws, regulations and administrative provisions of the Member States relating to the implementation of good clinical practice in the conduct of clinical trials on medicinal products for human use, OJ 2001 L 121/34 (Clinical Trials Directive) 25, 179, 188, 237, 238, 239, 247, 248–259, 268, 280, 281, 396, 407

Art 1 (2) 251, 252
Art 1 (4) 249
Art 2 251
Art 2 (e) 255
Art 3 252
Art 3 (2) (a) 253
Art 3 (2) (j) 252
Art 3 (1) 250
Art 4 254, 255
Art 4 (a), (b), (c), (g) 254
Art 4 (d), (e), (h), (i) 255
Art 5 254, 255
Art 5 (a), (b), (c), (e), (f) 254
Art 5 (d), (h) (g) 255
Art 6 253
Art 6 (1) 253
Art 6 (3) 253
Art 6 (3) (a)–(d) 253
Art 6 (3) (f) 253
Art 6 (3) (g) 253, 254
Art 6 (h), (i) 255
Art 7 256
Art 9 253, 256
Art 9 (1), (2) 253
Art 9 (6) 256
Art 10 253
Art 10 (c) 258
Art 11 256
Art 11 (1) (a)–(f) 257
Art 14 258
Art 14 258
Art 15 258
Art 16 (1), (2), (4) 257
Art 17 257
Art 17 (1) (a), (b), (d) 257
Art 17 (2) 258
Art 17 (3) (a) 258
Recital 10 237

Directive 2001/23/EC on the approximation of the laws of the Member States relating to the safeguarding of employees' rights in the event of transfers of undertakings, businesses or parts of undertakings or businesses, OJ 2001 L 82/16 195

Directive 2001/37/EC on the approximation of the laws, regulations and administrative provisions of the Member States concerning the manufacture, presentation and sale of tobacco products - Commission statement, OJ 2001 L 194/26 (Tobacco Manufacture, Presentation and Sale Directive; Tobacco Products Consolidation Directive) 96, 101, 103, 374, 375, 378, 379, 381, 383

preamble

Recitals 2, 3 375

Recital 27 377

Art 2 (1) 375

Art 2 (4) 375

Art 3 (1) 376

Art 3 (2) 376

Art 3 (3) 376

Art 5 (2) (a) 376

Art 5 (2) (b) 377

Art 5 (4) 376

Art 5 (5) 377

Art 5 (7) 377

Art 6 (a) 377

Art 6 (e) 377

Art 7 377

Art 8 376

Art 12 377

Art 12 (2) 377

Art 13 101

Art 13 (1) 377

Annex I 377

Directive 2001/83/EC on the Community code relating to medicinal products for human use, OJ 2001 L 311/67 214, 279, 286, 291, 300, 302, 303, 305, 306, 307, 313, 315, 345, 394

Art 1 (13) 300

Art 6 (1) 251, 289

Art 10 314

Art 10 (1) (a) (iii) 314

Art 17 315

Art 18 315

Art 27 316

Art 29 (3), (6) 316

Arts 32–34 290, 316

Art 40 299
Art 40 (2) 299
Art 41 299
Art 48 299
Art 49 299
Art 51 299
Art 54 303
Arts 54–57 303
Arts 59–60 304
Art 59 (1) (e) 304
Art 63 (1) 303
Art 87 305
Art 88 305
Art 88 (1) 429
Art 88 (3) 305
Art 89 (1) 306
Art 90 306
Art 89 (1) 306
Art 91 (1) 306
Art 94 306
Art 94 (1) 306
Art 95 306
Art 96 306
Art 102 300
Art 121 289
Art 121 (2) 316
Recital 2 288
Recital 3 288
Directive 2001/110/EC relating to honey, OJ 2002 L 10/47 351
Directive 2002/58/EC concerning the processing of personal data and the protection of privacy in the electronic communications sector (Directive on privacy and electronic communications), OJ 2002 L 201/37 160
Art 1 166
Directive 2002/98/EC setting standards of quality and safety for the collection, testing, processing, storage and distribution of human blood and blood components and amending Directive 2001/83/EC, OJ 2003 L 33/30 (Blood Safety Directive) 279, 336, 346–348, 392, 407, 422, 423
preamble
Recital 22 347
Art 2 (1) 346
Art 4 (2) 346, 396
Arts 5-8 346
Arts 11–13 346

Art 14 (1), (3) 346
Art 17 346
Art 18 346
Art 19 346
Art 20 347
Art 21 346
Art 23 346
Art 29 346
Art 32 346
Directive 2003/33/EC on the approximation of the laws, regulations and administrative provisions of the Member States relating to the advertising and sponsorship of tobacco products, OJ 2003 L 152/16 (new Tobacco Advertising Directive) 383, 384
Art 3 383
Art 4 383
Art 5 383
Art 8 383
Directive 2003/83/EC adapting to technical progress Annexes II, III and VI to Council Directive 76/768/EEC on the approximation of the laws of the Member States relating to cosmetic products, OJ 2003 L 238/23 285
Directive 2003/86/EC on the right of family reunion, OJ 2003 L 251/12 341
Directive 2003/88/EC concerning certain aspects of the organisation of working time, OJ 2003 L 299/9 194, 195
Directive 2004/23/EC on setting standards of quality and safety for the donation, procurement, testing, processing, preservation, storage and distribution of human tissues and cells, OJ 2004 L 102/48 (Tissue Directive) 280
Directive 2004/27/EC amending Directive 2001/83/EC on the Community code relating to medicinal products for human use, OJ 2004 L 136/34 313
Preamble
Recital 11 316
Art 1 (16) 315, 316
Art 8 (1) 314

Decisions

Decision 69/414/EEC setting up a Standing Committee for Foodstuffs, OJ L 1969 291/9 357
Decision 74/234/EEC relating to the institution of a Scientific Committee for Food, OJ L 1974 136/1 359
Decision 75/364/EEC setting up an Advisory Committee on Medical Training, OJ 1975 L 167/17 208
Art 2 208
Art 2 (2) 208
Art 2 (3) 208

Art 2 (4) 208
Art 5 209
Decision 85/195/EEC adopting a multiannual research action programme for the European Economic Community in the field of biotechnology (1985 to 1989), OJ 1985 L 83/1 63
Decision 85/368/EEC on the comparability of vocational training qualifications between the Member States of the European Community, OJ 1985 L 199/56 216
Decision 85/434/EEC setting up an Advisory Committee on pharmaceutical training, OJ 1985 L 253/43 212
Art 2 212
Decision 87/373/EEC laying down the procedures for the exercise of implementing powers conferred on the Commission, OJ 1987 L 197/33 50
Decision 87/516/EEC concerning the framework programme for Community activities in the field of research and technological development (1987 to 1991), OJ 1987 L 302/1 (Second Framework Programme) 240
Decision 88/351/EEC adopting a 1988 to 1989 plan of action for an information and public awareness campaign in the context of the "Europe against cancer" programme, OJ 1988 L 160/52 73
preamble 369
Decision 89/469/EEC concerning certain protection measures relating to bovine spongiform encephalopathy in the United Kingdom, OJ 1989 L 225/51 355
Decision 90/59/EEC amending Decision 89/469/EEC concerning certain protection measures relating to bovine spongiform encephalopathy in the United Kingdom, OJ 1990 L 041/23 355
Decision 90/200/EEC concerning additional requirements for some tissues and organs with respect to Bovine Spongiform Encephalopathy (BSE), OJ 1990 L 105/24 355
Decision 90/221/EEC concerning the framework Programme of Community activities in the field of research and technological development (1990 to 1994), OJ 1990 L 117/2 (Third Framework Programme) 240
Decision 90/238/EEC adopting a 1990 to 1994 action plan in the context of the "Europe against Cancer" programme, OJ 1990 L 137/31 370
Art 1 (2) 371
Decision 90/261/EEC amending Decision 89/469/EEC concerning certain protection measures relating to bovine spongiform encephalopathy (BSE) in the United Kingdom and Decision 90/200/EEC concerning additional requirements for some tissues and organs with respect to bovine spongiform encephalopathy, OJ 1990 L 146/29 355
Art 2 371
Decision 91/89/EEC making financial provision for a project relating to the inactivation of the agents of scrapie and bovine spongiform encephalopathy, OJ 1991 L 049/31 355

Decision 91/317/EEC adopting a plan of action in the framework of the 1991 to 1993 "Europe against AIDS" programme, OJ 1991 L 175/26 73, 337
Decision 91/505/EEC adopting a specific research and technological development programme in the field of biomedicine and health (1990 to 1994), OJ L 1991 267/25 ("Biomed 1") 242, 244, 245
Decision 92/290/EEC concerning certain protection measures relating to bovine embryos in respect of bovine spongiform encephalopathy (BSE) in the United Kingdom, OJ 1992 L 152/37 355
Decision 92/450/EEC 1992 amending for the third time Council Directive 82/894/EEC on the notification of animal diseases within the Community and temporarily amending the frequency of notification for bovine spongiform encephalopathy, OJ 1992 L 248/77 355
Decision 93/362/EEC concerning the continuation in 1994 of the 1990 to 1994 action plan in the context of the "Europe against Cancer" programme, OJ 1993 L 150/43 371
Decision 94/381/EC concerning certain protection measures with regard to bovine spongiform encephalopathy and the feeding of mammalian derived protein, OJ 1994 L 172/23 355
Decision 94/382/EC on the approval of alternative heat treatment systems for processing animal waste of ruminant origin, with a view to the inactivation of spongiform encephalopathy agents, OJ 1994 L 172/25 355
Decision 94/474/EC concerning certain protection measures relating to bovine spongiform encephalopathy and repealing Decisions 89/469/EEC and 90/200/EEC, OJ 1994 L 194/96 355
Decision 94/913/EC adopting a specific programme of research and technological development, including demonstration, in the field of biomedicine and health (1994 to 1998), OJ 1994 L 361/40 ("Biomed 2") 242, 245
Decision 1110/94/EC concerning the fourth framework programme of the European Community activities in the field of research and technological development and demonstration, OJ 1994 L 126/1 240, 244, 399
  Art 4 (1) 239
Decision 95/29/EC on the approval of alternative heat treatment systems for processing animal waste of ruminant origin, with a view to the inactivation of spongiform encephalopathy agents, OJ 1995 L 038/17 355
Decision 95/60/EC amending Decision 94/381/EC concerning certain protection measures with regard to bovine spongiform encephalopathy and the feeding of mammalian derived protein, OJ 1995 L 055/43 355
Decision 95/287/EC amending Decision 94/474/EEC concerning certain protection measures relating to bovine spongiform encephalopathy and repealing Decisions 89/469/EEC and 90/200/EEC, OJ 1995 L 181/40 355
Decision 1729/95/EC on the extensions of the "Europe against AIDS" programme, OJ 1995 L 168/1 337
Decision 96/239/EC on emergency measures to protect against bovine spongiform encephalopathy, OJ 1995 L 078/47 355

Decision 96/362/EEC amending Decision 96/239/EC on emergency measures to protect against bovine spongiform encephalopathy, OJ 1996 L 139/17 357
Decision 96/381/EEC approving the measures to be implemented as regards bovine spongiform encephalopathy in Portugal, OJ 1996 L 149/25 355
Decision 96/385/EC approving the plan for the control and eradication of bovine spongiform encephalopathy in the United Kingdom, OJ 1996 L 151/39 355
Decision 96/449/EC on the approval of alternative heat treatment systems for processing animal waste with a view to the inactivation of spongiform encephalopathy agents, OJ 1996 L 184/43 355
Decision 645/96/EC adopting a programme of Community action on health promotion, information, education and training within the framework for action in the field of public health (1996 to 2000), OJ 1996 L 095/1 75
Decision 646/96/EC adopting an action plan to combat cancer within the framework for action in the field of public health (1996 to 2000), OJ 1996 L 095/9 75
  Art 3 372
  Annex 372
Decision 647/96/EC adopting a programme of Community action on the prevention of AIDS and certain other communicable diseases within the framework for action in the field of public health (1996 to 2000), OJ 1996 L 095/16 75, 337
  Art 1 (2) 337
  Art 2 337
  Art 3 338
  Art 5 338
  Art 7 339
  Annex 338
Decision 102/97/EC adopting a programme of Community action on the prevention of drug dependence within the framework for action in the field of public health (1996-2000), OJ 1997 L 019/25 75
Decision 97/189/EC authorizing the Federal Republic of Germany and the French Republic to apply a measure derogating from Article 3 of the Sixth Directive 77/388/EEC on the harmonization of the laws of the Member States relating to turnover taxes, OJ 1997 L 080/20 355
Decision 97/312/EC approving the measures to be implemented as regards bovine spongiform encephalopathy in Ireland, OJ 1997 L 133/38 355
Decision 97/404/EC 1997 setting up a Scientific Steering Committee, OJ 1997 L 169/85 359
Decision 97/534/EC on the prohibition of the use of material presenting risks as regards transmissible spongiform encephalopathies, OJ 1997 L 216/95 355
Decision 97/579/EC setting up Scientific Committees in the field of consumer health and food safety, OJ 1997 L 237/18 359

Decision 1400/97/EC adopting a programme of Community action on health monitoring within the framework for action in the field of public health (1997 to 2001), OJ 1997 L 193/1 75
Decision 98/12/EC amending for the fourth time Council Directive 82/894/EEC on the notification of animal diseases within the Community and temporarily amending the frequency of notification for bovine spongiform encephalopathy, OJ 1998 L 4/63 355
Decision 98/256/EC concerning emergency measures to protect against bovine spongiform encephalopathy, amending Decision 94/474/EC and repealing Decision 96/239/EC, OJ 1998 L 113/32 355
Decision 2119/98/EC setting up a network for the epidemiological surveillance and control of communicable diseases in the Community, OJ 1998 L 268/1 335, 338
Decision 99/167/EC adopting a specific programme for research, technological development and demonstration on quality of life and management of living resources (1998 to 2002), OJ 1999 L 064/1
  Annex II 242
Decision 5/1999 of the EU-Republic of Slovenia Association Council of 3 November 1999 adopting the terms and conditions for the participation of the Republic of Slovenia in Community Programmes in the fields of social policy and health, OJ 1999 L 304/27 83
Decision 182/99/EC concerning the fifth framework programme of the European Community for research, technological development and demonstration activities (1998 to 2002), OJ 1999 L 26/1 240
  Article 1 242
  Annex II 242
Decision 372/99/EC adopting a programme of Community action on injury prevention in the framework for action in the field of public health (1999 to 2003), OJ 1999 L 046/1 75, 334
Decision 99/468/EC laying down the procedures for the exercise of implementing powers conferred on the Commission, OJ 1999 L 184/23 50
  Art 4 84
  Art 5 289
  Art 7 84, 289
Decision 99/534/EC on measures applying to the processing of certain animal waste to protect against transmissible spongiform encephalopathies and amending Commission Decision 97/735/EC, OJ 1999 L 204/37 355
Decision 2000/418/EC regulating the use of material presenting risks as regards transmissible spongiform encephalopathies and amending Decision 94/474/EC (notified under document number C(2000) 1735), OJ 2000 L 158/76 355
Decision 2000/520/EC pursuant to Directive 95/46/EC of the European Parliament and of the Council on the adequacy of the protection provided by the safe harbour privacy principles and related frequently asked questions issued by

the US Department of Commerce (notified under document number C(2000) 2441), OJ 2000 L 215/7 185
Decision 2001/497/EC on standard contractual clauses for the transfer of personal data to third countries, under Directive 95/46/EC (notified under document number C(2001) 1539), OJ 2001 L 181/19 184
Decision 2001/531/EC on standard contractual clauses for the transfer of personal data to third countries, under Directive 95/46/EC (notified under document number C(2001) 1539), OJ 2001 L 192/21
  Art 2 (1) 241
Decision 2002/2/EC pursuant to Directive 95/46/EC of the European Parliament and of the Council on the adequate protection of personal data provided by the Canadian Personal Information Protection and Electronic Documents Act (notified under document number C(2001) 4539), OJ 2002 L 2/13 185
Decision 2002/253/EC laying down case definitions for reporting communicable diseases to the Community network under Decision No 2119/98/EC of the European Parliament and of the Council (notified under document number C(2002) 1043), OJ 2002 L 86/44 331
Decision 2002/834/EC adopting a specific programme for research, technological development and demonstration: "Integrating and strengthening the European Research Area" (2002-2006), OJ 2002 L 294/1 247, 400
Decision 1513/2002/EC concerning the sixth framework programme of the European Community for research, technological development and demonstration activities, contributing to the creation of the European Research Area and to innovation (2002 to 2006), OJ L 2002 232/1 240, 241
  Recital 17 246
  Annex 1 247
Decision 1786/2002/EC 2002 adopting a programme of Community action in the field of public health (2003–2008) - Commission Statements, OJ 2002 L 271/1 75, 82, 84, 334, 337, 372
  Art 1 (2) 82, 373
  Art 2 82, 373
  Art 3 (2) (d) (v) 83
  Art 4 83, 373
  Art 5 (1) 83
  Art 7 82
  Art 9 83
  Art 9 (2) 84
  Art 13 82
  Annex 82, 373
    Annex 2.4 82
    Annex 2.5 84
    Annex 2.9 82
    Annex 3.1 82

Annex 3.4 83, 373
Annex 3.5 84

Soft law

Action Plan for skills and mobility, COM(2002) 72 final 61, 115, 427
Communication concerning the consequences of the judgment given by the Court of Justice on 20 February 1979 in case 120/78 ("Cassis de Dijon"), OJ 1980 C 256/2 55
Communication on the Free Movement of Foodstuffs within the Community, OJ 1989 C 271/3 353
Communication on blood self-sufficiency in the European Community, COM(93) 198 final 345
Communication covering the free movement of services across frontiers, OJ 1993 C 334/3 150
Communication on the framework for action in public health, COM(93) 559 final 244, 399
Communication on the Outlines of an Industrial Policy for the Pharmaceutical Sector, COM(93) 718 327
Communication adopting a programme of Community action on health promotion, information, education, and training within the framework for action in the field of public health COM(94) 202 final 75
Communication on blood safety and self-sufficiency in the European Community, COM(94) 652 final 345
Communication on the present and proposed Community role in combating tobacco consumption, COM(96) 609 final point 10 97
Communication on consumer health and food safety, COM(97) 183 final 104, 358, 363
Communication on food, veterinary and plant health control and inspection, COM(98) 32 final 360
Communication towards a European research area, COM(2000) 6 final 241
Communication on the future of health care and care for the elderly: guaranteeing accessibility, quality, and financial viability, COM(2001) 723 final 414
Communication on eEurope 2005: an information society for all – An Action Plan to be presented in view of the Sevilla European Council, 21–22 June 2002, COM(2002) 263 final 432
Communication on eEurope 2002: Quality Criteria for Health related Websites, Brussels, 29 November 2002, COM(2002) 667 final 307
Communication on consumer health and food safety and food, veterinary and plant health control and inspection, COM (2003) 52 final 363
Communication concerning the re-examination of Directive 93/104/EC concerning certain aspects of the organization of working time, COM(2003) 843 97

Communication on making healthcare better for European citizens: an action plan for a European e-Health Area, COM (2004) 356 427
Conclusions concerning AIDS, OJ 1987 C 178/1 337
Conclusions concerning AIDS, OJ 1988 C 197/8 337
Conclusions concerning AIDS and the place of work, OJ 1989 C 28/2 337
Conclusions regarding the prevention of AIDS in intravenous drug users, OJ 1989 C 185/3 337
Conclusions concerning AIDS, OJ 1989 C 28/1 337
Conclusions on self-sufficiency in blood in the European Community, OJ 1994 C 15/6 345
Conclusions on the future framework for Community action in the field of public health, OJ 1998 C 390/1 82
Conclusions on patient mobility and health care developments in the EU, OJ 2002 C 183/1 143
Opinion of the European Group on Ethics in Science and New Technologies to the European Commission, Ethical aspects of human tissue banking No 11, 21 July 1998 279
Recommendation 83/571/EEC concerning tests relating to the placing on the market of proprietary medicinal products, OJ 1983 L 332/11 285
Recommendation 87/176/EEC concerning tests relating to the placing on the market of proprietary medicinal products, OJ 1987 L 73/1 285
Recommendation 89/601/EEC concerning the training of health personnel in the matter of cancer, OJ 1989 L 346/1 370, 371
Recommendation 98/463/EC on the suitability of blood and plasma donors and the screening of donated blood in the European Community, OJ 1998 L 203/14 279, 345
  Para 14 345
Recommendation 2/2001 on certain minimum requirements for collecting data online in the European Union, 17 May 2001, 5020/01/EN/Final P6 432
Resolution on mutual recognition of diplomas, certificates and other evidence of formal qualifications, OJ 1974 C 98/1 204, 208, 216
  Para II 216
Resolution on the framework programmes for Community research, development and demonstration activities and a first framework programme 1984 to 1987, OJ 1983 C 208/1 63, 239, 240
Resolution on AIDS, OJ 1986 C 184/21 336
Resolution on a programme of action of the European Communities against cancer, OJ 1986 C 184/19 369
Resolution on compulsory gynaecological examination at the Dutch/German border, OJ 1991 C 106/13 150
Resolution on future action in the field of public health, OJ 1993 C 174/1 75, 78

Resolution on public health policy after Maastricht, OJ 1993 C 329/375 371, 372
Resolution concerning future guidelines for the "Europe against Cancer" programme following evaluation of it for the period 1987 to 1992, OJ 1994 C 15/1 371, 372
Resolution concerning the extension to the end of 1994 of the 1991 to 1993 plan of action in the framework of the "Europe against AIDS" programme, OJ 1994 C 15/4 337
Resolution on blood safety and self -sufficiency in the Community, OJ 1995 C 164/1 345
Resolution on orphan drugs, OJ 1995 C 350/3 245, 399
Resolution on the European health card, OJ 1996 C 141/104 61, 115, 427
Resolution on strategy towards blood safety and self-sufficiency in the European Community, OJ 1996 C 374/1 345
Resolution on the communication from the Commission to the Council and the European Parliament concerning scientific and technological research: a strategic part of the European Union's development cooperation with developing countries (COM(97) 174 C4-0207/97) OJ 1999 C 175/35 82
Resolution of on the future Community action in the field of public health, OJ 1999 C 200/1 82
Resolution on the promotion of mental health, OJ 2000 C 86/1 368, 434
Resolution on Human Cloning of 7 September 2000, B-0710, 0751, 0753, and 0764/2000, based on A5-0168/2000 273
Resolution of the European Parliament on the patenting of BRCA1 and BRCA2 ("breast cancer") genes, 4 October 2001 270
Resolution on amendment of the liability for defective products Directive, OJ 2003 C 26/2 312

Table of national provisions

Austria

Data Protection Act 2000 (BGB1 No 165/1999) 186

Federal Law of 23 January 1974 (*Bundesgesetzblatt* No 60, 1974) 110

Penal Code

ss 96–98 110

Reproductive Medicine Act 1992 275

Belgium

Constitution

Art 23 9

Crown Order (CO) nr 79 of 10 November 1967 191

Art 2 191

Law of 25 June 1938 191

Law of 8 December 1992 on privacy protection in relation to the processing of personal data 186

Law of 11 December 1998, implementing Directive 95/46/EC 186

Law on the Health Insurance System

Art 35 192

Penal Code (Code PÈnal, Title VII, Chapter 1)

ss 348–352 110

Czech Republic

Law on abortion, 20 October 1986 110

Denmark

Act on the processing of personal information (Act No 429, 31 May 2000) 186

Law No 350 of 13 June 1973 on the interruption of pregnancy (*Lovitidende for Kongeriget Danmark*, Part A, 6 July 1973, No 32, pp 993–995) 110

Medically Assisted Procreation Act 1997 275

Patients Rights Act 1998 24, 391

Finland

Constitution
Ch 2
s 19 9
Law No 239 of 24 March 1970 on the interruption of pregnancy 110
Law No 564 of 19 July 1978 110
Law No 572 of 12 July 1985 110
Medical Research Act 1999 274
Ordinance No 359 of 29 May 1970 on the interruption of pregnancy 110
Personal Data Act 523/1999 186

France

Bioethics Law 1994 275
Declaration of Human Rights 162
Law No 78/17 of 6 January 1978 187
Art 40 182
Law of 17 July 1978
Art 6 182
Law No 79-1204 of 31 December 1979 110
Law No 94-654 of 29 July 1994 148
Public Health Code relating to medical dossiers in health institutions
Art L 1112-1 182
Penal Code
Art 226-13 162

Germany

Beer Purity Law (Reinheitsgebot) 56
Bundes-Seuchengesetz
s 3 163
Embryo Protection Law (ESchG) 1990 275
Pharmaceuticals Act 1976 309
Treaty on German Unity 1990 401

Greece

Constitution
Art 9A 187
Civil Code
Art 57 168
Criminal Code
Art 232 163
Art 371 162
Law 2472/1997 on the Processing of Personal Data 186
Art 7, s 2 186

Law 2520/1940 163
Law 3089/2002 274
Law 4060/1929 163
Penal Code
ss 304–305 110
Presidential Decree 1383 of 1981 163
Royal Decree of 3 November 1950 163
Royal Decree 383 of 10 July 1972 163

Hungary
Constitution
Art 70D 8

India
Constitution
Art 39 (e), (f) 8
Arts 46, 47 8

Ireland
Constitution 153, 275
Art 40.3.3 65, 110, 149, 152, 401, 402
Health (Family Planning) Act 1979 401
Public Health (Tobacco) Act 2002 368
Tobacco Smoking (Prohibition) Regulations 2003, SI 2003/481 368

Italy
Constitution
Art 32 9
Decreto del Ministero della Sanita, 5 July 1975 163
Law No 458 of 26 June 1967 concerning the transplantation of kidneys from living donors 110
Law No 194 of 22 May 1978 on the social protection of motherhood and the voluntary termination of pregnancy (*Gazzetta Uficialee della Repubblica Italiana*, Part I, 2 May 1978, No 140, pp 3642–3646) 110
Leg Decree No 135 of 11 May 1999 186

Luxembourg
Constitution
Art 11 (5) 9

Malta
Criminal Code
ss 241–243A 401

Netherlands
Constitution
Art 22 (1) 9

Embryo Act September 2002 274
Law on the termination of pregnancy of 1 May 1981 110
Medical Treatment Contracts Act 1995
Art 457 162
Penal Code 162
Organ Donation Act (*Wet op de Orgaandonatie*) 1998 17, 422

Philippines
Constitution
Art II
s 15 8

Poland
Constitution
Art 68 8
Act on family planning, human embryo protection and conditions of permissibility of abortion 1993 147, 401

Portugal
Constitution
Art 64 (1) 9

Slovakia
Law on abortion 23 October 1986 110

South Africa
Constitution
Art 27 8

Spain
Constitution
Art 43 9

Sweden
Act of 1991 "Measures for Purposes of Research and Treatment Involving Fertilised Human Ova" 274
Communicable Diseases Act 1988 336
Health and Medical Care Act (18-982;763) 274
Personal Data Act 1998 186

United Kingdom
Access to Health Records Act 1990 171, 182, 186
Access to Medical Reports Act 1988 182
Access to Personal Files Act 1987 186

Consumer Protection Act 1987 310, 397
s 4 310
s 4(1) (e) 309
Data Protection Act 1984 186
Data Protection Act 1998 171, 175, 186
s 33(1) 177
Sch 1
para 2 177
Sch 3 177
Health Act 1999 192
Health and Social Care Act 2001 16
s 60 181
s 61 182
Human Fertilisation and Embryology Act 1990 3, 17, 147, 150, 151
s 24 150
s 41(2) (b) 151
Sch 3 150
Human Fertilisation and Embryology (Deceased Fathers) Act 2003 154
Human Organ Transplants Act 1989 17, 110
Human Rights Act 1998 3, 24, 148, 154
Human Tissue Act 1961 17, 422
Medical Act 1511–1512 189
Medical Act 1858 189
Medical Act 1983 191
National Health Service Reform and Health Care Professions Act 2002
s 25 192
Public Health Act 1848 330
Public Health (Control of Disease) Act 1984 331
Vaccine Damage Payments Act 1979 307

STATUTORY INSTRUMENTS

Data Protection Act 1998 (Commencement) Order 2000, SI 2000/183 186
Data Protection (Subject Access Modification) (Health) Order 2000, SI 2000/413 183
European Specialist Medical Qualifications Order 1995, SI 1995/3208 205
Health Service (Control of Patient Information) Regulations 2002, SI 2002/1438 reg 4 181
Human Fertilisation and Embryology (Research Purposes) Regulations 2001, SI 2001/188 274
Medicines for Human Use (Clinical Trials) Regulations 2004, SI 2004/1031 258
Public Heath Act (Infectious Diseases) Regulations 1985, SI 1985/434 331

Table of cases

A

A and others v National Blood Authority and another [2001] 3 All ER 289, (2001) 60 BMLR 1 310, 397

A-G v X [1992] 2 CMLR 277, [1992] ILRM 401, 15 BMLR 104 65, 152, 153, 398, 401

Albany International BV v Stichting Bedrijfspensioenfonds Textielindustrie Case C-67/96 [1999] ECR I-5751, [2000] 4 CMLR 446 322, 392

Algemene Transport-en Expeditie Onderneming van Gend en Loos NV v Nederlandse Belastingadministratie Case 26/62 [1963] ECR 1, [1963] CMLR 105 42, 220

Alpine Investments BV v Minister van Financien Case C-384/93 [1995] ECR I-1141 123

Angelopharm GmbH v Freie und Hansestadt Hamburg Case C-212/91 [1994] ECR I-171, 21 BMLR 80 251, 289

ANOZ Case C-156/01 [2003] ECR I-7045 115

AOK Bundesverband v Ichthyol-Gesellschaft Cases C-264/01, C-306/01, C-354/01 and C-355/01 [2004] All ER (D) 290 (Mar) 322, 393

Aragonesa de Publicidad Exterior SA and Publivia SAE v Departamento de Sanidad y Seguridao Social de la Generalitat de Cataluna Cases C-1/90 and C-176/90 [1991] ECR I-4151, [1994] 1 CMLR 887 91

Arantis v Land Berlin Case C-164/94 [1996] ECR I-135 228

Arcaro (criminal proceedings against) Case C-168/95 [1996] ECR I-4705, [1997] All ER (EC) 82 42

Artegodan GmbH v European Commissoin Cases T-76/00, T-83/00-T-85/00, T-137/00 and T-141/00 [2002] ECR II-4945, 72 BMLR 34 361

B

Badische Erfrischungs-Getränke GmbH & Co KG v Land BadenWürttemberg Case C-17/96 [1997] ECR I-4617, [1998] 1 CMLR 341 351

Baumbast v Secretary of State for the Home Department Case C-413/99 [2002] ECR I-7091, [2002] 3 CMLR 599 118, 340

Bayer AG v European Commission Case T-41/96 [2000] ECR II-3383, [2001] All ER (EC) 1 319

BECTU. *See* R (BECTU) v Secretary of State for Trade and Industry.
Belgian State v Humbel Case 263/86 [1988] ECR 5365, [1989] 1 CMLR 393 119, 120, 135
Bellon (criminal proceedings against) Case C-42/90 [1990] ECR I-4863 91, 92
Bergaderm. *See* Laboratoires Pharmaceutiques Bergaderm SA v EC Commission.
Bernàldez (Ruiz) (criminal proceedings against) Case C-129/94 [1996] ECR I-1829, [1996] All ER (EC) 741 42
Best v Wellcome Foundation Ltd [1994] 5 Med LR 81, 17 BMLR 111, Ir S Ct 282
Bestuur van het Algemeen Ziekenfonds Dreuthe-Platteland v Pierik (No 1) Case 117/77 [1978] ECR 825, [1978] 3 CMLR 343 115, 116
Bestuur van het Algemeen Ziekenfonds Dreuthe-Platteland v Pierik (No 2) Case 182/78 [1979] ECR 1977, [1980] 2 CMLR 88 116, 151
Bond van Adverteerders v Netherlands Case 352/85 [1988] ECR 2085, [1989] 3 CMLR 113 120
Borrell. *See* Colegio Oficial de Agentes de la Propiedad Immobiliaria v JL Aguirre Borrell.
Brandsma (criminal proceedings against) Case C-293/94 [1996] ECR I-3159, [1996] All ER (EC) 837 91
Brasserie du Pêcheur SA v Germany; R v Secretary of State for Transport, ex p Factortame Cases C-46 and 48/93 [1996] ECR I-1029, [1996] QB 404, [1996] 2 WLR 506, [1996] All ER (EC) 301 43, 220
Brenner v Manson 383 US 519, 86 SCt (1966) 265
Brunner v European Union Treaty [1994] 1 CMLR 57 65
Buet and Educational Business Services (EBS) v Ministère Public Case 382/87 [1989] ECR 1235, [1993] 3 CMLR 659 99
Burbaud v Ministère de l'Emploi et de la Solidarité Case C-285/01 [2003] 3 CMLR 635 211

C

Campus Oil Ltd v Minister for Industry and Energy Case C-72/83 [1984] ECR 2727, [1984] 3 CMLR 544 141
Carni. *See* Ligur Carni Srl v Unita Sanitarie Locali nos XV e XIX.
Cassis de Dijon. *See* Rewe-Zentral AG v Bundesmonopolverwaltung fr Branntwein.
Centrafarm BV and Adriaan De Peijper v Sterling Drug Inc Case 15/74 [1974] ECR 1147, [1974] 2 CMLR 480 45
Centrafarm BV v Winthrop Case 16/74 [1974] ECR 1183, [1974] 2 CMLR 480 45
CIA Security International SA v Signalson Case C-194/94 [1996] ECR I-220, [1996] All ER (EC) 557 42
CILFIT Srl and Lanificio de Gavardo v Ministry of Health Case 283/81 [1982] ECR 3415, [19839] 1 CMLR 472 175

Colegio Oficial de Agentes de la Propiedad Immobiliaria v JL Aguirre Borrell Case C-104/91 [1992] ECR I-3003 216

Compassion in World Farming. *See* R v Minister of Agriculture, Fisheries and Food, ex p Compassion in World Farming.

Conseil National de l'Ordre des Architectes v Dreessen Case C-31/00 [2002] ECR I-663, [2002] All ER (EC) 423 217

Coonan v Insurance Officer Case 110/79 [1980] ECR 1445 125

Costa v ENEL Case 6/64 [1964] ECR 585, [1964] CMLR 425 44

Cowan v Trésor Public Case 186/87 [1989] ECR 195, [1990] 2 CMLR 613 121

Customs and Excise Commissioners v Schindler Case C-275/92 [1994] ECR I-1039, [1994] QB 610, [1994] 3 WLR 103, [1994] 2 All ER 193 121, 123, 124, 150

D

De Peijper. *See* Officier van Justitie v De Peijper.

Deak. *See* Official National de l'emploi v Deak.

Debus (criminal proceedings against) Cases C-13/91 and C-113/91 [1992] ECR I-3617 92

Decker v Caisse de Maladie des Employées Prives Case C-120/95 [1998] ECR I-1831, [1998] All ER (EC) 673 45, 47, 80, 111, 125, 141, 194, 214, 228, 322, 393

Defrenne v Sabena (No 2) Case 43/75 [1976] ECR 455, [1981] 1 All ER 122 42

Delattre Case C-369/88 [1991] ECR I-1487, [1993] 2 CMLR 445 91, 251, 289, 320, 393

Denkavit Futtermittel GmbH v Minister Für Ernahrung Case 251/78 [1979] ECR 3369, [1980] 3 CMLR 513 92

Denmark v European Commission (Food Additives) Case C-3/00 [2003] ECR I-2643 352

Deutscher Apothekerverband v 0800 DocMorris and Waterval Case C-322/01 [2003] All ER (D) 213 (Dec) 47, 213, 322, 428, 429-431

Deutsche Paracelsus Schulen für Naturheilverfahren GbmH v Gräbner Case C-294/00 [2002] ECR I-6515 228

Dillenkofer v Germany Cases C-178-9, C-179/94, C-188/94 and C-190/94 [1996] ECR I-2553, [1997] QB 259, [1997] 2 WLR 253, [1996] All ER (EC) 917 43, 220

Distillers Co (Biochemicals) Ltd v Thompson [1971] AC 458, [1971] 2 WLR 441, [1971] 1 All ER 694 282

Duphar BV v Netherlands Case 238/82 [1984] ECR 523, [1985] 1 CMLR 256 111, 130, 194, 318, 322

E

EC Commission v Austria (Transparency Directive) Case C-424/99 [2001] ECR I-9285 324

EC Commission v Belgium (Clinical Biology Laboratories) Case 221/85 [1987] ECR 719, [1988] 1 CMLR 620 201

EC Commission v Belgium Case C-249/88 [1991] ECR I-1275, [1993] 2 CMLR 533, 23 BMLR 65 325
EC Commission v Denmark Case 252/83 [1986] ECR 3713, [1981] 2 CMLR 743 123
EC Commission v EC Council (Animal glands and organs) Case 131/87 [1989] ECR 3743 85, 93
EC Commission v EC Council (Beef Labelling) Case C-269/97 [2000] ECR I-2257 85, 86, 87, 93
EC Commission v EC Council (Tariff Preferences) Case 45/86 [1987] ECR 1483, [1988] 2 CMLR 131 73, 85
EC Commission v EC Council (Titanium Dioxide) Case C-300/89 [1991] ECR I-2867, [1993] 3 CMLR 359 85, 93, 100, 103
EC Commission v EC Council (Waste Directive) Case C-155/91 [1999] ECR I-939 85, 93, 103
EC Commission v France (Alcohol Advertising) Case 152/78 [1980] ECR 2299, [1981] 2 CMLR 743 91
EC Commission v France (Establishment of Doctors and Dentists) Case 96/85 [1986] ECR 1475, [1986] 3 CMLR 57 202, 203
EC Commission v France (Insurance Services) Case 22/83 [1986] ECR 3663 123
EC Commission v France (Re Tourist Guides) Cases C-154/89 [1991] ECR I-659 121, 123
EC Commission v France Case 96/85 [1986] ECR 1475, [1986] 3 CMLR 57 200
EC Commission v France Case C-344/89 [1992] ECR I-3245 91
EC Commission v France Case C-381/93 [1994] ECR I-5145, [1995] 2 CMLR 485 122
EC Commission v Germany (Beer Purity) Case 178/84 [1987] ECR 1227, [1988] 1 CMLR 780 47, 56, 92, 353
EC Commission v Germany (Lawyers' Services) Case 427/85 [1988] ECR 1123, [1989] 2 CMLR 677 124
EC Commission v Germany (Meat products) Case 153/78 [1979] ECR 2555, [1980] 1 CMLR 198 92
EC Commission v Germany Case 205/84 EC [1986] ECR 3755, [1987] 2 CMLR 69 123, 124
EC Commission v Germany Case C-290/90 [1992] ECR I-3317 251, 289
EC Commission v Germany Case C-62/90 [1992] ECR I-2575, [1992] 2 CMLR 549 213, 214, 320, 393
EC Commission v Greece Case C-154/00 [2002] ECR I-3879 312
EC Commission v Greece Case C-205/89 [1991] ECR I-1361, [1994] 2 CMLR 123 92
EC Commission v Greece Case C-293/89 [1992] ECR I-4577 91
EC Commission v Ireland Case 206/84 [1986] ECR 3817, [1987] 2 CMLR 150 123

EC Commission v Italy (Art Treasures) Case 7/68 [1968] ECR 617, [1969] CMLR 1 213
EC Commission v Italy (Curds) Case 35/84 [1986] ECR 545 91
EC Commission v Italy Case 39/72 [1973] ECR 101, [1973] CMLR 439 42
EC Commission v Italy Case 56/87 [1988] ECR 2919, [198] 3 CMLR 707 322
EC Commission v Italy Case C-202/99 [2001] ECR I-9319 206, 226, 399
EC Commission v Italy Case C-228/91 [1993] ECR I-2701 92
EC Commission v Italy Case C-307/94 [1996] ECR I-1011 226
EC Commission v Italy Case C-95/89 [1992] ECR I-4545 91
EC Commission v Luxembourg Case C-450/00 [2001] ECR I-7069 187
EC Commission v UK (Pasteurised Milk) Case 261/85 [1988] ECR 547, [1988] 2 CMLR 11 92
EC Commission v UK (Product Liability Directive) Case C-300/95 [1997] ECR I-2649, [1977] All ER (EC) 481 309, 310
EC Commission v UK (Turkeys) Case 40/82 [1982] ECR 2793, [1982] 3 CMLR 497 92
EC Commission v UK (UHT Milk) Case 124/81 [1983] ECR 203, [1983] 2 CMLR 1 47
Einberger v Hauptzollamt Freiburg (No 2) Case 294/82 [1984] ECR 1177, [1985] 1 CMLR 765 149
Elliniki Radiofonia-Tileorasi AE (ERT) Case C-260/98 [1991] ECR I-2925 406
Emmott v Minister for Social Welfare and A-G Case C-208/90 [1991] ECR I-4269, [1991] 3 CMLR 894 42
ERT. *See* Elliniki Radiofonia-Tileorasi AE.
European Commission v France (Medical Reagents) Case C-55/99 [2000] ECR I-11499 91, 320, 393
European Commission v France Case C-250/98 [1999] ECR I-2447 226
European Commission v France Case C-152/00 [2002] ECR I-3827 312
European Commission v Spain Case C-232/99 [2002] ECR I-4235 211, 226
European Parliament v EC Council (Transport of Waste) Case C-187/93 [1994] ECR I-2857, [1995] 2 CMLR 309 93, 103
European Parliament v EC Council (Linguistic Diversity) Case C-42/97 [1999] ECR I-869 103
European Parliament v EC Council (Radioactive contamination of foodstuffs) Case C-70/88 [1991] ECR I-4529 85, 94
European Parliament v EU Council (Edicom) Case C-271/94 [1996] ECR I-1689, [1996] 2 CMLR 481 85
European Patent Office Case No T19/90 [1990] 1 EPOR 4; [1990] 7 EPOR 501; OJ EPO 10/1992 261
Even. *See* Ministère Public v Even.
Eyssen. *See* Officier van Justitie v Koninklijke Kaasfabriek Eyssen.

F

F, Re [1990] 2 AC 1, [1989] 2 WLR 1025, [1989] 2 All ER 545 17, 150, 258
Factortame. *See* R v Secretary of State for Transport, ex p Factortame Ltd (No 2).

Farquhar v Murray (1901) 3 F 859, 9 SLT 45 11

Foster v British Gas plc Case C-188/89 [1990] ECR I-3313, [1991] 1 QB 405, [1991] 2 WLR 258, [1990] 3 All ER 897 42, 197, 220

Francovich and Bonifaci v Italy Cases C-6 and 9/90 [1991] ECR I-5357, [1993] 2 CMLR 66 43, 220

Frans-Nederlandse Maatschappij voor Biologische Producten BV (criminal proceedings against) Case 272/80 [1981] ECR 3277, [1982] 2 CMLR 497 47, 91

Freistaat Bayern v Eurim-Pharm GbmH Case C-347/89 [1991] ECR I-1747, [1993] 1 CMLR 616 213

G

GB-INNO-BM v Confederation du Commerce Luxembourgeois Case C-362/88 [1990] ECR I-667, [1991] 2 CMLR 801 121, 123

Gebhard v Consiglio dell'Ordine degli Avvocati e Procuration di Milano Case C-55/94 [1995] ECR I-4165, [1996] All ER (EC) 189 119, 123, 200

Geraets-Smits v Stichting Ziekenfonds VGZ, Peerbooms v Stichting CZ Groep Zorgverzekeringen Case C-157/99 [2001] ECRI-5473, [2002] QB 409, [2002] 2 WLR 154, [2003] All ER (EC) 481 45, 111, 117, 120, 122, 124, 125, 128, 129, 130, 131, 132, 134, 135, 137, 139, 140, 141, 144, 194, 393, 418

Germany v EC Commission Case C-359/92 (General Product Safety) [1994] ECR I-3681, [1995] 2 CMLR 461 94, 95

Germany v EC Commission Cases 281, 283-5, 287/85 [1987] ECR 3203 40, 70

Germany v European Parliament and Council (Deposit Guarantees) Case C-233/94 [1997] ECR I-2405 85, 93

Germany v European Parliament and Council (Tobacco Advertising) Case C-376/98 [2000] ECR I-8419, [2000] All ER (EC) 769 57, 94, 96–100, 101, 102, 103, 104, 105, 106, 181, 269, 278, 288, 375, 378, 382, 383, 411

Gouda. *See* Stichting Collectieve Antennevoorziening Gouda v Commissariaat voor de Media.

Gourmet International Products. *See* Konsumentombudsmannen (KO) v Gourmet International Products AB.

Gräbner. *See* Deutsche Paracelsus Schulen für Naturheilverfahren GbmH v Gräbner.

Grad v Finanzamt Traunstein Case 9/70 [1970] ECR 825, [1971] CMLR 1 42

Gravier v City of Liege Case 293/86 [1985] ECR 593, [1985] 3 CMLR 1 120

Grimaldi v Fonds des Maladies Professionnelles Case C-322/88 [1989] ECR 4407 61

Grzelczyk v Centre public d'Aide Sociale d'Ottignies-Louvain-la-Neuve Case C-184/99 [2001] ECR I-6193, [2000] All ER (EC) 385 118, 340

Guiot and Climatec (criminal proceedings against) Case C-272/94 [1996] ECR I-1905 121, 124

Gulling v Consel de l'Ordre des Avocats due Barreau de Colmar Case 292/86 [1988] ECR 111, [1990] 1 QB 234, [1989] 3 WLR 705 124, 203

H

H v Norway (1990) App No 170004/90 402

Haim v Kassenzahnärtzliche Vereinigung Nordrhein Case C-319/92 [1994] ECR I-425, [1994] 2 CMLR 169 231, 232

Harpegnies Case C-400/96 [1998] ECR I-5121 91

Hauptzollamt Bremerhaven v Massey-Ferguson Case 8/73 [1973] ECR 897 88, 103

Hauptzollamt Mainz v CE Kupferberg & Cie KG Case 104/81 [1982] ECR 3641, [1983] 1 CMLR 1 42

Heijn (Albert) BV Case 94/83 [1984] ECR 3263 91

Henning Veedfald v Arhus Amtskommune Case C-203/99 [2001] ECR I-3569, [2003] 1 CMLR 1217 308, 397

Hocsman (Hugo Fernando) v Ministre de l'Emploi et de la Solidarité Case C-238/98 [2000] ECR I-6623, [2000] All ER (EC) 899 232

Horvath v Hauptzollamt Hamburg-Jonas Case 50/80 [1980] ECR 385, [1982] 2 CMLR 522 149

Hünermund v Landesapothekerkammer Baden-Württemburg Case C-292/92 [1993] ECR I-6787 47

I

Idryma Koinonikon Asfaleseon (IKA) v Ionnidis Case C-326/00 [2003] ECR I-1703, [2004] QB 137, [2003] 3 WLR 1540, [2003] All ER (EC) 548, [2003] 1 CMLR 965 115, 117

IKA. *See* Idryma Koinonikon Asfaleseon (IKA) v Ionnidis.

Inizan v Caisse primaire d'assurance maladie des Hauts-de-Seine Case C-56/01 [2003] All ER (D) 398 (Oct) 132, 134, 135, 137, 140, 144, 393

Internationale Handelsgesellschaft mbH v Einfuhr und Vorratsstelle für Getreide und Futtermittel Case 11/70 [1970] ECR 1125 66, 167, 405

Inzirillo v Caisse d'Allocations Familiales de l'Arrondissement de Lyon Case 63/76 [1976] ECR 2057 118

J

Jany v Staatssecretaris van Justitie Case C-268/99 [2001] ECR I-8615, [2003] All ER (EC) 193, [2003] 2 CMLR 1 150

Johnson Case 224/84 [1986] ECR 1651 324

K

Keck and Mithouard Cases C-267/91 and 268/91 [1993] ECR I-6097, [1995] 1 CMLR 101 47, 429

Kemikalieinspektionen Toolex Alpha AB Case C-473/98 [2000] ECR I-5681 47, 91

Kempf v Staatssecretaris van Justitie Case 139/85 [1986] ECR 1741, [1987] 1 CMLR 764 120

Klopp. *See* Ordre des Avocats au Barreau de Paris v Klopp.

Köbler v Austria Case C-224/01 [2004] 2 WLR 976, [2004] All ER (EC) 23, [2003] 3 CMLR 1003 43, 64

Kohll v Union des Caisses de Maladie Case C-158/96 [1998] ECR I-1931, [1998] All ER (EC) 673, [1998] 2 CMLR 928 45, 47, 80, 120, 122, 124, 125, 126, 127, 128, 132, 134, 135, 141, 144, 157, 194, 214, 322, 393, 417, 418, 431

Konsumentombudsmannen (KO) v Gourmet International Products AB Case C-405/98 [2001] ECR I-1795, [2001] All ER (EC) 308 91

Kortmann. *See* Officier van Justitie v Kortmann.

Kupferberg. *See* Hauptzollamt Mainz v CE Kupferberg & Cie KG.

L

Laboratoires Pharmaceutiques Bergaderm SA v EC Commission Case T-199/96 [1998] ECR II-2805, 62 BMLR 179 361

Landeshauptstadt Kiel v Jaeger Case C-151/02 [2003] 3 CMLR 493, [2003] IRLR 804 196

Lawrie-Blum v Land Baden-Württemberg Case C-66/85 [1986] ECR 2121, [1987] 3 CMLR 389 200

Leclerc-Siplec. *See* Société d'Importation Edouard Leclerc-Siplec v TF1 Publicité SA.

Levin v Secretary of State for Justice Case 53/81 [1982] ECR 1035, [1982] 2 CMLR 454 120

Ligur Carni Srl v Unita Sanitarie Locali nos XV e XIX Cases C-277/91, C-318/91 and C-319/91 [1993] ECR I-6621 92

Lindqvist (criminal proceedings against) Case C-101/01 [2004] All ER (EC) 561, [2004] IP & T 469 167, 171

Loveday v Renton [1990] 1 Med LR 117 282

Luisi and Carbone v Ministero del Tesoro Cases 286/82 and 26/83 [1984] ECR 377 120, 121, 122, 149

M

Maria Victoria Gonzales Sanchez v Medicina Asturiana SA Case C-183/00 [2002] ECR I-3901 312

Marks & Spencer plc v Commissioners of Customs and Excise Case C-62/00 [2002] ECR I-6325, [2003] QB 866, [2003] 2 WLR 665 42

Marleasing SA v La Comercial Internacional de Alimentacion SA Case C-106/89 [1990] ECR I-4135, [1992] 1 CMLR 305 42

Marshall v Southampton and South West Hampshire Area Health Authority (Teaching) Case 152/84 [1986] ECR 723, [1986] QB 401, [1986] 2 WLR 780, [1986] 2 All ER 584 42

Marshall v Southampton and South West Hampshire Area Health Authority (No 2) Case C-271/91 [1993] ECR I-4367, [1994] QB 126, [1993] 3 WLR 1054, [1993] 4 All ER 586 42

Martinez Sala. *See* Sala v Freistaat Bayern.

Melkunie (CMC) BV Case 97/83 [1984] ECR 2367 91

Meroni & Co, Industrie Metallurgiche SpA v High Authority Case 9/56 [1957–58] ECR 133 50

Ministère Public v Auer Case 136/78 [1979] ECR 437, [1979] 2 CMLR 373 204

Ministère Public v Even Case 207/78 [1979] ECR 2019, [1980] 2 CMLR 71
118
Ministère Public v Mirepoix Case 54/85 [1986] ECR 1067, [1987] 2 CMLR 44
91
Ministère Public v Muller Case 304/84 [1986] ECR 1511, [1987] 2 CMLR 467
91, 92, 359
Mirepoix. *See* Ministère Public v Mirepoix.
MMR/MR Litigation: Sayers and others v Smithkline Beecham plc and others, Re [2002] EWHC 1280, [2002] All ER (D) 230 (Jun) 282
Monsanto Agricola Italia SpA v Perzidenza del Consiglio dei Ministri Case C-236/01 [2003] All ER (D) 95 (Sep) 361
Monteil and Samanni, Re Case C-60/89 [1991] ECR I-1547, [1992] 3 CMLR 425
91, 251, 289, 320, 393
Moore v University of California 793 P2d 479 Cal (1990) 263, 267
Moormann. *See* Oberkreisdirektor des Kreises Borken v Handelsondernening Moormann BV.
Motte Case 247/84 [1985] ECR 388, [1987] 1 CMLR 663 91, 92, 359
MS v Sweden (1997) 28 EHRR 313, (1997) 45 BMLR 133 163
Muller. *See* Ministère Public v Muller.
Müller-Fauré v Onderlinge Waarborgmaat-schappij OZ Zorgverzekeringen UA, van Riet v Onderlinge Waarborgmaat-schappij ZAO Zorgverzekeringen Case C-385/99 [2003] ECR I-4509 120, 122, 131, 132, 134, 135, 136, 137, 138, 140, 141, 144, 156, 393

N

Napp Pharmaceutical Holdings Ltd v Director General of Fair Trading (2002) 69 BMLR 69, CCAT 319
Netherlands v European Parliament and Council (Biotechnology Directive) Case C-377/98 [2001] ECR I-7079, [2002] All ER (EC) 97, [2001] 3 CMLR 1173
93, 262, 269, 407, 408
Nold (J) KG v EC Commission Case 4/73 [1974] ECR 491, [1974] 2 CMLR 3
25, 66, 167, 405

O

Oberkreisdirektor des Kreises Borken v Handelsondernening Moormann BV Case 190/87 [1988] ECR 4689, [1990] 1 CMLR 656 53, 92
Official National de l'emploi v Deak Case 94/84 [1985] ECR 1873 113
Officier van Justitie v De Peijper Case 104/75 [1976] ECR 613, [1976] 2 CMLR 271
91, 320, 393
Officier van Justitie v Koninklijke Kaasfabriek Eyssen Case 53/80 [1981] ECR 409, [1982] 2 CMLR 20 91
Officier van Justitie v Kortmann Case 32/80 [1981] ECR 251, [1982] 3 CMLR 46
91, 320, 393
Officier van Justitie v Sandoz Case 174/82 [1983] ECR 2445, [1984] 3 CMLR 557
91, 92

Open Door Counselling and Dublin Well Woman v Ireland (1992) 15 EHRR 244 402
Opinion 2/94, pursuant to Article 228(6) of the EC Treaty [1996] ECR I-1759, [1996] 2 CMLR 265 73
Ordre des Avocats au Barreau de Paris v Klopp Case 107/83 [1984] ECR 2971, [1985] QB 711, [1985] 2 WLR 1058 200
Ortscheit (Lucien) GmbH v Eurim-Pharm Arzneimittel GmbH Case C-320/93 [1994] ECR I-5243, [1995] 2 CMLR 242 91
Österreichischer Rundfunk. *See* Rechnungschof v Österreichischer Rundfunk.

P

Paraschi v Landesversicherungsanstalt Wrttemberg Case C-349/87 [1991] ECR I-4501, [1994] 2 CMLR 240 125
Parliament. *See* European Parliament.
Paton v UK (1980) 3 EHRR 408 402
Patrick v Ministre des Affairs Culturelles Case 11/77 [1977] ECR 1199, [1977] 2 CMLR 523 200
Pfizer Animal Health SA v European Council Case T-13/99 [2002] ECR II-3305 361
Pierik. *See* Bestuur van het Algemeen Ziekenfonds Dreuthe-Platteland v Pierik.
Piscitello v Instituto Nazionale della Previdenza Sociale (INPS) Case 139/82 [1983] ECR 1427, [1984] 1 CMLR 108 113
Pistre v Caisse Autonome Nationale de Compensation de l'Assurance Vieillesse des Artisans (Cancava), Poucet v Assurances Générales de France (AGF) and Caisse Mutuelle Régionale du Languedoc-Roussillon (Camulrac) Cases 159/91 and 160/91 [1993] ECR I-637 111, 194
Plaumann & Co v EC Commission Case 25/62 [1963] ECR 95, [1964] CMLR 29 407
Portugal v EU Council (India Development Cooperation) [Case C-268/94 1996] ECR I-6177, [1997] 3 CMLR 331 88, 90
Poucet and Pistre. *See* Pistre v Caisse Autonome Nationale de Compensation de l'Assurance Vieillesse des Artisans (Cancava), Poucet v Assurances Générales de France (AGF) and Caisse Mutuelle Régionale du Languedoc-Roussillon (Camulrac).
Pretty v UK (2002) 35 EHRR 1, [2002] 2 FCR 97, 66 BMLR 147 27
PreussenElektra AG v Schleswag AG Case C-379/98 [2001] ECR I-2099, [2001] All ER (EC) 330, [2001] 2 CMLR 833 47
Procureur de la République v Tissier Case C-35/85 [1986] ECR 1207, [1987] 1 CMLR 551 251, 289
Procureur du Roi v Dassonville Case 8/74 [1974] ECR 837, [1974] 2 CMLR 436 44, 47, 121, 429
Procureur du Roi v Debauve Case 52/79 [1980] ECR 833, [1981] 2 CMLR 362 379

Pubblico Ministero v Ratti Case 148/78 [1979] ECR 1629, [1980] 1 CMLR 96 42, 53, 92
R (on the application of BECTU) v Secretary of State for Trade and Industry Case C-173/99 [2001] ECR I-4881, [2001] 1 WLR 1313, [2001] All ER (EC) 647 61
R (on the application of British American Tobacco (Investments) Ltd) v Secretary of State for Health Case C-491/01 [2002] ECR I-11453, [2003] All ER (EC) 604, [2003] 1 CMLR 395 57, 99, 101, 102, 103, 104, 105, 378
R (on the application of H) v London North and East Region Mental Health Review Tribunal London [2001] EWCA Civ 415, [2002] QB 1, [2001] 3 WLR 512, 61 BMLR 163 25
R (on the application of Pretty) v DPP [2001] UKHL 61, [2002 1 AC 800, [2001] 3 WLR 1598, [2002] 1 All ER 1 25, 403
R (on the application of Rose) v Secretary of State for Health [2002] EWCHC 1593 (Admin) [2002] 2 FLR 962, 69 BMLR 83 25
R (on the application of Yvonne Watts) v Bedford Primary Care Trust and Secretary of State for Health [2003] EWHC 2228 (Admin), 77 BMLR 26 3, 120, 134, 135, 138, 157, 397, 409
R (on the application of Pfizer Ltd) v Secretary of State for Health [2002] EWCA Civ 1566, [2003] 1 CMLR 642, 70 BMLR 219 318, 326
R v Cambridge District Health Authority, ex p B [1995] 1 WLR 898, [1995] 2 All ER 129 109
R v Department of Health, ex p Source Informatics Ltd [2001] QB 424, [2000] 2 WLR 940, [2000] 1 All ER 786 CA 162, 174, 175, 177
R v Ethical Committee of St Mary's Hospital (Manchester), ex p H [1988] 1 FLR 512, [1988] Fam Law 165 109
R v Human Fertilisation and Embryology Authority, ex p Blood [1999] Fam 151, [1997] 2 WLR 806, [1997] 2 All ER 687 3, 65, 150, 151, 154, 389, 403
R v Kirk Case 63/83 [1984] ECR 2689, [1985] 1 All ER 453, [1984] 3 CMLR 522 66
R v Minister of Agriculture, Fisheries and Food and Secretary of State for Health, ex p Fedesa and others Case C-331/88 [1990] ECR I-4023, [1991] 1 CMLR 507 85, 86, 93
R v Minister of Agriculture, Fisheries and Food, ex p Compassion in World Farming Case C-1/96 [1998] ECR I-1251, [1998] All ER (C) 302 53
R v North West Lancashire HA, ex p A, D, and G [2000] 1 WLR 977, [2000] 2 FCR 525 109
R v Royal Pharmaceutical Society of Great Britain, ex p Association of Pharmaceutical Importers and others Cases 266 and 267/87 [1989] ECR 1295 91, 320, 393
R v Secretary of State for Health and others, ex p Imperial Tobacco Case C-74/99 [2000] ECR I-8599 97, 308

R v Secretary of State for Health, ex p Goldstein [1993] 2 CMLR 589 206, 399
R v Secretary of State for Health, ex p Pfizer Ltd [1999] 3 CMLR 875, 51 BMLR 189 318, 326
R v Secretary of State for Social Services, ex p Hincks (1980) 1 BMLR 93 109
R v Secretary of State for Transport, ex p Factortame (No 3) Case C-221/89 [1991] ECR I-3905, [1992] QB 680, [1992] 3 WLR 288, [19991] 3 All ER 769 200
R v Secretary of State for Transport, ex p Factortame Ltd (No 2) Case C-213/89 [1990] ECR I-2433, [1991] 1 AC 603, [1990] 3 WLR 818, [1991] 1 All ER 70 42, 45
Ramrath v Ministre de la Justice Case C-106/91 [1992] ECR I-3351, [1992] 3 CMLR 173 124
Ratti. *See* Pubblico Ministero v Ratti.
Rechnungschof v Österreichischer Rundfunk Cases C-465/00, C-138/01 and C-139/01 [2003] 3 CMLR 265 167, 168
Reina v Landeskreditbank Baden-Württemburg Case 65/81 [1982] ECR 33, [1982] 1 CMLR 744 118
Rewe-Zentral AG v Bundesmonopolverwaltung für Branntwein (Cassis de Dijon) Case 120/78 [1979] ECR 649, [1979] 3 CMLR 494 46, 55, 90, 200, 213, 352, 429
Reyners v Belgium Case 2/74 [1974] ECR 631, [1974] 2 CMLR 305 200
Rothmans Case T-188/97 [1999] ECR II-2463 50
Roussel Laboratoria BV v Netherlands Case 181/82 [1983] ECR 3849, [1985] 1 CMLR 834 322
Rutili v Minister for the Interior Case 36/75 [1975] ECR 1219, [1976] 1 CMLR 140 122, 202

S

Säger v Dennemeyer & Co Ltd Case C-76/90 [1991] ECR I-4221, [1993] 3 CMLR 639 121, 123, 124
Sala v Freistaat Bayern Case C-85/96 [1998] ECR I-2691, [1998] All ER (D) 206 118, 340
Salamander AG v European Parliament and Council Cases T-172/98 and 177-8/98 [2000] ECR II-2487, [2000] All ER (EC) 754 97
Sandoz Prodotti Farmaceutici SpA v EC Commission Case C-277/87 [1990] ECR I-45 319
Sandoz. *See* Officier van Justitie v Sandoz.
Schindler. *See* Customs and Excise Commissioners v Schindler.
Schloh v Auto Controle Technique SPRL Case 50/985 [1986] ECR 1855, [1987] 1 CMLR 450 91
Schumacher v Hauptzollamt Frankfürt am Main-Ost Case 215/87 [1989] ECR 617, [1990] 2 CMLR 465 213, 214, 320, 393, 431
SETTG. *See* Syndemos ton en Elladi Touristikon Kai Taxidiotikon Grafeion v Conselleria de Sanidad v Consumo de la Generalidad valenciana (SETTG).

SIMAP. *See* Sindicato de Medicos de Asistencia Publica (SIMAP) v Conselleria de Sanidad y Consumo de la Generalidad Valenciana.

Sindicato de Medicos de Asistencia Publica (SIMAP) v Conselleria de Sanidad y Consumo de la Generalidad Valenciana Case C-303/98 [2000] ECR I-7963, [2001] All ER (EC) 609 195, 196, 198

Snellers Autos BV v Algemeen Directeur van de Dienst Wegverkeer Case C-314/98 [2000] ECR I-8633 91

Societe d'Importation Edouard Leclerc-Siplec v TF1 Publicité SA Case 412/93 [1995] ECR I-179, [1995] All ER (EC) 343, [1995] 3 CMLR 422 47

Society for the Protection of the Unborn Child Ireland Ltd v Grogan Case C-159/90 [1991] ECR I-4685, [1991] 3 CMLR 849, 9 BMLR 100 65, 120, 121, 123, 149, 150, 152

Sodemare SA v Regione Lombardia Case C-70/95 [1997] ECR I-3395, [1998] 4 CMLR 667 111, 194, 200, 201, 322, 392

Sotgiu v Deutsche Bundespost Case 152/73 [1974] ECR 153 118

Spain v EU Council (Supplementary Patent Protection Certificate) Case C-350/92 [1995] ECR I-1985, [1996] 1 CMLR 415, 34 BMLR 192 95

SPUC. *See* Society for the Protection of the Unborn Child Ireland Ltd v Grogan.

Stauder v City of Ulm Case 29/69 [1969] ECR 419, [1970] CMLR 112 66, 167, 405

Steymann v Staatssecretaris van Justite Case 196/87 [1988] ECR 6159, [1989] 1 CMLR 449 120

Stichting Collectieve Antennevoorziening Gouda v Commissariaat voor de Media Case C-288/89 [1991] ECR I-4007 124

Stöber and Piosa Pereira v Bundesanstalt für Arbeit Cases C-4 & 5/95 [1997] ECR I-511 125

Syndemos ton en Elladi Touristikon Kai Taxidiotikon Grafeion v Conselleria de Sanidad v Consumo de la Generalidad valenciana (SETTG) Case C-398/95 [1997] ECR I-3091, [1998] 1 CMLR 20 132

T

Tankstation't Heukske VOF and JBE Boermans (criminal proceedings against) Cases C-400/92 and 402/92 [1994] ECR I-2199, [1995] 3 CMLR 501 47

Tarbuck, Blood, Blood, Blood v Secretary of State for Health (28 February 2003, unreported) 154

Tawil-Albertini v Ministre des Affaires Sociales Case C-154/93 [1994] ECR I-451, [1993] 1 CMLR 612 230, 231, 232

Tedeschi v Denkavit Commerciale srl Case 5/77 [1977] ECR 1555 91, 92

Ter Voort Case C-219/91 [1992] ECR I-5485, [1995] 2 CMLR 591, 30 BMLR 165 251, 289

Thieffry v Conseil de l'Ordre des Avocats a la Court de Paris Case 71/76 [1977] ECR 765, [1978] QB 315, [1977] 3 WLR 453, [1997] 2 CMLR 373 123, 200, 201

Tissier. *See* Procureur de la République v Tissier.
Tögel (Walter) v Niederosterreichische Gabietskrankenkasse Case C-76/97 [1998] ECR I-5357, [1998] 3 CMLR 768 137
Toolex Alpha. *See* Kemikalieinspektionen Toolex Alpha AB.

U

U v V [1997] 1 FLR 282 150
UK v EC Commission (BSE) Case C-180/96 [1998] ECR I-2265, [1998] 2 CMLR 1125 86, 355
UK v EC Commission Case C-180/96R [1996] ECR I-3903, [1996] 3 CMLR 1 77, 355, 361
UK v EC Council (Battery Hens) Case 131/86 [1988] ECR 905, [1988] 2 CMLR 364 93
UK v EC Council (Hormones in Beef) Case 68/86 [1988] ECR 855, [1988] 2 CMLR 543 85, 86, 93
UK v EC Council (Working Time) Case C-84/94 [1996] ECR I-5755, [1996] All ER (EC) 877, [1996] 3 CMLR 671 41, 85, 93, 94, 194
UK v EC Council Case C-131/86 [1988] ECR 905 86
UNECTEF. *See* Union National des Entraineurs et Cadres Techniques Professionnels du Football (UNECTEF) v Heylens.
Unilever Italia Case C-443/98 [2000] ECR I-7535 42
Unión de Pequeños Agricultores (UPA) v European Council Case C-50/00P [2002] ECR I-6677, [2003] QB 893, [2003] 2 WLR 795, [2002] All ER (EC) 893 43, 407
Union National des Entraineurs et Cadres Techniques Professionnels du Football (UNECTEF) v Heylens Case C-222/86 [1987] ECR 4097, [1989] 1 CMLR 901 216, 217
United Foods NV v Belgium Case 132/80 [1981] ECR 995, [1982] 1 CMLR 273 91, 92
UPA. *See* Unión de Pequeños Agricutores v European Council.
Upjohn Co and Upjohn NV v Farzoo Inc and Kortmann Case C-112/89 [1991] ECR I-1703, [1993] 1 CMLR 657, 14 BMLR 79 251, 289

V

Van Bennekom Case C-227/82 [1983] ECR 3883, [1985] 2 CMLR 692 251, 289
Van Binsbergen v Bestuur van de Defrijfsvereniging voor de Metaalnijverheid Case 33/74 [1974] ECR 1299, [1975] 1 CMLR 298 123, 124
Van Broekmeulen v Huisarts Registratie Commissie Case 246/80 [1981] ECR 2311, [19829] CMLR 9 209, 210
Van der Veldt (criminal proceedings against) [1994] ECR I-3537, [1995] 1 CMLR 621 92 Case C-17/93
Van Duyn v Home Office Case 41/74 [1974] ECR 1337, [1975] Ch 358, [1975] 2 WLR 760, [1975] 3 All ER 190, [1975] 1 CMLR 1
van Gend en Loos. *See* Algemene Transport-en Expeditie Onderneming van Gend en Loos NV v Nederlandse Belastingadministratie.

Vanbraekel v Alliance National des Mutualites Chretiennes (ANMC) Case C-368/98 [2001] ECR I-5363, [2002] 2 CMLR 425 45, 120, 122, 124, 127, 128, 129, 132, 134, 135, 137, 144, 157, 393

Vander Elst v Office des Migrations Internationales Case C-43/93 [1994] ECR I-3803, [1995] 1 CMLR 513 121

Vlassopoulou v Ministerium für Justiz, Bundes-und Europaangelegenlieten Baden-Württemberg Case C-340/89 [1991] ECR I-2357, [1993] 2 CMLR 221 201, 216, 217, 231

Von Colson and Kamann v Land Nordrhein-Westfalen Case 14/83 [1984] ECR 1891, [1986] 2 CMLR 430 42

W

W v Egdell [1990] Ch 359, [1990] 2 WLR 471, [1990] 1 All ER 835 163

Wachauf v Germany Case 5/88 [1989] ECR 2609, [1991] 1 CMLR 328 66, 406

Wagner Miret Case C-334/92 [1993] ECR I-6911 v Fonds de Garanatia Salarial 42

Webb (Alfred John), Re Case 279/80 [1981] ECR 3305, [1982] 1 CMLR 719 120

Winterwerp v Netherlands (1979) 2 EHRR 387 23

Wirth v Landeshaupstadt Hannover Case C-109/92 [1993] ECR I-6447 120

Witzemann v Hauptzollamt Munchen-Mitte Case C-343/89 [1990] ECR I-4477, [1993] STC 108 149

X

X v Y [1988] 2 All ER 648, (1987) 3 BMLR 1 172

Z

Z v Finland (1997) 25 EHRR 371, 45 BMLR 107 163

Part One

1

Introduction

I. Health law and the European Union

In 1996, a young British woman, Diane Blood, sought to use sperm which had been collected from her recently deceased husband, Stephen Blood, while he was critically ill with meningitis. Although Stephen and Diane Blood had discussed having a family, crucially, Stephen had not given written consent for the taking of his sperm. In English law, the use of the sperm was prohibited under the UK Human Fertilisation and Embryology Act 1990.[1] However, relying on Diane Blood's EU law right to receive medical treatment in another Member State,[2] the English Court of Appeal granted Diane Blood permission to receive the treatment she sought in Belgium. Diane Blood subsequently gave birth to a son, Liam.[3] In 2003, another British woman, Yvonne Watts, sought a hip replacement for her arthritic hip in France, to avoid an NHS waiting list.[4] She then attempted to reclaim the cost of her treatment from her local National Health Service Trust. The Trust refused, and Yvonne Watts brought an action in the English High Court, challenging their decision, claiming that it was *ultra vires*, contrary to provisions of the UK Human Rights Act 1998, and contrary to her free movement rights under EU law. She lost on the facts, but the case is currently subject to an appeal and has been referred to the European Court of Justice.

In both these situations, the law of the EU had a direct impact on the legal entitlements to health care of "citizens of the European Union". In the case of Diane Blood, EU law helped her to receive the medical treatment she sought, in the face of clear British law providing that such treatment would be illegal in the UK. The EU's legal regime came into conflict with the UK's regulatory regime on the matter, with the consequence that, for Diane Blood at least, the UK's regulatory regime ceased to

1 *R v Human Fertilisation and Embryology Authority, ex parte Blood* [1997] 2 All ER 687; and see generally T. Hervey, "Buy Baby: The European Union and Regulation of Human Reproduction" 18 OJLS (1998) 207; D. Morgan and R. Lee, "In the Name of the Father? Ex parte Blood: Dealing with Novelty and Anomaly" 60 MLR (1997) 840.

2 Articles 59 and 60 EC.

3 For further discussion of the *Blood* case, see chapter 4.

4 *R (on the application of Yvonne Watts) v Bedford Primary Care Trust, Secretary of State for Health* [2003] EWHC 2228 (Admin), 1 October 2003.

be applicable. This story led us to the subject of enquiry and main research question for this book.

Health is not an area which is traditionally regarded as falling within the remit of EU law. There is no single entity entitled "European health law". However, as the Diane Blood story made clear, EU law may have an effect on national health law and policy. We wondered to what extent, and in what ways, EU law might have such an effect. The deceptively simple question – "how does EU law affect national health law and policy?" – led us to a very wide-ranging enquiry. If one adopts a broad definition of health law and policy, scarcely any part of that field remains completely untouched by EU law. We are interested not simply in the kind of "hard legal" effect at issue in the cases of Diane Blood or Yvonne Watts, in which justiciable rights emanating from EU law change the health law of Member States. We are also interested in the many ways in which EU and national legal norms interact in the health field, to produce results that might not have been produced without the existence of the EU. Of course, it is not possible to determine clear cause and effect in this way. Changes to national health laws and policies may come about as a result of many pressures, ranging from local to global.[5] The EU institutions do not act in isolation from international bodies, such as the World Health Organisation or the Council of Europe, and, where appropriate, we have explored these interactions.[6] However, our principal aim was simply to elaborate, and seek to understand, the contribution of the institutions of the EU, with its unique legal order, to national health laws and policies in the Member States of the EU.

The Community's developing competence in the health field (Article 152 EC) formed a starting point for our analysis. However, it rapidly became clear that investigating the impact of activities of the EU institutions on health law and policy would involve consideration of many other areas of Community competence, including, at least potentially, the law of the internal market in goods and services, freedom of movement of persons (patients and medical professionals), the common agricultural policy, transport policy, environmental policy, consumer protection, competition policy, research and technological development, development cooperation, and even some elements of the employment strand of social policy.[7] We would also need to include discussion of the EU's power to finance activities, such as educational programmes or medical research, as a potential force for convergence of national health systems.

Our research question was not to determine whether there should be a "European health law", in the sense of a harmonised set of health care or medical entitlements, applicable across the whole of the EU, determined by institutions at EU level. It is

5 See, for example, R. Freeman and M. Moran, "Reforming Health Care in Europe" 23 *West European Politics* (2000) 35.

6 See generally S. Fluss, "The Development of National Health Legislation in Europe: The Contribution of International Organisations" 2 *European Journal of Health Law* (1995) 193.

7 For further elaboration, see chapter 3, nn 83–90.

important to emphasise that, in this book, we are not setting out an agenda of what the EU *should* engage in. Rather, we are attempting to examine just how the EU has engaged, is engaging, and is likely to engage, with health policy and, especially, health law.

Nor was our research question to determine whether there is such a "European health law". It is already clear that the EU does not currently have "its own" health law or policy in this sense. In fact, as will become clear, we regard such a conceptualisation of the EU's legal order as fundamentally misconceived and unhelpful. Rather, we prefer to conceptualise the EU as a "constitutionalised" non-national polity or system of governance, within which institutions and other actors interact to formulate policy, determine legal norms, and allocate resources. While national (and sub-national) institutions within this polity are the primary locus for formation of health law and policy, and indeed of delivery of health care entitlements, the EU institutions also have a role to play.

Of course there are significant differences between the Member States of the EU in the provision of health care and the organisation of its delivery, and these differences will increase as the EU enlarges towards the east.[8] Moreover, even *within* some Member States, such differences may exist, in particular where responsibilities for health care are devolved to regional or other sub-national institutions. These differences arise for many interrelated reasons, including the historical, social, political and cultural. Each Member State of the EU preserves its own national health policy, as part of its unique social policy. These differences translate into differences in approach with respect to regulation and to interpretation of legal measures supporting national health systems. However, at least at a level of abstraction, "fundamental values", such as the sanctity of life,[9] dignity,[10] autonomy,[11] privacy, justice, and solidarity,[12] may be said to underpin all health regimes within the EU although the interpretation of those values may differ considerably in practice.

One key element of the EU's role may be seen in the protection of such "European values" inherent in European national health systems, in the context of increasing international economic pressures. Although each Member State of the EU preserves its own unique national health policy, at a more abstracted level it may be possible

8 See below nn 95–101.

9 Respect for the sanctity of life is common across a wide range of jurisdictions and faiths, although what precisely constitutes "sanctity of life" has been the subject of much debate and discussion: see generally J. Glover, *Causing Death and Saving Lives* (Harmondsworth: Penguin, 1990); P. Singer, *Rethinking Life and Death; the collapse of our traditional ethics* (Oxford: OUP, 1995); J. Keown, "Restoring Moral and Intellectual Shape to the Law After *Bland*" 113 LQR (1997) 481.

10 Dignity itself is a notoriously difficult concept to define. For a comprehensive and incisive examination of the literature surrounding the definition of dignity and an attempt to refine a workable concept, see D. Beyleveld and R. Brownsword, *Human Dignity in Bioethics and Biolaw* (Oxford: OUP, 2001).

11 See e.g. J. Harris, *The Value of Life* (London: Routledge and Kegan Paul, 1985); R. Gillon, "Autonomy and Consent" in M. Lockwood, ed, *Moral Dilemmas in Modern Medicine* (Oxford: OUP, 1985).

12 For further discussion, and references to some relevant literature, see chapter 10.

to discern principles, values, preferences and orientations that are distinctively "European", as opposed to, say, American or Japanese. To the extent that such principles are articulated through EU measures, these elements of national health systems may find some protection from the encroachment of internationalisation. Some of these values may be given specifically legal protection in the EU's legal order, for instance, by seeking to articulate them as human rights, or by adopting cautious, risk-averse regulatory measures for key health determinants such as food. In this sense, *but in this sense only*, we would have to admit that we are broadly supportive of such an emerging "European health law".

Before we can begin our investigation, we need to set some parameters around our study. Before we can consider how EU law affects "health law" (or indeed, ultimately, whether we can discern the beginnings of a nascent "European health law"), we need to ascertain what we mean by "health law" for the purposes of our analysis. This is the task of this chapter. It is not a comparative law exercise, although we will draw upon comparative literature at various points in the discussion. Indeed, as we shall see, our conceptualisation of health law differs in several respects from the manner in which interactions between law and health are dealt with by some academic commentators in individual Member States.

The chapter proceeds as follows. First, we consider what we mean by "health". Second, the evolution in the law's engagement with health in Member States, and its engagement with biomedical ethics, is explored through selected examples. Third, we consider some of the definitional debates as to the disciplinary boundaries involved in the study of the relationship between law and health, as an academic discipline. Fourth, we suggest why "health law", rather than "medical law" or indeed "health care law", provides an effective starting point for considering the manner in which the EU engages in this area. All Member States of the EU have a body of "health law", even though it may not be explicitly recognised as such in the literature. Fifth, we consider fundamental components of health law. Finally, we outline the substantive examples which form the case studies discussed in this book.

II. What is health law?

We begin by considering just what exactly we mean by "health law". In a book which addresses itself to both health lawyers and EU lawyers, and seeks to explore the manner in which the EU is affecting health law in the Member States, we need, at the very least, to attempt to clarify what we mean by "health law". While the nature and the scope of the discipline of health law may seem obvious at first glance, its precise boundaries are in many respects rather fluid. A further difficulty in considering health law is that, although it is the case that many areas, which can be regarded as the component parts of the discipline, have been the subject of considerable legal regulation and academic commentary over decades,[13] there

13 And in some cases centuries.

is rightly a general perception that academic engagement with such issues is still a comparatively recent endeavour.

What is health?

What are health lawyers concerned with? The obvious answer is, "well, 'health', of course!" But what do we mean by "health" for these purposes? In the context of an important discussion of the "right to health", Montgomery outlined two possible conceptions of "health": the "engineering model" and the "social model".[14] The engineering model focuses on the repair of the "defective" human machine. At first sight, such an approach has the great advantage of producing a clear definition of good and ill health. However, as Montgomery himself notes, there are certain difficulties with such an approach. How does one identify when the "machine" becomes defective? Can we ascertain an optimum level of health? Sensitive and controversial classifications may result. For example, consider those who have difficulty conceiving, and seek access to modern reproductive technologies. Should we regard the infertile as "ill"?[15] Or, to take another example, does ascertaining an optimum state of health mean that those who believe that they are suffering trauma because they have a large nose or ears should be able to access cosmetic surgery to make them "beautiful"? As Kennedy so elegantly expressed it, illness,

> "a central concept of medicine, is not a matter of objective scientific fact. Instead it is a term used to describe deviation from a notional norm. So a choice exists whether to call someone ill. The choice depends upon the norm chosen and this is a matter of social and political judgment. As the great American scholar Oliver Wendell Holmes remarked at the end of the nineteenth century, 'the truth is that medicine, professedly founded on observation, is as sensitive to outside influences, political, religious, philosophical, imaginative, as is the barometer to the changes of atmospheric density'."[16]

The judgment of what constitutes illness, while inherently subjective, is something which, in the past, has been entrusted to the medical profession. But a medical professional determination of what constitutes ill health may not always be effective, conclusive, nor indeed necessarily appropriate.[17]

An alternative approach is to consider what constitutes "health" in the light of international statements such as that provided by the WHO and UNICEF Declaration of Alma Ata, 1978. This provides that:

> "health, which is a state of complete physical, mental and social well-being and not merely the absence of disease and infirmity, is a fundamental human right and that the

14 J. Montgomery, "Recognising a Right to Health" in R. Beddard and D. Hill, eds, *Economic, Social and Cultural Rights: Progress and Achievement* (Basingstoke: Macmillan, 1992); and see the further discussion in J. Montgomery, *Health Care Law* (Oxford: OUP, 2002), pp 2–4.

15 See further on this point J. Stone, "Infertility treatment: a selective right to reproduce?" in P. Byrne, ed, *Ethics and Law in Health Care and Research* (Chichester: John Wiley, 1990).

16 I. Kennedy, *The Unmasking of Medicine* (London: Allen and Unwin, 1981), pp 7–8.

17 See further Kennedy, above n 16, pp 10–11, 16.

attainment of the highest possible level of health is a most important worldwide social goal whose realisation requires the action of many other social and economic sectors in addition to the health sector."

Taking a broad notion of "health" as the basis for our consideration of health law has the advantage of including the legal rights encompassed by the engineering model. It also has the advantage that it extends beyond those legal measures, to link health law and policy to other social policy fields, such as poverty or social exclusion. Indeed, as Brazier and Glover comment, it may be the case that, in the future, health care law may be subsumed, at least to some extent, under social welfare law.[18] This is because a considerable amount of health care, especially in the context of its provision to vulnerable groups, such as the young, the elderly or those with learning disabilities, is provided at the interface between social care providers (both state and voluntary sector) and health care providers.

Nonetheless, such a broad model is potentially problematic. As Fluss has noted:

> "The WHO definition, partially taken up in Article 12 of the Covenant, expressed health in terms of well-being which again is a philosophical concept. In a large part of the world, living standards are so low, and life itself so precarious, that little more can be done to secure or to restore health other than to attempt to reduce disease or infirmity."[19]

Thus, even a broad definition of "health" may, in practice, lead to considerable problems regarding both the definition and the conceptualisation of the subject area of "health law". For example, if "health" is "a state of complete physical, mental and social well-being", how can we determine the practical content of any "right to health"? Such a "right to health" may be found in several international human rights Conventions,[20] including the Council of Europe's European Social Charter and Revised European Social Charter, and also in a number of national constitutions,[21]

18 M. Brazier and N. Glover, "Does Medical Law have a Future?" in D. Hayton, ed, *Law's Futures* (Oxford: Hart, 2000).

19 See above n 6.

20 See Universal Declaration of Human Rights 1948, Article 25; International Covenant on Economic, Social and Cultural Rights 1966, Article 12; Convention on the Elimination of all forms of Discrimination Against Women 1979, Article 12; Convention on the Rights of the Child 1989, Article 24; European Social Charter 1961, Articles 11 and 13; Revised European Social Charter 1996, Articles 11 and 13; Convention on Human Rights and Biomedicine 1997, Article 3; Additional Protocol to the American Convention on Human Rights in the Area of Economic, Social and Cultural Rights (Protocol of San Salvador) 1988, Article 10. See B. Toebes, *The Right to Health as a Human Right in International Law* (Antwerp: Intersentia/Hart, 1999); B. Toebes, "The Right to Health" in A. Eide, C. Krause and A. Rosas, eds, *Economic, Cultural and Social Rights* (The Hague: Kluwer, 2001), p 173.

21 See, for instance, Article 70 D of the Hungarian Constitution; Article 68 of the Polish Constitution; Article 27 of the South African Constitution; Articles 39 (e) and (f), 46 and 47 of the Indian Constitution; section 15 of Article II of the Philippines Constitution. See Toebes (2001), above n 20, p 174; A. den Exter and H. Hermans, eds, *The Right to Health in Several European Countries* (The Hague: Kluwer, 1999).

including, in the EU, Belgium,[22] Finland,[23] Italy,[24] Luxembourg,[25] the Netherlands,[26] Portugal,[27] and Spain.[28] As Gostin and Lazzarini have commented, there are dangers in a broad definition of a "right to health" because it is less likely to have clearly defined content than a narrower definition, and this could severely limit its practical impact.[29] They suggest that the WHO definition is not achievable and, even if it were limited to a reasonable rather than an absolute standard, there would be considerable practical difficulties of implementation. They propose an alternative approach, that the right to health may be regarded as:

> "[t]he duty of the state within the limits of its available resources to ensure the conditions necessary for the health of individuals and populations."[30]

As Gostin and Lazzarini note, many factors which have an impact on an individual's state of health, such as genetics, behaviour, over-population and climate, are (either totally or partially) beyond governmental control. However, they have argued that it is the state which possesses the power to ensure conditions under which people are healthy, and therefore it is the state which has a responsibility, within the limits of available resources, to intervene to prevent or reduce serious threats to the health of individuals and populations. Nonetheless, they recognise that the main disadvantage with such an approach is that it does not ensure a minimal standard of health. It also sanctions differential responses to threats to health, based upon available economic resources.

Notions of "health" vary according to temporal and geographical context. One need only look at global mortality rates, or mortality rates across time, to illustrate this. Health indicators are also closely linked to economic prosperity, both globally and within a particular state. The more wealthy enjoy better health, and also better health care. As a particular state becomes more wealthy, the provision of health

22 Article 23: "(1) Everyone has the right to lead a life in conformity with human dignity. (2) To this end, the laws, decrees and rulings alluded to in Article 134 guarantee, taking into account corresponding obligations, economic, social and cultural rights, and determine the conditions for exercising them. (3) These rights include, notably: ... (2) The right to social security, to health care and to social, medical and legal aid."

23 Chapter 2, section 19 (3): "The public authorities shall guarantee for everyone ... adequate social, health and medical services and promote the health of the population."

24 Article 32: "The Republic protects health as a fundamental right of the individual and as a concern of the collectivity and guarantees free care to the indigent."

25 Article 11 (5): "The law organises social security, health protection ...."

26 Article 22 (1): "The authorities shall take steps to promote the health of the population."

27 Article 64 (1): "Health: All have the right to health protection and the duty to defend it and to promote it."

28 Article 43: "(1) The right to health protection is recognised. (2) It is incumbent upon the public authorities to organise and watch over public health and hygiene through preventive measures and through necessary care and services. The law shall establish the rights and duties of all in this respect. (3) The public authorities shall foster health education, physical education, and sports. Likewise, they shall facilitate adequate utilisation of leisure."

29 L.O. Gostin and Z. Lazzarini, *Human Rights and Public Health in the AIDS Pandemic* (Oxford: OUP, 1997).

30 Gostin and Lazzarini, above n 29, p **.

services will change focus, to include elements such as cosmetic surgery that may be less closely related to "fixing the defective human machine". Gostin and Lazzarini's definition of the "right to health" recognises that conceptualisations of good health are dynamic in nature.

Further, it must be borne in mind that our conceptions of health are subject to constant revision due to technological developments. To try and identify one standard of "health", even across the (relatively homogenous) EU, is exceedingly difficult to undertake. It is particularly problematic in the light of the accession of states from central and Eastern Europe.[31] However, at the same time as noting this diversity, we need also to consider prospects for the development of a more consistent standard of "health", in the light of the developing globalisation of medicine and science.[32]

While the links between globalisation and health care are complex, it is certainly the case that globalisation may drive standards up. As Adlung has argued:

> "Globalisation in the form of increased mobility and enhanced information may prompt more governments to consider the case for domestic regulatory adjustment. Economic growth has enabled large segments of the population not only to compare their supply situation with that of other countries, but to act accordingly and, if need be, move abroad."[33]

While, in practice, such mobility tends to be amongst the affluent, the potential for the "race to the top" should not be underestimated, and can be also seen in terms of some of the debates regarding quality of health care provision, in the context of mobility of state-funded patients within the EU.[34]

Taking into account all of the above, for the purposes of this book, we regard "health" as centrally focussed upon the individual, and consequently upon an "engineering model". However, we are also inspired by the insight that the obligations of states to protect human health apply not only to the protection of the health of individuals, but also to the health of populations, and that "health" can be collectively determined. We recognise that the boundaries of individuals', and indeed societal, conceptions of "health" and "illness" are fluid, and in many instances highly subjective, and that this precludes an all-embracing definition of "health". We now turn to examine how "health law" has emerged as a discipline.

31 A first wave of 10 "accession states" (Cyprus, Czech Republic, Estonia, Hungary, Latvia, Lithuania, Malta, Poland, Slovak Republic and Slovenia) signed an Accession Treaty at Athens in April 2003. If ratified by all the accession states, and the current Member States of the EU, this will enter into force on 1 May 2004, at which point the EU will enlarge from the current 15 Member States to 25 Member States. The other "candidate states" Bulgaria and Romania aim to join the EU in 2007; Turkey still needs to strengthen its human rights protection. See further chapter 10.

32 D. Morgan, *Issues in Medical Law and Ethics* (London: Cavendish, 2001), pp 27–32 and see 8(3) *eurohealth* (2002) which devotes a major part of this issue to a discussion of globalisation.

33 R. Adlung, "Health services in a globalising world" 8(3) *eurohealth* (2002) 18.

34 See further chapter 4.

The evolution of law's engagement with health

Just why is the law concerned with health and its regulation? There are a number of reasons. First, the interface of law with health can be seen as a means of protecting the collective public interest. Public health law, considered in chapter 9, is a part of all legal systems. The state is concerned with the legal regulation of disease, and the use of legislative measures to detain individuals, because they are regarded as a danger to public health, has an ancient history.[35] As we shall see in chapter 6, health professional regulation has been undertaken for centuries across the Member States of the EU, bolstered by the state through legislative measures.

Nonetheless, it is still the case that "health law" is regarded as being a young academic discipline. The engagement of the law with legal regulation of health has speeded up dramatically across the various Member States of the EU over the last century. There are several perceptible triggers for this evolution of the discipline.

At a basic level, lawyers have become more interested in health because there was simply more litigation. Take, for example, the well-documented rise of medical malpractice litigation internationally. In his introduction to Giesen's treatise on *International Medical Malpractice Law* in 1988, Lord Kilbrandon quoted from the judgment given in a Scottish case, *Farquhar v Murray*, in 1901:[36]

> "This action is certainly one of a particularly unusual character. It is an action of damages by a patient against a medical man. In my somewhat long experience I cannot remember having seen a similar case before."

For the next 80 years, litigation across Europe against health professionals continued to be limited.[37] As Brazier and Glover note, discussing the English position:

> "Perusal of the Law Reports before 1980 will reveal no more than a handful of reported cases which address either the civil liability of doctors or how the law should respond to controversial problems of medical ethics."[38]

However, today the situation is very different from the early 1980s. Across Europe as a whole, the volume of litigation in the field of health care has increased significantly. This can be seen as a reflection of the experience in the US of malpractice litigation, where health litigation is "big business" and many lawyers have been

35 See generally L.O. Gostin, *Public Health Law: Powers, Duties and Restraints* (Berkley and Los Angeles: University of California Press, 2000), preface; L. Johnson, "Defining Public Health" and "Issues of Public Health; Infectious Diseases" in R. Martyn and L. Johnson, *Law and the Public Dimension of Health* (London: Cavendish, 2002).

36 *Farquhar v Murray* (1901) 3F, 859, 862, cited in D. Giesen, *International Medical Malpractice Law* (Tubingen: JCB Mohr (Paul Siebeck); Dordrecht, Boston, London: Martinus Nijhoff, 1988).

37 Kennedy and Grubb, in their introduction to *Principles of Medical Law* Ist ed. (Oxford: OUP, 1998), p vii, have also memorably commented that medical law "was once dominated by medical negligence actions and disciplinary cases arising out of the failure to adhere to the GMC's standards on the 'three A's': adultery, alcohol and advertising".

38 Brazier and Glover, above n 18.

branded "ambulance chasers". In the UK, there has been such a plethora of litigation involving treatment in the health care context that there are serious concerns that the NHS is facing a "malpractice crisis".[39] This position is reflected across many other European countries, where there has been an equivalent increase in litigation concerning clinical practice and related matters.[40]

Alongside the development of medical malpractice law, scholars became increasingly engaged with the ethical dilemmas of health care. In the UK context, Keown has commented that:

> "Unlike senior citizens such as equity and real property, medical law was conceived only in the latter half of the 20th century. The stimulus in this country was Glanville Williams' controversial *The Sanctity of Life and the Criminal Law* (1958). Suckled academically by Peter Skegg's excellent *Law, Ethics and Medicine* (1984) supplemented by Ian Kennedy's engaging articles collected in *Treat Me Right* (1988) the body of medical law has grown apace."[41]

"Ethics" has undoubtedly been an important driver in the development of the discipline.[42] As Montgomery has commented:

> "Traditionally medical lawyers have seen the relationship between ethics, law and medicine as a hierarchy. The purest discipline is ethics, the substance of which should be reflected in the law, which in turn should use its coercive aspects to bring medicine into line. Medical law is thus a species of applied medical ethics."[43]

The engagement of the medical profession with ethical principles has a long and ancient history which some root in such statements as the Hippocratic Oath in the days of Ancient Greece in around 420 BC.[44] Law has engaged with some of the great ethical dilemmas of clinical practice, such as abortion and euthanasia. As clinical practice itself developed rapidly over the last half century, so the ethical controversies have multiplied, and so, consequently, the engagement of bioethicists

39 See the discussion in M. Brazier, *Medicine, Patients and the Law* (London: Penguin, 3rd ed. 2003), chapter 7 "Malpractice Litigation". This has led to a review of clinical negligence compensation by the UK Chief Medical Officer, "Clinical Negligence: What are the Issues and Options for Reform?" (2002), http://www.doh.gov.uk/clinicalnegligencereform.

40 See J. Dute, "Medical Malpractice Liability. No easy solutions" 10(2) *European Journal of Health Law* (2003) 85.

41 J. Keown, "Review of 'The Principles of Medical Law'" [2000] CLJ 412. Both within and outside the UK, the influence of Kennedy's Reith lectures was undoubtedly also crucial: see further Kennedy, above n 16.

42 See, for example, J. McHale and M. Fox, *Health Care Law: Text and Materials* (London: Sweet and Maxwell, 1997), chapter 2.

43 J. Montgomery, "Time for a Paradigm Shift? Medical Law in Transition" 53 *Current Legal Problems* (2000) 363.

44 This reliance has, however, been the subject of some critical discussion. Thompson suggests that the Hippocratic Oath was not universally supported and only re-emerged in the nineteenth century as a means of medical practice enveloping itself in respectability; see further I.E. Thompson, "Fundamental ethical principles in health care" 295 BMJ (1987) 1461. For a discussion of the development of the discipline in the light of Hippocrates see J. Montgomery, "Medical Law in the Shadow of Hippocrates" 52 MLR (1989) 566.

and theologians[45] with lawyers and the law has increased. Should access to IVF be subject to legal regulation?[46] Should sex selection be allowed? Should children born through donor insemination be told the identity of the donor?[47] Should we regulate surrogacy?[48] When should artificial nutrition and hydration be withdrawn from a patient in PVS? Should a market in organs be introduced to increase supply? However, while there may be an engagement with ethical issues, nonetheless to attempt to align clinical practice with ethical precepts, and then to regulate on such a basis, is problematic, due to the divergence amongst bioethical commentators across a wide range of situations as to just what precisely is the appropriate ethical response to take. This is a problem which is acutely difficult in a single homogenous population, but with the cultural and religious diversity, both within and across Member States of the EU today, these problems are magnified. In spite of this, the engagement with ethical precepts continues to underpin the development of the area of health law, in particular in relation to deontological approaches through the application of human rights analysis. We return to this issue below.

Definitions: delineating the boundaries of a discipline

In the beginning, there was "medical law"?

Historically, the focus of health care provision in western societies has been upon care provided by the doctor. Doctors were the "professionals" responsible for the primary diagnosis and treatment of patients. Today across Europe, doctors continue to play a crucial "gatekeeping" role in terms of patients' access to medical services. For instance, UK patients cannot access hospital treatment (save in an emergency situation) without a referral from a primary physician – the registered medical practitioner. Once in hospital, the care process is directed by a clinician; frequently a senior physician – the consultant. This division between primary and secondary delivery of care is reflected in other Member States of the EU. So too is the dominance

45 For a few notable illustrations of this point, representing merely the tip of a vast iceberg: see, for example, T.L. Beauchamp and J.F. Childress, *Principles of Biomedical Ethics* (Oxford: OUP, 2001); J. Harris, *The Value of Life* (London: Routledge, 1985); R. Gillon, *Philosophical Medical Ethics* (Chichester: John Wiley and Sons, 1986).

46 See, for example, M. Warnock, *Making Babies: Is there a right to have children?* (Oxford: OUP, 2002).

47 See, for example, K. O'Donovan, "What shall we tell the children? Reflections on Children's Perspectives and the Reproduction Revolution" in R. Lee and D. Morgan, eds, *Birthrights; Law and Ethics at the Beginning of Life* (London: Routledge, 1989). One EU Member State (Sweden) does provide for a legal right of access to such information, although children are not required to be informed that they were conceived in this manner: see C. Gottlieb, O. Lalos and F. Lindblad, "Disclosure of Donor Insemination to the Child: the Impact of Swedish Legislation on Couples' Attitudes" 15 *Human Reproduction* (2000) 2052.

48 See, for example, M. Freeman, "Is Surrogacy Exploitative?" in S. McLean, ed, *Legal Issues in Human Reproduction* (Aldershot: Dartmouth, 1990); D. Morgan, "Surrogacy: An Introductory Essay" in R. Lee and D. Morgan, eds, *Birthrights: Law and Ethics at the Beginnings of Life* (London: Routledge, 1989); M. Brazier "Can You Buy Children?" 11 CFLQ (1999) 325; M. Freeman, "Does Surrogacy Have a Future After Brazier?" 7 *Medical Law Review* (1999) 1.

of the medical practitioner over her other health care counterparts.[49] While there has been a notable diversification in the nature of clinical care, with greater autonomy of action being afforded to other professional groups such as nurses,[50] this change has been gradual and comparatively recent.

This focus on the dominance of the doctor meant that it is unsurprising that, in those situations in which health care relationships engaged with the law, this was through the lens of the doctor-patient relationship, and in particular, where things went wrong, through civil law actions, or occasionally in the criminal law. This was reflected in the engagement in these issues by the academic community. The seminal comparative law text in this area, Giesen's *International Medical Malpractice Law*, was reflective of the dominance of the doctor in health professional negligence litigation.[51]

Law's engagement with health was predominantly cast in terms of the primary actors in the litigation process, and seen very much in terms of the interface between doctors and their legal obligations. In the UK, in their book *Medical Law: Text and Materials*, first published in 1991, Kennedy and Grubb defined the discipline as "medical law", and outlined its parameters in terms of the interrelationship between the patient and her doctor.[52] This was reflective of the involvement of the UK courts in the area which concerned, almost exclusively, the doctor-patient relationship. It also reflected the structure of health care delivery in the UK and the control of the medical profession. Similarly Morgan, in his book *Issues in Medical Law and Ethics*,[53] constructs the discipline in terms of naming, claiming and blaming.

This "medical law" approach is echoed in many texts across EU Member States. Nys' text *La Médicine et Le Droit*, published in 1995, (the first such book in two decades to be published in the French-speaking part of Belgium[54]) is primarily physician focused. While it discusses many of the doctor-patient issues to be found in standard UK texts, only in title XII is there discussion of the relationship of the physician with other health care professionals and health institutions. This approach is also reflected across other jurisdictions, for instance, in Ireland, Tomkin and Hanafin's book *Irish Medical Law* provides a traditional physician-patient focus.[55] In Sweden, Westerhäll's book, *Medical Law*, again focuses on the physician-patient

49 For further discussion of the subordinance of nurses in the health care structure, see J. Montgomery, "Doctors handmaiden's; the legal contribution" in S. McVeigh and S. Wheeler eds. *Law, Health and Medical Regulation* (Aldershot: Dartmouth, 1992); T. Murphy, "Bursting Binary Bubbles: Law, Literature and the Sexed Body" in J. Morison and C. Bell, eds., *Tall Stories? Reading Law and Literature* (Aldershot: Dartmouth, 1996).

50 See J. Montgomery, "Medicine, Accountability and Professionalism" 16 *Journal of Law and Society* (1989) 319.

51 Giesen, above n 36.

52 I. Kennedy and A. Grubb, *Medical Law: Text with Materials* (London: Butterworths, 1991 and 2000).

53 (London: Cavendish, 2001).

54 (Diagem: Kluwer Edit Juridiques, Belgique, 1995).

55 (Dublin: Round Hall Press, 1995); see also D. Madden, *Medicine, Law and Ethics in Ireland* (Dublin: Butterworths Law Ireland, 2002).

relationship with only some five pages being devoted to consideration of the interface with other professional relationships.[56] The approach is similar in Germany, in Laufs and Uhlenbruck's *Handbuch des Artzrechts.*[57]

The movement to "health law"

Alongside the term "medical law", two other terms have been increasingly used to define the discipline: "health care law" and "health law". Whilst use of the term "health law" is viewed by some legal scholars as a comparatively recent development, it is worth noting that the first national society of health law in Europe was founded in 1967.[58] Since 1977, the Regional Office of the World Health Organisation has developed a programme of health law. In 1994, the *European Journal of Health Law* was established. This replaced an earlier journal entitled *Medicine and Law* and its change in title reflected a perceived shift away from a focus on malpractice litigation.[59] Gradually textbooks have begun to refer to "health care law" or simply "health law" rather than to "medical law", although this still appears to be a primarily English development.[60] Health (as opposed to the doctor-patient relationship of medical law) is a matter – as we shall see in the next chapter – with which the EU is fundamentally concerned.

The narrow focus of "medical law" has been the subject of challenge by academic commentators.[61] It is argued that, while the regulation of the doctor-patient relationship is important, such a restricted focus in determining a field of socio-legal enquiry has the effect of excluding a number of other key areas, and is thus in danger of providing an unrepresentative approach of the legal regulation of health care delivery. Much of this debate appears to have been undertaken by UK commentators, and therefore the focus here is on UK sources. For example, as Sheldon and Thompson have argued, a "medical law" approach focuses on the doctor-patient relationship, at the expense of relationships with other medical professionals, such as nurses, occupational therapists and physiotherapists.[62] Brazier and Glover also regard the change in terminology as inevitable.[63] They emphasise the movement from an almost exclusive doctor-patient dynamic, certainly in the area of primary care, to the delivery of health care on a "team" basis. Today, patients entering hospital will have a multitude of treatment relationships with a range of health care providers. It is also the case that other professionals are replacing doctors in the provision of health care. For instance, in the UK context, the Labour

56 L. Westerhäll, *Medical Law: An Introduction* (Stockholm: Fritzes, 1994).
57 A. Láufs, W. Uhlenbruch and H. Genzel, *Handbuch des Artzrechts* (Munich: CH Beck, 2002).
58 H.J.J. Leenen, "The European Journal of Health Law: A New Publication" 1 *European Journal of Health Law* (1994) 1.
59 A. Carmi, "Health Law towards the 21st Century" 1 *European Journal of Health Law* (1994) 225.
60 Montgomery (2002), above n 14; McHale and Fox, above n 42.
61 Montgomery (2002), above n 14; Montgomery, above n 43.
62 S. Sheldon and M. Thompson eds. *Feminist Perspectives on Health Care Law* (London: Cavendish, 1998), Introduction.
63 Brazier and Glover, above n 18.

government has accepted the need for broadening prescribing rights across the health professions, and in particular for nurses.[64] Thus "health law" is concerned with the legal position where an individual receives health care in the context of team provision, not simply a one-to-one relationship between a patient and a doctor. Health law is concerned with the regulation of all health professionals, not simply doctors.

This criticism of "medical law" as a construct has not gone unnoticed. Interestingly, the UK academic commentators, Kennedy and Grubb, themselves seek to reconceptualise the discipline in the third edition of their textbook, stating that: "We see it as essentially concerned with the relationship between health care professionals (particularly doctors and to a lesser extent hospitals or other institutions) and patients."[65]

They go on to emphasise the ethical dimension of the discipline – respect for autonomy, consent, truth telling, confidentiality, respect for persons, respect for dignity and respect for justice. Moreover, they believe that medical law today has one unifying theme, namely that of human rights. As they go on to state: "the common law – that glorious concept of English law – is, in its application to medical law, rich with and informed by human rights notions."[66]

The elements of "health law"

"Health law" and "health care law"

In this section, we begin to outline what health law involves, and why a health law approach may provide us with a better mechanism for examining the involvement of the EU in health law and policy than "medical law" or even "health care law". Given that a medical law classification is clearly unduly limited, how then can we define what we mean by "health law"? The academic community in EU Member States does appear to believe that such a discipline exists. New journals, concerned with health law, have been established, such as the *European Journal of Health Law*, inaugurated in 1994. Meetings of academics examining health law matters are now commonplace, and indeed, in 2002, the World Health Law Conference was held in Maastricht.[67] Health care law is a subject of study in Universities in several EU Member States.[68] As we have noted, a number of academic commentators have sought to conceptualise this discipline in terms of "health care law". Here we consider the differences between health care law and health law, and why we suggest that, for the purposes of our research question in this book, the focus of the analysis is upon "health law" rather than "health care law".

64 Health and Social Care Act 2001; and see J. McHale, "Nurse Prescribing" 4(5) *Mental Health Care* (2001) 170.

65 Kennedy and Grubb, above n 52, p 3.

66 *Ibid*

67 H. Nys and F. van Wijmen "Maastncht 2002: Health law in an era of Globalisation" 9 *European Journal of Health law* (2002) 1.

68 For instance, the University of Maastricht, the Netherlands; the University of Athens, Greece; the University of Göteborg, Sweden.

Health care law is, generally, a composite of principles derivative from other legal disciplines, such as standard principles of criminal law (applicable, for instance, in the context of euthanasia) and of civil law (applicable in malpractice litigation). In Europe as a whole, in both common and civil law systems, the discipline of medical law itself has, primarily, evolved from the common law. As Fleming has commented, in civil law countries, this had the effect of being a "vast gloss overlaying a few exiguous Code articles".[69] In certain European countries, for example, Austria, Belgium, France, Germany, Greece and Italy, the regulation of the professional-patient relationship has been primarily contractual.[70] Health care law also has close links with principles of family law, in particular in relation to decisions about treatment of infants, children and incompetent adults, through, where applicable, a Member State's *parens patriae* jurisdiction.[71] There is, however, an increasing trend across Member States to enact specific laws which relate to health. For example, in the UK, the provision of modern reproductive technology is regulated by the Human Fertilisation and Embryology Act 1990. There are many pieces of legislation across Europe which regulate organ transplantation.[72] Legislation has recently been enacted in the Netherlands and Belgium concerning end of life decision-making and the legalisation of euthanasia.[73]

Montgomery's definition of "health care law", found in the second edition of his *Health Care Law* textbook, is as follows:

> "It embraces not only the practice of medicine, but also that of the non-medical health care professions, the administration of health services and the law's role in maintaining public health. It also means that the concept of 'law' in this context must be examined carefully. Legal rules in a strict sense as developed by Parliament and the courts, are not the only type of binding norm that is relevant to health care law."[74]

Montgomery's definition provided the inspiration for our own starting point in considering the effects of EU law on health law. However, we are defining the disciplinary boundaries in terms of "health law", rather than "health *care* law". It is important to emphasise here that we are not challenging the validity or the appropriateness of health care law itself as an academic discipline. Whilst, as we shall see, elements of standard medical or health care law jurisprudence resonate through this book, at the same time, "health law" has a somewhat different dimension. Montgomery's definition is rooted in structured health care, provided within a health care "system". The emphasis upon the "professional-patient" relationship

69 J.G. Fleming, "Comparative Law of Torts" 4 OJLS (1984) 235 at 241.

70 See Giesen, above n 36, p 9.

71 See for example in the English Context, *Re F* [1990] 2 AC 1.

72 See, for example, UK Human Tissue Act 1961, Human Organ Transplants Act 1989; Netherlands, Organ Donation Act (*Wet op de Orgaandonatie*) 1998; and see D. Price and H. Akeveld, eds, *Living Donation in the Nineties: European Medico-Legal Perspectives* (Leicester: Eurotold, 1994.

73 See, for example, J. De Haan, "The New Dutch Law on Euthanasia" 10 *Medical Law Review* (2002) 57.

74 Montgomery (2002), above n 14, p 4.

continues, and the professional in that professional-patient relationship is primarily the doctor. However, the role of the professional as health care provider and her relationship with her patients is simply one strand. Today, the provision of health care is rapidly becoming something which is considerably different. The patient is becoming a consumer. Health "products" are increasingly being made directly accessible. This may be through the deregulation of medicines, with more medicines being made available to patients in pharmacies "over the counter", or through "remote" prescribing using the internet.[75] The "gatekeeping" role of the doctor, or other health professional, is conspicuously absent. Indeed, it is difficult to identify a "carer" providing the "health care" in this type of situation.[76] Following this insight, "health law" includes the legal position with respect to those producing and marketing medicinal products, in a context in which they may (actually or potentially) interact directly with patients, without the intervention of the "gatekeeper" health professional. Indeed, different regulatory strategies may be needed in this context, in order to protect the "lay" patient.

Moreover, it is not simply medicinal *products* that may be accessed directly by patients, but also health care *services*. For instance, access to information regarding health and treatment, especially on the internet, is changing the nature of health care provision as we recognise it.[77] There is today no "medical" monopoly on clinical information. Telemedicine or, as it is now referred to by some commentators, 'e-health' allows patients to go further than on-line searches in electronic journals and on databases, to access *personalised* health information directly from a physician.[78]

The "patient as consumer" is increasingly commissioning health care services which are a world away from the accident and emergency unit of the local hospital. For example, there is a notable increase in the number of clinical procedures undertaken which, in the past, would not have been regarded as generally "therapeutic" in nature,[79] such as the increase in persons seeking access to cosmetic surgery to stave off the ageing process and prolong their viability in the workplace. This individual-provider relationship may initially be regarded as something which is firmly a matter for individual Member States rather than the EU institutions. However, as we shall see in this book, consumer protection, where products and services may be accessed easily across national boundaries, is something with which the EU is increasingly concerned. For example, health information privacy and the confidentiality of the clinician-patient relationship have been affected by the EU's Data

75 For further discussion of e-health see chapter 10, 426.

76 Can a company manufacturing pharmaceuticals, or medical devices, be said to be providing "health care" to a patient with whom it contracts as a consumer? Can the patient be said to be providing his or her own health care?

77 See, for example, H.D.C. Rosam Abbing "Internet, the Patient and the Right to Care for Health" 7 *European Journal of Health Law* (2000) 221.

78 P. Freddolini, "e-health for Europe: The possible and the practical" 8 *eurohealth* (2002) 5.

79 The drawing of the boundaries between therapeutic and non-therapeutic care constitutes a debate beyond the scope of this text, but serves to illustrate the problematic nature of effective regulation. The involvement of the EU with e-health is explored further in chapter 10.

Protection Directive[80] and may be affected, in the future, by the E-Commerce Directive.[81] Access to, and availability of, health care services are also affected by internal market law. This "consumerist" tendency in health care may also be particularly interesting in relation to the rise of fertility and transplantation tourism.[82]

The "empowerment" of patients and consequent "consumerisation" of health care provision calls for a different legal construction within which to understand relationships between providers and receivers of health care. The relationship between a patient and a public or quasi-public health care provider implies quite a different legal framework to that between a *consumer* of health care and what may still be a (quasi) public provider, or may indeed be a private actor in the market. Brazier and Glover have argued that such developments mean that the law needs to reconceptualise its approaches, regarding provision of publicly funded health care and the standards of such care.[83] Once the matter of health care is conceptualised as concerning consumers, and the regulation of providers acting within a market, albeit perhaps one that is highly regulated and involving significant interactions with the public purse, it becomes much easier to see that there may be a clear point of contact with EU law, concerned as it is with creating and sustaining the "single internal market" within the EU. It also clearly illustrates how restrictive a "medical" conceptualisation of the legal regulation of health has become.

A further difficulty with emphasis upon the relationships between health professionals and patients in defining the boundaries of the discipline of "health law" is that this obscures the fact that the legal regulation of health also concerns the regulation of scientific research. Interdisciplinary elements of health law, in particular where lawyers interact with ethicists and theologians, come strongly into play here. Current types of health research, such as embryonic and stem cell research, may not involve traditional health professional bodies at all. Yet, of course, the potential of the technological developments here is crucial in terms of health care and the protection of health. At the same time, such developments raise difficult ethical questions and form an important site for regulation.[84]

Public health law

Other elements of Montgomery's definition of health care law are, however, fundamental to our characterisation of "health law". Montgomery emphasises "the law's role in maintaining public health".[85] Although text books in medical and health law do make reference to the legal regulation of public health, public health has been notably downplayed in comparison with the engagement with, for instance,

80 Directive 95/46/EC, OJ 1995 L 281/31. See further chapter 5.

81 Directive 2000/31/EC, OJ 2000 L 178/1. See S. Callens, "Telemedicine and the E-Commerce Directive" 9 *European Journal of Health Law* (2002) 93.

82 See further chapter 4.

83 Above n 18.

84 See further chapter 7.

85 Above n 14.

malpractice or consent to treatment. Where public health is discussed, with the exception of certain aspects of disease transmission, in particular HIV and hepatitis B, it tends to be dealt with very separately. However, the move towards a "health law" focus includes an increasing interest in the use of law in a "proactive" mode, rather than simply as a reactive institution. Law can be used to protect health and to promote good health, rather than simply to determine liabilities when ill health strikes, or when the treatment of ill health goes wrong.

Gostin has suggested that there are five essential characteristics of "public" health law.[86] First, that of government, as the government has a power and a duty to protect the health of the public. Second, public health looks at the health of populations. Third, public health is concerned to address a relationship between the state and the population. Fourth, public health is concerned with the provision of population based services which are grounded in public health methodologies such as epidemiology. Fifth, public health authorities have power to coerce individuals and businesses for community protection. Public health law is one area which has, in the past, been the subject of comparatively limited discussion in legal commentaries, save a number of specific texts.[87]

Public health law, as conceptualised by Gostin, is, at its core, "the authority and responsibility of government to ensure the conditions for the population's health".[88] This, as we shall see later in this book, is a field where the institutions of the EU share competence with those of its Member States. Public health law is concerned with the regulation of risks to the health of the population. Public health interfaces with human rights considerations, notably in areas such as mental health and disease transmission. The very essence of public health law is that containment of many threats to public health within one jurisdiction is problematic. There is therefore an international dimension to the discipline as a whole.[89] Article 55 of the UN Charter makes reference to "higher standards of living" and to "solutions of international ... health, and related problems". The World Health Organisation plays a vitally important role in the resolution of health matters at a global level. The WHO drafts the international health regulations which have the aim of "ensuring maximum security against the international spread of disease with a minimum interference with world traffic"[90] and which operate in international law. These impose legal obligations in international law upon states, regarding issues such as disease notification, border restrictions and specific provisions regarding cholera, plague and yellow fever.

It is unsurprising then that disease control is one important aspect of legal regulation across Europe. It is also an issue with which the EU itself has become increasingly

86 Gostin, above n 35.

87 For instance, see M. Cazaban et al, *Santé Publique* (Paris: Masson, 2001).

88 Gostin, above n 35, p 327.

89 Y. Arai-Takahashi, "The role of international health law" in R. Martyn and L. Johnson, eds. *Law and the Public Dimension of Health* (London: Cavendish, 2001).

90 Foreword to the International Health Regulations.

concerned, as disease does not respect state boundaries. This is illustrated by the regulatory responses to HIV/AIDS and BSE/nv CJD in the EU context. There is an important interface between disease surveillance and privacy of health information.[91] The relationship between migration and disease control arises here also.

A further important element of "health law" is the use of law to promote good health. This includes, for instance, the communication of health information.[92] This is important, in the EU context, in relation to the debates regarding tobacco advertising and food labelling.[93] The extension of the definition of "health law" to include such matters is probably controversial as the discipline has developed to date. However, in the context of increasing budgetary stringency, states are seeking to use regulatory activity to attempt to prevent ill health and disease, as this is considerably cheaper than providing health care subsequently, when individuals become ill. So, for instance, lifestyle "contracts" may be used with patients with heart disease to attempt to stop them from smoking, to eat healthily and to take appropriate exercise. As biotechnology increases our knowledge of the interaction between genetics, lifestyle and disease, such regulatory or quasi-regulatory activity is likely to increase. The legal ramifications of such regulation, and in particular its interaction with human rights law, are likely to become an area of increasing interest for health lawyers.

Administration of health services: financing and resources

Montgomery also emphasises the law's role in the administration of health services. The precise boundaries of the discipline of health law across the Member States of the EU reflect the historical basis of health care delivery, and of the development of legal regulation and litigation on health matters in each particular state. One important context within which health regulation and litigation takes place is that of the different funding arrangements for health care across Europe as a whole.[94]

National public health care systems in the EU are said to fall into two broad types: national health services and social insurance systems.[95] National health services are funded by public taxation, and operate according to a benefits-in-kind system. They may be more or less centralised in terms of their administration.[96] In the UK, health care is still predominantly provided by the NHS, and funded through public

91 See further chapter 5.
92 See Gostin, above n 35, chapter 6.
93 See further chapter 9.
94 E. Mossialos et al, eds, *Funding Health Care: Options for Europe* (Buckingham: Open University Press, 2002).
95 A.P. Van der Mei, *Free Movement of Persons within the European Community: Cross-Border Access to Public Benefits* (Oxford: Hart, 2003), pp 224–226; W. Palm and J. Nickless, "Access to healthcare in the European Union" 7(1) *eurohealth* (2001) 13 at 14; Y. Jorens, "The Right to Health Care Across Borders" in R. Baeten, M. McKee and E. Mossialos, eds, *The Impact of EU Law on Health Care Systems* (Brussels: PIE Peter Lang, 2003).
96 In the EU, the UK and Ireland are said to operate a more centralised national health service. Italy, Portugal, Spain, Greece, Denmark, Sweden and Finland are said to operate more decentralised national health services; see Palm and Nickless, above n 95.

taxation. Since the introduction of the UK National Health Service by Aneurin Bevan in 1948, the principle has been one of health care free at the point of delivery. Whilst this principle has been weakened over time, through charges being levied for various NHS services, it is still a principle which underpins the system. In Greece, a National Health Service was established in 1983.[97] Other Member States operating a national health service include Ireland, Italy, Portugal, Spain, Denmark, Sweden and Finland.

National health social insurance systems are found in Belgium, Luxembourg, the Netherlands, Germany and France. Also, most of the accession and candidate states of Central and Eastern Europe have adopted social insurance systems.[98] Social insurance schemes are based upon the compulsory insurance of categories of persons (now expanded to include all, or virtually all, the population). Insurance premiums are usually income-related, and calculated on the basis of total annual expenditure.[99] Administratively speaking, health care schemes are often integrated into the general social security system. The administration of health insurance may be entrusted to public or semi-public bodies, such as sickness funds.[100] Interestingly, however, some states have changed or are in the process of changing from an insurance-based system to a taxation-based system.[101]

Alongside the operation of such systems, there is applicable jurisprudence concerning the relationships between health insurance funds, patients and providers of health care services. Buijsen has commented that:

> "one cannot maintain that health law consists of medical law and patient rights solely. Nowadays health lawyers also concern themselves with the way health care is financed. Therefore, health law consists of the rules and principles regarding the relationships between patients and health care providers (ie the law of health care provision) between health care providers (in the broadest sense) and health care financiers (ie the law of health care finance) and between health care financiers and their clients (ie the law of health care insurance)."[102]

This conceptualisation of the scope of health law may be seen to "fit" much better with the competencies of the EU, and the domain of the EU's legal order, as it encompasses commercial relationships, and may involve engagement with fields

97 M. Theodorou, "Recent Reforms in the Greek NHS" 8(2) *eurohealth* (2002) 29.

98 See WHO and European Commission, *Health Status Overview for Countries of Central and Eastern Europe that are Candidates for Accession to the European Union* (Copenhagen: WHO, 2002); J. Marrée and P. P. Groenewegen, *Back to Bismarck: Eastern European Care Systems in Transition* (Aldershot: Avebury, 1997); B. Deacon, "Eastern European welfare states: the impact of the politics of globalization" 10 *Journal of European Social Policy* (2000) 146.

99 Van der Mei, above n 95, p 224.

100 *Ibid*

101 A. Dixon and E. Mossialos, "Funding health care in Europe: recent experiences" in T. Harrison and J. Appleby, eds, *Health care UK* (London: Kings Fund, 2001). For a debate on the efficacy of the comparative approaches, see "Social Insurance the right way forward for health care in the United Kingdom" 325 BMJ (2002) 488.

102 M.A.J.M. Buijsen, "The Concept of Health Law", paper delivered at the 14th World Health Law Congress, Maastricht, (2002) 1. Jost also regards health care organisation and finance as a major area of health law. T. Jost *Readings in Comparative Health law and Bioethics* (Durham NC: Carolina Academic Press 2001)

such as competition law. We return to the law's engagement with financing and resource allocation within national health (insurance) systems in chapters 4 and 8.

Health and human rights

Although, as we have noted, health law has been affected considerably by ethical principles, some of the relevant debates have tended to be rather reactive and linked to specific technological developments. Nonetheless, there is some evidence that health law in the Member States of the EU is being fundamentally affected by one major general ethical framework which has been legitimated through legal developments, that of human rights analysis.[103] International human rights statements such as the UN Declaration, 1948 and the International Covenants on Civil and Political Rights and Economic, Social and Cultural Rights, 1966, have been influential in the development of health law and health policy.

Initially, the prominent human rights statements in Europe came from the Council of Europe, in particular the European Convention on Human Rights and Fundamental Freedoms 1950 (ECHR), rather than from the EU.[104] The ECHR has significant potential for affecting health law and health policy at individual state level, and a number of notable challenges on health matters have been brought over the years before the Commission and the Court of Human Rights at Strasbourg. For instance, persons with mental illness, particularly those who are compulsorily detained, are in a highly vulnerable situation, and it is particularly important that their rights should be respected.[105] There has been much litigation over the applicability of the ECHR to mental health,[106] and this has had considerable impact

103 See, in general, for example, Toebes, above n 20; Toebes, in Eide, Krause and Rosas, eds, above n 20; V. Leary, "The Right to Health in International Human Rights Law", 1 *Journal of Health and Human Rights* (1994) 3; J. Mann, L.O. Gostin et al, "Health and Human Rights" 1 *Journal of Health and Human Rights* (1994) 7; M. Brazier, "Rights and Health Care" in R. Blackburn, ed, *Rights of Citizenship* (London: Mansell, 1993); J. McHale, "Enforcing Health Care Rights in the English Courts" in R. Burchill, D. Harris and A. Owers, eds, *Economic, Social and Cultural Rights: Their Implementation in the United Kingdom* (Nottingham: University of Nottingham Human Rights Law Centre, 1999); A. Chapman, *Exploring a Human Rights Approach to Health Care Reform* (Washington DC: American Association for the Advancement of Science, 1993); L. Westerhäll and C. Phillips, eds, *Patients' Rights: Informed Consent, Access and Equality* (Stockholm: Nerenius and Santérus, 1994); J. Montgomery, "Recognising a Right to Health" in R. Beddard and D. M. Hill, eds, *Economic, Social and Cultural Rights: Progress and Achievement* (Basingstoke: Macmillan, 1992).

104 See further C. Overy and R. White, *The European Convention on Human Rights* (Oxford: OUP, 2003); A. R. Mowbray and D. J. Harris, *Cases and Materials on the European Convention on Human Rights* (London: Butterworths, 2001).

105 See generally, S.S. Herr, L.O. Gostin and H. Hongju Kerr, eds, *The Human Rights of Persons with Intellectual Disabilities* (Oxford: OUP, 2003); and E. Rosenthal and C. J. Sundram, "The Role of International Human Rights in Domestic Mental Health Legislation" 21 *New York Law School Journal of International and Comparative Law* (2002) **.

106 See for example, *Winterwerp v Netherlands* (1979–80) 2 EHRR 387; see further; L.O. Gostin, "Human Rights of Persons With Mental Disabilities" 23 *International Journal of Law and Psychiatry* (2000) 125; S. Herr, "Rights of Disabled Persons: International Principles and American Experiences" 12 *Columbia Human Rights Law Review* (1980) 1; O. Thorold, "The Implications of the European Convention on Human Rights for United Kingdom Mental Health Legislation" [1996] EHRLR 619; T.W. Harding, "The Application of the European Convention on Human

at national level. A more recent, and influential, Council of Europe document is the Convention on Human Rights and Biomedicine 1997,[107] although it should be noted that a number of EU Member States are not signatories to this Convention.[108] The concern to safeguard human rights in clinical research has been particularly notable post Nuremberg. This concern is reflected in international documents, such as the World Health Organisation and World Medical Assembly Declaration of Helsinki,[109] which sets out a series of basic principles for medical research.

The development of health law rights in the EU has also been fostered by the World Health Organisation (Europe). For example, in 1994, WHO Europe issued the Amsterdam Declaration on the principles of patients' rights in Europe.[110] In 1997, the WHO Regional Office for Europe established a patients' rights network, with the Centre for Health System Research in Warsaw, the Centre for Health Services Studies University of Kent, UK and the Nordic School of Public Health in Gothenberg. This has the aim of developing patients' rights legislation, in accordance with the Amsterdam Declaration.[111]

The Amsterdam Declaration has been highly influential upon the development of legislative statements of rights.[112] In 1994, only Finland had specific patients' rights legislation. However, subsequently a number of other European jurisdictions have enacted patients' rights legislation.[113] For example, in Denmark, the Danish Patients Rights Act 1998 makes very specific provisions for protection of rights to dignity, integrity and autonomy.[114] Other states have included patients' rights within existing legislation. In the UK, in the third edition of Kennedy and Grubb's *Medical Law*[115] the authors suggest that "medical law" is a subset of human rights law. In the UK, there is no legislative statement of patients' rights. However, the UK Human Rights Act 1998, which enables the UK courts to interpret English law in the light

Rights to the Field of Psychiatry" 12 *International Journal of Law and Psychiatry* (1989) 245; D. Hewitt, "Mental Health Law" in C. Baker, ed, *Human Rights Act 1998: A Practitioner's Guide* (London: Sweet and Maxwell, 1998).

107 And see also Council of Europe Steering Committee on Bioethics, Draft Additional Protocol to the Convention on Human Rights and Biomedicine, on Biomedical Research, Strasbourg, 23 June 2003, CDB1/INF(2003).

108 The Convention on Human Rights and Biomedicine has been ratified by Denmark, Greece, Portugal and Spain; also by Cyprus, Czech Republic, Estonia, Hungary, Lithuania, Romania, Slovak Republic and Slovenia. It has been signed, but not yet ratified, by Finland, France, Italy, Luxembourg, Netherlands and Sweden; also Latvia, Poland and Turkey. It has not been signed by Austria, Belgium, Germany, Ireland and the UK. See http://conventions.coe.int/.

109 See, for example, the Declaration of Helsinki, adopted by the World Medical Assembly, Helsinki, Finland, 1964. For discussion of a longer list, see D. Sprumont, "Legal Protection of Human Research Subjects in Europe" 6 *European Journal of Health Law* (1999) 25.

110 J. Martin, "The Principles of the Rights of Patients in Europe: A Commentary" 1 *European Journal of Health Law* (1994) 265.

111 See L. Fallsberg, "Patients' Rights in Europe: Where do we stand and where do we go?" 7 *European Journal of Health Law* (2000) 1.

112 L. Fallsberg, "Consequences of the Amsterdam Declaration: A Rights Revolution in Europe" 10 *European Journal of Health Law* (2003) 5.

113 The Netherlands, Norway, Lithuania, Denmark, France, Belgium and Austria.

114 L. Fallsberg, "Patients' Rights in the Nordic Countries" 7 *European Journal of Health Law* (2000) 123.

115 Kennedy and Grubb, above n 52.

of the ECHR, has meant that the UK courts are now able to articulate human rights principles overtly in their interpretation of health law, and there is a developing jurisprudence in this respect.[116]

However, whilst human rights discourse is clearly influential at a rhetorical level, and human rights undoubtedly underpin legal engagement with health, there are a number of difficulties with application of human rights analysis. First, the breadth of the provisions contained in human rights instruments may lead to problems of interpretation. Second, what happens when rights conflict may be seriously problematic. For example, in the context of abortion, human rights to privacy (of the mother) may conflict directly with rights based on the sanctity of life (of the embryo or foetus). Nonetheless, despite these and other problems, the application of human rights analysis will continue to have a crucial role to play in health law in the future, at the very least in terms of framing its discourse.

In the past, categorisation of health law as human rights law would not have sat easily with EU law. The EU's nascent human rights law had relatively modest beginnings, being particularly concerned with respect for rights of property.[117] However, questions of ethics formulated through the rhetoric of rights have increasingly informed EU health policy debate, as was the case, for example, in the debates regarding the regulation of clinical research through the Clinical Trials Directive[118] and the Directive on the Legal Protection of Biological Inventions.[119] EU health policy in relation to these Directives was undoubtedly influenced to some extent by statements such as the Council of Europe's Convention on Human Rights and Biomedicine, 1997.[120]

The EU now also has its own rights document, the Charter of Fundamental Rights of the European Union 2000 (EUCFR).[121] Although the status of the EUCFR is not entirely clear at present, as we shall discuss in chapter 10, it looks set to become part

116 For an illustration of the breadth of the issues to which the Act has been so far applied, see *R (on the application of Rose) v Secretary of State for Health* [2002] 2 FLR 962 (access to information regarding sperm donors); *R (on the application of Pretty) v DPP* [2002] 1 All ER 1 (end of life decision-making); *R (H) v London North and East Region Mental Health Review Tribunal* (2001) EWCA Civ 415 (powers of discharge of mental health review tribunals) (notably the first declaration of incompatibility in which the court held a statute incompatible with the Human Rights Act 1998); and see generally A. Garwood-Gowers, J. Tingle and T. Lewis, eds, *Healthcare Law: The Impact of the Human Rights Act 1998* (London: Cavendish, 2001).

117 See, for example, Case 4/73 *Nold v Commission* [1974] ECR 491.

118 Directive 2001/20/EC on the implementation of good clinical practice in the conduct of clinical, trials on medicinal products for human use, OJ 2001 L 121/34.

119 Directive 98/44/EC on the legal protection of biotechnological inventions, OJ 1998 L 213/13.

120 On the background to the Convention, and its scope, see P. Zilgalvis, "The European Convention on Human Rights and Biomedicine: Its Past, Present and Future" in Garwood-Gowers, Tingle and Lewis, above note 116.

121 There is a significant and growing literature on the EUCFR. For a starting point, see the contributions to volume 8 (1) *Maastricht Journal of European and Comparative Law* (2001); G. De Búrca, "The Drafting of the EU Charter of Fundamental Rights" 26 ELRev (2001) 126; and, with particular reference to social rights in the EUCFR, see C. Costello, ed, *Fundamental Social Rights: Current European Legal Protection and the Challenge of the EU Charter on Fundamental Rights* (Dublin: Irish Centre for European Law, 2001); T. Hervey and J. Kenner, eds, *Economic and Social Rights under the EU Charter of Fundamental Rights* (Oxford: Hart, 2003).

of binding EU Treaty law, if the Draft Constitutional Treaty (DCT) is adopted.[122] The EUCFR (and proposed DCT) contain a number of rights that may be referable to health care decision-making and to other matters of health law, including clinical research and public health.

Article 1 on human dignity may be said to be the basis of all elements of the right to health. Its close relative is Article 3 on the integrity of the person, which draws from and is stated to be consistent with[123] the European Convention on Human Rights and Biomedicine, 1997. This states that:

> "2. In the fields of medicine/biology the following must be respected:-
> free informed consent of the person concerned according to the procedures laid down by law,
> the prohibition of eugenic practices, in particular those aiming at the selection of persons,
> the prohibition on making the human body and its parts as such a source of financial gain,
> the prohibition of the reproductive cloning of human beings."

Article 2 safeguards the right to life. Article 4 provides for a prohibition on the infliction of torture and inhuman or degrading treatment or punishment. This may be applicable to decisions concerning consent to medical treatment. Article 7 contains the right to privacy in the context of private life. Article 8,[124] on the protection of personal data, may be relevant to data that medical professionals may hold on their patients, data with respect to medical research, and patients' entitlements to view their medical records.[125] Article 9 contains a provision safeguarding the right to marry and found a family, which may be particularly apposite to the debates

122 See, for example, C. McCrudden, "The Future of the EU Charter of Rights", Jean Monnet Papers, http://www.jeanmonnetprogram.org/papers/01/013001.html; M. Dougan, "The Convention's Draft Constitutional Treaty: A 'Tidying-Up Exercise' that Needs Some Tidying-Up of Its Own", Federal Trust Papers, http://www.fedtrust.co.uk/uploads/constitution/27–03.pdf; P. Craig, "What Constitution Does Europe Need? The House that Giscard Built: Constitutional Rooms with a View", Federal Trust Papers, http://www.fedtrust.co.uk/uploads/constitution/26–03.pdf; P. Eeckhout, "The EU Charter of Fundamental Rights and the Federal Question" 39 CMLRev (2002) 945; J. Schwarze, "Constitutional Perspectives of the European Union with Regard to the Next Intergovernmental Conference" 8 *European Public Law* (2002) 241; B. de Witte, "The Legal Status of the Charter: Vital Question or Non-Issue?" 8 MJ (2001) 81; J. Wouters, "Editorial" 8 MJ (2001) 3 and the other contributions to this special issue of the journal, volume 8(1); L. Betten, "The EU Charter on Fundamental Rights: a Trojan Horse or a Mouse?"17 IJCLLIR (2001) 151; B. Hepple "The EU Charter of Fundamental Rights" 30 ILJ (2001) 225; K. Lenaerts and P. Foubert, "Social Rights in the Case-Law of the European Court of Justice: the impact of the Charter of Fundamental Rights of the European Union on Standing Case-Law" 28 *Legal Issues of Economic Integration* (2001) 267; Lord Goldsmith, "A Charter of Rights, Freedoms and Principles" 38 CMLRev (2001) 1201.

123 See the Explanatory Memorandum to the Charter, CHARTE 4473/00 CONVENT 49.

124 Based on Article 286 EC, Directive 95/46/EC and also Article 8 of the ECHR and the Council of Europe Convention of 28 January 1981 for the Protection of Individuals with regard to Automatic Processing of Personal Data, which has been ratified by all Member States.

125 See further chapter 5.

regarding reproductive rights.[126] Article 10, on the freedom of conscience, belief and religion, may also be important to health care decisions such as in relation to the end of life.[127] Article 11, on freedom of expression, could be pertinent to whistleblowing in health care, and may prove important in the context of public health measures restricting freedom of information, especially advertising.[128] Article 13, on the freedom of the arts and sciences, may be relevant to medical research. Article 24, regarding the rights of the child, and their ability to express their views freely and have then taken into consideration in accordance with age and maturity, is important in health care. Similarly Article 25, emphasises the need to respect the ability of the elderly to lead a life, of dignity and independence and Article 26, concerning integration of persons with disabilities. Perhaps most importantly for our purposes, Article 35 provides that:

> "Everyone has the right of access to preventive health care and the right to benefit from medical treatment under the conditions established by national laws and practices. A high level of human health protection shall be ensured in the definition and implementation of all Union policies and activities."

All of these provisions should be seen in the context of Article 21, prohibiting any discrimination based on any ground such as sex, race, colour, ethnic or social origin, genetic features, language, religion or belief, political or other opinion, membership of a national minority, property, birth, disability, age or sexual orientation.

A human rights approach implies a conceptualisation of health law that includes legal provision for individual patients' entitlements, in the manner of their treatment, for instance, on rights to informed consent and bodily integrity. Such an approach also brings within the fold of health law, the rights of individuals used within clinical trials for new treatments and medicinal products. However, human rights have limitations as drivers of law and policy. Human rights provisions may be of rhetorical significance, particularly in policy-making debates, and, in some circumstances may assist in construction of specific legal instruments, or the determination of their legality. In other cases, however, their practical impacts are likely to be limited, as we shall see later in our discussion.[129]

III. Conclusion

In the early stages of writing this book, an academic colleague, on hearing of the expedition on which we were embarked, remarked, "European health law – there

126 See further the discussion in chapter 4.

127 See *Pretty v UK* (2002) 35 EHRR 1; and see, generally, on the prospect for conflicts on the basis of treatment decisions due to cultural beliefs, D. Pearl, "Legal issues arising out of medical provision for ethnic groups" in A. Grubb and M.J. Mehlman, eds, *Justice and Health Care: Comparative Perspectives* (Chichester: John Wiley and Sons, 1995).

128 See further, in the US context, where there has been considerable discussion of this issue, Gostin above n 35, chapter 6 "Health, Communication and Behaviour".

129 See chapter 2, p 63–67, and chapter 10, p 405–410.

isn't any ...". After further reflection he paused, and said: "No, no, sorry ... the subject is huge isn't it?" Indeed it is, and this provides us with our challenge, but at this point we also have to recognise our limitations.

Obviously, the law engages with "health". The attempt to try and delimit "health law" within the professional-patient relationship is, we have suggested, unduly restrictive, especially at a time when the patient can be increasingly seen as a consumer. To view health law in terms of the professional also obscures the interface between clinical care and the role of the scientist in health care development. Health law across EU Member States is concerned with a number of issues which have arisen consequent upon medical, technological or scientific developments. It is concerned with patient "rights" in relation to health care services; both civil and political rights, such as the right to life, privacy and freedom of religion; and also the more recent economic, social and cultural rights, such as the right to health itself. Health law is also concerned with the balance of rights and public interest in regulating risk, as shown notably in relation to public health. In addition, health law is concerned with resource allocation and financing of national health (insurance) systems.

One problem which we have not attempted to resolve in this book is whether "health law" itself is a term which is fundamentally too broad or too incoherent to be of any real practical or analytical use. Some may suggest that health law is simply a collection of existing legal principles, tacked together from different areas of academic scholarship, rather than one discrete entity worthy of study in itself. Whether this is the case or not, we suggest that the breadth of a subject by itself does not render it ineffective as a basis for analysis. The reification of divisions between subject areas within academic disciplines, including law, has led to considerable debate.[130] Moreover, as with "new" legal fields such as restitution, health law is still in a state of evolution. As academic commentators, we have a responsibility to be open to such changes and ready to respond to them. On the other hand, to document the full history and developments in the field of health law is beyond the scope of our book.

Nor could we provide an exhaustive account of all elements of EU law that have had an impact, or might have an impact, on health law, in its broadest definition. Rather, what we intend to do is to provide an overview as to how the EU interacts with health law, as defined in terms of its general themes, and then to focus on certain specific areas by way of illustration. The areas examined are those in which EU law appears to be particularly affecting health law in the Member States at present. It follows that the chapters in this book do not directly mirror those in standard health law textbooks. We should also say explicitly here that we are not being at all exhaustive in terms of reference to the effects of EU law on all elements of health

130 For example, in English law, the boundaries between tort and contract, and the development of restitution as a discipline: see, for instance, Lord Goff of Chieveley and G. Jones, *The Law of Restitution* (London: Sweet and Maxwell, 2002).

law in all the Member States of the EU. That would involve a massive comparative study, well beyond the scope of this book (and indeed these authors!).[131]

The structure of the book is as follows. Part One (the first three chapters) provides the context for the subsequent analysis. In this chapter, we have developed our definition of health law, drawing on existing literature in the field. We hope that our book will be of interest to both "health lawyers" and "EU lawyers", and we realise that there has been comparatively limited interaction between those disciplines to date. With this in mind, chapter 2 provides, in addition to an historical overview, an introduction, for those with no background in EU law, to the EU's unique legal order, its general principles, and institutions. Rather than reproducing a general EU law textbook, as far as possible, we have concentrated on those elements that health lawyers might find most interesting, in providing examples in this chapter. Thus, for instance, we have considered institutions that might not be covered in much detail in general EU textbooks.

Chapter 3 continues the focus on EU law, with an elaboration of Community competence in health, as set out in Article 152 EC. This provides that "Community action . . . shall be directed towards improving public health, preventing human illness and diseases, and obviating sources of danger to human health". However, our main research question – "how does EU law affect national health law and policy?" – cannot be answered simply by considering the powers of the EU institutions under Article 152 EC. If we define health law broadly, we need to consider the health elements in other policies and activities of the EU. We need to determine the impact (direct or indirect) of the EU law relating to such other policies, on national health law and policy in the Member States. This is the subject of Part Two, comprising chapters 4–9.

Chapter 4 considers individual access to health care services, with respect to individual rights and also standards applicable within national health care systems. The rights of patients to health care and medical treatment are affected by EU law on migrant workers and their families; the harmonisation and coordination of national social security systems; and also (as the Diane Blood and Yvonne Watts stories show) freedom of patients to move to receive health care services. These provisions entail relatively minor incursions on national health law, which are, however, significant for small groups of patients within the EU. More indirect impacts on health care standards may follow from the application of these provisions. Chapter 5 examines information privacy and data protection, considering the effect of EU law on health professional practice, through measures such as the Data Protection Directive. Chapter 6 considers the regulation of health professionals, in the context of their freedom of movement within EU law, in a system of "mutual recognition" of qualifications. Again, as the numbers of migrant workers are relatively small, the overall direct impact is generally fairly insignificant, save in a few key instances.

131 For a start, our linguistic abilities mean that the sources of reference for this book are limited to those available in the English language.

Indirect effects may be more wide ranging however, for example, the impact upon standards in professional practice, or on developments in professional ethical codes driven by the need to respond to diversity.

The regulation of medical research, through mechanisms such as determination of common standards, on matters such as the conduct of clinical trials, is considered in chapter 7. The role of the EU in financing medical research, and the indirect effects this may have for law and policy, is also considered here. Chapter 8 turns to the regulation of production and marketing of medical products, concentrating on the law relating to pharmaceuticals. Complex consumer protection measures have been adopted by the EU institutions in this field, dating back to the 1960s. Rules on product liability, promulgated at EU level, may determine the tortious relationships between pharmaceuticals producers and consumers of their products. Further, EU internal market law has an impact on the marketing of pharmaceuticals within the EU. Pharmaceuticals regulation plays a crucial "gatekeeping" role in terms of resource allocation within national health policies, and the impact, or potential impact, of EU law on, for example, (the prohibition of) direct-to-consumer marketing of these products within the EU, is discussed.

The EU is playing an increasingly significant role in the protection of public health. Chapter 9 considers this activity in a number of fields, with a detailed focus on the emerging EU food law, in particular concerning the BSE/nv CJD crisis. We also consider the EU's communicable diseases programmes, in particular Community activity on HIV/AIDS and the Community's role in health promotion, using the examples of regulation of tobacco and communicable diseases.

Part Three of the book consists of one final chapter. In chapter 10, we elaborate the various roles of law in the interactions between EU and national level institutions in the formation of health law and policy. We seek to draw some general conclusions on our initial research question, by reference to a "spectrum" of different types of effect that EU law has (or potentially has) on national health law and policy. This spectrum allows us to predict likely effects of EU law in areas of health law that we were not able to explore in detail in the substantive chapters, although, of course, the robustness of such predictions will need to be tested by future research. We conclude with a brief discussion of possible directions for new development in our subject – health law and the EU.

2

Historical, legal and institutional contexts

I. Introduction: what is the European Union?

The question this book sets out to answer is: "how – to what extent and in what ways – does EU law affect health law and policy?" Chapter 1 offered an indication of what we (and others) mean by "health law and policy". This chapter turns to the other part of the question: EU law. It is obviously impossible to develop an understanding of the impacts of EU law on health law and policy without a contextualised understanding of the legal system of the EU. We hope that this book will be of interest to a diverse group of readers, many of whom may have no background in EU law. This chapter therefore provides an introduction to the EU's legal order, its general principles and its institutions.[1] The aim is to provide a framework within which the more detailed analyses offered by subsequent chapters may be placed. This framework provides historical context; it also aims to elucidate the legal structures and institutional mechanisms of the EU.

The legal order of the EU is unique. It differs from both the national legal systems of its component Member States and from traditional international law. It is also a legal order with a clearly articulated dominant purpose: that of "integration" of the markets, economies, and (ultimately) related policies of its Member States. "Integration", in this context, does not mean simple centralisation of powers or harmonisation of laws, but refers to a diverse array of mechanisms by which the EU achieves its integrative aims. Further, the EU's legal order is relatively unstable, certainly when compared to the constitutional settlements of its component Member States, in the sense of being subject to significant "constitutional" changes over short periods of time.[2] It follows that merely to describe the state of EU law at a particular moment is an exercise limited in utility. Rather, what is needed is an

1 More detailed accounts may be found in P. Craig and G. De Búrca, *EU Law: Text, Cases and Materials* (Oxford: OUP, 2003); S. Weatherill, *Cases and Materials on EU Law* (Oxford: OUP, 2003); T. Hartley, *The Foundations of European Community Law* (Oxford: OUP, 2003); J.H.H. Weiler, *The Constitution of Europe* (Cambridge: CUP, 1999); J. Shaw, *Law of the European Union* (Basingstoke: Palgrave, 2000).

2 See B. de Witte, "The Closest Thing to a Constitutional Conversation in Europe: The Semi-Permanent Treaty Revision Process" in P. Beaumont, C. Lyons and N. Walker, *Convergence and Divergence in European Public Law* (Oxford: Hart, 2002). However, it all depends on what is meant by "constitutional" changes: see J.H.H. Weiler, "In defence of the status quo: Europe's

understanding of the EU and its legal order as an unfolding *process*: or as Pierson so neatly puts it, "What one makes of the EU depends on whether one examines a photograph or a moving picture."[3]

The original "European Economic Community" (with its sister communities the European Coal and Steel Community and the European Atomic Energy Community), set up in the 1950s, had six Member States.[4] Subsequent enlargements led to a Community of 15 by 1995,[5] and future enlargements, to include Central and Eastern European states, and also to the south, are set to take place in 2004[6] and 2007.[7] The constitutive document of what is now the European Community[8] is the Treaty of Rome of 1957 (EC Treaty), which, on its face, is a measure of international law, setting obligations and objectives agreed by its Member States. However, crucially, the EC Treaty also establishes common "supranational" administrative, legislative and judicial institutions, with which its Member States share the task of achieving these objectives. The original EC Treaty was significantly amended in 1986 by the "Single European Act", which primarily aimed to set in train the completion of the "single market" or "internal market" by the end of 1992. Subsequent amendments have taken place following a process of "Intergovernmental Conferences" (IGCs), whereby the Heads of State and Government of the Member States agree various (greater or lesser) changes to the Treaty text. In 2002, following the

constitutional *Sonderweg*" in J.H.H. Weiler and M. Wind, eds, *European Constitutionalism Beyond the State* (Cambridge: CUP, 2003), p 9.

3 P. Pierson, "The Path to European Integration: a Historical Institutionalist Analysis" 29 *Comparative Political Studies* (1996) 123 at 127. For elaboration of the idea of the EU's "constitution" as process, see J. Shaw, "Postnational constitutionalism in the European Union" 6 *Journal of European Public Policy* (1999) 579.

4 Belgium, France, Germany, Italy, Luxembourg and the Netherlands.

5 In addition to the original six, Denmark, Ireland and the UK acceded in 1973; Greece in 1980; Spain and Portugal in 1986; and Austria, Finland and Sweden in 1995. The reunification of Germany in 1990 also in effect added the former German Democratic Republic.

6 Negotiations for membership of Cyprus, the Czech Republic, Estonia, Hungary, Poland and Slovenia began in 1998, and for membership of Bulgaria, Latvia, Lithuania, Malta, Romania and the Slovak Republic in 2000. An EU strategy to prepare Turkey for accession was also launched in the late 1990s. Membership criteria (on stability of democratic institutions, protection of the rule of law, human rights and minorities; the existence of a functioning market economy, the capacity to cope with competitive market forces within the EU; adoption of the Community *acquis*, and ability to take on the conditions of membership of the EU, including the aims of economic and monetary union – the "Copenhagen criteria") were established by the European Council meeting at the Copenhagen summit in June 1993. An Accession Treaty, applying to Cyprus, the Czech Republic, Estonia, Hungary, Latvia, Lithuania, Malta, Poland and Slovak Republic and Slovenia, was signed at Athens in April 2003. This provides that those 10 countries will become full members of the EU on 1 May 2004, if all the parties to the Treaty (the new Member States and the existing Member States) have ratified the Treaty according to their respective constitutional requirements (Accession Treaty 2003, Article 2).

7 The European Council in Copenhagen in December 2002 agreed to support the objective of Bulgaria and Romania to join the EU in 2007. Turkey needs to make further progress towards the Copenhagen criteria. Enlargement of the EU is discussed further in chapter 10, pp 414–421.

8 The "Economic" part of the title was formally dropped in 1993 when the Treaty on European Union came into force.

"Laeken Declaration" in December 2001,[9] an additional process for reform was instituted in the establishment of the "Convention on the Future of the European Union", a body made up of a wide range of governmental, parliamentary and other representatives, whose task was to "consider questions about the future development of the EU and to identify possible answers". This body produced a "Draft Treaty establishing a Constitution for Europe" (DCT).[10] This will form the basis of the 2003-04 IGC negotiations for a new composite Treaty, replacing both the EC Treaty and the Treaty on European Union.[11]

The "European Union" came into being after the Member States agreed, in the Treaty of Maastricht 1992 (the Treaty on European Union), to establish it. The European Union (EU) has been characterised as an "umbrella" or "temple" structure, supporting three "pillars" of activity. It is based on the framework of the (renamed) European Community (the "first pillar"), and shares its institutions. The EU comprises this first pillar, and two further "pillars", consisting in cooperation between the Member States on common foreign and security policy; and police and judicial cooperation in matters of criminal law. These latter pillars have only very limited effects on health law and policy (cooperation in the field of combating drug abuse, through the fight against drugs and crime, is probably the most significant area likely to have such an effect).[12] Most of this book is concerned with the impact of the law of the "first pillar" of the EU on health law and policy. Technically speaking, then, this is "Community law". However, the term "EU law" has gained currency as a generalised descriptor for the whole legal order and in particular its institutional and constitutional dimensions. Therefore, "EU law" is the term we adopt in this book. However, where more specific "European Community" elements are at issue, we will revert to the more technically legally accurate terminology, for instance in the discussion of "Community competence".

Even this brief introduction illustrates that there are many ways of conceptualising the EU. To generalise, these may be seen as falling into two camps: those which stress the features of the EU as an international organisation; and those which stress the features of the EU as a constitutionalised legal order, or system of governance.[13] We recognise the value and importance of the first of these conceptualisations. An understanding of the EU's effects on health law and policy would be incomplete if it ignored the fact that the EU has many hallmarks of an international organisation,

9 Laeken Declaration on the Future of the European Union, adopted by the Heads of State and Government at the Laeken Summit, 14–15 December 2001, http://www.europa.eu.int/futurum/documents/offtext/doc151201_en.htm. This declaration sets out what, in the view of its authors at least, are the main current challenges for the EU.

10 Available at http://european-convention.eu.int/. The DCT is discussed further in chapter 10, pp 404–411.

11 See further chapter 10.

12 See, for example, G. Estivenart, ed, *Policies and Strategies to Combat Drugs in Europe* (Dordrecht: Martinus Nijhoff, 1995).

13 For an introduction to the various theoretical approaches to the EU, see B. Rosamund, *Theories of European Integration* (Basingstoke: Macmillan, 2000).

in particular where the Treaty reform process is concerned.[14] It is also important to include in our analysis circumstances where the Member States are acting technically outside the formal legal competence of the Community, but nevertheless use the institutional structures of the EU to agree common positions. These technically bind the Member States only in ordinary international law, but the context of the integration process and the support of the EU institutions may give these agreements a different significance. For instance, the Ministers of State for Health, meeting within the Council of Ministers, included on their agenda matters concerning AIDS and HIV from the mid-1980s, long before the Community had any formal legal competence in the field.[15] The fact of this common action may have been one important element in persuading the Heads of State and Government to agree the Treaty provisions that eventually gave the EU institutions some formal powers in the health field.

However, as is probably already clear from the discussion so far, our approach is to focus on the EU as a constitutionalised legal order or system of governance. In our view, seeing the EU as a system of governance is more appealing as a framework for analysis of the wide-ranging influence and effects the EU has within its geographical territory and beyond, including those on health law and policy. Further, we favour a conceptualisation of the EU as a *multilevel* system of governance in which norms are promulgated through interactions between sub-national, national, EU, and transnational institutions and actors. The benefits and drawbacks of such an approach have been widely discussed in the political science literature.[16] Its core assumptions are that policy-making in the EU cannot be understood simply as determined by the preferences of national governments, and that the political arenas, within which such preferences are formed, are not "nested" solely within states, but are interconnected across state boundaries.[17] From policy initiation, through

14 But see above on the Constitutional Convention. See also the significant literature on the role of the Court in "constitutionalising" the Treaty, especially J.H.H. Weiler, "The Transformation of Europe" 100 *Yale Law Journal* (1991) 2403; and A. Stone Sweet, *Governing with Judges: Constitutional Politics in Europe* (Oxford: OUP, 2000), especially pp 160–193.

15 See further chapter 9.

16 For proponents of a multilevel governance perspective, see L. Hooghe and G. Marks, *Multilevel Governance and European Integration* (Lanham: Rowman & Littlefield, 2001); S. Leibfried and P. Pierson, "European Social Policy" in H. Wallace and W. Wallace, eds, *Policy-Making in the European Union* (Oxford: OUP, 2000); P. Schmitter, "Imagining the Future of the Euro-Polity with the Help of New Concepts" in G. Marks et al, eds, *Governance in the Emerging European Union* (London: Sage, 1996); S. Leibfried and P. Pierson, "Semi-Sovereign Welfare States: Social Policy in a multitiered Europe" in S. Leibfried and P. Pierson, eds, *European Social Policy: Between Fragmentation and Integration* (Washington: Brookings, 1995); F. Scharpf, "Community and Autonomy: Multi-Level Policy-Making in the European Union" 1 *Journal of European Public Policy* (1994) 219; G. Marks, "Structural Policy in the European Community" in A. Sbragia, ed, *Euro-Politics: Institutions and Policy-Making in the "New" European Community* (Washington: Brookings, 1992), p 191. As a starting point for a critique of such an approach, see Rosamund, above n 13; and see, in particular, the work of Moravcsik, for instance, A. Moravcsik, "Preferences and Power in the European Community: A Liberal Intergovernmental Approach" 31 JCMS (1993) 473.

17 See Hooghe and Marks, above n 16, pp 2–29.

decision-making, to implementation and adjudication, actors other than national governments have significant influences on the EU's law and policy. Fundamentally, such a "governance" perspective on the EU, while not denying that national governments and national arenas are important, accords an influential explanatory role to the independent agency of supranational institutions, such as the Commission and the European Court of Justice.[18] This focus on supranational institutions, including judicial institutions, places significant emphasis on the roles of law, and in particular judge-made law, in the integration process.[19]

Of course, it is not necessarily possible to define with precision whether a particular actor or institution "belongs" to the sub-national, national, EU or indeed transnational level. For instance, an "EU level" scientific committee, say, the Scientific Committee on Food, is made up of "national" experts, who may also act for "transnational" bodies, such as those that form the UN *Codex Alimentarius* system.[20] Indeed the very notion of "levels" may be seen as implying a hierarchy (with the EU as the "top" or "central" level), which we would seek to reject.[21] However, our primary research question – how does EU law affect health law and policy? – requires a focus on the "EU-level" elements of the system, which would be more difficult to achieve were we to adopt a strictly heterarchical model of the EU's legal order. Moreover, the metaphor of levels, though limited, as every model must be, may be particularly appealing to lawyers. For instance, in exercising its judicial review function, the law adopts such a notion of different levels, or arenas,[22] operating on

18 For a starting point on "new institutionalism" in EU studies, see Rosamund, above n 13; and P. Craig, "The Nature of the Community: Integration, Democracy and Legitimacy" in P. Craig and G. de Búrca, eds, *The Evolution of EU Law* (Oxford: OUP, 1999); K. Armstrong and S. Bulmer, *The Governance of the Single European Market* (Manchester: MUP, 1998); K. Armstrong, "Legal Integration: Theorizing the Legal Dimension of European Integration" 36 JCMS (1998) 155; K. Armstrong, "The New Institutionalism" in P. Craig and C. Harlow, eds, *Lawmaking in the European Union* (Deventer: Kluwer, 1998).

19 See, for example, A.-M. Burley and W. Mattli, "Europe before the Court: a Political Theory of Legal Integration" 47 *International Organization* (1993) 1; K. Alter and S. Meunier-Aitsahalia, "Judicial Politics in the European Community: European Integration and the Path-breaking *Cassis de Dijon* Decision" 26 *Comparative Political Studies* (1994) 535; E. Stein, "Lawyers, Judges and the making of a Transnational Constitution" 75 *American Journal of International Law* (1971) 1; A. Stone Sweet, "From free trade to supranational policy: the European court and integration" in W. Sandholtz and A. Stone Sweet, eds, *European Integration and Supranational Governance* (Oxford: OUP, 1998). In so far as we consider the impact of rules and norms in the construction of the EU, and its identity, our position may also be said to resonate with a "constructivist" approach to European integration studies. See T. Christiansen, K.E. Jorgensen and A. Wiener, "The social construction of Europe" 6 *Journal of European Public Policy* (1999) 528; A. Wiener, "Editorial: Evolving Norms of Constitutionalism" 9 ELJ (2003) 1.

20 See P. Gray, "The Scientific Committee for Food" in M. Van Schendelen, *EU Committees as Influential Policy-Makers* (Aldershot: Dartmouth, 1998), pp 81, 83.

21 K. Armstrong, *Regulation, Deregulation, Reregulation* (London: Kogan Page, 2000), p 55: "Traditional hierarchical images of European governance tend to operate within simplified notions of that system of governance in the sense that decision-making is understood as taking place at 'national' or 'Community' level. In reality, governance takes place within linked networks of decision-making, drawing on human resources from national, European and international settings; harnessing public and private actors; and utilising different sources of knowledge."

22 See N. MacCormick, *Questioning Sovereignty* (Oxford: OUP, 1999).

the basis of the "legal fiction" that acts of governance are attributable to one level or another, and thus reviewable in courts at one level or another.[23]

Further, a multilevel governance perspective avoids the rather uncritical "Europhile" stance on allocation of competencies that sometimes characterises EU legal literature.[24] This view of the EU's legal order tends to describe as "progress" all allocation of law-making power to the EU institutions, and conversely to bemoan the retention of powers at national levels. Such a mindset ignores important questions concerning the locus of law-making within an increasingly diverse legal order, increasingly distant from those it seeks to regulate. Fundamentally, by concentrating only on the *locus* for decision-making, it diverts attention from the important question of whether the relevant policy *outcomes* are "good" or "bad", from a normative perspective by reference, say, to a particular socio-economic constitutional model, or to a particular notion of democratic governance. Although we are not taking a particular normative perspective with respect to the constitutional model appropriate for the EU in this book, our evaluation of the impact of EU law on health law and policy, ultimately concerned with the allocation of social goods, may raise future research questions along those lines. Perhaps more importantly, the uncritical "allocation of competencies" perspective, by assuming that allocation of law-making power to the EU institutions is beneficial, tends to assume that EU-level harmonised policy solutions (and legislation) are the most appropriate mechanism for integration or mode of regulation. This approach fails to consider significant "new" modes of governance within the EU.[25] Such new modes of governance move beyond the "classic" Community method of harmonisation, and seek to allow for participation, power-sharing, coordination between local, regional, national and EU-level actors, diversity, decentralisation, deliberation, flexibility, revisability, experimentation and knowledge creation.[26] Thus, for instance, new governance includes considering the possible benefits of regime competition within a quasi-federal legal order.[27]

23 For discussion of the significance of this in the context of regulation of genetically modified foods, see T. Hervey, "Regulation of Genetically Modified Products in a Multi-Level System of Governance: Science or Citizens?" 10 *Review of EC and International Environmental Law* (2001) 321.

24 For a striking example of this, see Lord Slynn of Hadley, "Preface" in D. O'Keeffe and P. Twomey, eds, *Legal Issues of the Maastricht Treaty* (Chichester: Wiley Chancery, 1994): "the papers in this book . . . are written, as I see it, by lawyers who are wholly in favour of the aims of the Community and of developing integration (union) . . . "

25 See Commission, *European Governance: A White Paper* COM(2001) 428 final. Such modes of governance are elaborated and subjected to critical analysis in the contributions to the special issue of the *European Law Journal*, Volume 8, No 1, edited by Scott and Trubek. See also the on-line papers from the Jean Monnet Symposium, *Mountain or Molehill: A Critical Appraisal of the Commission White Paper on Governance*, http://www.jeanmonnetprogram.org/papers/01/.

26 J. Scott and D.M. Trubek, "Mind the Gap: Law and New Approaches to Governance in the European Union" 8 ELJ (2002) 1. For further information on one of these new methods of governance, the "open method of coordination", see chapter 10, pp 412–414.

27 See, in this respect for instance, D. Chalmers, "The Single Market: From Prima Donna to Journeyman" in J. Shaw and G. More, eds, *New Legal Dynamics of European Union* (Oxford: Clarendon, 1995); C. Barnard, "Social Dumping and the Race to the Bottom: Some Lessons for the EU from Delaware" 25 ELRev (2000) 57.

Moreover, and fundamentally, a dichotomous legalistic conceptualisation of law and policy-making in the EU (law is made either at EU level or at national level)[28] *simply fails to capture the actual processes* by which law is made and implemented in many areas of EU activity. For instance, in the regulation of clinical research and of marketing of pharmaceuticals, the policy-making process involves interactions between national civil servants, Commission officials, and technical experts, meeting in various fora including the European Medicines Evaluation Agency, national authorisation authorities, the International Conference on Harmonisation and the World Health Organisation's International Conferences of Drug Regulatory Authorities.[29] In so far as it ignores the implementation phase of law and policy-making, such a legalistic conception ignores activities of national actors even in core areas of Community law, such as internal market law.[30] It also fails to take seriously the very real impact of "soft law",[31] the "open method of coordination"[32] and other mechanisms of persuasion in the integration process, such as the impact of EU-level financial support.[33] Thus, for all these reasons, we conceptualise the EU's legal order as that of a multilevel system of governance.

II. What does the European Union do?

The aims, goals and values of the European Union and of the European Community are found in the preambles and introductory sections of the EC Treaty and the Treaty on European Union (TEU). For instance, the TEU and the EC Treaty refer to the creation of an "ever closer union" among the peoples of Europe.[34] The objectives of the EU include the promotion of economic and social progress, high employment and balanced and sustainable development; the implementation of

28 For a striking example of such a conceptualisation, see the work of Toth: for instance, A. Toth, "A Legal Analysis of Subsidiarity" in D. O'Keeffe and P. Twomey, eds, *Legal Issues of the Maastricht Treaty* (Chichester: Wiley Chancery, 1994).

29 See further chapters 7 and 8.

30 See Armstrong and Bulmer, above n 18; T. Daintith, ed, *Implementing EC Law in the UK: Structures for Indirect Rule* (Chichester: Wiley, 1995).

31 For discussion of soft law, see, for instance, K.C. Wellens and G.M. Borchardt, "Soft Law in European Community Law" 14 ELRev (1989) 267; J. Kenner, "The EU Employment Title and the 'Third Way': Making Soft Law Work?" 15 *International Journal of Comparative Labour Law and Industrial Relations* (1999) 33.

32 See further chapter 10. See, for instance, E. Szyszczak, "The New Paradigm for Social Policy: A Virtuous Circle" 38 CMLRev (2001) 1125; Kenner, above n 31; E. Szyszczak, "The Evolving European Employment Strategy" in J. Shaw, ed, *Social Law and Policy in an Evolving European Union* (Oxford: Hart, 2000); C. De La Porte, "Is the Open Method of Coordination Appropriate for Organising Activities at European Level in Sensitive Policy Areas?" 8 ELJ (2002) 38; K. Armstrong, "Tackling Social Exclusion through OMC: Reshaping the Boundaries of EU Governance" in T. Börzel and R. Cichowski, eds, *State of the Union: Law, Politics and Society* (Vol 6) (Oxford: OUP, 2003); S. Regent, "The Open Method of Coordination: A New Supranational Form of Governance?" 9 ELJ (2003) 190; F. Scharpf, "The European Social Model: Coping with the Challenges of Diversity" 40 JCMS (2002) 645.

33 For discussion of the relationship between the role of law in "classic" theories of integration, and under the open method of coordination, see Armstrong, above n 32.

34 Article 1 TEU; Preamble EC.

a common foreign and security policy, including a common defence policy; and the maintenance and development of an area of freedom, security and justice, in which the free movement of persons is assured in conjunction with external border controls on persons.[35] Article 2 EC sets out the "task" of the EC:

> "The Community shall have as its task, by establishing a common market and an economic and monetary union and by implementing common policies or activities ... to promote throughout the Community a harmonious, balanced and sustainable development of economic activities, a high level of employment and of social protection, equality between men and women, sustainable and non-inflationary growth, a high degree of competitiveness and convergence of economic performance, a high level of protection and improvement of the quality of the environment, the raising of the standard of living and quality of life, and economic and social cohesion and solidarity among Member States."

These generalised statements give some idea of the overall mission of the EC and EU, but these do not necessarily reflect substantive EU law, especially during earlier stages of its development. Here the pursuit of the integration process through the development of the "single" or "internal" market – "an area without internal frontiers in which the free movement of goods, persons, services and capital is ensured"[36] – formed a substantial part of the endeavours of the EU – a role which it plays to this day. The internal market is to be established through integration by law, and the legal provisions that thus promote the integration process enjoy an enduring centrality within EU law. However, as we shall see, over time, the discourse defining EU law as concerned with *integration* of markets has been overlaid by a discourse about EU law as a system of *governance*.[37] This shift in the language of EU law appears to have at least two implications. First, although the EU's system of governance may be primarily concerned with the integration of markets, this is not to be integration at the expense of "good governance", in the sense of legitimate, transparent or accountable law and policy-making.[38] Second, implicit in a "governance" perspective is the notion that the "internal market" is not simply an "economic" construct,

35 Article 2 TEU.

36 Article 14 (2) EC.

37 Armstrong and Bulmer, above n 18; F. Scharpf, *Governing in Europe: Effective and Democratic?* (Oxford: OUP, 1999); G. Majone, *Regulating Europe* (London: Routledge, 1996); G. Majone, "A European regulatory state?" in J. Richardson, ed, *European Union: power and policy-making* (London: Routledge, 1996); G. Marks, L. Hooghe and K. Blank, "European Integration from the 1980s: State-Centric *v* Multi-Level Governance" 34 JCMS (1996) 3; G. Marks et al, *Governance in the European Union* (London: Sage, 1996); J. Richardson, "Policy-making in the EU: Interests, Ideas and Garbage Cans of Primeval Soup" in J. Richardson, ed, *European Union: power and policy-making* (London: Routledge, 1996); S. Hix, "The Study of the European Community: The Challenge to Comparative Politics" 17 *West European Politics* (1994) 1; M. Jachenfuchs, "Theoretical Perspectives on European Governance" (1995) 1 ELJ 115; J. Peterson, "Decision-Making in the European Union: Towards a Framework for Analysis" 2 *Journal of European Public Policy* (1995) 1; special issue of the *European Law Journal*, Volume 8, No 1, edited by Scott and Trubek; Commission, *European Governance: A White Paper* COM(2001) 428 final.

38 See further above p 36 and below pp 50–51 and 64.

divorceable from the broader social contexts in which it operates. This notion may in fact be traced to the original EEC Treaty, which established, in addition to the internal market provisions, a number of "common policies" for the EC. Best known among these is probably the common agricultural policy,[39] but as the EU has developed through time these have expanded to include common policies in diverse areas such as competition; economic and monetary affairs; transport; industrial affairs; employment; social policy, including education and health; consumer protection; the environment; research and development; "economic and social cohesion" (by which is meant the EU's main redistributive functions, administered through the European Regional Development Fund and the European Social Fund); and overseas development. A number of these common policies and activities of the EU have effects, more or less direct, on national health law and policy.

One way of considering what the EU actually does is to look at its budget.[40] The EU has had autonomous sources of revenue since the 1970s. Even after successive reforms, the largest share of the EU's expenditure (about 45%) remains committed to the common agricultural policy, with about 35% of expenditure on economic and social cohesion. The next largest budgetary item is aid to applicant countries and external development aid, taking up around 8%. The administrative expenditure of the institutions represents around 5%. This leaves only 7% of the overall budget for internal policies, within which the major EU spending in the field of health falls. Looking at the budget also gives an impression of the size of the EU's enterprise. The idea, at times perpetuated by the British media, of swathes of "Brussels bureaucrats" is a gross exaggeration. In fact, the European Commission employs fewer people than a large county council in England.[41] The EU budget represents only a fraction of levels of public spending in the Member States. It is obvious from this that the EU, as currently constituted, cannot possibly replace health spending in the Member States. The EU's redistributive interventions in the health field are small-scale, in the totality of health spending across the EU as a whole. However, they may nevertheless be significant, especially at the margins, for instance, where EU funds are made available for activities for which there is little support among national administrations, such as in the case of research into "orphan medicines", for the treatment of conditions affecting very small proportions of the populations of the Member States. Financial support may promote integration through encouraging certain types of activities over others by granting them finance in addition to that available at national or sub-national level. Indirect

39 For an introduction, see E. Rieger, "The CAP" in W. Wallace and H. Wallace, eds, *Policy-Making in the European Union* (Oxford: OUP, 2000). See also K.A. Ingersent, A.J. Rayner and R.C. Hine, *The Reform of the Common Agricultural Policy* (Basingstoke: Macmillan, 1998). For discussion of the law of the CAP (although now rather dated), see J.A. Usher, *Legal Aspects of Agriculture in the EU* (Oxford: Clarendon Press, 1998); and M. Cardwell, *The European Model of Agriculture* (Oxford: OUP, forthcoming 2004).

40 For an introduction to the EU budget, see B. Laffan and M. Shackleton, "The Budget" in H. Wallace and W. Wallace, eds, *Policy-making in the European Union* (Oxford: OUP, 2000).

41 A. Hayes, "The EU and Public Health beyond the Year 2000" 4 *eurohealth* (1998) 2.

pressures for change at national level may arise as a result.[42] However, given that the EU's budgetary powers are distinctly weak, it is not surprising that the EU's main influence, in the field of health among others, has been in *regulation*, rather than redistribution.[43]

Second, then, in understanding what the EU actually does, we need to consider the EU's law and policy-making or regulatory activities. The legislative institutions of the EU have limited competence. In legal terms, this means that the EU institutions may act only where the founding Treaties have given them power to act. This is encapsulated in the principle of "conferred powers", set out in Article 5 (1) EC, which provides that "the Community shall act within the limits of the powers conferred upon it by this Treaty and the objectives assigned to it therein". Treaty provisions granting power to the EU institutions to take regulatory action (to enact EU law) are known as "legal basis provisions".[44] A legal basis provision is also necessary for non-regulatory action, such as the disbursement of the budget, or other administrative acts. Legal basis provisions set out the fields in which the EU institutions may act, and also, importantly, as we shall see, the procedures by which they may so act. Action taken outside the powers given by these legal basis provisions is unlawful, and acts so taken may be annulled by the European Court of Justice.[45]

However, this very straightforward-sounding position is made more complex by three further considerations. First, the Court has accepted a notion of *implied* competence, where the Treaty does not explicitly grant a power, but requires the achievement of an objective.[46] Second, in very many fields of action, including health, the Community does not have exclusive competence to act, but shares this competence with the Member States.[47] In those circumstances, the Treaty provides that Community action is limited to that which "cannot be sufficiently achieved by the Member States" acting alone and therefore can be better achieved by the Community, by reference to the "scale or effects" of the action.[48] Further, Community action is limited by the principle of proportionality: it must not go beyond what

42 For example, outside the health field, in education, the Erasmus and Socrates programmes supporting migration of students within the EU played a role in prompting changes to national education policy: see J. Shaw, "From the Margins to the Centre: Education and Training Law and Policy" in P. Craig and G. de Búrca, *The Evolution of EU Law* (Oxford: OUP, 1999).

43 Majone, above n 37; Majone, in J. Richardson, ed, above n 37.

44 Article 253 EC requires that a statement of reasons must be given by the EU institutions for each piece of secondary legislation enacted. This statement includes a reference to the relevant legal basis provision in the Treaty.

45 Under the procedures set out in Article 230 EC or Article 234 EC.

46 Cases 281, 283–5, 287/85 *Germany v Commission* [1987] ECR 3203.

47 On exclusive competence compare A. Toth, "A Legal Analysis of Subsidiarity" and J. Steiner, "Subsidiarity under the Maastricht Treaty" in D. O'Keeffe and P. Twomey, eds, *Legal Issues of the Maastricht Treaty* (London: Chancery, 1994); see also S. Weatherill, "Beyond Preemption? Shared Competence and Constitutional Change in the European Community" in O'Keeffe and Twomey, eds, above.

48 Article 5 (2) EC; and see Protocol No 30 on Subsidiarity and Proportionality, annexed by the Treaty of Amsterdam to the EC Treaty, 1997.

is necessary to achieve its objectives.[49] Third, the precise scope of a particular legal basis provision may be unclear. This is particularly so for the "catch-all" legal basis provision found in Article 308 EC, which provides that:

> "if action by the Community should prove necessary to attain, in the course of the operation of the common market, one of the objectives of the Community and this Treaty has not provided the necessary powers, the Council shall, acting unanimously on a proposal from the Commission, and after consulting the European Parliament, take the appropriate measures."

Thus the precise extent of Community competence may, for all these reasons, be the subject of significant political disagreement; disagreement which may be resolved through legal discourse.[50]

The fact that the legal basis also sets out the relevant procedure for regulatory action may result in the adoption of Community legislation on some surprising legal basis provisions. For instance, the Working Time Directive, which sets out maximum working hours and provides for paid holidays and rest periods,[51] was enacted on the basis of what was then Article 118a EC. This gave the EU institutions power to adopt legislation to ensure "health and safety at work". The reason for the choice of legal basis was that the procedure under Article 118a EC provided for only a qualified majority of Member States voting in Council in favour of the proposal. The UK government, which had opposed the proposal in Council, subsequently challenged the Working Time Directive, arguing that Article 118a was the wrong legal basis for the measure, and that in fact a procedure involving a unanimous vote for the proposal in the Council (thus effectively granting the UK a veto on the measure) should have been chosen. The resolution of the matter before the European Court of Justice[52] turned on the interpretation of the term "health and safety". The Court adopted a broad notion, drawing explicitly on the World Health Organisation's definition of health as a "state of complete physical, mental and social well-being that does not consist only in the absence of illness or infirmity".[53] Thus working hours fell within the notion of health and safety in Article 118a, and the Working Time Directive was valid. As we will see throughout the book, measures of

49 Article 5 (3) EC. For discussion of proportionality and subsidiarity, see G.A. Bermann, "Proportionality and Subsidiarity" in C. Barnard and J. Scott, *The Law of the Single European Market: Unpacking the Premises* (Oxford: Hart, 2002).

50 In particular, through judicial review litigation before the European Court of Justice, Article 230 EC. See further chapter 3.

51 Directive 93/104/EC. Incidentally, these apply equally to health care professionals, which has caused problems in some Member States such as the UK, where junior doctors' hours were longer than those prescribed by the Directive.

52 Case C-84/94 *UK v Council (Working Time)* [1996] ECR I-5755.

53 Para 15. Preamble to the Constitution of the World Health Organization as adopted by the International Health Conference, New York, 19–22 June 1946; signed on 22 July 1946 by the representatives of 61 States (Official Records of the World Health Organization, No 2, p. 100) and entered into force on 7 April 1948.

EU law affecting health law and policy have been adopted on a number of different legal bases, and these are elaborated in chapter 3.

Overall, then, what the EU does is to promote economic (and to a greater or lesser extent, depending upon the context, social and even political) integration partly through its redistributive powers, but largely through its regulatory activities, in the adoption and implementation of EU law. Generally speaking, EU law is adopted by EU-level institutions, and implemented by institutions at national level. The legislative acts of the EU institutions are known as "secondary sources" of EU law (the primary sources being the founding Treaties). Secondary sources of EU law include "hard" or binding legal measures, such as regulations, directives and decisions. A regulation is a measure of general application, "binding in its entirety and directly applicable in all Member States", and a decision is binding on those to whom it is addressed.[54] The term "directly applicable" in this context means that regulations and decisions take legal effect in the legal systems of Member States without the need for intervening action on the part of national legislatures or executives. Further, the European Court of Justice has found that certain provisions of both primary and secondary EU law have "direct effect", that is they are enforceable at the suit of individuals, before the national courts of the Member States.[55] Directives are said to be "binding as to the result to be achieved", but to "leave to the national authorities the choice of form and methods".[56] In fact, interpretation of this provision by the European Court of Justice,[57] and the practice of adopting detailed directives, that leave very little discretion to national authorities in terms of their mode of adoption, means that directives also have significant legal effects in Member States, both where they have been implemented in national legal orders[58] and also in circumstances where national authorities fail to implement them, or fail to implement them correctly.[59] Secondary sources of EU law also include a wide

54 Article 249 EC.

55 Case 26/62 *Van Gend en Loos* [1963] ECR 1; Case 43/75 *Defrenne v SABENA (No 2)* [1976] ECR 455; Case 39/72 *Commission v Italy* [1973] ECR 101; Case 9/70 *Grad v Finanzamt Traunstein* [1970] ECR 825; Case 104/81 *Kupferberg* [1982] ECR 3641; Case 41/74 *Van Duyn v Home Office* [1974] ECR 1337; Case 148/78 *Ratti* [1979] ECR 1629; Case 152/84 *Marshall v Southampton and South West Hampshire Area Health Authority* [1986] ECR 723. For discussion, see, for example, P. Pescatore, "The Doctrine of Direct Effect: An Infant Disease of Community Law" 8 ELRev (1983) 155; P. Craig, "Once upon a time in the west: Direct Effect and the Federalization of EEC Law" 12 OJLS (1992) 453; S. Prechal, "Does Direct Effect still Matter?" 37 CMLRev (2000) 1047.

56 Article 249 EC.

57 Case 41/74 *Van Duyn* above n 55; Case 148/78 *Ratti* above n 55; Case 152/84 *Marshall* above n 55; Case C-188/89 *Foster v British Gas* [1990] ECR I-3313.

58 Case C-62/00 *Marks & Spencer v Commissioners of Customs and Excise* [2002] ECR I-6325.

59 See also the Court's doctrines of "indirect effect" (Case 14/83 *Von Colson and Kamann v Land Nordrhein-Westfalen* [1984] ECR 1891; Case C-106/89 *Marleasing* [1990] ECR I-4135; Case C-334/92 *Wagner Miret* [1993] ECR I-6911; Case C-168/95 *Arcaro* [1996] ECR I-4705); "incidental effect" (Case C-194/94 *CIA Security* [1996] ECR I-220; Case C-129/94 *Bernàldez* [1996] ECR I-1829; Case C-443/98 *Unilever Italia* [2000] ECR I-7535); the requirement of adequacy of remedies (Case 14/83 *Von Colson* above; Case C-213/89 *Factortame* [1990] ECR I-2433; Case C-208/90 *Emmott* [1991] ECR I-4269; Case C-271/91 *Marshall v Southampton and South West Hampshire Area Health Authority (No 2)* [1993] ECR I-4367; Case C-50/00P *UPA v Council* [2002]

variety of measures of "soft" or non-binding law, which, though lacking formal legal force, may nevertheless have significant effects in practice.[60]

III. What methods of governance does the European Union employ?

The EU utilises a number of different methods of governance in fulfilling its integrative aims. The method used depends upon a number of factors, including the policy field at issue, and the likelihood of securing agreement and cooperation from relevant national institutions.[61] Different methods of governance have enjoyed more or less significance at different periods in the evolution of the EU. Within a particular policy field, a number of different methods may be used simultaneously or sequentially, and interactions between the methods are therefore also important. For our purposes,[62] we divide the EU's methods of governance into six:

- deregulation;
- "old style" harmonisation;
- "new approach" harmonisation;
- regulatory coordination;
- "soft" coordination; and
- financial incentives.

Of these, the first four involve the achievement of European integration through the agreement of binding legal norms. Because of the nature of the EU's legal order, these norms are enforceable not simply by the Member States as parties to the founding Treaties, but also by individual litigants. This gives a significant influence to courts (both national courts and the European Court of Justice) in the EU's legal order.

ECR I-6677); and "state liability" (Cases C-6 & 9/90 *Francovich and Bonifaci v Italy* [1991] ECR I-5357; Cases C-46 & 48/93 *Brasserie du Pêcheur* [1996] ECR I-1029; Cases C-178-9 & 188-90/94 *Dillenkofer* [1996] ECR I-2553; Case C-224/01 *Köbler* [2003] ECR I-(30th September 2003, nyr in ECR). For discussion, see, for example, P. Craig, "Directives: Direct Effect, Indirect Effect and the Construction of National Legislation" 22 ELRev (1997) 519; G. de Búrca, "Giving Effect to Community Directives" 55 MLR (1992) 215; R. Craufurd-Smith, "Remedies for Breaches of EC Law in National Courts: Legal Variation and Selection" in P. Craig and G. de Búrca, eds, *The Evolution of EU Law* (Oxford: OUP, 1999); F. Snyder, "The Effectiveness of European Community Law" 56 MLR (1993) 19; W. van Gerven, "Of Rights, Remedies and Procedures" 37 CMLRev (2000) 501; P. Craig, "Once More unto the Breach: The Community, the State and Damages Liability" 109 LQR (1997) 67; W. van Gerven, "Bridging the Unbridgeable: Community and National Tort Laws after *Francovich* and *Brasserie*" 45 ICLQ (1996) 507.

60 F. Snyder, "The Effectiveness of European Community Law: Institutions, Processes, Tools and Techniques" 56 MLR (1993) 19 at 32; see further below.

61 This perspective draws on a view of the EU institutions as "purposeful opportunists", see in particular L. Cram, *Policy-making in the EU: conceptual lenses and the integration process* (London: Routledge, 1997).

62 Of course, as is the case with any model, the "fit" with real life governance may be imprecise. For an alternative typology, see B. Duncan, "Health Policy in the European Union: How it's made and how to influence it" 324 BMJ (2002) 1027.

Deregulation

The EC Treaty envisages the unfettered movement of factors of production within the territory of the EU (originally the "common market", now the "single" or "internal market"[63]), and puts in place legal mechanisms to ensure the necessary economic integration to create that single market. One mechanism used is deregulation. The Treaty prohibits all customs duties, quantitative restrictions on imports, exports, and "measures having equivalent effect" on goods moving between the Member States.[64] Restrictions on the freedom to provide services, and on the free movement of capital within the Community, are also prohibited.[65] Workers must be allowed to move freely within the Community in order to take up employment;[66] and (unjustified) restrictions on the freedom of establishment of the self-employed (including professionals) and companies are prohibited.[67]

The use of deregulation as a method of governance, and to promote integration and the formation of a single market, is illustrated by the Treaty provisions concerning free movement of goods. These have been held by the European Court of Justice to be directly effective. Directly effective provisions confer rights upon individuals within the Member States, which become part of their "legal heritage".[68] This is a key element of the unique nature of the EU's legal order. EU law is more than ordinary international law, agreed between and binding upon sovereign states. EU law creates rights and obligations in respect of individuals within those states, and takes effect within national legal orders. National courts are obliged to give effect to directly effective provisions of Community law as if they were provisions of national law.[69] Thus such a right in EU law may be relied upon as a cause of action, or as a defence, in legal proceedings before national courts in the Member States. It follows that individuals may bring legal proceedings, before their own courts or the courts of other Member States, in order to challenge any remaining customs duties or quantitative restrictions on imports or exports, or "measures having equivalent effect", that stand in the way of the single market. The term "measures having equivalent effect" has been given a broad interpretation by the European Court of Justice, and covers, according to the *Dassonville* test, "all trading rules enacted by Member States which are capable of hindering, directly or indirectly, actually or potentially, intra-Community trade".[70] Such national measures, if they breach the Treaty provisions, must, according to the European Court

63 On the evolution of the single market, see P. Craig, "The Evolution of the Single Market" in C. Barnard and J. Scott, eds, *The Law of the Single European Market: Unpacking the Premises* (Oxford: Hart, 2002).

64 Articles 23, 24, 28 and 29 EC.

65 Article 49 EC; Article 56 EC.

66 Article 39 (1), (3) EC.

67 Article 43 EC.

68 Case 26/62 *Van Gend en Loos* above n 55, para 11.

69 Case 26/62 *Van Gend en Loos* above n 55; Case 6/64 *Costa v ENEL* [1964] ECR 585.

70 Case 8/74 *Procureur du Roi v Dassonville* [1974] ECR 837.

of Justice, be held by national courts to be inapplicable, in accordance with the EC Treaty.[71]

The Treaty provisions on free movement apply to all goods and services that form part of the national economies of the Member States. The fact that provision of a good or service forms part of a national health care system is not sufficient in itself to remove it from the application of EU law.[72] So, for example, importers of pharmaceuticals have relied on directly effective EU law to challenge barriers to free movement of these medicinal goods. Wide differences in prices of pharmaceuticals in different Member States (arising largely from differences in arrangements for the purchase of pharmaceuticals by national authorities) were underpinned by holders of intellectual property rights, such as patents and trade marks, in the pharmaceuticals, preventing the "parallel import" of the goods from a Member State in which they are cheap into a Member State in which they are more expensive. The price differentials were sufficient to attract parallel importers, who sought to rely on the EC Treaty in order to challenge the exercise of such intellectual property rights in these circumstances. The parallel importer "Centrafarm" has been a particularly insistent litigant in this respect. Its litigation began in the early 1970s, with challenges to patents and trademark rights that were being relied on to prevent the parallel import into the Netherlands of various pharmaceuticals. Although the EC Treaty provides that it is without prejudice to the rules in Member States governing property ownership,[73] and that protection of industrial and commercial property is an exception to the principle of free movement of goods,[74] the European Court of Justice held that once the intellectual property right has been "exhausted", and the product placed on the market in one Member State, to inhibit parallel imports constitutes an unjustified breach of EU law on the free movement of goods.[75] Thus one barrier to the creation of a single market in pharmaceuticals was removed in accordance with the application of directly effective deregulatory EU law.

One of the benefits of deregulation from the point of view of the institutions of the EU is that it moves the detailed working out of the processes of integration from the highly visible political arena, where differences in approach may be extremely difficult to reconcile, to the judicial arena, where solutions are reached by an "impartial" body, relatively shielded from public scrutiny. Here, respect for the rule of law and the authority of courts help to ensure compliance with EU-level norms. This is particularly so where it is *national* courts that actually apply EU

71 Case C-213/89 *Factortame* [1990] ECR I-2433. This doctrine of "supremacy" of EU law has posed problems for national constitutional courts, in particular with respect to the protection of fundamental human rights: see the discussion below.

72 See Case C-120/95 *Decker* [1998] ECR I-1831; Case C-158/96 *Kohll* [1998] ECR I-1931; Case C-368/98 *Vanbraekel* [2001] ECR I-5363; Case C-157/99 *Geraets-Smits* [2001] ECR I 5473.

73 Article 295 EC (ex Article 222 EEC).

74 Article 30 EC (ex Article 36 EEC).

75 Case 15/74 *Centrafarm v Sterling Drug* [1974] ECR 1147; Case 16/74 *Centrafarm v Winthrop* [1974] ECR 1183.

law, which is the case with directly effective provisions. However, deregulation, as a mode of governance or integration strategy, also has limits. The Member States of the EU do not have a tradition of neo-liberal economics with which classical market deregulation is associated. Rather, the Member States of the EU have tended to reflect more of a "social market" tradition, in which public intervention in the free operation of markets is accepted and indeed expected. Such intervention may be presented either as required to prevent various "market failures" (social values as "market perfecting or correcting"), or as to promote values of social justice as ends in themselves.[76]

Deregulatory EU internal market law prohibits measures having equivalent effect to quantitative restrictions on imports or exports. Such measures may apply only to imported goods. However, they may be measures that are equally applicable to domestically produced and imported goods, but have a disproportionate impact on imported goods.[77] In principle, for instance, a national rule with the objective of protecting health, such as a rule banning certain additives in foodstuffs, could breach the Treaty provisions on the free movement of goods, being a measure capable of hindering, directly or indirectly, actually or potentially, intra-Community trade. This deregulatory thrust of the provisions on the free movement of goods posed a potential risk to health policy within the Member States, as individual traders might rely on directly effective rights in EU law to undermine the substantive content of national health policies. Moreover, unfettered movement of goods might pose hazards to health in the Member States, for instance, if dangerous goods, or disease-carrying goods, moved without regulatory checks and were marketable throughout the territory of the EU.

EU law provides a number of responses to these potential threats to health. First, there is a limited exception in the EC Treaty from the general principle that goods are allowed to move freely within the common market. This is now found in Article 30 EC, which provides, *inter alia*, that the Treaty "shall not preclude prohibitions or restrictions on imports . . . justified on grounds of . . . the protection of health and life of humans, animals or plants . . . ". However, such prohibitions must be justified in accordance with the principle of proportionality,[78] and may not "constitute a means of arbitrary discrimination or a disguised restriction on trade between Member States". So, for example, the Court has rejected arguments raised

76 On deregulation, the internal market and the EU's socio-economic constitution, see, for instance, M. Poiares Maduro, *We The Court: The European Court of Justice and the European Economic Constitution* (Oxford: Hart, 1998); Scharpf, above n 37; on social law in particular, see S. Deakin, "Labour Law as Market Regulation" in P. Davies et al, eds, *European Community Labour Law: Principles and Perspectives* (Oxford: Clarendon, 1996); G. Majone, "Which social policy for Europe?" in Y. Mény, P. Muller and J.-L. Quermonne, eds, *Adjusting to Europe: The impact of the European Union on national institutions and policies* (London: Routledge, 1996); W. Streek, "Neovoluntarism: A New European Social Policy Regime?" 1 ELJ (1995) 31.

77 Sometimes termed "distinctly applicable" and "indistinctly applicable" measures: see J. Steiner, *Textbook on EEC Law* (London: Blackstones, 1988) p 63. See Directive 70/50/EEC, OJ Sp Ed (I) p 17; Case 120/78 *Cassis de Dijon* [1979] ECR 649.

78 The restriction on trade must be no more than is necessary to meet its objective.

by Member States to the effect that a second set of health checks is required for goods already checked in the Member State of origin.[79] However, where this is not the case, the European Court of Justice has been relatively generous in its interpretation of the health protection exemption in Article 30 EC. For instance, national legislation laying down a general prohibition on the use of tricholoroethylene – a carcinogenic substance – (with a system of individual exemptions) is justified under Article 30 EC.[80]

The second response is a Court-developed exception to the free movement rules. Some national measures that do have an effect on intra-Community trade within the *Dassonville* test nevertheless have been held by the Court to fall outside the scope of EU law entirely. In particular, rules relating to selling arrangements, which restrict market access equally to domestically produced and imported goods, are not covered by EU law on free movement of goods.[81] Further, the Court has accepted that some national measures, again technically falling within *Dassonville*, or its equivalent with respect to free movement of persons, freedom of establishment or the free supply and receipt of services, may be justified by a legitimate public interest.[82] Such public interests include protection of human health, and other grounds closely related to national health policies, such as protection of the environment,[83] consumer protection[84] and the safeguarding of the financial balance of national social security schemes.[85]

The third response of EU law to the threats to public interests, such as maintaining health protection from the deregulatory impact of single market law, is to move the site of regulation. Different health protection standards imposed at national level create a barrier to the creation of a single market, as goods or services moving across borders must meet a dual standard, both that of the "home" and the "host" State. Harmonised standards, promulgated at EU level and applicable in all Member States, may achieve the dual objective of protecting health and creating the single market.[86]

79 Case 124/81 *Commission* v *UK (UHT Milk)* [1983] ECR 203; Case 272/80 *Frans-Nederlandse Maatschappij voor Biologische Producten* [1981] ECR 3277.

80 Case C-473/98 *Toolex Alpha* [2000] ECR I-5681.

81 Cases C-267 & 268/91 *Keck* [1993] ECR I-6097; Cases C-140 & 402/92 *Tankstation* [1994] ECR I-2199; Case C-292/92 *Hünermund* [1993] ECR I-6787; Case 412/93 *Leclerc-Siplec* [1995] ECR I-179; Case C-322/01 *Deutscher Apothekerverband v 0800 DocMorris and Waterval* [2003] ECR I-(11 December 2003 nyr in ECR). This exception would presumably cover national rules, for instance relating to the sale of dangerous goods, or restricting the sale of pharmaceuticals.

82 For further discussion, see J. Scott, "Mandatory or Imperative Requirements in the EU and the WTO" in C. Barnard and J. Scott, eds, *The Law of the Single European Market: Unpacking the Premises* (Oxford: Hart, 2002).

83 Case C-379/98 *PreussenElektra* [2001] ECR I-2099.

84 Case 178/84 *Commission v Germany (Beer Purity)* [1987] ECR 1227.

85 Case C-120/95 *Decker* above n 72, para 39; Case C-158/96 *Kohll* above n 72, para 41.

86 However, there is a fundamental asymmetry in EU law between deregulation (or "negative integration") supported by enforceable primary EU law, and reregulation (or "positive integration") which is reliant upon legal competence of the EU institutions to act, and the political will to reach agreement among the governments of the Member States meeting in Council. See J.H.H. Weiler, "The Community System: The Dual Character of Supranationalism" 1 YEL (1982) 267;

"Old style" harmonisation

The EC Treaty responds to the potential threat to health protection posed by the internal market in goods by making provision for a limited regulatory response to the deregulatory mechanisms of internal market law. The establishment of supranational legislative institutions in the EEC Treaty allowed sufficient allocation of sovereign powers to the EU level, and the setting up of procedures necessary to develop such regulatory standards. The main legislative institutions are the European Commission, the Council of Ministers and the European Parliament.[87]

The European Commission is made up of a President,[88] a college of Commissioners,[89] and a permanent staff, divided into directorates general (DGs), each responsible for a particular policy area. The Commission plays both legislative and administrative roles in the EU. It enjoys a significant agenda-setting power in the legislative process in that it alone may initiate legislative proposals. The Council of Ministers is the central law-making body in the EU. It is composed of the relevant ministers of the Member States, depending upon the subject matter under discussion. The original EEC Treaty envisaged that decision-making in Council would be undertaken unanimously, effectively giving each Member State a veto, with a gradual transfer to qualified majority voting as the integration process proceeded.[90] This has happened to quite a large extent, although many key areas are still subject to unanimity in Council (for example, agriculture), and Member States can still use their veto as a diplomatic weapon (for instance, John Major's use of the veto in

Scharpf, above n 37, pp 51–83; S. Weatherill, *Law and Integration in the European Union* (Oxford: Clarendon, 1995); F. Scharpf, *A New Social Contract? Negative and Positive Integration in the Political Economy of European Welfare States* EUI Working Paper RSC 96/44, 1996; R. Dehousse, "Integration *v* Regulation? On the Dynamics of Regulation in the European Community" 30 JCMS (1992) 383.

87 For further information, see J. Peterson and M. Shackleton, *The Institutions of the European Union* (Oxford: OUP, 2002). There are also two consultative institutions that play a part in the EU legislative process, the Economic and Social Committee, and the Committee of the Regions.

88 Following the Treaty of Nice, appointed by a qualified majority of the European Council, and approved by the European Parliament.

89 Following the Treaty of Nice, appointed by a qualified majority of the European Council, and approved by the President. Individual Commissioners must resign if the President so requests, after obtaining the collective approval of the Commission. The European Parliament can force the resignation of the Commissioners collectively, on a motion of censure carried by two-thirds majority of the votes cast, and including a majority of MEPs.

90 The precise details of qualified majority voting have varied through time, in particular depending on the number of Member States. With 15 Member States, after the Treaty of Amsterdam 1997, France, Germany, Italy and the UK had 10 votes each; Spain had eight; Belgium, Greece, the Netherlands and Portugal had five each; Austria and Sweden had four each; Denmark, Finland and Ireland had three each and Luxembourg had two. For QMV the majority needed is 62 votes out of a possible 87. After a great deal of wrangling over several years, the Treaty of Nice altered this with effect from 1 January 2005, largely to deal with the prospect of enlargement, see Protocol on Enlargement of the EU, Article 3. However, the rules on qualified majority voting will be revised again when the Accession Treaty, Athens, 2003 enters into force: see Act concerning the Conditions of Accession, Article 12. (The Act forms an integral part of the Treaty, see Accession Treaty, Article 1 (2).) The Draft Treaty establishing a Constitution for Europe (DCT) proposes yet another change ("the majority of Member States, representing at least three fifths of the population of the Union"), Article I-24 (1) DCT. For further information on the DCT, see chapter 10.

response to perceived non-cooperation of other Member States in resolving the BSE crisis).[91] The European Parliament, directly elected by the citizens of the EU, originally enjoyed only a consultative role in the legislative process. However, subsequent Treaty amendments have increased the Parliament's role to one of "co-legislator" with Council in most policy areas, and "co-decision" has become the general rule.[92]

The EC Treaty now provides that legislation be adopted by a number of different procedures, each giving different powers to different institutional actors. The original EEC Treaty provided for only the "basic procedure", whereby the Commission proposes a measure, the European Parliament is consulted, and the Council adopts it. The Commission and the European Court of Justice ensure compliance with and, where necessary, legal enforcement of such agreed norms.

It will be remembered that the EU institutions have no general competence to enact legislation. A specific "legal basis" for any act of the institutions must be given by the Treaties. The original EEC Treaty gave power to the institutions to enact EU-level harmonised measures, *inter alia*, to protect legitimate interests that might be threatened by the common market. Old Article 100 EEC provided that:

> "The Council shall, acting unanimously on a proposal from the Commission, and after consulting the European Parliament . . . , issue directives for the approximation of such laws, regulations or administrative provisions of the Member States as directly affect the establishment or functioning of the common market."

This provision remains unchanged in the EC Treaty, renumbered as Article 94 EC. Measures adopted on the basis of Article 94 EC, in addition to their common market objectives and effects, might also include elements that have the effect of protecting health. Other legal basis provisions for old style harmonisation include what is now Article 308 EC, discussed above.

For example, extensive regulatory measures applicable to the manufacture, marketing and sale of pharmaceuticals were enacted as early as the 1960s to ensure protection of patients as consumers across the EU. Directive 65/65/EEC[93] is the earliest EU-level measure with the aim of harmonising safety and efficacy standards for medicinal products. The measure was enacted in response to the Thalidomide tragedies of the early 1960s.[94] It required Member States to enact laws to ensure that new medicinal products could not lawfully be marketed on their territories

91 See T. Salmon, "The Structures, Institutions, and Powers of the EU" in J. Gower, ed, *The European Union Handbook* (London and Chicago: Fitzroy Dearborn, 2002). This is specifically at IGCs, where the veto is threatened to block Treaty changes.

92 See D. Earnshaw and D. Judge, "From Co-operation to Co-decision: The European Parliament's path to legislative power" in J. Richardson, ed, *European Union: power and policy making* (London: Routledge, 1996); S. Boyron, "The Co-Decision Procedure: rethinking the constitutional fundamentals" in P. Craig and C. Harlow, *Law-Making in the European Union* (The Hague: Kluwer, 1998).

93 OJ 1965 P 22/369; OJ Sp Ed 1965–6 p 24. Now amended and consolidated by Directive 93/39/EEC, OJ 1993 L 214/22.

94 See chapter 8.

without the approval of a competent regulatory body. Thus the first stage in harmonisation was simply to provide for equivalent national regulatory institutions. More detailed harmonisation provisions for the criteria and procedures according to which approval may be given by national regulatory bodies for new medicinal products followed. These provisions are now contained in the Commission's (nine-volume) publication "The Rules Governing Medicinal Products within the European Union".[95]

The technical requirements for testing of new medicinal products are regularly updated, in the light of scientific developments. Technically speaking, this is carried out by the Commission, in accordance with power delegated for this purpose by Council. However, in reality, a system of "comitology"[96] has grown up, under which the Commission exercises its delegated legislative powers[97] on the approval of a committee, comprised of representatives of national executives.[98] This compromise (without basis in the original EEC Treaty) allows the effective governance of the EU through its supranational institutions, while at the same time securing representation of national interests within the law and policy-making process.[99] Several different types of committee procedure exist, giving more or less power to national representatives over the Commission's final decision, and some providing for intervention of Council. The comitology system has been heavily criticised, in particular on the basis of its lack of transparency[100] and its exclusion of the European Parliament.[101] It is, however, a firmly fixed feature of EU governance.

95 The "Eudralex collection", http://www.pharmocos.eurdra.org/.

96 For an explanation of the four models used to conceptualise comitology (regulatory (Majone); deliberative (Joerges and Neyer); heterarchical network (Ladeur); and administrative supranationalist/principal-agent (Lindseth)), see Armstrong, above n 21. See also C. Joerges and J. Neyer, "From Intergovernmental Bargaining to Deliberative Political Processes: The Constitutionalisation of Comitology" 3 ELJ (1997) 273, who call for an approach to comitology that transcends the law/politics disciplinary divide.

97 See Case 9/56 *Meroni* [1957-58] ECR 133; K. Lenaerts, "Regulating the Regulatory Process: Delegation of Powers within the European Community" 18 ELRev (1993) 23. Comitology is, of course, an example of "multi-level" governance in the EU: see W. Wessels, "Comitology: fusion in action. Politico-administrative trends in the EU system" 5 *Journal of European Public Policy* (1998) 209.

98 See Decision 87/373/EC, OJ 1987 L 197/33; Decision 99/468/EC, OJ 1999 L 184/23.

99 For examples, see chapter 6, pp 208–209; chapter 8, pp 290–295; chapter 9, pp 357, 359–360.

100 But see Case T-188/97 *Rothmans* [1999] ECR II-2463.

101 See C. Harlow, *Accountability in the European Union* (Oxford: OUP, 2002), especially chapter 3; M. Andenas and G. Türk, eds, *Delegated Legislation and the Role of Committees in the EC* (The Hague: Kluwer, 2000), especially G. Schäfer, "Linking Member State and European Administrations – The Role of Committees and Comitology" and A.E. Toeller and H.C.H. Hofmann, "Democracy and the Reform of Comitology" therein; C. Joerges and E. Vos, *EU Committees: Social regulation, law and politics* (Oxford: Hart, 1999), especially G. Ciavarini Azzi, "Comitology and the European Commission" therein; E. Vos, "The Rise of Committees" 3 ELJ (1997) 210; K. St Clair Bradley, "The European Parliament and Comitology: On the Road to Nowhere" 3 ELJ (1997) 230; R. Pedler and G. Schäfer, eds, *Shaping European Law and Policy: The Role of Committees in the Political Process* (Maastricht: European Institute of Public Administration, 1996); K. St Clair Bradley, "Comitology and the Law: Through a glass, darkly" 29 CMLRev (1992) 691.

The EU has also established a number of scientific committees[102] and independent "agencies"[103] to assist with the economic, technical or scientific side of its regulatory activities, and to promote the credibility that comes with the appointment of specialist policy advisors, insulated from short-term political exigencies. The management board of such agencies (comprised of representatives of national executives and the Commission) sets guidelines and adopts the work programme for the agency, under the responsibility of its executive director, who is usually appointed by the Council of Ministers. Agencies use technical or scientific committees, comprised of experts in the particular field, and networks of partners within the EU, to provide information necessary for determining effective regulatory choices. For instance, the European Food Safety Authority provides scientific advice on all matters related to food safety, by carrying out risk assessments in any area of the human food chain.[104] Many of the criticisms of the comitology system apply also to EU agencies,[105] although significant efforts have been made to make such agencies more "citizen friendly". A key task of the European Food Safety Authority is to communicate directly with the public on matters within its remit.

In addition to the single market in goods, the EC Treaty also sets up a single market in the other factors of production: persons, services and capital. The free movement of persons proved much more difficult to attain than that of goods. Again, the Treaty makes provision for exceptions to the general rules. Article 48 EEC (now renumbered Article 39 EC) provides for freedom of movement for workers, "subject to limitations justified on grounds of public policy, public security or public health" and similar provisions apply to freedom of establishment (Article 56 EEC, now Article 46 EC) and freedom to provide and receive services (Article 66 EEC, now Article 55 EC).

These measures are elaborated in secondary legislation. For instance, Directive 64/221/EEC[106] applies to workers, the self-employed and recipients of services.[107] The Directive permits Member States to exclude nationals of other Member States

102 See, for example, M.P.C.M. Van Schendelen and R.H. Pedler, "Are EU Committees Influential?" and P. Gray, "The Scientific Committee for Food" in M.P.C.M. Van Schendelen, ed, *EU Committees as Influential Policy-Makers* (Aldershot: Dartmouth, 1998).

103 As Majone points out, these are not regulatory agencies in the normal sense, as they do not have powers of rule-making, adjudication and enforcement normally associated with such agencies: see G. Majone, "Functional Interests: European Agencies" in J. Peterson and M. Shackleton, eds, *The Institutions of the European Union* (Oxford: OUP, 2002); Harlow, above n 101, especially chapter 3; R. Dehousse, "Misfits: EU Law and the Transformation of European Governance" in C. Joerges and R. Dehousse, eds, *Good Governance in Europe's Integrated Market* (Oxford: OUP, 2002), pp 216–223.

104 http://europa.eu.int/agencies/efsa/index_en.htm.

105 See Majone, above n 103; G. Majone, "The Credibility Crisis of Community Regulation" 38 JCMS (2000) 273; G. de Búrca, "The Institutional Development of the EU: A Constitutional Analysis" in P. Craig and G. de Búrca, eds, *The Evolution of EU Law* (Oxford: OUP, 1999); E. Vos, "Reforming the European Commission: What Role to Play for EU Agencies" 37 CMLRev (2000) 1113.

106 OJ Sp Ed 1963–4 p 117. There is currently a proposal to consolidate the EU legislation on the free movement and residence entitlements of EU citizens and their families, see COM(2001) 257 final and COM(2003) 199 final, Council political agreement reached in September 2003.

107 Directive 64/221/EEC, Article 1.

from entry to their territory on certain harmonised health grounds. Article 4 of the Directive provides that the only diseases or disabilities justifying exclusion of an individual are those listed in the Annex to the Directive. The Annex defines "diseases which might endanger public health" as WHO-designated contagious diseases, tuberculosis, syphilis and "other infectious diseases or contagious parasitic diseases if they are the subject of provisions for the protection of nationals of the host country". This Directive allows exclusion of a non-national *only* at the point of entry. Once a residence permit has been granted on the basis of Treaty provisions concerning free movement of workers, the host Member States' national health service is responsible for a non-national who contracts such a disease, on the same terms as nationals, in accordance with the principle of non-discrimination on grounds of nationality.[108]

In addition to the deregulatory Treaty provisions, in order to secure free movement for workers (in particular professionals) it was necessary to tackle obstacles posed by different national educational systems, each issuing their own qualifications. The old approach to harmonisation of qualifications concentrated on enacting EU-level legislation requiring host Member States to recognise educational qualifications achieved in other Member States, by agreeing harmonised requirements for professional training. The EU institutions took a sectoral approach, according to which a separate mutual recognition directive was required for each branch of each profession. A number of Directives applicable to health professionals were enacted, covering doctors,[109] dentists,[110] pharmacists,[111] nurses[112] and midwives.[113] These Directives set out a detailed agreed core of requirements for professional training in each profession, and abolish restrictions on freedom of establishment based on the fact that a professional qualification was gained in a Member State other than that in which the professional wishes to practise. National authorities giving authorisation to health professionals practising within their territory are obliged to recognise qualifications gained in another Member State.[114]

To summarise, "old style" harmonisation involves the promulgation of detailed harmonised regulatory norms at EU level. In the health field, such norms provide protection for human health in the context of what would otherwise be a deregulated single market. Once the EU-level norms have been adopted, the general rule is that national authorities are precluded from adopting provisions in the field, even if

108 Article 6 EEC, now Article 12 EC. The entitlements to health care of migrant workers within the EU are governed by Regulation 1408/71/EEC, OJ Sp Ed 1971 II p 416; see chapter 4.
109 Directives 75/362/EEC, OJ 1975 L 167/1 and 75/363/EEC, OJ 1975 L 167/14.
110 Directives 78/686/EEC, OJ 1978 L 233/1 and 78/687/EEC, OJ 1978 L 233/10.
111 Directives 85/432/EEC, OJ 1985 L 253/34 and 85/433/EEC, OJ 1985 L 253/37; pharmacists do not, however, have an automatic right to establish a pharmacy in another Member State, as some Member States control the geographical distribution of pharmacies. See further chapter 6.
112 Directives 77/452/EEC, OJ 1977 L 176/1 and 77/453/EEC, OJ 1977 L 176/8.
113 Directives 80/154/EEC, OJ 1980 L 33/1 and 80/155/EEC, OJ 1980 L 33/8.
114 These directives are now consolidated in Directive 2001/19/EC, OJ 2001 L 206/1. See further chapter 6.

those provide greater health protection. The implication is that an Article 30 EC justification is no longer available.[115] The EU is said to have "occupied the field" or "pre-empted" national competence – to the exclusion of national regulatory activity. This has raised some concerns, in particular where Member States wish to have higher health protection standards than provided for in EU-level norms.[116] For instance, health experts in the accession state of Poland have expressed concern about the EU's regulation of tobacco advertising, on the basis that Poland's extremely restrictive regime, recognised by the WHO and internal assessments as improving standards of health in Poland by reducing tobacco-related illness, will no longer be permissible once Poland accedes to the EU.[117]

Other problems arise from the processes by which old style harmonisation measures are adopted. The need for agreement of governments of all Member States in Council places a significant "drag" on the system. Agreement on detailed standards in these EU-level intergovernmental fora is a slow and difficult process, and may lead to situations in which regulation cannot keep pace with technological developments or developments in scientific understanding. Where new health threats arise, such as HIV/AIDS or BSE/nvCJD, and therefore regulatory responses are required relatively quickly, old style harmonisation may not be an appropriate mode of governance. Something more flexible is needed, and this may be found in other methods of governance employed by the EU, including "new approach" harmonisation.

"New approach" harmonisation

The context for the development of "new approach" harmonisation is the significant loss of momentum in the pace of adoption of EU-level legislation during the late 1960s and 1970s. This was in no small measure due to the "Luxembourg Accords", a compromise ending French President de Gaulle's "empty chair policy", under which French ministers boycotted all Community business in Council. The Luxembourg Accords effectively gave the government of each Member State a veto over any vote to be taken in Council. The effect of this was to paralyse the legislative process. Moreover, it had become apparent that the single market, which according

115 See, for example, Case 190/87 *Moormann* [1988] ECR 4689 on health inspections for poultry meat, where the Court held that the existence of EU-level measures harmonising such inspections meant that an Article 30 EC defence was no longer available; Case 148/78 *Ratti* above n 55 on Directive 73/173/EEC on packaging and labelling of dangerous substances, where the Court held that national rules requiring more information on the packaging than required by the Directive were inapplicable; see also Case C-1/96 *Compassion in World Farming* [1998] ECR I-1251. But see the procedure in Article 95 (4) EC, discussed below.

116 See further chapter 8, p 320.

117 See A. Gilmore and W. Zatonski, "Free trade versus the protection of health: the implications of EU accession for tobacco consumption in Poland?" 8 *eurohealth* (2002) 31; and compare E. Delcheva, "Implementing EU tobacco legislation in Bulgaria: Challenges and opportunities" 8 *eurohealth* (2002) 34. However, as the Tobacco Advertising Directive 98/43/EC is based on Article 95 EC, there is presumably the option of application for an exemption under Article 95 (4) EC.

to the original Treaty of Rome should have been in place by 1972,[118] was still far from a reality. Hidden barriers to its completion, in the form of disparate national regulatory regimes, remained.

However, by the beginning of the 1980s, the economic and political climate had changed sufficiently for the governments of the Member States to be open to a relaunch of the integration project.[119] The appointment of the dynamic Jacques Delors as President of the European Commission may have been the final element needed to set in motion the next phase of European integration. Delors hit on the idea of uniting interested actors (not only the governments of the Member States, but also representatives of economic and social elites; industry, commerce, trades unions and so on) behind a single concept: the completion of the single market by the end of 1992. The Commission's "White Paper" on the completion of the internal market[120] comprised a list of measures which needed to be enacted, in order to remove the physical, technical and fiscal barriers to trade in the Community. It was adopted unanimously by the meeting of the European Council (comprised of the Heads of State/Government and Foreign Ministers of the Member States) at Milan in June 1985, and an Intergovernmental Conference was called, in order to discuss the amendments to the Treaty needed to complete the single market. This treaty amendment – termed the "Single European Act" – was adopted by the governments of the Member States in February 1986.

One key element of the Treaty amendments introduced by the Single European Act was the provision of new legal bases for Community action, crucially enabling enactment of legislation without the need for unanimity in the Council of Ministers. This effectively removed the national veto, and the Luxembourg Accords have fallen into abeyance. Thus no single Member State could now block proposed legislation in many policy areas, including regulation required to protect and promote human health in the context of the single market. A new legal basis provision, now modified and renumbered Article 95 EC, was inserted into the EC Treaty, according to which, in order to achieve the completion of the "internal market", Council (in response to a Commission proposal), acting by qualified majority voting procedures, and cooperating with the European Parliament, shall adopt harmonisation measures "which have as their object the establishment and functioning of the internal market". Article 95 (3) specifically provides that the Commission, in proposing such measures, shall "take as a base a high level of protection" in measures concerning "health, safety, environmental protection and consumer

118 Article 8 (1) EEC: "The common market shall be progressively established during a transitional period of 12 years"; Article 8 (6) EEC: "nothing in the preceding paragraphs shall cause the transitional period to last more than 15 years after the entry into force of this Treaty."

119 Explanations for the success of the single market project vary: see overview in Craig and de Búrca, above n 1, chapter 28; W. Sandholtz and J. Zysman, "1992: Recasting the European Bargain" [1989] *World Politics* 95; contrast A. Moravcsik, "Negotiating the Single European Act: National Interests and Conventional Statecraft in the European Community" 45 *International Organization* (1991) 19.

120 COM(85) 310.

protection". Thus the basis for EU-level harmonisation measures protecting such health interests – provided that they are necessary to complete the internal market and ensure its proper operation – was laid down in the Treaty. The new legislative procedure, with qualified majority voting, allowed the EU institutions, especially the Commission and European Parliament, to reassert themselves, after the dominance of the governments of the Member States that had characterised the previous decade or so.[121]

Parallel developments in the judicial arena also had a significant effect on the integration process at this stage. In a key ruling, *Cassis de Dijon*,[122] the European Court of Justice established the principle of "mutual recognition", according to which goods lawfully produced and marketed in one Member State (the home state) must be accepted in all other (host) Member States, unless the host state can justify a more restrictive rule by reference to a legitimate public interest.[123] *Cassis de Dijon* concerned, in part, the protection of health. German food regulations provided that a drink marketed as "cassis" (a blackcurrant liqueur) must have an alcohol content of 25%. Cassis de Dijon was lawfully produced and marketed in France, with an alcohol content of 15–20%. The German government argued, *inter alia*, that the fixing of the minimum alcohol content at 25% was justified by the need to avoid the proliferation of alcoholic drinks with a low alcohol content on the German market, since, in its view, such products may more easily induce an unhealthy tolerance towards alcohol than more highly alcoholic drinks. The Court was not convinced, pointing out that a very wide range of drinks with a low alcohol content were already permitted on the German market, and in any case, most drinks with a high alcohol content are consumed in a form diluted by mixers. The Court concluded that:

> "There is therefore no valid reason why, provided that they have been lawfully produced and marketed in one of the Member States, alcoholic beverages should not be introduced into any other Member State."[124]

The Commission took up the opportunity presented by the ruling in *Cassis de Dijon* in a Commission communication,[125] which made it clear that the Commission took the view that import prohibitions going beyond the scope of the principle of mutual recognition were contrary to the law of the internal market. One of the

121 Subject to Article 95 (4) EC.

122 Case 120/78 [1979] ECR 649.

123 *Cassis de Dijon* is also often seen as the foundation of a principle of "home state control" in EU law. However, this is probably to overstate the case: see K. Armstrong, "Mutual Recognition" in C. Barnard and J. Scott, eds, *The Law of the Single European Market: Unpacking the Premises* (Oxford: Hart, 2002), who argues (at pp 233–235) that *Cassis* is authority only for the proposition that the principle of mutual recognition applies to police *host* state controls. See also Craig and de Búrca, above n 1, pp 636–639.

124 Para 14.

125 Commission Practice Note on Import Prohibitions: Communication from the Commission concerning the consequences of the judgment given by the Court of Justice on 20 February 1979 in Case 120/78 "*Cassis de Dijon*", OJ 1980 C 256/2.

duties of the Commission is to ensure compliance by Member States with Community law. Article 226 EC provides a procedure by which the Commission may first deliver a reasoned opinion on alleged non-compliance on the part of the Member State, and then, if this fails to have the desired effect, to bring the Member State before the Court.[126] So, for instance, the Commission successfully challenged the German *Reinheitsgebot* (Beer Purity Law), on the basis that it was not necessary to protect health, as the German government claimed.[127] The Commission is aided in this respect by the "Transparency Directive", which requires Member States to notify all new technical standards to the Commission before they are adopted.[128] However, the Article 226 EC enforcement procedure is limited in that the Commission has few resources with which to police all activities of Member States, and, perhaps more importantly, cannot afford to adopt too confrontational an approach with governments of the Member States, whose support the Commission needs to carry out its other duties effectively. In this respect, private litigation is more important than Commission action in cementing the key principles of the internal market.

The Court and Commission enunciated the key principle of mutual recognition in the context of what is now Article 28 EC on free movement of goods, which, it will be remembered, is also enforceable before national courts. Thus all national courts are also obliged to uphold this principle. This meant that the need for harmonised regulatory measures at EU level, in order to complete the internal market, and at the same time safeguard external values, such as protection of health, was significantly reduced. Rather than reaching an agreed EU level standard on, say, safe additives to cheese, each Member State was free to set its own standards, applicable to its domestic cheese producers, provided that it allowed cheese lawfully produced in other Member States to be marketed in its territory. If it did not do so, it could be forced to comply with Treaty law by private litigation. A system of competition between national regulatory regimes within the Community was thus established. Within that system, the protection of consumer health was to be guaranteed by the labelling of products, in theory allowing consumers the "choice" of regulatory regimes, through the selection of freely available competing products.[129] EU-level regulation was thus, at least in theory, required only in cases where an external imperative mandated intervention at that level to prevent competition between the

126 Since the TEU, the Court has had power, under Article 171 (2) EC, in the event of continued failure on the part of a Member State to comply with a ruling against it under Article 226 EC, to order the payment of a lump sum or penalty payment.

127 Case 178/84 *Commission v Germany (Beer Purity,* above n 84). See further chapter 9, n 140. For a detailed analysis, see J. Scott and E. Vos, "The Juridification of Uncertainty" in C. Joerges and R. Dehousse, eds, *Good Governance in Europe's Integrated Market* (Oxford: OUP, 2002), pp 262–264.

128 Directive 83/189/EEC, OJ 1983 L 109/8.

129 See H. Von Heydebrand u. d. Lasa, "Free Movement of Foodstuffs, Consumer Protection and Food Standards in the EC: Has the Court of Justice got it wrong?" 16 ELRev (1991) 391 for a critical perspective on labelling; see also C. MacMaolain, "Free Movement Of Foodstuffs, Quality Requirements and Consumer Protection: Have the Court and the Commission Both Got It Wrong?" 26 ELRev (2001) 413.

national regulatory regimes operating in a manner detrimental to public interests. The EU-level regulation required is only to set a minimum standard to protect such interests; so, for instance, to prohibit unequivocally dangerous additives in cheese.

The Commission took up the logic of this position, signalling its new strategy in the White Paper on completing the internal market.[130] This new approach to harmonisation was to be based on drawing a distinction between "what it is essential to harmonise, and what may be left to mutual recognition of national regulations and standards".[131] Legislative harmonisation is to be limited to "essential health and safety requirements", which will apply to all Member States, and conformity with which will secure access to the single market.[132] National authorities are permitted to go beyond these minimum standards by setting higher levels of protection, applicable to nationally produced goods, subject only to the ceiling of the Treaty rules on free movement.[133] There is also a Treaty-based procedure,[134] in accordance with Article 95 (4) EC, by which Member States may seek permission from the Commission to maintain national regulatory norms applicable to imported goods, after the adoption of an EU-level harmonisation measure. Such a national measure must be based on "major needs referred to in Article 30", which, of course, include the protection of human health.[135] Article 95 (4) EC has recently been successfully used by Denmark to maintain national measures governing food additives that were more restrictive than those set by the relevant EU-level directive.

Thus, in the case of new approach harmonisation, there is no "field occupation" by the EU, but rather both national and EU-level norms are applicable. Further, non-state corporate actors are involved in the regulatory process by the elaboration of "European industry standards".[136] These help manufacturers demonstrate conformity with essential requirements and allow inspection to test for such

130 COM(85) 310.
131 COM(85) 310, para 65.
132 Ibid.
133 See S. Weatherill, "Pre-emption, Harmonisation and the Distribution of Competence" in C. Barnard and J. Scott, eds, *The Law of the Single European Market: Unpacking the Premises* (Oxford: Hart, 2002). If a Member State wishes to apply such higher protective standards to *imports*, the implication of the rulings in Case C-376/98 *Germany v Parliament and Council (Tobacco Advertising)* [2000] ECR I-8419 and Case C-491/01 *R (British American Tobacco (Investments) Ltd) v Secretary of State for Health* [2002] ECR I-11453 (discussed in chapter 3), it must use the procedure in Article 95 (4) EC; see Weatherill, above n 1, pp 636–637.
134 The details of the procedure are set out in Article 95 (4)–(10) EC. The Commission must examine the request within six months, and must consider amendments to the EU-level harmonisation measure. In the case of a specific problem on public health, the Commission must immediately examine whether a proposal to alter existing EU law should be brought to Council.
135 It also includes protection of the environment or working environment, see Article 95 (4) EC.
136 The main standardisation bodies are the European Committee for Standardisation (CEN), the European Committee for Technical Standardisation (CENELEC), and the European Telecommunications Standards Institute (ETSI). CEN's Healthcare Sector Forum coordinates the production of European standards with respect to health care products, for instance, sterilisers for medical purposes, respiratory and anaesthetic equipment, chemical disinfectants and antiseptics, standardising fittings for medical devices, harmonising medical devices nomenclature, tissue engineering in medical devices, and quality systems for medical device manufacturers.

conformity. By involving specialist elites in particular sectors in the development of such standards, they allow for development of consensus on appropriate standards, even at times of rapid technological change and developments in scientific understanding.

A good example of a new approach directive, with relevance in the health field, is Directive 88/378/EEC on toy safety.[137] This provides for harmonised essential consumer health and safety requirements to be met by all toys placed on the internal market. Users of toys must be protected against health hazards and risk of physical injury when toys are used, bearing in mind the normal behaviour of children.[138] Toys meeting these requirements must be allowed to circulate freely in the EU.[139] A European standard (CE mark) is to be set by EU-level standardisation bodies, and administered by national bodies. Though this is not in itself mandatory, toys meeting the European standard must be presumed to meet the essential requirements of the Directive. A procedure for modification of the standards, in the event that, with developments in scientific knowledge, they are no longer appropriate to protect essential health and safety requirements, is established. The procedure involves the Standing Committee set up under the Transparency Directive (a "comitology" element), the Commission, and the standardisation bodies. Member States are also entitled to withdraw from the market toys that might jeopardise the health or safety of consumers, due to shortcomings in the standards. Member States so doing must inform the Commission, which again must inform the Standing Committee.

The Toy Safety Directive illustrates the extent to which new approach harmonisation promotes both national regulatory autonomy and the interests of relevant business and industry elites. Although the minimum regulatory requirements are set at EU-level, by Directive, the standards are developed by private standardisation bodies. Concerns have been raised about the extent to which other elements of civil society, in particular consumers, can access the law-making procedures under the new approach. These concerns raise questions of legitimacy that go to the heart of the EU's constitutional order, with its central internal market aim. Member States retain significant control over the enforcement of the Directive, at least with respect to national producers or importers, in that national bodies determine compliance with these standards. However, Member States must mutually recognise the granting of market access by competent national bodies in other Member States. This involves a degree of mutual trust, the lack of which it is sometimes alleged is a significant drawback in the new approach to harmonisation. Moreover, any detailed negotiations over the match of the standards to the essential health and safety requirements set out in the Directive are to be carried out in the context of the Transparency Directive Standing Committee.

137 OJ 1988 L 187/1.
138 Article 2; Annex II, Recital 1.
139 Article 4.

"New approach" harmonisation thus involves the determination at EU level only of a floor of minimum standards required to protect essential health and safety interests. Member States remain free to set higher regulatory standards with respect to home producers or providers of goods and services, but must recognise standards of other Member States, provided they meet the EU minimum requirements. Compliance with these may be proved by reference to "European standards" agreed and promulgated by industry experts. Detailed determination of the EU requirements and modification of these, and of the European standards, takes place through interactions between the Commission, EU committees, the Council, standardisation bodies, and national competent authorities. The system has a high degree of flexibility and gives considerable protection to national interests, allowing for different determinations of appropriate regulatory response (for instance, arising from different assessments of what constitutes appropriate risk) within each Member State. However, in order for the integration process to work, the system requires significant levels of mutual trust between national administrations. Where such trust is lacking, further methods of governance will be required to secure the integration process. One such method is the use of regulatory coordination.

Regulatory coordination

As we have seen, simple mutual recognition, along with new approach minimum harmonisation, can be an effective mode of governance for the EU. However, in some circumstances, these mechanisms alone are insufficient. For instance, there may be insufficient trust between national administrations. Or there may be a significant lack of "fit" between national systems, such that mutual recognition provides only limited opportunities for the freedom of movement mandated by the internal market. In these circumstances, EU law may leave intact these separate national systems, but also make mandatory their coordination, so as to safeguard the aims of the EU. Such mandatory coordination takes a number of forms. Its key elements are the preservation of separate national systems, but the use of law to ensure that this has as minimal a negative impact on the internal market as is possible, given the need to protect external interests, such as health, within that context. Although essentially designed to accommodate diversity, regulatory coordination may, over time, prompt voluntary convergence of disparate national systems.

For example, the rules regulating marketing approval of pharmaceuticals brought into effect a certain element of EU-level, old-style harmonisation in the field. However, power to approve new pharmaceuticals before their entry to the market remained at national level. There are various reasons for this, not least the fact that, as national health (insurance) systems are the main purchaser of pharmaceuticals in the Member States, the approval of a new pharmaceutical product (such as Viagra) may have significant resource implications for national health (insurance) systems. The fact that approval remained at national level constituted a practical inhibition on a single market in pharmaceuticals, as, in order to market such a new product across the EU, national approvals must be successfully sought from each Member State. This problem was alleviated somewhat by the establishment of a committee for proprietary medicinal products (CPMP),[140] comprised of national experts and members of the Commission, which administered a system of coordination of national approvals, according to which other Member States must in effect provide a good reason for non-approval of a medical product approved in one Member State.[141] This may be seen as an early example of mutual recognition. However, even under this procedure, separate approvals still have to be sought for each Member State, a costly and time-consuming process. Given the sensitivity of the regulation of pharmaceuticals, because of the potentially drastic consequences of inappropriate risk assessment, simple application of the principle of mutual recognition was not politically possible. Rather, a new "decentralised procedure" was established,[142] according to which a producer of a medicinal product authorised in one Member State could, using a procedure involving the CPMP, *require* extension of this authorisation to two or more other Member States. The first Member State is required to provide an assessment report for the relevant product: other Member States must make a decision on approval within 90 days. Approval may be refused only on grounds of quality, safety or efficacy. Provision is made for arbitration in the CPMP, in the event of refusal. The CPMP thus provides an institutional forum for mandatory coordination of national approval systems. In the context of this regulatory coordination, some commentators predict that the gradual convergence of national approval systems will take place over time.[143]

Neither old nor new-style harmonisation provides the full spectrum of regulatory frameworks necessary for the freedom of movement of human "factors of production" within the EU. Neither the legal orders of the Member States, nor that of the EU, regard human beings as simply factors of production, and the legal framework promoting their freedom of movement reflects this. For instance, each Member State, in its welfare settlement, provides a system of social security for workers, in the event of various risks (unemployment, old age, accident or injury, illness) befalling them. So that free movers do not suffer detriment in respect of social security entitlements consequent upon their moving from home to host Member State, a system of regulatory coordination of social security systems has been established. A genuine free movement of persons could not be achieved without guaranteeing such migrants, and their families, a right to obtain, *inter alia*, health care under the national health service of the host Member State to which they moved. EU-level regulatory measures aim to achieve this not through harmonisation

140 Directive 75/319/EEC, OJ 1975 L 147/1.

141 See J. Gardner, "The European Agency for the Evaluation of Medicines and European Regulation of Pharmaceuticals" 2 ELJ (1996) 48.

142 Regulation 2309/93/EC, OJ 1993 L 214/1; Directive 93/39/EC, OJ 1993 L 214/22.

143 Gardner, above n 141, at 59–60.

(which would be to set up a "common European welfare law"), but through the mandatory coordination of national social security systems. The principal coordination instruments are Regulation 1408/71/EEC[144] and Regulation 574/72/EEC.[145] Among other social security matters, they cover entitlement of migrant workers to access the national health service of the host Member State. Entitlement is to the level of health care (for instance, coverage of services by the national health system, level of co-payment) provided for nationals in the competent Member State.[146] These entitlements are legally enforceable, before national courts, according to the direct applicability and direct effect of EU law, discussed above.[147] A complex system of transfer of payments between national social security systems underpins Regulation 1408/71/EEC, essentially aiming to ensure that Member States do not bear the financial burden of providing social security to persons who are not contributing or have not previously contributed to their economies. Thus, under this system, the social security system of each Member State remains intact, but systems must be coordinated where they are applied to (the relatively small number of) migrant employees and migrant professionals and other self-employed persons.

"Soft" coordination

In addition to binding or regulatory coordination, the EU uses a number of mechanisms of non-binding or soft coordination. These persuasive norms take a number of forms, including resolutions, recommendations, opinions, notices, communications, action programmes or plans, declarations and communiqués. Measures of soft law may be significant forces in the integration process for a number of reasons. They may provide an interpretative reference point for measures of hard law.[148] They may promote convergence through articulation of agreed statements of good practice and recommendations, against which national policies are measured,[149] eventually prompting voluntary changes to bring national systems in line with an agreed "European norm". They may carve out areas of "Community concern", where formal legal competence is lacking, thus paving the way for future

144 OJ 1971 L 149/2; OJ Sp Ed 1971 II p 416.

145 OJ 1972 L 74/1. These were adopted to replace the early Regulations 3 and 4, which were a product of intergovernmental agreement, and were subsequently adopted as Community law.

146 See further chapter 4.

147 The Commission has proposed an electronic "European health card", to replace the existing E111 form, as evidence of the legal entitlements of free movers (workers, students, holiday-makers) to emergency health care treatment in host Member States, see Council Resolution on a European health card, OJ 1996 C 141/104; Commission Action Plan to remove obstacles to EU workers' mobility by 2005, COM(2002) 72 final.

148 See, for example, Case C-322/88 *Grimaldi* [1989] ECR 4407; and more recently the opinion of the Advocate General in Case C-173/99 *BECTU* [2001] ECR I-4881.

149 For example, the "open method of coordination", in the context of employment policy, see Szyszczak, above n 32.

developments in action taken by EU institutions, sometimes ultimately leading to the enactment of binding and directly effective EU-level legal provisions.[150]

Such "soft law" norms have always been a part of EU law and policy-making, but have received increased attention in the context of a turn to "new" methods of governance in the EU from the late 1990s onwards.[151] The need to adopt such "new" governance methods was highlighted by the Commission in its White Paper on European Governance.[152] New methods of governance may be said to include governance through partnership,[153] and the social dialogue,[154] and also the "Open Method of Coordination" (OMC). The OMC process, originally established in the context of coordination of "broad economic policy guidelines" and a "European employment strategy", uses soft law mechanisms of guidelines (agreed by the Member States), exchange of best practice, benchmarking of national standards against those of the best performing Member States, and national action plans according to which Member States' national policies are to converge on these guidelines. The OMC process was subsequently applied to social inclusion and pensions, and a similar process exists in the environmental sphere.[155] One of the key benefits of OMC is that it is able to accommodate significant differences in welfare policies between the Member States, and yet also move towards integration.[156] Proposals currently under consideration envisage an umbrella OMC on social protection, which will include social inclusion, pensions and "health care and long term care for the elderly".[157]

Financial incentives

Although, as we have seen, the EU's budget is modest, the EU institutions have also used the provision of financial incentives to promote the integration process. This is governance through "carrots" rather than "sticks" – the notion of "we fund

150 See Cram, above n 61, pp 107–111. For examples in the areas of sex equality and racism/xenophobia see, respectively, C. Hoskyns, *Integrating Gender* (London: Verso, 1996); R. Geyer, *Exploring European Social Policy* (Cambridge: Polity, 2000), pp 164–171.

151 See Scott and Trubek, above n 26.

152 COM(2001) 428 final.

153 See, for instance, the discussion of partnership in the context of EU structural funding, in Scott and Trubek, above n 26.

154 For further information, see C. Barnard, *EC Employment Law* (Oxford: OUP, 2000), pp 85–104; J. Kenner, *EU Employment Law: From Rome to Amsterdam and beyond* (Oxford: Hart, 2002), pp 105–108, 235–291.

155 Entitled "Environmental Policy Integration"; see further, A. Lenschow, "New Regulatory Approaches in 'Greening' EU Policies" 8 ELJ (2002) 19.

156 See De La Porte, above n 32.

157 See Commission, *Strengthening the social dimension of the Lisbon strategy: Streamlining open coordination in the field of social protection* COM(2003) 261 final. The Council's High Level Group on Patient Mobility and Healthcare, due to report in early 2004, is also considering how or whether health and long-term care should be inserted into the OMC on social protection, see europa.eu.int/comm./ dgs/health_consumer/library/press/press301_en.pdf and http://europa.eu.int/comm./dgs/ health_consumer/library/press/press301_en.pdf. See further chapter 10.

what we like" so as to encourage more of the same.[158] Thus, for instance, the EU has funded programmes aimed at combating cancer and AIDS/HIV. In December 2002, the Commission announced that an EU-funded research team had created a new effective drug to treat malaria.[159] The EU, through its research and technology policy, has funded medical research since the mid-1980s.[160] A key element of these programmes is the sharing of best practice across borders, and the forging of networks in particular fields, in order to provide a forum for shared knowledge and expertise. Again, over time, it may be that the experiences of collaboration may feed into national policy processes, thus prompting gradual convergence. In participating in EU-wide research projects, experts from each Member State are exposed to other Member States' different approaches and alternative regulatory conceptualisations with respect to the field concerned. These experts may often be relatively powerful within the policy-making process in their own Member State. Their interaction – facilitated by the EU institutions' allocation of financial support – may help to promote a gradual convergence of approaches within the EU. In the long term, these horizontal relationships may prove to be as significant as any EU-level regulatory activity. Furthermore, EU level financial support may lead to the adoption of principles or values that eventually feed through to EU level legislation. The current debate over funding of stem cell research under the Sixth Framework Programme may provide an example of this phenomenon.[161]

IV. Courts and fundamental rights

Having considered the various types of governance method used by the EU in its regulatory activity, the chapter concludes with an overview of the roles played by courts, in particular through the articulation and enforcement of "fundamental rights" in the process of European integration. This provides the final element of the contextual background within which our overall research question – how does EU law affect national health law and policy? – is approached. In addition to the legislature's regulatory activities, courts have played a significant role in the construction of the EU's constitutionalised legal order.[162] As we have seen, the European Court of Justice has the power to determine the validity of acts of the EU institutions, in accordance with its jurisprudence under Article 230 EC and Article 234 EC. Acts may be invalid for lack of competence, misuse of powers, incorrect legal basis or infringement of another essential procedural requirement, or for "breach of this Treaty or of any rule of law relating to its application". Such rules of law include

158 What the EU does not fund is also relevant; see further chapter 7.
159 Commission Press Release IP/02/1878, 13 December 2002.
160 See Council Resolution on the first framework programme of research, OJ 1983 C 208/1; Decision 85/195/EEC establishing a multiannual research action plan in the field of biotechnology, OJ 1985 L 83/1, which included the use of biotechnology in health care.
161 See chapter 7.
162 See, for instance, Weiler, above n 86; Weiler, above n 14; Stone Sweet, above n 14, pp 153–193.

"general principles" of law, held by the Court to be inherent in the legal orders of all Member States, such as various fundamental human rights, including those recognised in the Council of Europe's European Convention on Human Rights and Fundamental Freedoms 1950, and the EU's own Charter of Fundamental Rights 2000 (EUCFR).

Further, as we have already mentioned, the European Court of Justice has articulated a number of "constitutional principles"[163] of EU law, with respect to its interactions with national legal orders, none of which is made explicit in the EC Treaty.[164] The Court has found that EU law penetrates directly into legal systems of the Member States (direct applicability), and that it is enforceable by individuals before national courts (direct effect). Further, to secure the aims of the Treaty, EU law takes priority over conflicting national law (supremacy). The duty of fidelity to the aims of the EC Treaty, found in Article 10 EC, applies to all national bodies, be they legislative, executive or judicial. These principles have been developed in the context of the Court's power to give authoritative interpretations of EU law under Article 234 EC. The procedure provided for by Article 234 EC involves a reference from a national court to the European Court of Justice for a "preliminary ruling" in a case before the national court concerning a question of EU law, before final resolution of the case at the national level. Thus the "constitutional principles" enunciated by the European Court of Justice have been given effect in national legal orders by national courts. The Article 234 EC procedure cuts both ways.[165] On the one hand, it requires national courts to apply EU law within their own legal orders – embodying the idea that "every national court is an EU court". On the other hand, under Article 234 EC, national courts retain an important "gatekeeping" control, in that they are the ultimate arbiters of any litigation, and indeed of whether to refer to the European Court of Justice at all.[166]

Problems have arisen, however, with respect to the interactions of the principle of supremacy of EU law, as articulated by the European Court of Justice, and unalterable provisions of national constitutions, as interpreted by national constitutional courts. What happens if "supreme" EU (internal market) law undermines a fundamental national constitutional provision, in particular a fundamental human right? This question goes to the heart of questions concerning the legitimacy of the EU as a polity exercising powers once exclusively held by the democratically legitimated sovereign entities of its Member States.[167] One way of resolving such a

163 See Shaw, above n 1, pp 28, 422–458; B. de Witte, "Direct effect, supremacy and the nature of the Legal Order" in P. Craig and G. de Búrca, eds, *The Evolution of EU Law* (Oxford: OUP, 1999).

164 But see Article I-10 of the Draft Treaty establishing a Constitution for Europe (DCT).

165 See, in general, T. Tridimas, "Fragmentation, Efficiency and Defiance in the Preliminary Reference Procedure" 40 CMLRev (2003) 9.

166 But see Case C-224/01 *Köbler* above n 59, in which the Court held, for the first time, that a national supreme court (the Supreme Court of Austria) should have referred a case under Article 234 EC (or rather, should not have withdrawn a reference).

167 Obviously, this question goes beyond the scope of this book. For a starting point on the (copious) literature on the subject, see Craig and de Búrca, above n 1, chapter 4; Craig, in Craig and de Búrca,

conflict is for national constitutional courts to reinterpret their national constitutional provisions so as to guarantee supremacy of EU law. So for instance, in the *X* case,[168] a pregnant woman successfully challenged an injunction preventing her from leaving Ireland for a period of nine months. She argued, *inter alia*, that, as a medical treatment, abortion is a "service"[169] and freedom to provide and receive services is guaranteed by EU law. The injunction was effectively preventing her from exercising her EU rights. At first instance, the injunction, based on provisions of the Irish Constitution[170] was upheld. Although abortion is a "service" in EU law, the injunction was justified by the public policy of the deeply held moral conviction on the "right to life of the unborn", as expressed in the Irish constitution. On appeal, however, the injunction was discharged, on the grounds that the lower court had not correctly interpreted the relevant constitutional provision.[171] A similar reinterpretation of national law occurred before the UK Court of Appeal in the *Blood* case, discussed in chapter 1.

However, reinterpretation of national constitutional provisions cannot resolve all such conflicts. It cannot be regarded as entirely accurate simply to assert that supremacy of EU law enjoys the support of all judicial bodies within the EU under all circumstances.[172] However, for our purposes, what is important in this context is

eds, above n 18 pp 23–50; the essays collected in A. Arnull and D. Wincott, eds, *Accountability and Legitimacy in the European Union* (Oxford: OUP, 2002); Scharpf, above n 37; Weiler, above n 1; the essays collected in Weiler and Wind, above n 2, especially M. Poiares Maduro, "Europe and the constitution: what if this is as good as it gets?" therein; N. Walker, ed, *Sovereignty in Transition* (Oxford: Hart, 2003).

168 *Attorney General v X and others* [1992] ILRM 401.

169 This had been established by the European Court of Justice in Case C-159/90 *SPUC v Grogan* [1991] ECR I-4685.

170 Article 40.3.3: "The State acknowledges the right to life of the unborn and, with due regard to the equal right to life of the mother, guarantees in its laws to defend and vindicate that right."

171 See F. Murphy, "Maastricht: Implementation in Ireland" 19 ELRev (1994) 94 at 97–99.

172 See, for example, U.R. Haltern and J.H.H. Weiler, "The Autonomy of the Community Legal Order Through the Looking Glass" 37 *Harvard International Law Journal* (1996) 411; Craig and de Búrca, above n 1, pp 285–315; J.H.H. Weiler, "Does Europe Need a Constitution? Reflections on Demos, Telos and the German Maastricht Decision" 1 ELJ (1995) 219; J. Wouters, "National Constitutions and the EU" in D. O'Keeffe, ed, *Judicial Review in EC Law* (The Hague: Kluwer, 2000). See, in particular, the ruling of the German Federal Constitutional Court in *Brunner v The European Union Treaty* [1994] 1 CMLR 57; and the commentary provided in U. Everling, "The Maastricht Judgment of the German Federal Constitutional Court" 14 YEL (1994) 1; M. Herdegen, "Maastricht and the German Constitutional Court: Constitutional Restraints for an Ever Closer Union" 31 CMLRev (1994) 235; N. MacCormick, "The Maastricht-Urteil: Sovereignty Now" 1 ELJ (1995) 259; M. Zuleeg, "The European Constitution under Constitutional Constraints: The German Scenario" 22 ELRev (1997) 19. On the position in other Member States, see, J. Dutheil de la Rochère, "The Attitude of French Courts towards ECJ Case Law" in D. O'Keeffe, ed, *Judicial Review in EC Law* (The Hague: Kluwer, 2000); G. Gaja, "New Developments in a Continuing Story: The Relationship between EEC Law and Italian Law" 27 CMLRev (1990) 401; E. Magarris "The Principle of Supremacy of Community Law – The Greek Challenge" 23 ELRev (1998) 179; P. Oliver, "The French Constitution and the Treaty of Maastricht" 43 ICLQ (1994) 1; R. Petriccione, "Italy: Supremacy of Community Law over National Law" 11 ELRev (1986) 320; H. Rasmussen, "Confrontation or Peaceful Co-existence? On the Danish Supreme Court's Maastricht Ratification Judgment" in D. O'Keeffe, ed, *Judicial Review in EC Law* (The Hague: Kluwer, 2000); P. Roseren, "The Application of Community Law by French Courts from

the Court's attempt to accommodate supremacy and the protection of fundamental human rights. The Court has done so by reference to the "general principles" of EU law.[173] This has enabled the Court to find that what appear to be clashes between EU norms and national constitutional provisions protecting fundamental rights can be resolved by reinterpretation of the EU norms to incorporate fundamental rights,[174] or by finding invalid any EU norms that do not respect such fundamental rights.[175] Thus according to the Court, fundamental human rights as guaranteed by national constitutional provisions are also implicit in the EU's legal order. The language of rights carries significant normative power, in particular with respect to relationships between individuals and repositories of collective power, typically states, but also non-state polities such as the EU. As we saw in chapter 1, human rights may exert some influence within the field of health law, in particular in framing its discourse. It is possible, therefore, that fundamental human rights recognised in the health field might constrain action of the EU institutions, or of the Member States when implementing EU law.[176]

As we saw in chapter 1, an important reference point in determining which such fundamental rights are recognised in EU law is the Charter of Fundamental Rights of the European Union 2000 (EUCFR).[177] By no means the first attempt to incorporate a "Bill of Rights" into EU law, the Charter initiative came from the German Presidency of the EU in 1999, following up a number of reports on human rights commissioned by the EU in the late 1990s.[178] The EUCFR is a "solemn proclamation" of the European Parliament, Council and the Commission, that is, a measure of soft law. Its influence within the EU's legal order is therefore, at least at present,[179] indirect. However, the Charter imposes obligations on the

1982–1993" 31 CMLRev (1994) 315; A.G. Tesauro, "Community Law and National Courts: An Italian Perspective" in D. O'Keeffe, ed, *Judicial Review in EC Law* (The Hague: Kluwer, 2000).

173 See, for example, Case 29/69 *Stauder v City of Ulm* [1969] ECR 419; Case 11/70 *Internationale Handelsgesellschaft* [1970] ECR 1125; Case 4/73 *Nold v Commission* [1974] ECR 491.

174 Case 29/69 *Stauder v City of Ulm* above n 173.

175 Case 11/70 *Internationale Handelsgesellschaft* above n 173.

176 Case 63/83 *R v Kirk* [1984] ECR 2689; Case 5/88 *Wachauf v Germany* [1989] ECR 2609.

177 There is a significant and growing literature on the EUCFR. For a starting point, see the contributions to Vol 8(1) *Maastricht Journal of European and Comparative Law* (2001); G. de Búrca, "The Drafting of the EU Charter of Fundamental Rights" 26 ELRev (2001) 126; and, with particular reference to social rights in the EUCFR, see C. Costello, ed, *Fundamental Social Rights: Current European Legal Protection and the Challenge of the EU Charter on Fundamental Rights* (Dublin: Irish Centre for European Law, 2001); T. Hervey and J. Kenner, eds, *Economic and Social Rights under the EU Charter of Fundamental Rights* (Oxford: Hart, 2003).

178 See Comité des Sages Report on Civic and Social Rights, 1996; P. Alston, M. Bustelo and J. Heenan, eds, *Leading by Example: A Human Rights Agenda for the European Union for the Year 2000* (Florence: European University Institute, 1998); P. Alston, ed, *The EU and Human Rights* (Oxford: OUP, 1999); Report of the Expert Group on Fundamental Rights, *Affirming Fundamental Rights in the European Union: Time to Act*, February 1999. See further de Búrca, above n 177.

179 The Draft Treaty establishing a Constitution for Europe (DCT), available at http://european-convention.eu.int/, has proposed that the EUCFR be included in the Treaty, in Part II. See further chapter 10.

EU institutions, and may be found to be an expression of pre-existing "general principles" of EU law. It may be used to interpret provisions of EU law. The Charter takes its inspiration from various sources, in particular the European Convention on Human Rights and Fundamental Freedoms 1950 (ECHR), and provides that where rights in the Charter correspond to provisions of the ECHR, the meaning and scope of those rights is to be the same as laid down in the ECHR.[180] As we noted in chapter 1, several provisions of the EUCFR may be important in the field of health.[181] The extent to which the rights articulated in the EUCFR may have an impact on health policy in the EU and its Member States is currently unclear, but the Charter remains an important site for possible future developments.[182]

V. Conclusions

This chapter has set out a typology of modes of governance utilised by the EU, within which its various effects on national health law and policy may be analysed. The EU promotes the integration process, or governs, by a number of methods, which may be categorised as: deregulation; "old style" harmonisation; "new approach" harmonisation; regulatory coordination; soft coordination; and providing financial incentives. This typology will form the basis for the analysis in subsequent chapters of this book, in which a number of examples from substantive law are considered.

The main primary sources, and types of secondary sources, of EU law have been set out, and their legal status within the legal orders of the Member States has been explained. In addition, the key regulatory institutions of the EU, relevant to health law and policy – the Commission, Council of Ministers, European Council, European Parliament, committees and agencies – have been introduced. As our focus is the impact of EU *law* on health law and policy, attention has been drawn to the significant influences of courts – both national courts and the European Court of Justice – on the processes of governance in the EU. These have primarily taken place in the context of the deregulatory mode of governance, and in the articulation of "fundamental rights" as inherent in the EU's legal order. This latter development must be seen in the broader context of the development of the EU as a "constitutionalised" system of governance, within which conflicts between national and EU-level "constitutional" norms must be somehow accommodated. The eventual outcome of the 2004 IGC on the Draft Constitutional Treaty will be yet another step along the road.

180 Article 52 (3) EUCFR.
181 See chapter 1, pp 25–27.
182 See T. Hervey, "The right to health in European Community Law" in T. Hervey and J. Kenner, eds, *Economic and Social Rights under the EU Charter of Fundamental Rights* (Oxford: Hart, 2003); see further chapter 10.

Any understanding of the EU as a law-making entity must be firmly based on the idea of the EU as a polity with limited competences. The EU may not lawfully act without an appropriate "legal basis", in the EC Treaty or TEU, for its action. Acts taken outside the EU's formal legal competence may be subject to challenge by means of judicial review. EU-level acts that may influence health law and policy may be taken on a number of different legal bases, and it is to these that the next chapter turns.

3

Community competence in the field of health

I. Introduction[1]

As we noted in chapters 1 and 2, health law is concerned with "rights" of individuals, for instance, to access elements of health care, or to particular standards of treatment in the health care context, or even to health protection. Health law is also centrally concerned with the legal construction of *responsibilities* – primarily that of the state in relation to the provision of health care services or in the area of safeguarding public health. However, in general, as is recognised by international and national (constitutional) law,[2] national governmental institutions hold a primary responsibility for health care provision, health protection and promotion of health within their territories. In the case of the Member States of the EU, however, this responsibility for health is not located solely with national institutions, but may in some circumstances lie with the institutions of the EU, or in interactions between national and EU institutions. The notion of legal responsibility is constructed in EU law by reference to the powers or "competence" of the Community.[3] This chapter therefore considers Community competence in the field of health.

The general context here – the allocation of competence within the EU's system of governance – is very much a matter of current concern for the EU, as reflected in the Laeken Declaration and the Draft Treaty Establishing a Constitution for Europe (DCT).[4] This concern relates to the overall questions of legitimacy of the

1 This chapter is partly based on T. Hervey, "Community and National Competence in Health after *Tobacco Advertising*" 38 CMLRev (2001) 1421.

2 See chapter 1, nn 20–28.

3 Of course, "competence" is not entirely contiguous with "responsibility". In some circumstances, the EU institutions may simply have a permissive competence (that is, they *may* act); whereas in others they may have a mandatory competence (that is, they *must* act). The notion of legal "responsibility" appears to be closer to mandatory competence than permissive competence. On the difference between "powers" and "competence" (clearer in other official languages of the EU), see G. de Búrca and B. de Witte, "The Delimitation of Powers between the EU and its Member States" in A. Arnull and D. Wincott, eds, *Accountability and Legitimacy in the European Union* (Oxford: OUP, 2002), pp 204–205.

4 Laeken Declaration on the Future of the European Union, adopted by the Heads of State and Government at the Laeken Summit, 14–15 December 2001, http://www.europa.eu.int/futurum/documents/offtext/doc151201_en.htm; and Draft Treaty establishing a Constitution for Europe, available at http://european-convention.eu.int/. For general discussion of Community

EU's "constitutionalised" legal order that were raised in chapter 2. The formal legal position is that the legislative institutions of the EU have (and have always had) limited competence. The institutions may act only where the founding Treaties (the EC Treaty and the Treaty on European Union[5]) give them formal legal power to act.[6] Treaty provisions that grant such competence are known as "legal basis" provisions. Where there is no appropriate legal basis provision, or where an act has been adopted on the wrong legal basis, the act may be the subject of judicial review before the European Court of Justice, and may be set aside as unlawful. Such legal basis provisions thus may constrain the actions taken by the institutions, in terms of both their form and their substance.[7] Therefore, one important element in arriving at an understanding of the impact of the EU legal order on health law and policy in the Member States is the structure of the relevant legal basis provisions in the EC Treaty. This chapter aims to examine these legal basis provisions in some detail.

However, the formal legal position does not tell the whole story. The precise extent of Community competence is not always easy to determine, for a number of reasons. Community competence includes *implied competence*, where the Treaty does not grant an explicit power, but requires the achievement of an objective.[8] Competence in a particular field is rarely exclusively allocated to the EU institutions, but is most often *shared* with national institutions, leading to boundary disputes about the proper limits of Community competence, expressed in legal terms by reference to the principles of subsidiarity and proportionality.[9] Some legal basis provisions may be expressed in very *general* terms, leaving doubt as to their precise scope in a particular context.[10] The European Court of Justice has not developed a complete doctrine of the allocation of powers between Member States and EU institutions.[11] All of these elements contribute to a situation in which the EU institutions may be charged with taking advantage of "creeping competence" – the extension of Community competence into ever wider areas, including health. The Laeken Council charged the Convention on the Future of the European Union with clarifying and simplifying

competence, see, for example, P. Craig and G. de Búrca, *EU Law: Text, Cases and Materials* (Oxford: OUP, 2003), pp 122–138; S. Weatherill, *Cases and Materials on EU Law* (Oxford: OUP, 2003), pp 45–68; T. C. Hartley, *The Foundations of European Community Law* (Oxford: OUP, 2003), pp 105–118; de Búrca and de Witte, above n 3; U. di Fabio, "Some Remarks on the Allocation of Competences between the European Union and its Member States" 39 CMLRev (2002) 1289; S. Weatherill, "Pre-emption, Harmonisation and the Distribution of Competence" in C. Barnard and J. Scott, *The Law of the Single European Market: Unpacking the Premises* (Oxford: Hart, 2002).

5 As noted in chapter 2, for our purposes the EC Treaty forms the main focus of enquiry.

6 See Article 5 (1) EC.

7 The imperative to act is also subject to the principles of subsidiarity and proportionality: see Article 5 (2) and (3) EC.

8 Cases 281, 283–5, & 287/86 *Germany v Commission* [1987] ECR 3203.

9 Article 5 (2) and (3) EC. See chapter 2, pp 40–41.

10 See, in particular, Article 308 EC. Along with Article 95 EC, this is explicitly mentioned in the Laeken Declaration as a possible site for adjustment by the Constitutional Convention; see de Búrca and de Witte, above n 3, p 204.

11 See de Búrca and de Witte, above n 3, p 201. De Búrca and de Witte contrast the position with respect to other elements of European constitutional law, where the Court has developed quite comprehensive jurisprudence.

the provisions on Community competence, and the Draft Treaty Establishing a Constitution for Europe (DCT) proposes a number of changes.[12] This chapter shows how, in the field of health as in other fields, such (essentially political) disputes concerning the allocation of competences may be resolved by reference to legal discourse, in particular judicial review of acts of the EU institutions.

In addition to establishing the *fields* in which the EU institutions may act, legal basis provisions also provide the *forms* that those acts may take, and the *procedure* by which they may be adopted. Legal basis provisions may refer to the adoption of "measures", allowing the EU institutions a wide choice of different types of legislative act, or they may specify which type of measure may be adopted, say directives,[13] or provisions of soft (non-binding) law. It will be remembered that different types of EU acts have different effects in national legal orders.[14] Legal basis provisions may explicitly preclude acts which have the effect of harmonising national laws.[15] Further, legal basis provisions state which legislative procedure is to be used in the adoption of a particular act. The determination of a particular procedure grants different powers to the EU institutions.[16] Two components are particularly relevant: the voting rules in the Council of Ministers, and the role of the European Parliament. Voting in Council may be by unanimity, effectively granting the government of each Member State a veto over any proposal, or it may be by qualified majority, in which case a "blocking minority" of Member States is needed to oppose a proposal. The European Parliament may simply have the right to be consulted, or may have the power of "co-legislature" with Council, in which case it enjoys an ultimate veto.[17] The context within which critical assessment of the EU's legislative procedures takes place is the more general debate about the legitimacy of the EU as a polity that now exercises some of the law-making functions once reserved to the democratically legitimated governments of its Member States.[18]

12 See Laeken Declaration on the Future of the European Union, above n 4 (see further chapter 2, n 9); Articles I-9 – I-17 DCT. For further information on the DCT, see chapter 10. For discussion of the proposals of the DCT in this respect, see M. Dougan, "The Convention's Draft Constitutional Treaty: a 'Tidying Up Exercise' that needs some Tidying-Up of its Own", Federal Trust online papers, http://www.fedtrust.co.uk/uploads/constitution/27_03.pdf; P. Craig, "What Constitution does Europe need? The House that Giscard Built: Constitutional Rooms with a View", Federal Trust online papers, http://www.fedtrust.co.uk/uploads/constitution/26_03.pdf.

13 Such as the original Article 100 EEC, now Article 94 EC: see chapter 2, p 49.

14 According to the Treaty, Regulations are "binding in their entirety and directly applicable in the Member States"; directives are "binding as to the result to be achieved" but leave the method of achieving this result to national authorities. The European Court of Justice has developed a sophisticated jurisprudence concerning the effects of various provisions of secondary Community law in the national legal orders of the Member States, see, chapter 2, pp 42–43.

15 Such as Article 152 EC: see below.

16 There are six main different legislative procedures set out in the Treaty, see Craig and de Búrca, above n 4, pp 140–148.

17 This was used by the European Parliament for the first time on 1 March 1995 in rejecting the first proposed Directive on the Legal Protection of Biotechnological Inventions COM(88) 496 final; see further chapter 7.

18 As we noted in chapter 2, this question goes beyond the scope of this book. For a starting point on the (copious) literature on the subject, see the literature cited in chapter 2, n 167.

In particular, the increased use of qualified majority voting, and the consequent gradual loss of the veto in Council, beginning with the Single European Act, and continuing through the Treaty reforms at Maastricht, Amsterdam and Nice, has proved to be a site of conflict between governments of the Member States and the EU institutions.[19]

The EC Treaty has an explicit legal basis provision concerned with health, in Article 152 EC.[20] However, in order to explore the extent to which EU law affects national health law and policy in the Member States, we must also consider the effect of measures based on other legal basis provisions, that might also affect health policy. Following the Treaty, and as reflected in the various textbooks on the subject,[21] EU law is constructed in terms of various policy fields, such as internal market law, competition law, agricultural law, environmental law, and so on. In order to understand the effects of EU law on national health law and policy, these existing "constructs" of EU law must be reconceptualised from the point of view of health. We cannot answer our research question by using the traditional categories of EU law; rather we need to look across these pre-established categories to see how various diverse policies as articulated and promulgated at EU level may affect health law and policy in the Member States. Part of the context of that enquiry is the scope of the legal basis provisions in those other fields.

Among those fields of EU law, the law of the internal market enjoys a central place in the EU's legal order. As we saw in chapter 2, a fundamental aim of the EU is to integrate the markets of its Member States, though the legal mechanisms of deregulation and re-regulation. The enforceability of the Treaty provisions on free movement of the factors of production has played a key role in this respect. However, the legal basis provisions provided in the Treaty to ensure the establishment and functioning of the common (Article 94 EC, ex Article 100 EEC) and internal market (Article 95 EC, ex Article 100a EEC) have also played a crucial role. They will therefore form a central part of our analysis.

II. Article 152 EC

Historical context

Until the Treaty of Maastricht, EU institutions had no explicit competence in the field of health. There has nevertheless been EU-level activity in the field since the

19 See, in general, on "legal basis litigation", A. Charlesworth and H. Cullen, "Diplomacy by Other Means: The Use of Legal Basis Litigation as a Political Strategy by the European Parliament and Member States" 36 CMLRev (1999) 1243.

20 The DCT proposes some amendments to this provision, see Article III-179 DCT, see further chapter 10.

21 See, for instance, Craig and de Búrca, above n 4; Weatherill, above n 4; D. Wyatt and A. Dashwood, *European Union Law* (London: Sweet and Maxwell, 2000); D. Chalmers and E. Szyszczak, *European Union Law Vol II: Towards a European Polity?* (Aldershot: Ashgate, 1998).

late 1970s.[22] Its legal basis is unclear and its legality may be dubious,[23] but, as it was broadly uncontentious, no party with *locus standi* has sought to challenge any of the measures adopted. Article 2 EEC stated that one of the "objectives" of the Community was the "raising of the standard of living". This was interpreted by some to imply that health protection was one of the aims of the Community. If this were so, action could lawfully be taken by the EU institutions on the "general" legal basis of Article 235 EEC (now Article 308 EC).[24]

This broad interpretation of Articles 2 and 235 EEC underpinned some subsequent activity involving coordination of policies between the Member States in the field of health, predating the inclusion of specific legal basis provisions on health in the Treaty. For instance, the Europe against Cancer programme[25] was established in 1989, and the Europe against AIDS programme[26] in 1991. As the enactment of these measures pre-dated any formal legal competence on the part of the Community to take such action, the legal basis presented in Decision 88/351/EEC on Europe against Cancer is simply "the Treaty establishing the EC".

An explicit legal basis provision for health – Article 129 EC (now amended and renumbered Article 152 EC) – was not introduced into the EC Treaty until the amendments made by the Treaty of Maastricht took effect in 1993. The introduction of Article 129 EC into the Treaty may have been due to a perception that some problems relating to health policy were not amenable to resolution solely within

22 For instance, the Europe against Cancer programme (Decision 88/351/EEC of the Council and Representatives of the Governments of the Member States meeting within Council, OJ 1988 L 160/52), which encompassed anti-tobacco campaigns, improvements in nutrition, protection against carcinogenic agents, promotion of screening policies, provision of information to the public and professionals, and research; and the Europe against AIDS programme (Decision 91/317/EEC of the Council and Ministers of Health of the Member States adopting a plan of action in the framework of the "Europe against AIDS" programme, OJ 1991 L 175/26), which encompassed training provision, information exchange on services, research and measures to promote the safety of blood. See further, M. McKee, E. Mossialos and P. Belcher, "The Influence of European Law on National Health Policy" 6 *Journal of European Social Policy* (1996) 263 at 265; H.D.C. Roscam Abbing, "European Community and the Right to Health Care" in A.F. Casparie, H. Hermans and J.H.P. Paelinck, eds, *Health Care in Europe After 1992* (Aldershot: Dartmouth, 1992), p 24.

23 Article 5 EC (ex 3b) provides that the Community shall act within the limits of the powers conferred upon it by the Treaty. The EU institutions are obliged to state the legal basis on which they base legislative acts, see Case 45/86 *Commission v Council (Tariff Preferences)* [1987] ECR 1483. Although Article 308 (ex 235) EC grants a residual power to the institutions to act where necessary to attain one of the objectives of the Treaty, where the Treaty has not provided the necessary powers, the Court has made it clear that this does not involve a limitless competence: see *Opinion 2/94* [1996] ECR I-1759.

24 A. Verwers, "Towards a New EC Health Policy?" *Uniting Public Health in Europe* (European Public Health Association, 1992), p 12, cited in A.P. Van der Mei and L. Waddington, "Public Health and the Treaty of Amsterdam" 5 *European Journal of Health Law* (1998) 129 at 132–133. See further below.

25 Decision 88/351/EEC of the Council and Representatives of the Governments of the Member States meeting within Council, OJ 1988 L 160/52.

26 Decision 91/317/EEC of the Council and Ministers of Health of the Member States adopting a plan of action in the framework of the "Europe against AIDS" programme, OJ 1991 L 175/26. See further, McKee, Mossialos and Belcher, above n 22, at 265.

national borders. For instance, governments of Member States may have felt a shared concern with respect to various threats to public health, such as new diseases including HIV/AIDS. Alternatively, or additionally, the new Treaty provision may have been introduced to prevent further extension of a perceived "creeping competence" of the EU into health matters, reflected in the EU's health-related activities to date.[27] Article 129 EC may be seen as representing a compromise between those governments of Member States who did not want any EU mandate on health, and those who wanted to go further. Article 129 EC was seen by some as setting limits to the expansion of EU-level activities in the health field, which had occurred in the past without any specific legal basis. For others, it was a mere formalisation of what was already taking place.[28] Ultimately, the proper construction of Article 152 (ex 129) EC is a matter for the European Court of Justice, in the context of its jurisprudence on competence and legal basis, and this is explored below.

Article 129 EC provided that "the Community shall contribute towards a high level of human health protection by encouraging cooperation between Member States, and, if necessary, lending support to their action". Action of the EU institutions was to be directed towards a number of specified areas, in particular major health scourges (including drug dependence); research into causes and transmission of these diseases; and provision of information and education on health. The matters covered by Article 129 EC (and now by Article 152 EC) are thus essentially concerned with *public* health, in the sense of health protection and promotion of good health carried out on a *collective* basis, rather than *individual* health-related entitlements.[29] It appears that these matters were seen as more appropriate for EU-level activity than responsibilities for health care of individuals; relationships between individual recipients of health care, health care providers and health care funders; or the organisation of national health (insurance) systems. In fact, however, as we shall see, elements of community competence appear to go beyond at least a narrow definition of public health, and may in some circumstances encroach on individually-based health entitlements.

The impact of various EU policies and activities, in particular the law of the internal market,[30] on public health may also help to explain the focus on public health and its inclusion in the Treaty. To this end, Article 129 EC also provided that health protection requirements are to form a constituent part of the EU's other policies. The "weak mainstreaming"[31] objective of Article 129 EC required that in policy areas not directly related to health, due regard should nevertheless be given to

27 It is difficult to discern the reasons for a particular Treaty revision, as detailed records of summit meetings, at which Treaty revisions are agreed, are not made public. The notion of "creeping competence" is explicitly mentioned as one of the challenges for the EU in the Laeken Declaration, above n 4.

28 McKee, Mossialos and Belcher, above n 22, at 267.

29 See discussion in chapter 1, pp 19–21.

30 See discussion in chapter 2, pp 44–47.

31 Also known as "integration".

health issues.[32] The presence of this objective in the Treaty arguably set health policy on the road to being established as a general EU policy. Such a conclusion is underpinned by the inclusion of the raising of "the quality of life" among the objectives of the Community (Article 2 EC) and a "contribution to the attainment of a high level of health protection" among the Community's activities (Article 3 (o) EC).[33]

The insertion of Article 129 EC into the Treaty of Rome established health as what is known as a "flanking policy" in the EU: an area in which activities of the EU institutions are limited to coordination, and harmonisation of national laws is explicitly excluded from Community competence. Member States are thereby placed under an obligation to liaise with the Commission and to coordinate policies and programmes in the areas referred to above. Thus national health policy in these matters may not lawfully develop in a vacuum, but multi-level coordination is required. The Commission was formally granted a general power of initiative to propose measures which will promote cooperation between the Member States in those areas. Article 129 formed a legal basis on which Council and Parliament may adopt "incentive measures" according to the co-decision procedure, or recommendations, by qualified majority on a proposal from the Commission, in order to contribute to the achievement of the objectives set out in the provision. In fact, as we have seen, this grant of formal competence to take such action post-dated actual activities at EU level, and put them on a firmer legal footing.

The competence of the Community in the field of health was expressed at greater length in 1993 in the Council Resolution on future action in the field of public health.[34] The 1993 Council Resolution was fleshed out by a number of official Commission action programmes, including the first action programme for health promotion, information, education and training in the field of public health.[35] The health programmes proposed on AIDS, cancer, drug dependence and health promotion were implemented in 1996;[36] the fifth programme, on health monitoring, was implemented in 1997.[37] The final three programmes – on injury prevention; rare diseases; and pollution-related diseases were adopted in 1999.[38] These programmes support a number of projects covering, for instance, exchange of information and personnel, training, pilot projects, information campaigns, and networking of organisations and experts.

32 Van der Mei and Waddington, above n 24, at 133.
33 Van der Mei and Waddington, above n 24, at 133; citing Verwers, above n 24, p 12; COM(95) 196 final.
34 OJ 1993 C 174/1.
35 COM(94) 202 final.
36 Decision 646/96/EC, OJ 1996 L 95/9; Decision 647/96/EC, OJ 1996 L 95/16; Decision 102/97/EC, OJ 1997 L 19/25; Decision 645/96/EC, OJ 1996 L 95/1.
37 Decision 1400/97/EC, OJ 1997 L 193/1.
38 Decision 372/99/EC, OJ 1999 L 46/1. Repealed by Decision 1786/2002/EC adopting a programme of Community action in the field of public health (2003–2008), OJ 2002 L 271/1.

The elements of Article 152 EC

Originally, it appears that there was no intention to amend Article 129 EC in the 1996 IGC, which culminated in the Treaty of Amsterdam.[39] However, it seems that the BSE/nvCJD crisis – which made it clear that some threats to health merit a response at European level – galvanised the governments of the Member States into taking some action in that respect.[40] The result was the new Article 152 EC. A number of changes of emphasis from Article 129 EC should be noted.

Article 152 EC provides:

> "(1) A high level of human health protection shall be ensured in the definition and implementation of all Community policies and activities.
>
> Community action, which shall complement national policies, shall be directed towards improving public health, preventing human illness and diseases, and obviating sources of danger to human health. Such action shall cover the fight against the major health scourges, by promoting research into their causes, their transmission and their prevention, as well as health information and education.
>
> The Community shall complement the Member States' action in reducing drugs-related health damage, including information and prevention.
>
> (2) The Community shall encourage cooperation between the Member States in the areas referred to in this Article and, if necessary, lend support to their action.
>
> Member States shall, in liaison with the Commission, coordinate among themselves their policies and programmes in the areas referred to in paragraph 1. The Commission may, in close contact with the Member States, take any useful initiative to promote such coordination.
>
> (3) The Community and the Member States shall foster cooperation with third countries and the competent international organisations in the sphere of public health.
>
> (4) The Council, acting in accordance with the procedure referred to in Article 251 and after consulting the Economic and Social Committee and the Committee of the Regions, shall contribute to the achievement of the objectives referred to in this Article through adopting:
>
> (a) measures setting high standards of quality and safety of organs and substances of human origin, blood and blood derivatives; these measures shall not prevent any Member State from maintaining or introducing more stringent protective measures;
> (b) by way of derogation from Article 37, measures in the veterinary and phytosanitary fields which have as their direct objective the protection of public health;
> (c) incentive measures designed to protect and improve human health, excluding any harmonisation of the laws and regulations of the Member States.

39 See W. Dommers, "Europese Integratie en volksgesondheit: handel noopt tot handelen" in H.D.C. Roscam Abbing and G. Van Berkenstijn, eds, *Gezondheidsbeleid in Europa* (Houten: Bohn Stafleu Van Loghum, 1995), p 46, cited in Van der Mei and Waddington, above n 24, at 134.

40 See chapter 9, pp 354–357.

The Council, acting by a qualified majority on a proposal from the Commission, may also adopt recommendations for the purposes set out in this Article.

(5) Community action in the field of public health shall fully respect the responsibilities of the Member States for the organisation and delivery of health services and medical care. In particular, measures referred to in paragraph 4 (a) shall not affect national provisions on the donation or medical use of organs and blood."

The first element of Article 152 EC is now the mainstreaming element, to the effect that health protection must be considered in the implementation of all other Community policies and activities. This is consonant with new provisions in Articles 2 and 3 EC, to the effect that the Community's tasks include "raising of the standard of living and quality of life" and activities include "a contribution to the attainment of a high level of health protection". Health interests must now be taken into account when pursuing potentially competing goals in other policy areas. The bolstering of the mainstreaming element in Article 152 EC is said to be[41] in response to the arguments of the UK government in Case C-180/96-R *UK v Commission*,[42] concerning the emergency measures taken against BSE.[43] On a broad reading, Article 152 EC might require extra weight to be given to health goals, or indeed might render measures in other areas unlawful if a "high level of human health protection" cannot be guaranteed.[44]

The obligation of the EU institutions has been strengthened from a requirement to "contribute" to ensuring a high level of protection of human health, to the duty to "ensure" a high level of health protection in all Community activities. Similarly, the requirement that "Community action shall be directed towards *improving* public health" (italics added) suggests an extension from the Article 129 EC formulation of simply "contributing" to a high level of human health protection. Moreover, Community activities are no longer limited to *prevention* of disease, but have expanded to include *promotion* of good health.[45] Article 152 (1) EC states that Community action "shall be directed towards improving public health, preventing human illness

41 R. Geyer, *Exploring European Social Policy* (Cambridge: Polity, 2000), p 175.

42 [1996] ECR I-3903.

43 The UK argued that the measures (banning the export of bovines, meat from bovines and products obtained from bovines liable to enter the animal feed or human food chain, or materials destined for use in pharmaceuticals or cosmetics) were adopted on the basis of economic measures and the need to reassure consumers and protect the beef market. The UK sought an interim suspension of the ban with respect to various products for which the risk of BSE was not established or had been eliminated by national measures. Essentially, the UK argued that the ban was not justified for such products. The Court took the view that the potentially (at the relevant time, the link between BSE and nvCJD was not clear) serious harm to public health posed by BSE did justify the measures. Implicit in the Court's reasoning was the position that the protection of public health is a fundamental duty of the EU institutions, which cannot be disregarded in the pursuit of the common agricultural policy (para 63). This implicit position was made more explicit by the "strong mainstreaming" of public health protection in all Community policies, effected at Amsterdam.

44 Van der Mei and Waddington, above n 24, at 134.

45 Van der Mei and Waddington, above n 24, at 135.

and diseases and obviating sources of danger to human health". The reference to the major health scourges, and health information and education remains. Drug-related health damage[46] has its own indent, again with an emphasis on prevention, rather than repression.[47] The new wording of Article 152 (1) EC reflects a refocusing of EU policy, towards health promotion and the broader determinants of good health, from the direction suggested by the wording of old Article 129 EC. This refocus, if not change, of policy direction appears to have emanated from old DG V[48] of the European Commission,[49] rather than from the governments of the Member States. However the Treaty expression of the change of focus reflects an acceptance by the governments of the Member States that this is an appropriate direction for EU health policy. The refocus is significant, as it suggests an acceptance of the indivisibility of health promotion from health protection in the formation of health policy. It follows that the Community may have competence not only in health protection matters, such as disease control, as at issue in for instance the BSE/nvCJD affair, but also in matters of health promotion, such as restricting the advertising of tobacco.

Further, the wording of Article 152 (1) may suggest a move away from a solely "public health" competence for the EU institutions. "Improving public health" and "obviating sources of danger to human health" are centrally concerned with collective health protection and promotion. However, "preventing human illness and diseases" may at least potentially involve a concern with the individual. This may be particularly so as knowledge and understanding of the genetic make-up of an individual, and its relationship to diseases, increases. Further, the notion of "preventing diseases" may suggest a "defective human machine" model of health,[50] and may be more susceptible to an objective definition than that of "preventing human illness". "Illness" is a concept that may be defined only by reference to the subjective notion of "well-ness", and thus may suggest a "social" model of health, which has a wider ambit of concern, including for instance the relationship of health to poverty and social exclusion.[51] The inclusion of the phrase "preventing human illness" in Article 152 EC may thus constitute an extension of the scope of Community competence from that in Article 129 EC.

46 Presumably this means damage to health arising from illicit drugs; otherwise Community action could include matters such as damage arising from authorised pharmaceuticals, or from the use of drugs in clinical trials.

47 H.D.C. Roscam Abbing, "Public Health in the Treaty of Amsterdam" 5 *European Journal of Health Law* (1998) 171 at 172.

48 The responsibility for public health protection has now been transferred to DG Health and Consumer Protection.

49 The 1993 Council Resolution on future action in the field of public health, OJ 1993 C 174/1, suggested that the priority areas for EU action were drug dependence, cancer, AIDS and other communicable diseases, health data, information, accidents and injuries, pollution-related diseases, and rare diseases. The Commission's action programmes suggested a slight refocusing of policy from the position of the Council, towards health promotion and the broader determinants of good health. See McKee, Mossialos and Belcher, above n 22, at 266.

50 See chapter 1, p 7.

51 Ibid.

Article 152 (2) sets out the division of tasks and powers between the Member States and the EU institutions in the field of public health. The duty of cooperation on the part of the Member States remains unchanged. The provision makes it clear that, in accordance with the principle of subsidiarity, the main powers in the health field remain firmly with the Member States. This is underlined by subparagraph 5. The EU institutions are entitled to act only if "added European value" will result from the action. This point is taken up in the proposed new public health programme, discussed below.

Article 152 (4) sets out the procedures by which the EU institutions may act in the health field, and delimits the types of measures that may be enacted. Two types of legislation are envisaged: "measures" (Article 152 (4) (a) and (b)) and "incentive measures" (Article 152 (4) (c)). "Incentive measures" explicitly preclude harmonisation provisions; however, "measures" implicitly include harmonising regulations, directives or other acts. This is a development from Article 129 EC, which gave power to enact only "incentive measures" designed to protect and improve human health. Article 152 EC adds to the pre-Amsterdam wording competence to adopt measures in two further areas. These are "measures setting high standards of quality and safety of organs and substances of human origin, blood and blood derivatives" and "measures in the veterinary and phytosanitary fields which have as their direct objective the protection of public health" (Article 152 (4) (a) and (b) EC). In one sense, these provisions, especially those in Article 152 (4) (b) EC, are not an extension of Community competence, as they refer to areas of well-established EU policy. These latter provisions are an extension of (or rather a derogation from) the powers given to the EU institutions in Article 37 EC to effect the common agricultural policy. Their inclusion is apparently due to the BSE/nvCJD crisis. The provision removes from the scope of the common agricultural policy veterinary and phytosanitary measures which are primarily concerned with human health protection.[52] Significantly, a different legislative procedure (co-decision, rather than the basic procedure of Article 37 EC) is to be used.[53] This procedure gives more power to the European Parliament, and may be directly related to the Parliament's condemnation of the Council and Commission over the BSE affair.[54]

The provisions in Article 152 (4) (a) EC are more obviously an extension of the power of the EU institutions. Their presence in the Treaty may be explained by various health scandals concerning blood and human organs, such as the distribution and transfusion of HIV-infected blood and blood products.[55] It may also be relevant that an embryonic "market" in human blood, organs and other

52 Van der Mei and Waddington, above n 24, at 137.

53 Although Council is to act by qualified majority under Article 37 EC, the role of the European Parliament is consultative only, rather than the co-decision role envisaged in Article 152 EC. For further discussion, see below.

54 See further chapter 9.

55 J. Abraham and G. Lewis, *Regulating Medicines in Europe: Competition, expertise and public health* (London: Routledge, 2000), pp 73–75; Van der Mei and Waddington, above 24, at 137.

substances is emerging in the EU. Using the ordinary internal market provisions, including those on free movement of goods and consumer protection, to regulate this "market" is politically and ethically sensitive in many Member States, as these substances are neither conceptualised as "goods" nor the object of ordinary commerce or consumption. However, "consumers" of these "goods" do need to be protected within the EU's legal order. These and other ethical concerns about the use of blood and human organs are also reflected in the Council of Europe's Convention on Human Rights and Biomedicine, signed in Oviedo in April 1997, especially in its Protocol on Transplantation of Organs and Tissues of Human Origin,[56] and in ongoing work by the WHO.[57] Article 152 EC gives power to Council and Parliament to enact the necessary protective regulations as public health measures, although the measures may well be modelled on existing internal market consumer protection regulation. EU-level requirements will set only a "minimum floor" of regulatory protection, and Member States are free to enact higher standards if they wish. Again, the subsidiarity principle is invoked with a specific exclusion in sub-paragraph 5 for "national provisions on the donation or medical use of organs and blood". This refers to the differences in national legal systems concerning donor consent.[58]

Article 152 (5) EC provides that "Community action in the field of public health shall fully respect the responsibilities of the Member States for the organisation and delivery of health services and medical care". This is an explicit statement on the application of the principle of subsidiarity in the health field. Presumably, the main concern of the Member States is the preservation of national competence over the financing of national health systems.[59] The wording suggests a conceptualisation of health policy in terms of a more or less stark dichotomy between the regulation of general "public" health matters, regulating the broader determinants of good health, prevention of disease and promotion of good health (a matter for shared Community and national competence) and the regulation of medical services, health care and private relationships between patients, medical professionals and funding bodies (a matter for Member States). However, this apparent dichotomy belies the much more complex reality in terms of the regulation of health, as we saw in chapter 1. It follows that the wording of Article 152 EC does not in itself reflect the reality of the impact of EU law on the health law and policy of the Member States. A broader

56 Strasbourg, 24 January 2002.

57 See especially the work of the WHO Task Force on Organ Transplantation, and the WHO, *Guiding Principles on Human Organ Transplantation* (Geneva: WHO, 1991), reprinted in *International Digest of Health Legislation* (1991).

58 See Roscam Abbing, above n 47, at 172 and also see further the discussion in chapter 9, pp 346–348; and chapter 10, pp 421–426.

59 Community law may have an *indirect* impact on the financing of national health systems, through the enforcement of the directly effective provisions on free movement of goods and services, and competition law. See, in particular, Case C-120/95 *Dekker* [1998] ECR I-1831 and Case C-158/96 *Kohll* [1998] ECR I-1931, as discussed in T. Hervey, "Social solidarity: a buttress against internal market law" in J. Shaw, ed, *Social Law and Policy in an Evolving European Union* (Oxford: Hart, 2000).

reading of Community competence in the health field, as that field interacts with other areas of EU activity, is needed.

In the final analysis, what is perhaps most significant about new Article 152 EC is that it gathers together powers and activities of the EU institutions in the health field in a much more coherent and logical manner than the pre-Amsterdam Treaty provisions. The EU can perhaps now truly be said to have its own (admittedly extremely modest) (public) health policy, which interacts with those at national level in the Member States. The details of that policy are a matter for elaboration among the institutions of the EU.

Secondary legislation adopted on the basis of Article 152 EC

The Commission lost no time in responding to its new duties under Article 152 EC. In April 1998, in view of the proposed new provisions of the Treaty of Amsterdam, the Commission launched a debate on a new direction for EU public health policy.[60] The Commission took the view that the existing public health strategy was in need of fundamental revision. The differentiated strategy, with eight separate programmes, was administratively inefficient and inflexible, in terms of responding to new developments in health status within the EU, such as the emergence of nvCJD, challenges arising from the EU's changing demographic profile,[61] and the process of enlargement of the EU. It was difficult to avoid overlap between the programmes, and to show clear "added value" with very small budgets and a focus on small-scale projects with relatively short time frames.

The Commission therefore proposed an EU public health policy comprising three strands: improving information for the development of public health; reacting rapidly to threats to health; and tackling health determinants through health promotion and disease prevention. The basic principles of the proposed new strategy were to make the best use of the limited resources available at EU level; to concentrate on a limited number of priorities; to emphasise the improvement of health; to be sufficiently flexible to respond to new developments; and to be credible and convincing from the point of view of citizens of the EU, reflecting their concerns. The Commission suggested that one way forward would be to adopt a single "framework instrument" providing for subsequent adoption of separate instruments for each strand. This would have the benefit of creating a single budgetary heading, with an administrative structure to apportion funding between the strands.

60 COM(98) 230 final.

61 Since 1970, life expectancy at birth for women in the EU has risen by 5.5 years, and for men by almost 5 years. A girl born in 1995 can expect to live well over 80 years, a boy to nearly 74 years: COM(98) 230 final, p 1. As a consequence of increasing life expectancies, more people are suffering from health problems related to old age, such as Alzheimer's Disease and other degenerative disorders. It was estimated that by 2000, 8 million people in the EU would be affected by Alzheimer's Disease: COM(98) 230 final, p 2.

The Council and the European Parliament (and also the Economic and Social Committee, and the Committee of the Regions) responded positively to the Commission's 1998 proposals.[62] These institutions also took the view that a single overall framework programme would be the best way forward. The proposal for a Decision of Council and Parliament adopting the new public health framework was first put forward by the Commission in the summer of 2000,[63] and, duly amended during the course of the legislative process, was finally adopted in September 2002.[64] Part of the reason for the length of the legislative process was negotiations over the budget size for the programme.[65] The new public health framework programme repealed the existing eight public health programmes,[66] and runs from 1 January 2003 to 31 December 2008.[67]

The three priorities of the 1998 consultation – improving health information and knowledge; responding rapidly to health threats; and addressing health determinants – are maintained, and set out as general objectives in Article 2 of the Decision. Each general objective is to be pursued by "actions" from among those listed in the Annex of the Decision, organised by reference to the three general objectives of Article 2 of the Decision. The detail here reflects topical concerns of the health systems of the Member States, at least those related to "public" health elements on disease prevention and promotion of the underlying determinants of good health. For instance, rapid response to health threats includes exchange of information on strategies to counter health threats from physical, chemical or biological sources in emergency situations, including those relating to terrorist acts.[68] The legacy of the events in the US on 11 September 2001 is clearly the inspiration for inclusion of this provision. Other examples include developing strategies for reducing antibiotic resistance,[69] implementing strategies on life-style related health determinants,[70] and exchanging information on genetic determinants and the use

62 Council conclusions of 26 November 1998 on the future framework for Community action in the field of public health, OJ 1998 C 390/1; Council resolution of 8 June 1999, OJ 1999 C 200/1; European Parliament Resolution A4-0082/99 of 12 March 1999, OJ 1999 C 175/35; Opinion of the ECOSOC of 9 September 1998, OJ 1998 C 407/26.

63 COM(2000) 285–2 final.

64 Decision 1786/2002/EC, OJ 2002 L 271/1. European Parliament first reading Report, 4 April 2001, A5-0104/2001; modified Commission proposal, COM(2001) 302 final; Council common position 31 July 2001; European Parliament second reading Report, 12 December 2001, A5-0420/2001; Joint Text approved by Conciliation Committee 15 May 2002, C5-0204/2002. Provision was made for the existing programmes to continue until the unified start date, see Decision 521/2001/EC, OJ 2001 L 79/1.

65 The Commission's original proposal set the budget at € 300 million; at its first reading, the European Parliament proposed € 500 million; Council responded with a suggestion of € 280 million; the European Parliament came down to € 380 million in its second reading; the final amount agreed by the Conciliation Committee is € 312 million: Decision 1786/2002, Article 7.

66 Decision 1786/2002/EC, Article 13.

67 Decision 1786/2002/EC, Article 1 (2).

68 Decision 1786/2002/EC, Annex 2.4.

69 Decision 1786/2002/EC, Annex 2.9.

70 Decision 1786/2002/EC, Annex 3.1.

of genetic screening.[71] This latter is an example of the extension of Community competence beyond a narrow notion of public health, towards elements of health policy focused more on the individual rather than collective activity.[72]

The "actions" are to be implemented by EU-level support for "activities", in cooperation with the Member States. "Activities" may implement all or part of an action, and may be combined. The complex arrangement of "objectives", "actions" and "activities" reflects a compromise position between those legislative actors who wished to place more constraints on the funding of the EU public health programme, and those who valued flexibility.[73] "Activities" fall into four categories, related to: monitoring and rapid reaction systems; health determinants; legislation; and consultation, knowledge and information. The last includes matters such as developing and maintaining networks for exchange of information on best practice in public health and the effectiveness of health policies.[74] The programme is open to participation by the candidate countries of Central and Eastern Europe, Cyprus, Malta and Turkey.[75]

The rationale for EU-level intervention, in the context of a field in which the main responsibilities for organisation and delivery of health care rest with the Member States, remains that of "added value". The requirement to integrate public health in other Community activities and policies will be carried out by a number of specific measures. Article 4 of the Decision envisages "joint actions" with related Community programmes and actions, such as those in "consumer protection, social protection, health and safety at work, employment, research and technological development, internal market, information society and information technology, statistics, agriculture, education, transport, industry and environment".

The detailed running of the programme is to be carried out by the Commission, through the comitology process.[76] Decisions are therefore to be made by an

71 Decision 1786/2002/EC, Annex 3.4.

72 Although of course exchange of large-scale collections of genetic information, such as that pertaining to Iceland's population used by deCODE Genetics of Reykjavik, or the UK's Biobank (http://www.ukbiobank.ac.uk), would presumably be included.

73 Broadly speaking, the European Parliament sought greater flexibility, while the Council sought to impose constraints on the disbursement of EU finances for the public health programme.

74 Decision 1786/2002/EC, Article 3 (2) (d) (v).

75 Each country's participation is governed by a decision of the "Association Council" appertaining to that country. See, for example, Decision No 5/99 of the EU-Republic of Slovenia Association Council, OJ 1999 L 304/27. The countries of Central and Eastern Europe are permitted to complement their own financial contributions to the programmes with PHARE funding, some 10% of which is reserved for community action programmes, including public health. Originally set up in 1989, in response to the "velvet revolution", PHARE is the main pre-accession instrument for assisting the ten candidate countries in Central and Eastern Europe to prepare for membership of the EU. In 2000–06, PHARE is providing some € 11 billion of co-financing for institution building through "twinning" of civil servants and technical assistance, and for investment to help applicant countries in their efforts to strengthen their public administrations and institutions, to promote convergence with the EU's extensive legislation, and to promote economic and social cohesion. See http://www.europa.eu.int/comm/enlargement/faq/.

76 Decision 1786/2002/EC, Article 5 (1); Article 9.

"Advisory Committee", or a "Management Committee" composed of representatives of the Member States, and chaired by the Commission, in accordance with Decision 99/468/EC,[77] Articles 4 and 7.[78]

The European Parliament sought to include various provisions related to medical services and health care systems, but these were rejected by Council. Some did not survive the conciliation process at all, such as Parliament's proposal that "patients' rights" should be promoted. This is in spite of the fact that the EU Charter of Fundamental Rights, "solemnly proclaimed" in 2000, provides that everyone has the right to respect for his or her physical and mental integrity, and specifically that, in the fields of medicine and biology, "free and informed consent" of the person concerned must be respected,[79] and that everyone has the right of access to preventive health care and the right to benefit from medical treatment under national law.[80] Other parliamentary proposals appear in the final text in a significantly watered-down form. For instance, Parliament wished to stress the role of the programme in contributing to the development of minimum quality standards with respect to health care as well as "public health". This remains among the "actions" as developing methods to evaluate the quality and efficacy of health *promotion* (not health care provision) strategies and measures.[81] Council also rejected Parliament's proposal for work on an EU-wide vaccination strategy. What remains is an "action" on exchanging information on national vaccination and immunisation strategies.[82] As these examples show, the governments of the Member States were at pains to maintain the dichotomy, reflected in the wording of Article 152 EC, between the broader determinants of good health ("public health") and provision of medical services and health care. To a large extent, the text adopted in Decision 1786/2002/EC on the EU public health programme maintains this distinction, which, as we noted above, may be problematic.

III. Other legal bases

Common policies as legal basis: "mainstreaming" of health protection

As we explained above, to conceptualise Community competence in the health field as solely that arising from Article 152 EC would be misleading. The obligation to "mainstream" the protection of health in all EU policies now finds expression in Article 152 (1) EC. A more complete picture of the Community's power to adopt measures that have an impact on human health protection or promotion in the Member States must therefore take account of the various EU policies that have implications for such health protection and promotion. These include the

77 OJ 1999 L 184/23.
78 Decision 1786/2002/EC, Article 9 (2).
79 Article 3 (1) and (2) EUCFR.
80 Article 35 EUCFR.
81 Decision 1786/2002/EC, Annex 3.5.
82 Decision 1786/2002/EC, Annex 2.5.

common agricultural policy,[83] transport,[84] environmental policy,[85] consumer protection,[86] competition policy,[87] research and technological development,[88] development cooperation,[89] and even some elements of the employment strand of social policy.[90] Thus, measures with health implications have lawfully been adopted on the basis of Treaty provisions such as Article 37 (ex 43) EC on the common agricultural policy, Article 71 (ex 75) EC on the common transport policy, Article 137 (ex 118a) EC on social policy, Article 133 (ex 113) EC on the common commercial policy, Article 153 (ex 129a) EC on consumer protection, Article 175 (ex 130s) EC on environmental policy, and Article 181 (ex 130y) EC on development cooperation.

Such legal basis provisions may lawfully be utilised to achieve health protection or promotion aims, where such aims are incidental to the core aim or effect of the measure and the legal basis chosen is appropriate for this core aim. The European Court of Justice has consistently held[91] that the choice of legal basis is a matter of legal principle, not political expediency, and must be based on objective factors, subject to judicial review. These factors include, in particular, the aim and content of the measure.[92] More specific legal bases are to be preferred over general ones.[93] Thus, for instance, the Court has held in a number of rulings that Article 37 (ex 43) EC is a proper legal basis for health protection measures in the field of food law, as these form part of the common agricultural policy.[94]

83 The CAP has implications for food safety, a major determinant of public health, and cause of illness.

84 Matters such as road safety contribute to public health.

85 Matters such as air and water quality are major determinants of public health, as may be the presence of substances hazardous to human health in the environment.

86 Food law would be a major component of health related consumer protection law, but other areas, such as cosmetics, could also be included.

87 The use of competition law to attack anti-competitive agreements, such as those granting intellectual property rights to subsidiaries or the enforcement of intellectual property rights by dominant firms, applied to the pharmaceuticals industry, may have implications for the pricing of pharmaceuticals and other medical goods within the Member States, thus affecting health care provision.

88 The Community supports programmes of research and technological development, to encourage the competitiveness of European industry, in various fields, including health.

89 Measures aimed at health promotion, for instance, HIV prevention and drug abuse control, may form part of a contribution to economic and social development in "third countries".

90 Legislation protecting workers from workplace hazards and occupational illness and accidents makes a contribution to health protection.

91 Case 45/86 *Tariff Preferences* [1987] ECR 1493, para 11; Case C-300/89 *Commission v Council (Titanium Dioxide)* [1991] ECR I-2867; Case C-70/88 *Parliament v Council (Radioactive contamination of foodstuffs)* [1991] ECR I-4529; Case C-155/91 *Commission v Council (Waste Directive)* [1999] ECR I-939; Case C-84/94 *UK v Council (Working Time)* [1996] ECR I-5755.

92 Case C-300/89 *Commission v Council (Titanium Dioxide)* above n 91, para 10; Case C-84/94 *UK v Council (Working Time)* above n 91, para 25; Case C-233/94 *Germany v Parliament and Council (Deposit Guarantees)* [1997] ECR I-2405, para 12; Case C-269/97 *Commission v Council (Beef Labelling)* [2000] ECR I-2257, para 43.

93 See, for example, Case C-271/94 *Parliament v Council (Edicom)* [1996] ECR I-1689.

94 Case 68/86 *UK v Council (Hormones in Beef)* [1988] ECR 855; Case C-131/87 *Commission v Council (Animal glands and organs)* [1989] ECR 3743; Case C-331/88 *R v Minister of Agriculture, Fisheries and Food and Secretary of State for Health, ex parte Fedesa and others* [1990] ECR I-4023;

For example, in *Beef Labelling*,[95] the Court considered a challenge to Regulation 820/97/EC establishing a system of registration of bovine animals and regarding the labelling of beef and beef products. Adopted in response to the BSE crisis, this Regulation set up a traceability and labelling system for beef, in order to reassure consumers that the meat they buy presents no health risk. The Commission had originally proposed a legal basis of Article 100a (now 95) EC (the internal market legal basis provision), but the Council adopted the measure on the basis of Article 43 (now 37) EC. This had the effect of excluding the European Parliament from involvement, as Article 43 EC provided only for consultation of Parliament, whereas Article 100a provided for the co-decision procedure. The Commission argued that "recourse to Article 100a of the Treaty was justified by the fact that the principal objective of the contested decision is the protection of human health, referred to in Article 129 EC, and that the Parliament must, in such an important field, be able to participate in the legislative process".[96] The Commission's position was difficult, as the Court had held in a number of previous rulings,[97] applying its rule that a more specific legal basis should be preferred over a general one, that Article 43 EC should be chosen as legal basis over Article 100 EC where the rules at issue concerned the production and marketing of agricultural products. In response to this argument, the Commission pointed to the evolution of the Treaty, and made a connection between the evolving powers of the European Parliament, culminating in Parliament's status as "co-legislator" in the co-decision procedure, the internal market provision (Article 100a EC, now Article 95 EC) under which Parliament enjoyed such status, and the introduction of the explicit health competence in Article 129 EC. The Commission's claim was that the authors of the Treaty intended to impose the co-decision procedure for the matters referred to in Articles 129 and 100a of the Treaty. Therefore, to preserve an exception for measures intended to protect public health when those measures concern agricultural products would be anomalous.[98] It seems clear that the context here was the serious mismanagement by Council and the Commission of the BSE crisis,[99] and the desire to provide legitimacy in such matters by involvement of the European Parliament.

The Court did not accept the Commission's argument. Rather, the Court preferred Council's view that, having regard to the aim and content of the measure,[100] its principal purpose was not the protection of public health, but the re-establishment

Case C-180/96 *UK v Commission (BSE)* [1998] ECR I-2265; Case C-269/97 *Commission v Council (Beef Labelling)* above n 92.

95 Case C-269/97 *Commission v Council (Beef Labelling)* above n 92.

96 Para 9.

97 Such as Case C-68/86 *UK v Council (Hormones in Beef)* above n 94; Case C-131/86 *UK v Council* [1988] ECR 905; Case C-331/88 *for Fedesa* above n 94.

98 Paras 13–15.

99 See Report on alleged contraventions or maladministration in the implementation of Community law in relation to BSE, without prejudice to the jurisdiction of the Community and national courts, 7 February 1997, A4-0020/97. See further, chapter 9.

100 Para 43.

of stability in the beef market. The public health element was secondary.[101] Therefore, as the regulation was intended primarily to achieve the objectives of the common agricultural policy, Article 43 EC was the correct legal basis.

The Commission's "evolution of the Treaty" argument was rejected, on the grounds that the choice of legal basis must be assessed at the time the provision was adopted. Although this meant that the argument could not apply in *this* case, it may be significant that the Court did not reject it on principle. The Court's statement may suggest that the proper legal basis for *later* secondary legislation may be assessed in the light of such Treaty amendments. However, it appears that this argument has not yet been made before the Court in such a case, so an assessment of its merits must wait for subsequent proceedings. Given that a specific legal basis is to be preferred over a general one, and Article 152 (4) (b) EC appears to be more specific than Article 37 EC, at least for health-related agricultural measures, the role of the European Parliament may now be more secure, as Article 152 EC provides for the use of the "co-decision" procedure. Interestingly, in *Beef Labelling*, the Court *was* prepared to read a strong mainstreaming obligation into Article 43 EC itself, even though the case preceded the entry into force of Article 152 EC. The Court stated that efforts to attain the objectives of the common agricultural policy cannot disregard requirements relating to the public interest such as the protection of consumers or human health.[102]

Therefore, specific legal basis provisions in particular policy areas such as agriculture, transport, the environment, consumer protection, competition, development cooperation, or employment, may be used to enact provisions of EU law having an effect on health policy, provided that the core aim of the provision is found in the policy field reflected in the legal basis. Where the provision is essentially concerned with "setting high standards of quality and safety of organs and substances of human origin, blood and blood derivatives" (consumer protection) and "measures in the veterinary and phytosanitary fields which have as their direct objective the protection of public health" (agriculture), Articles 152 (4) (a) and (b) EC must be used in preference to Articles 153 and 37 EC. However, where such specific legal basis provisions are used, the obligation to "mainstream" the protection of health in Article 152 (1) EC applies. Although the Court has not yet ruled on the matter, it is possible that failure to respect the "mainstreaming" obligation would render the measure invalid.

Article 308 EC: health protection as a Community objective

In addition to establishing Community competence in the health field through "mainstreaming" of health in other policies, the possibility of utilising Article 308 EC as the legal basis for health protection or promotion measures should be considered. Article 308 EC provides that "if action by the Community should prove necessary

101 Para 28.
102 Paras 48–49.

to attain . . . one of the objectives of the Community and the Treaty has not provided the necessary powers, the Council shall, acting unanimously . . . take the appropriate measures". The Treaty provides that the objectives of the Community include "the raising of the standard of living and quality of life". Thus, were the term "quality of life" construed appropriately, Article 308 EC could constitute a proper legal basis for health protection measures.

One bar to using Article 308 EC is the Court's constant view that, if available, a more specific legal basis provision must be preferred over a more general one.[103] Article 308 EC is the most general legal basis provision in the EC Treaty. However, the Court has held, in a different context, that the mere fact that another, more specific legal basis provision has given the power to adopt *non-binding* measures (*in casu*, to make a recommendation) does not preclude the use of Article 308 EC to enact *binding* measures. In *Massey-Ferguson*,[104] the Court considered whether Regulation 803/68/EEC had been validly adopted on the basis of Article 235 (now 308) EC. The Regulation concerned the value of goods for customs purposes. A specific legal basis provision (Article 27 EEC (now repealed)) provided that during the first stage of the establishment of the common market, in setting up the common customs tariff, the Commission was to make recommendations to Member States on the steps to be taken to approximate national provisions on customs matters. However, in spite of this provision, the Court held that Article 235 EC was a valid legal basis for the Regulation.

It will be remembered that Article 152 EC provides a legal basis only for "incentive measures" and cooperation between the Member States, rather than harmonisation of national laws (save the exceptions in Article 152 (4) (a) and (b) EC). Thus, if an analogy can be drawn between the power to make recommendations and the power to promote cooperation and adopt incentive measures, applying *Massey-Ferguson* it would seem that the existence of Article 152 EC would not necessarily prevent Council from lawfully adopting harmonised health measures on the basis of Article 308 EC.[105] It might be objected that Article 152 EC explicitly excludes harmonisation, whereas old Article 27 EEC did not. However, the exclusion of harmonisation was clearly *implicit* in old Article 27 EEC. Whether such a distinction is relevant has not yet arisen before the Court.

However, the relationship between Article 152 EC and other legal basis provisions, by implication including Article 308 EC, has arisen in a different context in *Portugal v Council (India Development Cooperation)*.[106] This concerned Portugal's objection to the adoption of the Community Development Cooperation Agreement with India, on the basis of Article 130y (now 181) EC. Portugal claimed that such an Agreement needed recourse to Article 235 (now 308) EC. The Portuguese

103 See above, n 93.

104 Case 8/73 *Hauptzollamt Bremerhaven v Massey-Ferguson* [1973] ECR 897.

105 Of course, the need to find unanimity in Council under Article 308 EC may form a significant *political* barrier to such a measure.

106 Case C-268/94 *Portugal v Council (India Development Cooperation)* [1996] ECR I-6177.

challenge concerned various elements of the Agreement, but one such element (Article 19) concerned the health promotion provision of drug abuse control. Cooperation between the EU and India in this respect was to include training, education, health promotion and the rehabilitation of addicts. The Court stated that the Portuguese arguments raised "the question of the extent to which an agreement concluded between the EU and a non-member country and adopted on the basis of Article 130y (now 181) EC may lay down provisions on specific matters without there being any need to have recourse to other legal bases, or indeed to the participation of the Member States in the conclusion of the agreement".[107] The Court pointed out that if this approach were taken, it would have the effect of rendering the competence and procedure prescribed in Article 130y (now 181) EC nugatory. Rather, the main objectives and the content of the Agreement must determine its proper legal basis.

As far as the drug abuse control provisions were concerned, Portugal argued that Article 129 (now 152) EC "does not constitute a legal basis enabling the Community to assume powers of decision; Community action must be limited to measures of encouragement or to adopting recommendations".[108] For Portugal, this meant that the Community lacked the necessary internal competence in health to mandate the external competence necessary for the Agreement to be adopted by the EU institutions alone, rather than as a "mixed agreement".[109] The Council noted that there were already several internal Community acts concerned directly or indirectly with drug abuse control, without any challenge to their legal basis.[110] The doctrine of parallel competences meant the Community possesses the same power in external matters. The Court held that "drug abuse control cannot . . . be excluded from the measures necessary for the pursuit of the objectives referred to in Article 130u [now Article 177] EC, since production of narcotics, drug abuse and related activities can constitute serious impediments to economic and social development".[111] The Court then looked at the content of Article 19 of the Agreement, and concluded that it concerned an intent to cooperate, within the respective competences of the Community and India. The relevant measures of cooperation could all be linked to development cooperation objectives.[112] Article 130y (now 181) EC was therefore an appropriate legal basis, and there was no need for a mixed agreement.

107 Para 35.
108 Para 57.
109 A "mixed agreement" in EU law is an international agreement to which both the EU and the Member States are parties, because the competence to adopt the agreement is shared between the EU and its Member States. They are often politically contentious, and are legally complex. See A. Dashwood and C. Hillion, eds, *The General Law of EC External Relations* (London: Sweet and Maxwell, 2000); D. McGoldrick, *International Relations Law of the European Union* (London: Longman, 1997); D. O'Keeffe and H. Schermers, eds, *Mixed Agreements* (The Hague: Martinus Nijhoff, 1983); M. Cremona, "The Doctrine of Exclusivity and the Position of Mixed Agreements in the External Relations of the Community" 2 OJLS (1982) 393.
110 This in itself is, of course, not a guarantee of legality in the way that unsuccessful legal basis challenges to such measures would be.
111 Para 60.
112 Para 63.

Thus it follows from *India Development Cooperation* that the existence of Article 152 EC in itself does not preclude the use of other legal bases to achieve health promotion objectives. Presumably this also applies to the use of Article 308 EC.[113]

The internal market

Health and the internal market

We have noted that various EU policies and activities may have implications for health. Of these, the internal market is crucially important, because of its "constitutional" position in the EU's legal order.[114] Any social policy regime within the EU (and this would include health policy) must now take its place within the "constitutional" construct of the internal market, the law of which has been one of the fundamental drivers of the integration process.

As we saw in chapter 2, the Treaty of Rome envisaged the unfettered movement of factors of production within the territory of the EEC (the "common market"), and put in place the legal mechanisms to ensure the necessary economic integration to create that common market. Furthermore, the Court has established[115] the principle of "mutual recognition", according to which goods lawfully produced and marketed in one Member State must be accepted in all Member States. In principle, therefore, a national measure with the objective of protecting public health might breach the Treaty provisions on the free movement of goods. The competence of Member States to enact such health protection measures may thus be limited by the law of the internal market.

However, it has been recognised in EU law that this deregulatory thrust of the provisions on the free movement of goods might pose a potential risk to health policy within the Member States, as individual traders might rely on directly effective provisions in EU law to undermine the substantive content of national health protection measures. Moreover, unfettered movement of goods might pose hazards to health in the Member States, for instance, if dangerous goods, or disease-carrying goods, moved without regulatory checks and were marketable throughout the EU.

113 This may change if the Draft Constitutional Treaty is adopted, as the Laeken Declaration, above n 4, implies that the governments of the Member States may be seeking to constrain the use of Article 308 EC.

114 The relationships between internal market law, the EU's "constitution" and social regulation in general are already well explored in the literature. See, by no means exclusively, F. Scharpf, "The European Social Model: Coping with the Challenges of Diversity" 40 JCMS (2002) 645; F. Scharpf, *Governing in Europe: Effective and Democratic?* (Oxford: OUP, 1999); C. Joerges, "European Economic Law, the Nation State, and the Maastricht Treaty" in R. Dehousse, ed, *Europe after Maastricht: An Ever Closer Union* (Munich: Beck, 1994); M. Poiares Maduro, *We the Court* (Oxford: Hart, 1998); M. Poiares Maduro, "Striking the Elusive Balance between Economic Freedom and Social Rights in the EU" in P. Alston, ed, *The EU and Human Rights* (Oxford: OUP, 1999); M. Poiares Maduro, "Europe and the Constitution: What if this is as good as it gets?" in J.H.H. Weiler and M. Wind, *European Constitutionalism Beyond the State* (Cambridge: CUP, 2003); G. Majone, *Regulating Europe* (London: Routledge, 1996); S. Weatherill, *Law and Integration in the European Union* (Oxford: Clarendon, 1995); J.H.H. Weiler, "The Transformation of Europe" 100 *Yale Law Journal* (1991) 2403.

115 Case 120/78 *Cassis de Dijon* [1979] ECR 649.

One response to the potential threats to public health posed by internal market law was a limited exclusion to the general principle that goods are allowed to move freely within the common market. This is found in Article 30 (ex 36) EC, which provides, *inter alia*, that the Treaty "shall not preclude prohibitions or restrictions on imports . . . justified on grounds of . . . the protection of health and life of humans . . . ". The provision has been relied upon to justify national measures such as those concerning health risks arising from food, (for instance, the prohibition or restriction of the use of additives in food and feed,[116] the testing of food products to ensure compliance with health standards,[117] restrictions on the use of pesticides and biocides,[118] restrictions on alcohol, in particular alcohol advertising[119]); from the use of dangerous products;[120] from pharmaceuticals and other medicinal products;[121] and also measures promoting road safety.[122] However, the Treaty provides that such measures may not "constitute a means of arbitrary discrimination or a disguised restriction on trade between Member States".

The European Court of Justice has said that "the health and life of humans rank foremost among the property or interests to be protected by Article 30 [ex Article 36] of the Treaty".[123] Member States enjoy a significant level of discretion in the determination of the level of protection to be granted to the health of their population. Where there is no international scientific consensus on the potential health hazard posed by a substance, the Court is prepared to grant Member States the benefit of the doubt.[124] Differences between national populations may be taken into account in determining appropriate national health protection rules.[125]

However, the justification in Article 30 EC is subject to the proviso in the last sentence, which the Court has held imposes a condition of proportionality on

116 See, for example, Case 5/77 *Tedeschi v Denkavit* [1977] ECR 1555; Case 53/80 *Eyssen* [1981] ECR 409; Case C-42/90 *Bellon* [1990] ECR I-4863.

117 See, for example, Case 132/80 *United Foods* [1981] ECR 995; Case 97/83 *Melkunie* [1984] ECR 2367; Case 35/84 *Commission v Italy (Curds)* [1986] ECR 545.

118 See, for example, Case 272/80 *Frans-Nederlandse Maatschappij* [1981] ECR 3277; Case 94/83 *Albert Heijn* [1984] ECR 3263; Case 54/85 *Mirepoix* [1986] ECR 1067; Case C-293/94 *Brandsma* [1996] ECR I-3159; Case C-400/96 *Harpegnies* [1998] ECR I-5121.

119 See, for example, Case 152/78 *Commission v France (Alcohol Advertising)* [1980] ECR 2299 (in which the Court found, however, that the rules constituted an arbitrary discrimination in trade between Member States); Cases C-1 & 176/90 *Aragonesa* [1991] ECR I-4151; Case C-405/98 *Gourmet International Products* [2001] ECR I-1795.

120 See, for example, Case C-473/98 *Toolex Alpha* [2000] ECR I-5681.

121 See, for example, Case 104/75 *De Peijper* [1976] ECR 613; Case 32/80 *Kortmann* [1981] ECR 251; Cases 266 & 267/87 *R v Royal Pharmaceutical Society of Great Britain* [1989] ECR 1295; Case C-369/88 *Delattre* [1991] ECR I-1487; Case C-60/89 *Monteil and Samanni* [1991] ECR I-1547; Case C-320/93 *Ortscheit* [1994] ECR I-5243; Case C-55/99 *Commission v France (Medical Reagents)* [2000] ECR I-11499.

122 See, for example, Case 50/85 *Schloh* [1986] ECR 1855; Case C-314/98 *Snellers* [2000] ECR I-8633.

123 See Case C-473/98 *Toolex Alpha* above n 120; Case C-320/93 *Ortscheit* above n 121.

124 Case 53/80 *Eyssen* above n 116; Case 174/82 *Sandoz* [1983] ECR 2445; Case 97/83 *Melkunie* above n 117; Case 247/84 *Motte* [1985] ECR 3887; Case 304/84 *Muller* [1986] ECR 1511; Case 178/84 *Commission v Germany (Beer Purity)* [1987] ECR 1227; Case C-42/90 *Bellon* above n 116.

125 See Case 304/84 *Muller* above n 124; Case C-95/89 *Commission v Italy* [1992] ECR I-4545; Case C-293/89 *Commission v Greece* [1992] ECR I-4577; Case C-344/89 *Commission v France* [1992] ECR I-3245.

national health protection measures. Member States must show that there is a risk to public health,[126] that the measure concerned must actually have the aim and effect of protecting public health,[127] and must not constitute more of an incursion on trade between Member States than is necessary.[128] Furthermore, recourse by national authorities to Article 30 EC ceases to be justified where EU-level measures put in place harmonised provisions to secure public health protection in the relevant field.[129]

The approach of the European Court of Justice to the health protection justification under Article 30 EC appears to suggest that competence in this field belongs with Member States, not the EU institutions. However, particularly as the legislative pace increased with the 1992 programme, this position became increasingly unsustainable. As EU-level internal market measures had an increasing impact on national measures aimed at protecting human health, the need for a recognition that health concerns must become a part of those EU-level measures became more pressing. Indeed the Court has said that the purpose of Article 30 EC is not to reserve certain matters to the exclusive jurisdiction of the Member States, but merely to allow Member States a derogation in circumstances justified by interests such as public health protection.[130] Thus a second response to the potential problems posed for public health through the development of internal market law was given Treaty expression in Article 100a (3) EEC, now Article 95 (3) EC.

The relationship between health and the internal market probably first came to the fore during the Delors' Commission and the promulgation of the 1992 programme for the completion of the internal market. As we saw in chapter 1, in the Single European Act, putting in place the measures necessary for the 1992 programme, a new Article 100a EEC (now 95 EC) was inserted into the Treaty. According to this provision, in order to achieve the completion of the internal market, Council (in response to a Commission proposal), acting by qualified majority voting procedures, and cooperating with the European Parliament,[131] shall adopt harmonisation measures "which have as their object the establishment and functioning of the internal market". Article 95 (3) EC specifically provides that the

126 Case C-17/93 *Van der Veldt* [1994] ECR I-3537; Case C-205/89 *Commission v Greece* [1991] ECR I-1361; Case C-228/91 *Commission v Italy* [1993] ECR I-2701.

127 See Case 40/82 *Commission v UK (Turkeys)* [1982] ECR 2793; Case C-42/90 *Bellon* above n 116; Cases C-13 & 113/91 *Debus* [1992] ECR I-3617.

128 Case 174/82 *Sandoz* above n 124; Case 247/84 *Motte* above n 124; Case 304/84 *Muller* above n 124; Case 178/84 *Commission v Germany (Beer Purity)* above n 124; Case 261/85 *Commission v UK (Pasteurised Milk)* [1988] ECR 547.

129 Case 5/77 *Tedeschi v Denkavit* above n 116; Case 148/78 *Ratti* [1979] ECR 1629; Case 251/78 *Denkavit* [1979] ECR 3369; Case 190/87 *Moormann* [1988] ECR 4689; Cases C-277, 318 & C-319/91 *Carni* [1993] ECR I-6621; Case C-17/93 *Van der Veldt* above n 126.

130 Case 153/78 *Commission v Germany (Meat products)* [1979] ECR 2555. The Court regards rules the effect of which is a "double inspection" in Member State of dispatch and Member State of destination as particularly suspect: see, for example, Case 132/80 *United Foods* [1981] ECR 995; Case 251/78 *Denkavit* above n 129.

131 Article 95 EC now provides for the "co-decision" procedure.

Commission, in proposing such measures, shall "take as a base a high level of protection" in measures concerning "health, safety, environmental protection and consumer protection". Thus the basis for EU-level harmonisation measures protecting such health interests – provided that they are necessary to complete the internal market or ensure its proper operation, or both – was laid down in the Treaty. This provision is reflected, expressly or implicitly, in other legal bases in the Treaty, such as Article 37 (ex 43) EC on the common agricultural policy, Article 71 (ex 75) EC on the common transport policy, Article 133 (ex 113) EC on the common commercial policy, Article 153 (ex 129a) EC on consumer protection, Article 175 (ex 130s) EC on environmental policy, and Article 181 (ex 130y) EC on development cooperation. As we saw above, the obligation to "mainstream" the protection of health in all EU policies now finds expression in Article 152 (1) EC: this obligation applies equally to the internal market.

Just as other legal basis provisions in the Treaty do not provide *carte blanche* to the EU institutions to adopt measures essentially aimed at the protection of human health, neither may the EU institutions utilise Article 95 EC in this way. If Article 95 EC is the proper legal basis, the "core" or "principal aim" of the measure must be to establish or maintain the internal market.[132] In a number of judicial review proceedings concerning secondary legislation promoting or protecting health, the Court has been asked to rule on a choice of legal basis between the internal market and other legal basis provisions. Many of these concern the choice between the internal market and the common agricultural policy, and there the Court has favoured the specific Treaty provisions in the agricultural field over the more general provisions relating to the internal market. For instance, in *UK v Council (Hormones in Beef)*,[133] the Court held that although Directive 85/649/EEC prohibiting the use in livestock farming of certain substances having a hormonal action has an aspect concerned with the harmonisation of national legislation with a view to protecting consumer and public health, it regulates conditions for the production and marketing of meat with a view to improving its quality, and therefore the Council had the power to adopt it on the basis of Article 43 EC.[134]

The Court has also been concerned with choice of legal basis between internal market and environmental policy, and again, in general, has favoured environmental bases over Article 95 EC. So, in the *Waste Directive*[135] and *Waste Shipments*[136] cases, the Court found that the aim and content of the measures (Directive 91/156/EEC

132 See Case C-300/89 *Titanium Dioxide* above n 91, para 10; Case C-155/91 *Waste Directive* above n 91, paras 19–21; Case C-84/94 *Working Time* above n 91, para 25; Case C-233/94 *Deposit Guarantees* above n 92, para 12; Case C-269/97 *Beef Labelling* above n 92, para 43; Case C-377/98 *Netherlands v Parliament and Council (Biotechnology Directive)* [2001] ECR I-7079, para 27.

133 Case 68/86 *Hormones in Beef* above n 94.

134 See also Case 131/86 *UK v Council (Battery Hens)* [1988] ECR 905; Case C-131/87 *Commission v Council (Animal glands and organs)* above n 94; Case C-331/88 *Fedesa* above n 94.

135 Case C-155/91 *Waste Directive* above n 91.

136 Case C-187/93 *Parliament v Council (Waste Shipments)* [1994] ECR I-2857.

on waste and Regulation 259/93/EEC on shipments of waste respectively) was to protect human health and the environment. Any effect on the internal market was merely ancillary. Article 130s (now 175) EC was the proper legal basis.

In the *Working Time Directive* case,[137] the Court was faced with a challenge brought by the United Kingdom to the Working Time Directive 93/104/EC, which lays down minimum harmonised requirements on the organisation of working time, and is based on Article 118a (now 137) EC. The Court reiterated that the choice of legal basis must be based on objective factors which are amenable to judicial review, and that these factors include, in particular, the aim and content of the measure. The Directive has an incidental effect of contributing towards creating the social dimension of the internal market. But this does not mean that its principal aim is not the protection of health and safety of workers. Article 118a (now 137) EC is the appropriate legal basis for measures whose principal aim is the protection of the health and safety of workers, notwithstanding the ancillary effects which such measures may have on the establishment and functioning of the internal market. The Court reached a similar conclusion in a case concerning health and safety under the European Atomic Energy Community Treaty.[138]

However, where the choice of legal basis has been between what is now Article 95 EC and Article 94 or Article 308 EC, at least until 2000,[139] the Court has been relatively generous in drawing the boundaries of Article 95 EC, including in cases concerning the use of Article 95 EC for measures with perhaps more than an incidental health protection aim or effect. For example, the General Product Safety Directive 92/59/EEC grants a power to the Commission to adopt a decision requiring Member States to withdraw a certain consumer product from the market or restrict its marketing, where the product presents a serious and immediate risk to the health and safety of consumers. Article 9 effectively empowers the Commission to take decisions replacing those which the national authorities have taken in order to ensure compliance with national legislation transposing the directive. Germany argued that the Community was not competent to enact Article 9 of the Directive on the basis of Article 100a (now 95) EC.[140]

The Court held that the General Product Safety Directive is a measure of "horizontal" harmonisation, establishing general safety requirements for all consumer

137 Case C-84/94 *Working Time* above n 91.

138 Case C-70/88 *Parliament v Council (Radioactive contamination of foodstuffs)* [1991] ECR I-4529, concerning Regulation 3954/87/EEC laying down maximum permitted levels of radioactive contamination of food and feed, following a nuclear accident or other radiological emergency. The measure was based on Article 31 of the European Atomic Energy Community (EAEC) Treaty. Parliament claimed the proper legal basis should have been Article 100a EEC. The Court held that the aim of the measure was to establish uniform safety standards to protect the health of workers and of the general public, as provided in Article 2(b) EAEC. The regulation has only the incidental effect of harmonising the conditions of the free movement of goods within the Community. Therefore, the correct legal basis had been chosen.

139 See Case C-376/98 *Germany v Parliament and Council (Tobacco Advertising)* [2000] ECR I-8419.

140 Case C-359/92 *Germany v Commission (General Product Safety)* [1994] ECR I-3681.

products. The Commission's power in Article 9 is a last resort measure, to act in cases where a product puts consumers in serious and immediate jeopardy, and where Member States differ with respect to the health protection measures adopted or planned with regard to that product. Such measures would prevent the product from moving freely within the EU, if, say, they provided different levels of consumer protection.[141] Free movement of goods can be secured only if product safety requirements do not differ significantly from one Member State to another. A high level of protection can be achieved only if dangerous products are subject to appropriate measures in all Member States.[142] The approximation of general laws may not always be sufficient to ensure the unity of the market. Thus Article 100a (now 95) EC includes Council's power to lay down measures relating to a specific product or class of products. These are included in the concept of "measures for approximation" of legislation.[143] Thus, according to the Court, the EU institutions are empowered to use Article 95 EC to create EU-level institutional structures to protect consumer health.[144] This is a recognition that health protection is not simply guaranteed in the EU through the derogation to national authorities under Article 30 EC: the EU institutions, through the instrumentalisation of other policies, including that of creating and maintaining the internal market, must also play a role in this respect.

Similarly, the Court adopted a broad notion of the extent of Article 95 in the *Supplementary Patent Protection Certificate* case.[145] Regulation 1768/92/EEC on the creation of a supplementary protection certificate for medicinal products extends the duration of patent protection, to take into account the time it takes to procure a marketing authorisation for a new pharmaceutical product. The Regulation was based on Article 100a (now 95) EC. Spain challenged the use of Article 100a, claiming that the measure should have been based on Article 100 or Article 235 EC, and pointing out that the Treaty explicitly preserves the power of the Member States to regulate intellectual property rights.[146]

The Court held that the Regulation was intended to prevent the heterogeneous development of national laws, which would be likely to create obstacles for the free movement of pharmaceuticals within the EU. Harmonising measures were necessary to deal with disparities between the laws of the Member States where such disparities are liable to create or maintain distorted conditions of competition.[147] Harmonising measures are also necessary to deal with disparities between the laws of Member States in so far as such disparities are liable to hinder the free movement of goods within the EU.[148] This measure aimed at removing disparities which would

141 Para 33.
142 Para 34.
143 Para 37.
144 See Weatherill, above n 4, p 602.
145 Case C-350/92 *Spain v Council (Supplementary Patent Protection Certificate)* [1995] ECR I-1985.
146 See Article 295 (ex 222) EC and Article 30 (ex 36) EC.
147 Para 32.
148 Para 33.

hinder the free movement of pharmaceuticals. The Regulation took all the interests at stake into account, including those of public health. Article 100a EC was a valid legal basis in those circumstances.

The Court departed from this rather generous construction of Article 95 EC as a proper legal basis for provisions having an effect on health protection in its seminal ruling in the *Tobacco Advertising* case. As this case appears to represent a "high water mark" in the Court's case law, it is discussed in some detail here.[149]

The *Tobacco Advertising* ruling

The question of choice of legal basis arises mainly in proceedings where two possible specific legal basis provisions are at issue. However, logically, it also applies where the choice is between a specific legal basis provision and Article 308 (ex 235) EC, and, indeed, where the choice is between Community competence and national competence.[150] This was the issue in *Tobacco Advertising*.

The background to the case is as follows. Directive 98/43/EC[151] on tobacco advertising and sponsorship provided that all forms of advertising and sponsorship of tobacco products[152] were to be banned within the EU.[153] The Tobacco Advertising Directive was hotly contested in both the European Parliament[154] and in Council.[155] Considerable economic interests were involved in its implementation. Eight of the 15 Member States produce tobacco.[156] In addition, all the Member States rely on

149 For further discussion, see K. Lenaerts, "Bricks for a Constitutional Treaty of the European Union: Values, Objectives and Means" 27 ELRev (2002) 377 at 387; G. de Búrca, *Setting Constitutional Limits to EU Competence?* Francisco Lucas Pires Working Papers Series on European Constitutionalism, Working Paper 2001/02; Hervey, above n 1; T. Hervey, "Up in Smoke: Community (anti) tobacco law and policy" 26 ELRev (2001) 101; C. Hillion, "Tobacco Advertising: if you must, you may" 60 CLJ (2001) 486; P. Syrpis, "Smoke without Fire: The Social Policy Agenda and the Internal Market" 30 ILJ (2001) 271; J. Usher, "Annotation of Case C-376/98" 38 CMLRev (2001) 1519; Editorial, "Taking the limits of competences seriously" 37 CMLRev (2000) 1301. For an interpretation of the *Tobacco Advertising Directive* ruling, from the point of view of a solicitor acting for British American Tobacco, in the context of Directive 2001/37/EC on the manufacture, presentation and sale of tobacco products, see S. Crosby, "The New Tobacco Control Directive: An Illiberal and Illegal Disdain for the Law" 27 ELRev (2002) 177. Crosby's implicit notion of the internal market is of a neo-liberal, deregulatory and permissive order, quite at odds with the notion of the internal market as inspired by "social market" traditions, which we would argue are reflected in the Treaty and the jurisprudence of the European Court of Justice, see above, and also chapter 2.

150 See Opinion of AG, Case C-376/98 *Germany v Parliament and Council (Tobacco Advertising)* [2000] ECR I-8419, para 61.

151 Directive 98/43/EC, OJ 1998 L 213/9.

152 Save communications for professionals within the tobacco trade; the presentation of tobacco products at point of sale; advertising aimed at specialist tobacco retailers; publications containing advertising for tobacco products which are published and printed in third countries, where those publications are not intended for the Community market; and the use, to advertise non-tobacco products, of brand names (or trademarks, emblems or other distinctive features) already used in good faith for both tobacco products and for other goods or services.

153 Directive 98/43/EC, Article 4.

154 See, for example, Written Questions No 1005/98, OJ 1998 C 323/104; 1020/98, OJ 1998 C 354/52; 1091/98, OJ 1998 C 323/112; E-2072/99, OJ 2000 C 219 E/84.

155 It took no fewer than ten meetings of the health Council before the Directive was adopted.

156 Greece, Italy, France, Spain, Portugal, and, to a lesser extent, Austria, Belgium and Luxembourg.

taxation of tobacco products.[157] The printed media rely heavily on revenue from tobacco advertising. The Council common position on the Directive was finally reached by a qualified majority of health ministers on 4 December 1997, with Germany and Austria voting against, and Spain and Denmark abstaining. Had the UK continued in its opposition, the Directive would not have been adopted: the new Labour government under Blair, with its commitment to a national ban on tobacco advertising, made possible the change of position of the UK health minister.[158] Given the contentious nature of the Tobacco Advertising Directive, and the fact that it was adopted by a very narrow margin in Council, it is not surprising that interested parties sought to challenge its validity through legal means, once the political routes had been exhausted.[159] The challenge came from Germany, and also from private litigants seeking judicial review through Article 234 EC.[160]

Germany and Imperial Tobacco (the applicants) argued that the institutions of the EU were not competent to enact the Directive, and, even if they were, they used the wrong legal basis.[161] It was argued first that the Directive is truly a measure for the protection of public health, not an internal market measure. As we have seen, Article 129 EC – the relevant legal basis for public health measures (now 152 EC) – explicitly excludes harmonisation measures such as the Tobacco Advertising Directive. As evidence regarding the true aim of the Directive, the applicants pointed to the references to the Europe against Cancer programme, various recitals and deleted recitals referring to public health, the fact that health ministers had handled the adoption process, and the statements and press releases of those responsible for the process. Second, it was argued that in any event the Directive was not a valid internal market measure. There is no significant inter-state trade in the EU in the advertising services and products concerned, therefore the *de minimis* test was not met. Tobacco advertising is highly state-specific, and there is no true EU-wide market in tobacco brands. The effect of the Directive was not to enhance the free movement of services and goods, but rather to restrict freedom to trade in advertising-related goods and services. Total restriction of an economic activity is not consistent with promotion of free movement of goods and provision of services. Worse, the Directive divided the internal market along national lines, as it had the effect of preventing new brands from entering national markets. Finally, it was

157 See COM(96) 609 final, point 10.

158 See R. Watson, "Europe agrees complete ban on tobacco advertising by 2006" 315 BMJ (1997) 1559.

159 A number of private litigants sought to challenge the validity of the Directive in Cases T-172 & 177-8/98 *Salamander et al v European Parliament and Council* [2000] ECR II-2487 but the pleas of inadmissibility raised by Parliament and Council were accepted by the Court of First Instance.

160 Case C-376/98 *Tobacco Advertising* above n 150; and Case C-74/99 *R v Secretary of State for Health and others, ex parte Imperial Tobacco* [2000] ECR I-8599.

161 The applicants also raised arguments based on subsidiarity, proportionality, breach of Article 30 (now 28) EC, the right to property and to pursue an economic activity, freedom of expression, and inadequate reasoning. These arguments were subsidiary to the main issue of competence of the institutions of the EU.

argued that the Directive distorted competition in the related but separate markets in which there are diversification products, such as clothes and toiletries.

The European Parliament and Council, joined by France, Finland, the UK and the Commission (the defendants) submitted the following responses. They pointed out that there is some cross-border trade in services and goods in tobacco advertising, in that multinational companies have uniform brands, images, slogans and themes for their tobacco products. Moreover, the defendants pointed out that the quantification of the extent of the prohibition could not be calculated solely on the basis of the situation in a Member State such as Germany, in which advertising activity had previously been subject to a relatively liberal regime. Widely varying restrictions on tobacco advertising in the different Member States constituted a barrier to the provision of advertising services and to the free movement of goods. Therefore there was a need to introduce an EU-level measure to harmonise the national regulations in question. The Directive had achieved this, coupled with setting a high standard of consumer and health protection, as the institutions were required to do by Article 100a (3) EC. The defendants pointed out that Article 100a EC did not require the completion of the internal market through unchecked liberalisation of national rules. Article 100a EC also permitted regulation of the internal market, in their view, even when such regulation did not have a liberalising effect. Moreover, the defendants pointed out that the Directive does not amount to a total prohibition of tobacco advertising. The exemptions in Article 5 of the Directive (point of sale advertisement) and Article 3 (diversification products) implied that tobacco advertising would continue to be lawful in those forms. The Directive merely created a level playing field for those remaining permitted areas of tobacco advertising.

The Court began its analysis by pointing out that the national measures affected by the Directive are to a large extent inspired by public health policy objectives.[162] This, for the Court, appeared to imply that the Directive itself had a public health policy objective. The Court went on to point out that Article 129 (4) EC explicitly excluded any harmonisation of national laws designed to protect and improve public health.[163] Other articles of the Treaty could not be used as a legal basis to circumvent that restriction on Community competence.[164] The Court then turned to the legal basis of the Directive, the internal market provisions. Article 100a EC, read together with Article 3 (c) (now 3 (1) (c)) and Article 7 a (now 14) EC, is a legal basis for measures intended to improve the conditions for the establishment and functioning of the internal market.[165] Article 100a EC is thus a constricted legal basis provision; it is not a general legal basis provision granting the EU legislature power to regulate the internal market. Such a conclusion is based on both the wording of the provisions cited, and also the principles of attribution of powers

162 Para 76.
163 Para 77.
164 Para 79.
165 Para 83.

and of subsidiarity.[166] Therefore, a measure based on Article 100a EC must have as its object the improvement of the conditions for the establishment and functioning of the internal market.[167] It followed, according to the Court, that the question for the Court was whether the Directive in fact pursued the objectives stated by the EU legislature.[168] The Court therefore proceeded to examine in more detail first the stated objective of the Directive, and second its actual effects.

In assessing the objective of the Directive, the Court carried out a textual analysis, referring to provisions in the preamble (Recitals 1 and 2) and in the Directive itself. The Court pointed out that the Directive regulated all advertising for tobacco products, save that for professionals in the tobacco trade, advertising in sales outlets and publications for third countries.[169] The Court also drew attention to the diversification products provision in Article 3 (2), and to the exemption for Member States in Article 5 EC allowing the adoption of stricter requirements as necessary to protect the health of their populations.[170]

On the free movement point, the Court accepted that obstacles to the free movement of goods and the freedom to provide services could arise from disparities between national laws on the advertising of tobacco products. In the case of press products, for instance, the trend in national legislation to greater restrictions on the advertising of tobacco products in the printed press is likely to give rise to obstacles to the free movement of the printed media.[171] However, such restrictions did not apply to all types of products in, on or through which tobacco products are advertised. In particular, the prohibition of advertising of tobacco products on posters, parasols, ashtrays, and other articles used in hotels and cafes, and the prohibition of advertising spots in cinemas in no way helps to facilitate trade in those products. Moreover, the Court pointed out, the Directive did not promote free movement of products in conformity with its provisions.[172] Given the provision in Article 5 EC, Article 3 (2) of the Directive could not be construed to mean that where diversification products meet the conditions of the Directive, they may move freely in all Member States, including those in which national law prohibits such products.[173]

166 Article 5 EC.
167 Para 84.
168 Para 85.
169 Article 3 (5).
170 Paras 92–94.
171 Para 97.
172 Para 101.
173 Para 102–104. The implication of paras 101–104 appears to be that a measure based on Article 95 EC (or presumably Article 94 EC) must remove the possibility for the application of stricter national rules, based for example on the protection of human health, or other grounds in Article 30 EC, to imports (contrast Case 382/87 *Buet* [1989] ECR 1235; see also Case C-491/01 *R (British American Tobacco (Investments) Ltd) v Secretary of State for Health (Directive on Tobacco Manufacture, Presentation and Sale)* [2002] ECR I-11453, paras 74 and 75, discussed below). It appears that Member States may apply such stricter rules to nationally produced goods, but must rely on the procedure in Article 95 (4) EC (see chapter 2, p 57) if they seek to apply such rules to imports. See Weatherill, above n 4, pp 636–637.

On the point concerning elimination of distortion of competition, the Court followed its previous ruling in *Titanium Dioxide*[174] concerning the *de minimis* rule. Where a directive is adopted on the basis of Article 100a EC, its effect must be to eliminate an *appreciable* distortion of competition within the internal market.[175] Otherwise, the effect would be to grant the EU institutions a virtually unlimited competence under Article 100a EC. While it is true that undertakings in the advertising market established in Member States which impose fewer restrictions on tobacco advertising are at an advantage in terms of economies of scale and increase in profits, the effects of this advantage on the conditions of competition are "remote and indirect" and do not give rise to appreciable distortions in competition.[176] The Court agreed with the submissions of the Commission, the UK and Finland to the effect that national rules on tobacco sponsorship of sports do give rise to considerable repercussions on the conditions of competition for firms associated with sponsored sports events, with events being relocated in the light of the introduction of a prohibition of sponsorship in national law. However, this did not justify the *general* prohibition enacted in the Directive.

In terms of the market for tobacco products themselves, the Court stated that the Directive is not likely to remove appreciable distortions of competition in that sector.[177] In Member States where tobacco advertising is restricted, tobacco companies have to resort to other methods, in particular price competition, in order to influence their market share in that Member State. However, this does not constitute a distortion of competition, merely a restriction on the forms of competitive activity that may be used.

Thus, the Court concluded, the Directive was not properly enacted on the basis of Articles 100a, 57 (2) and 66 EC. As partial amendment of the Directive was not practical, without the Court amending provisions of the Directive, the Directive as a whole was annulled.

Community competence in health after *Tobacco Advertising*

The *Tobacco Advertising* case is the first (and only to date) in which the Court has ruled that the Community lacks competence to adopt a health protection measure, rather than holding that a measure has been adopted on the wrong legal basis. There seems little doubt, in any event, that in *Tobacco Advertising*, the Court has moved a step closer to fulfilling an explicit role as a constitutional court for the EU. From the point of view of Community competence in health, the ruling reinforces what is clear from the Treaty provisions: there are "constitutional" limits to the scope of lawful EU activity in the health field. However, it appears that the *Tobacco Advertising*

174 Case C-300/89 [1991] ECR I-2867.
175 Para 106.
176 Para 109.
177 Para 112.

case represents a "high water mark" in the Court's jurisprudence in this respect. Subsequent case law has apparently returned to the pattern of the previous case law discussed above. The final part of this chapter considers the current position.

Subsequent to the *Tobacco Advertising* ruling, the Court, in *BAT and Imperial Tobacco*,[178] considered a challenge to another measure of internal market law relating to the manufacture, presentation and retail of tobacco in the EU, Directive 2001/37/EC.[179] This sets maximum acceptable tar, nicotine and carbon monoxide yields for cigarettes manufactured or marketed in the EU, and requires that the packaging of tobacco products must carry specified warnings about the health dangers of smoking. The Advocate General specifically addressed the question of whether a measure which is also intended to safeguard public health can lawfully be based on Article 95 EC. Again rejecting the "core aim" approach, the Advocate General took the view that where a barrier to trade arises, Article 95 EC gives the EU institutions power to adopt harmonisation legislation to remove this barrier. This is so irrespective of the "principal reason" for action on the part of the EU legislature.[180] Indeed, the realisation of the internal market may mean that protection of a public interest, such as public health, takes place at EU level,[181] as the EU moves from deregulatory to reregulatory means of integration. Here the "real reason" for the adoption of the measure is the protection of the public interest, but Article 95 EC is the proper legal basis if the measure is directly connected to removing a barrier to inter-state trade.[182] The Advocate General concluded that Directive 2001/37/EC is validly adopted on the basis of Article 95 EC.[183]

The Court followed the conclusion of its Advocate General. The Court found that, provided that the conditions for recourse to Article 95 EC are fulfilled (the measure must genuinely have the object of improving the conditions for the establishment or functioning of the internal market), it does not matter that public health protection is a decisive factor in the content of the legislation concerned.[184] In this case, differences between (existing or likely future) national laws on the manufacture, presentation and sale of tobacco products constitute obstacles to the free movement of goods.[185] The Directive guarantees the free movement of goods that comply with its provisions.[186] It does not matter that the Directive has a public

178 Case C-491/01 *BAT and Imperial Tobacco (Directive on Tobacco Manufacture, Presentation and Sale)* above n 173.
179 OJ 2001 L 194/26. See further chapter 9.
180 Case C-491/01, Opinion of AG, para 100.
181 Case C-491/01, Opinion of AG, para 106.
182 Case C-491/01, Opinion of AG, paras 106–109.
183 In fact, the measure has a dual legal basis, Article 95 EC and Article 133 EC, the latter being applicable to the Directive's application to tobacco products manufactured in the EU and exported to other countries.
184 Case C-491/01, para 62, citing Case C-376/98 *Tobacco Advertising* above n 150.
185 Paras 64–67.
186 Directive 2001/37/EC, Article 13.

health protection element; on the contrary, this is required by Article 95 (3).[187] The Court also found that the Directive does not breach the principles of subsidiarity or proportionality.[188]

In addition to confirming the limited nature of Community competence in health, the rulings in *Tobacco Advertising* and *BAT and Imperial Tobacco* are also indirect confirmation that health protection is not a matter simply of national competence. Rather, the protection of human health must be guaranteed by both national and EU-level institutions. It should be remembered in this respect that if the allocation of responsibility for protection of human health is not clear, then human lives might be at risk. One of the main reasons for the failure of the EU to respond appropriately to the BSE crisis before nvCJD claimed human lives was that division of responsibility between national and EU-level institutions was unclear.[189] Thus, to the extent that the current position leaves this division of responsibilities unclear, this must be regarded as unsatisfactory.

It remains unclear whether the Community's tasks and activities, as set out in Article 2 and 3 EC, include an implicit general competence in the health field, applicable, of course, only where, under the principle of subsidiarity, EU-level action is necessary to protect human health. Such circumstances may be rare, but as the BSE situation shows, not unknown. In *Tobacco Advertising*, the Court stated that the explicit exclusion in Article 152 (4) EC of any harmonisation of national laws designed to protect and improve public health could not be circumvented by the use of other articles of the Treaty as legal basis.[190] It is not clear, however, whether the Court's statement in paragraph 79 to the effect that the restriction on Community competence in Article 152 EC cannot be circumvented applies also to Article 308 EC. The issue of whether a health protection provision could lawfully be adopted on the basis of Article 308 EC was not before the Court in *Tobacco Advertising* nor was it at issue in *BAT and Imperial Tobacco*. The proposed Draft Constitutional Treaty (DCT)[191] appears to clarify the position, providing, in Article I-17 DCT (the proposed successor to Article 308 EC), that "provisions adopted on the basis of this article may not entail harmonisation of Member States' laws or regulations in cases where the Constitution excludes such harmonisation", which would include "protection and improvement of human health",[192] although not "common safety concerns in public health matters".[193]

In terms of challenges brought by Member States, this is of little practical interest, as Article 308 EC (and the proposed Article I-17 DCT) requires unanimity in Council. It is not inconceivable, however, that a future challenge may be brought

187 Para 79.
188 Paras 177–185; paras 122–141.
189 See further chapter 9.
190 Paras 77–79.
191 See chapter 2, pp 32–33; and see further chapter 10.
192 Article I-16 DCT, Article III-179 (5) DCT. See further chapter 10.
193 Article I-13 (2) DCT.

(for instance, by the European Parliament, or by a private litigant, under the Article 234 EC procedure) to a health measure adopted on the basis of Article 308 EC, or even to an existing measure already adopted on the basis of Article 235 EC. The Court would then have to consider whether its ruling in *Massey-Ferguson*[194] is applicable in the situation where a Treaty amendment exists which explicitly provides that there is no Community competence to harmonise in the field of health.[195]

One significant contribution of *Tobacco Advertising* to the Court's legal basis jurisprudence is to illustrate the limits of the "core aim" approach to determination of the proper legal basis of a provision. On their face, both the Tobacco Advertising Directive and the Directive on Tobacco Manufacture, Presentation and Sale appeared to have both a health protection or promotion aim and an internal market aim. Following a choice of legal basis analysis would in those circumstances be effectively fruitless, especially given that Article 95 (3) requires that health protection be an indivisible element of internal market legislation. The Court had in fact already accepted in *Titanium Dioxide*[196] that there may be circumstances in which a measure has two equal aims, reflected in its content, corresponding to two different legal bases. In those circumstances, choice of legal basis approach, focussed on the "core aim" of the relevant measure, to determining the proper legal basis is profoundly unhelpful.

In both *Tobacco Advertising* and *BAT and Imperial Tobacco*, the Advocate General concerned began his detailed analysis by explicitly rejecting the "core aim" approach previously adopted by the Court in a number of choice of legal basis challenges to EU-level legislation.[197] For the Advocates General, the correct mode of analysis of the issue was not to set the internal market aims and content of the Directive against its public health aims and content. Article 95 (3) makes it clear that concerns such as those for public health may be pursued at the same time as internal market aims. Such concerns may be "indissociable" from internal market objectives. The issue was not whether health protection figured prominently in the motivation for the adoption of the Directives concerned, but simply whether the internal market, on its own, constituted a sustainable legal basis.

In *Tobacco Advertising*, the Court began its analysis with the *assumption* that the Tobacco Advertising Directive was a health protection measure. The Court appears to have reached this position on the basis that the national measures affected by the Directive are to a large extent inspired by public health policy objectives.[198] Given the interrelationships between health policy and other policies, both at national and EU level, as evidenced by previous choice of legal basis case law concerning

194 Case 8/73 *Massey-Ferguson* above n 104.
195 Save the exceptions in Article 152 (4) (a) and (b) EC.
196 Case C-300/89 *Titanium Dioxide* above n 91.
197 See, for example, Case C-155/91 *Waste Directive* above n 91; Case C-187/93 *Parliament v Council (Transport of Waste)* [1994] ECR I-2857; Case C-42/97 *Parliament v Council (Linguistic Diversity)* [1999] ECR I-869.
198 See para 67.

measures with health protection aims or effects, and by the Treaty provisions on mainstreaming public health, this appears to be profoundly unsatisfactory. Many measures may have both health protection aims and other aims. The mere effect on national health protection measures is insufficient to allow objective categorisation of a particular measure. The reasoning by which the Court rejected a choice of legal basis analysis lacks the nuance of that of the Advocate General. The same might be said for the *BAT and Imperial Tobacco* ruling. Here, rather than beginning from an assumption that the measure was a health protection measure, the Court appeared to begin from the assumption that the measure was an internal market measure. The Court did not discuss the claimants' arguments based on the exclusion in Article 152 (4) (c) EC.[199]

In *Tobacco Advertising*, the Court did explicitly discuss the provision in (then) Article 129 (4) EC, which excluded any harmonisation of national laws designed to protect and improve public health.[200] The Court stated that other articles of the Treaty could not be used as a legal basis to circumvent that restriction on Community competence.[201] This is perhaps a curious beginning, as it appears to circumscribe the powers and duties of the institutions under a well-established legal basis provision, Article 100a (now 95) EC, in terms of a more recent Treaty addition, Article 129 (now 152) EC. One reading of this element of the Court's reasoning would suggest that the powers of the institutions under Article 100a EC were reduced at Maastricht, when Article 129 EC was added to the Treaty. On this reading, the governments of the Member States used the Treaty reform process to "tweak" Community competence, in order to prevent the further expansion of EU-level activities in the field of health.[202] The alternative reading, of course, is that Article 100a EC has never been a proper legal basis for measures in the public health field, unless these actually have the effect of establishing or maintaining the internal market.

Further, the Court may have missed an opportunity to consider, in *Tobacco Advertising* and in *BAT and Imperial Tobacco*, the extent to which Community competence in the health field has evolved, and any implications this may have for the proper construction of Article 95 EC (and indeed other legal basis provisions where health protection may be an inherent part of the relevant policy). This evolution is reflected in the Treaty provisions and also in increased EU activity in the health field.[203] In particular, the lack of discussion of Article 95 (3) EC and the duty to

199 These arguments are simply noted in para 43 of the judgment.

200 Para 77.

201 Para 79.

202 See also Opinion of Advocate General Geelhoed, in Case C-491/01 *BAT and Imperial Tobacco* above n 173, paras 110–114, in which he takes the view that Article 152 EC *complements* the already existing Treaty powers such as Article 95 EC.

203 See, for instance, in addition to the activities already discussed, the establishment of a "European Food Safety Authority", in order to protect those within the EU from food-related hazards to health; Commission *Green Paper on Food Law* COM(97) 176; *Communication on Consumer Health and Food Safety* COM(97) 183 final; *White Paper on Food Safety*, adopted on 12 January

"mainstream" public health protection, as set out in Article 152 (1) EC, appears disappointing.[204] However, in *Tobacco Advertising*, given the Court's conclusion that the Tobacco Advertising Directive could not properly be considered to be an internal market provision, logically there was no "mainstreaming" at issue. In a sense, the mainstreaming of health in the Tobacco Advertising Directive was its downfall: health was so central to the provision that it ceased to be an internal market measure. Read thus, the Court's ruling indicates that health can be "mainstreamed too far". Article 95 (3) EC also has its limitations. This has implications for the nature of internal market legislation – it must facilitate free movement of the factors of production or remove an appreciable distortion of competition within the internal market – which were made clear by the Court.

The Court's comments in *Tobacco Advertising* about the specificity of Article 95 EC are interesting in the light of its earlier choice of legal basis rulings in which Article 95 EC was regarded as more general than other legal basis provisions, such as those for the common agricultural and environmental policies.[205] *Tobacco Advertising* confirms that Article 95 EC is not a general legal basis provision in the sense of Article 308 EC. The argument to the effect that Article 95 EC permits a general *regulation* of the internal market appears to have been roundly rejected, and this is confirmed in *BAT and Imperial Tobacco*. It appears then that there is a continuum of generality of legal basis provisions in the Treaty, with Article 308 EC as the most general, Article 95 EC being more specific, but not as specific as other legal bases. It follows that where measures with an element of health protection may lawfully be enacted on the basis of such other more specific provisions, they must be so enacted. Where the internal market can be a proper legal basis for such measures, Article 95 EC must be used. Article 308 EC may only be used as a basis for health protection measures as a last resort, if at all. This may have implications for the involvement of the European Parliament – still excluded as co-legislator from the Article 308 EC procedure – in the determination of EU health policy.

IV. Conclusions

Community competence in the field of health has evolved significantly, especially since the inception of the 1992 programme. While it is clear that the main responsibility for health protection and promotion remains with national authorities, the EU institutions are also obliged to contribute to the protection of human health. The Treaty envisages that such contribution is to be based on the provision in Article 152 EC. The Draft Treaty Establishing a Constitution for Europe (DCT) keeps this

2000; Regulation 178/2002/EC, laying down general principles and requirements of food law, establishing a European Food Safety Authority, and laying down procedures for food safety, OJ 2002 L 31/1. See further chapter 9.

204 Contrast the discussion of Advocate General Geelhoed in the later case C-491/01 *BAT and Imperial Tobacco* above n 173, paras 97–114.

205 See cases cited above.

provision relatively unchanged in Article III-179 DCT. The EC Treaty also recognises that the protection of human health forms a component part of many other EU policies and activities.

The powers and responsibilities of the EU institutions in the health field have been clarified by the Court's ruling in *Tobacco Advertising*. In particular, as the Court confirmed in *Tobacco Advertising*,[206] if Article 95 EC is to be the legal basis for a measure of EU-level secondary legislation, the measure concerned must actually have the object and effect of establishing or maintaining the functioning of the internal market. However, various questions, in particular the role of Article 308 EC in the protection of human health, remain unresolved at present.

Chapters 1, 2 and 3 set out the contextual background to our project: the determination of the extent to which, and the ways in which, EU law affects health law and policy in the Member States. Armed with an overview of the concerns of "health law", the activities of the EU and the characteristics of its legal order, and an understanding of the EU as a body with limited competence, we are now in a position to turn to the substance of our discussion. This takes the form of various case studies, divided into five chapters, on various matters in which EU law has affected, or has the potential to affect, elements of national health law. The first of these considers the application of EU law to patients' abilities to access health care services.

206 Case C-376/98 *Tobacco Advertising* above n 150.

Part Two

4

Access to health care services

I. Introduction

In this chapter and the next, we consider two of the areas which would, in standard health law jurisprudence, be frequently considered as falling within the boundaries of "patient rights" (for instance, to confidentiality, protection of personal autonomy and dignity, consent to treatment, and so on) and the right to access health care services. As we noted in chapter 1, while it is the case that the law of the EU may, in some respects, affect those issues which are to be commonly found in health law textbooks, such issues are not neatly categorised under the "headings" of health law.[1] Nonetheless, as we have seen already, there are certain areas in which the EU appears to be having an impact on health law in the Member States. One such area is that of access to health care services, as illustrated by the Diane Blood and Yvonne Watts stories with which we began this book.[2]

In the case of access to health care services, the subject of this chapter, in many respects, the use of rights language in this context can be seen as something of a misnomer. A claim by an individual of a "right" to access health care services is wholly dependent upon the particular service being available. Where services are state funded, this depends on the resources available. Competing rights claims may arise. This is probably why there has been notable judicial unwillingness at national level to become embroiled in disputes concerning resource allocation.[3] A further consideration is that health services are dependent upon varying degrees of clinical control, as to whether they are regarded as being clinically suitable. Patients

1 This obviously precluded organisation of our book into substantive chapters mirroring those of a standard health law textbook.

2 See chapter 1, p 1.

3 In the UK, for example, in *R v Secretary of State for Social Services, ex parte Hincks* (1980) 1 BMLR 93, Lord Denning commented that, "It cannot be supposed that the Secretary of State has to provide all the latest equipment. As Oliver LJ said in the course of argument, it cannot be supposed that the Secretary of State has to provide all the kidney machines which are asked for, or for all the new developments such as heart transplants in every case where people would benefit from them"; and see also *R v Cambridge DHA, ex parte B* [1995] 1 WLR 898 and *R v Ethical Committee of St Mary's Hospital (Manchester), ex parte H* [1988] 1 FLR 512; although see also *R v North West Lancashire HA, ex parte A, D, and G* [2000] 1 WLR 977. See further D. O'Sullivan, "The allocation of scarce resources and the right to life under the European Convention on Human Rights" [1998] *Public Law* 389.

attempting to claim the ability to access certain health care services may be rejected on the basis that a particular service is not clinically indicated. Rather than relying on an enforceable "right" to access health care services, national health (insurance) services are structured with the aim of ensuring clear lines of responsibility for planning, management and delivery of health care services on the basis of clinical need, sometimes with consequences in public law where such responsibilities are not met. Further, mechanisms of quality control, designed to ensure that health care services meet appropriate standards, may be set down. These include regulation of medical professionals, including their recognition as such and permission to practise within national health (insurance) systems;[4] complaints mechanisms; and "soft law" statements of best practice or the quality standards which health care providers are expected to strive to attain.

Where a health service is provided in the private sector, the extent to which the "gatekeeping" of access to health care services by medical professionals or by national health insurance providers operates may be more limited. Nonetheless there may still be some control as the result of the application of professional ethical codes, which may be mandated through legislation. Alternatively it may be the case that, even where services are provided privately, restrictions in national law may limit their availability on public health or public policy grounds. Illustrations of this include abortion,[5] organ transplantation[6] and various genetic tests.[7]

The details of the legal entitlements of individual patients to access health care services within the EU are essentially determined by national law. All the Member States of the EU have a public national health (insurance) system ensuring near

4 See further chapter 6.

5 See, for example, Austria: Penal Code, sections 96–98, Federal Law of 23 January 1974 *Bundesgesetzblatt* No 60, 1974; Belgium: Code Pénal, Title VII, Chapter 1, sections 348–352; Czech Republic: Law on abortion, 20 October 1986; Denmark: Law No 350 of 13 June 1973 on the interruption of pregnancy (*Lovitidende for Kongeriget Danmark*, Part A, 6 July 1973, No 32, pp 993–995); Finland: Law No 239 of 24 March 1970 on the interruption of pregnancy, as amended by Law No 564 of 19 July 1978 and Law No 572 of 12 July 1985, Ordinance No 359 of 29 May 1970 on the interruption of pregnancy; France: Law No 79-1204 of 31 December 1979 and related laws (*Journal Officiel*, No 1, 1 January 1980, p 3); Greece: Penal Code, sections 304–305; Italy: Law No 194 of 22 May 1978 on the social protection of motherhood and the voluntary termination of pregnancy (*Gazzetta Ufficiale della Repubblica Italiana*, Part I, 2 May 1978, No 140, pp 3642–3646; Netherlands: Law on the termination of pregnancy of 1 May 1981; Slovakia: Law on abortion 23 October 1986 (all taken from the website of the Berkman Center for Internet and Society, Harvard); Irish Constitution, Article 40.3.3.

6 So, for example, in the UK the Human Organ Transplants Act 1989 places particular limitations on organ donation in the case of genetically related donors and criminalises the sale of human organs: see generally D. Price, *Legal and Ethical Issues of Organ Transplantation* (Cambridge: CUP, 2000); similar limitations apply in Italy (Law No 458 of 26 June 1967 concerning the transplantation of kidneys from living donors) – preference is given to transplants from living related donors and transplants may only be undertaken from other persons where a patient does not have any of the blood relatives specified in the legislation or where these exist but are not available or suitable. In addition, persons who act as intermediaries regarding donation of a kidney for payment may be subject to prosecution. See further L. Nielson, "Living Organ Donors – Legal Perspectives from Western Europe" in D. Price and H. Akeveld, eds, *Living Donation in the Nineties: European Medico-Legal Perspectives* (Leicester: Eurotold, 1991).

7 Human Genetics Commission, *Genes Direct* (London: HGC, 2003).

universal access to comprehensive service,[8] although the details and mechanisms of provision, and the precise entitlements of patients to medical treatment and health care within each system, vary considerably.[9] Article 152 (5) EC provides that "Community action in the field of public health shall fully respect the responsibilities of the Member States for the organisation and delivery of health services and medical care". The European Court of Justice has regularly observed that "Community law does not detract from the powers of the Member States to organise their social security systems",[10] which includes their national health (insurance) systems.

However, these provisions of national law are affected by EU law in several ways, through both legislation promulgated at EU level and litigation based on directly effective provisions of Community law. This chapter considers the impact of such measures of EU law on the right to access health care services; on standards applicable in the provision of such services; and any implications for resource allocation. The relevant body of case law is that of the European Court of Justice on the entitlements of patients to cross-border health care. Patients may seek health care services in a Member State different from their own for a number of reasons, for instance, where value for money, waiting times, or other elements of quality of care (standards), or the particular health care service available (rights to access a particular type of health care service) differ from Member State to Member State. The latter is discussed in terms of the particular example of "reproductive tourism", which poses special difficulties because of its interface with ethical and religious concerns.[11]

8 It is estimated that approximately 95% of the EU population is covered by a public health (insurance) system: see A.P. Van der Mei, *Free Movement of Persons within the European Community: Cross-Border Access to Public Benefits* (Oxford: Hart, 2003), p 222. As far as accession and candidate countries are concerned, as Central and Eastern European states have moved from the centralised state budget financed "Semashko system" of health care to systems based on social insurance, some gaps in coverage have come to light. See further, J. Marrée and P.P. Groenewegen, *Back to Bismarck: Eastern European Care Systems in Transition* (Aldershot: Avebury, 1997); B. Deacon, "Eastern European welfare states: the impact of the politics of globalization" 10 *Journal of European Social Policy* (2000) 146.

9 See Y. Jorens, "The Right to Health Care Across Borders" in R. Baeten, M. McKee and E. Mossialos, eds, *The Impact of EU Law on Health Care Systems* (Brussels: PIE Peter Lang, 2003); R. Freeman, *The Politics of Health in Europe* (Manchester: MUP, 2000); R.B. Saltman, J. Figueras and C. Sakallarides, eds, *Critical Challenges for Health Care Reform in Europe* (Buckingham: Open University Press, 1998); M. McCarthy and S. Rees, *Health Systems and Public Health Medicine in the EC* (London: Royal College of Physicians, 1992); J. Elola, A. Daponte, and V. Navarro, "Health indicators and the organization of health care systems in Europe" 85 *American Journal of Public Health* (1995) 1397.

10 Case 238/82 *Duphar* [1984] ECR 523, para 16; Cases 159 & 160/91 *Poucet and Pistre* [1993] ECR 637, para 6; Case C-70/95 *Sodemare* [1997] ECR I-3395, para 27; Case C-120/95 *Decker* [1998] ECR I-1831, para 21; Case C-158/96 *Kohll v Union des Caisses de Maladie* [1998] ECR I-1931, para 17; Case C-157/99 *Geraets-Smits and Peerbooms* [2001] ECR I-5473, para 44. This phrase has begun to "acquire the status of a catechism": see G. Davies, "Welfare as a Service" 29 *Legal Issues of Economic Integration* (2002) 27.

11 Another example would be that of "end of life tourism"(or "death tourism"), where national provisions with respect to the end of life differ between Member States. It is believed that, at present, only a limited number of persons have availed themselves of such provisions. There have been instances of UK citizens travelling to Switzerland to end their life: see, for example, C. Dyer "Swiss Parliament may ban suicide tourists" 326 BMJ (2003) 242.

Litigation here falls into the category of "deregulation", in terms of our typology set out in chapter 2. However, the litigation in these areas takes place in the context not only of the relevant directly effective and essentially deregulatory Treaty provisions on freedom to provide and receive services, but also the legislative framework for coordination of national social security schemes in the event of free movement of persons. The interface between this legislation and the relevant case law, and the modes of governance represented by each (regulatory coordination and deregulation), is considered in detail.

II. Access to health care services

Before we turn to a discussion of the effect of EU law on entitlements to health care services, we need to set out in some detail the relevant legal provisions on free movement, and explain their interpretation by the European Court of Justice and application in the context of health care. This may be familiar ground for EU lawyers, but we hope it will assist health lawyers in understanding the principles behind the relevant EU law, which were not developed with health care in mind.

Free movement of patients

Migrant patients as migrant workers

Creation of the internal market, one of the central aims of the EU, requires provisions ensuring mobility of labour. If people are to move around the EU in order to work, then provision must be made for their protection in the event of the traditional social security risks, including illness, befalling them. Yet, as we have seen, responsibility for such protection remains with the Member States, and there is no EU-level social security or health system. However, if no EU-level provision were made at all, potential migrant workers might be dissuaded from moving, on the grounds that they and their families might lose social security entitlements, including rights to health care and medical treatment in the event of illness, if they did so. The answer of the EU's legislative institutions to this problem is the system of regulatory coordination of national social security systems, set out in Regulation 1408/71/EEC,[12] as amended,[13] and supporting legislation.[14]

The technical operation of this system is the subject of many detailed rules and numerous interpretative rulings of the European Court of Justice.[15] The personal

12 OJ 1971 L 149/2; OJ Sp Ed 1971 II p 416.

13 Regulation 1408/71/EEC is amended regularly. Readers are referred to CELEX, http://www.europa.eu.int/celex_en.htm, the online source of EU legislation, for the latest text.

14 Regulation 574/72/EEC, OJ 1972 L 74/1.

15 See, for instance, L. Luckhaus, "European Social Security Law" in A. Ogus and N. Wikeley, eds, *The Law of Social Security* (London: Butterworths, 1995); C. Barnard, *EC Employment Law* (Oxford: OUP, 2000), pp 299–328; and the regular reviews of case law on Regulation 1408/71/EEC in the *Common Market Law Review*.

scope of the Regulation is governed by Article 2 (1): it currently extends to employed or self-employed persons, civil servants, students, and pensioners, who are citizens of the EU,[16] or nationals of "third countries" legally resident within the EU,[17] or stateless persons or refugees resident in a Member State, and their families[18] and survivors.[19] The concept of "employed or self-employed" in this context is defined by reference to affiliation to and insurance under a national social security scheme.[20] The material scope of the Regulation is governed by Article 4. This draws a broad distinction between national social *security* benefits – which are covered by the Regulation – and "social and medical *assistance*" – which is not. The test for whether a benefit constitutes "social or medical assistance" has been developed by the European Court of Justice. The Court considers whether the benefit accrues as of right, consequent upon a period of employment or affiliation under a social security scheme (more likely to constitute "social security"), or whether there is an element of means-testing (more likely to constitute "social assistance").[21] The Regulation applies to all legislation concerning, *inter alia*, sickness, invalidity and maternity benefits, whether as part of a contributory, non-contributory, or special non-contributory scheme.[22]

Broadly, the system established by Regulation 1408/71/EEC is based on four overarching principles. These are the principle of non-discrimination on grounds of nationality; the principle of aggregation or apportionment of benefit rights; the exportability of benefits from Member State to Member State; and the "single state" rule in terms of affiliation, liability to contribute and benefit entitlement.[23] Thus, where a Member State makes the acquisition of sickness benefits conditional upon completion of periods of employment, insurance or residence, such periods in another Member State must be aggregated to periods completed in the host Member State, and treated as though they were periods in that Member State.[24] Migrant workers must be entitled to equal treatment with nationals in terms of access to and benefits provided under national health (insurance) systems, where these fall within the scope of the Regulation.[25] Each migrant worker (and his or her family) is the responsibility of a "competent Member State", in which the worker is insured at the time of the application for benefit, or would be entitled to health care benefits (sickness or maternity benefits, in the terms of the Regulation) if

16 That is, hold the nationality of a Member State of the EU; Article 17 (ex 8) EC.
17 "Provided that they . . . are in a situation which is not confined in all respects within a single Member State": see Regulation 859/2003/EC, OJ 2003 L 124/1, Article 1.
18 But see Case 94/84 *Deak* [1985] ECR 1873.
19 See further, D. S. Martinsen, "Who Has the Right to Intra European Social Security? – From Market Citizens to European Citizens and Beyond" *Annual of German and European Law* (forthcoming 2004).
20 Not by reference to an EU-level definition determined by the European Court of Justice.
21 See, for instance, Case 139/82 *Piscitello v INPS* [1983] ECR 1427.
22 Regulation 1408/71/EEC, Article 4 (1) (a) and (b), Article 4 (2), Article 4 (2a).
23 Regulation 1408/71/EEC, Articles 3; 18 (1), 38, 45, 64, 67; 72; 10 (1); Articles 12 (1) and 46 (3).
24 Regulation 1408/71/EEC, Article 18 (1).
25 Regulation 1408/71/EEC, Article 3 (1).

resident in the Member State concerned.[26] In principle, then, the "competent Member State" is the state in which the worker is employed. Where a migrant worker resides in a Member State other than the competent Member State,[27] he or she is entitled to receive, in the Member State of residence, in the event of illness or maternity:

> "(a) benefits in kind provided on behalf of the competent institution by the institution of the place of residence in accordance with the provisions of the legislation administered by that institution as though he were insured with it;
> (b) cash benefits provided by the competent administration in accordance with the legislation which it administers."[28]

Remembering that in this context an "employed or self employed" migrant worker means a person who is insured under a social security scheme of one of the Member States, Regulation 1408/71/EEC also applies to retired persons and their families. Special provisions of the Regulation apply to persons entitled to a pension under the legislation of one or more Member States.[29] Such a person, who is entitled to benefits under the legislation of one of these Member States, and who is staying in the territory of a Member State other than that of his or her residence, shall receive benefits in kind provided by the host Member State, the cost being borne by the competent Member State or cash benefits provided by the competent Member State, or if the two relevant Member States agree, by the host Member State on behalf of the competent Member State.[30] "Benefits" in this context includes health care benefits, either in the form of health insurance benefits ("cash benefits") or health care services given free at the point of access ("benefits in kind"). A typical migration pattern for such retired persons is from northern to southern "sunshine"[31] Member States and one might expect significant numbers of retired persons accessing the health care systems of southern Member States, with the cost being borne by "competent" northern Member States, with consequent impact on the capacity of the health care systems of the host southern Member States. In fact, it seems that those retired persons who access public health care schemes in their host Member State (rather than relying on private medical insurance alone), tend to relocate back to their (northern) home states later in their retired life, when their health may

26 Regulation 1408/71/EEC, Article 1 (o) (i) and (ii).
27 Special rules apply to frontier workers and members of their families: see Regulation 1408/71/EEC, Article 20.
28 Regulation 1408/71/EEC, Article 19 (1).
29 Regulation 1408/71/EEC, Articles 27–34b.
30 Regulation 1408/71/EEC, Article 31.
31 Havighurst discusses the effects of this migration pattern in the United States, observing that the "sunshine states" of California and Florida reduced welfare benefits in an attempt to avoid an influx of poor people: see C. Havighurst, "American Federalism and American Health Care: Lessons for the European Community" in H.E.G.M. Hermans, A.F. Casparie and J.H.P. Paelinck, *Health Care in Europe after 1992* (Aldershot: Dartmouth, 1992), p 42. In the EU context, see K. Sieveking, "The Significance of the Transborder Utilisation of Health Care Benefits for Migrants" 2 *European Journal of Migration and Law* (2000) 143.

be failing,[32] perhaps because they feel more confident in the health care services available in the "competent" (northern) Member State. Where such patients do not relocate, but remain resident in the host Member State, yet seek medical treatment in the competent Member State, the state of residence must authorise the treatment.[33]

The principle of exportability of benefits from Member State to Member State is incomplete in the context of sickness and maternity benefits under Regulation 1408/71/EEC. An insured person whose condition necessitates immediate benefits during a stay in the territory of another Member State is entitled to benefits in kind provided by the host state, in accordance with its legislation, as though he or she were insured in the host state.[34] This covers *emergency* medical treatment for those on temporary stays in another Member State, such as for work, study, or holidays, and is currently administered through the E111 system.[35] However, for retired persons, the relevant equivalent provision of the Regulation, Article 31, makes no equivalent requirement with respect to their state of health. Under that provision, benefits must be provided irrespective of whether the illness manifested itself suddenly during the stay in the host state, making immediate treatment necessary.[36]

Further, according to Regulation 1408/71/EEC, a Member State may *authorise* the receipt by an individual national of that Member State of a particular medical treatment in another Member State where it is available, at the expense of the home Member State.[37] The Regulation originally provided that authorisation "may not be refused where the treatment in question cannot be provided for the person concerned within the territory of the Member State in which he resides".[38] In *Pierik (No 1)*[39] the European Court of Justice applied these rules in the context of physiotherapeutic treatment for a rheumatic ailment, where the individual concerned had already received treatment in Germany, and a medical expert in the Netherlands

32 In fact, many such migrants, while resident in host Member States, also returned regularly for short visits to their home Member States to access public health care benefits and services, such as prescription medicines, there. See P. Dwyer, "Retired EU Migrants, healthcare rights and European social citizenship" 23 *Journal of Social Welfare and Family Law* (2001) 311.

33 Case C-156/01 *ANOZ* [2003] ECR I-7045.

34 Regulation 1408/71/EEC, Article 22 (1) (a).

35 The Commission has proposed an "electronic health card", to replace the E111 and other forms: see Council Resolution on the European health card, OJ 1996 C 141/104; Commission Action Plan to remove obstacles to EU workers' mobility by 2005, COM(2002) 72 final. The European electronic health insurance card will be adopted in 2008, replacing the paper-based forms that citizens need for health treatment when in other Member States. The Commission envisages that: "Such cards could feature added functionalities, such as medical emergency data and secure access to personal health information. Combined with other developments, this could bring greater efficiency to health information management, continuity of care across Europe, and greater security and control for users over their health data." See http://europa.eu.int/information_society/eeurope/2005/all_about/ehealth/text_en.htm. For further discussion of the "e-health" action plan, see chapter 10.

36 Case C-326/00 *IKA v Ioannidis* [2003] ECR I-1703. See V. Hatzopoulos, "Case note on Case C-326/00 *IKA v Ioannidis*" 40 CMLRev (2003) 1251.

37 Regulation 1408/71/EEC, Article 22 (1) (c).

38 Regulation 1408/71/EEC, Article 22 (2).

39 Case 117/77 [1978] ECR 825.

was of the opinion that no treatment available in the Netherlands would be as effective as the treatment sought. The ruling suggests that an individual seeking medical treatment according to a procedure which is not available in his or her own Member State could rely on Regulation 1408/71/EEC to *require* his or her Member State's national health insurance to meet the cost. However, a subsequent ruling on the same issue as *Pierik (No 1)* suggests that the Court would perhaps have been unlikely to interpret Regulation 1408/71/EEC to this very broad effect. In *Pierik (No 2)*[40] the Court was asked to deal with the question of whether Regulation 1408/71/EEC applied where the home Member State *deliberately* excluded a medical treatment from its national health service, on cost-containment or "medical-ethical" grounds. Although the facts of Pierik's case did not require the Court to consider this issue,[41] the submissions of the Commission suggest that Member States are permitted to refuse authorisation, for instance, for treatments "seriously contrary to the ethical rules prevailing" in its jurisdiction, on the grounds that Member States retain competence to regulate public morality.[42]

In any event, Article 22 (2) of Regulation 1408/71/EEC was subsequently amended by the EU legislature.[43] It now provides that authorisation:

> "may not be refused where the treatment in question is among the benefits provided for by the legislation of the Member State on whose territory the person concerned resides, and where he cannot be given such treatment within the time normally necessary for obtaining the treatment in question in the Member State of residence, taking account of his current state of health and the probable course of the disease."

The aim of the amendment was to make clear that patients do not have the right under Regulation 1408/71/EEC to claim financial support from their home Member State for treatments received in another Member State which are not available, or not publicly funded, in the home Member State. The amendment also aimed to prevent patients from circumventing waiting lists in the home Member State by claiming an EU law "right to be treated" in another Member State.[44] The intention of the legislature, it seems, was to reassert that control over the authorisation procedure remains firmly at the discretion of the Member States, and is not the subject of individually enforceable rights in EU law. The amended provision makes clear that patients do not have a *right* to obtain authorisation for types of treatment not included in the competent Member State's insurance package, nor can they rely on Article 22 (2) to circumvent waiting lists in that state. The decision on authorisation is for national authorities, not the patient him- or herself.[45] A patient only has the

40 Case 182/78 [1979] ECR 1977.
41 Case 182/78 *Pierik (No 2)* above n 40, para 10; see also Advocate General's Opinion, para 2.
42 See P. Watson, *Social Security Law of the European Communities* (London: Mansell, 1980), p 258.
43 OJ 1981 L 275/1.
44 Van der Mei, above n 8, p 256.
45 Jorens, above n 9, pp 92–93.

right to authorisation where delayed treatment would be "medically unacceptable", taking into account only their *current* state of health.[46] In all other circumstances, then, authorisation may be lawfully refused by the competent Member State, thus preventing a full "exportability" of publicly funded health care benefits from Member State to Member State. In general, authorisation is given only in exceptional cases, although practice varies somewhat from Member State to Member State.[47] Again, however, a different provision, Article 31 of Regulation 1408/71/EEC, applies to retired persons. Member States may not make enjoyment of benefits under that provision subject to an authorisation procedure.[48]

Thus it follows that migrant *workers* from other Member States (and their families, and others that fall within the personal scope of Regulation 1408/71/EEC) may impose burdens on national social welfare systems, including national health systems. Generally, of course, this is not particularly problematic. The overall numbers of migrant workers within the EU are small.[49] Crucially, migrant workers by definition either are currently contributing or have contributed to the host Member State's national welfare systems, including its national health system, and/or at least to the system of another Member State, from whom the host Member State can claim reimbursement for its outlay. The regulatory coordination system of Regulation 1408/71/EEC ensures that Member States who finance social security entitlements, including in the health field, are reimbursed from the Member State(s) into which social insurance and/or tax payments have been made. For instance, Article 36 of Regulation 1408/71/EEC provides that benefits in kind provided by one Member State on behalf of another in accordance with the regulation "shall be fully refunded".

46 Contrast the position under Case C-157/99 *Geraets-Smits and Peerbooms* above n 10: see below. See Van der Mei, above n 8, p 256; A. P. Van der Mei, "Cross-Border Access to Health Care within the European Union: Some Reflections on *Geraets-Smits and Peerbooms* and *Vanbraekel*" 9 MJ (2002) 1 at 17.

47 The total spent on cross-border treatments is around 0.1–0.2% of total public spending on health care in the EU: see R. Busse, "Border-crossing patients in the EU" 8(4) *eurohealth* (2002) 19; and R. Busse, "Consumer choice of healthcare services across borders" in R. Busse, M. Wismar and P.C. Berman, eds, *The European Union and Health Services: The Impact of the Single European Market on Member States* (Amsterdam: IOS Press, 2002). For instance, Member States such as Sweden, France and the UK traditionally granted authorisation only very rarely, for instance, where waiting lists were deemed "too long". At the other end of the spectrum, Luxembourg and Belgium grant authorisation relatively often. Some Member States, such as Denmark, Germany, Greece, Ireland, Netherlands and Portugal, grant authorisation for types of treatment (often new treatments) which are not available in their own country: W. Palm, J. Nickless, H. Lewalle and A. Coheur, *Implications of Recent Jurisprudence on the Coordination of Health Care Protection Systems* Summary Report produced for DG Employment and Social Affairs (Brussels: AIM, 2000); Van der Mei, above n 8, p 256; E. Mossialos and M. McKee, *EU Law and the Social Character of Health Care* (Brussels: PIE Peter Lang, 2002), pp 84–85; Jorens, above n 9, p 91. At least some Member States, for example, Denmark, have recently changed their practice, in the light of the Court's jurisprudence discussed below: see D.S. Martinsen, "National Impacts of Institutionalising Social Security Rights for Migrants in the European Union" EUI Working Papers, Law No 2003/13, http://www.ive.it/PUB/law 03-13.pdf.

48 Case C-326/00 *IKA v Ioannidis* above n 36.

49 For statistics, see, for example, http://www.ilo.org/public/english/bureau/stat/portal/topics.htm#migr and http://www.oecd.org/document/36/0,2340,en_2825_494553_2515108_1_1_1_1,00.html.

However, the provision in Article 22 of Regulation 1408/71/EEC does not tell the whole story in terms of entitlements to publicly funded cross-border receipt of health care services within the EU, as we shall shortly see. The reason for this is that the EU-level system of regulatory coordination of national social security systems, including health systems, set out in Regulation 1408/71/EEC, operates within the context of relevant provisions of *harmonised* EU-level laws, both of a deregulatory and re-regulatory nature. Where a person seeking cross-border access to health care services is a worker, Regulation 1612/68/EEC,[50] Article 7 (2) provides that migrant (EU citizen) workers and members of their families shall enjoy the same "social and tax advantages" as national workers. Such "social advantages" have been defined broadly by the Court, and would clearly include access to national health service provision, on the same basis as national workers.[51] Further, Article 18 (ex 8a) EC provides that citizens of the EU shall have the right to move and reside freely within the territory of the EU, "subject to the limitations and conditions laid down by this Treaty and by the measures adopted to give it effect".[52] The provisions on free movement of EU citizens are elaborated in secondary legislation. For instance, the "residence directives"[53] grant EU citizens (who need not be workers) a right of residence in Member States other than that of which they are a national. However, this provision does not encompass an entitlement to access publicly funded health care in the host state, as it is provisional upon the migrant EU citizen having sufficient resources to avoid becoming a burden on the social and medical assistance schemes of the host Member State.[54]

Further, and crucially, provisions of secondary EU legislation such as Regulation 1408/71/EEC cannot undercut provisions of primary EU law, in particular Treaty provisions on freedom of movement for workers[55] and, most importantly for our purposes, freedom to provide and receive services.[56] Such freedom of movement is effected, *inter alia*, by application of the principle of non-discrimination

50 OJ Sp Ed 1968 II p 475.

51 The Court adopted a broad approach to "social advantages" in Case 207/78 *Even* [1979] ECR 2019. In the context of benefits related to health, see, for example, Case 63/76 *Inzirillo* [1976] ECR 2057, concerning a disability allowance; and Case 65/81 *Reina* [1982] ECR 33, concerning a childbirth loan.

52 The Court is currently developing a line of jurisprudence exploring the contours of this exception, see Case C-85/96 *Martinez Sala* [1998] ECR I-2691; Case C-184/99 *Grzelczyk* [2002] ECR I- 6153; Case C-413/99 *Baumbast* [2002] ECR I-7091. See C. Jacqueson, "Union Citizenship and the Court of Justice: Something New Under the Sun" 27 ELRev (2002) 260.

53 Directive 90/366/EEC, OJ 1990 L 180/30 (replaced by Directive 93/96/EC, OJ 1993 L 317/59); Directive 90/365/EEC, OJ 1990 L 180/28; and Directive 90/364/EEC, OJ 1990 L 180/26. There is currently a proposal to consolidate the EU legislation on the free movement and residence entitlements of EU citizens and their families: see COM(2001) 257 final and COM(2003) 199 final, Council political agreement reached in September 2003.

54 Of course, for most EU citizens, that is, those who are workers, their entitlements under Regulation 1408/71/EEC will fulfil this requirement.

55 Article 39 EC.

56 Article 49 EC.

on grounds of nationality[57] and by prohibiting "restrictions" on the freedom of movement.[58] Thus the Court has held that Regulation 1408/71/EEC provides only part of the story with respect to the individual entitlements of patients to access health care services in the EU, and in particular that migrant patients may in certain circumstances rely on the directly effective Treaty provisions on freedom to provide and receive services.[59] Here the migrant is not moving for work, but specifically for receipt of medical treatment or services. The safeguards for the home and host Member States of the regulatory coordination system of Regulation 1408/71/EEC do not apply. It follows that there is scope here for deregulatory EU law to have a more profound effect on national health systems. It is to these individual entitlements to health care under EU law that we now turn.

Migrant patients as recipients of services

Article 49 EC provides that "restrictions" on the freedom to provide services within the EU "shall be prohibited". "Services", according to Article 50 EC, in this context are those activities of an industrial, commercial, artisanal or professional character "normally provided for remuneration, insofar as they are not governed by the provisions related to freedom of movement for goods, capital and persons".[60] Article 54 EC provides that if Member States maintain restrictions on the freedom to provide services, these must be applied without discrimination on grounds of nationality or residence. Four components of this provision require further elaboration: the concept of remuneration; the application of the provision to recipients, rather than providers, of services; the definition of a restriction; and the possibility of justifying such restrictions on free provision and receipt of services.

In order to fall within the Treaty, a service must be provided for ***remuneration***. This means there must be an economic or financial link between the service provider and the recipient of the service. The essential characteristic of remuneration is that it constitutes consideration for the service in question.[61] This requirement reflects the function of the provisions on freedom to provide services; that is the economic aim of establishing the internal market. The Court has explicitly held that privately remunerated medical services fall within the Treaty provisions on freedom

57 Article 39 (2) EC. Regarded as a "general principle" of EU law by the European Court of Justice: see, for example, Case 152/73 *Sotgiu v Deutsche Bundespost* [1974] ECR 153; and given expression in the Treaty in Article 12 (ex 6) EC.

58 Article 49 (1) EC.

59 See also V. Hatzopoulos, "Killing National Health and Insurance Systems but Healing Patients?" 39 CMLRev (2002) 683 at 696.

60 The services provisions are expressly stated by the Treaty to be subordinate to those relating to free movement of goods, capital and persons. The Treaty provisions on freedom to provide services are closely related to those on freedom of establishment. See Case C-55/94 *Gebhard* [1995] ECR I-4165, para 22.

61 Case 263/86 *Belgian State v Humbel* [1988] ECR 5365, para 17.

to provide services.[62] Further, the requirement of economic activity is interpreted generously by the Court.[63] Moreover, the Court has held that remuneration need not come directly from the recipient of the services.[64] This suggests that medical treatment paid for by a sickness insurance fund, or a charitable organisation, could fall within the Treaty concept of services. The Court has confirmed this by finding that "remuneration" is present in the provision of some forms of publicly funded medical services. In certain circumstances, medical treatment or health care reimbursed under a national social security scheme may fall within Article 49 EC.[65] For instance, this is so where treatment is paid for by the patient, but reimbursed by a public sickness insurance fund, and provided extramurally "outside any hospital [i.e. public] infrastructure".[66] It is also the case where *intramural* treatment (within a hospital) is reimbursed by a national sickness insurance fund, even where such reimbursement is on the basis of regulated pre-set scales of fees.[67]

In the case of services funded directly by the state, financed by public taxation, it would seem that the necessary "economic link" between service provider and recipient is not present. For instance, the Court has ruled that state-financed education is not a service in the sense of the Treaty.[68] However, the decisive factor is not the nature of the service itself, but the manner in which its provision is financed.[69] Thus, there is no general exclusion for "welfare provision" such as health care, from the Treaty provisions on freedom to provide services. The Court has not yet ruled on the application of the Treaty to the provision of health care services under a national health system financed largely by public taxation.[70]

On a literal interpretation, the provisions in Articles 49 and 50 EC are concerned with the freedoms (or rights) of service *providers*. They do not appear to establish a right for individuals to travel to another Member State, to *receive* services. However, the European Court of Justice, through its interpretative jurisprudence, has extended the provisions of the Treaty to encompass recipients of services. This jurisprudence is controversial, precisely because it has the effect of extending the scope of the

62 Cases 286/82 & 26/83 *Luisi and Carbone* [1984] ECR 377, para 16. This ruling was confirmed in respect of the medical treatment of abortion in Case C-159/90 *SPUC v Grogan* [1991] ECR I-4685.

63 See Case 196/87 *Steymann* [1988] ECR 6159; see also, in the case of free movement of workers, Case 53/81 *Levin* [1982] ECR 1035 and Case 139/85 *Kempf* [1986] ECR 1741.

64 Case 352/85 *Bond van Adverteerders* [1988] ECR 2085.

65 Case C-158/96 *Kohll* above n 10.

66 Case C-158/96 *Kohll* above n 10, para 29.

67 Case C-157/99 *Geraets-Smits and Peerbooms* [2001] ECR I-5473, paras 55–58; Case C-368/98 *Vanbraekel* [2001] ECR I-5363, para 42; Case C-385/99 *Müller-Fauré and van Riet* [2003] ECR I-4509.

68 Case 263/86 *Belgian State v Humbel* above n 61; Opinion of the Advocate General in Case 293/86 *Gravier* [1985] ECR 593.

69 Case 279/80 *Webb* [1981] ECR 3305. Thus the Court has held that privately funded education does fall within the scope of the Treaty, see Case C-109/92 *Wirth* [1993] ECR I-6447.

70 The English High Court has ruled that the principles developed by the Court in *Geraets-Smits* and *Müller-Fauré* do apply in the context of the UK NHS, funded largely through public taxation: see *R (on the application of Yvonne Watts) v Bedford Primary Care Trust and Secretary of State for Health* [2003] EWHC 2228 (Admin), 1 October 2003; see further below.

Treaty beyond its literal wording, to which the Member States have agreed. In *Luisi and Carbone*[71] the Court held that the entitlement of a service recipient to go to the Member State where the service was provided was a necessary corollary of the right of the provider to provide the service in the recipient's Member State. The Court stated that:

> "the freedom to provide services includes the freedom for the recipients of services to go to another Member State in order to receive a service there, without being obstructed by restrictions . . . "

The term ***"restriction"*** in the sense of Article 49 EC has been further defined by legislation and by the Court. The General Programme for the abolition of restrictions of freedom to provide services[72] sets out various "prohibited restrictions" on the provision of services. Title III, A provides that:

> "any requirements imposed, pursuant to any provision laid down by law, regulation or administrative practice, in respect of the provision of services are also to be regarded as restrictions where, although applicable irrespective of nationality, their effect is exclusively or principally to hinder the provision of services by foreign nationals."

This is a generous test, similar to the *Dassonville* test with respect to free movement of goods, which provides that "all trading rules enacted by Member States which are capable of hindering, directly or indirectly, actually or potentially, intra-Community trade" are unlawful.[73] Restrictions on the freedom to provide services have also been given a broad interpretation by the Court. The essence of the Court's approach is to consider the potential for the restriction to inhibit inter-Member State provision of services.[74] For instance, compliance with regulatory conditions required for establishment in the Member State in which the service is provided, licensing or qualifications requirements,[75] restrictions on advertising,[76] and requirements to make social security contributions to the Member State in which the service is provided[77] may all constitute "restrictions". As the freedom to receive services is a corollary of the freedom to provide services, the Court's interpretation of "restrictions" in cases concerning freedom to provide services applies by analogy. Therefore, prohibited restrictions would clearly include physical restrictions, measures which made it impossible or excessively difficult in practice for the

71 Cases 286/82 & 26/83 above n 62, para 16; see also Case 186/87 *Cowan* [1989] ECR 195.
72 OJ 002 pp 32–35, 15 January 1962; OJ English Special Edition Series II, Vol IX, p 3.
73 Case 8/74 *Procureur du Roi v Dassonville* [1974] ECR 837. See further chapter 2.
74 See Case 186/87 *Cowan* above n 71, paras 15–17; Case C-76/90 *Säger v Dennemeyer* [1991] ECR I-4221, para 12; Case C-43/93 *Vander Elst* [1994] ECR I-3803, para 14; Case C-272/94 *Guiot and Climatec* [1996] ECR I-1905, para 10.
75 Case C-154/89 *Commission v France (Re Tourist Guides)* [1991] ECR I-659.
76 By analogy with Case C-362/88 *GB-INNO-BM* [1990] ECR I-667; Case C-76/90 *Säger* above n 74, paras 12–14; Case C-275/92 *Schindler* [1994] ECR I-1039, paras 43–44; see also Case C-159/90 *Grogan* above n 62.
77 Case C-272/94 *Guiot and Climatec* above n 74.

person to receive the service sought,[78] and also any other measures which have the effect of making the provision of services between the Member States more difficult than the provision of services purely within one Member State.[79] It follows that application of the prior authorisation rules under Regulation 1408/71/EEC can be a "restriction" in the sense of Article 49 EC, for instance where it is subject to the requirements that the treatment be "normal within the professional circles concerned" in the home Member State, and that the treatment be a "medical necessity", meaning that adequate treatment cannot be obtained without undue delay in hospitals in the home Member State that have a contractual relationship with the sickness fund.[80] Where the application of the prior authorisation rules under Regulation 1408/71/EEC results in a lower level of cover where treatment is received in another Member State to that in which the patient is insured, this also constitutes a restriction in the sense of Article 49 EC.[81]

Freedom to provide and receive services in EU law is not a right without exceptions. Restrictions on the freedom to provide and receive services may be *justified* in various circumstances. The Treaty provides a limited exemption for discriminatory restrictions on the freedom to provide or receive services on the grounds of "public policy, public security and public health".[82] These three grounds of exemption are also reflected in the Treaty provision on free movement of workers, Article 39 (3) EC.[83] The Court's jurisprudence on either provision may be read as applying to the other. The main thrust of that jurisprudence is to limit the restrictions on the freedom of movement as much as possible in their scope. The grounds of exemption do not provide a wide discretion to Member States to preserve national policies. Rather, Member States must show a clear, objective and proportionate imperative of public policy, public security or public health. More importantly, the interpretation of the exemption provisions is a matter of EU, not national law, to be determined by the European Court of Justice.[84] Any suggestion that the exemption is being relied on to protect national interests from competition from other Member States

78 For instance, in Cases 286/82 & 26/83 *Luisi and Carbone* above n 62, a prohibition on export of foreign currency above a certain amount was held to restrict the freedom to receive services, as it prevented the transfer of currency necessary to pay for services received (including medical treatment) in another Member State.

79 Case C-381/93 *Commission v France* [1994] ECR I-5145, para 17; Case C-158/96 *Kohll* above n 10, para 33; Case C-368/86 *Vanbraekel* above n 67, para 45; Case C-157/99 *Geraets-Smits and Peerbooms* above n 10, para 61.

80 Case C-157/99 *Geraets-Smits and Peerbooms* above n 10, paras 60–69; Case C-385/99 *Müller-Fauré* above n 67, paras 37–44.

81 Case C-368/86 *Vanbraekel* above n 67, para 45.

82 Article 55 EC, referring to Article 46 (1) EC.

83 The grounds are also found in the Directives extending residence rights to non-nationals not exercising Treaty rights; Directive 90/365/EEC, OJ 1990 L 180/28; Directive 93/96/EEC, OJ 1993 L 317/59; Directive 90/364/EEC, OJ 1990 L 180/26.

84 Case 36/75 *Rutili* [1975] ECR 1219. However, the application of the exemption in a particular case would be a matter for the tribunal of fact, at national level, albeit operating under a duty to apply EU law (Article 234 EC; Article 10 EC).

is generally regarded by the Court as being evidence that the exemption is not justified.[85]

Where restrictions on the freedom of movement are not measures directly discriminating on grounds of nationality, but are equally applicable to nationals and non-nationals, these may still be unlawful "restrictions" in the sense of Article 49 EC. This will be so where they have the effect (or potential effect) of restricting the freedom to provide or receive services.[86] The exemptions in Articles 39 and 46 EC probably apply to such indirectly discriminatory measures. However, in addition, there is a further means of justification of such national regulatory measures, developed by the Court in its jurisprudence. This is necessary because, as mentioned above,[87] the Treaty of Rome does not envisage a completely deregulated single market,[88] but rather recognises that there are differences between national regulatory regimes, and that some national regulation is justified in the public interest.[89] Therefore, the freedom to provide services (and the other freedoms) needs to be reconciled with legitimate national regulatory measures, for instance, those concerned with consumer protection. The European Court of Justice has established a legal means by which this balance may be effected, by permitting indirectly discriminatory restrictions on the freedom to provide services, provided they are justified in pursuance of an ***objective public interest.***[90] Four conditions must be met before a non-discriminatory restriction on the freedom to provide services can be justified, and therefore held not to constitute an infringement of EU law.[91] The restriction must be applied in a non-discriminatory manner.[92] There must be imperative reasons

85 See also Directive 64/221/EEC, OJ 1964 L 56/117, Article 2 (1), which provides that the grounds of exemption may not be used to serve economic ends.

86 Examples would include national rules effectively requiring service providers to be established in a particular Member State (Case C-154/89 *Commission v France (Re Tourist Guides)* above n 75) and obstacles impinging on the economic activity itself, such as restrictions "liable to prohibit or otherwise impede" the activities of a provider of services established in another Member State where the services were lawfully provided – including advertising (Case C-76/90 *Säger* above n 62, paras 12–14; Case C-275/92 *Schindler* above n 74, paras 43–44; Case C-159/90 *Grogan* above n 76, referring to Case C-362/88 *GB-INNO-BM* above n 76).

87 See chapter 2.

88 See, with respect to services in particular, S. Weatherill, *Law and Integration in the European Union* (Oxford: Clarendon, 1995), p 256; D. Edward, "Freedom of Movement for the Regulated Professions" in R. White and B. Smythe, eds, *Current Issues in European and International Law* (Festschrift for F. Dowrick) (London: Sweet and Maxwell, 1990), p 40.

89 Weatherill, above n 88, pp 252–261.

90 The origins of this approach in the area of services lie in Case 33/74 *Van Binsbergen* [1974] ECR 1299, in which the Court held: " ... taking into account the particular nature of the services to be provided, specific requirements imposed on the person providing the service cannot be considered incompatible with the Treaty where they have as their purpose the application of ... rules justified by the general good ... which are binding upon any person established in the State in which the service is provided ..." See also Case 71/76 *Thieffry* [1977] ECR 765, para 15; Case C-384/93 *Alpine Investments* [1995] ECR I-1141.

91 See Case C-55/94 *Gebhard* above n 60, para 37; Case 22/83 *Commission v France (Insurance Services)* [1986] ECR 3663; Case 252/83 *Commission v Denmark* [1986] ECR 3713; Case 205/84 *Commission v Germany* [1986] ECR 3755; Case 206/84 *Commission v Ireland* [1986] ECR 3817.

92 If distinctions are made on the basis of nationality, then the measure can only be justified under the grounds set out in Articles 39 and 46 EC.

relating to the public interest (mandatory requirements), the public interest must not be already protected by the state of establishment (equivalence),[93] and the restriction must not be disproportionate to its ends (proportionality).[94]

The Court has not set out a precise definition of "public interest" in this context. Nor is there a fixed list of mandatory requirements, justifying non-discriminatory restrictions on the freedom to provide services, freedom of establishment or free movement of workers. The Court has recognised various interests, for instance, the application of professional rules, including those relating to the organisation of professions, qualifications, or professional ethics, for the public good,[95] the social protection provided by national social security systems,[96] the financial viability of such social security systems,[97] and consumer protection.[98] The public interest justification is by implication wider than the public policy exemption of Articles 39 and 46 EC. The existence of these mandatory requirements, or the question of whether a justifiable public interest worthy of protection is present, is a matter of EU law, not national law. Thus the European Court of Justice is empowered to decide whether national regulatory rules imposing restrictions on the freedom to provide or receive services serve a legitimate public interest. The matter of public interest becomes an EU matter, not one determined solely within the scope of competence of the Member States.

Freedom to receive health care services

Having set out the relevant EU law with respect to the freedom to provide and receive services across borders within the EU, we now turn to consider the application of these provisions to the receipt of medical treatment and other health care services across borders in the EU. Whereas the system under Regulation 1408/71/EEC implies that such cross-border medical treatment is essentially at the discretion of the national authorities in the competent home Member State, reliance on the directly effective Treaty provision of Article 49 EC implies an enforceable *right* held by patients in the EU to access cross-border health care services. In order to understand the application of the Treaty to public national health (insurance) schemes in the Member States, it is first necessary to establish some understanding of the different types of such schemes currently found in the EU, and the scope of their operation.

93 See, for example, Case C-272/94 *Guiot and Climatec* above n 74.

94 See, for example, Case 427/85 *Commission v Germany (Lawyers' Services)* [1988] ECR 1123, para 26.

95 Case 33/74 *Van Binsbergen* above n 90, para 14; Case 292/86 *Gulling* [1988] ECR 11, para 29; Case C-106/91 *Ramrath* [1992] ECR I-3351.

96 Case C-272/94 *Guiot and Climatec* above n 74.

97 Case C-120/95 *Decker* above n 10; Case C-158/96 *Kohll* above n 10; Case C-157/99 *Geraets-Smits and Peerbooms* above n 67; Case C-368/86 *Vanbraekel* above n 10.

98 Case 205/84 *Commission v Germany* above n 91, para 30; Case C-288/89 *Gouda* [1991] ECR I-4007, para 27; Case C-76/90 *Säger* above n 74, para 15; Case C-275/92 *Schindler* above n 76, para 58.

Public health care systems in the EU make different provision in terms of the entitlements of patients under each system.[99] These entitlements are determined by three factors: who is covered by the system; the types of treatment available under the system; and the range of providers from whom the patient is entitled to receive health care under the system.[100] All Member States have limited the benefits that patients can receive under their public health care systems.[101] Member States also limit the providers to which a patient has access under the system.[102] National public health care systems in the EU are said to fall into two broad types: social insurance systems and national health services.[103] Social insurance schemes are based upon the compulsory insurance of categories of persons (now expanded to include all, or virtually all, the population). Insurance premiums are usually income related, and calculated on the basis of total annual expenditure.[104] Administratively speaking, health care schemes are often integrated into the general social security system. The administration of health insurance may be entrusted to public or semi-public bodies, such as sickness funds.[105] Social insurance schemes may be further subdivided into reimbursement schemes, in which patients have to pay for care, and are reimbursed subsequently by their sickness fund; and benefits-in-kind schemes, in which patients receive care essentially free (to them)[106] from health providers, who are then paid directly by the relevant health insurance institutions.[107] National health services are funded by public taxation, and operate according to a benefits-in-kind system. They may be more or less centralised in terms of their administration.[108]

99 See above n 9.

100 J. Nickless, "*Smits-Peerbooms:* Clarification of *Kohll* and *Decker*?" 7(4) *eurohealth* (2001) 7. The Court has confirmed that, in the absence of EU-level harmonisation, it is for each Member State to determine the conditions concerning the right or duty to be insured with a social security scheme, see Case 110/79 *Coonan* [1980] ECR 1445, para 12; Case C-349/87 *Paraschi* [1991] ECR I-4501, para 15; Case 158/96 *Kohll* above n 10, para 18; and the conditions for entitlement to benefits, see Cases C-4 & 5/95 *Stöber and Pereira* [1997] ECR I-511, para 36; Case 158/96 *Kohll* above n 10, para 18; Case C-157/99 *Geraets-Smits and Peerbooms* above n 10, para 45.

101 For instance, more "luxury" types of treatment, such as cosmetic surgery, dentistry or physiotherapy, are often excluded. All Member States limit medical and pharmaceutical products available under their public health care systems, either by means of "positive" or "negative" lists. See Van der Mei, above n 8, p 225.

102 For instance, by requiring the patient to choose only from those providers with whom their insurer has negotiated a contract, or to have prior authorisation for treatment from a "non-contracted" provider; or by limiting access to specialist medical professionals by means of general practitioners exercising a "gatekeeper" role. See Van der Mei, above n 8, p 225.

103 Van der Mei, above n 8, pp 224–226; W. Palm and J. Nickless, "Access to healthcare in the European Union" 7(1) *eurohealth* (2001) 13 at 14; Jorens, above n 9.

104 Van der Mei, above n 8, p 224.

105 Ibid.

106 Patients may have to make a small individual contribution (co-payment) towards costs.

107 In the EU, Belgium, France and Luxembourg are said to operate a reimbursement social insurance system; Austria, Germany and the Netherlands to operate a benefits-in-kind social insurance system; see Palm and Nickless, above n 103.

108 In the EU, the UK and Ireland are said to operate a more centralised national health service. Italy, Portugal, Spain, Greece, Denmark, Sweden and Finland are said to operate more decentralised national health services: see Palm and Nickless, above n 103.

The analysis of the Court's jurisprudence on the receipt of health care services across borders in the EU, and, in particular, interventions by governments of the Member States before the Court in later cases, has tended to proceed on the basis of this division into "social insurance" and "public taxation" national health systems, with a further subdivision being made between reimbursement and benefits-in-kind systems. To some extent, this is also reflected in the reasoning of the Court itself. However, it is important to realise that such a categorisation has a limiting effect on the analysis. The categories represent only "ideal types". In practice it may be more difficult than the model implies to distinguish between them. All national health care systems in the EU rely on a mix of revenue sources, including compulsory or social insurance, user charges and voluntary or private insurance, with taxation playing some role in all systems.[109] Further, as Member States face similar challenges to their national health (insurance) systems, they may "borrow" solutions from other states, leading to a certain amount of convergence.[110] It follows that firm conclusions on the application of EU law to the health care funding provisions within a particular Member State cannot be drawn by simply drawing distinctions on the basis of a binary social insurance-public taxation model.

The right to publicly funded cross-border health care services on the basis of Article 49 EC was first explicitly confirmed in *Kohll*,[111] in the context of a reimbursement social insurance scheme. Mr Kohll (a Luxembourg national) challenged the refusal of authorisation for his daughter to receive dental treatment in Trier, Germany. Kohll's doctor recommended treatment by an orthodontist established there, but the social security medical supervisors refused to authorise payment for the treatment from the social security fund. Only one orthodontist established in Luxembourg would have been able to give the treatment, thus the daughter would have had to wait much longer if she were to receive treatment there, rather than in Germany.

The Court held that the "special nature of certain services does not remove them from the ambit of the fundamental principle of freedom of movement".[112] Treatment was to be provided for remuneration by an orthodontist, established in another Member State "outside any hospital infrastructure".[113] Thus the application of Articles 59 and 60 EC (now Articles 49 and 50 EC) on provision of services was not excluded in this case. Luxembourg raised a number of justifications, including the need to guarantee the quality of medical services, and the need to control health

109 See E. Mossialos et al, eds, *Funding Health Care: options for Europe* (Buckingham: Open University Press, 2002), pp 3–11. Mossialos et al have developed a typology of three "clusters" of health care funding, with France, Germany and the Netherlands at around 80% social insurance and 10–15% taxation; Greece and Belgium at around 30–40% social insurance and 30–40% taxation and Portugal, Italy, Switzerland, Spain, the UK, and Denmark at around 0–15% social insurance and 60–80% taxation. It is clear that the groupings of Member States differ under this approach to that described above: see above n 103–108.

110 Jorens, above n 9, p 84.

111 Case C-158/96 *Kohll* above n 10.

112 Case C-158/96 *Kohll* above n 10, para 20.

113 Case C-158/96 *Kohll* above n 10, para 29.

expenditure. The Court pointed out that taking up and pursuing the professional activities of doctor and dentist have been subject to EU-level harmonisation since the 1970s,[114] and thus held that the quality of medical services was guaranteed. The Court also accepted the argument of Mr Kohll, that he was asking for reimbursement only at the Luxembourg rate, and so application of the free movement rules presented no threat to the financial stability of the social security scheme.[115] Justification in this case was therefore not established.

The *Kohll* decision left a great deal of uncertainty with respect to the application of Article 49 EC to national health (insurance) systems. For instance, did the ruling apply only where reimbursement was used as the funding mechanism, or could it also apply to benefits-in-kind schemes? Could the principles in *Kohll* be applied to systems funded more heavily through public taxation? Did the ruling apply to hospital, as well as extramural, care? In what circumstances might a threat to the financial stability of a national social security scheme justify a restriction on the freedom to provide and receive publicly funded health care services across borders? What other justifications might be available, and in what circumstances? It is not surprising, therefore, that further litigation followed. In July 2001, the Court decided two further cases on cross-border receipt of health care, and these were followed by a decision in another two cases in May 2003, and one in October 2003. These cases concerned claims against the Belgian, Dutch and French social insurance health systems, and again concerned challenges to refusals to authorise cross-border medical treatment under Regulation 1408/71/EEC.

The *Vanbraekel* case concerned a Belgian national, who sought orthopaedic surgery for bilateral gonarthrosis (a disease of the knees).[116] The patient was insured under the Belgian social insurance system, with a sickness fund called the Alliance nationale des mutualités chrétiennes (ANMC). She sought authorisation from the ANMC for the treatment to be carried out in France. Belgian law provided that authorisation under Article 22 of Regulation 1408/71/EEC was only to be given in very exceptional cases, where an expert medical specialist certified that the treatment was not available in Belgium, and specified exactly where,[117] and for what period of time, treatment would be given in another Member State. Authorisation was therefore refused, on the grounds that the patient did not have a supporting opinion from a doctor practising in a national university institution. In fact, the patient went ahead with the operation in France, and then sought reimbursement from the ANMC. An expert report subsequently sought by the national court determined that the patient's condition necessitated treatment abroad. The ANMC was therefore ordered to reimburse the costs of treatment. However, the costs came to FRF 38 608.99 if the reimbursement was calculated according to French legislation;

114 See further chapter 6.
115 Case C-158/96 *Kohll* above n 10, para 37.
116 Case C-368/86 *Vanbraekel* above n 67.
117 In which institution, or under which medical professional.

but FRF 49 935.44 if calculated according to Belgian legislation. This amounted to a difference of nearly € 1700. The question then arose of which scheme was the correct basis for the calculation: the scheme under which the patient was insured, or the scheme under which the treatment took place? This question was referred to the European Court of Justice.[118]

The Court, going further than *Kohll*, held that Article 49 EC applies to hospital care.[119] The Court then found that if a person has a lower level of cover when medical treatment is received in another Member State, than if given the same treatment in the Member State of insurance, this is a "restriction" in the sense of Article 49 EC.[120] The Court considered, but rejected, a number of possible justifications for the restriction.[121] The Court went on to find that, where the amount of reimbursement is less if calculated according to the scheme of the Member State of treatment than if calculated according to the scheme of the competent Member State, the sickness insurance fund must grant additional reimbursement covering that difference.[122]

The Court was also asked whether, in such circumstances, the competent Member State is permitted to limit the amount to be reimbursed, for instance in accordance with its rules on types of treatment available under its public health insurance scheme. It will be remembered that Article 36 of Regulation 1408/71/EEC provides that benefits in kind provided by one Member State on behalf of another in accordance with the regulation "shall be fully refunded". Did the application of Article 49 EC mean that the competent Member State was obliged to refund in full health care services carried out in another Member State, on the basis of an entitlement in Article 49 EC, in the terms provided by the *host* Member State? The Court held that this is not the case. A full refund in the sense of Article 36 of Regulation 1408/71/EEC is only for services carried out *on behalf of the competent Member State.* This implies that it is for the competent Member State to set the terms on which reimbursement is available.

Kohll and *Vanbraekel* concerned the application of Article 49 EC to health care systems where reimbursement is the norm. The question of whether the principles established in those cases apply also to social insurance systems where provision of benefits-in-kind is the norm arose in *Geraets-Smits and Peerbooms*, in 2001,[123] although in a context in which patients insured under such a scheme were seeking reimbursement. The patients, both Dutch nationals, sought reimbursement from their sickness funds for the costs of hospital treatment incurred in Germany

118 Under the Article 234 EC preliminary rulings procedure: see chapter 2.

119 Case C-368/86 *Vanbraekel* above n 67, paras 38–43.

120 Case C-368/86 *Vanbraekel* above n 67, paras 44–45.

121 The risk of seriously undermining the financial balance of a social security system (para 47; see Case C-158/96 *Kohll* above n 10, para 41); the objective of maintaining a balanced medical and hospital service open to all (para 48; see Case C-158/96 *Kohll*, para 50); to maintain treatment capacity or medical competence on the national territory, so as to safeguard the health, or even life, of the population (para 49; Case C-158/96 *Kohll*, para 51).

122 Case C-368/86 *Vanbraekel* above n 67.

123 Case C-157/99 *Geraets-Smits and Peerbooms* above n 10.

and Austria respectively. Mrs Geraets-Smits received multidisciplinary treatment for Parkinson's disease at a hospital in Germany. The rules of the Dutch sickness fund provided that care to be reimbursed is that to be determined "in accordance with what is normal in the professional circles concerned", which in practice meant professional circles in the Netherlands. The treatment received by the patient was not regarded as such "normal" treatment and thus reimbursement was refused. Reimbursement was also refused on the grounds that satisfactory treatment for Parkinson's disease was available in the Netherlands, and there was thus no "medical necessity" for the treatment in Germany. Mr Peerbooms (aged 35) fell into a coma after a road accident, and was transferred from the Dutch hospital originally treating him to a hospital in Austria. There he received special intensive therapy, using neurostimulation. This therapy was only available on an experimental basis in the Netherlands, and not available for patients over the age of 25 years. Reimbursement was sought, and refused on the grounds that as adequate treatment could have been given by a provider in the Netherlands with whom the sickness fund had a contractual relationship, there was no "medical necessity" for the treatment. Furthermore, the treatment carried out in Austria was not regarded as "normal" in Dutch professional circles.

As in *Vanbraekel*, the Court confirmed that Article 49 EC applies to hospital care.[124] The Court explicitly rejected the argument, raised by a number of governments of Member States before the Court, that a benefits-in-kind sickness insurance scheme, where hospitals are usually paid directly by the sickness insurance funds, in accordance with agreed pre-set fees established through their contractual relationships, cannot constitute an economic activity in the sense of Articles 49 and 50 EC.[125] The Court pointed out that in these cases, the patients had in fact paid the health care providers directly, and then sought reimbursement from their sickness insurance funds. The Court went on to find that the requirements that treatment be "normal in the professional circles concerned" and that treatment must be a "medical necessity", meaning that adequate treatment could not be given in a hospital with which the sickness fund has a contractual relationship, are "restrictions" in the sense of Article 49 EC.[126]

On the question of justification, the Court reaffirmed that the possible risk of seriously undermining the financial balance of a social security system, the need to maintain a balanced medical and hospital service open to all, and the need to maintain medical capacity and professional competence to safeguard the health or life of the national population, might all constitute legitimate public interest justifications for a restriction on the freedom to provide services.[127] The Court found that the prior authorisation requirement, according to which if treatment by a non-contracted care provider was to be reimbursed, a prior authorisation

124 Case C-157/99 *Geraets-Smits and Peerbooms* above n 10, paras 47–59.
125 Paras 55–58.
126 Paras 60–69.
127 Paras 72–75.

was needed, was "necessary and reasonable".[128] This was on the basis that such a requirement allowed for necessary planning of hospital provision in the Member State concerned, to ensure sufficient and permanent access for the population of that Member State to a balanced range of high-quality hospital treatment. It also allowed for control of costs, consonant with prevention of inefficient use of financial, technical and human resources. If patients could simply seek treatment with health care providers with whom their sickness funds had no contractual relations, all planning and cost-control would be impossible.[129] This is so whether the non-contracted providers were established in the Netherlands, or elsewhere in the EU. However, the Court noted that while EU law does not therefore in principle preclude a system of prior authorisation for reimbursement of care carried out by non-contracted providers, the detailed operation of such a system must be justified by reference to overriding public interest considerations, and must meet the principle of proportionality.

The Court then considered the two conditions under the Dutch prior authorisation rules. With regard to the condition that the treatment must be considered "normal in the professional circles concerned", the Court reaffirmed that it is for Member States to decide what medical treatment and health care provision falls within the scope of their public national health (insurance) system.[130] However, when exercising that power, Member States must comply with EU law. So a prior authorisation scheme "cannot legitimise discretionary decisions taken by the national authorities which are liable to negate the effectiveness of provisions of Community law, in particular those relating to a fundamental freedom".[131] It follows that prior authorisation schemes must be based on objective, non-discriminatory criteria, known in advance, which circumscribe the discretion of national authorities administering the scheme. There must also be scope for an expeditious, and judicially reviewable, decision, within such a scheme.[132] The Dutch rule at issue referred to the views of professional circles in the Netherlands. Interestingly the Court held that this did not comply with the above criteria: rather only an authorisation system based on "what is sufficiently tried and tested by international medical science" would comply.[133] With regard to the condition that the treatment must be "medically necessary" for prior authorisation to be granted with respect to treatment received from a provider with which the sickness insurance fund had no contractual relations, the Court noted that this applied whether the relevant healthcare provider was situated within or outside the Netherlands. Therefore, the Court found that such a requirement would be justified, provided that the condition is interpreted to mean that authorisation may be refused only if "the same or equally effective treatment" can

128 Para 80.
129 Para 81.
130 See Case 238/82 *Duphar* [1984] ECR 523.
131 Case C-157/99 *Geraets-Smits and Peerbooms* above n 10, para 90.
132 Para 90.
133 Para 94.

be given, "without undue delay", from a healthcare provider with which the sickness fund has a contractual relationship.[134] Furthermore, in making this determination, the national authorities must take into account both the patient's medical record at the time authorisation is sought *and* the patient's past medical history.

In *Müller-Fauré and Van Riet*,[135] the Court confirmed its rulings in *Geraets-Smits and Peerbooms*. Ms Müller-Fauré received dental treatment while on holiday in Germany, and on her return sought reimbursement from the Dutch "Zwijndrecht" mutual sickness insurance fund, which under normal circumstances grants insured persons benefits-in-kind in the form of free (to the patient) medical treatment, not reimbursement of costs incurred for medical treatment. This was refused on the grounds that no exceptional circumstances justified reimbursement of her costs. Likewise, Ms Van Riet sought authorisation from her sickness insurance fund (the "Amsterdam fund") to have an arthroscopy performed in a Belgian hospital, because the treatment could be carried out much sooner in Belgium. This was refused, but in the meantime, Ms Van Riet had the procedure carried out in Belgium and subsequently sought reimbursement. The Dutch national court referred to the European Court of Justice on the question whether the Dutch system, which provided that, where treatment is sought from a health care provider with whom the insurance fund has not entered into an agreement, prior authorisation[136] is required, was compatible with EU law.

The Court restated its conclusion in *Geraets-Smits and Peerbooms* that such a system constitutes a barrier to the freedom to provide services.[137] The Court went on to explore further the question of objective justification. It reiterated that the protection of public health constitutes a legitimate justification in these circumstances. Thus the objective of maintaining a high-quality, balanced medical and hospital service open to all, and of ensuring medical capacity and professional competence can justify restrictions on the freedom to provide services.[138] In this instance, the justification put forward was inextricably linked to the way in which the Dutch social security system is financed and to the control of expenditure under the Dutch national health (insurance) system.[139] This raised a second possible justification, again also accepted in the previous jurisprudence, the risk of seriously undermining the financial balance of the social security system. Here the Court in *Müller-Fauré* drew a distinction between intramural and extramural health care. With respect to extramural care, the Court found no evidence that removal of the requirement for prior authorisation would result in a risk of seriously undermining the financial balance of the social security system.[140] By contrast, with respect to hospital services,

134 Para 103.
135 Case C-385/99 *Müller-Fauré* above n 67.
136 Such authorisation is granted only where it is a medical necessity.
137 Case C-385/99 *Müller-Fauré* above n 67, paras 37–45, 103.
138 Paras 67–69.
139 Para 71.
140 Paras 93–98.

again following *Geraets-Smits and Peerbooms*, if insured persons were entitled to use the services of hospitals with which their sickness insurance fund had no agreement (whether those hospitals were situated in the Netherlands or another Member State), "all the planning which goes into the system of agreements in an effort to guarantee a rationalised, stable, balanced and accessible supply of hospital services would be jeopardised at a stroke".[141] Where the Court went further than in *Geraets-Smits and Peerbooms*, however, was with respect to what is a legitimate ground on which prior authorisation could be refused under the Dutch system. The Court considered the criterion of "without undue delay", holding that such an assessment must be based on an assessment of the individual patient's medical condition. Further, a refusal to grant prior authorisation based not on fear of wastage resulting from hospital over-capacity, but solely on the ground that there are waiting lists within that Member State for the hospital treatment concerned, cannot amount to a proper justification.[142] This is because arguments to the effect that such waiting lists are necessary, at least as argued before the Court in this case, amounted in the view of the Court to no more than a consideration of a "purely economic nature",[143] which can never justify a restriction on a fundamental freedom in EU law.[144]

The Court had another opportunity to confirm its rulings in *Vanbraekel*, *Geraets-Smits and Peerbooms*, and *Müller-Fauré and Van Riet* in October 2003. The *Inizan* case[145] again concerned a refusal, this time by a French sickness insurance fund (the Caisse primaire d'assurance maladie des Hauts-de-Seine), to reimburse treatment in a German hospital sought by Ms Inizan, resident in France. According to national law, such reimbursement was subject to prior authorisation, which would only be given if the same or equally effective treatment to that sought could not be carried out on the home territory without undue delay. Ms Inizan sought a particular package of multidisciplinary pain treatment, available in Germany, but the French authorities found that equivalent treatments were available in France, without any undue delay. The Court reiterated that the prior authorisation rule would be *prima facie* a restriction on the freedom to provide and receive services under Article 49 EC.[146] However, such a rule, in the case of hospital treatment, would be justified,[147] so long as it is based on objective non-discriminatory criteria, and based on a procedural system which is easily accessible, and subject to judicial review.[148]

The Court was also specifically asked in *Inizan* whether Article 22 of Regulation 1408/71/EEC is valid, in the light of the application of Article 49 EC to free

141 Para 82
142 Para 92.
143 Ibid.
144 Para 72, citing Case C-398/95 *SETTG* [1997] ECR I-3091 and Case C-158/96 *Kohll* above n 10.
145 Case C-56/01 *Inizan v Caisse primaire d'assurance maladie des Hauts-de-Seine* [2003] ECR I-(23 October 2003, nyr in ECR).
146 Para 54.
147 Para 56, citing Case C-157/99 *Geraets-Smits and Peerbooms* above n 10, paras 76–80, and Case C-385/99 *Müller-Fauré* above n 67, paras 76–81.
148 Para 57.

movement of patients. The Court explained that Article 22 does not regulate in any way the reimbursement by competent Member States, at their home rates, of costs incurred in receiving medical treatment in another Member State.[149] What Article 22 does is to confer an entitlement, in certain circumscribed circumstances, to medical treatment provided by the host Member State on behalf of the competent Member State, in accordance with the legislation of the host Member State, as if the patient were resident in the host Member State.[150] The competent Member State then must reimburse the host Member State, under Article 36 of Regulation 1408/71/EEC.[151] Thus Article 22 helps to facilitate the free movement of persons, including patients, by granting additional rights (to be compensated according to the tariffs in the host Member State) to those available under Article 49 EC.[152] In any event, the Community legislature is not prohibited from attaching conditions to the rights of freedom of movement for workers.[153] Therefore, Article 22 of Regulation 1408/71/EEC remains valid.[154]

Thus Member States remain free to determine the content and scope of entitlements to medical treatment under their public national health (insurance) systems, *provided that* this is effected in such a way that any restrictions on free movement are objective, non-discriminatory on the basis of nationality or residence, subject to judicial review and interpreted in a non-discriminatory EU context.[155] A scheme that allows patients to visit "any orthodontist in Luxembourg" must be interpreted to mean "any orthodontist in the EU". "Normal in the professional circles concerned" means "normal according to accepted international medical practice". "Any non-contracted provider" means "any non-contracted provider anywhere in the EU", and it should be equally easy to obtain treatment from a non-contracted provider in another Member State and from a non-contracted provider in one's home Member State. Where national health (insurance) systems operate on the basis of negative or positive lists of pharmaceuticals or other medical products that may be accessed under the system, these must be drawn up without discrimination on grounds of nationality.[156] Where a national system allows exceptional use of non-contracted or private providers,[157] this must extend to providers established in other Member States. Extramural healthcare that does not have any effect on the financial stability

149 Para 19.
150 Para 20.
151 Ibid.
152 Para 22.
153 Para 23.
154 Para 26.
155 See Nickless, above n 100 at 9.
156 For instance, the same product but with a different name in another Member State must be included.
157 For instance, in Spain, a patient injured significantly nearer to a private hospital than a hospital contracted to the national health system is treated in the private hospital, which is then reimbursed in full by the national health service; see J. Nickless, "The Internal Market and the Social Nature of Health Care" in R. Baeten, M. McKee and E. Mossialos, eds, *The Impact of EU Law on Health Care Systems* (Brussels: PIE Peter Lang, 2003), p 68.

of the home Member State's scheme may be procured in another Member State without prior authorisation, but the amount to be reimbursed is only that available had the healthcare been received in the home Member State. It may therefore be more beneficial to the patient to seek prior authorisation, in which case reimbursement is of the cost of the treatment according to the Member State in which it was received.[158] Intramural (hospital) care may still be subject to prior authorisation, provided it meets the requirements above, and in particular the basis for the prior authorisation is not simply based on the existence of waiting lists on the national territory.[159] The amount to be reimbursed is also calculated according to the rules of the home Member State, apparently even if that means that the patient pockets the difference.[160]

Thus the cross-border patients litigation has had an effect at the margins on Member States' ability to determine the terms under which patients may access health care services under their public national health (insurance) systems. Certain national rules in this respect may be unlawful, under directly effective EU law. National rules may also have to be adjusted, in order to be viable, if their interpretation means opening of access to health care across borders in ways that are not consonant with national priorities, for instance those related to cost-containment, such as the rule in *Kohll* restricting access only to Luxembourg orthodontists. However, the restrictions placed by EU law on national discretion in this respect remain fairly minimal. Overall, Member States retain discretion over the scope and organisation of their public national health (insurance) systems.

A number of questions remain unresolved after *Vanbraekel*, *Geraets-Smits and Peerbooms*, *Müller-Fauré and Van Riet* and *Inizan*. Further litigation is to be expected. It is still unclear whether the rulings apply to national health systems that are funded by a greater proportion of public taxation than social insurance. At least one national court, the English High Court, thinks that they do. In *R (on the application of Yvonne Watts) v Bedford Primary Care Trust and Secretary of State for Health*,[161] Munby, J considered a claim by Yvonne Watts, who, facing a delay in receiving a hip replacement operation, first sought permission to receive the treatment abroad and have it paid for by the national health authority (Bedford Primary Care Trust), and on refusal, subsequently travelled to France for the operation, and claimed reimbursement from the Trust or the Secretary of State for Health. Watts failed on the facts, as she was unable to show that she faced an "undue delay", as, at the time she had the operation abroad, she was facing a delay of only three to four months.[162] What is important here, though, is that Munby J, applying the judgments in *Geraets-Smits* and *Müller-Fauré*, held that, in principle, the application

158 According to Article 22 of Regulation 1408/71/EEC; see Jorens, above n 9, pp 99, 111–114.

159 Case C-385/99 *Müller-Fauré* above n 67, para 92.

160 See Jorens, above n 9, pp 114–116.

161 [2003] EWHC 2228 (Admin), 1 October 2003.

162 The UK High Court did find that a delay of one year, for such an operation, where the patient suffered considerable pain and mobility difficulties, would be "undue": [2003] EWHC 2228 (Admin) at para 158.

of Article 49 EC in the context of a right to be reimbursed for the cost of medical treatment obtained abroad remains the same irrespective of whether the reimbursement comes from a national health insurance fund or from a national budget.[163]

However, the interpretation of the English High Court of the judgments in *Geraets-Smits* and *Müller-Fauré* relies heavily on the distinction between reimbursement systems and benefits-in-kind systems, rather than engaging directly with the differences between social insurance health systems and health systems funded by public taxation. The Court has not explicitly considered the operation of the principles developed in *Kohll*, *Vanbraekel*, *Geraets-Smits and Peerbooms*, *Müller-Fauré and Van Riet* and *Inizan* in a national health system funded largely by public taxation.[164] The English High Court's ruling places considerable emphasis on the statement of the European Court of Justice at the very end of its ruling in paragraph 103 of *Müller-Fauré*, to the effect that "as has already been made clear in paragraph 39 above, a medical service does not cease to be a provision of services because it is paid for by a national health service . . . or by a system providing benefits in kind . . . ".[165] Munby J read "national health service" here to mean a national health system like the UK's NHS. Unfortunately, this is not quite what paragraph 39 actually says: it merely states that simply because a national health (insurance) system operates on the basis of benefits-in-kind, this does not take its operation outside the scope of Article 49 EC.[166] There is definitely scope here for future litigation.[167]

Whatever national courts may make of the health care rulings, it is not easy to reconcile the earlier public education rulings of the Court with the more recent cases on health care provision.[168] It seems that simply asserting that a state has a "public duty" to provide a particular welfare service, or that the money came from the "public purse", as the Court did in the education case of *Humbel*,[169] is insufficient to bring the matter outside the scope of Article 49 EC.[170] Commentators such as Davies,[171] van der Mei[172] and Flear[173] argue that neither the link between the payer

163 [2003] EWHC 2228 (Admin) at paras 105, 107–110.

164 McHale and Bell think the principles unlikely to apply in the UK context: see J. McHale and M. Bell, "Traveller's checks" *Health Service Journal*, 23 May 2002, pp 39–41. See also C. Garcia de Cortazar, "*Kohll* and *Decker*, or That is Somebody Else's Problem" 6 *European Journal of Health Law* (1999) 397 with respect to Spain.

165 [2003] EWHC 2228 (Admin) at paras 104–105.

166 The relevant part of para 39 reads, ". . . the fact that the applicable rules . . . provide, as regards sickness insurance, for benefits in kind rather than reimbursement does not mean that the medical treatment in question falls outside the scope of the freedom to provide services guaranteed by the EC Treaty."

167 The case is currently subject to an appeal and has been referred to the European Court of Justice.

168 See Hatzopolous, above n 59 at 692–693, who is particularly critical of the Court's (lack of) reasoning in *Geraets-Smits/Peerbooms* in this respect; N. Bernard, "A 'New Governance' Approach to Economic, Social and Cultural Rights in the EU" in T. Hervey and J. Kenner, *Economic and Social Rights under the EU Charter of Fundamental Rights: A Legal Perspective* (Oxford: Hart, 2003), pp 249–253.

169 Case 263/85 *Belgian State v Humbel* above n 61.

170 Davies, above n 10 at 32–33.

171 Davies, above n 10, at 33–34.

172 Van der Mei, above n 8, pp 313–315, especially p 314.

173 M. Flear, Case note on *Müller-Fauré*, 41 CMLRev (2004) 209.

and the recipient, nor the fact of an identifiable payment for a particular service, provide the crucial defining factor for application of Article 49 EC. Rather, the Court's earlier jurisprudence suggests that whether welfare is a service depends on whether it is organised according to a system where payer and provider are separate, independent institutions. This introduces a "market-like model" to the provision of welfare, and in particular involves a structure where there is an element of choice either for the payer or for the recipient of the welfare service, or both. If this analysis is correct, a monopoly state provider of free-to-recipients health care would not fall within EU law. This is probably the case whether the system is funded as a national health service or through insurance. A unitary public insurance system, characterised by subsidisation and compulsory membership, probably has insufficient elements of choice. However, if Member States use market models to improve efficiency in provision of public services, and justify the structure of their healthcare provision in terms of choice for "consumers" of such care,[174] the scope for application of Article 49 EC to such welfare services increases.[175] So, for instance, a system characterised by a variety of social insurance sickness funds, perhaps some or all of which are unsubsidised, and of a semi-private nature, would fall within EU law.

Second, the difference between intramural and extramural treatment will need further elaboration. The Court noted the difficulty of drawing this distinction in *Müller-Fauré*, but this was not at issue in those proceedings.[176] What is the status of so-called "policlinical treatment", which is in practice carried out in a hospital, but need not be so?[177] Is it relevant that a particular treatment is carried out extramurally in another Member State?[178] What about outpatient care? What about combined treatments?[179] Third, with respect to prior authorisation rules, still permitted for intramural treatment, there is scope for litigation over the term "normal treatment"

174 See, for example, the UK health service reforms of the 1990s (see D. Hughes, "The Reorganisation of the NHS – The Rhetoric and the Reality of the Internal Market" 54 MLR (1991) 88; R. Flynn and G. Williams, *Contracting for Health: Quasi Markets and the NHS* (Oxford: OUP, 1997); W. Ranade, "Reforming the British National Health Service: all change, no change?" in W. Ranade, ed, *Markets and Health Care: A Comparative Analysis* (Harlow: Longman, 1998)); and the Dutch health service reforms following the Dekker Report in 1987 (R. Robinson, "Managed competition: health care reform in the Netherlands" in W. Ranade, ed, *Markets and Health Care: A Comparative Analysis* (Harlow: Longman, 1998)). For an overview, see Freeman, above n 9, pp 66–74; Saltman, Figueras and Sakellarides, above n 9; C. Barker, *The Health Care Policy Process* (London: Sage, 1996), pp 151–157; R.B. Saltman, "A conceptual overview of recent health care reforms" 4 *European Journal of Public Health* (1994) 287. Contrast the Swedish case: see R.B. Saltman, "Health reform in Sweden: the road beyond cost containment" in W. Ranade, ed, *Markets and Health Care: A Comparative Analysis* (Harlow: Longman, 1998). See the special issue of the *European Journal of Public Health* Vol 5(3), 1995.

175 Davies concludes that the current structure of the British NHS, a centralised benefits-in-kind national health system, but divided into funds and providers, would probably not be a system with sufficient independence between the relevant institutions to fall within Article 49 EC. See Davies, above n 10, at 36–37.

176 Case C-385/99 *Müller-Fauré* above n 67, para 75.

177 E. Steyger, "National Health Care Systems Under Fire (but not too heavily)" 29 *Legal Issues of Economic Integration* (2002) 97.

178 Flear, above n 173.

179 Ibid.

with regard to international medical science. This standard implies that national courts applying the directly effective Treaty provisions, or the European Court of Justice, must consider medical practice outside the EU. Particularly with relatively new treatments, there is likely to be considerable room for difference among professional opinion, and patients are likely to exploit this, as seen in the *Vanbraekel*, *Geraets-Smits and Peerbooms* and *Inizan* cases. Given the cultural contingency of health care, even within the relatively homogenous EU, this may be very difficult to resolve.[180] The concept of "the same or equally effective treatment" is similarly likely to be the subject of significant disagreement, which again we can expect to be resolved through litigation. Likewise, and particularly where there are waiting lists, in spite of some clarification in *Müller-Fauré*, there is scope for disagreement over what constitutes "undue delay". The Court has said this needs to be defined on a case-by-case basis, with reference to the probable trajectory of the disease, the patient's medical history, and also matters such as pain control or the nature of the patient's disability, in particular where these make it difficult for the patient to continue to work.[181]

Finally, the elements of justification will need further elaboration. It is not entirely clear whether Member States may lawfully make it more difficult for providers in other Member States to obtain contracts with sickness insurance funds, on the basis that this is justified by need to maintain capacity, and if so, under what circumstances.[182] The Court considered that an "outflow of patients" reliant upon Article 49 EC, leading to "logistical and financial wastage",[183] might jeopardise the maintenance of an adequate, balanced and permanent supply of high-quality hospital treatment, and thus restrictive prior authorisation rules may be justified in some circumstances. What is a sufficiently high "outflow of patients" to trigger this justification? If patients go abroad to circumvent waiting lists, surely that will lead to an *improvement* in the provision for those remaining at home, rather than "wastage"? This argument was accepted by the English High Court in the *Watts* case discussed

180 Mossialos and McKee, above n 47, p 99; Steyger, above n 176; for examples of difference in healthcare practice between Member States of the EU, see C.G. Helman, *Culture, Health and Illness* (Oxford: Butterworth-Heinemann, 2000), pp 60, 180.

181 Case C-385/99 *Müller-Fauré* above n 67, para 90. Mossialos and McKee, above n 47, p 99, posit that "undue delay" should now be interpreted in the patient's favour, rather than the national authority's. Flear, above n 173, points out that the Court in *Müller-Fauré* takes the view that the assessment is to be made not simply on the basis of medical need alone, but also by reference to matters such as "for example" the patient's ability to work. What other matters are relevant, for instance, the impact of the delay on the patient's family life – is not yet clear.

182 Nickless, above n 100, and above n 157, p 68 thinks not: "it should be just as easy for a foreign provider to obtain a contract as it is for a domestic one". There are no hard and fast rules on the application of EU public procurement rules to providers of health care services (see Hatzopoulos, above n 59, at p 716). It appears that the European Court of Justice has held that the public procurement rules may apply to social security institutions when they contract with service providers: see Case C-76/97 *Tögel* [1998] ECR I-5357.

183 Case C-157/99 *Geraets-Smits/Peerbooms* above n 10, para 106; Case C-385/99 *Müller-Fauré* above n 67, para 91.

above.[184] Munby J took the view that, as patients take advantage of their rights in EU law to travel abroad for medical treatment where they face "undue delay" at home, the UK NHS would move from a position of under-capacity to one of adequate or balanced capacity. However, this does not take account of the use of hospital waiting lists as a mechanism to contain national health spending. Obviously, short-term costs would be increased where patients travel abroad for treatment, as those treatments would have to be covered in that financial year, in addition to the treatments undertaken for other patients in the home Member State. This has implications for financial planning for national health authorities. In the longer term, however, these would be offset by the fact that a patient who had already travelled abroad for a treatment would not require the treatment at home in the following financial year. Of course, some patients actually die before they can receive treatment, and in their case, if such patients were to travel abroad, the national health service would have to fund treatment that they might never have had to meet. In reality, however, the majority of critically ill patients are unlikely to be able to travel abroad for treatment.

In any event, the details of justification are likely to vary from situation to situation, and may even depend upon analysis of actual movements of patients across borders, and their financial implications, in particular if the Court continues with its quantitative approach[185] to justification. In *Müller-Fauré*, the Court appeared to take the view that, taking into account various factors limiting cross-border treatments in practice, with respect to non-hospital services, there was unlikely to be any significant impact on the financing of the Dutch social security system. Does this imply that, if in the future the number of patients seeking cross-border, non-hospital treatments increased significantly, so that there was a true jeopardy to the financing of the system, then restrictions on such movements would at that point be justified?[186] Again, this suggests that further litigation will be necessary to resolve disputes at the margins.

Impact on access to health services and wider implications

Assessment of the case law on free movement of patients based on Article 49 EC varies. Many commentators, particularly after *Kohll*, extrapolating from the terms of the judgment, considered possible worst-case scenarios.[187] Criticisms focussed in particular on the impact on the stability and internal balance of national health

184 *Watts* above n 161, at para 148: "... the idea that, if given the chance so many NHS patients will go abroad to be treated that the NHS will face the spectre of *overcapacity*, with resultant logistical or financial wastage, seems to me to be wholly unproven".

185 Jorens, above n 9, p 110.

186 A point noted by Flear, above n 173: "Paradoxically, the more patients exercise their right, the more cause there is for limiting it."

187 This is particularly so for press comments, see Steyger, above n 176; see, for example, "EU patients entitled to treatment abroad" *Irish Times*, 13 July 2001; "Ruling frees NHS patients to seek treatment abroad" and "A healthy opportunity" *The Sunday Times*, 15 July 2001; "NHS may pay for EU care" *Independent on Sunday*, 15 July 2001; see also Garcia de Cortazar, above n 163, and the views of the German government as cited in Sieveking, above n 31.

(insurance) systems, and the viability of their social goals.[188] This applies to both competent Member States, whose ability to restrict consumption of health care services is reduced by the effect of the rulings, and host Member States. Certain host Member States, for instance, those Member States that provide higher standards of service, better value for money and a greater choice for patients, or whose medical profession enjoys a high reputation, might experience an unpredictable influx of patients. This may have an impact on standards of national health care provision for nationals, for instance longer waiting lists. As a worst-case scenario, if such pressures reached extreme levels, there might be a temptation on the part of the national authorities of those states to reduce the quality of service provided, in order to discourage such "medical tourism". Were this to happen, it would represent a classic deregulatory "race to the bottom". As we will shortly see, it appears that such assessments are probably unduly pessimistic.

More specifically, the rulings are seen by some commentators to have a detrimental effect on health care planning and capacity maintenance,[189] both crucial to the sustaining of quality standards and values of social equity in health care provision. States calculate their health care needs by reference to their populations. Too much movement of patients might result in overburdening of some hospitals, and corresponding under use of others, possibly leading to closures. This could jeopardise the social principle of effective health care accessible to all, which underpins the national health (insurance) systems of all Member States. The ability of patients to access (and be reimbursed for) innovative treatments that might not be recognised as reimbursable within their home state may imply a loss of control over the reimbursement of such new and "unproven" treatments. The ruling in *Geraets-Smits/Peerbooms* certainly seems to imply a loss of control at the national level over the assessment of what is regarded as a "normal" treatment for a particular condition. This may take on a particular complexion in the new Central and Eastern European Member States,[190] due to become part of the EU on enlargement in 2004 and 2007. Given the significantly lower average incomes in the accession states, one might expect movements to be fairly minimal.[191] However, particularly at the borders, there might be exceptions to this principle. Also, at least among the wealthier citizens of the new Member States, the fact that many treatments are not available in their home Member State may well encourage patients to seek treatments elsewhere in the EU. If the new Member State could not show that the same or equally effective

188 R. Baeten, "European Integration and National Healthcare Systems: a challenge for social policy" 8 *infose*, November 2001, pp 1–2; Jorens, above n 9.

189 See Jorens, above n 9, pp 87-88; 99–100.

190 The Central and Eastern European accession countries have adopted social insurance health systems: see Marrée and Groenewegen, above n 8; WHO and European Commission, *Health Status Overview for Countries of Central and Eastern Europe that are Candidates for Accession to the European Union* (Copenhagen, WHO, 2002).

191 No data on likely movements from Central and Eastern European states is currently available: see A.P. den Exter, "Legal Consequences of EU Accession for Central and Eastern European Health Care Systems" 8 ELJ (2002) 556 at 563.

treatment to that sought could be carried out on the home territory without undue delay, it might not be able to rely on a prior authorisation rule.[192] It follows from *Geraets-Smits/Peerbooms* that decisions about cost-effectiveness in terms of determining which treatments are to be reimbursed within a particular national health (insurance) system may no longer be kept within the "closed" national system, with its own "home-grown" experts, but must be subject to exogenous assessment. Ultimately, the decision to reimburse certain types of treatment, and not others, in the context of limited overall resources for health care, constitutes a choice to allocate resources to meet the health care needs of one part of the population rather than another. In the new Member States, such resource allocation is even more sensitive, as the amounts available for spending on the national health system are restricted.[193] Accession states are, if such a thing is possible, even more concerned about cost containment within their health care systems than the existing Member States.[194] The prospect of many patients seeking cross-border health care on the basis of *Kohll*, at the expense of the national health insurance systems, is worrying to the governments of those countries.[195] This may influence the Court's assessment of the justifications with respect to maintaining the balance of a social security system.

The same reasoning applies to the use of EU law by litigants seeking to avoid waiting times for health care services under their national health (insurance) systems. States use hospital waiting lists in effect as a tool to constrain spending. Waiting lists also arise as a logical consequence of policy decisions about resource allocation. Again, the ruling in *Müller-Fauré*, that a refusal to authorise hospital treatment in another Member State *solely* on the grounds that there are waiting lists for the treatment concerned in the home Member State does not constitute a justification for a restriction on the freedom to provide services, implies a loss of control at national level over the use of hospital waiting lists. The ability of certain (litigious) patients to utilise EU law in circumstances such as those arising in *Geraets-Smits* and *Müller-Fauré* may be regarded as an inappropriate judicial interference with political processes. In general, then, these kinds of pressures may jeopardise the overall structure of national health (insurance) systems, and their financial and administrative arrangements.

However, the overall impact of such EU rules on the Member States' discretion to specify the scope and organisation of their national health systems is likely to be limited. This is partly because restrictions on freedom to provide and receive

192 See Case C-56/01 *Inizan* above n 145.

193 Central and Eastern European states are spending a falling proportion of their GDP on social policy, of which health care is a significant component. See Z. Ferge, "Welfare and 'Ill-fare' Systems in Central and Eastern Europe" in R. Sykes, B. Palier, and P.M. Prior, eds, *Globalization and European Welfare States: Challenges and Change* (Basingstoke: Palgrave, 2001), p 148; A. Inotai, "The 'Eastern Enlargements' of the EU" in M. Cremona, ed, *The Enlargement of the European Union* (Oxford: OUP, 2003).

194 Most new Member States have taken recent steps to reduce burdens on their health care systems, for instance, by limiting types of treatment available under the national social health insurance systems.

195 den Exter, above n 191 at 562.

services may be *justified* in EU law, in accordance with protection of "objective public interests". A consideration of a purely economic nature cannot constitute such an objective public interest. But the Court has held that preserving the financial viability of national social security systems constitutes such an objective public interest, provided that the requirements of equivalence (the public interest is not already protected in the other Member State) and proportionality (the rule in question does not restrict trade more than is necessary to meet its ends) are met.[196] Although the precise application of the rules on justification in this area awaits further litigation, it seems likely that courts applying internal market law will protect the objective public interest in each Member State maintaining an efficiently structured and effectively financed national health (insurance) system.

Particular criticism is aimed at the assumption of the Court in *Kohll* that the mutual recognition of qualifications directives imply a similar standard of health care across the EU. Although these directives have gone some way to harmonise training requirements for certain medical professionals,[197] the harmonisation is far from complete. Not all health care professions are subject to the sectoral directives, which specify minimum levels of education and training. Moreover it is highly questionable whether patients will be aware that the substantive requirements laid down by the directives are only a minimum. In the context of team care, the activities of those covered by the sectoral directives are dependent upon skills of some types of health professional not included. Member States may recognise medical diplomas from non-Member States. Perhaps most significantly, the directives only apply to initial training, and not to continuous education as part of quality control programmes.[198] Jorens considers further whether different quality standards with respect to treatment in hospitals could be used to justify a refusal to reimburse, on the grounds that Member States may justify additional national regulatory measures if these are essential for protection of public health.[199] He concludes that, while there is harmonisation of quality standards for *licensing* of medical professionals, there is no equivalent EU-level legislation for quality standards with respect to the practice of hospital care in general. Therefore, in his view, a justification for restrictions on freedom to provide services could be present here. Alternatively, this could conceivably lead to pressure for articulation of agreed standards at EU level, perhaps through soft law mechanisms such as codes of practice.

However, other commentators have pointed to possible benefits of EU cross-border contracting for health care services.[200] Such cross-border provision could

196 Case C-120/95 *Decker* above n 10; Case C-158/96 *Kohll* above n 10; Case C-157/99 *Geraets-Smits/Peerbooms* above n 10; Case C-368/86 *Vanbraekel* above n 67; Case C-385/99 *Müller-Fauré* above n 67.

197 See further chapter 6.

198 J. Nickless, "Were the European Court of Justice decisions in *Kohll* and *Decker* right? 7(1) *eurohealth* (2001) 16; see also Jorens, above n 9, p 96.

199 Jorens, above n 9, pp 96–97, citing Case C-72/83 *Campus Oil* [1984] ECR 2727.

200 See, for example, Mossialos and McKee, above n 47, pp 102–103; Palm and Nickless, above n 103, S. Agasi, "Cross border healthcare in Europe: a perspective from German patients" 8(1) *eurohealth* (2002) 37.

be beneficial in a number of specific instances, such as in border regions,[201] for highly specialised treatments in centres of excellence, and in foreign tourist centres. More generally, cross-border provision could be used by patients wishing to gain access to higher quality care than available in their home Member State, to reduce costs of co-payments, and to alleviate waiting lists. There is some evidence that Member States are already funding treatment packages for their patients to travel to other Member States as a means of alleviating waiting lists.[202] It is also the case that at least some of the Central and Eastern European accession and candidate states are seeking to promote the opportunity for the existing Member States to authorise access to highly specialised elements of health care provision in those states at competitive rates.[203] The effects that this, and similar developments, may have on standards applicable to health care professionals will be discussed in chapter 6. Where a Member State's home capacity does not meet the health needs of its population – as may be the case for some of the Central and Eastern European accession and candidate states[204] – authorised movements, under Regulation 1408/71/EEC, may help. This does assume, however, that health care budgets are able to meet the costs.[205] Of course, whatever the position in theory, the practical reality is such that such a benefit would be limited to patients with sufficient independent means to pay up-front for cross-border health care services, even if they were subsequently reimbursed for at least part of the overall cost.[206] For Member States with over-capacity, access from patients in other Member States could result in a more efficient use of resources.[207] Overall, the jurisprudence of the Court may be seen as moving towards empowering individuals to opt out of inadequate or delayed local treatment. This may have the resultant effect of improvements in the standards of care available locally. For instance, the use by the Irish Western Health Board of a national fund to purchase treatment in hospitals at home and abroad has been criticised by medical professionals and politicians in Ireland. They take the view that the fund's resources would be better used in public hospitals in Ireland, in particular through keeping wards open and recruiting more nurses.[208] This

201 See A. Coheur, "Integrating care in the border regions" 7(4) *eurohealth* (2001) 10; R. Busse, "Border-crossing patients in the EU" 8(4) *eurohealth* (2002) 19 at 20–21.

202 An illustration of this is the UK; see McHale and Bell, above n 164; and for an empirical evaluation of such initiatives, see K. Lowson, P. West, S. Chaplin, J. O'Reilly, *York Health Economic Consortium Document; Final Report; Evaluation of Treating Patients Overseas* (York: YHEC, 2002). Interestingly, the UK government suggested that the measures they were taking to send patients to other Member States were linked to the developments in EU law.

203 See, for example, T. Albrecht, "Opportunities and challenges in the provision of cross border care: View from Slovenia" 8(4) *eurohealth* (2002) 8; Busse, above n 201, at 20.

204 The legacy of the pre-"velvet revolution" health care systems remains in those states. In particular, hospital facilities have been poorly maintained and suffer from lack of investment in new technology. See Marrée and Groenewegen, above n 8, p 17.

205 Busse, above n 201, at 20.

206 A. Cabrai, " Cross-border medical care in the European Union – Bringing down a first wall" 24 ELRev (1999) 387; Busse, above n 201, at 20.

207 Agasi, above n 200, at 37–40; Nickless, above n 157, pp 81–82.

208 E. Donnellan, "Medical Fund for treatment abroad is 'a nonsense' says consultant" *Irish Times*, 3 February 2003.

would imply a corresponding improvement in standards in those national public hospitals.

Finally, several commentators have criticised the effect of law-making through litigation, and raised the question of whether a legislative response at EU level might be prompted by the rulings. An amendment to Regulation 1408/71/EEC would be insufficient, as the rulings rely on the directly effective *primary law* of the EC Treaty.[209] The consensus required for a Treaty amendment is almost certainly not present. But most agree that some sort of response is necessary, in order to deal with at least some of the issues arising from the rulings.[210] In particular, questions of quality control, equivalence of medical practice, and continuing education and training of medical professionals, need to be addressed. A further issue is that the rulings imply that reimbursement for certain treatments for particular diseases may no longer be justified solely by reference to national professional opinion. Jorens sees this as a first step towards establishing "European" standards for health care delivery.[211] Hatzopoulos suggests that EU legislation coordinating the conditions under which health care services are to be organised by the Member States, in line with the case law, is needed.[212] Nys takes this even further, expressing the view that the rulings pave the way for development of a harmonised "package" of comparable health services available to all within the EU.[213] While these examples may, at first sight, suggest that the jurisprudence may trigger a radical restructuring of health care services, in practice it appears likely that any movement towards EU-wide provision of health care standards would be effected, not through the adoption of binding harmonisation measures, but rather through the "soft law" open method of coordination.[214]

Despite the extensive interest by academics and policy-makers in the Court's jurisprudence on the free movement of patients, to date the impact of the rulings has been relatively limited. This is perhaps to be expected. In determining the reality of cross-border treatment provision, fundamental practical considerations arise. First, the rulings will be unlikely to apply in the context of emergency treatment. Second, a

209 For further discussion of the relationship between Regulation 1408/71/EEC and the EC Treaty see Jorens, above n 9.

210 T. Van der Grinten and M. de Lint, "The impact of Europe on healthcare: The Dutch case" 7(1) *eurohealth* (2001) 19; Nickless, above n 157, pp 81–82.

211 Jorens, above n 9, p 109.

212 Hatzopoulos, above n 59, at 728.

213 H. Nys, "Comparative health law and the harmonisation of patients' rights in Europe" 8 *European Journal of Health Law* (2001) 317.

214 See chapter 2 for an explanation. See Conclusions of the Council and of the Representatives of the Member States meeting in the Council of 19 July 2002 on patient mobility and health care developments in the EU, OJ 2002 C 183/1, which establishes a Commission-led "high level process of reflection"; Commission, *Strengthening the social dimension of the Lisbon strategy: Streamlining open coordination in the field of social protection* COM(2003) 261 final; The Council's High Level Group on Patient Mobility and Healthcare, europa.eu.int/comm./dgs/health_consumer/library/press/press270_en.pdf and http://eurpoa.eu.int/comm/dgs/health_consumer/library/press/press301_en.pdf. The High Level Group is due to report in early 2004, and is considering how or whether health and long-term care should be inserted into the OMC on social protection. See further chapter 10.

patient's physical condition may preclude them from travelling any major distance. Third, even where travel is a realistic prospect, other hurdles may deter access to health care services. Language barriers, travel expenses, and uncertainty with respect to follow-up treatments, and, where necessary, protection from risk, pose significant obstacles to cross-border treatments.[215] Fourth, there are considerable potential difficulties regarding issues of legal liability should treatment procedures go awry[216] and this may prove a significant deterrent.

III. "Reproductive tourism"

So far in this chapter we have primarily been concerned with those individuals who may make the decision to move around the EU for health care services either because a particular therapy is not available in their home state because it is a new experimental therapy (*Geraets-Smits/Peerbooms; Inizan*) or where an individual is seeking access to care which can be more rapidly (*Kohll; Van Riet*) or more cheaply (*Vanbraekel*) provided in another Member State, or where the patient believes it will be provided at a higher standard (*Müller-Fauré*). However, in some situations, an individual may seek provision of health care services because they are unavailable in his or her own Member State, due to the fact that the home Member State has chosen to limit the provision of such services on what can primarily be regarded as being "ethical" grounds, rather than grounds concerned with resource allocation. Within a particular Member State, there may be a cultural or religious perspective, which may be opposed to certain health care services or the use of certain technologies. This may be inherent in national law, and possibly even expressed within the constitution of that Member State. To what extent do EU law rights to freedom of movement affect the entitlements of individuals within the Member States to access ethically controversial treatments that are available in some Member States of the EU, but not in others? Does EU law affect an individual's ability to access such health services, in the sense of an enforceable entitlement to treatment? This question is explored through the example of "reproductive tourism".

One area in which there is a wide divergence in the approach taken to treatment across Member States is that of modern reproductive technologies. This is an area that is underpinned by considerable ethical discourse concerning the "right to reproduce".[217] The advent of new reproductive technologies gave hope to many infertile couples, but at the same time it gave rise to acute ethical dilemmas regarding the extent to which individuals can claim to have reproductive rights. While

215 Mossialos and McKee, above n 47, pp 85–86; Agasi, above n 200, at 37–40.

216 See McHale and Bell, above n 164, p 41.

217 J.A. Robertson, *Children of Choice* (Princeton: Princeton University Press, 1994); J. Stone, "Infertility Treatment: A Selective Right to Reproduce" in P. Byrne, ed, *Ethics and Law in Health Care and Research* (Chichester: John Wiley, 1990); M. Warnock, *Making Babies* (Oxford: OUP, 2002); R. Cook, B.M. Dickens and M.F. Fathalla, *Reproductive Health and Human Rights: Integrating Medicine, Ethics and Law* (Oxford: Clarendon Press, 2003).

considerable support was given to infertile married couples seeking treatment, it was less clear to what extent the technology should be made available to others. The boundaries of treatment provision led to debate around whether access should be made available to single women, postmenopausal women and to gay men to enable them to commission surrogates to bear their genetically related children. More recent technological developments have led to debates regarding embryo screening and the use of cloning technologies.

The scope of a "right to reproduce" is problematic. Some support is found for such a right in international human rights statements.[218] For example, in the context of the European Convention on Human Rights, Article 8, on the right to privacy, and Article 12, on the right to marry and found a family, may be used to support such claims (the scope of the latter however delimits those who may seek to claim access to reproductive services). There is now an argument that developments in the EU may support the "right to reproduce" discourse, in particular through the application of the EU Charter of Fundamental Rights and Freedoms (EUCFR). Millns has suggested that the EUCFR, with its provisions relating to respect for human dignity, is applicable, as it "offer[s] an interesting combination of classical and innovative rights, the former guaranteeing the right to life while the latter expressly addresses the advent of new technologies by proclaiming a right to physical and mental integrity".[219] She goes on to suggest that "[i]n this respect, it seems that the conceptualisation of fundamental rights contained within the Charter goes well beyond the strict service-based approach set out in Blood".[220] She also suggests that the reference made in Articles 2 and 3 EUCFR to the right to life and the right to physical and mental integrity "explicitly addresses the advent of new reproductive technologies".[221] While these may be possible bases for such a claim, they may also be highly problematic.[222] Dignity, for example, is a notoriously uncertain concept to pin down; and moreover the right to physical and mental integrity is also very general.[223] However, Millns does not make reference to other provisions of the EUCFR which may be more pertinent here; in particular Article 7 EUCFR contains the right to privacy in the context of private life and Article 9 EUCFR contains a provision safeguarding the right to marry and found a family.

218 See, for example, the discussion regarding the implications for human rights discourse in relation to the European Convention on Human Rights in the context of reproductive rights: J. Ramsey, "Regulating Surrogacy – A Contravention of Human Rights?" 5 *Medical Law International* (2000) 45.

219 S. Millns, "Reproducing inequalities; assisted conception and the challenge of legal pluralism" 24 *Journal of Social Welfare and Family Law* (2002) 19 at 32. "Respect for human dignity" also appears as the first of the "Union's values" in the Draft Treaty establishing a Constitution for Europe, Article I-2 DCT.

220 Millns, above n 219, at 32.

221 Ibid.

222 The legal status of the EUCFR gives rise to additional problems in this respect – see the discussion in chapters 2 and 10.

223 For an extensive discussion of the issues, see D. Beyleveld and R. Brownsword, *Human Dignity* (Oxford: OUP, 2002).

The diversity of approach to the regulation of reproduction across Member States has been a major factor in encouraging the development of what is termed "reproductive tourism"[224] or "fertility tourism".[225] As Pennings has commented, the reasons for undertaking reproductive tourism include that:

> "a type of treatment is forbidden by law for moral reasons; a treatment is not available because of lack of expertise or equipment (like pre-implantation genetic diagnosis (PGD)); a treatment is not available because it is not considered safe enough (for the moment); certain categories of patients are not eligible for assisted reproduction; the waiting lists are too long in the home country; and the costs to be paid by the patients are too high in their home country."[226]

While reproductive tourism is becoming a global phenomenon, for our purposes (given our focus on the extent to which EU law may affect health law and policy within the Member States of the EU) we will concentrate on movements of individuals seeking access to modern reproductive technologies within the EU. Modern reproductive technologies are the subject of quite widely differing systems of regulation across the EU,[227] or may even in some respects remain relatively unregulated in some Member States, reflecting ethical choices and values of national societies. The variety of regulatory approaches is likely to increase on the enlargement of the EU to include Central and Eastern European states.[228] Much of this regulation is in a state

224 G. Pennings, "Reproductive tourism as moral pluralism in motion" 28 *Journal of Medical Ethics* (2002) 337.

225 It should be noted that the implications of the use of this term – "tourism" – suggests some kind of leisure pursuit, which some might find offensive in the context of fertility treatment.

226 Pennings, above n 224.

227 For a recent illustration, see the proposed reform of the Italian laws concerning assisted reproduction which, if enacted, would limit use of IVF to sterile heterosexual couples in a stable relationship, and which would ban all genetic screening of embryos; see F. Turone, "Italy to pass new law on assisted reproduction" 328 BMJ (2004) 9. Proposed restrictions include making such technologies only available to married couples. See further, regarding the regulation of this area, R. Lee and D. Morgan, *Human Fertilisation and Embryology: Regulating the Reproductive Revolution* (Blackstones: London, 2001), chapter 11; E. Jackson, *Regulating Reproduction: Law, Technology and Autonomy* (Oxford: Hart Publishing, 2001); M. Freeman, "Medically Assisted Reproduction" in I. Kennedy and A. Grubb, eds, *Principles of Medical Law* (Oxford: OUP, 1998), chapter 10; M. Latham, *Regulating Reproduction: A Century of Conflict in Britain and France* (Manchester: MUP, 2002); C. MacKellar, ed, *Reproductive Medicine and Embryological Research: A European Handbook of Bioethical Legislation* (Edinburgh: European Bioethical Research, 1998); D. Langdridge and E. Blyth, "Regulation of assisted conception services in Europe: Implications of the new reproductive technologies for the family" 23 *Journal of Social Welfare and Family Law* (2001) 45; L. Nielsen, "Legal Consensus and Divergence in Europe in the Area of Assisted Conception – Room for Harmonisation" in D. Evans and N. Pickering, *Creating the Child: The ethics, law and practice of assisted procreation* (The Hague: Martinus Nijhoff, 1996); D. Morgan and L. Nielsen, "Dangerous Liaisons: Reproduction and European Ethics" in S. Wheeler and S. McVeigh, eds, *Law, Health and Medical Regulation* (Aldershot: Dartmouth, 1992).

228 Most of the accession states and the other Central and Eastern European candidate countries have a fairly laissez faire or liberal perspective on the regulation of human reproduction. For instance, in Bulgaria, the Czech Republic, Estonia, Hungary, Latvia, Lithuania, Romania, the Slovak Republic and Slovenia, abortion rates are three times the EU average: see WHO and European Commission, above n 190, p 20. Poland is an exception to this trend, where abortions are lawful only in cases of severe risk to the mother's health, high risk of significant foetal abnormality or where the

of flux,[229] with legislatures attempting to keep pace with the rapid technological developments, and fruits of research into human reproduction, over the past couple of decades. There is no one universal approach to difficult ethical issues arising with respect to various techniques of modern reproductive technology such as cloning, sex selection and pre-implantation genetic diagnosis. Three basic underlying orientations for national positions on the regulation of human reproduction may be identified. States may take a position promoting maximum freedom of choice for individuals, implying a minimum threshold of (protective) regulation, and a wide construction of the "right to reproduce". Alternatively, states may place an emphasis on protection of children-to-be issuing from assisted conception, or protection of other societal interests, leading to a significantly higher level of regulation and indeed prohibition of some activities. Third, states may seek to protect individuals seeking access to these technologies due to concerns regarding the safety of particular techniques and the perceived vulnerability of individuals and couples seeking access to such services, particularly in a situation in which treatment services are sought after individuals or couples have suffered from infertility problems over many years. Each of these basic orientations, and various positions in between, is reflected in national regulatory regimes in the EU. This diversity in approach makes modern reproductive technologies one obvious area in which patients may seek treatment in another Member State of the EU.

The UK provides an example of a Member State in which the provision of modern reproductive technology is the subject of relatively comprehensive regulation.[230] In 1990, the UK Human Fertilisation and Embryology Act was enacted, following a major review of the area by Dame Mary Warnock.[231] Today modern reproductive technologies are the subject of regulation by a statutory body, known as the Human Fertilisation and Embryology Authority (HFEA).[232] Clinics involved in the provision of fertility treatment services and embryo research are required to be licensed by the HFEA. The HFEA produces a code of practice as the basis for clinics' operation, although on many issues, such as selection of individuals for treatment services, clinics are given a considerable degree of discretion in relation to the provision of services. Nonetheless, the HFEA takes a restrictive

pregnancy is the result of an illegal act such as a rape: see Polish Act on family planning, human embryo protection and conditions of permissibility of abortion 1993; Ruling of the Polish Constitutional Tribunal, 28 May 1997; available at http://www.federa.org.pl/english/abortion.htm and http://www.federa.org.pl/english/consrib.htm. As for Malta, where regulation is also restrictive, Protocol No 7, annexed to the Accession Treaty 2003, provides that "Nothing in the Treaty on European Union, or in the Treaties establishing the European Communities, or in the Treaties or Acts modifying or supplementing those Treaties, shall affect the application in the territory of Malta of national legislation relating to abortion".

229 It is extremely difficult to find accurate up-to-date statements of legal developments in other Member States, therefore it is quite possible that some legal developments have been missed in the analysis below.

230 Another such example is Spain.

231 *Report of the Committee of Inquiry into Human Fertilisation and Embryology* (Cmnd 9314, 1983).

232 See Lee and Morgan, above n 227; and M. Brazier, "Regulating the Reproduction Business" 7 *Medical Law Review* (1999) 166.

approach in relation to the provision of certain controversial technologies, such as sex selection. So, for example, in 2001 the HFEA refused to sanction treatment of a Scottish couple, Alan and Louise Masterton, whose only daughter had been killed in a bonfire night accident. The Mastertons wanted to use pre-implantation gender selection to enable them to have another daughter (they already had several sons). While the couple considered a challenge under the UK Human Rights Act 1998, they ultimately sought treatment in Italy.[233] In contrast to the UK, in Belgium there is little regulation of human reproduction. There, some 30% of the patients who are receiving IVF treatment come from abroad.[234] While, in the UK, the HFEA were opposed to sex selection, the *Guardian* newspaper reported that English couples had been seeking the use of sex selection facilities in a Belgian clinic.[235] HFEA have now confirmed their ban on sex selection, save for serious sex-related disorders.[236]

Another example involving cross-border movement to Belgium is noted by Pennings. Significant numbers of patients seeking fertility treatment come to Belgium from France. This is arguably in no small part due to the tighter regulatory structure in France, where treatment is available only in relation to a *projet parental.* Treatment is allowed in the context of a couple (man and woman) who are alive, married or who can establish that they have cohabited for a period of at least two years, and are of reproductive age. The treatment is to be provided to alleviate infertility or to prevent the transmission of a serious disease.[237] Further, in Belgium, fresh oocytes can be used, which increases the success rate. (Though in contrast it has been noted that in France there are other advantages not available in certain other EU countries, namely that fertility treatment is publicly funded.[238]) Pennings also notes that other groups of patients seeking treatment in Belgium are from Germany, where egg donation, embryo donation, posthumous use of sperm and surrogate motherhood are also forbidden[239] and also from the Netherlands due to the age limitations which are operational there[240] and the fact that sperm cannot be used if this has been surgically obtained.

In 1994, a 59-year-old British woman travelled to Italy to receive IVF treatment. She subsequently gave birth to twins. This incident led to the then UK health minister, Virginia Bottomley, calling for action at EU level to restrict such movements. This was supported by Philippe Douste-Blazy, a former member of the European

233 BBC News "Rise of the Fertility Tourist" http://news.bbc.co.uk/1/health/1205247.

234 College of Physicians Reproductive Medicine and the Belgian Register for Assisted Procreation Verslag 1998–99, Brussels: College of Physicians Reproductive Medicine and the Belgian Register for Assisted Procreation, 2001.

235 "Parents Pay to Choose Baby's Sex" *Guardian*, 8 September 2002.

236 Human Fertilisation and Embryology Authority, *Sex Selection: options for regulation* (2003) http://www.hfea.gov.uk.

237 Law 94-654 of 29 July 1994; and see discussion in Lee and Morgan, above n 227, pp 278–279.

238 Latham, above n 227; and see generally Brazier, above n 232.

239 See Lee and Morgan, above n 227, p 280.

240 It appears that in practice an age limit of 40 is adopted; see Lee and Morgan, above n 227, p 280.

Parliament and Mayor of Lourdes, who talked of the dangers of IVF tourism.[241] Nonetheless, in the years that followed, explicit EU-level legislative measures, or soft law provisions, or even political statements on this issue have been conspicuous by their absence. Rather, involvement of the EU institutions has been largely concentrated in the area of Treaty provisions on freedom to provide services, and litigation based on such provisions. As we saw above, privately remunerated medical treatment falls within the concept of "services" in this context.[242]

The legitimacy of the use of EU law regarding the provision of medical services in controversial areas arose in the case of *Society for the Protection of the Unborn Child (Ireland) Ltd v Grogan*.[243] In this case, a Students' Union at an Irish University was distributing information regarding the availability of abortion services in Member States where the termination of pregnancy, in contrast to the position in Ireland, was lawful. The Society for the Protection of the Unborn Child objected and claimed that Article 40.3.3 of the Irish Constitution was applicable. This states that:

> "The State acknowledges the right to life of the unborn and, with due regard to the equal right to life of the mother, guarantees in its laws to respect, and as far as practicable, by its laws to defend and vindicate that right."

A reference was made by the Irish High Court to the European Court of Justice under the Article 234 EC preliminary reference procedure. While this reference was criticised by the Irish Supreme Court, they did not otherwise interfere. The students claimed that distribution of the materials was supported by the application of Article 59 (now 49) EC. Although in that particular case, the European Court of Justice was not required to find on the substantive issue, holding that restriction of distribution of advertising material by a body unconnected with the provider of the service was not a "restriction" in the sense of Article 59 (now 49) EC,[244] the Court did confirm that, in principle, the medical treatment of abortion constitutes a "service" in the sense of the Treaty.

The *Grogan* case also raised the issue of whether services which are illegal or immoral as a matter of national law or policy may constitute services in the sense of the EC Treaty. It seems clear that activities that are prohibited in every Member State, such as sale of unlawful drugs, do not fall within the provisions of EU law.[245] However, where some Member States permit an economic activity, and others do not, those national prohibitions do not have the effect of removing the services from

241 See further R. Watson, "Focus: Brussels Which 'Europe' should deal with ethical issues?" 308 BMJ (1994) 362.

242 Cases 286/82 & 26/83 *Luisi and Carbone* above n 62, para 16. What exactly constitutes "privately remunerated" in this context is as yet not precisely determined; see discussion above at n 62–70.

243 Case C-159/90 [1984] ECR 377.

244 Case C-159/90 *Grogan* above n 243, para 24.

245 See Case 294/82 *Einberger* [1984] ECR 1177; Case 50/80 *Horvath v Hauptzollamt Hamburg-Jonas* [1980] ECR 385; Case C-343/89 *Witzemann* [1990] ECR I-4477.

the scope of EU law.[246] EU law would therefore extend to various medical services relating to human reproduction, for instance all forms of assisted conception.[247] Adoption services, and the service of surrogate motherhood, if remunerated, could also fall within EU law. EU law could cover the provision of contraception and abortion services.

The implications of EU legal principles in the context of access to reproductive technologies are further illustrated by the decision of the English Court of Appeal in *R v Human Fertilisation and Embryology Authority, ex parte Blood*[248] – the Diane Blood case noted in chapter 1.[249] Stephen and Diane Blood planned to have a family. However, Stephen Blood contracted meningitis. While in a coma and sustained on a life support machine, sperm was taken from him. He died four days after the onset of meningitis. Subsequently Diane Blood sought use of the sperm. This was refused by the HFEA, the body charged with the regulation of infertility treatment under the UK Human Fertilisation and Embryology Act 1990. The reasons given were that, first, Stephen Blood had not given his consent to the removal, storage and subsequent use of the sperm. The Human Fertilisation and Embryology Act 1990, Schedule 3, requires that consent must have been given both to the storage of gametes and embryos and their subsequent use. Here, obviously, there had been no such opportunity for consent to be given. Second, there was in this case a further, fundamental issue, namely the legality of the removal of the sperm from the comatose Stephen Blood. The removal of the sperm was a non-therapeutic procedure. After the decision of the House of Lords in *Re F* in 1990,[250] the legitimacy and the legality of the performance of non-therapeutic procedures on mentally incompetent adults was thrown into question. The removal of sperm was thus almost certainly unlawful under existing national law.

Diane Blood sought to have the sperm exported to enable her to receive treatment in Belgium. This was refused by the HFEA, who informed her that storage of the sperm was in contravention of the Human Fertilisation and Embryology Act 1990, and that, in addition, they would not make a direction under section 24 of the 1990 Act permitting export of the sperm. Counsel for Mrs Blood argued that the free

246 See Case C-159/90 *Grogan* above n 243, paras 16–21; Case C-275/92 *Schindler* above n 76; and, in the context of the EU-Poland Association Agreement, Case C-268/99 *Jany* [2001] ECR I-8615. See also the Commission's Interpretative Communication covering the free movement of services across frontiers, OJ 1993 C 334/3, and the Resolution of the European Parliament on compulsory gynaecological examination at the Dutch/German border, OJ 1991 C 106/13. Whether it would be sufficient for an activity to be lawful in just one Member State has not yet been ruled on by the Court.

247 J. Parsons, "Assisted Conception: The State of the Art" in Evans and Pickering, eds, above n 227, pp 15–27.

248 [1997] 2 All ER 687.

249 T. Hervey, "Buy Baby; The European Union and Regulation of Human Reproduction" 18 OJLS (1998) 207; D. Morgan and R. Lee, "In the Name of the Father? *Ex parte Blood*: Dealing with Novelty and Anomaly" 60 MLR (1997) 840. See also *U v V* [1997] 1 FLR 282.

250 [1990] 2 AC 1.

movement provisions of the EC Treaty should be taken into account. In particular, it was argued that Articles 59 and 60 EC (as they then were) justified the export of the sperm.

The Court of Appeal held that Article 59 (now 49) EC was applicable. The rules on free movement of services were applicable where the principles of free movement relating to goods, persons or capital were not engaged. As we saw above, while restrictions may be imposed in relation to the exercise of such rights, to comply with EU law these must be legitimate, in that they must be non-discriminatory, justified by an imperative public interest requirement, suitable for attaining the objectives to be pursued, and proportionate. In the *Blood* case, the HFEA had failed to take into account a relevant consideration, namely Diane Blood's rights under EU law. The Court of Appeal also held that the HFEA were wrong to take into account the fact that permitting export of the sperm would create a precedent for later cases, as this was a unique case. Following the Court of Appeal judgment, the HFEA reconsidered their decision and authorised the export of the sperm.

It is interesting to note, as Kennedy and Grubb have highlighted, the fact that the storage of sperm in this case without written consent appeared to be unlawful and thus a criminal offence under section 41(2)(b) of the 1990 Act.[251] Here it would seem that the application of principles of EU law on free movement to the *export* of the sperm effectively undermined provisions of national criminal and civil law with respect to the *storage* of the sperm.[252] Criminal law is not an area that is generally affected by EU law, except in certain specific circumstances such as those relating to policing. The *Blood* case may therefore imply an unexpected impact of EU law on national law relating to the regulation of human fertility and medical treatment more generally. However, it should be noted that, in fact, the legality of the removal of the sperm in this case was ultimately side-stepped as an issue, and not argued in the proceedings. Presumably if it had been, the imperative public interest in maintaining national provisions of criminal law with respect to assault could have constituted a proportionate justification for the restriction on the freedom to provide services.

It follows, therefore, that individual entitlements to fertility treatment cannot be entirely constrained within national borders within the EU. National rules on rights to treatment cannot prevent citizens of the EU seeking treatment elsewhere in the EU, no matter how unethical or immoral such treatment may be seen in the home state, provided it is acceptable in another Member State. The provision in Regulation 1408/71/EEC, Article 22, amended in response to the *Pierik (No 2)* ruling,[253] has been circumvented by the application of the directly effective Treaty provisions on freedom to receive services. Two sets of questions follow. One relates

251 I. Kennedy and A. Grubb, *Medical Law* (London: Butterworths, 2000), p 1304.

252 Removal of the sperm would have amounted to the tort of battery which is both an offence in criminal law and actionable in the civil law of tort.

253 See discussion above n 40–42.

to the ability of Member States to continue with their national policies, in terms of potential litigation based on the Treaty provisions. The second relates to potential broader, indirect, impacts of free movement on national health law and policies with respect to human reproduction.

With respect to the first, most of the relevant "fertility tourism" takes place in the context of private treatment, and so public interest justifications with respect to the burdens on the public purse, the organisation of national health (insurance) schemes and the need for planning, management and capacity building that are at issue in the general litigation on free movement of patients do not apply with the same force.[254] It may be that, in some circumstances, such justifications related to resource allocation may be relevant. For instance, in the case of the 59-year-old woman travelling to Italy to receive IVF treatment, had the UK sought to prevent this free movement, might the Court have been sympathetic to an argument to the effect that the long-term burden on national health and social services once the mother and her children returned home justified a restriction on free movement? However, such an argument would have to meet the hurdle of proportionality and it might be very difficult to show that a hindrance to any free movement at all would be a proportionate response, especially given the fact that a mother who can afford to seek private IVF treatment is likely to be able to afford to support any children and to make financial provision for their future.

The case of *Grogan* led to a great deal of speculation with respect to the extent to which the (essentially economic) principles of EU law should be permitted to undermine ethical principles, especially those enshrined in national constitutions.[255] This debate goes to the heart of matters central to the EU's "constitutional" law, discussed in chapter 2. *Grogan* was followed by the *X* case,[256] in which a pregnant Irish woman successfully challenged an injunction preventing her from leaving the country for a period of nine months. She argued, *inter alia*, that, as a medical treatment, abortion is a "service" in the sense of Articles 59 and 60 EC.[257] The injunction was effectively preventing her from exercising her rights in EU law. At first instance, the injunction, based on Article 40.3.3 of the national Constitution, was upheld. Although abortion is a "service" in EU law, the injunction was *justified* by the public policy of the deeply held moral conviction on the right to life of the unborn, which is expressed in the Irish Constitution. On appeal, though, the injunction was

254 Of course, if Member States revise their provisions on what human reproductive treatment is available under the national health (insurance) system, this will change. The UK government announced in summer 2003 that it is intending to fund IVF treatment for couples where the woman is under 39 years of age.

255 Subsequent to *Grogan*, Protocol No 17, which reads, "Nothing in the Treaty on European Union, or in the Treaties establishing the European Communities, or in the Treaties or Acts modifying or supplementing those Treaties, shall affect the application in Ireland of Article 40.3.3 of the Constitution of Ireland", was annexed to the Treaty on European Union.

256 *Attorney General v X and others* [1992] ILRM 401.

257 This had been established by the European Court of Justice in Case C-159/90 *Grogan* above n 243.

discharged, on the grounds that the lower court had not correctly interpreted the relevant constitutional provision.[258]

This review of litigation where the parties have sought to undermine national legal provisions, including those enshrined in national constitutions, concerning the regulation of human reproduction, by relying on EU law, shows that, to date, little concrete success can be reported in that respect. Diane Blood was permitted to export Stephen Blood's sperm to Belgium, but in the UK, national law permits assisted conception after death of the gamete donor, provided the relevant consent has been given, so the case cannot be said to undermine national law on human reproduction.[259] However, the potential for such litigation remains. The application of EU law in such circumstances, where (often politically controversial) ethical choices have been given legal force within states, constitutes an archetypal situation of conflict of competence between national and European regulatory regimes. These competence issues arise where there is "friction" between national and EU-level regulation, and are reflected in debates in the European Union concerning sovereignty of the Member States and subsidiarity in regulation within the EU system of governance.[260] The potential of EU law to undermine legally enshrined national ethical choices raises the question of whether *deregulatory* EU-level rules relating to the internal market are best equipped to fulfil the function of legal enforcement of these types of moral or ethical choices made by European society or societies. Thus far, however, no move has been made to *re-regulate* the field of human reproduction as a whole at EU level (though there has been considerable controversy regarding reproductive cloning: see the discussion in chapter 7). This is probably the case for two reasons: first, because the possibility of justification of restrictions on freedom to receive services is intrinsic to the internal market regime; and second, because in practice it is *national* courts that apply the relevant EU law. This last point is crucial. In *X*, in the final analysis, the matter was resolved as a matter of national constitutional law. National courts are the "gatekeepers" of the extent to which potential litigation in such controversial areas is likely to prove successful. Member States are therefore unlikely to be significantly hindered in the continuation of their disparate policies with respect to human reproduction by litigation based on EU free movement law.

Second, then, we need to consider the extent to which the application of EU legal principles, such as those of free movement, may have a broader, indirect impact upon health law with respect to human reproduction. Areas such as abortion may

258 See F. Murphy, "Maastricht: Implementation in Ireland" 19 ELRev (1994) 94 at 97–99.

259 The only issue that the application of EU law may be said to have undermined is the national law concerning consent, with respect to mentally incompetent adults. In itself, this is not a legal restriction of reproductive treatment, but rather a general common law principle concerning procedures involving those lacking capacity.

260 See further the discussion in chapter 2. See Weatherill, above n 88, p 225. It is not clear whether the European Court of Justice is bound by the principle of subsidiarity: see G. de Búrca, "The principle of Subsidiarity and the Court of Justice as an Institutional Actor" 36 *Journal of Common Market Studies* (1998) 217.

be identified as matters on which consensus and coherent policy across EU Member States is highly unlikely. However the question arises as to whether the ability of individual citizens of the EU to obtain access to services such as abortion or infertility services of a type not available at home – perhaps reproductive cloning or certain forms of embryo selection – will, over the long term, have an effect at individual Member State level and lead to consequent reform of health care policy.[261]

This question may be explored by considering the broader impact of the *Blood* case. From the point of view of the individual patient, Diane Blood was able to undergo treatment in Belgium and subsequently to give birth to two children over a five-year period. But did the litigation have a substantial impact upon those legal principles which were raised in the case itself and the reason why she wanted to access treatment services beyond the borders of the UK? The EU law issues here run alongside the fundamental issues regarding the illegality of the removal of the sperm. Following the *Blood* case, the whole question of consent to use and storage of sperm was the subject of further consideration in the UK in a review commissioned by the UK government and chaired by Professor Sheila McLean.[262] She recommended that the requirement of written consent should remain, but that there may be certain exceptional circumstances in which the removal of gametes from an unconscious person may be deemed to be in their best interests. She proposed that there should be amendments to the law to allow HFEA to waive the requirements for written consent in such cases. She also recommended that, in the case of posthumous conception where the child was born as the result of use of the gametes from the woman's husband/partner, the existing legal position should be amended to enable the name of the husband to be included on the birth certificate (at the time, the child was deemed in English law to be fatherless). In 2000, Yvette Cooper, UK Minister for Public Health, announced that the government intended to change the law. However, despite attempts by Debra Shipley MP to introduce a private member's bill, nothing was done.[263] Diane Blood gave birth in 2002 to a second child, again conceived through use of her dead husband's sperm in a clinic in Belgium. She subsequently brought proceedings under the UK Human Rights Act 1998, relying on Article 8 ECHR, to enable Stephen Blood's name to be placed on the birth certificates of both her children.[264] At the hearing, the government conceded that there was a potential conflict with Article 8 ECHR, and this resulted in the passage of the Human Fertilisation and Embryology (Deceased Fathers) Act 2003, bringing UK law into line with Article 8 ECHR.

261 See generally on this Hervey, above n 249, p 221.

262 S. McLean, *Review of the Common Law Provisions Relating to the Removal of Gametes and of the Consent Provision in the Human Fertilisation and Embryology Act 1990* (London: DOH, 1998).

263 UK Human Fertilisation and Embryology (Amendment) Bill 2000.

264 *Tarbuck, Blood, Blood, Blood v Secretary of State for Health*, 28 February 2003, before Sullivan J in the English High Court, unreported. See http://www.rpc.co.uk/main/..%5Cpdf%5CinHealth%20Apr%2003.pdf.

In EU Member States other than the UK, the relative ease with which reproductive services not available at home may be accessed in another EU Member State also appears to have had a minimal effect upon the alteration of national policy. While in Ireland there was a referendum on abortion in 2002, some of the questions in the referendum militated in favour of new *restrictions* upon the existing legal position, rather than a radical reform prompted by comparisons with other EU Member States, and convergence of approach. It can be speculated in such controversial areas as to what extent the availability of reproductive tourism may mean that individual Member States, rather than easing the national regulatory regime, in practice may be enabled to *retain* their restrictions, precisely because individual citizens can access such services in other EU Member States.[265] If this is so, the overall impact of EU internal market law on human reproduction may actually be to shore up diversity in legal responses, with the wide range of different regulatory approaches adopted across the EU acting as a safety valve for political pressures at home. Unless the phenomenon of reproductive tourism expands *greatly*, there are unlikely to be sufficient pressures either for EU-level action, or for change at national policy levels, to overcome the significant political inertia in such a controversial area.

That does not mean however that upon *all* issues which have a controversial ethical element, the EU will be prepared totally to stand aside and allow Member States to make regulatory choices between which "consumers" (at least those who are prepared and financially able to move between Member States) may choose freely. As we shall see when we consider the interface between EU law and clinical research, in some controversial areas, such as cloning, the institutions of the EU have not been slow to signal displeasure at certain activities, and to seek to (re-)regulate these at EU level.[266]

From the point of view of individual access to health care services, the application of EU free movement law to the example of reproductive tourism, shows that, in the EU context, individuals' ability to access certain treatments or health care services is not solely determined by national law. Provided an individual is willing and (financially) able to travel, a Member State cannot prevent citizens of the EU seeking reproductive services elsewhere in the EU, no matter how unethical or immoral such treatment may be seen in the home state, provided it is acceptable in another Member State. EU law has thus had a (limited) effect on patients' rights to access health care services. However, this effect is limited by the ability to justify restrictions on the freedom to provide and receive services by reference to public interest and public policy grounds, and by the fact that litigation strategies, in order to undermine successfully national policy positions based on ethical or religious considerations, must pass the "gatekeepers" of the national courts.

265 What applies in respect of Ireland's position on abortion may have similar effects on the new Member States of Poland and Malta, on accession. Both these states restrict lawful abortions, see above n 228, and see further chapter 10.

266 See further chapter 7.

IV. Conclusions

This chapter has considered the impact of EU law on the access of individual patients to health care services, in terms of both the types of treatment and the standards of care to which patients are entitled. The overall conclusion is that, while such access to health care services is primarily a matter for national law, this cannot be entirely isolated from the application of EU law. Patients' access to health care services is subject to some elements of "multilevel governance" in the EU context.

One of the most important practical consequences arising from the case law on freedom to receive health care services arises from the dynamic of the impact and application of (deregulatory) internal market law. This may render some aspects of the entitlements of patients under national health care policies not formally unlawful, but not viable in practice. This may arise, for instance, from the financial drain placed on national policies by requiring non-discriminatory treatment of all citizens of the European Union (EUCs) or migrant EUC workers, or because of the loss of control over supply implied by freedom to provide and receive welfare goods and services across frontiers. Control over supply is a classic mechanism for ensuring control over welfare costs, including health care costs, in all Member States. This point has been reiterated strongly by governments of several Member States in the most recent litigation, the *Müller-Fauré* case, but the Court has, at least thus far, been fairly sceptical about these arguments. Thus, litigation processes may constrain policy options for national or sub-national governments, not by making policies formally unlawful, but by rendering some options politically undesirable. In other words, governments of Member States of the EU no longer maintain total control over the terms on which access to health care services is organised within their territory.

There may be problems with this conclusion from a policy point of view. A more fundamental criticism of the free movement case law in this context – often implicit rather than explicit – is that it may be regarded as inappropriate to apply internal market rules *at all* to the health care sector.[267] The healthcare "market" is not an ordinary market, for a number of reasons. There are significant asymmetries of information between the "consumer" (patient) and the "provider" (medical professional, health (insurance) system). Because of subsidisation, patients rarely pay the full price of treatment, and so there is little incentive to reduce consumption.

Further, the notion of a "right" to health care,[268] and consequent obligation upon the state, implies, if not a bare minimum of access to health care irrespective of the patient's means, at least a notion of equality of access for all. When welfare

267 See, for example, Nickless, above n 157, p 79; Davies, above n 10, at 40; Hatzopoulos, above n 59, pp 684–685.

268 Found in the Constitutions of several Member States; the Charter of Fundamental Rights of the European Union, Article 35; and various international instruments; see further chapter 1; T. Hervey, "The right to health in EU law" in T. Hervey and J. Kenner, eds, *Economic and Social Rights under the EU Charter of Fundamental Rights* (Oxford: Hart, 2003).

states were originally set up, this was achieved by their territorial application, and "closedness" to the outside, as a positive measure of social solidarity among the nation.[269] Cross-border entitlements to health care, on the basis of EU law, are likely to prove most beneficial to certain patients. Patients seeking cross-border medical treatment, for instance, to benefit financially from the rule in *Vanbraekel* with respect to reimbursement, are likely to be those who have at their disposal all the necessary information for making a rational choice.[270] *Vanbraekel* implies that patients able to access and interpret the information necessary to compare costs of treatment in different Member States may actually make a profit at the expense of their social insurance system. Such patients are likely to be well educated, and thus probably better paid, and generally wealthier than others within their Member State. Patients have to meet their own travel costs, which may favour those living nearer to borders.

The development of the case law in the area may also, as we have noted, have an impact upon the standards of health care across Member States. The willingness to look beyond the individual Member State to what is the appropriate European or international standard is an important development. This process may eventually become formalised in an "open method of coordination".[271] A further important impact arises in the context of the provision of ethically controversial services. It remains to be seen whether the long-term implications are in terms of aligning types of health care service provision (convergence); or whether, in particular regarding certain very ethically controversial services, the "safety valve" effect of individuals being able to bypass national restrictions by travelling to other Member States, while their home state maintains the *status quo*, allows retention of diversity.

In the final analysis, something more profound may be occurring on an incremental basis through the application of EU internal market law. One construction is that the notion of a "right to health care", and underlying welfare notions of solidarity and the provision of health care for all, on an equal basis, regardless of means, may be undermined by the application of market models to health care systems in the Member States.[272] On the other hand, taking into account this case law, the Court may be seen to be articulating a notion of social solidarity as a

269 Davies, above n 170, at 40.

270 Jorens, above n 9, pp 100, 114. Of course, high-profile cases such as that of Yvonne Watts in the UK are likely to increase patient awareness of the possibilities of cross-border treatment. Following the ruling in that case, it was reported that a pensioner, Robert Towner, was among those relying on the ruling to seek treatment abroad. His wife, Maggie Towner, was reported as saying that the couple were "inspired" by the *Watts* judgment: "if it wasn't for this woman's case, we wouldn't have known anything about this": see http://news.bbc.co.uk/1/hi/health/, 3 October 2003.

271 See chapter 2; see further chapter 10.

272 Van der Mei makes a slightly different point, with respect to the ruling in *Kohll*, pointing out that "better off" patients are more likely to benefit from the ruling, as, under that ruling, a difference in price for health services between the competent Member State and the Member State providing the service would have to be found by the patient. See A. P. Van der Mei, "Cross Border Access to Medical Care within the European Union" 5 MJ (1998) 277 at 297.

fundamental exception to the application of internal market rules.[273] "Solidarity", though undefined in this context, is stated by the Draft Treaty establishing a Constitution for Europe to be one of "the Union's values".[274] Here then, the Court's version of EU internal market law is seen not as undermining, but rather as *shoring up* the "European value" of social solidarity. We return to these issues in the concluding chapter.

273 See Hatzopoulos, above n 59, at 720–727; T. Hervey, "Social solidarity: a buttress against internal market law" in J. Shaw, ed, *Social Law and Policy in an Evolving European Union* (Oxford: Hart, 2000), 31.

274 Article I-2 DCT: "The Union's values. The Union is founded on the values of respect for human dignity, liberty, democracy, equality, the rule of law and respect for human rights. These values are common to the Member States in a society of pluralism, tolerance, justice, solidarity and non-discrimination."

5

Data protection and health information privacy

I. Introduction

Health information privacy is one aspect of the right to privacy.[1] Wacks regards the notion of "personal information" as essential to such a right. This he defines as being:

> "those facts, communications or opinions which relate to the individual and which it would be reasonable for him to regard as intimate or sensitive and therefore to want to withhold or at least to restrict their collection, use and circulation."[2]

Much of the Anglo-American legal discourse concerning privacy in the common law tradition derives from a crucially influential article in the 1890 *Harvard Law Review*.[3] The authors of this article, Warren and Brandeis, examined US case law and suggested that elements of this case law, such as defamation, copyright and breach of confidence, culminated in recognition of a right to privacy, which they regarded as being a "right to be left alone". Health information is today commonly regarded as an important part of an individual's right to information privacy, and indeed information worthy of particular protection. Information privacy in the health context is integrally linked to the perceived inherent sensitivity of health information. In this chapter, we explore the effects of EU law on rights to privacy in health contexts, which include both health care and clinical research settings.[4]

As we noted in chapter 1, there is no "European health law" in the sense of a harmonised set of health care or medical entitlements, applicable across the whole of the EU, determined by institutions at EU level, and indeed many elements of "health law" are not the subject of EU regulation. There is therefore no "European health privacy directive". However, information privacy is an area of health law where *general* measures of EU law have a particular impact. The perceived

1 A. Westin, *Privacy and Freedom* (New York: Atheneum, 1967).

2 R. Wacks, *Personal Information Privacy and the Law* (Bodley Head: London 1989), p 26.

3 "The Right to Privacy" 4 *Harvard Law Review* (1890–91) 193.

4 It should be emphasised that this chapter is not a general chapter examining health care confidentiality, as might be found in a health law text; rather it considers the applicable EU legal principles regarding the control of personal health information through legal safeguards primarily in the context of data protection and the impact of EU law on the use of personal health information at national level.

need to safeguard information privacy interests in general, and health privacy interests in particular, is reflected in the Data Protection Directive 95/46/EC,[5] a measure of "old style" harmonisation – in terms of our typology of modes of governance[6] – which has affected patients' rights within the EU. A number of other directives concerning data protection, particularly where data are held or disseminated electronically, may also be relevant here.[7] Privacy rights are also contained in the EU Charter of Fundamental Rights and Freedoms 2000, a measure of "soft law".[8]

We begin the chapter by considering why health information privacy may be regarded as particularly important. Second, we consider briefly various international and EU measures reflecting a concern with privacy protection in health contexts. These include general statements, such as the EU Charter of Fundamental Rights and Freedoms, 2000. Such measures form an important point of reference for the construction of more detailed legal provisions, both at national and EU level. In the main substantive part of the chapter, we focus upon the Data Protection Directive, as an illustration of an EU-level measure that has had an effect upon the Member States' regulation of health information privacy.

Why safeguard health information privacy?

Long before more recent academic discourse in terms of health information privacy, health professional ethical codes had emphasised the special and sensitive nature of health information, and the consequent need for confidentiality in the health care context. Safeguarding information privacy considerations in the context of health is still today integrally bound up with notions of the sensitivity and confidentiality of health information. While the terms "health information privacy" and "health care confidentiality" are related, it is, nonetheless, important to note that they also have distinct characteristics. Gostin helpfully defines health information privacy as:

> "An individual's claim to control the circumstances in which personal health information is collected, used, stored and transmitted."[9]

5 OJ 1995 L 281/31. Replacement Article 31 from 20 November 2003, Regulation 1882/2003/EC, OJ L 284/1. Proposal for a Regulation on the exercise of powers of implementation COM(2001) 789 final, OJ 2001 C 75/385.

6 See chapter 2.

7 See, in particular, Directive 2002/58/EC concerning the processing of personal data and the protection of privacy in the electronic communications sector, OJ 2002 L 201/37; Directive 2000/31/EC on certain legal aspects of information society services (the "E-Commerce Directive"), OJ 2000 L 178/1.

8 The Draft Treaty establishing a Constitution for Europe (DCT) proposes that the EUCFR be incorporated into the Treaty, as Part II, as a kind of "Treaty within a Treaty": see M. Dougan, "The Convention's Draft Constitutional Treaty: a 'Tidying Up Exercise' that needs some Tidying-Up of its Own", Federal Trust online papers, http://www.fedtrust.co.uk/uploads/constitution/27_03.pdf. See further chapter 10.

9 See, for example, L. Gostin, *Public Health Law: Power, Duty and Restraint* (Berkeley, Los Angeles: University of California Press, 2000), p 128.

He defines confidentiality as being:

> "A form of health informational privacy that focuses on maintaining trust between two individuals engaged in an intimate relationship, characteristically a physician-patient relationship."

Gostin then goes on to comment:

> "Confidentiality is a person's claim to keep private the secrets exchanged in the course of that relationship, enforced not simply to respect the person whose confidences are divulged but also to underscore the importance of relationships of trust."[10]

Thus, although the notions of privacy and confidentiality are distinct, a perceived need to safeguard information privacy encompasses particular concerns to safeguard sensitive personal information, such as health information. Information privacy does not replace notions of confidentiality; rather it can be seen as complementing and enhancing them. Of course, in practice, the nature and dimension of health care confidentiality has expanded considerably, as we shall see below. However, these two definitions provide a useful succinct delineation of the concepts.

The history of patient confidentiality can be traced back to at least the Hippocratic Oath of Ancient Greece, which included the statement that:

> "Whatsoever things I see or hear concerning the life of men, in my attendance on the sick or even apart therefrom, which ought not to be noised abroad, I shall keep silence thereon, counting such things as sacred secrets."

From the days of Hippocrates, health care professional codes of ethics across jurisdictions have included statements regarding the need to maintain the confidentiality of patient information. Two main reasons are advanced for this. First, confidentiality is promoted for utilitarian purposes,[11] namely that, without the assurance of confidentiality, patients would be discouraged from coming forward to seek treatment. This may be particularly the case where patients seek treatment in the case of illness which may be regarded as particularly sensitive, should this illness become widely known; examples include HIV/AIDS and mental illness. As Gillon has stated:

> "people's better health, welfare, the general good and overall happiness are more likely to be attained if doctors (and we would add, nurses) are fully informed by their patients, and this is more likely if doctors undertake not to disclose patients' secrets."[12]

10 Gostin, above n 9, p 128.

11 See generally J.V. McHale, *Medical Confidentiality and Legal Privilege* (London: Routledge, 1993), chapter 3; G. Laurie, *Genetic Privacy* (Cambridge: CUP, 2002).

12 See also R. Gillon, *Philosophical Medical Ethics* (Chichester: John Wiley, 1985); and R. Gillon "Medical Ethics; Four Principles Plus Attention to Scope" 309 BMJ (1994) 184, where he makes virtually the same point.

Second, the maintenance of health professional confidentiality is supported on deontological grounds, including the right to privacy. The importance of the ethical mandate of confidentiality, and the need for health professionals to maintain the confidence of sensitive patient information, is illustrated by the fact that breach of such ethical requirements has been subject to professional disciplinary sanctions in Member States across the EU. In addition, both civil and criminal law in these states have upheld the obligation of patient confidentiality. For example, in France, breach of confidentiality is an offence under the Penal Code.[13] So, for example, the Court of Appeal in Paris held that disclosure, by his doctor, of the confidential medical information relating to former President Mitterrand constituted an infringement of the French Declaration of Human Rights, and that such disclosure was not justified by either the public interest or press freedom.[14] In the Netherlands, medical secrecy is mandated in criminal law in the penal code, and in civil law through Article 457 of the Medical Treatment Contracts Act 1995.[15] In the UK, doctor-patient confidentiality has been recognised as safeguarded under the common-law remedy of breach of confidence[16] and protection of patient confidentiality is increasingly being regarded as inherent in the patient's right to privacy.[17] In Greece, breach of confidentiality is a criminal offence under Article 371 of the Greek Criminal Code (CrC).[18]

Thus, there is explicit protection given to health information privacy across the Member States of the EU, and also implicit protection given to health care information, through the application of national laws concerning confidentiality. Nonetheless, whilst the need to safeguard such information (whether derived directly from a privacy justification or through the protection given to health care confidentiality) is universal, it is subject to considerable limitations in practice. A general privacy right, or a more specific confidentiality right, is almost

13 Article 226–13: "The disclosure of any secret information confided to a person in connection with his/her social position or profession or on the grounds of a temporary office or mission, will be punished with imprisonment of one year and a fine of 15,000 Euros." This provision applies expressly to professionals who were listed in the preceding Criminal Code which had made explicit reference in Article 378 to the medical profession. See further the discussion in S. Michalowski, *Medical Confidentiality and Crime* (Aldershot: Ashgate, 2003), chapter 4.

14 Cited in T. Kienle, "New forms of medical data collection – should be complemented by a new European privacy standard?" 8 *European Journal of Health Law* (2001) 27 at 29; and see A. Dorozynski, "Mitterand Book Provokes Storm in France" 312 BMJ (1996) 201.

15 See further discussion in T. Hooghiemstra, "The Implementation of Directive 95/46/EC in the Netherlands with Special Regard to Medical Data" 9 *European Journal of Health Law* (2002) 219.

16 *X v Y* [1988] 2 All ER 648 (QB); *W v Egdell* [1990] 1 All ER 835 (CA); and see generally M. Brazier, *Medicine Patients and the Law* (London: Penguin 3rd edn, 2003), chapter 3; J.K. Mason, R.A. McCall Smith and G. Laurie, *Law and Medical Ethics* (London: Butterworths, 6th edn, 2002), chapter 8; J. Montgomery, *Health Care Law* (Oxford: OUP, 2002), chapter 11; A. Grubb, *Kennedy and Grubb Medical Law* (Oxford: OUP, 2000).

17 *R v Department of Health, ex parte Source Informatics Limited* [2001] QB 424 (CA).

18 See discussion in M. Canellopoulou-Bottis, "The Implementation of the European Directive 95/46/EC in Greece and Medical/Genetic Data" 9 *European Journal of Health Law* (2002) 207 at 214.

invariably the subject of explicit limitations. For example, health professionals' ethical codes routinely contain provisions permitting breach of confidentiality, for example, because this is in the "public interest"; because information is needed in the course of a criminal investigation; or where it is perceived that disclosure of that information is necessitated because it is in that patient's best interests. In addition, legal protection given to professional-patient confidentiality is frequently qualified by legal principles which either permit or, on occasions, mandate disclosure. Across the EU, a broad range of exceptions are recognised. Public health grounds are a common reason allowing disclosure, with numerous examples across states requiring disclosure in the case of notifiable diseases.[19] Investigation of crime is another common reason why principles of confidentiality may be overridden. In Greece, doctors have a legal obligation to inform the public authorities where they suspect a criminal offence has been committed.[20]

At times, national law permits discretionary disclosure by health professionals. For example, in the UK, under the equitable remedy of breach of confidence, which is the basis for safeguarding the confidentiality of health care and other confidential information, the obligation of confidentiality may be outweighed on the basis that it is in the public interest to disclose. A public interest test has been adopted by the UK courts, with reference to professional ethical guidelines, such as those of the doctors' statutory regulatory body, the General Medical Council.[21]

All Member States thus recognise that health information is of particular sensitivity, is regarded as confidential in nature and worthy of particular protection. In many states, confidentiality is safeguarded through explicit recognition of a privacy right.[22]

II. Rights to health information privacy in international and EU law

In the European context, the right to privacy is recognised in Article 8 of the European Convention on Human Rights 1950 (ECHR).[23] More recently, the Council of

19 For example, in Greece, there are some 48 notifiable diseases, which include chickenpox, diphtheria and encephalitis: Law 4060/1929; Law 2520/1940; Royal Decree of 3 November 1950; Royal Decree 383 of 10 July 1972; Presidential Decree 1383 of 1981. In Germany, the Bundes-Seuchengesetz, section 3 lists communicable diseases. Italy has a variety of laws concerning communicable diseases, 71 diseases are made notifiable under the Decreto del Ministero della Sanità, 5 July 1975. See further, J. Harris, *Communicable Diseases, Lifestyles and Personal Responsibility: Ethics and Rights Final Report* (Brussels: European Commission, 1999), chapters 6 and 7.

20 Article 232 CrC.

21 See, for example, *W v Egdell* above n 16.

22 See Michalowski, above n 13; and Laurie, above n 11.

23 See, for example, *Z v Finland* (1997) 25 EHRR 371; *MS v Sweden* (1997) 45 BMLR 133.

Europe's Convention on Human Rights and Biomedicine, 1997, provides in Article 10 that:

> "1. Everyone has the right to respect for private life in relation to information about his or her health.
> 2. Everyone is entitled to know any information collected about his or her health. However the wishes of individuals not to be so informed shall be observed.
> 3. In exceptional cases, restrictions may be placed by law on the exercise of the rights contained in paragraph 2 in the interests of the patient."

This Convention has been ratified by a number of Member States of the EU.[24]

The need to safeguard the privacy of personal health information is particularly pertinent in the light of current technological developments in the health field. The development of electronic health records has led to concerns regarding the increasing availability of such information, with the associated need for safeguards to be introduced to reduce the prospect of unauthorised access to such information. Developments in genetics are proceeding apace, and, in the future, large amounts of information regarding an individual's potential to develop illness or disability is likely to be revealed through genetic testing.[25] Whilst this can be seen as an incredible advantage to an individual, in terms of obtaining treatments or trying to avert the onset of illness, making such information widely accessible may have some notable drawbacks. Considerable concern has surrounded the prospect for unauthorised uses being made of genetic information, in particular in the context of insurance and employment.[26] This concern has led to various international statements on the human genome, such as the UNESCO Universal Declaration on the Human Genome and Human Rights 1997.[27] Measures have been adopted in various EU Member States, and numerous proposals for law reform are under consideration.[28] The Council of Europe, in Recommendation No R(97) 5, made special provision regarding genetic information. This recommendation states that:

> "4.7 Genetic data collected and processed for preventive treatment, diagnosis or treatment of the data subject or for scientific research should only be used for these purposes or to allow the data subject to take a free and informed decision on the matters.
> 4.8 Processing of genetic data for the purposes of a judicial procedure or a criminal investigation should be the subject of a specific law offering appropriate safeguards."

24 See chapter 1, n [108].

25 See, for example, Mason, McCall Smith and Laurie, above n 16. See also chapter 7.

26 See, for example, O. O'Neill, "Insurance and Genetics: The Current State of Play" 61 MLR (1998) 716; Nuffield Council on Bioethics, *Genetic Screening: Ethical Issues* (1993); House of Commons Science and Technology Select Committee, *Genetics and Insurance* (Cm 5286, 2001); European Group on Ethics, *Opinion No 18 on ethical aspects of genetic testing in the workplace* (July 2003) http://europa.eu.int/comm/european_group_ethics.

27 http://www.unesco.org/shs/human_rights/hrbc.htm.

28 See, for example, in the UK context, the Human Genetics Commission Report *Inside Information*, (London HGC 2002); and K. Liddell "Did the Watchdog Bark, Bite, Whimper? The UK Report on the Use of Personal Genetic Information" 9 *European Journal of Health Law* (2002) 243.

These various international and European provisions, as well as national laws on the subject, have helped to shape the relevant provisions of EU law concerning privacy with respect to health information.

Privacy concerns are inherent in discussions regarding the use of health information across jurisdictions. Given the perceptibly enhanced importance of privacy safeguards in the "information society", it is thus unsurprising that the right to privacy itself, and in particular information privacy, is explicitly recognised in legal instruments at the EU level. If personal data are to move within the EU, as part of the internal market, then EU-level re-regulatory norms are justified by the need to protect privacy interests.

In EU law, rights to privacy appear in a measure of "constitutionalised" soft law and also in secondary legislation. The EU Charter of Fundamental Rights and Freedoms 2000 (EUCFR) provides protection for individual privacy, in Article 6 EUCFR ("Everyone has the right to respect for his or her private and family life, home and communications") and Article 8 EUCFR on protection of personal data. This latter provides:

> "1. Everyone has the right to the protection of personal data concerning him or her.
> 2. Such data must be processed fairly for specified purposes, on the basis of the consent of the person concerned or some other legitimate basis laid down by law. Everyone has the right of access to data which has been collected concerning him or her, and the right to have it rectified.
> 3. Compliance with these rules shall be subject to control by an independent authority."

As we saw in chapter 2, the EUCFR is a non-binding soft law document. Its provisions do not, at least at present,[29] form the source of enforceable rights *per se.* However, its provisions may be used in the interpretation of measures of binding law, or may be regarded as an expression of the "general principles" of EU law, which courts must respect where they interpret or apply EU law.[30]

Safeguards given to the privacy of patient information have been enshrined in EU law as part of the more general data protection safeguards contained in Directive 95/46/EC[31] on the protection of individuals with regard to the processing of personal data (the Data Protection Directive). The Data Protection Directive forms the main focus of this chapter.

Increasingly, personal data concerning individuals, including health care records, is being held electronically. While this facilitates transference of information (in the health care context, amongst clinical providers, health care managers, or insurance institutions), it also gives rise to considerable potential problems with regard to unauthorised collection of information and access to such information. This is a problem identified both within and outside the EU. The Data Protection Directive

29 The Draft Treaty establishing a Constitution for Europe, available at http://european-convention.eu.int/, has proposed that the EUCFR be included in the Treaty, in Part II.
30 See further below, and in chapter 10.
31 OJ 1995 L 281/31.

is supplemented here by Directive 2002/58/EC on privacy and electronic communications, which particularises and complements the Data Protection Directive.[32] The EU has also adopted a Directive on "e-commerce", Directive 2000/31/EC.[33] The E-Commerce Directive harmonises national law with respect to "information society services", including commercial communications, electronic contracts, and codes of conduct.[34] Thus, it applies to on-line services such as on-line medicine.[35] As Callens notes, it also extends more broadly to "for example, the use of electronic cancer registration files by physicians who pay a fee for accessing the file, the setting up of a web site of a physician promoting his activities, the sending of medical information among physicians for compensation".[36] The E-Commerce Directive provides that where professionals offer "information society services", Member States must ensure that this is done in compliance with national professional rules regarding, *inter alia*, professional secrecy.[37] Member States and the Commission are to encourage professional associations to adopt EU-level codes of conduct to this effect.[38] We return to consider the E-Commerce directive in a little more detail in chapter 10 below.[39]

III. The Data Protection Directive

Introduction

Directive 95/46/EC (the Data Protection Directive) was adopted with the aim of harmonisation of information privacy. The Directive is based on Article 100a (now 95) EC, and, as explained in its preamble, is justified by the fact that differences between Member States in levels of protection of the right to privacy, with regard to the processing of personal data, may prevent the transmission of such data between Member States, and may thus constitute an obstacle to the pursuit of economic activities at EU level, distort competition and generally hinder the achievement of the internal market.[40] Interestingly, whilst the aim of safeguarding privacy here can be seen in terms of economic activity, there is also another dimension – the fundamental rights dimension of the Directive – to which, as the Commission has noted, Article 8 of the EU Charter of Fundamental Rights and Freedoms gives added emphasis.[41]

32 Directive 2002/58/EC, Article 1.
33 Directive 2000/31/EC on certain legal aspects of information society services, in particular electronic commerce in the internal market, OJ 2000 L 178/1.
34 Directive 2000/31/EC, Article 1 (2).
35 For further discussion of so-called "e-health", see chapter 10.
36 S. Callens, "Telemedicine and the E-Commerce Directive" 9 *European Journal of Health Law* (2002) 93 at 95.
37 Directive 2000/31/EC, Article 8 (1).
38 Directive 2000/31/EC, Article 8 (2).
39 See chapter 10, p 432–433.
40 Directive 95/46/EC, preamble, Recitals 7 and 8.
41 Commission, *First Report on the Implementation of the Data Protection Directive* 95/46/EC COM(2003) 265 final, p 4.

The Directive aims to ensure that the level of protection of the rights and freedoms of individuals with regard to data protection is equivalent in all Member States.[42] As noted in Recital 10, EU-level harmonisation in this area must not result in any lessening of the protection afforded by national laws concerning the right to privacy. Therefore the Directive is not a minimum harmonisation provision, but constitutes a complete harmonisation (or "field occupation") of the area.[43] The Directive thus represents a measure of "old style" harmonisation, in terms of our typology set out in chapter 2. However, Member States do retain a certain "margin for manoeuvre"[44] in implementing the Directive. Although the Directive sets out basic principles and standards with respect to the lawfulness of data processing, it is left to the Member States to set the precise conditions within which such processing is lawful.[45] Member States are authorised to maintain or introduce particular rules for specific situations. There is nothing to prevent a Member State from extending the scope of its national implementing legislation to cover areas that are excluded from the scope of the Directive.[46]

The Directive sets a high harmonised standard of protection.[47] This is effected by reference to fundamental human rights, and rights language permeates the text of the Directive as a whole. Recitals 1 and 2 of the preamble to the Directive refer only to fundamental rights, and the establishment and functioning of the internal market, mentioned for the first time in only Recital 3, are explicitly stated to require "not only that personal data should be able to flow freely from one Member State to another" but also that "the fundamental rights of individuals should be safeguarded". Article 1 (1) of the Directive provides that:

> "Member States shall protect the fundamental rights and freedoms of natural persons and in particular their right to privacy, with respect to the processing of personal data."

The fact that rights language is inherent in the Directive, and its overall structure, which, as we will see, begins from the premise that certain information is intrinsically private, may have implications in terms of its interpretation by national courts and the European Court of Justice. In interpreting measures of EU law, courts must have regard to the "general principles" of EU law, which include fundamental rights.[48] The Court has already referred extensively to the ECHR and the jurisprudence of the European Court of Human Rights in interpreting the Data Protection Directive.[49] This jurisprudence may be applicable, for instance, in assessing justifications for

42 Directive 95/46/EC, preamble, Recital 8.
43 See Case C-101/01 *Lindqvist* [2004] All ER(EC) 561 (nyr in ECR), para 96.
44 Directive 95/46/EC, preamble, Recital 9.
45 Directive 95/46/EC, Article 5.
46 Provided, of course, that no other provision of Community law precludes it; see Case C-101/01 *Lindqvist* above n 43, para 98.
47 Recital 10.
48 See, for example, Case 29/69 *Stauder v City of Ulm* [1969] ECR 419; Case 11/70 *Internationale Handelsgesellschaft* [1970] ECR 1125; Case 4/73 *Nold v Commission* [1974] ECR 491.
49 Cases C-465/00, C-138/01 & C-139/01 *Österreichischer Rundfunk* [2003] 3 CMLR 265 (nyr in ECR), paras 64–94.

interference with fundamental rights to privacy, within the terms of the Directive. The Court has referred expressly to the jurisprudence of the European Court of Human Rights on proportionality, and "margin of appreciation" in this respect.[50] Interestingly, the Court has not referred to the EUCFR in this context.[51] Presumably, the incorporation of the EUCFR into the Treaty, as proposed by the Draft Treaty establishing a Constitution for Europe, would make a difference in terms of the Court's points of reference in the future.[52]

As Cannellopolou-Bottis notes, Greece, which held the Presidency of the European Council during the passage of the Directive, played an important part in the decision to adopt harmonised standards on data protection at EU level.[53] This is perhaps unsurprising, given that, in Greece, safeguards for clinical confidentiality have been in existence since the days of Hippocrates. Greece itself had already ratified the Council of Europe's Convention of 1981 for the Protection of Individuals with Regard to the Automatic Processing of Personal Data.[54] Furthermore there was already a specific provision regarding protection of personality in Article 57 of the Greek Civil Code.

Processing of personal data

The Data Protection Directive applies to the "processing" of "personal data". "Processing" means:

> "any operation or set of operations which is performed upon personal data, whether or not by automatic means, such as collection, recording, organisation, storage, adaptation or alteration, retrieval, consultation, use, disclosure by transmission, dissemination or otherwise making available, alignment or combination, blocking, erasure or destruction."[55]

"Personal data" is any information which relates to an identified or identifiable natural person. This is a person who can be directly or indirectly identified as an individual, by reference, to an identification number, or to one or more factors which relate to a person's physical, physiological, mental, economic, cultural or social identity.[56]

The Directive covers processing of data both by computer (automatic means),[57] but also by other means "which form part of a filing system or are intended to form part of a filing system".[58] In the health care context, this would therefore include

50 Cases C-465/00, C-138/01 & C-139/01 *Rundfunk* above n 49, paras 82–88.

51 Cases C-465/00, C-138/01 & C-139/01 *Rundfunk* above n 49, para 56, notes the UK government's submission to the effect that the EUCFR was of no relevance in the case, in spite of the fact that the national court making the reference under Article 234 EC had referred to the EUCFR. The Court makes no comment on this submission.

52 See further chapter 10.

53 See above n 18.

54 L 2068/1992, as cited in Cannellopolou-Bottis, above n 18.

55 Directive 95/46/EC, Article 2 (b).

56 Directive 95/46/EC, Article 2 (a).

57 Directive 95/46/EC, Article 3 (c).

58 Directive 95/46/EC, Article 3(1).

hospital records, records held by medical professionals operating outside a hospital context, and records with respect to medical research, provided that that data is sufficiently individualised and is held in some sort of systematic manner. The data need not be held in electronic form, and so the traditional manual filing systems of health care practitioners are covered.[59]

The Directive requires Member States to ensure that processing of personal data is carried out under lawful conditions, and to define those conditions more precisely, within the confines of the relevant part of the Directive.[60] Member States must ensure adherence to various principles relating to "data quality", in particular that personal data must be processed fairly and lawfully;[61] be collected for specific, explicit and legitimate purposes[62] and shall not be subject to further processing in an incompatible manner;[63] be adequate, relevant, and not excessive, in relation to the purposes for which they are collected or processed;[64] be accurate and up-to-date;[65] and enable the identification of data subjects for no longer than is necessary.[66] These provisions are "directly effective", that is, they may be relied on by individuals before their national courts, in a claim against an "emanation of the state".[67] National legislative exceptions to these provisions are permitted in a number of situations including where justified by national security, defence, public security, investigation of criminal offences, or breaches of ethics for regulated professions, important national economic interests; and the protection of the data subject or the rights and freedoms of others.[68]

Ordinary personal data

The Directive allows the "legitimate processing" of personal data. The Directive envisages two types of personal data: ordinary personal data and "special" personal data. For our purposes, the provisions with respect to the latter are more pertinent. With respect to the former, ordinary personal data, the basic position is that data may only be legitimately processed if the person concerned has unambiguously given consent.[69] However, data processing may also be legitimate in a number of further circumstances where consent may be implied, for instance, if processing is needed to perform a contract which has been undertaken with the data subject[70] or

59 See S. Callens, "The Privacy Directive and the Use of Medical Data for Research Purposes" 2 *European Journal of Health Law* (1995) 309 at 314.

60 Directive 95/46/EC, Article 5.

61 Directive 95/46/EC, Article 6 (1) (a).

62 Directive 95/46/EC, Article 6 (1) (b).

63 Directive 95/46/EC, Article 6(1) (b) provides that: "Further processing of data for historical, statistical or scientific purposes shall not be considered as incompatible provided that Member States provide appropriate safeguards."

64 Directive 95/46/EC, Article 6 (1) (c).

65 Directive 95/46/EC, Article 6 (1) (d).

66 Directive 95/46/EC, Article 6 (1) (e).

67 Cases C-465/00, C-138/01 & C-139/01 *Rundfunk* above n 49, para 101. On "direct effect" see further chapter 2, n 55.

68 Directive 95/46/EC, Article 13 (1).

69 Directive 95/46/EC, Article 7 (a).

70 Directive 95/46/EC, Article 7 (b).

is necessary in order to protect the vital interests of the data subject.[71] Further, data processing may be legitimate, without the explicit consent of the subject concerned, on public interest grounds, such as where processing is necessary for the national public authority charged with determining the purposes and means of processing of personal data ("the controller" in the terms of the Directive[72]) to comply with its legal obligations,[73] or is necessary for the performance of a task carried out is the public interest or exercise of official authority.[74] Finally processing may be undertaken under Article 7 (f) where:

> "necessary for the purposes of the legitimate interests pursued by the controller or by the third party or parties to whom the data are disclosed, except where such interests are overridden by the interests or fundamental rights and freedoms of the data subject which require protection under Article 1(1)."

The data subject may object to the processing of data pertaining to him under Article 7 (e) and (f).[75]

Special data

The Directive makes particular provision concerning the processing of "special data". "Special categories of data" are defined as being "personal data revealing racial or ethnic origin, political opinions, religious or philosophical beliefs, trade-union membership, and ... data concerning health or sex life".[76] The basic position in relation to this data, according to Article 8 (1) of the Directive, is that its processing is to be prohibited by Member States. However, in practice, the Directive operates to permit processing where there is compliance with at least one of a long list of exceptions. These include where explicit consent has been given;[77] where processing is required by national employment law;[78] in so far as authorised by national law providing for appropriate safeguards, where processing is necessary to meet the vital interests of the data subject or a third party and the data subject is physically or legally incapable of consenting;[79] where "processing is carried out in the course of its legitimate activities with appropriate guarantees by a foundation, association or any other non-profit seeking body with a political, philosophical, religious or trade union aim";[80] where data has been manifestly made public by the data subject;[81] and where it is necessary for legal proceedings.[82] Member States may add to this list of exemptions "for reasons of substantial public interest", by law or decision of

71 Directive 95/46/EC, Article 7 (d).
72 Directive 95/46/EC, Article 2 (d).
73 Directive 95/46/EC, Article 7 (c).
74 Directive 95/46/EC, Article 7 (e).
75 Directive 95/46/EC, Article 14 (a).
76 Directive 95/46/EC, Article 8 (1).
77 Directive 95/46/EC, Article 8 (2) (a).
78 Directive 95/46/EC, Article 8 (2) (b).
79 Directive 95/46/EC, Article 8 (2) (c).
80 Directive 95/46/EC, Article 8 (2) (d).
81 Directive 95/46/EC, Article 8 (2) (e).
82 Ibid.

supervising authority.[83] A specific exemption is provided where data processing is required in a health care context and we discuss this further below.[84]

The provisions of the Data Protection Directive obviously have a particular application in the context of health care.[85] Health care information is included in the category of special personal data as defined by the Directive. The Court has confirmed that "data concerning health" is a wide category, and includes "information concerning all aspects, both physical and mental, of the health of an individual".[86] The Directive is silent on the issue as to whether the Directive applies to information after the death of the data subject, and it appears that it does not extend to cover the deceased. This is in contrast to the situation in the ethical codes of many health professionals across the EU, according to which patient confidentiality continues beyond the grave.[87] Thus, in the UK, the Data Protection Act 1998 repealed almost all of the Access to Health Records Act 1990 (which, as the name suggests, regulated patients' access to their health records – whether manual or electronic) but left unrepealed the provisions of that Act which applied to the health records of deceased persons.

The Directive's "special categories of data" include "data concerning health". The basic position, in Article 8 (1), is that the processing of such sensitive personal data is prohibited. There is an implicit assumption that health data is different and sensitive. The assumption that health data is sensitive is interesting. Whilst this is in accord with traditional approaches to confidentiality, namely to assume that all health care information is *prima facie* confidential, the extent to which all health information is necessarily regarded as sensitive is perhaps questionable. The sensitivity of such information is highly relative. Some health care information may be unlikely to be "sensitive" because the existence of the ailment is rarely regarded as such, and in any case may be obvious – the person who has broken their leg in a car accident, for example.[88] Other conditions may be regarded as

83 Directive 95/46/EC, Article 8 (4).

84 Directive 95/46/EC, Article 8 (3); see further below.

85 See, for example, T. Hooghiemstra, "Introduction to the Special Privacy Issue" 9 *European Journal of Health Law* (2002) 181; S. Brillon, "The European Data Protection Legislation and the Medical Records", in S. Callens, ed, *E-Health and the Law* (London, The Hague, New York: Kluwer Law International, 2003).

86 Case C-101/01 *Lindqvist* above n 43, para 50.

87 See, for example, the UK statutory medical professional regulatory body guidance, which provides that "You still have an obligation to keep personal information confidential after a patient dies. The extent to which confidential information may be disclosed after a patient's death will depend on the circumstances. These include the nature of the information, whether the information is already public knowledge or can be anonymised and the intended use to which the information will be put. You should also consider whether the information may cause distress to, or be of benefit to, the patient's partner or family": General Medical Council, *Confidentiality* (London: GMC, 2000), para 40. See also the discussion in Mason, McCall Smith and Laurie, above n 16, pp 267–270.

88 In Case C-101/01 *Lindqvist* above n 43, the Court held that a reference on a website to the fact that a named individual had sustained a foot injury, and therefore worked half-time on medical grounds, constituted "data concerning health".

being, by their very nature, inherently sensitive, such as HIV/AIDS[89] or mental illness.[90] In both these instances, the wide recognition of the need for sensitivity is related to the fact that those who are HIV positive and the mentally ill have, sadly, suffered from stigmatisation. In between, there are a range of issues which one individual may regard as very sensitive and acutely confidential, and others not, for example, gynaecological conditions. The approach of the Directive is very much one of assumption that all information is sensitive, but that exceptions may be recognised. This is in line with health care professional ethical codes across jurisdictions. In contrast, an innovative response to privacy issues would have been to avoid making such assumptions, but rather to enable greater focus on individual choice in determining the legitimacy and the parameters of individual disclosure of information. In the past it has been suggested that one approach to health care confidentiality is that of the adoption of a process of "negotiated confidentiality" which is utilised in social work practice.[91] However, realistically, in practice a personalised and particularly sophisticated approach would be time consuming and, arguably, disproportionately expensive.

Anonymisation

The Data Protection Directive includes a number of provisions with respect to anonymisation (or "depersonalisation") of data. We have already noted Article 6 (1) (e), which provides that personal data must be:

> "kept in a form which permits identification of data subjects for no longer than is necessary for the purposes for which the data were collected or for which they are further processed."

The implication of this provision is that data should be anonymised wherever possible. As the terms of the Directive apply only to "identified or identifiable natural persons",[92] the implication is that, once data are anonymised, the data fall outside of its personal scope and that, for example, the provisions concerning subject access are no longer applicable. However, the Directive does not specify what exactly constitutes anonymised data.

89 So, for example, the English courts have been prepared to stop publication of the identities of two general practitioners with AIDS in a national newspaper: *X* v *Y* above n 16, where Rose J. emphasised the need for confidentiality in such a situation, as otherwise patients who were HIV positive or with AIDS would be deterred from seeking treatment. The fear that information concerning their HIV positive status would be made public was noted as an important factor in patients not coming forward for treatment in the US in the early years of the spread of HIV/AIDS.

90 Nonetheless, even in these situations, the precise boundaries of confidentiality may prove problematic, due to other countervailing interests which may militate in favour of disclosure; see further, for example, C. Cordess, ed, *Confidentiality and Mental Health* (London: Jessica Kingsley Publishers, 2001).

91 I. Thompson, "The Nature of Confidentiality" 5 *Journal of Medical Ethics* (1979) 57; P. Sieghart "Professional Ethics for Whose Benefit?" 8 *Journal of Medical Ethics* (1982) 25.

92 Directive 95/46/EC, Article 2 (a).

One approach to defining anonymous data is offered by Gostin. Anonymous data is:

> "Data with all identifiers stripped, with no reasonable means to associate the information with a specific person."[93]

This can be contrasted with "linkable data" where data is not immediately identifiable, but there is some prospect of linkage of data to an identifiable individual, because there is a "key" which is held by a third party. The Directive is unclear as to whether anonymisation encompasses both Gostin's "anonymous" and "linkable data". The Directive applies where a person is "identifiable": identifiable by whom? Is data anonymous where it is encoded, and the person handling the data does not possess the code? Does the fact that the data is linked in some way mean that it is still pertaining to an "identifiable" natural person? In France, certainly in 1995, the answer to this question was clearly yes. Even if identification is possible only in theory, where a medical professional communicates data to a researcher, the data is covered by the relevant national legal provisions.[94] Anonymity is subject to an absolute test. However, the explanatory document accompanying the proposal for the Data Protection Directive[95] and the original draft proposals[96] suggest that a test of proportionality is envisaged by the Directive. It has also been argued that proportional anonymity of data or samples is sufficient to ensure compliance with international standards concerning anonymisation.[97] Thus an individual is not "identifiable" under the Directive if identification would involve a disproportionate amount of time or effort. This was also the case in Dutch and German law, according to which data, for which a researcher has no access to the code to individualise them, do not fall within data protection laws.[98] While this may be seen as a pragmatic solution, nonetheless, as Laurie has noted, anonymisation itself may be insufficient as a privacy safeguard at a practical level if "for example, anonymisation procedures are inadequate, without review or otherwise defective in their protection of individual interests".[99] The fact that the original proposal included a specific provision on "depersonalisation",[100] which now no longer features in the Directive,[101]

93 See Gostin, above n 9, p 130.

94 See Callens, above n 59 at 315, citing the French *Commission Nationale de L'Informatique et des Libertés*.

95 Explanatory Memorandum OJ 1995 C 93/3. See Callens, above n 59, at 315.

96 COM(90) 314 final and COM(92) 442 final.

97 See Laurie, above n 11, p 295; and Council of Europe's Recommendation on Regulations for Automated Medical Databanks, No R(81)1 and Council of Europe Recommendation on the Protection of Medical Data, 1997, No R(97)5.

98 Callens, above n 59, at 315.

99 Laurie, above n 11, p 295.

100 Draft Article 2 (b) of COM(92) 442 final provided a definition of "depersonalised" data, which specifically included a reasonableness test: "except at the price of an excessive effort in terms of staff, expenditure and time".

101 The proposal to remove it may be traced to the European Parliament's first reading: see European Parliament Report A3-0010/92, Amendment No 13.

coupled with a strong interpretation of the Directive in terms of the provisions of the EUCFR, to which reference must be made in interpreting secondary EU law, might be read as implying an absolute, rather than a proportionality, test in this respect. This would broaden the scope of the Directive significantly, particularly in terms of health data, including genetic data, used for research purposes.[102]

Irrespective of which definition of anonymised data is adopted, it follows that the Directive envisages limited subject access where the data have been anonymised,[103] or even excludes a right to such access at all. This may be problematic in terms of respect for the privacy of the individual – a premise on which the Directive was predicated. Does anonymity itself make a difference to privacy rights? Are privacy interests adequately protected once information is anonymised? One interpretation suggests that they are. Gostin has argued that, generally, release of anonymised data does not compromise privacy, because individuals cannot be identified.[104] Nonetheless, he does comment that there may be concerns relating to "group privacy". He gives, as an example of this, publication by a researcher of anonymised information where this infringes "group interests", which can arise if there is genetic research concerning sickle cell anaemia, with consequent impact in relation to African Americans, or Tay Sachs disease, in the case of Ashkenazi Jews. The UK Human Genetics Commission considered anonymisation in their report, *Inside Information*, in 2002,[105] and noted that there is the possibility that individuals may be "protective" of genetic information, even if anonymised.

In the UK context, the English Court of Appeal considered the use of anonymised information in *R v Department of Health, ex parte Source Informatics Limited.*[106] In this case, a company sought to collect information from pharmacists about the prescribing habits of general practitioners. Data, including the identity and quantity of the drug prescribed, and the general practitioner's name, was collected, although the company did not collect the names of patients or other identifying information. The Court of Appeal sanctioned this use of data. They indicated that patients do not have any proprietary interest in the prescription form itself. As long as their personal privacy interests were not put at risk, they had no right to control that information.[107] The use of anonymised information could, in fact, be regarded as protecting the patients' privacy, rather than undermining it. This decision has not passed without critical comment,[108] and it remains to be seen whether this approach is followed by the courts in subsequent cases.

In *Source Informatics*, the Court of Appeal briefly considered the Data Protection Directive. At the time of the case, the implementing measure, the UK Data

102 See further below.
103 This is clearly reflected in the terms of Recital 26.
104 Gostin, above n 9, p 129.
105 Above n 28, p 24.
106 [2001] QB 424 (CA).
107 *Source Informatics* above n 106
108 See, for example, D. Beyleveld and E. Histed, "Anonymisation is not Exoneration" 4 *Medical Law International* (1999) 69.

Protection Act 1998, was not in force. Simon Brown LJ considered the definition of personal data under Article 2 of the Directive, and also the provisions regarding processing of health data under Article 8. One issue which the court was asked to consider was whether anonymisation itself constituted processing under Article 2 (b) of the Directive. The issue was whether the Directive applied to the process of anonymisation, even if it did not apply once the data had been anonymised. Simon Brown LJ, while indicating that this was not "the appropriate occasion to attempt a definitive ruling on the scope of Council Directive (95/46/EC)", commented that "common sense and justice" dictated that the Directive applied neither to anonymised data itself, *nor* to the process of anonymisation. Moreover, he stated that:

> "By the same token, that the anonymisation of data is, in my judgment, unobjectionable here under domestic law, so too, I confidently suppose, would it be regarded by other Member States."[109]

The significance of this last statement was that this certainty removed the need to refer the question of interpretation of the scope of the Directive to the European Court of Justice under Article 234 EC.[110] However, as Grubb has commented, such an assumption is problematic. He suggests that the breadth of the Data Protection Directive may indeed extend to anonymised information.[111] He argues that Article 2 (b), which defines processing very broadly to cover any operation which is performed on personal data, could encompass the process of anonymisation.[112]

Consent and special data

Given that the Data Protection Directive was rooted in the perceived need to safeguard individual privacy, it is unsurprising that the Directive emphasises the need for consent. A focus on consent is reflected in several of its provisions.[113] The need to ensure that consent has been obtained where data is held and processed is also reflected in Article 8 EUCFR, which provides that data must be processed fairly for specified purposes on the basis of the consent of the person concerned, or some other legitimate basis.

The main exception to Article 8 (1) of the Directive, which provides that processing of "special categories" of data is prohibited, is Article 8 (2) (a). This states

109 *Source Informatics*, above n 106, para 45.

110 See Case 283/81 *CILFIT* [1982] ECR 3415, para 16: "... the correct application of Community law may be so obvious as to leave no scope for any reasonable doubt as to the manner in which the question raised is to be resolved. Before it comes to the conclusion that such is the case, the national court or tribunal must be convinced that the matter is equally obvious to the courts of the other Member States ...." On the Article 234 EC preliminary rulings procedure, see chapter 2.

111 A. Grubb, "Breach of Confidence: Anonymised Information" *8 Medical Law Review* (2000) 115 at 117.

112 Grubb, above n 111, at 118.

113 See, in general, C. Dierks, "Data Subject's Consent and Cross-Border Data Processing" in S. Callens, ed, *E-Health and the Law* (London, The Hague and New York: Kluwer Law International, 2003).

that processing of such special data, which includes data concerning health, is lawful where the data subject has given his consent to the processing of those data. Consent in this circumstance must be explicit, according to the Directive. It need not, as one early draft proposal of the Directive suggested, be written consent.[114] While one argument which has been advanced is that consent would not be voluntary consent, if given as part of receiving a service, as in the case of medical treatment, this interpretation has been doubted.[115] It thus appears that this provision would cover the situation where a competent adult gives permission for his medical records to be "processed", for instance, shared among various health care professionals, in the context of the provision of care in a hospital setting.[116]

What if a patient lacks capacity to give consent? A patient arriving in the accident and emergency department may be temporarily incapacitated, and thus unable to provide consent for collection and processing of his personal data needed in order to facilitate emergency treatment necessary to save his life. The Directive takes account of this type of situation in Article 8 (2) (c), which provides that, where the data subject is incapable of giving consent, data processing is still lawful where "necessary to protect the vital interests of the data subject".[117] Health care provision is clearly a "vital interest" of the data subject (the patient) in this context.

The concept of consent in the Directive is understood to be "informed consent". Article 2 (h) states that consent means "any freely given specific and informed indication of his wishes by which the data subject signifies his agreement to personal data relating to him being processed". This can also be implied from the provision in Article 6 that data may be collected only for "*specific*, *explicit* and legitimate purposes", and from the provision in Article 7 (a) that consent must be given "unambiguously". None of these could be the case if consent were not informed consent. The preamble to the Directive also refers to "informed consent" in Recital 70. The Directive does not, however, clarify the precise boundaries of what constitutes "informed consent". Earlier drafts attempted to do so.[118] In practice, across Member States, there is considerable divergence as to the constituent elements of the notion of informed consent in relation to consent to treatment.[119] The Directive does not attempt to harmonise this element of national health law.

114 See OJ 1990 C 277/3.

115 UK Information Commissioner, *Use and Disclosure of Health Data: Guidance on the Application of the Data Protection Act 1998* (Wilmslow: Information Commissioner, 1998), p 18.

116 See below regarding problems of data sharing at 178.

117 See also Directive 95/46/EC, Recital 31.

118 See, for instance, Report of the European Parliament A3-0010/92, amendment to draft Article 12, which suggested that the giving of consent under the Directive would be valid only if the data subject were supplied with information with respect to the purposes of the collection of the data and the types of personal data about the data subject stored or intended to be stored; and information with respect to the type of use and, where appropriate, the types of potential recipients of the personal data. It was also proposed that there should be an explicit provision to the effect that the consent of the data subject must be obtained whenever the purpose of the data processing changed.

119 See H. Nys, "Comparative health law and the harmonisation of patients' rights in Europe" 8 *European Journal of Health Law* (2001) 317.

Moreover, although the Data Protection Directive may be interpreted as permitting implied consent in the case of "ordinary data" (Article 7 (a) refers merely to "unambiguously given" consent), the wording of the Directive with respect to "special categories of data" (which include data concerning health) is more tightly drawn. Article 8 (2) provides that the prohibition on processing of such special data shall not apply where the data subject has given his *explicit* consent. So, for example, the data at issue in *Source Informatics* was sensitive clinical data. One of the criteria of Schedule 3 to the UK Data Protection Act 1998, namely that of the requirement of "specific consent", obviously cannot have been established, and it is questionable whether the disclosure would fall within the other medical purposes of this section. The provision in Article 8 (3) of the Directive would not seem to apply to the processing of data by a third-party private actor, unless this was "required for the purposes of preventive medicine, medical diagnosis, the provision of care or treatment or the management of health care services". As Grubb notes:

> "Only the latter purpose – 'management of healthcare services' – could conceivably have applied on the facts of *Source Informatics.* But arguably it does not since the processing was not for management purposes but rather for the commercial purposes of the pharmaceutical companies who wished to track GP prescribing habits."[120]

A further issue that arose in *Source Informatics* was the use of data, initially obtained for one purpose, for a "secondary" purpose.[121] Under the UK Data Protection Act, Schedule 1, paragraph 2, following the Data Protection Directive, Article 6 (1) (b), this is not allowed. But, as Grubb notes, it is the case that secondary use may occur if the UK Information Commissioner or patients are informed. In addition, section 33(1) of the UK Act permits processing for research purposes, which includes statistical purposes. This is permitted under the Directive.[122] However, Grubb suggests that the section which is headed "research, history and statistics" is not intended to cover all statistical purposes, but only where research is included, which was not the case here.[123] It is remains to be seen whether such an interpretation would be followed by the English courts in the future, or whether, were a reference made to the European Court of Justice, it would follow such an approach.

Further exceptions allowing disclosure

Article 8 (3) of the Directive sets out a number of further exceptions to the general principle in Article 8 (1) to the effect that processing of "special categories" of data is prohibited. It provides that:

> "Paragraph 1 shall not apply where processing of the data is required for the purposes of preventive medicine, medical diagnosis, the provision of care or treatment or the

120 Grubb, above n 111.
121 W. Lowrance, *Learning from Experience: Privacy and the Secondary Use of Data* (Oxford: Nuffield Trust, 2002).
122 Directive 95/46/EC, Article 6 (1) (b).
123 Grubb, above n 111, at 120.

management of health-care services and where those data are processed by a health professional subject under national law or rules established by national competent bodies to the obligation of professional secrecy or by another person also subject to an equivalent obligation of secrecy."

This provision recognises that obligations of privacy and confidentiality in the area of health care are rarely stated in absolute terms. Health care professional ethical codes routinely allow disclosure of personal data in the context of treatment.[124] Data may need to be shared between professionals forming a health care team, in the context of providing a package of health care to a patient. Nevertheless, patients are frequently unaware of exactly how wide these boundaries of disclosure are.[125] The sanctioning of disclosure in relation to the management of health services, where there may be extensive disclosure of patient information without that individual's knowledge, is equally controversial. The Directive seems to imply that the principle of health professional-patient confidentiality may extend to other persons who operate in the broader context of health care delivery. These would presumably also include health insurance companies, if these form part of the national health (insurance) system. The Directive does nothing to alter the position that potentially wide boundaries operate with respect to disclosure of personal health data within the context of national health (insurance) systems. The only observation that might be made in this respect is the fact that the Directive conceptualises the processing of sensitive personal data in a health care context as an exception, rather than the rule. This may underline the importance of health information privacy and consequently increase the need to justify exceptions to that right.

Article 8 (3) also highlights the fact that the Directive enables Member States to exercise a considerable degree of discretion in the implementation of the Directive, where this relates to their own codes of professional-client confidentiality. Further, Article 8 (4) provides that Member States may also create exemptions on grounds of "substantial public interest". Laurie has commented that:

> "What those public interests are, or may be, is discernible in large part from the general tenor of the Directive, which makes special provisions among others for national security, the investigation and prosecution of crimes, legitimate journalistic activities, and research."[126]

Of these, research activities are likely to be of most relevance in the health context, and the question of research use of data subjects' information is considered below.

124 General Medical Council, *Confidentiality* (London: GMC 2000). See http://www.gmc-uk.org/standards/secret.htm#Introduction.

125 See M. Siegler, "Medical Confidentiality – a decrepit concept" 307 *New England Journal of Medicine* (1982) 1518; and generally McHale, above n 11 chapter 4.

126 Laurie, above n 11, p 253.

Clinical research and public health monitoring

The application of the Directive in the context of clinical and scientific research, especially epidemiological research, has proved particularly controversial. Clinical or scientific researchers may seek to access existing clinical records from the treating physician or health body, rather than directly from the patients themselves. The Directive is fundamentally ill-fitted to this situation. First of all, the very structure of the Directive has been criticised. Given the considerable exceptions applicable to the processing of health data, why does the Directive begin with a prohibition? Callens takes the view that it would be more appropriate to allow the processing of health data under certain conditions, or to limit the principle of prohibition to communication of health data, rather than all types of processing.[128]

Various members of the research community have been particularly critical of the consent provisions of the Directive. If taken literally, the requirement for consent, before data is collected, would seem to impede research using health data collected from young children, or adults who are mentally incompetent to give consent. The exemption provision in Article 8 (3) would not apply to such a situation, as research cannot be said to be "preventive medicine, medical diagnosis, the provision of care or treatment or the management of health-care services". Neither can the situation be said to fall clearly within the exemption in Article 8 (2) (c), as medical research, particularly of a speculative nature, cannot be said to be "*necessary* to protect the vital interests of the data subject": such research may be desirable, but cannot be said to be necessary. It would seem that Member States would need to fall back on Article 8(4) of the Directive (the "substantial public interest" exemption) to allow such data to be collected and processed. This would be consistent with the general thrust of regulation of clinical research in the EU, seen for instance in the Clinical Trials Directive,[129] which requires consent to be obtained from an appropriate person, be that a parent or other "legal representative".

Furthermore, it was suggested that much of the information held in banks of health information, such as cancer registries, could contravene the national legislation implementing the Data Protection Directive, as this was information that was transferred and used without explicit consent having been sought or given, and where none of the other grounds in Article 7 or 8 of the Directive appeared to be applicable.[130] The prospect of having to seek consent from large numbers of

127 See E.G. Knox, "Confidential medical records and epidemiological research" 304 BMJ (1992) 727; E. Lynge, "Misguided Directive on confidential data: a threat to epidemiology" 308 BMJ (1992) 490.

128 Callens, above n 59 at 320.

129 Directive 2001/20/EC on the approximation of the laws, regulations and administrative provisions of the Member States relating to the implementation of good clinical practice in the conduct of clinical trials on medicinal products for human use, OJ 2001 L 121/34. See further chapter 7.

130 These concerns were initially voiced in the early stages of the drafting of the Directive: see, for example, C. Vanchieri, "New EC privacy directive worries European epidemiologists" 83 *Journal of the National Cancer Institute* (1993) 1022; and, discussing the final Directive, see J. Strobl, E. Cave and T. Walley, "Data Protection Legislation: Interpretation and Barriers to Research" 321 BMJ (2000) 890.

individuals, many of whom might be very difficult to trace, or who might indeed no longer be alive, posed considerable logistical problems, and might involve prohibitive costs.

However, the Directive appears to take this potential problem into account. For a start, if the personal scope of the Directive covers only the living, then the processing of data, for instance, genetic data, held over very long periods of time, as part of medical research projects, will not fall foul of the Directive. Second, as we saw above, where data is anonymised, it appears that the data falls outside the scope of the Directive, as it does not pertain to an "identified or identifiable" individual. Further, Article 6 provides that personal data must be collected for specified purposes, and the implication is that consent is given for the processing of data for those purposes only. However, Article 6 goes on to provide that:

> "Further processing of data for historical, statistical or scientific purposes shall not be considered as incompatible provided that Member States provide appropriate safeguards."[131]

This is potentially a controversial provision in the health care context. It can be argued that, whilst persons may be happy for their data to be used for one scientific purpose, for instance, for one particular clinical research project, they may not be happy for that same data to be used for another clinical research project, perhaps because they disagree with its aims. There may be particular concerns regarding the use of such data for commercial purposes. It would thus be unwise to presume that consent to process the data can necessarily be implied in such circumstances.[132]

It may be practically problematic to enforce requirements to seek consent for further use of health research data, in a situation in which information is held for long periods of time – perhaps because it forms part of a genetic database. The Directive attempts to tackle the potential problems with long-term preservation of data with its provision in Article 6 (1) (e) to the effect that data must be:

> "kept in a form which permits identification of data subjects for no longer than is necessary for the purposes for which the data were collected or for which they are further processed. Member States shall lay down appropriate safeguards for personal data stored for longer periods for historical, statistical or scientific use."

However, as we saw above, the mere anonymisation of data may not always be sufficient to preserve an individual's rights to privacy or confidentiality.

In some situations, information may come into the hands of health researchers from third parties. Here, Article 11 (1) is applicable. This states that, in such a situation, where the data is recorded, or no later than when the data is first disclosed, the data subject shall be informed of the controller's identity, purposes of the processing, and relevant further information, including the categories of data covered.

131 Directive 95/46/EC, Article 6(1)(b).
132 See below.

Interestingly, in the light of the above discussion, we should also note Article 11 (2) which provides that:

> "Paragraph 1 shall not apply where, in particular for processing for statistical purposes or for the purposes of historical or scientific research, the provision of information proves impossible or would involve a disproportionate effort or if recording or disclosure is expressly laid down by law. In these cases Member States shall provide appropriate safeguards."

This provision makes the disclosure requirement subject to a proportionality test.

A further problem with the Directive in terms of health research is that it does not actually promote the transfer of data within the EU's internal market. Such data transfer is often needed for research purposes, for instance for large-scale epidemiological projects, the setting up of research registers, pharmacovigilance and clinical trials. The Directive leaves so many options to Member States to provide other exceptions to the processing of health data that a fully harmonised system in this context will not result from the Directive.[133] Callens takes the view that Member States are likely to impede the free movement of health data on the grounds of the protection of the right to privacy,[134] in accordance with different national traditions on the interpretation of that right in concrete situations. However, such an approach may be to downplay the perceived importance to Member States of facilitating clinical and scientific research. Indeed the need for "free movement of data" within the EU constituted the driving force behind the adoption of the Data Protection Directive in the first place.

The other situation, relevant to health care, where the Data Protection Directive might cause difficulties is public health monitoring, for instance, of infectious diseases. Article 8 (4) of the Directive deals with this type of situation, as it provides that Member States may create exemptions from the Directive on grounds of "substantial public interest". So, for instance, in the UK, the Westminster Parliament has enacted section 60 of the Health and Social Care Act 2001.[135] This provision enables the Secretary of State to introduce secondary legislation to allow the disclosure of confidential patient information, where this relates to the diagnosis of communicable diseases and other public health risks, for the identification of trends in such diseases or risks, and to control their spread.[136] The regulations adopted in the UK provide for monitoring and management of outbreaks of communicable diseases, incidents relating to disease exposure, delivery, safety and efficacy of vaccination programmes

133 See Brillon, above n 85, p 96. We might speculate whether this Directive is therefore valid, in the terms of the *Tobacco Advertising* ruling (Case C-376/98 *Germany v Parliament and Council (Tobacco Advertising)* [2000] ECR I-8419). One of the problems with the Tobacco Advertising Directive, according to the Court, was that it did not promote the free movement of products in conformity with its provisions (para 101). See chapter 3, n 172.

134 Callens, above n 59, at 323, 325.

135 See discussion of this provision in P. Case, "Confidence Matters: The Rise and Fall of Informational Autonomy in Medical Law" 11(2) *Medical Law Review* (2003) 208.

136 Health Service (Control of Patient Information) Regulations 2002, SI 2002/1438, reg 4.

and any adverse reactions to vaccinations and medicines. The regulations also apply to disclosure of information that concerns risks of infection arising from food or the environment, which includes water supplies. Finally, the regulations concern provision of information to persons regarding communicable disease diagnosis and risk of infection. A "Patient Information Advisory Group" was established, with the aim of advising the Secretary of State as to whether the presumption of consent should be overridden under the regulations.[137] It seems that such a provision is permissible under Article 7 (f) and Article 8 (4) of the Directive. Nonetheless, the provision has come under criticism. For example, as Case has suggested, its terms are extremely broad:

> "It is not only the breadth of information which can be caught under these provisions that is cause for concern, but also the persons to whom access may extend. The new regulations extend access to such records to anyone 'employed or engaged by a government department or other public authority' in communicable disease surveillance."[138]

This provision illustrates that the Directive may prove to have only limited utility, in terms of safeguarding privacy in some controversial instances.

Control rights for data subjects

For many years, there was considerable debate as to whether patients should be entitled to access their own health records.[139] This argument was based upon paternalistic concerns about the prospect of psychological or indeed, on occasions, physical harm which might result from such disclosure. Gradually over time, however, in various EU Member States, legislation was passed sanctioning, or even requiring, such disclosure. The legal approaches varied. For example, in France, disclosure of patient information is through the doctor appointed by the patient,[140] while, in contrast, in the UK, patients themselves could exercise access rights.[141] Where information is held about patients falling within the personal scope of the Directive, as "data subjects", they are now given explicit access rights in accordance with EU law.

The Directive grants data subjects ("identified or identifiable natural persons"[142]) control rights over their personal information. Article 10 provides that the data controller shall provide data subjects with details of the identity of the data

137 Health and Social Care Act 2001, section 61.

138 Case, above n 135, at 231.

139 See, for example, A.P. Ross, "The Case Against Showing Patients Their Records" 292 BMJ (1986) 578.

140 Article 40 of Law No 78/17 of 6 January 1978; Article 6 of the Law of 17 July 1978 (concerning measures for improving relations between government and the general public); Article L 1112-1 Public Health Code relating to medical dossiers in health institutions; see J. Bossi, "European Directive of October 24 1995 and Protection of Medical Data; The Consequences of the French Law Governing Data Processing and Freedoms" 9 *European Journal of Health Law* (2002) 201 at 204.

141 See, for example, in the UK, Access to Medical Reports Act 1988; Access to Health Records Act 1990.

142 Directive 95/46/EC, Article 2 (a).

controller,[143] purposes of processing[144] and also any appropriate further information,[145] which includes access rights and also the right to rectify the information held. Article 11 applies where the data have not been obtained from the data subject, and applies similar requirements where the data are first disclosed. Data subjects are also entitled to confidentiality and security of data processing.[146] The data subject has the right to object to the processing of data about him under Article 14. Article 12 provides that a data subject must be given:

"(a) without constraint at reasonable intervals and without excessive delay or expense:

- confirmation as to whether or not data relating to him are being processed and information at least as to the purposes of the processing, the categories of data concerned, and the recipients or categories of recipients to whom the data are disclosed;
- communication to him in an intelligible form of the data undergoing processing and of any available information as to their source;
- knowledge of the logic involved in any automatic processing of data concerning him at least in the case of [certain] automated decisions . . . ;[147]

(b) as appropriate the rectification, erasure or blocking of data the processing of which does not comply with the provisions of the Directive, in particular because of the incomplete or inaccurate nature of the data;
(c) notification to third parties to whom the data have been disclosed of any rectification, erasure or blocking carried out in compliance with (b), unless this proves impossible or involves a disproportionate effort."

Member States may restrict the scope of the rights in Article 12 where necessary to safeguard, *inter alia*, the data subject himself.[148] The Directive requires that such provisions must be the subject of *legislation*, so presumably simply a provision of a professional ethical code would not comply with the Directive in this respect. However, if legislation so provides, access to one's own medical records may still be restricted in cases where harm would be caused by such access, in accordance with the Directive. This is the situation, for instance, in the UK. Although UK law has recognised the principle of patient access to health records since 1990, this principle has always been subject to limitations on therapeutic grounds. These limitations have been incorporated in the measures introduced by the UK to fulfil its obligations under the Data Protection Directive. For example, in the UK, the Data Protection (Subject Access Modification) (Health) Order 2000 provides some limitations to

143 Directive 95/46/EC, Article 10(a).
144 Directive 95/46/EC, Article 10(b).
145 Directive 95/46/EC, Article 10(c).
146 Directive 95/46/EC, Article 16; Article 17.
147 These are outlined in Article 15, as decisions which produce legal effects concerning the data subject or significantly affect him or her, and which are based solely on automated processing of data intended to evaluate certain personal aspects relating to him or her, such as his performance at work, creditworthiness, reliability, conduct, etc. It is conceivable that this might include decisions with respect, for instance, to health insurance.
148 Directive 95/46/EC, Article 13 (1) (g).

patient access to health records, in a situation where permitting access would be likely to cause serious harm to the physical or mental health or condition of the patient, or of any other person.[149] Where information is sought on behalf of the data subject, then access can be denied where information was provided on the basis that it was not to be disclosed to the applicant, or where data was derived from an examination and investigation which the data subject had consented to, on the basis that the information would not be disclosed. Thus, whilst it is the case that privacy rights are enhanced through the Directive, the right to privacy is circumscribed by paternalism where there is a perceived clinical need to safeguard the interests of the patient.

Implementation and compliance with the Directive

While the Directive emphasises the need to safeguard privacy, in practice the Directive works in conjunction with existing safeguards to privacy and to confidentiality at national level. However, the Directive also poses specific obligations on Member States with respect to national compliance with its provisions. For instance, each Member State is to have a "controller" – a public authority or agency which determines the purposes and the means of processing of personal data within that Member State. The Directive provides for monitoring of data by independent supervisory authorities under Article 28. These supervisory authorities are to have powers of consultation, intervention, and also effective powers of investigation. They must be able to engage in legal proceedings, where national laws, adopted to implement the Directive, have been violated. Provisions on judicial remedies, and sanctions for breach of the relevant legal measures, are included.[150]

Where data controllers intend to undertake data processing, they must notify the supervisory authority of this fact.[151] Member States may exclude this notification requirement in situations which, taking account of the data to be processed, are unlikely to affect adversely the rights and freedoms of data subjects. Some requirements, such as prior checks and publicising of processing information, are left primarily to the Member State to determine. Where data is transferred to non-EU states, then arrangements are to be made to ensure that the use of the data is in fact subject to adequate protection.[152]

In terms of the implementation of the Directive, Article 27 provides that Member States and the European Commission are required to promote both national and EU-level codes of conduct in relation to specific sectors. As Kuitenbrouwer comments:

> "This is in line with the modern approach to the internet of both the EU and OECD, be it that of late the emphasis has shifted somewhat from self-regulation pure and simple to 'co-regulation' with a pronounced input from the government."[153]

149 SI 2000/413.

150 Directive 95/46/EC, Articles 22–24.

151 Directive 95/46/EC, Article 18.

152 See Commission Decision 2001/497/EC on standard contractual clauses for the transfer of personal data to countries under Directive 95/46/EC, OJ 2001 L 181/19.

153 F. Kuitenbrouwer, "Privacy and Its Fallacies" 9 *European Journal of Health Law* (2002) 173 at 174.

This approach fits well with the turn to "new" modes of governance, seen in the EU from the late 1990s. Soft law, such as a code of conduct, is promulgated to ensure standards are met, but without the intervention in national competence implied by detailed "old style" harmonising regulatory measures.[154]

Transfer of data outside the EU

Article 25 of the Data Protection Directive provides that Member States:

> "shall provide that the transfer to a third country of personal data which are undergoing processing or are intended for processing after transfer may take place only if, without prejudice to compliance with the national provisions adopted pursuant to the other provisions of this Directive, the third country in question ensures an adequate level of protection."

The Commission may determine that the protection granted by a particular third country is "adequate" in the terms of the Directive.[155] Moreover, in a situation in which the Commission finds that such a third country does not ensure an adequate degree of protection, then Article 25(4) provides that: "Member States shall take the measures necessary to prevent any transfer of data of the same type to the third country in question."

Knoppers and Fecteau have commented that this provision has been of considerable practical importance in the context of international pharmacogenetic trials.[156] They suggest that:

> "This is because the norms governing medical data specifically are often directed at the health sector (usually public, except in the US) and not those of commercial companies doing research in the private sector which fall under personal data legislation. Given the research involvement of the commercial sector in medical research, such an 'extra territorial' effect of personal data protection is important."[157]

IV. Conclusions

What has been the impact of the Data Protection Directive on patients' rights to confidentiality and privacy? Across the EU, there has been a differential response to the Directive. This has been subject to recent criticism by the Commission.[158] In its First Report "Concerning the Implementation of the Directive", in 2003, the Commission commented that, in a number of instances, there were indications of non-compliance with Community law, concerning those provisions which give

154 See chapter 2.

155 Directive 95/46/EC, Article 25 (6). It has done so with respect to the "Safe Harbor Privacy Principles" published by the US Ministry of Commerce (Decision 2000/520/EC, OJ 2000 L 215/7) and Canadian law (Decision 2002/2/EC, OJ 2002 L 2/13); see Brillon, above n 85 and A. Charlesworth, "Dataprivacy in cyberspace" in L. Edwards and C. Waelde, *Law and the Internet* (Hart Publishing: Oxford, 2000).

156 B.M. Knoppers and C. Fecteau, "Human Genomic Databases: A Global Public Good?" 10 *European Journal of Health Law* (2003) 27.

157 Knoppers and Fecteau, above n 156, at 29.

158 Commission, *First Report from the Commission on the Implementation of the Data Protection Directive 95/46/EC* COM (2003) 265 final, p 11.

little discretion to individual Member States. The Commission specified the following illustrations: the grounds for legitimate processing under Article 7; sensitive data under Article 8 (1); information to data subjects under Article 10; exceptions under Article 13; and exceptions concerning transfer of information to third countries. It commented that discussions were to be held with Member States with the intention of agreed solutions being reached.[159] Interestingly, the Report also noted problems with enforcement, which included lack of resources, "patchy compliance by data controllers", and the fact that data subjects had "low level awareness" of their rights.[160]

As we have seen, legislative measures adopted at EU-level and individual litigation concerning, directly or more indirectly, the provision of national health care services may have the effect of rendering some national laws and policies inconsistent with EU law, which precludes national governments from pursuing those policies or maintaining in place those laws. Member States must, for instance, now ensure that the standards required by the Data Protection Directive on the processing of personal data are applied with respect to personal data "processed" (collected, held, used, disseminated) in the health care context. While most Member States adopted new legislative provisions in order to comply with the Directive,[161] implementation of the

159 This may be a preliminary, informal stage in what may eventually become enforcement proceedings under Article 226 EC; see further chapter 2.

160 Commission, above n 41, p 12.

161 Countries which have now implemented the Directive include Austria (Data Protection Act 2000, BGB1 No 165/1999); Finland (Personal Data Act 523/1999); Italy (Leg Decree No 135 of 11.05.99); Sweden (Personal Data Act 1998); Greece (Law 2472/1997); Belgium (Law of 8 December 1992 on privacy protection in relation to the processing of personal data as modified by the law of 11 December 1998, implementing Directive 95/46/EC); Denmark (The Act on the processing of personal information, Act No 429, 31 May 2000, in force 1 July 2000). Germany is amending the existing law and in addition working at fundamental reform of the law of data protection. In the UK, the government passed the Data Protection Act 1998. Prior to 2000, access to health care records was regulated predominantly under the Access to Health Records Act 1990 and the Data Protection Act 1984. The Access to Health Records Act 1990 and Access to Personal Files Act 1987 applied to manually stored records, whilst the Data Protection Act 1984 related to those records which were stored electronically. The position however changed in 2000, when the remaining provisions of the Data Protection Act 1998 were brought into force: see UK Data Protection Act 1998 (Commencement) Order 2000, SI 2000/183; and see generally I. Lloyd, *A Guide to the Data Protection Act 1998* (London: Butterworths, 1998). The 1998 Act has repealed the Data Protection Act 1984, Access to Personal Files Act 1987 and most of the Access to Health Records Act 1990. The new 1998 Act covers both electronic and manual health records. In Greece, a law was passed implementing the Directive, Law 2472/1997 "On the Processing of Personal Data". The law itself refers to medical data as being "sensitive" data. As Cannellopolou-Bottis notes, this is a different interpretation from that of the Directive's use of the word "special categories of data": Cannellopoulou-Bottis, above n 18, at 208. Many of the categories for processing mirror those of the Directive. Where consent is given for processing under Article 7, section 2, this must be informed, and also explicit, consent. The processing of data must be undertaken subject to a licence issued by a new body created by the law, the Greek Authority of Data Protection. This body is independent of the government. Headed by a Supreme Court Justice, it is comprised of five members. This is an influential organisation which may, for example, be involved in the development of ethical codes. Failure to comply with the legislation may result in criminal or civil sanctions. In addition, the regulatory body, the Authority of the Protection of Personal Data, is able to impose administrative sanctions. These include withdrawal of licences and fines. In addition, the Greek Constitution was amended to provide in Article 9A that "Everyone has the

Directive was delayed in several Member States, and this led to formal infringement proceedings being brought.[162]

Overall, the Data Protection Directive has affected, to some extent, the terms in which patients' rights to confidentiality and privacy are respected in the EU, at least in connection with the "processing" of data on their health. The Directive's fundamental rights approach has made it more difficult for Member States to adopt paternalistic models of regulation, under which data with respect to a patient is kept from him "for his own good", or is communicated to a patient only by the intermediary medical professional. The Directive purports to be based on an underlying requirement of consent to all "processing" of data, but the leeway given to Member States in its detailed implementation may actually undermine this in certain circumstances, as the example of the UK illustrates. Moreover, the Directive fails to engage with other possible assaults *in practice* on the privacy of individual patients. While the mechanisms for protection of privacy may be in place and the rhetoric operational, the efficacy of some national measures implementing the Directive has been subject to question. In practice if, for example, a person seeks indemnification for health expenses from an insurance fund, they will inevitably have to disclose relevant information to the insurers.[163] This kind of problem is likely to become more common as genetic information becomes more widely available. Furthermore, the protection offered by the Directive and national implementing measures is dependent upon the relevant infrastructure being in place. The Data Protection Directive is part of the "acquis communautaire" to be implemented by new Member States before accession.[164] However, questions remain about infrastructure and, in particular, human resources capacity to implement its provisions effectively in Central and Eastern European accession states.

A further difficulty in implementation of the Directive, in the broader health context, is that the Directive concerns only "data" and information privacy. In practice, however, where clinical research is undertaken, both information and

right to the protection of the collection, processing and use, especially by electronic means, of personal data as the law provides".

162 In the case of France, Luxembourg, Germany, Ireland and the Netherlands, this led to the Commission bringing proceedings before the European Court of Justice for failure to notify them of all measures, the third stage of formal infringement procedures under Article 226 EC. A finding was made against Luxembourg (Case C-450/00 *Commission v Luxembourg* [2001] ECR I-7069) but it did subsequently implement legislation. France to date has still not implemented. A draft law was introduced in 2001: see Bossi, above n 140. This amends the existing Law No 78-17 of 6 January 1978 which concerned data processing and will provide patients with access rights to their own health records, in contrast to the existing position where, as we noted above, disclosure is required through the use of a physician intermediary. See, in general, *Fifth Annual Report on the Situation Regarding the Protection of Individuals with regard to the processing of personal data and privacy in the community and in third countries* Article 29 Data Protection Working Party SD19/01/EN WPL16, 2002; and *First Report from the Commission on the Implementation of the Data Protection Directive 95/46/EC* COM (2003) 265 final.

163 See, citing the example of Greece, Cannellopoulou-Bottis, above n 18, at 216.

164 Indeed, some Central and Eastern European Member States used the Data Protection Directive as a model for completely new data protection legislation.

physical samples may be stored together in a large genetic database. The absence of a single regulatory regime governing research use of information and of samples may lead to considerable practical difficulties for researchers. So, for example, at Member State level, this may mean that one legal regime governs the retention and use of samples, and a totally separate regime applies to the use of information.[165] The logical consequence of regulatory developments such as the Data Protection Directive and the Clinical Trials Directive, discussed in chapter 7 below, may be that there is an emerging need for a specific EU-level regime, which relates to the use of both data and physical research materials in the health research context. Such a regime could be based on the need to ensure cross-border mobility of data and physical research material, within a "single European research area".[166]

165 In the UK context, see, for example, the discussion of the legal regulation of genetic databases by P. Martin and J. Kaye, *The Use of Biological Sample Collections and Personal Medical Information in Human Genetic Research* (London: Wellcome Trust, 1999).

166 See further chapter 7.

6

Regulation of health care professionals

I. Introduction

The regulation of health care professionals has a long and ancient history.[1] The teaching and practice of physic and surgery dates from the days of Hippocrates and the works of Galen (131–201 AD). The Salerno School, a group which had settled in Salerno in Italy in AD 900, not only taught medicine but, it is believed, was the first to confer doctorates.[2] Overt occupational control is illustrated through the operation of licensing procedures observable in certain European countries as long ago as the sixteenth century.[3] Today, statutory regulation of health professional bodies is common across EU Member States.[4] Our concern in this chapter is with the extent to which EU law has affected such regulation. As we will see, such effects have so far been limited, marginal and mainly indirect. They will probably remain so, unless significant cross-border movements of patients alter the political imperative for Member States to coordinate or even harmonise their regulatory standards.

Before we explore interactions between the EU's legal order and those of its Member States in the regulation of health care professionals, we need, briefly, to develop some parameters concerning who is a "health care professional", and set out what elements constitute the "regulation" of such health care professionals. Our starting point here is that "health care professional" is a broader category than that of "doctor".[5] Different approaches have been advanced for identifying professions, including the health care profession.[6] Such approaches may concentrate on the

1 J. Jacobs, *Doctors and Rules: A Sociology of Professional Values* (New Jersey: Transaction Publishing, 1999).

2 Jacobs, above n 1, p 89.

3 For example, in England and Wales, the first Medical Act was passed by Henry VIII in 1511–1512. This Act provided that it was an offence to practice medicine without a degree or a Bishop's licence, although it was only much later that the practice of medicine was regulated over the UK as a whole. In 1858, the Medical Act established the General Medical Council with the task of supervising a register of the medically qualified – a task which it continues until this day.

4 See for example, M. Moran and B. Wood, *States, Regulation and the Medical Profession* (Buckingham: Open University Press, 1993); R. Freeman, *The politics of health in Europe* (Manchester: MUP, 2000), especially chapter 6.

5 But it probably does not include every person to whom a patient might go for health care or health advice, for instance, it would not include tarot card reader.

6 See, for instance, Moran and Wood, above n 4.

"normative" elements of professional regulation, the "traits" common to professions, or may hold that professionalism can be seen as a mode of regulatory occupational control.[7] Elements of each are useful. The "normative" approach suggests that professions are distinguishable through a well-developed ethical code. Certainly, from Hippocrates onwards, ethical codes have been a distinguishing feature of clinical practice. However, given the huge range of trades which today have some form of code, this approach may be insufficient to distinguish "professionals". Following the "trait" approach, professions are defined through a process of examining those occupations that assert professional status, to see whether common characteristics, such as the type of work and methods of entry to a profession, can be discerned. However, the number of such groups renders the task of distilling unifying features almost certainly impossible.

According to the "regulatory" approach, professions are identified by reference to the special regulatory controls that are imposed on those practising a particular profession. Such special regulation is justified, *inter alia*, by the particular nature of the job:

> "Occupations like medicine are in particular need of a professional status according to this view because of the nature of the job. Medicine is an intrusive business, involving examination of the most intimate and sensitive matters. Ideas of professionalism – of special ethical codes, of unusual care of clients – help make intrusion acceptable."[8]

The regulatory approach thus focuses on the public interest imperatives that drive professional regulation. This also highlights another feature of professional regulation: the centrality of politics to the regulatory process.[9] It follows that the "regulatory contract" between state and profession, the mix of state regulation and self-regulation through professional bodies, and the substance of the relevant rules, may differ considerably between jurisdictions.[10] This forms an important context within which EU-level rules concerning professionals (including health care professionals) must take effect. In particular, the strong differences of approach between jurisdictions have a particular resonance within the context of "creating the EU internal market in persons", as we shall see below.

Within Member States of the EU, health care professions are regulated in many respects. Entry to professions, and the use of professional titles, is restricted to those who have completed initial, and, in many cases, advanced education and training, and who therefore hold a professional qualification. Remaining within a health

7 See, in particular, E. Friedson, *Profession of Medicine: A Study of the Sociology of Applied Knowledge* (New York: Dodd Mead, 1988).
8 Friedson, above n 7, p 25.
9 See Moran and Wood, above n 4, p 25.
10 For discussion of the relations between health professionals and the state in a number of European countries, see T. Johnson, G. Larkin and M. Saks, eds, *Health Professions and the State in Europe* (London: Routledge, 1995); see also E. Segest, "Consumer Protection and the Free Movement of Medical Practitioners in the European Union" 4 *European Journal of Health Law* (1997) 267; J. Lonbay, "The Free Movement of health care professionals in the European Community" in R. Goldberg and J. Lonbay, eds, *Pharmaceutical Medicine, Biotechnology and European Law* (Cambridge: CUP, 2000), p 45.

care profession is limited to those fit to practise. There may be requirements to undertake continuous professional training. The boundaries of practice are determined,[11] for instance, by reserving the powers to prescribe or dispense medicines,[12] or to carry out particular medical procedures, to certain health care professionals. Conditions of employment of health care professionals within national health (insurance) systems, for instance covering pay, are determined by factors other than market forces. The obligations of the health care professional to the state, and, conversely limitations on her private practice, may be formalised. Limitations may be placed on health care professionals established in their own practices, for instance, on the numbers of patients they may have on their lists, or which gifts may be properly received from patients. Ethical principles, such as a duty of confidentiality, respect for patients' dignity and autonomy, and a duty to act in the patient's best interest, are maintained, often through membership of professional bodies.[13] Further, standards of appropriate conduct towards patients may be prescribed, perhaps in the form of codes of conduct, covering matters such as courtesy, or improper relationships with patients. Standards of professional competence are established, beyond the requirements of contractual relationships and non-contractual liability of negligent health care professionals to their patients.[14] These standards may

11 For instance, whether health care professionals may practise alternative and complementary medicine.

12 In this context, see the example of the development of the nursing profession. Nursing history illustrates that nurses have been long subject to regulation, but in past centuries regulation took the form of directions and constraints rather than the maximisation of professional autonomy. Nurses were historically regarded as "doctors handmaidens" (see J.R. Montgomery, "Doctor's Handmaidens: The Legal Contribution" in S. Wheeler and S. McVeigh ed. *Law, Health and Medical Regulation* (Aldershot: Dartmouth, 1992)). One of the catalysts for the modern conceptualisation of nursing was the work of Florence Nightingale, who emphasised that nurses were to be managed by nurses. Across jurisdictions today, there is a movement towards granting nurses greater degrees of professional autonomy of action; an enhanced or expanded role. This is something which has led to considerable heated debate amongst nurses themselves, notably in relation to the development of nurse practitioners. See, for example, D. Wicks, *Nurses and Doctors at Work* (Buckingham: Open University Press, 1998). In the UK, enhanced prescription powers have been a particular source of controversy. These are regarded by some nurses as a logical development in professional practice, whilst other nurses resist attempts to thrust them into a medical role with the aim of cutting costs. See J. McHale, "A review of the legal framework for nurse prescribing" 1(3) *Nurse Prescribing* (2003) 107.

13 In the UK, for example, doctors are regulated through the General Medical Council under the Medical Act 1983. This body is not only concerned with the registration of practitioners, but promulgates an ethical code and implements professional disciplinary procedures. In Belgium, doctors are regulated through the Order of Physicians, initially established by the Law of 25 June 1938 and now regulated through the Crown Order (CO) nr 79 of 10 November 1967. See, for example, R. Schepers, H. Nys, P. Mokos and I. Van Bael, "Controlling Medical Doctors in Belgium", paper presented to the 14th World Congress on Medical Law, Maastricht, August 2003, pp 256–261. The Order is constituted through a national council, ten provincial councils and two councils of appeal. All medical practitioners are required to be entered upon the register of the Order: Article 2 CO nr 79. Practitioners are subject to rules of professional conduct and may be disciplined by, in the first instance, the provincial councils, with provision for appeal to the appeal council.

14 For an accessible discussion of contractual and non-contractual relationships between patients and their doctors in the UK context, see M. Brazier, *Medicine, Patients and the Law* (London: Penguin, 2003), especially chapters 3 and 6; A. Grubb, "Duties in Contract and Tort" in I. Kennedy and A. Grubb, eds, *Principles of Medical Law* (Oxford: OUP, 1998).

interact with state-imposed quality control parameters, covering matters such as standard operating procedures and protocols, adherence to which is expected.[15] Some Member States have attempted to impose duties appertaining to respect for the public purse,[16] or to restrict the numbers of health care professionals that may establish themselves in a particular state.[17] Different Member States use different mechanisms, and a different mix of self-regulation and state regulation, to protect patients from substandard practice on the part of health care professionals.[18] These

15 There is an observable trend across a number of Member States for the state to be increasing its involvement in the regulation of health care provision, as opposed to leaving matters to self-regulation through professional bodies. This trend is linked to a concern regarding standards and quality in health care. This may affect the actions of individual professionals if, for example, constraints are imposed on the quality of health care external to those imposed by the professional bodies. Illustrations of this trend include the Commission for Health Care Improvement in the UK (soon to become the Commission for Healthcare Audit and Inspection), a statutory body established under the UK Health Act 1999 which has a wide remit to review the provision of health care services, and considerable investigatory powers. In addition, the provision of treatments in the UK is subject to the National Institute of Clinical Excellence, which produces guidelines as to treatment procedures and regarding those drugs that should be funded through the NHS. Major restructuring of mechanisms for reviewing quality in health care in the UK is currently underway, following an inquiry chaired by Professor Ian Kennedy into the cardiac paediatric unit at Bristol Royal Infirmary: see further J. McHale, "Quality and Safety in Health Care: A role for the Law?" *Quality and Safety in Health Care* (2002) p 88. One of the bodies established consequent upon this inquiry, and the criticism levied at the vast proliferation of professional guidelines, is the Council for the Regulation of Health Professionals, which is to have the power to investigate complaints regarding the regulatory bodies' exercise of their jurisdiction; see UK National Health Service Reform and Health Care Professions Act 2002, section 25.

16 In Belgium, the "Medical Control Service" is established under the Health Insurance System and includes a Committee for Medical Control of the Belgian National Institute of Sickness and Disability Insurance (l'Institut national d'assurance maladie-invalidité, "INAMI"). This body is comprised of physicians and of magistrates. It has the task of evaluating quality of medical care. This is in line with Article 35 of the Belgian Law on the Health Insurance System which imposes a "duty of economy" on doctors. They are required to undertake skilful medical treatment in the patient's interests and with regard to the "means disposed of by society". There is a prohibition upon the prescription of examinations and treatments which are too expensive or upon the performance of procedures which are superfluous. Whether treatments fall within the categories of too expensive or superfluous is determined by reference to the perspective of the "reasonable physician" in the same circumstances. Interestingly, it appears that the committee is involved in a very small number of cases and indeed this number appears to be declining. Schepers and Casparie have noted that there are considerable difficulties with the system as it currently stands. There appears to be resistance from physicians regarding such regulation. Moreover the rules and the norms which the formal institutions are intended to apply are in fact "ill-defined and impractical". Furthermore, it is suggested that the Committee for Medical Control is influenced both by the medical trade unions and the sickness funds with their own political interests. See generally R. Schepers and A.F. Casparie, "Continuity or discontinuity in the self-regulation of the Belgian and Dutch medical professions" 19(5) *Sociology of Health and Illness* (1997) 580.

17 For instance, in Germany, the numbers of pharmacists are limited.

18 For instance, some Member States, such as Finland, place a heavier reliance on prevention of poor practice, rather than repression. This allows for a greater range of possibilities for redress, such as statements, instructions and guidelines, many of which do not involve disciplinary measures against a particular health care professional. See H.D.C. Roscam Abbing, "The Right of the Patient to Quality of Medical Practice and the Position of Doctors in the EU" 4 *European Journal of Health Law* (1997) 347 at 354–357; A.C. Oostermann-Meulenbeld, "Quality Regulation on Professional Health Care Practice in the European Community" (1993/1) *Legal Issues of European Integration* 61 at 72–75. Other Member States place a greater reliance on repressive measures. There are

elements of regulation of health care professionals are a matter of national law, set at Member State level. Most are unaffected by EU law, and remain a matter of national competence.

Although the nature of health care may itself in principle suggest "professionalism", in practice, while there is a vast proliferation of health care practitioners, that does not itself necessarily equate with their recognition as "professionals". Some health care providers have struggled for recognition as "professionals" and others are yet to be recognised as such. Providers of less well-established or innovative health care services, for instance, practitioners of complementary and associated professions, such as various forms of psychotherapy, may not (yet) be subject to state regulation. If "health care professional" is to be defined by reference to a regulatory framework, then these practitioners, by definition, are not "health professionals", at least in that state. This may be because the state itself is unwilling to afford the provider with the explicit recognition and legitimacy which regulation provides. A further reason may be the influence of *existing* health professional bodies and their concerns over boundary disputes. Indeed, as Friedson has commented, professionalisation of health care practice can be regarded as control over that part of the labour market, by excluding other potential providers of health care.[19]

As we will see in this chapter, the EU has left the matter of what is and is not a (health care) profession to national regulatory structures. Over time, however, the EU has moved from engagement with health professionals in *particular individual* professional categories (or "sectors" in the EU terminology) defined by regulation of entry requirements (sectoral professional qualifications) towards an approach that simply requires a minimum regulation of entry to a profession at national level, for an activity to fall within the EU rules. Nevertheless, the relevant EU rules apply only where there is some national regulation of a profession *qua* profession. Aspiring professions cannot use EU law in itself to move towards professional recognition. That matter also remains a matter of national competence.

II. The impact of EU law on health care professional practice

This chapter considers the involvement of the EU in the regulation of health care professionals. But this must be seen in the context of the extent to which individual

differences in terms of the availability of professional conduct procedures across professional bodies' complaints procedures, who may bring a claim for civil or criminal liability, what remedies are available and so on. In the UK, for example, while disciplinary proceedings may be brought, for instance, in the context of the medical profession to the professional conduct committee, the extent to which these procedures legitimated through statute have been effective has been subject to question and indeed there is now general overarching scrutiny of professional practice through the Council for the Regulation of Health Care Professions. See further Brazier, above n 14, pp 10–17; J.K. Mason, R.A. McCall Smith, G. Laurie, *Law and Medical Ethics* (London: Butterworths, 6th edn, 2002), pp 13–20; J. Montgomery, *Health Care Law* (Oxford: OUP, 2nd edn, 2002), chapter 6.

19 Friedson, above n 7.

Member States autonomously regulate their own national health (insurance) systems. In general, the regulation of health care professionals is a matter of national competence. National control over health care professionals and professional bodies is motivated not only by a desire to protect the health and lives of patients as the "consumers" of health care services, and, with respect to public health, of all residents of the state, but also by a desire to control costs, as the state is the primary purchaser of such services within the Member States of the EU. The regulation of the "organisation and delivery of health services and medical care" falls within the Member States' responsibility, in accordance with Article 152 (5) EC. The European Court of Justice has regularly observed that "Community law does not detract from the powers of the Member States to organise their social security systems",[20] which includes their national health (insurance) systems.

It follows that the impact of EU law on the regulation of health care professionals is mainly of an indirect nature. EU law has an effect only at the margins of national regulation of health care professionals, and is constrained by the limited Community competence in this field. We consider two examples here, EU employment law and EU law on freedom to provide services, before turning to the principal area in which EU law has affected health care professionals, that of mutual recognition of qualifications in the context of free movement of persons.

EU employment law

Health care professionals, who are also employees or workers in the sense of EU employment law, are subject to measures of EU employment law based on Article 137 EC and its precursors in the Treaty, especially Article 118a EC. Article 137 EC now provides a legal basis for the adoption of directives setting minimum requirements (new approach harmonisation) in various employment-related fields, in particular health and safety at work and working conditions. The significance of Article 118a EC was that it provided for qualified majority voting in Council, which led to the adoption of measures of EU employment law that were not supported by the governments of all Member States.[21] Such measures only occasionally make special provision for health care professionals, but, provided that health care professionals satisfy the status of "employee" or "worker", simply treat them as all other workers are treated. [22] So, for instance, EU secondary legislation on health and safety at

20 Case 238/82 *Duphar* [1984] ECR 523, para 16; Cases 159 & 160/91 *Poucet and Pistre* [1993] ECR I-637, para 6; Case C-70/95 *Sodemare* [1997] ECR I-3395, para 27; Case C-120/95 *Decker* [1998] ECR I-1831, para 21; Case C-158/96 *Kohll* [1998] ECR I-1931, para 17; Case C-157/99 *Geraets-Smits and Peerbooms* [2001] ECR I-5473, para 44. This phrase has begun to "acquire the status of a catechism": see G. Davies, "Welfare as a Service" 29 *Legal Issues of Economic Integration* (2002) 27.

21 The best-known example of this is the Working Time Directive, Directive 93/104/EC, OJ 1993 L 307/18, now repealed and replaced by Directive 2003/88/EC, OJ 2003 L 299/9; challenged (unsuccessfully) by the UK in Case 84/94 *UK v Council (Working Time)* [1996] ECR I-5755.

22 Other sectors, such as transport, regularly enjoy special exemptions from measures of EU employment law. For instance, the Working Time Directive, Directive 93/104/EC exempts seafarers entirely from its provisions (Article 1 (3)) and allows Member States to derogate from its provisions in the case of managing executives, family workers and religious officials.

work,[23] employment rights in the event of restructuring of employers' enterprises,[24] and non-discrimination on grounds of sex,[25] racial or ethnic origin, religion or belief, age, disability or sexual orientation[26] applies to employment in the health care field, just as in other fields.

In some circumstances, the fact that the general EU employment law provisions have not been tailored to the health care profession may cause difficulties in a Member State. For instance, Spanish legislation provided for a 40-hour working week for staff in primary health care teams (which was within the terms of the Working Time Directive, Directive 93/104/EC[27]), but this was without prejudice to work that such staff were required to undertake as a result of being on call. In rural districts, because small numbers of staff were covering relatively large geographical areas, the maximum annual hours on call was set at 850,[28] with a view to the progressive reduction of this total. This provision was challenged by the Sindicato de Médicos de Asistencia Pública (SIMAP) on the grounds that, in accordance with the Working Time Directive, working time should not exceed 48 hours, including overtime, in any period of seven days (over a total of four months)[29] and night work should not exceed eight hours in any period of 24 hours.[30] The European Court of Justice confirmed that the Working Time Directive applies to workers in primary health care teams.[31] The Court went on to find that time spent "on call" where the worker was required to be present at the place of employment fell within the scope of the Directive, as did time actually providing health care, in circumstances where the worker was "on call" in the sense of it being possible to contact her, but not actually present at the place of employment.[32] If national authorities wish to rely on the provisions in the Working Time Directive allowing Member States to derogate from certain of its provisions in the case of activities involving the need for continuity of service, in particular "services related to the reception, treatment

23 See the Framework Directive on Health and Safety at Work, Directive 89/391/EEC, OJ 1989 L 183/1; replacement Article 17 from 20 November 2003 by Regulation 1882/2003/EC, OJ 2003 L 284/1; and the discussion of the EU's legal framework on health and safety at work in C. Barnard, *EC Employment Law* (Oxford: OUP, 2000), chapter 6.

24 See, for example, Directive 77/187/EEC, OJ 1977 L 61/126 on the transfer of undertakings, and the discussion of the EU's legal framework on employees' rights in EU law on the restructuring of enterprises (now repealed and replaced by Directive 2001/23/EC, OJ 2001 L 82/16) in Barnard, above n 23, chapter 7.

25 See, for example, Directive 76/207/EEC, OJ 1976 L 39/40 on equal treatment on the ground of sex in employment, as amended, and the discussion of the EU's legal framework on sex equality in employment in Barnard, above n 23, chapter 4. Such legislation would now be based on Article 141 EC.

26 See Directive 2000/43/EC, OJ 2000 L 180/22 on race discrimination; Directive 2000/78/EC, OJ 2000 L 303/16 on forbidden grounds of discrimination in the labour market. Such legislation is based on Article 13 EC.

27 OJ 1993 L 307/18. Now consolidated in Directive 2003/88/EC, OJ 2003 L 299/9, to enter into force on 2 August 2004.

28 In comparison with the maximum of 425 hours per year set for other staff.

29 Directive 93/104/EC, Article 6.

30 Directive 93/104/EC, Article 8.

31 Case C-303/98 *SIMAP* [2000] ECR I-7963, para 38.

32 Case C-303/98 *SIMAP* above n 31, para 52.

and/or care provided by hospitals or similar establishments",[33] they must do so explicitly.

In the *SIMAP* case, the professionals concerned were present at the place of employment and available for work during the on-call time that constituted working time for the purposes of the Working Time Directive. Where the professionals were on call in the sense of being contactable, but not actually working or present at the place of work, this time fell outside "working time" in the sense of the Directive. What about the situation where an on-call hospital doctor is present in the hospital, contactable, but actually asleep? In a case involving a hospital doctor in Kiel, Germany, the Court confirmed that, for the purposes of the Working Time Directive, time spent on call in such circumstances counts as working time.[34] It is irrelevant that the hospital makes a room with a bed available for the doctor to rest in during quiet periods. The fact that the doctor is required to be present at the place of work and available immediately should the need arise is decisive. This clarification may have an impact on hospital practices in a number of Member States.

In the UK and Irish contexts, the Working Time Directive has been criticised by health care professionals and providers of health care as being insufficiently sensitive to the traditional practices of the British and Irish national health systems, and in particular to causing capacity problems as junior doctors may no longer work the long hours that have historically formed part of their training. Such criticisms led to an amendment of the Directive in 2000.[35] Member States may now derogate from the Directive's provisions in respect of maximum weekly working time in the case of doctors in training, for a transitional period of five years from 1 August 2004, with a possible extension of three further years.[36] This is "to take account of difficulties in meeting the working time provisions with respect to their responsibilities for the organisation and delivery of health services and medical care".[37] Nonetheless in the UK the controversy continues. Implementation of the Directive apparently means that, by 2009, junior hospital doctors' hours will be cut by 25%. The British Medical Association chairman, James Johnson, stated that the consequence of the Directive would be to place general practitioners under pressure not to admit patients to hospital and may have the result that hospitals will close.[38] In the Netherlands, hospitals were given until 1999 to implement the Directive. An order in Council allowed a more flexible application of the Directive and there were certain exceptions provided for some groups such as doctors in training and junior doctors. However, inspections of hospitals by the inspection body of the Netherlands Ministry of Social Affairs and Employment found that there was a serious problem with compliance with the Directive by hospitals. Reasons suggested for this included the time taken

33 Directive 93/104/EC, Article 17 (2.1) (c) (i).

34 Case C-151/02 *Landeshauptstadt Kiel v Jaeger* [2003] ECR I-(9 september 2003, nyr in ECR).

35 Directive 2000/34/EC, OJ 2000 L 195/41.

36 Directive 2000/34/EC, Article 1, consolidated in Directive 93/104/EC, Article 17.

37 Directive 93/104/EC, Article 17 (2.4) (a).

38 Z. Kmietowicz, "Emergency service under threat from working time directive" 327 BMJ (2003) 184.

to complete the necessary paperwork with no consequent financial incentives and difficulties in identifying what constituted "working time".[39] The Working Time Directive is directly effective as against an "emanation of the state",[40] and therefore can be enforced in national courts. It may be that litigation is necessary to change the working conditions of some health care professionals to be consistent with the provisions of the Directive. However, in anticipation of such litigation, Member States may rely on an explicit sector-specific opt out from the maximum 48-hour working week, relying on Article 18(1)(b)(i) of the Directive.[41]

EU law on provision of services

Health care professionals who provide a "service", in the sense of EU law, are also subject to measures of EU law based on Article 95 EC on completion and maintenance of the internal market or on Article 47 (2) EC on self-employment and Article 55 EC on provision of services.[42] Where health professionals move to another Member State to provide services, the cross-border provision of health care services may cause tensions with national provision, where cross-border service provision means that health care workers carrying out the same jobs, side-by-side, may have different terms and conditions of employment, arising in part from different cultures in professional practice. The Posted Workers Directive 96/71/EC[43] aims to guard against the perceived risks of "social dumping" where cheaper labour is used to provide a service in a Member State, thus potentially undermining the arrangements for employment rights and other elements of social protection, such as collective bargaining arrangements, in the host Member State. The Directive provides that posted workers must be guaranteed the host Member State's terms and conditions of employment, in respect of certain core matters, such as working periods and minimum rates of pay. However, the Directive leaves other terms and conditions of employment to the employment law of the home Member State. When various British hospitals contracted nurses from Spain, where there are high levels of unemployment among nurses, to deal with the problem of British under-capacity,[44] tensions arose over the different conditions of work of the Spanish nurses and British nurses working alongside them.[45] For instance, an NHS Trust in the North West of

39 F. Sprangers, "The Dutch Experience of implementing the European Working Time Directive" 325 BMJ (2002) 71.

40 See Case C-188/89 *Foster v British Gas* [1990] ECR I-3313. A hospital or other employer that formed part of the national health (insurance) system would fall within this category.

41 This requires "agreement" from the employee, and is subject to a record-keeping and reporting obligation on the employer. France has introduced such legislation in the health sector, although this allows for time off in lieu. Germany, Netherlands and several new Member States are considering sectoral opt outs, see COM(2003) 843.

42 For a discussion of the principles of EU law in this respect, see chapter 4.

43 Directive 96/71/EC, OJ 1996 L 18/1.

44 On the shortage and oversupply of nurses, see J. Irwin, "Migration patterns of nurses in the EU" 7 *eurohealth* (2001) 13.

45 BBC News, 20 March 2001, 27 February 2002, http://www.bbc.co.uk/1/hi/health. See also the discussion in C. Ludvigsen and K. Roberts, *Health Care Policies and Europe: the implications for practice* (Oxford: Butterworth-Heinemann, 1996), p 146.

England employed 21 Spanish nurses, four of whom were on secondment. Those four seconded claimed, relying in part on the *SIMAP* case, that Spanish working hours applied to them. The Trust, relying on the Directive, took the view that British law applied. The case was eventually settled by virtue of ending the secondment, re-employing the four nurses on a different basis, and paying overtime rates for extra hours worked.[46]

Provision of health care services by health care professionals across borders within the EU is likely to be affected by the current proposal to amend and consolidate the EU's directives on mutual recognition of the regulated professions.[47] The proposal provides that Member States may not restrict, for any reason relating to professional qualifications, the free provision of services in another (host) Member State, where the service provider is legally established in a (home) Member State for the purposes of practising the same professional activity there, and has done so for at least two years.[48] A "service provider" is defined for these purposes as a professional who provides the service for not more than 16 weeks per year in the host Member State. Presumably, a professional could offer services in a succession of host Member States, each period lasting less than 16 weeks. It might then be possible for such a professional to "slip through the net" of regulation in the home Member State of establishment, as that Member State would have no incentive to control the activities of a professional who was not in fact practising on the territory of the home Member State. A number of bodies in the UK health profession, and also patient groups, have raised concerns to this effect about the proposal, and these have been taken up by the European Parliament.[49] The concern focuses around patient safety. Doctors and other health care professionals would be able to work in a Member State for 16 weeks per year, without being subject to that state's regulatory system for health care professionals. It remains to be seen, if the proposal is adopted in its current form, whether this concern turns out to be anything other than a purely hypothetical situation. Would a health professional seek only 16 weeks' employment per year in a particular Member State, perhaps moving on to another Member State for the next 16 weeks, and a third for the rest of the year? This would seem to be appealing only to a particularly enterprising individual, who did not mind significant personal disruption. Maybe this would be a concern in the "sunshine" Member States, such as Spain, Portugal or Greece, if health care professionals, say from Germany or the UK, moved to those Member States to provide health care for holiday-makers during the holiday season.

At least at present, in the absence of well-established "e-commerce" in the health field in the EU,[50] it seems unlikely that significant numbers of professionals will offer

46 Thanks to Stephen Hardy for providing details of this dispute.

47 Proposal for a Directive of the European Parliament and the Council on the recognition of professional qualifications, COM(2002) 119 final, amended by COM(2004) 317 final.

48 Proposed Directive COM(2002) 119 final, Article 5.

49 "EU work plan 'puts patients at risk'", 18 July 2002, http://www.bbc.co.uk/1/hi/health; "EU rejects foreign doctors plan", 27 November 2003, http://www.bbc.co.uk/1/hi/health.

50 Such "e-commerce" may develop in the future: see further chapter 10.

health care *services* across borders within the EU, creating situations where the health care professional is established in (and subject to the professional regulatory regime of) a Member State other than that to which the patient belongs. Apart from the examples we considered in chapter 4, where the *patient* moves to receive health care services in another Member State,[51] the most likely movement across borders within the EU in this context is health care professionals seeking to *establish* themselves in a Member State other than that in which they have qualified. This involves a different body of EU law from that at issue in the exercise of the freedom to provide services. It is to this matter that we now turn.

III. EU law and entry into professional practice in Member States

As we saw above, regulation of health care professionals includes setting terms and conditions on entry into professional practice, through requiring health care professionals to hold a professional qualification. As a matter of EU law, control over education systems is largely a matter of national competence,[52] so where health care professional qualifications are regulated, these qualifications will be peculiar to the Member State in which they were acquired. However, one of the most important bodies of EU law that affects the regulation of health care professionals in the Member States is that which ensures the freedom of movement of professionals within the EU, moving not to provide services, but to *establish* themselves permanently in the host Member State. We first set out the main principles of this body of EU law, before turning to their specific application in the field of health.

EU law on freedom of establishment, including Treaty provisions, secondary legislation, and the jurisprudence of the European Court of Justice, is concerned with ensuring the internal market in persons, including professionals, working within the EU. From the point of view of the EU, the measures aim to prohibit "restrictions" on the freedom of establishment that might impede the establishment or functioning of the internal market. Where such measures are applied to health care professionals, this may indirectly affect the national regulation of health care professionals within the Member States. These effects are the main concern of the remainder of this chapter.

Freedom of establishment: Treaty provisions

Where a (health care) professional[53] seeks to practice in a Member State other than that of which she is a national, or other than that in which she is entitled to practise, the Treaty provisions on freedom of establishment may apply. Article 43 EC provides that "restrictions on the freedom of establishment of nationals of a Member State

51 But see further below p 234–235, on the possibility of cross-border provision of health care services, and see further chapter 10, p 426–433.

52 Community competence in the field of education and training is limited: see Articles 149 and 150 EC which provide that any harmonisation of the content of education or vocational training is explicitly prohibited.

53 Who is a "citizen of the European Union" or of an EEA state – see below for the position of "third country" nationals.

in the territory of another Member State shall be prohibited", and requires that the right to take up and pursue activities as a self-employed person is to be under the conditions laid down for the pursuit of such activities applicable to nationals by the host Member State.[54] This provision is directly effective, and thus may be relied upon by an individual in proceedings before national courts, in order to tackle national regulatory measures that impede freedom of establishment, irrespective of whether EU-level harmonising or coordinating directives or other measures have been adopted.[55] Thus, the Treaty provisions of freedom of establishment represent an essentially deregulatory mode of governance.[56]

The Court has defined "***establishment***" as "the actual pursuit of an economic activity through a fixed establishment in another Member State for an indefinite period",[57] where presence in another Member State is "stable and continuous".[58] Permanence is thus a key feature of establishment, as distinct from the provision of services, which implies a temporary basis.[59] Establishment also denotes independence of activity. Where work is carried out "for and under the direction of another person",[60] the free movement of workers regime applies, rather than that relating to freedom of establishment.

Originally, the Treaty provisions on freedom of establishment were conceived as simply excluding discrimination on grounds of nationality.[61] However, following the *Cassis de Dijon* ruling[62] concerning the free movement of goods, the freedom of establishment jurisprudence was gradually developed so that any ***restrictions*** on access to the market of a host Member State in which a professional seeks to establish herself, even if not directly discriminatory on grounds of nationality, may fall foul of the Treaty provisions.[63] However, unlike the case of "restrictions" in the sense of provision of services,[64] in the case of freedom of establishment, it appears that there must still be some link with the non-discrimination principle. But, at least in terms

54 The principle of non-discrimination on grounds of nationality, see Article 12 EC.
55 Case 2/74 *Reyners v Belgium* [1974] ECR 631; Case 71/76 *Thieffry* [1977] ECR 765; Case 11/77 *Patrick* [1977] ECR 1199.
56 See our typology of modes of governance set out in chapter 2, p 43.
57 Case C-221/89 *R v Secretary of State for Transport, ex parte Factortame (No 3)* [1991] ECR I-3905.
58 Case C-70/95 *Sodemare v Regione Lombardia* [1997] ECR I-3395.
59 Case C-55/94 *Gebhard v Milan Bar Council* [1995] ECR I-4165. Drawing from the Court's jurisprudence, a presumption of a time period of 16 weeks per year will be set by the proposed new Directive; see further below; see COM(2002) 119 final, proposed Article 5.
60 Case C-66/85 *Lawrie-Blum* [1986] ECR 2121.
61 See the reasoning in *Reyners*, above n 55, to the effect that a requirement that a lawyer must have Belgian nationality to practise as an advocate was found to be a breach of Article 52 EEC (now Article 43 EC). See P. Craig and G. de Búrca, *EU Law* (Oxford: OUP, 2002), pp 783–787; D. Chalmers and E. Szyszczak, *European Union Law: Towards a European Polity?* (Dartmouth: Ashgate, 1998), p 368.
62 Case 120/78 [1979] ECR 649. See discussion in chapter 2.
63 See, for example, Case 107/83 *Klopp* [1984] ECR 2971; Case 96/85 *Commission v France* [1986] ECR 1475; and especially Case C-55/94 *Gebhard* above n 59. See also Craig and de Búrca, above n 60, p 776; but see G. Marenco, "The Notion of Restriction on the Freedom of Establishment and Provision of Services in the Case law of the Court" 11 YEL (1991) 111.
64 See chapter 4.

of access to a profession, the Court has gradually developed the non-discrimination principle in this context, so that it now includes both direct, and indirect, discrimination. Therefore where national rules *de facto* place nationals of another Member State at a disadvantage, for instance, by imposing upon them a "double burden" of regulatory requirements with which to comply, these may fall foul of the Treaty provisions.[65] In the case of professional activity, such a restriction may include the requirement to hold a professional qualification from the host Member State. Where the professional holds an equivalent qualification in the home Member State, if the host Member State refuses to recognise that qualification, this may be a "restriction" in the sense of the Treaty provisions on freedom of establishment. Thus in *Thieffry*,[66] refusal of access to the training stage for the legal profession of *avocat* in France, on the basis that the applicant held a degree from another Member State (Belgium),[67] was a restriction on the freedom of establishment. In *Vlassopoulou*,[68] the Court held:

> "...even if applied without any discrimination on the basis of nationality, national requirements concerning qualifications may have the effect of hindering nationals of the other Member States in the exercise of their right of establishment ...That could be the case if the national rules in question took no account of the knowledge and qualifications already acquired by the person concerned in another Member State."[69]

Thus restrictions on *access* to the market of the host Member State by a professional seeking to establish herself there are defined relatively broadly in the Court's jurisprudence. The position with respect to restrictions on the *pursuit* of a particular profession remains less clear, and it seems that some discrimination on grounds of nationality is still necessary if national regulatory measures are to fall within the terms of the Treaty.[70]

As is the case with freedom to provide and receive services,[71] restrictions on the freedom of establishment in EU law may be ***justified*** in a number of circumstances. The Treaty itself provides for two types of exemption: exercise of official authority,[72] and the traditional exemptions for "public policy, public security and public health".[73] The former applies to professions concerned with the exercise of the prerogative powers of the state, such as the judiciary,[74] and so could not be relied upon with respect to the health care profession.

65 Case C-340/89 *Vlassopoulou* [1991] ECR I-2357.
66 Case 71/76 *Thieffry* above n 55.
67 Which had actually been recognised as equivalent to a French law degree.
68 Case C-340/89 *Vlassopoulou* above n 65.
69 Para 15.
70 Case 221/85 *Commission v Belgium (Clinical Biology Laboratories)* [1987] ECR 719; Case C-70/95 *Sodemare* above n 58.
71 As we saw in chapter 4.
72 Article 45 EC.
73 Article 46 EC.
74 Case 2/74 *Reyners* above n 55.

As we noted in chapter 4, the latter three grounds of exemption are also reflected in the Treaty provision on free movement of workers, Article 39 (3) EC,[75] and the Court's jurisprudence may probably be read across both provisions. The main thrust of that jurisprudence is to limit the restrictions on the freedom of movement as much as possible. The grounds of exemption do not provide a wide discretion to Member States to preserve national policies. Rather, Member States must show a clear, objective and proportionate imperative of public policy, public security or public health. More importantly, the interpretation of the exemption provisions is a matter of EU, not national, law to be determined by the European Court of Justice.[76] Any suggestion that the exemption is being relied on to protect national interests from competition from other Member States is generally regarded by the Court as being evidence that the exemption is not justified.[77] The public health ground is also elaborated with respect to residence in Directive 64/221/EEC,[78] which lists those diseases that justify a refusal of entry on the grounds of public health.[79] Whether a Member State might seek to rely on the Treaty ground of public health to restrict access to health care professions in other circumstances arose in *Commission v France (Establishment of Doctors and Dentists)*.[80] There the Court held that national rules prohibiting doctors and dentists from practising in France where they were already established in another Member State, unless they relinquished that registration in the Member State of origin, were not, in these circumstances, justified on public health grounds. This was the case because the French rules were disproportionate to the aim in question. Logically, then, the protection of public health, were it applied in a proportionate and non-discriminatory manner, could in some circumstances constitute a justification for a restriction on the freedom of establishment.

Where restrictions on the freedom of movement are not measures directly discriminating on grounds of nationality, but are equally applicable to nationals and non-nationals, these may still be unlawful "restrictions" in the sense of Article 43 EC. However, a further means of justification of such national regulatory measures, is necessary in EU law, because, as already discussed in chapter 2, the Treaty of Rome does not envisage a completely deregulated single market,[81] but rather

75 The grounds are also found in the Directives extending residence rights to non-nationals not exercising Treaty rights: Directive 90/365/EEC, OJ 1990 L 180/28; Directive 93/96/EC, OJ 1993 L 317/59; Directive 90/364/EEC, OJ 1990 L 180/26.

76 Case 36/75 *Rutili* [1975] ECR 1219. However, the application of the exemption in a particular case would be a matter for the tribunal of fact, at national level, albeit operating under a duty to apply EU law (Article 234 EC; Article 10 EC).

77 See also Directive 64/221/EEC, OJ 1964 L 56/117, Article 2 (1) which provides that the grounds of exemption may not be used to serve economic ends.

78 OJ Sp Ed 1964 No 850/64, p 117. Council reached political agreement on the proposal for a Directive on the free movement and residence of EU citizens and their family members in September 2003 and this was approved by the European Parliament on 10 March 2004. This proposal will repeal and replace Directive 64/221/EEC.

79 See Directive 64/221/EEC, Annex.

80 Case 96/85 [1986] ECR 1475.

81 See, with respect to freedom of establishment in particular, D. Edward, "Freedom of Movement for the Regulated Professions" in R. White and B. Smythe, eds, *Current Issues in European and International Law* (Festschrift for F. Dowrick) (London: Sweet and Maxwell, 1990), p 40.

recognises that there are differences between national regulatory regimes, and that some national regulation is justified in the public interest.[82] Therefore, the freedom of establishment must be reconciled with legitimate national regulatory measures. The European Court of Justice has established a legal means by which this balance may be effected, by permitting indirectly discriminatory restrictions on the freedom to provide services, provided they are justified in pursuance of an ***objective public interest***.

So, for instance, in *Commission v France (Establishment of Doctors and Dentists)*,[83] the Court considered as possible justification the "concern that individuals enjoy the most effective and complete health protection possible", "the need to ensure continuity of medical treatment" and considerations of "medical ethics".[84] Although the Court found that such concerns did not, in fact, justify the particular restrictions in the circumstances of the case, such aims would apparently constitute potential objective public interests. In *Gullung*,[85] the Court held that the requirement that lawyers must be registered at a bar must be regarded as lawful in EU law, provided that such registration is open to all EU citizens without discrimination. The Court observed that such a requirement "seeks to ensure the observance of moral and ethical principles and the disciplinary control of the activity of lawyers, and thus constitutes an objective worthy of protection".[86] Such objective public interests would presumably also apply in the case of registration requirements for health care professionals. However, as Scott has pointed out, the precise contours of the concept of objective public interest are difficult to discern with precision.[87]

The Treaty provisions alone are insufficient to ensure freedom of movement for professionals within the EU. In addition to the Treaty provisions, there is a significant body of secondary EU law which attempts, with varying degrees of success, to make the "internal market" in professionals a reality. Some of this secondary law applies to health care professions, and it is to these measures that we now turn.

The sectoral (professional) directives

Article 44 EC provides that "in order to attain freedom of establishment as regards a particular activity, the Council . . . shall act by means of directives".[88] The relevant procedure is now the co-decision procedure, which involves qualified majority

82 S. Weatherill, *Law and Integration in the European Union* (Oxford: Clarendon, 1995), pp 252–261.

83 Above n 80.

84 Paras 10 and 14.

85 Case 292/86 [1988] ECR 111.

86 Para 29.

87 J. Scott, "Mandatory or Imperative Requirements in the EU and the WTO" in C. Barnard and J. Scott, eds, *The Law of the Single European Market: Unpacking the Premises* (Oxford: Hart, 2002), pp 269–294.

88 See, for instance, Directive 73/148/EEC, OJ 1973 L 172/14, which provides a right of entry and residence for those wishing to establish themselves in the territory of another Member State, along with their families.

voting in Council, and a significant role for the European Parliament.[89] Further, in order to make it easier for professionals to pursue activities as self-employed persons across the EU, Article 47 (1) EC gives the EU institutions a legal basis for adoption of directives on the mutual recognition of diplomas, certificates and other evidence of formal qualifications. This in itself is insufficient to provide for sufficient coordination of (health care) professions to ensure freedom of establishment,[90] but is supplemented by Article 47 (2) EC which provides for mandatory coordination of national regulatory regimes. Further, a specific mention is made in the Treaty of the application of these rules to "medical and allied and pharmaceutical professions".[91] Article 47 (3) EC provides that in the case of these professions, "the progressive abolition of restrictions shall be dependent upon coordination of the conditions for their exercise in the various Member States". This provision has been in the Treaty of Rome since its inception, and indicates the sensitivity of the application of EU law to the regulation of health care professionals, whose primary concern is with the fundamental interests of human health and indeed life.[92]

The EU institutions initially approached the problem of freedom of movement for professionals[93] by adopting "sectoral" directives, each addressed to a particular profession or sector. These directives apply to freedom of establishment, and also to free movement of workers. The relevant directives cover the professions of doctor (including, as later amended, general practitioner),[94] dentist,[95]

89 However, at earlier stages in the history of the EU, the "basic" procedure (Commission proposes, Council decides unanimously, Parliament is only consulted) was the relevant procedure.

90 See J. Lonbay, "The Mutual Recognition of Professional Qualifications in the EC" in R. Hodgin, ed, *Professional Liability: Law and Insurance* (London: LPP Professional Publishing, 1999), p 9.

91 The "medical and allied professions" cover those professionals concerned with human life and health: see Case 136/78 *Ministère Public v Auer* [1979] ECR 437. "Allied" professions probably include those whose activities are covered by national health (insurance) care systems, independent practitioners of traditional therapeutic treatment and those undertaking health care activities under the control of medical practitioners. They may also include alternative and complementary therapists, hospital attendants, social workers and medical technicians. See Lonbay, in Goldberg and Lonbay, eds, above n 10, p 55.

92 See the argument advanced by the Commission and supported by the Advocate General in Case 136/78 *Auer* above n 91.

93 For an early provision of soft law, see the Resolution on mutual recognition of diplomas, certificates and other evidence of formal qualifications of 6 June 1974, OJ 1974 C 98/1.

94 The sectoral system for doctors was contained in Directive 75/362/EEC, OJ 1975 L 167/1 "concerning the mutual recognition of diplomas, certificates and other evidence of formal qualification in medicine, including measures to facilitate the effective exercise of the right of establishment and freedom to provide services"; and Directive 75/363/EEC, OJ 1975 L 167/14 "concerning coordination of provisions laid down by law, regulation or administrative action in respect of activities of doctors". Further minimum levels of training for general practitioners were introduced through Directive 86/457/EEC, OJ 1986 L 267/26. The legislation is now consolidated in Directive 93/16/EEC "to facilitate the free movement of doctors and the mutual recognition of their diplomas, certificates and other evidence of formal qualifications", OJ 1993 L 165/1, as amended.

95 The sectoral system for dentists is contained in Directive 78/686/EEC, OJ 1978 L 233/1 on "the mutual recognition of diplomas, certificates and other evidence of formal qualifications of practitioners of dentistry, including measures to facilitate the effective exercise of the right of establishment and freedom to provide services"; and Directive 78/687/EEC, OJ 1978 L 233/10 on "the coordination of provisions laid down by law, regulation or administrative action in respect

pharmacist,[96] midwife,[97] and nurse responsible for general care.[98] It appears that the health care profession was tackled first by the Commission, as it was perceived as "easier" to provide for mutual recognition of qualifications in such a discipline, based on "international science", than professional disciplines such as law, that are specific to a particular state. Of course, such a perspective makes light of significant differences in medical opinion, practice and culture, both between and also within the health care professions in the Member States of the EU.

The essential aim of the sectoral directives was to enable the automatic recognition in all Member States of a licence to practise a profession in one Member State. Each sector was originally the subject of two different directives. The first of these provided an EU-level definition of the minimum requirements for education and training required to pursue the professional activities concerned. Where the content of a Member State's education and training requirements does not meet these minima, they must be adjusted in order to comply with EU law.[99] The impact of the sectoral directives on national law, therefore, was (at least potentially) to affect national rules on entry to particular health care professions. However, because the provisions in these directives were expressed in very general terms, each Member State could, in effect, ensure that any adjustment required to its own national system was minimal or non-existent. There are, however, some examples of significant national adjustments mandated by the sectoral directives. For instance, the UK was

of the activities of dental practitioners", as amended by Directive 2001/19/EC, OJ 2001 L 206/1. See also OJ 1978 C 202, Statement on the Directive concerning the coordination of provisions laid down by law, regulation, etc., on the activities of dental surgeons.

96 The sectoral system for pharmacists is contained in Directive 85/432/EEC, OJ 1985 L 253/34, concerning the coordination of provisions laid down by law, regulation or administrative action in respect of certain activities in the field of pharmacy; and Directive 85/433/EEC, OJ 1985 L 253/37 concerning the mutual recognition of diplomas, certificates and other evidence of formal qualifications in pharmacy, including measures to facilitate the effective exercise of the right of establishment relating to certain activities in the field of pharmacy, as amended by Directive 2001/19/EC, OJ 2001 L 206/1.

97 The sectoral system for midwives is contained in Directive 80/154/EEC, OJ 1980 L 33/1 concerning the mutual recognition of diplomas, certificates and other evidence of formal qualifications of practitioners of midwifery; and Directive 80/155/EEC, OJ 1980 L 33/8 concerning the coordination of provisions laid down by law, regulation, or administrative action in respect of the activities of midwives, as amended by Directive 2001/19/EC, OJ 2001 L 206/1.

98 The sectoral system for nurses responsible for general care is contained in Directive 77/452/EEC, OJ 1977 L 176/1 on "the mutual recognition of diplomas, certificates and other evidence of formal qualifications of nurses responsible for general care, including measures to facilitate the effective exercise of this right of establishment and freedom to provide services"; and Directive 77/453/EEC, OJ 1977 L 176/8 on "the coordination of provisions laid down by law, regulation or administrative action in respect of the activities of nurses responsible for general care", as amended by Directive 2001/19/EC, OJ 2001 L 206/1.

99 Thus, for instance, in the UK, the European Specialist Medical Qualifications Order 1995, SI 1995/3208 allowed for the introduction of a "certificate in specialist medical training". Prior to this, the UK system did not recognise "specialists" as such, but rather consultants. See Lonbay, in Goldberg and Lonbay, eds, above n 10, p 65. All the Central and Eastern European candidate countries are modifying their laws to provide for mutual recognition of professional qualifications. See Commission *Reports on Progress towards Accession by each of the Candidate Countries* (1998–), available on http://www.europa.eu.int/comm/enlargement/.

obliged to recognise "specialist medical training". Previously, the UK's system was structured in terms of general practitioners and "consultants". The UK admitted in the High Court that the procedure for the award of specialist medical accreditation was in breach of the sectoral "doctors directive".[100] Italy has recently been required by the European Court of Justice to cease making the exercise of dentistry conditional on holding two diplomas (in dentistry and general medicine), and registrations with two professional bodies.[101]

The second directive simply contained a list of the diplomas awarded in the Member States which satisfy these requirements. Thus, the system allows for automatic general recognition of a qualification that meets the EU-level minimum standard, without the need to assess each migrant professional on an individual basis. The impact here was to require some penetration of the national profession by professionals from other Member States who, by definition, had been subject to different (home state) regulatory requirements on entry to the profession. In order to appreciate the application of the sectoral directives in practice, two such sectors, concerning doctors and pharmacists, are now considered in a little detail.

Doctors

The mutual recognition of doctors' qualifications was originally covered in Directive 75/362/EEC[102] and Directive 75/363/EEC.[103] These have subsequently been amended and to some extent consolidated by Directive 93/16/EEC,[104] and further amended in Directive 2001/19/EC.[105] There is currently a proposal before the European Parliament and Council that will, if adopted, consolidate all secondary legislation on mutual recognition of qualifications, and repeal all previous legislation.[106] Directive 93/16/EEC applies to the activities of doctors working in a self-employed or employed capacity who are nationals of the Member States.[107] Article 2 provides that each Member State shall recognise the diplomas, certificates and other evidence of formal qualifications in medicine awarded to nationals of Member States by the other Member States. These qualifications are listed, country by country, in what is now Annex A. Member States must give "such qualifications, as far as the right to take up and pursue the activities of a doctor is concerned, the same effect in its territory as those which the Member State itself awards".[108]

100 Lonbay, in Goldberg and Lonbay, eds, above n 10, p 79; and see *R v Secretary of State for Health, ex parte Goldstein* [1993] 2 CMLR 589.
101 See Case C-202/99 *Commission v Italy* [2001] ECR I-9319. This decision was partly on the basis of the sectoral directives, but relied also on the general Treaty provisions discussed above.
102 OJ 1975 L 167/1.
103 OJ 1975 L 167/14.
104 OJ 1993 L 165/1. Directive 93/16/EEC did not, however, repeal the earlier provisions.
105 OJ 2001 L 206/1. This provision is part of the "Simpler Legislation for the Single Market (SLIM) Initiative", which formed part of the movement towards better law-making in the EU: see Commission, *Better Law-Making 1998 – A Shared Responsibility* COM(98) 715 final.
106 COM(2002) 119; see further below.
107 Directive 93/16/EEC, Article 1.
108 Directive 93/16/EEC, Article 2.

Similarly worded provisions follow for the mutual recognition of diplomas, certificates and other evidence of formal qualifications in specialised medicine, where such specialisms are common to all Member States.[109] Where a specialism is common to two or more Member States, equivalent provisions apply.[110] Authorisation to practise in the host Member State must be given "as soon as possible and not later than three months after presentation of all documents".[111] Member States must allow professionals to use their academic title of the Member State of origin.[112] Certification of good repute or good character, or of good physical or mental health, from the Member State of origin must be accepted by the host Member State.[113] Further, the home Member State is required to share with the host Member State information on disciplinary action in the case of serious professional misconduct and criminal offences.[114]

Impact on medical training

Member States must ensure that doctors hold a diploma, certificate or other evidence of formal qualifications in medicine, as listed in Article 3 of the Directive. Such a qualification must guarantee that during training, the person concerned has acquired:

> "(a) adequate knowledge of the sciences on which medicine is based and a good understanding of the scientific methods including the principles of measuring biological functions, the evaluation of scientifically established facts and the analysis of data;
>
> (b) sufficient understanding of the structure, functions and behaviour of healthy and sick persons, as well as relations between the state of health and physical and social surroundings of the human being;
>
> (c) adequate knowledge of clinical disciplines and practices, providing him with a coherent picture of mental and physical diseases, of medicine from the points of view of prophylaxis, diagnosis and therapy and of human reproduction;
>
> (d) suitable clinical experience in hospitals under appropriate supervision".[115]

The training period must be at least six years or 5,500 hours, and must be given under the supervision of a university.[116] Special provisions are made for the various medical specialisms covered by the Directive.[117] These minimum requirements are phrased in fairly general language, for instance referring to "adequate" knowledge, "sufficient" understanding, and "suitable" clinical experience. The Directive thus,

109 Directive 93/16/EEC, Article 4 and Annexes B and C.
110 Directive 93/16/EEC, Article 5 and Annexes B and C.
111 Directive 93/16/EEC, Article 15.
112 Directive 93/16/EEC, Article 10. Provision is made for the circumstance where the academic title used in the Member State of origin may be confused in the host Member State with an academic title requiring additional training.
113 Directive 93/16/EEC, Articles 11 and 13.
114 Directive 93/16/EEC, Article 12.
115 Directive 93/16/EEC, Article 23 (1).
116 Directive 93/16/EEC, Article 23 (2).
117 Directive 93/16/EEC, Articles 24, 25, 26, 27 and Annex C.

in practice, gives the Member States significant discretion in designing their own training schemes for doctors.

The scheme of Directive 93/16/EEC is, therefore, an example of mandatory coordination of national regulatory regimes, but also contains elements of "new approach" harmonisation, in particular the principle of mutual recognition and the setting of a minimum floor of standards that each Member State's regulatory regime must meet. Further, the EU scheme for mutual recognition of the professional qualifications of doctors is underpinned by a system of advisory committees. This was originally recommended by Council in its 1974 Resolution on the mutual recognition of diplomas, certificates and other evidence of formal qualifications.[118]

Advisory Committee on Medical Training

At the same time as the adoption of Directives 75/362/EEC and 75/363/EEC, the EU institutions adopted Decision 75/364/EEC[119] setting up an Advisory Committee on Medical Training (ACMT). Citing the Council's earlier Resolution of 1974,[120] Decision 75/364/EEC, Article 2 states that the task of the ACMT was "to help to ensure a comparably demanding standard of medical training in the EC, with regard both to basic training and further training". Article 2(2) elaborates on the ways in which such a goal is to be achieved. It shall involve:

> "exchange of comprehensive information as to the training methods and the content, level and structure of theoretical and practical courses provided in the Member States;
>
> discussion and consultation with the object of developing common approaches to the standard to be attained in the training of doctors and, as appropriate, to the structure and content of such training; [and]
>
> keeping under review the adaptation of medical training to developments in medical science and teaching methods."

The opinions and suggestions of the ACMT were to be communicated to the Commission and the Member States[121] and broad provision was given for the ACMT to "advise the Commission on any matter which the Commission may refer to it in relation to medical training".[122]

The ACMT consisted of three experts (and substitutes) from each Member State. Of these three experts, one was from the "practising profession", one from the "medical faculties of the universities", and one was an "expert from the competent authorities of the Member States". All three representatives were nominated by the Member State concerned, and duly appointed by the Council.[123] The chair of the ACMT was elected by the committee itself, from its own membership. The only

118 Council Resolution on the mutual recognition of diplomas, certificates and other evidence of formal qualifications, OJ 1974 C 98/1.
119 OJ 1975 L 167/17.
120 Above n 118.
121 Decision 75/364/EEC, Article 2 (3).
122 Decision 75/364/EEC, Article 2 (4).
123 Decision 75/364/EEC, Article 3 (3).

role that the Commission played in the workings of the ACMT was a consultative one, with the chair, in the drawing up of the ACMT's meeting agendas.[124] It appears that the Commission ceased to fund the ACMT in 1999.[125] A Commission proposal of that year[126] suggests that the advisory committees for the sectoral directives are now obsolete, as they have effectively completed their mandate, and the Commission needs no further advice on the issue of training requirements for health care professionals covered by the sectoral directives.[127] The Council has not acted on the Commission's proposal to abolish the advisory committees.

General practice and reform of the Doctors Directive

In spite of the committee system, one of the problems of the approach taken in the sectoral directives is that the details of the legislation require significant negotiation at the level of the EU institutions. This makes the legislative process slow, causing difficulties where reform of the legislation is needed to respond to developments in health care practice in the Member States. Here, the European Court of Justice may play a role in creating an incentive for governments of Member States to reach agreement in Council, by exercising its interpretative power, and making reform more appealing to the governments of the Member States. This may be illustrated by the *Van Broeckmeulen* case.[128]

The original Doctors Directives made no provision for mutual recognition of diplomas in general practice as a speciality. Van Broeckmeulen, a Dutch national, undertook his medical training in Belgium. He wished to practise as a general practitioner in the Netherlands, but was prevented from so doing by the Dutch authorities, on the grounds that he had not followed specific courses in general practice, as he would have done under the Dutch scheme for doctors' training. The national tribunal (the Dutch registration committee) asked the European Court of Justice whether a Member State may make the practice of general medicine, by the holder of a diploma awarded in another Member State and recognised by virtue of the provisions of Directive 75/362/EEC, subject to the completion of a period of additional training, where this condition is also imposed upon its own nationals. The Directive did not contain any rules on the recognition of specialist training for general practice. However, recent thinking had shown that general medicine was a specific discipline akin to the specialised disciplines,[129] hence the Dutch rules requiring further specific training for general practitioners. In spite of clear concerns

124 Decision 75/364/EEC, Article 5.

125 See M.M. Mäkinen and M. Äärimaa, "The challenge of professional freedom" 7 *eurohealth* (2001) 16; T. Richards, "Germany turns away UK trained GP" 322 BMJ (2001) 384 (17 February). Confirmed by personal correspondence with the authors from DG Internal Market on 1 December 2003.

126 COM(99) 177 final.

127 Whether this can really be the case, especially in the context of enlargement of the EU, is debatable. See the views of the NGO umbrella organisation the Standing Committee of European Doctors/Comité Permanent des Médecins Européens, http://www.cpme.be/.

128 Case 246/80 *Van Broekmeulen* [1981] ECR 2311.

129 Para 22.

expressed by the Dutch registration committee that the freedom of establishment should not interfere with the responsibilities of the Member States to set the best possible standards of patient care, the Court held that:

> "... a national of a Member State who has obtained a diploma listed under Article 3 of the Directive in another Member State and who, by that token, may practise general medicine in that other Member State is entitled to establish himself as a general practitioner in the Member State of which he is a national, even if that Member State makes entry to that profession by holders of diplomas of medicine obtained within its own borders subject to additional training requirements."[130]

The Court reached this conclusion through a structural analysis of the provisions of Directive 75/362/EEC. As the Court pointed out, the Directive distinguished between the recognition of diplomas of medicine (in Articles 2 and 3) and recognition of diplomas of specialised medicine (Articles 4 to 8). It is only in so far as the training of specialists is concerned that Member States are permitted, under Article 8, to impose additional training requirements. General practice was not recognised as a speciality within the Directive. Therefore, the Court reasoned, it must come under the provisions of the Directive relating to general medicine, and not to specialists.

The Court's judgment prompted legislative reform in Directive 86/457/EEC on specific training in general medical practice.[131] The basic operation of the Directive, in summary, was achieved through three Articles. Article 1 of the Directive states that each Member State "which dispenses the complete training referred to in Article 1 of Directive 75/363/EEC" within its territory shall institute specific training in general medical practice. The minimum requirements for such training are then specified in Articles 2 and 3. The Directive thus effectively overturns the impact of the Court's decision in *Van Broekmeulen*, where the Court did not allow a Member State to impede freedom of movement for a health care professional on the basis of the failure in the Directive to cover the speciality of general medical practice. The Directive thus appeases the concerns of the Netherlands and other Member States that recognised general medical practice as a speciality, by recognising general medical practice as a speciality in the context of EU mutual recognition of qualifications legislation. The preamble to the Directive obviously does not explicitly identify this as the thinking behind the Directive, but rather seeks to justify the Directive's adoption on the basis of keeping up with trends in scientific knowledge and research. The Preamble refers to the "benefit to patients" which will result from a recognition of the status of general practitioner as a specialist status, and also of the contribution to an improvement in health care generally, "particularly by developing a more selective approach to the consultation of specialists, use of laboratories and other highly specialised establishments and equipment".[132] In order to emphasise the

130 Para 27.
131 OJ 1986 L 267/26. Subsequently amended by Directive 2001/19/EC, Article 14 (12) and (13).
132 Para 5 of the preamble.

benefits of this development – of recognising the status of general practitioner as a specialist status – the preamble also notes that improved training for general medical practice will "upgrade the status of the general medical practitioner". This may have implications for health care of patients, as an upgrade in the status of general practitioners may well correlate with better conditions and better facilities for such general practitioners, perhaps resulting, overall, in better care for patients.[133]

In spite of the sectoral Doctors Directive, some doctors continue to experience practical difficulties in having their qualifications recognised in other Member States. The Commission receives a steady drip of complaints to this effect.[134] For instance, in 2001, a general practitioner, Dr Schenck, who had undertaken his undergraduate training in Germany but had then worked in the UK since 1995 and had completed a general practitioner vocational course, found he was unable to persuade the German medical authorities to accept his qualification. There was speculation that the reason for the German approach was due to an oversupply of doctors in Germany at the time. Some such complaints are taken before the European Court of Justice, either by the Commission under Article 226 EC,[135] or by individuals before national courts, through the preliminary ruling procedure in Article 234 EC.[136] Where a complaint reaches this stage, of course, a finding against a Member State will oblige that Member State to alter its national regulatory structures to comply with its duties in EU law.[137]

Pharmacists

The Pharmacists Directives, Directive 85/432/EEC[138] and Directive 85/433/EEC,[139] achieve almost exactly the same function as the Doctors Directives, described above. Directive 85/432/EEC lays down the obligation on Member States to grant mutual recognition to qualifications gained in other Member States[140] which meet certain minimum requirements.[141] As with Directive 75/363/EEC for doctors, Directive 85/432/EEC concerning pharmacists applies to both employed and self-employed

133 See J. Hermesse, H. Lewalle and W. Palm, "Patient Mobility Within the European Union" 7(3 Supplement) *European Journal of Public Health* (1997) 4 at 9; and H. Hermans, "Patients' Rights in the European Union" 7(3 Supplement) *European Journal of Public Health* (1997) 11.

134 F. Klemperer, "Working abroad as a doctor" in G. Eysenbach, ed, *Medicine and Medical Education in Europe: The Eurodoctor* (Stuttgart: Thieme, 1998).

135 See, for instance, Case C-232/99 *Commission v Spain* [2002] ECR I-4235, in which it was held that by systematically requiring certain migrant doctors to take part in the national competition procedure for "Médico Interno Residente" without taking their specialist medical training into account, Spain was breaching its obligations under the Doctors Directive.

136 See, for instance, (although this case does not concern a doctor, but another professional working in the health sector) Case C-285/01 *Burbaud* [2003] ECR I, (9 September 2003 nyr in ECR) in which a Portuguese national successfully sought entry to the French public hospital service on the basis of her qualifications as hospital administrator obtained in Portugal.

137 For discussion of Article 234 EC, Article 226 EC, and the relationship between EU law and national law of the Member States, see chapter 2.

138 OJ 1985 L 253/34.

139 OJ 1985 L 253/37.

140 Directive 85/432/EEC, Article 1.

141 These are laid down in Directive 85/432/EEC, Article 2.

pharmacists. Directive 85/433/EEC specifies the diplomas and qualifications of each Member State which satisfy the requirements of Directive 85/432/EEC, and which thus must be recognised by each Member State. The Pharmacists Directives have also been amended by Directive 2001/19/EC, and will, of course, also be consolidated in the new proposed Directive, if it is adopted.

As with the Doctors Directives, the pharmacists directives make provision for a specialist committee to assist in the interpretation of "difficulties" in the mutual recognition rules.[142] To this end, the Advisory Committee on Pharmaceutical Training was established by Decision 85/434/EEC.[143] The task of the committee, which was comprised of three experts from each Member State (representing the pharmaceutical body, education and an expert from the pharmaceutical authorities), appointed for three years, was specified in Article 2. It was "to help to ensure a comparably high standard of pharmaceutical training in the Community" through the "exchange of comprehensive information as to the training methods and the content, level and structure of theoretical and practical courses provided in the Member States", and through "discussion and consultation with the object of developing a common approach to the standard to be attained in the training of pharmacists and, as appropriate, to the structure and content of such training".

One significant difference between the sectoral scheme for pharmacists and that for doctors is that the principle of freedom of establishment contained in the Pharmacists Directives does not automatically include the right to become the holder of a pharmacy.[144] Thus, the position with respect to pharmacists' freedom of establishment in the EU is more limited than that of doctors. The difference may be explained by the fact that the number of pharmacies is restricted in some Member State territories, as a cost containment measure of national health (insurance) law.[145]

Further, the Pharmacists Directives do not set an exhaustive definition of the activities of pharmacists. Rather, they simply set out the minimum conditions for qualification to carry out a range of defined activities carried out by members of the pharmaceutical profession. These are:

> "the preparation of the pharmaceutical form of medicinal products;
> the manufacture and testing of medicinal products;
> the testing of medicinal products in a laboratory;
> the storage, preservation and distribution of medicinal products at the wholesale stage;
> the preparation, testing, storage and supply of medicinal products in pharmacies open to the public;
> the preparation, testing, storage and dispensing of medicinal products in hospitals;
> the provision of information and advice on medicinal products."[146]

142 Directive 85/432/EEC, Article 6.
143 OJ 1985 L 253/43. The Commission also proposed the abolition of this committee in COM(99) 177 final: see above n 126.
144 See Directive 85/433/EEC, Article 2(2).
145 See Oostermann-Meulenbeld, above n 18, at 67; and Lonbay, above n 10, at 69.
146 Directive 85/432/EEC, Article 1 (2).

Interactions with free movement of pharmaceuticals

One interesting dimension to the Pharmacists Directives is the extent to which the European Court of Justice has relied upon them in its jurisprudence concerning the free movement of goods. The combination of the Treaty provisions on free movement of goods as applied to pharmaceuticals moving across borders, and the Pharmacists Directives, has resulted in some undermining, at the fringes, of national regulatory measures aimed, ostensibly, at consumer protection, but probably in actuality also at capacity maintenance of the pharmaceutical industry. This jurisprudence has arisen in the context of individual patients relying on EU Treaty law to secure the free movement of pharmaceuticals across borders, in circumstances where national law prohibited such movement.

As we noted in chapter 2, the measures of primary EU law establishing the internal market in goods are found in the EC Treaty, Articles 23–25 (ex 9–16) and 28–31 (ex 30–36) EC. Pharmaceuticals and other medical products fall within the definition of "goods" in EU law.[147] Restrictions on the free movement of goods may be justified by reference to protection of human health,[148] or to other objective public interests, such as consumer protection,[149] although such justifications are subject to the principle of proportionality.

The Court has found that the prohibition of private imports of pharmaceuticals, for personal use, does not meet the proportionality test. Such a prohibition was in place in Germany, and its compatibility with EU law was successfully challenged in *Schumacher*.[150] Heinz Schumacher, a German resident, ordered, for his personal use from a French pharmacy, a medicinal product Chophytol, used to treat dyspepsia and as a diuretic. Chophytol was authorised to be marketed in both France and Germany, and was available over-the-counter in both Member States. However, the price for the product was higher in Germany than in France.[151] As German law prohibited the private importation of pharmaceuticals, the customs authorities refused entry to the product. Schumacher challenged this as contrary to the EU law provisions on the free movement of goods.

147 Case 7/68 *Commission v Italy (Art Treasures)* [1968] ECR 617, in which "goods" are defined as "products which can be valued in money and which are capable, as such, of forming the subject of commercial transactions".

148 Article 30 (ex 36) EC.

149 Case 120/78 *Cassis de Dijon* [1979] ECR 649.

150 Case 215/87 [1989] ECR 617. See also Case C-62/90 *Commission v Germany* [1992] ECR I-2575; Case C-347/89 *Freistaat Bayern v Eurim-Pharm* [1991] ECR I-1747; and Case C-322/01 *Deutscher Apothekerverband v 0800 DocMorris and Waterval* (11 December 2003 nyr in ECR), discussed in chapter 10.

151 The pharmaceuticals market is characterised by a number of unusual characteristics. In particular, the fact that price setting is undertaken by public regulatory authorities, rather than through the normal interplay of market forces, has led to the situation where the prices obtaining for a particular pharmaceutical product vary widely between the Member States, in some instances by as much as 500%: see L. Hancher, "The European Pharmaceutical Market: problems of partial harmonisation" 15 ELRev (1990) 9. Within the internal market, "parallel importers" have sought to take advantage of this situation, by purchasing pharmaceuticals wholesale in one Member State (such as Greece, Spain or Portugal) where their price is fixed at a low rate, and exporting them to a high price Member State (such as Germany, the UK, the Netherlands or Denmark) in order to return a profit. See further chapter 8.

The German government argued that the measure was justified on public health grounds. Consumer protection was guaranteed by restricting the sale of pharmaceuticals only to authorised retailers within Germany. It was argued that the entire system of consumer and health protection would be jeopardised, if private individuals were free to import pharmaceuticals. That freedom might give rise to abuses which it would be impossible to control, and to the misuse of pharmaceuticals. Further, it would also facilitate evasion of the rules on national authorisation for pharmaceuticals, contained in Directive 65/65/EEC, as amended.[152]

The Court gave this argument short shrift. The Court pointed out that the purchase of a pharmaceutical product in a pharmacy in another Member State provides a guarantee equivalent to that provided by the German rules. This, according to the Court, is all the more the case, given that pharmacists' professional qualifications within the EU have been the subject of harmonisation in the mutual recognition of diplomas directives.

Although this is not articulated in the ruling, one function of the German rules at issue in *Schumacher* may have been to protect the prices of pharmaceuticals in Germany, which are traditionally higher than those in many other Member States, in order to protect national capacity in the pharmaceutical industry. The ruling in *Schumacher* had the effect of rendering such national rules inapplicable, because of their incompatibility with EU law. The provision on mutual recognition of qualifications of professionals is a crucial facet of the development of EU law in this direction. One argument used (legitimately) by Member States to maintain control over aspects of their social welfare systems, and in particular the health care field, was the need to protect the beneficiaries of that scheme by means of a closed system applying nationally determined professional standards and rules on qualifications to providers of health care services. The mutual recognition of qualifications directives, as understood by the Court, undercut that argument. The Court implies from the directives that Member States have accepted that the educational and professional standards applied to health care professionals in any other Member State must be sufficient to protect "consumers" of health care benefiting from corresponding health care services in their own Member State.[153] There are, as we will see below, problems with this assumption, as the EU system of mutual recognition of qualifications leaves significant space for difference in quality standards, and therefore differences in protection of patients, between the Member States. However, the Court does not appear to be prepared to recognise these problems in the context of free movement of pharmaceuticals. Thus an indirect effect of the Pharmaceuticals Directives may have been to undermine some national measures concerning

152 Now repealed and replaced by Directive 2001/83/EC: see further chapter 8.

153 See Case C-62/90 *Commission v Germany* above n 150; Case 215/87 *Schumaker* above n 150; see also, in the context of free movement of the "health care goods" spectacles, Case C-120/95 *Decker* above n 20. This is the companion case to Case C-158/96 *Kohll* above n 20 on the freedom to provide and receive cross-border medical services, see further, chapter 4.

importation of pharmaceuticals, aimed at supporting a national pharmaceutical industry, as part of a broader national health policy.

Sectoral directives: conclusions

The EU's involvement in the regulation of health care professionals by means of the sectoral directives is limited by reference to Community competence, which is essentially confined to what is necessary for creating a "single market" in persons. The approach of the sectoral directives is to combine the mutual recognition element of new approach harmonisation, and the setting of minimum standards, with the mandatory coordination of national regulatory regimes. This makes for a slow regulatory process, as agreement must be reached (through committee structures) on the minimum training standards appropriate for each health care professional specialism, in a context of differing cultures and practices across the EU. The advisory committee structure is cumbersome and, at least in the view of the Commission, inefficient.[154]

In a few cases, the regulatory process may have been speeded up by activity of the European Court of Justice, applying the deregulatory Treaty provisions, which made EU-level coordination more desirable for governments of Member States. Such case law also played a role in prompting further EU-level legislation, first in the form of the "general" directives on mutual recognition of professional qualifications, and, second, in the form of a proposal[155] to consolidate this entire area of law.

The general directives on mutual recognition of qualifications

The complexity, slowness and inflexibility of the sectoral system prompted the Commission to consider a more flexible means of enabling EU citizens to have their qualifications recognised in other Member States, thus enabling them to establish themselves in a place other than the Member State in which their qualification was obtained. The process of reform leading up to the system of "general" directives on mutual recognition of qualifications was a rather long one. The directives which resulted – Directive 89/48/EEC[156] and Directive 92/51/EEC[157] – were not intended to supplant the sectoral directives, but rather, preserve what the sectoral directives had achieved, and apply only to other "regulated" professions which were not covered by the sectoral directives. Thus, in the context of the health care professions, they apply, for example, to paramedics, chiropodists, art and music therapists,

154 For further discussion of the "virtues and vices" of the sectoral system, see K. Armstrong, "Mutual Recognition" in C. Barnard and J. Scott, eds, *The Law of the Single European Market: Unpacking the Premises* (Oxford: Hart, 2002), pp 254–256.

155 COM(2002) 119 final.

156 OJ 1989 L 19/16, as amended by Directive 2001/19/EC, OJ 2001 L 206/1.

157 OJ 1992 L 209/25, as amended by Directive 2001/19/EC, OJ 2001 L 206/1.

speech therapists, orthoptists, or physiotherapists,[158] who are not subject to specific sectoral schemes themselves. These directives will also be repealed by the proposed consolidation Directive, if it is adopted.[159]

The roots of the system of general directives may be traced to Council's 1974 Resolution on the mutual recognition of formal qualifications.[160] The Council "expresse[d] the wish that future work on the mutual recognition of diplomas, certificates and other evidence of formal qualifications be guided by the desire for a flexible and qualitative approach", and that future work in the area of mutual recognition would be based upon flexible and qualitative criteria, with the Directives resorting as little as possible to prescriptive detailed training requirements.[161] This is in direct antithesis to the approach under the system of sectoral directives. In June 1984, the Fontainebleau European Council urged the Commission to develop a method for universal recognition of higher education diplomas. The Commission responded in its White Paper of June 1985, in which it proposed a general approach to cover all professions where the rules had not been harmonised.[162] A reform to the sectoral system was anticipated by Decision 85/368/EEC,[163] which set up a system for the comparability of vocational training qualifications between skilled workers in the Member States. The purpose of this Decision, however, was not to lead to the legal recognition of certificates, diplomas and qualifications, but rather to simplify the procedures for applying mutual recognition.

It was not, however, until the latter part of the 1980s that the EU institutions adopted the first of two general directives which were intended to supplement the sectoral system on mutual recognition of qualifications. These directives may have been in part a response to decisions of the European Court of Justice on the application of the Treaty provisions to mutual recognition of qualifications. For instance, in *UNECTEF v Heylens*,[164] the Court held that EU law requires that where employment is dependent on the possession of a diploma, it must be possible to obtain judicial review of a decision of national authorities to refuse to recognise a diploma from another Member State, and reasons must be given for such a refusal. Although Member States are entitled to specify conditions for access to a profession that is not the subject of EU-level legislation on mutual recognition of diplomas, such conditions may not discriminate on the grounds of nationality.[165] Rather, an objective analysis of the comparability of the foreign diploma and that of the host Member State must

158 Over 1450 physiotherapists relied on the general directive in the first four years of its operation, 1991–94: see Commission, *Report to the European Parliament and the Council on the State of Application of the General System for the Recognition of Higher Education Diplomas* COM(96) 46.

159 COM(2002) 119 final.

160 Above n 118.

161 Para II of the Resolution.

162 Para 93 of the White Paper.

163 OJ 1985 L 199/56.

164 Case C-222/86 [1987] ECR 4097.

165 See also Case C-340/89 *Vlassopoulou* above n 65, para 8; Case C-104/91 *Borrell* [1992] ECR I-3003.

be undertaken.[166] These principles are reflected in the general mutual recognition directives. In 1988, the Council adopted Directive 89/48/EEC on a "general system for the recognition of higher-education diplomas awarded on completion of professional education and training of at least three years' duration".[167] This was followed in 1992 with Directive 92/51/EEC on a "second general system for the recognition of professional education and training to supplement Directive 89/48/EEC".[168] Each of the two Directives follows basically the same approach. The later directive covers education and training programmes other than those covered by the three-year higher education requirement of the first general directive.[169]

Between them, Directives 89/48/EEC and 92/51/EEC cover all regulated occupations, professions and titles not covered by the sectoral directives.[170] They introduce a novel form of mutual recognition of national qualifications, which is not dependent on prior coordination of these qualifications at EU level. The guiding principle behind these Directives is one of "mutual trust".[171] The essence of the general scheme is that a national of a Member State may not be refused, on the grounds of inadequate qualifications, the right to take up or pursue an activity which is regulated in that Member State under the same conditions as nationals, if he or she has acquired corresponding qualifications in another Member State. However, recognition under the general directives is not automatic, as under the sectoral directives. Under the general scheme, it is not necessary to explore in detail whether a particular activity counts as a particular profession, but rather once any national regulation of entry to the profession is in place, the activity concerned in principle falls within the general directives.

As the EU institutions themselves point out, in an official summary of Directive 89/48/EEC,[172] the general scheme grants recognition to the "end product", that is, to fully qualified professionals who have already received any professional training in addition to their university diplomas. Where there are major differences in education and training, or in the structure of a profession, compensation mechanisms,

166 Case C-222/86 *UNECTEF v Heylens* above n 164, para 17. See also Case C-31/00 *Conseil National de l'Ordre des Architectes v Dreessen* [2002] ECR I-663; here, the applicant's qualification was, through oversight, not included within the relevant sectoral directive, and thus could not be subject to mutual recognition through the legislation. However, the principles of *Vlassopoulou* and *Heylens* applied to require the host Member State to examine the applicant's knowledge and qualifications according to objective standards, and to give full and proper reasons for the non-recognition of the qualification.

167 OJ 1989 L 19/16.

168 OJ 1992 L 209/25.

169 It applied to diplomas awarded after a post-secondary course, other than higher education courses covered by Directive 89/48/EEC, which lasted for at least one year and which qualified the holder to take up a regulated profession; and certificates awarded after educational or training courses other than post-secondary courses of one year's duration, or after a probationary or professional period, or after vocational training, which qualified the holder to take up a regulated profession.

170 There are also a number of "transitional" directives on mutual recognition of qualifications.

171 See J. Pertek, "Free Movement of Professionals and Recognition of Higher Education Diplomas" 12 YEL (1999) 293 at 312.

172 Bulletin of the European Communities, EC 6-1988, 11.

in the form of an adaptation period or an aptitude test, are provided for in the Directives. These are applied at *national*, not EU, level. However, where a Member State requires professionals to complete an adaptation period or to take an aptitude test, the Member State must first examine whether the knowledge acquired by the professional in the course of his or her experience is such that it fully or partly covers the difference in duration between the professional's education and training and that required in the host Member State.[173]

Thus, the general system, unlike its sectoral predecessor, does not automatically guarantee the mutual recognition of specialised qualifications – it only provides a "starting point" for a person wishing to practise a particular trade or profession. Under the general scheme, the Member States are able to scrutinise and control particular qualifications, and where they deem fit, national authorities may set additional requirements of adaptation periods or aptitude tests.[174] According to Pertek,[175] there is a clear preference in the Member States to use an aptitude test rather than the slightly easier adaptation period in order to correct any apparent deficiencies in educational training or qualifications. Therefore the general Directives are an example of some elements of "new approach" harmonisation, but instead of minimum requirements being set at EU level, national authorities effect regulatory control using the adaptation periods or aptitude tests. National authorities retain greater control over access to regulated professions under the general system. The model adopted is quite different from that applicable under the sectoral directives.

Assessment of the sectoral and general directives

Certainly, the sectoral directives, and probably also the general directives, have resulted in a somewhat increased number of health care professionals moving around the EU.[176] The theory is that barriers to movement arising from separate education and training systems, leading to qualifications that are only nationally recognised, have been removed by the sectoral directives. This has allowed health care professionals, in particular those in Member States where there is overcapacity in their particular specialism, to practise in other parts of the EU.[177] Member States suffering from under-capacity could take the opportunity provided by the system to recruit professionals from other Member States to fill health care professional roles,

173 Directive 2001/19/EC, Articles 1 (3) and 2 (2).

174 Craig and de Búrca, above n 60, p 240.

175 Pertek, above n 170, at 293.

176 For figures on the UK position, see Lonbay, in Goldberg and Lonbay, eds, above n 10, pp 66–67; Oostermann-Meulenbeld, above n 18, at 68; C. Jinks, B.N. Ong and C. Paton, "The mobility of doctors and nurses – a United Kingdom case study" in R. Busse, M. Wismar and P.C. Berman, eds, *The European Union and Health Services* (Amsterdam: IOS Press, 2002). See also Committee of Senior Officials on Public Health, *Statistical Tables Relating to the Migration of Doctors in the Community from 1997 to 1998* (Brussels: European Commission, 1998).

177 For examples, see Ludvigsen and Roberts, above n 44, p 146; G. Eysenbach, "Medicine in Europe" in G. Eysenbach, ed, *Medicine and Medical Education in Europe: The Eurodoctor* (Stuttgart: Thieme, 1998), p 10; J. Poulsen, "Medical Manpower in Europe" in G. Eysenbach, ed, *Medicine and Medical Education in Europe: The Eurodoctor* (Stuttgart: Thieme, 1998), p 29.

confident that such professionals at least meet the EU-agreed minimum training requirements, or that any disparities are compensated for by adaptation periods or aptitude tests administered at the national level.

While, in theory, mobility of health care professionals is facilitated by EU law, in practice, movement of health care professionals between Member States remains relatively low.[178] The extent to which there is a market for health professionals outside individual Member States' jurisdictions can vary considerably.[179] Language may prove a considerable barrier, as may differences in culture and bureaucracy. Movement of health care professionals is greatest between Member States with a shared language,[180] and/or cultural similarities in the organisation of their health systems.[181] In practice, it appears that the largest movement of health professionals across the EU is into the UK, which is made easier by the fact that English is a language studied and spoken so widely, including among the international medical community.[182] There are other reasons why movement to the UK may be regarded as attractive: the excellence of the training, the generous provision of study leave and of support in relation to courses and conferences have all been cited as reasons.[183] Outside these exceptions, however, it appears that little significant use has been made of the opportunities provided by EU law for Member States to recruit health care professionals from other Member States, in particular where they suffer from occupational capacity shortfalls.[184] Neither have significant numbers of health care professionals taken advantage of the opportunity to work in another Member State. These two effects appear to be for a number of reasons.

Probably most importantly, movement of health care professionals is particularly sensitive due to the nature of the professional service provided. Where patients'

178 For instance, the total number of doctors who practise in a Member State other than the one in which they obtained their qualification is typically fewer than 2000 per year. See Committee of Senior Officials on Public Health, above n 176.

179 See Eysenbach, ed, above n 176; F. Klemperer, "How To Do It: Work in the European Union" 312 BMJ (1996) 567; M. McKee, E. Mossialos and P. Belcher, "The Influence of European Law on National Health Policy" 6 *Journal of European Social Policy* (1996) 263 at 273; J. Finch, "Professional Recognition and Training of Doctors: The 1993 EC Directive" 2 *European Journal of Health Law* (1995) 163.

180 Such as Belgium and France or the UK and Ireland.

181 In particular, between the Scandinavian Member States.

182 See Eysenbach, ed, above n 176, p 10; McKee, Mossialos and Belcher, above n 179 at 273–274; Ludvigsen and Roberts, above n 44, pp 117–118.

183 C. Herzmann, " European doctors in the UK" 326 BMJ (2003) 9.

184 Health care professionals holding qualifications from Member States where there is an oversupply of members of that particular profession could be deployed in Member States where capacity problems are being experienced. For instance, Italy, Germany and Spain have traditionally had an oversupply of doctors, and the UK is undersupplied: see Lonbay, in Goldberg and Lonbay, eds, above n 10, pp 64–65; Poulsen, above n 176, pp 27–28. Several of the accession countries in Central and Eastern Europe have an over-supply of specialist doctors: see J. Marrée and P.P. Groenewegen, *Back to Bismarck: Eastern European Care Systems in Transition* (Aldershot: Avebury, 1997), pp 17–22; WHO and European Commission, *Health Status Overview for Countries of Central and Eastern Europe that are Candidates for Accession to the European Union* (Copenhagen: WHO, 2002).

health, or even lives, are at issue, there remains a strong public interest in retaining control by keeping health care professionals "home grown". Inadequate levels of professional service in the health care field cannot simply be compensated financially. Therefore, the mutual trust on which the EU-level directives are in theory based may be difficult to realise in practice. The sectoral directives are based on the formulation of rather general or imprecise definitions in respect of minimum training. This imprecision has been criticised,[185] as the vague terms used to define standards cannot guarantee quality in training practice or outcomes.[186] ***Lack of trust*** in (or downright suspicion of) professional qualifications from another Member State on the part of national authorities may mean that health care professionals find it difficult to assert their rights in EU law under the sectoral or general directives.

The directives on mutual recognition of professional qualifications may prove very ***difficult to enforce.***[187] If a Member State fails to recognise a listed qualification on the grounds that it does not meet the standards laid down by the relevant directive, or to adopt procedures that effectively do not treat a listed qualification as equivalent to a national qualification,[188] a number of legal challenges to that position may be envisaged. Where directives are directly effective, they can be enforced before a national court. Where they lack direct effect,[189] alternative enforcement routes would have to be considered. The most lengthy, and least useful from the point of view of a migrant health care professional, is an Article 226 EC enforcement action by the Commission.[190] This procedure requires the willingness of the Commission to take up the case and is time-consuming. It would thus be ineffective in the short term to assist the plight of the health care professional who wishes to establish herself in a territory other than the Member State of which she is a national. However, the general effect of a ruling against a Member State under Article 226 EC would require legislative reform for the Member State to comply with its obligations in EU law. Another possible route for legal challenge would be through the principle of state liability for breach of EU law, the so-called *Francovich* procedure.[191] Here, where a Member State fails to comply with EU law, and an individual suffers loss through a "sufficiently serious" breach, damages may be recovered.[192] If the training course were listed in the Annex to the relevant directive, such a breach would occur if a Member State refused to recognise the qualification. Dr Schenck's case[193] seems,

185 See, for example, N. Green, T. Hartley and J. Usher, *The Legal Foundations of the Single European Market* (Oxford: OUP, 1991), at chapter 12 generally, particularly p 160.
186 Green, Hartley and Usher, above n 184, p 160.
187 *Ibid.*
188 For an example, see P. Cawston, "Getting a job in France is difficult" 312 BMJ (1996) 1611.
189 For instance, if the terms are insufficiently clear and precise, Case 26/62 *Van Gend en Loos* [1963] ECR 1, or if the professional seeks to enforce against a body that is not an "emanation of the state": see Case C-188/89 *Foster v British Gas* above n 40. See further chapter 2.
190 See, for instance, Dr Schenk's case, and the other examples discussed above.
191 Cases C-6 & 9/90 *Francovich and Bonifaci v Italy* [1991] ECR I-5357.
192 Cases C-46 & 48/93 *Brasserie du Pêcheur* [1996] ECR I-1029; Cases C-178-9/94, C-188/94 and C-190/94 *Dillenkofer* [1996] ECR I-4845; Case C-5/94 *Hedley Lomas* [1996] ECR I-2553.
193 See above p 211.

at least on its face, to fit this situation. However, a causal link between that failure to recognise the qualification and damage to the health care professional would have to be shown, which might prove difficult. To the extent that the sectoral directives lack direct effect, and that other remedies for their enforcement by health care professionals may be incomplete, therefore, the sectoral scheme fails to ensure that the opportunities provided by freedom of movement of health care professionals may be enjoyed (by such professionals, but also by recipients of health care) within the EU.

Furthermore, in terms of the sectoral directives, the lack of trust noted above is exacerbated by the extremely slow pace of the legislative procedure. It has proved extremely difficult to generalise the training for health care professionals sufficiently to reach agreement on a minimum harmonised level of training requirements. A system of automatic mutual recognition ***lacks flexibility***, as it requires all the Member States to agree that the activities performed by a particular profession in their territory are sufficiently equivalent to those carried out by members of that profession in all of the other Member States.[194] This is simply not the case in many circumstances. For example, as a consequence of the EU sectoral directives on dentists, both Italy and Austria had to introduce "dentists" as a distinct profession within their systems. The flexibility problems within the system are likely to become even more intractable on the enlargement of the EU, set to take place in 2004 and 2007.[195]

The inflexibility of the system in terms of legislative reform may lead to reification of particular professions at the moment in time when their particular sectoral directive was finally agreed. It then may become systemically difficult to effect changes necessary to respond to altered scientific understanding, notions of best practice and so on. The sectoral directives attempted to overcome this through the system of committees administering their provisions. However, increased numbers of Member States have meant unwieldy committees, and this is probably part of the reason the Commission has ceased to use committees such as the ACMT.[196] The Commission's

194 Lonbay, above n 10, p 57.

195 In Central and Eastern European candidate states, health care workers suffer from low morale, arising from under-investment in infrastructure and also from low levels of pay (comparable to average skilled blue-collar workers). There is an oversupply of highly specialised physicians. See Marrée and Groenewegen, above n 184. These factors may lead health care professionals from these new Member States to seek employment, or to establish themselves, in the existing Member States, after accession. However, anecdotal evidence at least suggests that such movements are unlikely to be "seismic": see S. Nicholas, "Movement of health professionals: Trends and enlargement" 8(2) *eurohealth* (2002) 11. For the provisions amending the doctors and pharmacists directives, and recognising relevant professional qualifications of the accession states, see the Act concerning the conditions of accession of the Czech Republic, the Republic of Estonia, the Republic of Cyprus, the Republic of Latvia, the Republic of Lithuania, the Republic of Hungary, the Republic of Malta, the Republic of Poland, the Republic of Slovenia and the Slovak Republic and the adjustments to the Treaties on which the European Union is founded – Annex II: List referred to in Article 20 of the Act of Accession –2. Freedom of movement for persons – C. Mutual recognition of professional qualifications – III. Medical and paramedical activities, OJ 2003 L 236/258.

196 See above n 124.

proposed reform of the mutual recognition of qualifications envisages just one advisory "committee on the recognition of professional qualifications".[197] This obviously could not carry out the detailed work that was carried out by the subject specialist committees in the past. This proposal has been strongly criticised by the professional regulatory bodies, on the grounds that the quality management role played by the ACMT would effectively be dismantled.[198] There is some suggestion that the professional regulatory bodies might take on this role themselves, but this would be outside the EU framework.

Further, although the committee system may allow for incremental change, what remains almost impossible, even with the specialist committees, is fundamental, or non-incremental, change, that may involve reconceptualisation of the basis of practice of a whole profession. So, with respect to the pharmacists profession, Furet argues, that, given developments in the pharmaceutical industry, in particular arising from biotechnology, a re-thinking of pharmacy as a whole, and therefore pharmaceutical training, is necessitated, and this is impeded by the EU's sectoral system on mutual recognition of qualifications.[199] The same might be said of the profession of nursing, which has seen increased specialisation since the nurses directives were first adopted.[200] Thus an indirect impact of EU law may be to impede the development of health care professions in a way that ultimately would be beneficial to patients.

Quality in health care and professional training

More generally, the failure of Member States to take advantage of the mutual recognition of qualifications directives to solve national capacity problems probably arises from the failure of the directives to take sufficient account of genuine concerns about ***quality standards*** of health care, in the name of promoting freedom of movement and creating the internal market. This is, of course, a function of Community competence in this field. Article 47 EC would probably not be a valid legal basis for EU legislation harmonising professional rules covering standards of health care provision within the Member States. It allows only for EU law to have a limited impact on regulation of health professionals by harmonising training standards. Article 95 EC might be a possible legal basis for more wide-reaching patient (consumer)

197 COM(2002) 119 final, Articles 20 (5) and 54 (2).

198 See M.M. Mäkinen, "The challenge of professional freedom" 7(4) *eurohealth* (2001) 16; Standing Committee of European Doctors/Comité Permanent des Médecins Européens, "Joint Statement of the Sectoral Professions in the context of the legislative debate on the proposal of the European Parliament and of the Council on the Recognition of Professional Qualifications, COM(2002) 119 final", http://www.cpme.be/policy.htm; European Union of Medical Specialists (UEMS), "Future of the Doctors Directive 93/16", July 2001, http://www.uems.be/d-0142-e.htm. The UEMS is the representative organisation of all medical specialists in the EU; its aim is the harmonisation and improvement of the quality of medical specialist training and practice. See Eysenbach, in Eysenbach, ed, above n 176, pp 13–14.

199 M.D. Furet, "The mutual recognition of diplomas in pharmacy within the European Union" 7 *Sciences et Techniques Pharmaceutiques Pharma Pratiques* (1997) 162 at 164.

200 See above n 97.

protection legislation, if it could be shown to be necessary for the establishment and functioning of the internal market,[201] but to date no proposal based on Article 95 EC to this effect has been promulgated. At least in their rhetoric (but perhaps only so?), the EU institutions appear to be increasingly alive to the tension between freedom of movement and patient protection. For instance, the preamble to Directive 93/16/EEC, the main aim of which is firmly focussed on the establishment of the internal market, states that such a goal is to be achieved whilst also recognising advances in medical science, which have "increasingly widened the gap between medical research and teaching on the one hand and general medical practice on the other". The goals of improving the status of doctor and of elevating the standard of patient care are explicitly mentioned in the preamble not only as desirable objectives, but also as *consequences* of improving training for general medical practice across the Member States. It appears that such goals did not form a crucial element of the rationale for the earlier sectoral directives.

However, rhetoric aside, one possibility is that the very approach of the EU sectoral and general directives on mutual recognition of qualifications may undermine standards of health care in the Member States.[202] The point is that it is not the aim of the directives to protect patients and ensure quality of care.[203] They are provisions of EU law aimed at promoting the freedom of movement of persons. The provisions of the directives on minimum training requirements are not framed in terms of granting directly effective rights to patients, and thus could not be enforced by an individual who received sub-standard care from a health care professional who had moved between Member States in reliance upon the directive. Effectively, once a course of training is included in the Annex to the relevant sectoral directive, it becomes accepted that that course of training meets the minimum standards set out in the directive, and legal challenge of that position is not possible. The sectoral directives operate on the assumption that health care training and education in particular professions is basically equivalent across all Member States. It has, however, been forcefully pointed out that this is clearly not the case. For instance, in the UK, in the 1990s, trainees were managing and operating on about 210 patients with trauma before becoming fully qualified; whereas in Sweden, Finland, the Netherlands and France the average number was around 30 patients.[204] Opinion differs as to whether this is a significant difference.[205] Differences in training provision exist between existing Member States, and problems relating to lack of equivalence

201 See further chapter 3.

202 Lonbay, in Goldberg and Lonbay, eds, above n 10; Roscam Abbing, above n 18, at 352; S. Brearley, "Harmonisation of specialist training in Europe: is it a mirage?" 311 BMJ (1995) 297.

203 Nys has argued for the harmonisation of patients' rights in the EU: see H. Nys, "Comparative health law and the harmonisation of patients' rights in Europe" 8 *European Journal of Health Law* (2001) 317.

204 See P.R. Eldridge, "Junior Doctors Hours" 308 BMJ (1993) 417, cited in J. Finch, "Professional Recognition and Training of Doctors" 2 *European Journal of Health Law* (1995) 163 at 171.

205 See J. Poulsen, "Junior Doctors Hours and EC draft directive on working hours" 307 BMJ (1993) 1158, "the quality of postgraduate training is not ensured simply by long hours", cited in Finch, above n 203, at 170.

of standards are only likely to increase on further enlargement of the EU. Further, there is no procedure at EU level for checking the quality of training standards and providers of training against agreed common standards. National quality assurance procedures are deemed to be sufficient.

Moreover, and fundamentally, the sectoral directives also operate on the assumption that ***initial training*** of sufficient quality is an adequate guarantor of good practice in the health care profession. The directives fail to address the different approaches of Member States in determining what amounts to sub-standard medical practice and what are appropriate corrective measures in this circumstance.[206] The original sectoral directives made no provision with respect to continuing professional development. In an effort to ensure that medical training keeps up with modern trends in medicine, and in recognition of the necessity for ongoing professional training throughout the whole of a professional career, Directive 2001/19/EC inserts into Directive 93/16/EEC a provision which stipulates that continuing training shall ensure that the persons who have completed their studies can "keep up with progress in medicine".[207] However, this provision may be of little benefit, as the Directive provides no further guidelines for Member States in this regard, leaving such an aspect of training, ultimately, at the discretion of Member States. Indeed, this provision may even have the effect of creating further diversity across the Member States in their medical training, as, inevitably, there could be huge discrepancies in ways in which Member States fulfil this obligation.

A practical problem is the ***lack of transparency*** in the form of documentation in order to keep track of doctors who, due to poor professional records, "shop" around the EU.[208] Although, as noted above, the sectoral directives provide that the home Member State is required to share with the host Member State information on disciplinary action in the case of serious professional misconduct and criminal offences,[209] this is limited to cases where disciplinary action has been taken. Further, there is no requirement on the host Member State to share information with the home Member State, or indeed other Member States in which such a professional may seek to establish herself. Other serious matters relating to professional conduct are not subject to a mandatory requirement to be communicated, even between host and home Member States. The relevant provisions only state that, with respect to good character or good repute[210] including provisions for disciplinary action in respect of serious professional misconduct or criminal convictions:[211]

> "where a host Member State has detailed knowledge of a serious matter which has occurred, prior to the establishment of the person concerned in that state, outside its

206 Roscam Abbing, above n 18, at 350–353.

207 Article 14 (9).

208 See examples given in E. Segest, "Consumer Protection and the Free Movement of Medical Practitioners in the European Union" 4 *European Journal of Health Law* (1997) 267 at 269–270.

209 Directive 93/16/EEC, Article 12.

210 Directive 93/16/EEC, Article 11.

211 Directive 93/16/EEC, Article 12.

territory, and which is likely to affect the taking up within its territory of the activity concerned, it *may* inform the Member State of origin."[212]

These provisions are obviously too weak to guarantee good practice in medical professionals moving around the EU. For instance, a permissive provision (a host Member State ... *may* ...) is not as effective in protecting patients as a mandatory provision would be.[213] Further, it is not clear whether the provisions apply only to a restriction, suspension or removal of a health care professional's registration, or whether they include other disciplinary measures, such as a warning, or attaching conditions to a licence to practise. Different Member States use different mechanisms, and a different mix of self-regulation and state regulation, to protect patients from substandard practice on the part of health care professionals.[214] Perceptions as to what constitutes professional misconduct may thus vary widely, and these considerations are not taken into account in the sectoral directives. This has led some commentators to condemn the sectoral directives as putting market mechanisms and economic considerations before patients' interests.[215] Indeed, there is evidence to suggest that even these weak provisions are not being complied with.[216] An EU-wide database holding information on professional misconduct, and other concerns relating to quality of care provided by health care professionals, would help to alleviate these concerns, but no such database is provided for in the current legislation. The proposed new Directive does not appear to even require the exchange of information on professional misconduct, providing simply that:

> "Where the competent authority of a host Member State ... prohibits the pursuit of [a] profession in the event of serious professional misconduct or a criminal offence, that State shall accept as sufficient evidence, in respect of nationals of Member States wishing to pursue that profession in its territory, the production of documents issued ... in the Member State of origin showing that those requirements are met."[217]

There is, therefore, no duty imposed by the Directive on the home Member State of origin to communicate evidence of serious professional misconduct or criminal offences. The burden is on the host Member State to request information showing the absence of such professional misconduct.

212 Emphasis added. This remains unchanged in the proposed amendment: see COM(2002) 119 final, Article 46 (2).

213 This problem is reflected elsewhere in the sectoral and general directives, see Segest, above n 207, at 270.

214 See above n 15, 16 and 18. Such differences are then reflected in the numbers of disciplinary procedures against health care professionals in the sense of the directives, which do not take account of disparity in approach among Member States.

215 See Roscam Abbing, above n 18, at 359; H.D.C. Roscam Abbing, "Main Issues and Findings of the Symposium" in *Quality of Medical Practice and Professional Misconduct in the European Union* (Symposium, Amsterdam, 1997), 4 *European Journal of Health Law* (1997) 273.

216 Roscam Abbing, above n 215 cited by Lonbay in Goldberg and Lonbay, eds, above n 10, p 64 n 129.

217 Proposed Directive COM(2002) 119 final, Annex VII (d).

The system of advisory committees is fundamental to the sectoral directives. The committees provided a forum for exchange of information on the training of health care professionals. They were supposed to keep abreast of developments in medical science, and see that these are reflected in the various training programmes recognised under the directives. They were also supposed to keep the directives up to date. There was doubt from various quarters as to whether the committees, as structured and administered, were able to achieve this. Certainly the medical profession considered that there was insufficient administrative support and too few meetings for the committees to operate effectively.[218] As we have seen, the Commission has effectively frozen the operation of the ACMT since 1999. In 1997, power was delegated to the Commission to update the lists of recognised specialist qualifications and minimum duration of the training for each,[219] using a normal "comitology" procedure. As Lonbay points out, however, this did not really resolve matters, as the logjam simply moved to the implementation stage, with Member States being unable to keep up with the pace of legislative reform.[220]

The size of the committees was unwieldy in practice. With three members and substitutes for each Member State, the current committees were already at 90 members. Enlargement of the EU without reform would see a situation with committees of 120 or more members. This is simply impractical. Further, the frequency with which members were reappointed (every three years) makes for lack of continuity, and thus reduces effectiveness.

Perhaps more significantly, the advisory committee system raises profound questions of accountability and transparency. There are no patients' or other users' representatives on the committees. The proposed new "general" committee would not have space for such interest groups.[221] Save the availability of a very few of their reports on the internet,[222] there is no public access to their activities. The Commission is obliged only to consult advisory committees; they do not represent the strong articulation of national interests in the EU legislative process in the way that

218 UK Royal College of General Practitioners, response to SLIM Questionnaire, Commission, *Positions and Replies Adopted by Professional Associations and Member States in Reply to Commission Questions on the SLIM Project for the SLIM Team on the Mutual Recognition of Professional Diplomas*, DGXV – E2/ZPS D (96) XV/E/68572/96 (Brussels: Commission, 1996), cited in Lonbay, in Goldberg and Lonbay, eds, above n 10, pp 57 and 67; Brearley, above n 201, at 297.

219 Directive 97/50/EC, OJ 1997 L 291/35.

220 Lonbay, in Goldberg and Lonbay, eds, above n 10, pp 67–68. One indicator of implementation problems is the number of cases successfully brought by the Commission against various Member States for failure to implement the sectoral directives. See, for example, Case C-307/94 *Commission v Italy* [1996] ECR I-1011; Case C-250/98 *Commission v France* [1999] ECR I-2447; Case C-202/99 *Commission v Italy* [2001] ECR I-9319; Case C-232/99 *Commission v Spain* [2002] ECR I-4235. The Commission also commenced infringement actions in 2001 against Greece (opticians) and Austria (physiotherapist, occupational therapist, speech therapist) for failure to comply with the general directives, Directive 92/51/EEC and Directive 89/48/EEC.

221 COM(2002) 119 final, Article 54 (2).

222 See, for instance, Advisory Committee on Medical Training, *Fifth Report on Conditions for Specialist Training* (ACMT, 2001), http://www.uems.be/. This report, of a sub-committee of the ACMT, was produced without any support from the Commission.

"regulatory committees" do. Thus advisory committees lay emphasis on "efficiency" of results and representing collective interests of elites.[223] Where advisory committees are "embedded" in the decision-making process, their influence may be significant.[224] As Gehring shows, in the context of environmental regulation, if Member States ultimately retain decision-making power in Council, as is currently the case with the mutual recognition of qualifications directives, they may be more likely to entrust negotiation to experts in the field rather than ministers concerned with protecting national interests. However, in the context of health care professionals, the "experts" in the relevant field do not include a wide range of users of health care provision, and represent training schemes and professional cultures that are deeply nationally embedded and themselves reflect national interests, rather than an "international scientific" approach.

Minor changes were made to the sectoral directives in various amending acts during the 1990s, but, in essence, they did not address these substantial problems with the system, and were really only cosmetic and correctional amendments to the lists of qualifications originally included.[225] It was not until the SLIM process that meaningful consideration was given to amending the sectoral directives facilitating the free movement of health care professionals within the EU.[226] However, neither the SLIM amendments nor the proposed new consolidating Directive do a great deal to address many of the problems outlined above, since they maintain the essential features of the system as currently established.

Difficulties with the general directives

Many of the problems with respect to the operation in practice of the sectoral directives apply also to the general directives. Like the sectoral directives, the general directives also operate on the assumption that health care training and education in particular professions is basically equivalent across all Member States, which is not the case. However, whereas the sectoral directives at least provide for minimum standards (however generously drafted) to be agreed at EU level, the general directives do not provide even that guarantee, but simply leave it to national level to check the quality of training, and compensate where training provision is found wanting.[227] The general directives leave significant control in the hands of national authorities in deciding whether a professional is actually permitted to practise in a host Member State. Yet, the position that professional training is equivalent across the EU appears to be shared by the EU legislature and Court alike. For instance, the

223 See J. Neyer, "The Comitology Challenge to Analytical Integration Theory" in C. Joerges and E. Vos, eds, *EU Committees: Social Regulation, Law and Politics* (Oxford: Hart, 1999), p 221.

224 See M. Gehring, "Committees in European Environmental Process Regulation" in C. Joerges and E. Vos, eds, *EU Committees: Social Regulation, Law and Politics* (Oxford: Hart, 1999), pp 199–204.

225 For example, in the case of Directive 93/16/EEC: see Directive 97/50/EC, OJ 1997 L 291/35; Directive 98/21/EC, OJ 1998 L 119/15; Directive 98/63/EC, OJ 1998 L 253/24; and Directive 99/46/EC, OJ 1999 L 139/25.

226 See Directive 2001/19/EC, OJ 2001 L 206/1.

227 See Lonbay, in Goldberg and Lonbay, eds, above n 10, p 64.

Court stated in *Decker* that an optician in another Member State provides guarantees equivalent to those afforded on the sale of a pair of spectacles by an optician established in the national territory.[228]

The general system is insufficient to promote freedom of establishment of health care professionals not covered under the sectoral system.[229] Difficulties in promoting such freedom of movement arise from a combination of the complex mechanisms of the general system and the ability of national authorities to place a restrictive interpretation on its provisions. For instance, there was a reluctance at national level to acknowledge that an activity is "regulated" within the meaning of the directives.[230] Interactions with the sectoral directives make it difficult to determine whether there is compliance with EU law, and some professions may slip through the net. For instance, the Court considered an Austrian law intended to counter the activities of German training institutions which established themselves in Austria and intensively advertise training as a "Heilpraktiker" ("lay health practitioner"). Heilpraktikers are recognised in Germany, but in Austria they are not permitted to carry out diagnosis, treatment or alleviation of human illness. The Court held that Heilpraktikers are not covered by the Doctors Directive 93/16/EEC, nor are they a "regulated profession" in Austria in the sense of Directive 92/51/EC.[231]

Further, there are significant difficulties with putting the basic principle behind the general system – that of mutual trust – into full effect. Some of these difficulties arise from different definitions of the extent of a particular profession, which we noted above.[232] For instance, some Member States recognise a "denturist" (a dental technician who makes, fits, and repairs dentures directly for the public) as a separate profession, whereas in others the activities of denturists are reserved to dentists.[233] In some Member States, certain activities such as osteopathy, chiropractic or alternative medicine are restricted to doctors, whereas in others, persons who are not qualified as doctors may be licensed to carry out these activities.[234]

It is not surprising, then, that Member States consider countervailing and controlling measures to be justified in the case of most, if not all, health care professions under the general system. Moreover, the general system is also imperfect in completing freedom of movement for persons with specialist qualifications in the EU,

228 Case C-120/95 *Decker* above n 20, para 43.

229 See Pertek, above n 170, at 320–322.

230 Here, Pertek uses the example of the activities of engineer in Belgium: see Pertek, above n 170, at 320. As we saw in the introduction to this chapter, the very concept of "regulated profession" was problematic in any event; and see Case C-164/94 *Arantis v Land Berlin* [1996] ECR I-135, where the Court discussed this concept, and concluded that geology was an "unregulated profession".

231 Case C-294/00 *Gräbner* [2002] ECR I-6515.

232 Ludvigsen and Roberts, above n 44, pp 138–142.

233 F. Du Pré, "Public and Private Harmonisation of Vocational Qualifications in the EU: The Case of the Denturists" 3 *European Journal of Health Law* (1996) 273.

234 For example, in Austria, Belgium, France and Italy only doctors may practise osteopathy or chiropractic; in Denmark, Finland and the UK, chiropractors need not be qualified as doctors, in Finland and the UK osteopaths need not be so qualified.

as not even all regulated professions fell within the regime. The general system carries with it the risk that decision-making power is being exercised in a purely discretionary manner by national authorities. Consequently, it would be difficult for a migrant professional to challenge a Member State's decision. Last, there is a perceived difficulty with the choice of the competent authority, as the fear existed that if the designated competent authority represented the profession, there may be a tendency towards protectionism of "home" professionals or hostility towards migrants.

However, from the point of view of recipients of health care within the Member States, these "drawbacks" in the general system may actually be seen as beneficial. For instance, the ability of Member States to insist upon adaptation periods or aptitude tests may help to guarantee appropriate standards of care. However, concerns may be raised about the "equivalence" of qualifications, even supplemented by nationally administered aptitude tests or adaptation periods, where no attempt at establishing EU-level minimum standards has been made. Thus, for instance, a health care professional such as a chiropodist may have a much longer qualification period and more intensive training in some Member States ("more stringent" Member States) than in others ("less stringent" Member States).[235] The prospect of health care professionals gaining qualifications in "less stringent" Member States, where the cost of training is, therefore, cheaper, and then establishing themselves in "more stringent" Member States, raises the spectre of "social dumping". If a health care professional has had a shorter qualification period and less intensive training, and therefore a smaller time and money investment in her training, she can afford to charge lower prices for her health care services. Unless differences in qualifications are explicitly drawn to the attention of consumers, they may be attracted to the cheaper professionals who have qualified in "less stringent" Member States. This would be so in respect of private patients seeking health care, but also may be so in the case of bodies within national health (insurance) systems purchasing health care services in a climate of cost containment. Therefore, over time, higher standards in the "more stringent" Member States may be jeopardised by the influx of providers from other Member States. However, given the focus in many Member States on standards within health care professions, it seems unlikely that this would actually prove to be the case.[236]

Overall, then, the mutual recognition of qualifications directives has had only a limited effect on national regulatory structures applying to health care professionals within each Member State. As a matter of EU law, Member States must ensure that their professional training schemes meet the standards set down in the sectoral directives. Given the fact that the sectoral directives frame these standards

235 For example, UK chiropodists may legally obtain and administer local anaesthetics and carry out minor surgical procedures, and this is reflected in their training. In some EU Member States, chiropodists are not allowed to breach intact skin: correspondence with the authors from the Director of Education, UK Society of Chiropodists and Podiatrists, 25 November 2002.

236 See discussion on regime competition in chapter 2, p 36 and 56.

in relatively general terms, this is unlikely to have significant effects on national law.[237] Otherwise, the potential opportunity to create a "single market" in health care professionals, with the effect of significant numbers of health care professionals exercising freedom of movement within the EU, is as yet largely unrealised. Member States have relinquished some control over professional regulation, by recognising health care qualifications gained in another Member State, but the effects of this remain marginal. Most of the sites for professional regulation within the Member States remain untouched by the mutual recognition of qualifications regime.

Non-EU citizens and qualifications from non-EU states

Neither the sectoral nor the general directives on mutual recognition of qualifications apply to nationals of states other than Member States of the EU. Nor did they originally apply to qualifications obtained outside of the EU.[238] Member States are encouraged to recognise diplomas and other evidence of formal qualifications obtained by citizens of the EU in non-Member countries by Recommendation 89/49/EC,[239] but this is a measure of soft law, and is not binding or enforceable. There is no equivalent "hard" law to the general or the sectoral directives on mutual recognition of qualifications. Nationals of non-EU states who are established in the Member States of the EU have no rights, under secondary EU legislation, of mutual recognition or permission to practise as self-employed persons. Thus, even if a non-EU national has obtained a qualification in one of the Member States which is contained within the Directives, she lacks any rights under EU law to recognition of her qualifications, or to establishment. The only exception to this is for EEA nationals.[240]

Nevertheless, relying on the provisions of primary Treaty law, relatively recent jurisprudence of the European Court of Justice has made considerable inroads into national competence to regulate the recognition of extra-EU qualifications. This is particularly significant in the field of health care professionals, because of the relatively large numbers of health care professionals holding such qualifications practising in certain of the Member States. For instance, many doctors trained in India or Pakistan practise in the UK, and many trained in Latin America practise in Spain or Portugal.[241]

The Court first considered the issue in *Tawil-Albertini*,[242] concerning a French national who possessed Lebanese dental qualifications. His qualifications had been

237 For instance, the accession state of Poland only had to implement major changes with respect to professional training for nurses, and to change the title of "doctor of dentistry" to "dentist", see M. Zajac, "EU Accession: Implications for Poland's Healthcare Personnel" 8(4) *eurohealth* (2002) 13.

238 Under Directives 89/48/EEC and 92/51/EEC, however, a diploma awarded within the EU may in certain instances take into account education or training obtained outside the EU.

239 OJ 1989 L 19/24.

240 See Annex VII to the EEA Agreement.

241 See McKee, Mossialos and Belcher, above n 179, at 272.

242 Case C-154/93 *Tawil-Albertini v Ministre des Affaires Sociales* [1994] ECR I-451.

recognised by the Belgian, UK and Irish authorities, but not by those in France, where Abdullah Tawil-Albertini wished to practise. The Member States were required to recognise the qualifications listed in Directive 78/686/EEC[243] on the mutual recognition of dental qualifications (the Dentistry Directive), but, of course, this Directive did not include any qualifications obtained outside of the EU. Tawil-Albertini argued however that his qualification fell within the terms of the Directive, as it had been recognised elsewhere in the EU (in Belgium) as equivalent to the Belgian diploma. His argument failed, with the Court ruling that the Directive did not require Member States to recognise diplomas, certificates and other evidence of formal qualifications which did not testify to dental training acquired in one of the Member States of the EU.[244] The Court categorically stated that recognition by a Member State of qualifications awarded by non-Member States did not bind other Member States.[245] This did not, however, preclude Member States from remaining free, in accordance with their own rules, to authorise holders of qualifications obtained in non-EU states to take up and pursue the activities of a dental practitioner.[246] The Court justified its ruling by reference to the fact that the mutual recognition of qualifications in dentistry awarded by the Member States was based on the guarantees provided by the application of minimum training criteria, and that, regarding relations with non-EU states, such co-ordination of legislation on training could be established only by agreements concluded between the states concerned.[247] Whilst concerned with the Dentistry Directive, the reasoning of this ruling would seem to apply in the case of the other sectoral Directives.

However, if a Member State does recognise a qualification obtained outside of the EU, it must take into account, in its assessment of whether a national training period has been fulfilled, of any practical training or experience obtained in another Member State. This was established by the Court in *Haim*,[248] relying on its earlier judgment in *Vlassopoulou*.[249] The applicant in *Haim* had been authorised to practise as a dentist in Germany, despite the fact that he did not hold one of the qualifications listed in the Dentistry Directive. Upon his application to work within a social security scheme in Germany, he was told that he would have to complete a further two-year preparatory training period. The Court upheld his argument that his experience working for eight years as a dentist in a similar Belgian scheme must be taken into account in calculating any necessary preparatory training. According to the Court:

> "A Member State which receives a request to admit a person to a profession to which access, under national law, depends upon the possession of a diploma or a professional qualification must take into consideration the diplomas, certificates and other

243 OJ 1978 L 233/1.
244 Case C-154/93 *Tawil-Albertini* above n 242, para 15.
245 Para 13.
246 Para 12.
247 Paras 11–12.
248 Case C-319/92 *Haim* v *Kassenzahnärtzliche Vereinigung Nordrhein* [1994] ECR I-425.
249 Case C-340/89 *Vlassopoulou* above n 65.

> evidence of qualifications which the person concerned has acquired in order to exercise the same profession in another Member State by making a comparison between the specialised knowledge and abilities certified by those diplomas and the knowledge and qualifications required by the national rules.
>
> By application of that same principle, it should be considered in the present case that the competent national authority, in order to verify whether the training period requirement prescribed by the national rules is met, must take into account the professional experience of the plaintiff in the main proceedings, including that which he has acquired during his appointment as a dental practitioner of a social security scheme in another Member State."[250]

More recently, in *Hocsman*,[251] the Court confirmed that:

> "where, in a situation not regulated by a directive on mutual recognition of diplomas, a Community national applies for authorisation to practise a profession access to which depends, under national law, on the possession of a diploma or professional qualification, or on periods of practical experience, the competent authorities of the Member State concerned must take into consideration *all* the diplomas, certificates and other evidence of formal qualifications of the person concerned *and his relevant experience*, by comparing the specialised knowledge and abilities certified by those diplomas and that experience with the knowledge and qualifications required by the national rules."[252]

The reference to "all" diplomas is a deliberate reference to qualifications gained in non-EU states. Thus the Treaty principle of non-discrimination may aid EU citizens seeking mutual recognition of qualifications obtained in non-EU states, at least in certain circumstances.

The principles developed by the European Court of Justice now find reflection in the secondary legislation. Directive 2001/19/EC, preamble, Recital 6 highlights the role of the Court's jurisprudence in the process of amending the EU's secondary legislation on mutual recognition of professional qualifications:

> "According to the case-law of the Court of Justice of the European Communities, Member States are not required to recognise diplomas, certificates and other evidence of formal qualifications which do not testify to training acquired in one of the Member States of the Community [reference is here made to the *Tawil-Albertini* case]. However, Member States should take into account professional experience gained by the person concerned in another Member State [reference is here made to the *Haim* case]. That being so, it should be stipulated in the sectoral Directives that *recognition by a Member State of a diploma, certificate or other evidence of formal qualification* awarded to a nurse responsible for general care, dental practitioner, veterinary surgeon, midwife, architect, pharmacist or doctor on completion of education and training in a third country and

250 Case C-319/92 *Haim* above n 248, paras 27–28.

251 Case C-238/98 *Hocsman v Ministre de l'Emploi et de la Solidarité* [2000] ECR I-6623. The case concerned Directive 93/16/EEC.

252 Case C-238/98 *Hocsman* above n 251, para 40, emphasis added.

professional experience gained by the person concerned in a Member State *constitute Community elements which the other Member States should examine*."[253]

The Directive adds to the sectoral directives a requirement to examine diplomas, certificates and other evidence of formal qualifications obtained outside of the EU, where such diplomas have been recognised by at least one Member State. Professional experience undergone in another Member State must also be examined. Member States have three months in which to examine this evidence, and must give a reasoned decision at the end of that period.[254] However, the Directive leaves unchanged the position of nationals of non-EU states.

IV. Conclusions

The involvement of the EU with the regulation of professional practice in Member States is thus largely[255] in terms of provisions on access to a health care profession. Even within that constraint, individual Member States are left with significant discretion in terms of the precise boundaries of professional qualifications. Member States retain control over the many other sites for regulation of health care professionals, as outlined above. In practice, as we have seen, this means that there is still considerable regulatory divergence across Member States, driven by the political imperatives which apply to individual Member State regulation.[256] In general, the effects of EU law on the regulation of health care professionals have so far been limited, marginal and mainly indirect.

We have noted that, whilst permitting this divergence across Member States is in line with the EU's general approach in allowing operational discretion to Member States, and simply obliging "mutual recognition" of home state control, it nonetheless may give rise to considerable practical difficulties in terms of the recognition of professional qualifications. While, in principle, EU institutions have a role to play in terms of the development of the detailed provision of educational qualifications, at present this seems to be virtually non-existent, as the Commission has embarked on a different approach to the mutual recognition of qualifications of medical professionals. This is controversial, not least as it appears to downplay concerns about quality control of professional education. Other EU involvement in day-to-day regulation of professional practice is largely through the application of employment law provisions and, as we noted above in the context of the Working Time Directive, this has also proved to be controversial.

Following a consultation exercise in 2002,[257] as we noted above, the Commission produced a draft consolidation Directive which seeks to completely revise, and

253 Emphasis added.

254 Directive 2001/19/EC, Article 14 (16), amending the Doctors Directive; Article 12 (5), amending the Pharmacists Directive.

255 Also, EU employment law may affect medical professionals who fall within the personal scope of the relevant provisions: see above.

256 See Moran and Wood, above n 4.

257 http://www.europa.eu.int/comm/internatioal_market/en/qualifications/02-02-06cons_res.pdf.

replace, all of the general and sectoral directives on mutual recognition.[258] The proposed new Directive is aimed at consolidating and streamlining the vast array of secondary legislation in the field, and at bringing about "greater liberalisation in the field of freedom to provide services rather than the field of establishment, to seek to develop partnership between the public and private sectors through the professional bodies, and to provide a more central role for the competent authorities". Craig and de Búrca take the view that the Commission, through this proposed Directive, is attempting to strengthen its own role vis-à-vis national professional bodies and educational institutions, rather than leave such mediation in the hands of advisory committees.[259] If this is correct, then it heralds a huge shift in the way in which this area of EU law has traditionally developed, and it remains to be seen, if the proposal comes to full fruition, whether this will improve the system of mutual recognition of qualifications in the EU and result in greater mobility of health care professionals.

There has already been some controversy regarding the proposed Directive. In the UK, for example, health and social care regulators have argued that the new proposals may result in harm to patient safety, noting, for example, the element of the proposal that health professionals be allowed to practise in another Member State for a period of up to four months per year without having been registered with the host Member State's regulating authority.[260] In Ireland, the health regulatory bodies – the Medical Council, Dental Council, Opticians Board and the Pharmaceutical Society of Ireland – all called upon the Tanaiste to stop the proposed Directive, which would enable health practitioners to practise in Ireland without any registration there. They were concerned that a health professional who had been struck off in another Member State could practise in Ireland without having registered.[261] Whether the proposal is adopted in its current form remains to be seen. The European Parliament has already registered its objection to this element of the proposal.[262]

There is no Community competence to regulate health professionals in the absence of a connection with either employment law (if the health care professional concerned is an employee) or the internal market, be that through freedom of movement of workers, freedom of establishment or freedom to provide services. The fact that few health care professionals establish themselves in Member States other than that in which they qualify means that there is probably insufficient imperative to improve the legal provisions on mutual recognition of qualifications, to deal with the significant problems associated with those measures, outlined above.

A potential site for future developments may be the freedom to provide services. This may come from one or both of two possible directions. First, if health care

258 COM (2002) 119, amended COM (2004) 317 final. The Directive does not, however, apply to services and establishment for lawyers.

259 Craig and de Búrca, above n 60, p 782.

260 R. Watson, "GMC opposes EU proposal to allow greater freedom of movement for doctors" 325 BMJ (2002) 795 – see above under the discussion of freedom to provide services.

261 http://www.nursingboard.ie/ABANews/Directive19NOV02.html.

262 See above.

professionals take advantage of the technological developments of the "information society",[263] and seek to provide health care services remotely, perhaps through "tele-prescribing", "tele-consultation" and on the internet, a significant market in cross-border health care services may emerge. If this were to be the case, the imperative for EU involvement might increase significantly, as each Member State would lose control over the regulation of the health care professionals to whom "its" patients were turning for health care advice and services. The free cross-border provision of services would need to be sufficiently underpinned by consumer protection measures, to mitigate the potentially problematic operation of an unregulated single market in this field. Such a situation might provide the impetus for EU-level harmonised consumer protection measures, or at least for the coordination of national standards.

Second, an impetus for EU-level regulation might arise if significant numbers of patients exercise their rights in EU law, or the opportunities EU law provides, for cross-border receipt of health care services by travelling to another Member State to receive health care services there. The relevant EU law is discussed above in chapter 4. If significant numbers of patients followed in the footsteps of Yvonne Watts, and sought health care services in another Member State, that implies that the home Member States are accepting the host Member States' regulatory controls over the professional standards that apply to the health care professionals providing services for "their" patients. One could then imagine the possibility for EU law to intervene to set regulatory standards at EU level. Or perhaps the proposed "open method of coordination" on health could be used as a method of soft coordination to move towards such agreed standards.[264] For instance, Nys takes the view that the cross-border movement of patients requires the establishment of EU-level professional standards.[265] Alternatively, subnational responses, for instance contractual provisions between health care financers and providers in home and host Member States, may be envisaged.

Member States with excess capacity, especially the accession states, might actively seek such cross-border patients. At least some of the new Central and Eastern European Member States are seeking to promote the opportunity for the existing Member States to authorise access to highly specialised elements of health care provision in the new Member States at competitive rates.[266] There is evidence that such cross-border migration already takes place, for instance, patients going from Austria to Hungary for dental services.[267] In order to make such an opportunity

263 See discussion in chapter 10.

264 See further chapter 10.

265 Nys frames his argument in terms of harmonised "patients' rights": see Nys, above n 203. See also, more generally, D. Banta, "Quality of healthcare in Europe – an introduction" 6(5) *eurohealth* (2000–01) 18; I. Kalo, "Development of quality of health systems in Europe" 6(5) *eurohealth* (2000–01) 20.

266 See, for example, T. Albrecht, "Opportunities and challenges in the provision of cross border care: View from Slovenia" 8(4) *eurohealth* (2002) 8; R. Busse "Border crossing patients in the EU" 8(4) *eurohealth* (2002) 19, at 20.

267 Nicholas, above n 195.

appealing, host Member States might choose to reframe their standards of professional regulation, towards a kind of "European consensus" on standards. The effect of EU internal market law here is indirect. These scenarios are, however, a matter for the future.

7

The regulation of clinical research

I. Introduction

This chapter considers the ways in which the EU has become involved in the regulation of clinical research. The concerns of health lawyers with clinical research generally focus on the legal protection given to the rights of the subjects of (or participants in) clinical trials, in the light of a recognition that states have responsibilities to ensure protection of such rights.[1] Post Nuremberg, the legal regulation of research activity has also been seen as a matter of particular concern for international bodies. One of the main drivers in this area is the need to ensure that research practices are ethical.[2] This is reflected in a series of influential statements made by international bodies, such as the World Health Organisation and World Medical Assembly Declaration of Helsinki,[3] and, in a European context, the Council of Europe in its Convention on Human Rights and Biomedicine 1997, and more recently in its draft Additional Protocol on Clinical Research.[4] In the EU context, Community competence to regulate the rights of research subjects can be seen, for example, in various provisions within the Clinical Trials Directive, discussed below. The legal basis of this Directive is Article 95 EC, and Recital 10 explains that harmonised administrative provisions for the conduct of clinical trials are needed

1 On the legal regulation of clinical research, see generally M. Brazier *Medicine, Patients and the law* (London: Penguin, 3rd edn, 2003), A. Grubb, *Kennedy and Grubb Medical Law* (London: Butterworths, 2000), chapter 14; J.K. Mason, R.A. McCall Smith and G. Laurie, *Law and Medical Ethics* (London: Butterworths, 6th edn, 2002), chapters 19 and 20; J. Montgomery, *Health Care Law* (Oxford: OUP, 2002), chapter 14; M. Fox, "Clinical Research and Patients: the Legal Perspective" in J. Tingle and A. Cribb, *Nursing Law and Ethics* (Oxford: Blackwell Scientific, 2002); J. McHale and M. Fox, *Health Care Law: Text and Materials* (London: Sweet and Maxwell, 1997), chapter 10.

2 There is a vast literature on the ethics and consequent legal regulation of clinical research, see, for example, C. Foster, *The ethics of medical research on humans* (Cambridge: CUP, 2001); J.K.M. Gevers, "Medical Research and the Law: A European Perspective" 2 *European Journal of Health Law* (1995), 97.

3 See, for example, Declaration of Helsinki, adopted by the World Medical Assembly, Helsinki, Finland, 1964. For discussion of a longer list, see D. Sprumont, "Legal Protection of Human Research Subjects in Europe" 6 *European Journal of Health Law* (1999) 25.

4 Council of Europe Steering Committee on Bioethics, Draft Additional Protocol to the Convention on Human Rights and Biomedicine, on Biomedical Research, Strasbourg, 23 June 2003 CDB1/INF(2003).

in order to ensure effective conduct of such trials in the EU. However, in spite of its apparent harmonisation-based rationale, the Clinical Trials Directive contains a number of provisions with an ethical dimension, and is to some extent framed in a human rights idiom, with particular reference to rights to physical and mental integrity, and privacy.

Another focus for health lawyers interested in the regulation of clinical research is that of the perceived need to regulate on the basis not of rights of individuals, but of a collective notion of the public interest and also public safety. Here the concern is with modes of regulation that ensure research is carried out in matters in which there is a clear public interest, for instance, in developing drugs to combat diseases for which there is currently no effective cure, rather than developing more drugs to combat diseases for which there are already established effective treatments. Regulation is also required to ensure that trials are carried out responsibly and with due regard to health and safety, and that members of the general public (in addition to research subjects) are not endangered by the conduct of a clinical trial.

However, the involvement of the EU and its Member States in research practices and their regulation can be seen as having a third dimension; namely that of fostering research development and the research industry. The logic of the single internal market would seem to suggest a "single research area". Cross-EU research is seen here as directly benefiting European industry and employment, and enabling European companies to compete in global markets. The Treaty provides, in Article 163 EC, that "the Community has the objective of strengthening the scientific and technological bases of Community industry and encouraging it to become more competitive on an international level". This is to be carried out in cooperation with the institutions of the Member States, and research and technological development is a policy field in which the EU is to support and complement activities carried out at a national level.[5] The EU's support for research is carried out principally on the basis of multi-annual "framework programmes", which disburse EU funding for various research activities. The EU is also becoming involved in the process of "technology transfer",[6] concerning the interface between the more theoretical elements of research and its industrial or commercial applications.

In the context of clinical research, a "single research area" would seem to imply clinical research taking place with subjects across several or all Member States of the EU, with the implicit economies of scale and benefits in terms of considering a wide range of research subjects. However, in practice, although the pharmaceutical industry is a global industry, many trials of new pharmaceuticals are still carried out within national boundaries. Nevertheless, the EU plays an important role in fostering cross-EU research in the way in which it facilitates funding of clinical research through the Commission's Directorate General for Research. The EU supports

5 Article 164 EC.

6 See, for instance, the "Innovation and SME Programme", http://www.cordis.lu/innovation-smes/home.html.

clinical research that has an EU dimension, favouring projects with partners in different Member States, where clear "European added value" is given by carrying out the research, for instance, if it could not be carried out effectively within national boundaries.[7]

The Commission also issues various policy statements (measures of "soft law") regarding particularly controversial clinical trials, such as those concerning cloning. These soft law measures may have implications for the disbursement of EU research funding. They may also have other indirect effects on national and EU regulatory measures, for instance, through setting expectations for convergence towards a particular regulatory approach or standard, or creating "path dependence" or otherwise constraining the policy options within the frame in the regulation of a particular area of research. This impact of EU law may increase as EU and national policy-makers grapple with controversial research practices, in particular those involving biotechnology.

Inevitably there are tensions between these various dimensions of the regulation of clinical and health-related research. Interestingly, it is the ethical dimensions that appear to be increasingly coming to the fore in debates within the EU. For example, this is illustrated by the inclusion of the incompetent participant in clinical trials under the Clinical Trials Directive; the patenting of life forms under the Directive on the Legal Protection of Biotechnological Inventions; and the various measures concerning cloning and stem cell research. In this chapter, we examine each of these legal provisions in turn. However, we turn first to a consideration of the way in which research activities are co-ordinated and financed by the EU institutions.

II. Co-ordinating and funding clinical research activities

The EU's activities concerning coordination and funding of medical research across the EU take place in the context of the EU's general research and technological development policy. The EU Commissioner responsible for research is currently Philippe Busquin.[8] The Research Commissioner oversees the DG for Research, which develops the EU's research policy, and administers the "Framework Programmes" for research funding, and the Joint Research Centre (also a DG of the Commission), which is responsible for providing research and advice to support EU policy-making. Accountability of the Commission to the European Parliament and Council of Ministers, with respect to these activities, is implied by the requirement that the Commission's annual report to Parliament and Council includes information on research and technological development activities.[9]

7 See Council Resolution of 25 July 1983, establishing the First Framework Programme, OJ 1983 C 208/1: "Community action can be justified where it presents advantages (added value) in the short, medium or long term from the point of view of efficiency and financing or from the scientific and technical point of view as compared with national activities."

8 See further http://europa.eu.int/comm/commissioners/busquin./index-en.html.

9 Decision 1110/94/EC, OJ 1994 L 126/1, Article 4 (1).

The EU's "Framework Programmes" provide the principal mechanism of dispensing research funding to cross-EU research projects.[10] Medical and health research is also funded under the auspices of the EU's public health programmes, discussed in chapter 3. The EU is currently on its Sixth Framework Programme, which runs from 2002 to 2006.[11] Funding administered through the Framework Programmes has been directed towards a number of health and health-related research areas. The First Framework Programme (1984–87)[12] included under objective 6 "improving safety and protecting health". This modest beginning was expanded in the Second and Third Framework Programmes (1987–91; 1991–94).[13] For our purposes, two elements of objective 4 "Life sciences and technologies" are most significant: Biotechnology; and Biomedical and Health Research ("Biomed 1"). Under Biomed 1, the focus was on research into economically and socially significant diseases (in particular cancer, AIDS, cardiovascular disease and mental illness), ageing, disabilities and workplace health problems. Analysis and sequencing of the human genome was also included. These were carried through to "Biomed 2", under the Fourth Framework Programme (1994–98),[14] which also added research into evaluating new pharmaceuticals; biomedical engineering, including medical devices; rare or "orphan" diseases; research on health systems and "research on bio-medical ethics, to address general standards for the respect of human dignity and the protection of the individual in the context of bio-medical research and its clinical application".

The Fifth Framework Programme[15] was operational in the period 1998–2002. Research under this programme was concentrated in four main areas or "thematic priorities" (in contrast to the 13 objectives in the previous programme). Of these, thematic objective 1 "Quality of life and management of living resources" ("Life Quality") was the strand of EU funding relevant to health-related research. Elements of five of the "key actions" under Life Quality were relevant: control of infectious diseases, including development of vaccines; research into the role of food in promoting health; new or innovative health-related processes or products; environmentally influenced diseases and allergies; and age-related health problems. There were also a number of "generic activities" under Life Quality, all of which are relevant to health-related research. These are research into chronic and degenerative diseases, cancer, diabetes, cardiovascular diseases and rare diseases; research into genomes and diseases of genetic origin; neurosciences; public health and health services; research related to persons with disabilities; bioethics; and socio-economic aspects of life science and technologies. Under the Fifth Framework Programme, the

10 This looks set to continue in the future, if the relevant provisions of the proposed Draft Treaty establishing a Constitution for Europe are adopted, see Article III-149 DCT ff. For further discussion of the DCT, see chapter 10.

11 Decision 1513/2002/EC, OJ 2002 L 232/1.

12 Council Resolution of 25 July 1983, OJ 1983 C 208/1.

13 Decision 87/516/EEC, OJ 1987 L 302/1; Decision 90/221/EC, OJ 1990 L 117/28.

14 Decision 1110/94/EC, OJ 1994 L 126/1.

15 Decision 182/99/EC, OJ 1999 L 26/1.

EU funded contributions to a wide variety of research projects relevant to health. To give just a few examples,[16] the programme provided funding for clinical trials of cognitive enhancers on the elderly, in particular those with Alzheimer's Disease; research into AIDS and other infectious diseases; and the development of various genetics research, such as bio-informatics, which is technology used, for example, to discover the function of genes and how genes express.[17]

The Sixth Framework Programme, 2002–06,[18] focuses on the development of the "European Research Area": a border-free zone for research, in which resources are efficiently deployed to improve both employment and competitiveness in the EU.[19] The creation of a European Research Area was endorsed by the European Council at the Lisbon summit in March 2000. Philippe Busquin, the European Commissioner for Research, has stated that the Sixth Framework Programme, "has been designed above all to be a structuring instrument for making the European Research Area happen".[20] The European Research Area is intended to coordinate research activities with the aim of creating a research and innovation equivalent of the single or common market for goods and services. This ties EU research policy closely to the notion of a "single research area" in which research funded by the EU directly benefits European industry, and enables European companies to compete in global markets.[21] On 26 April 2000, Philippe Busquin launched a European Group on Life Sciences consisting of 13 members with pre-eminence in life sciences and related applications,[22] to advise on this process. In addition, the European Commission, under the auspices of the Research Commissioner, has established a European Research Advisory Board which met for the first time on 26 September 2001.[23] This body is comprised of 45 members: including 20 members proposed by the European Science Foundation drawn from science and academia and 20 members from the Union of Industrial and Employers Confederation of Europe. Its role is to:

> "advise the Commission on design and implementation of Community policy in research and technological development. In this context the Committee will pay particular attention to the realisation of the European research area and the use of policy instruments such as the Community research and technological development framework programmes."[24]

16 For a complete list of projects funded under the Framework Programmes, see the Cordis database, http://www.cordis.lu/.
17 Press Release "Genomes: knowing more; discovering faster – Boosting Europe's capability in bioinformatics", http://europa.eu.int/comm/research/press/2001/pr1605enhtml.
18 Decision 1513/2002/EC, OJ 2002 L 232/1.
19 See Commission Communication *Towards a European Research Area* COM(2000) 6 final.
20 P. Busquin, "Towards a European dialogue between science and society" 8(1) *eurohealth* (2001–02) 5.
21 There is currently a proposal to establish a European Research Council, with a budget of about € 2 billion, to stimulate basic, strategic and investigator driven research in the EU. See R. Watson, "Pressure grows for EU to set up a European Research Council" 327 BMJ (2003) 768 (4 October).
22 http://europa.eu.int/comm/research/life-sciences legls/index_en.html
23 Decision 2001/531/EC establishing the European Research Advisory Board, OJ 2001 L 192/21.
24 Decision 2001/531/EC, Article 2 (1).

Research aims in this new programme are concentrated in more discrete areas than in the past. Of the five specific programmes envisaged under the Sixth Framework Programme, that most relevant to medical research is programme 1, entitled "Integrating and strengthening the European Research Area, including the thematic priorities". Two of the "thematic priorities" are particularly relevant for health: priority 1 on "life sciences, genomics and biotechnology for health"[25] and priority 5 on "food safety and risks to health".[26] In the medical field, the objectives of priority 1 include the development of patient-orientated strategies regarding prevention and management of disease; living and ageing healthily; research into childhood diseases; and confronting the major communicable diseases linked to poverty. Further, the Commission's Director of Life Sciences Research, within DG Research, has indicated that the facilitation of efficient health care systems is a priority policy area in the EU.[27]

To give a flavour of the types of health-related or medical research projects that have been funded by the EU, we now consider in a little more detail such projects in the field of AIDS/HIV. Under Biomed 1 and 2,[28] the EU has supported viro-immunological research, research into the genetics, biology and structure of the HIV virus, research into the development of a "European Vaccine against AIDS", development of anti-viral drugs, and clinical research centring on trials for AIDS treatment regimes. The AIDS research programme also includes an element of behavioural, socio-economic and health services research which aims to identify the most effective methods of health care delivery.[29] Life Quality under the Fifth Framework Programme included control of infectious diseases among its key areas for action.[30] The goal of this action was to combat established, new or re-emerging infectious diseases linked to old, new or mutated agents in humans or animals. The relevant Decision[31] clearly indicates that this would include development of vaccines, including clinical trials, research into new or improved strategies for identification and control of infectious diseases, development of diagnostic tests, immunological research, and public health matters, such as surveillance, management and prevention of infectious diseases. Thus the Fifth Framework Programme

25 Budget € 2.255 billion.

26 Budget € 685 million.

27 P. Belcher, "Interview with Dr Octavi Quintana: Director of 'Life Sciences: Research for Health' Directorate General for Research, European Commission" 8(3) *eurohealth* (2002) 1.

28 Decision 91/505/EC adopting a specific programme of research and technological development in the field of biomedicine and health (1990–1994) "Biomed 1", OJ 1991 L 267/25; Decision 94/913/EC adopting a specific programme of research and technological development, including demonstration, in the field of biomedicine and health (1994–1998) "Biomed 2", OJ 1994 L 361/40. Originally, the Community's research endeavours in the field were under the programmes in "Medical Health and Research (MHR) 1–4", from 1978–90. For further information, see C. Altenstetter, "European Union responses to AIDS/HIV and policy networks in the pre-Maastricht era" 1 *Journal of European Public Policy* (1994) 413 at 418–420.

29 Altenstetter, above n 28, at 421.

30 Decision 99/182/EC, Article 1 and Annex II; Decision 99/167/EC, OJ 1999 L 64/1, Annex II.

31 Decision 99/167/EC, Annex II.

allowed continued EU-level support for the kinds of research projects and activities in the AIDS/HIV field previously financed from the EU budget.

The relevant "thematic priority" under the Sixth Framework Programme for HIV/AIDS research is "life sciences, genomics and biotechnology for health". The objectives of this "thematic priority" include the development of "improved patient-oriented strategies for the prevention and management of disease" and to combat cancer and "the major communicable diseases linked to poverty".[32] This would include research aimed at combating HIV/AIDS, explicitly named along with malaria and tuberculosis, and thus the previously maintained EU-level support for such activity has again been brought forward. The EU subsequently announced support[33] for a long-term partnership between the EU and developing countries to support development of new medicines and vaccines against HIV/AIDS, malaria and tuberculosis. The European and Developing Countries Clinical Trials Partnership brings together EU Member States, Norway and a number of developing countries, especially in Africa, with industry, in a joint effort to combat these poverty-related diseases.[34]

The EU's role in supporting such scientific research is based on the notion inherent in the concept of "subsidiarity",[35] meaning in this context that the EU will finance only "added value" to national endeavours. Thus, typically, EU finances cover only travel and accommodation expenses of research teams from co-operating research institutions in the Member States, in order to enable EU-level meetings of networks of researchers. These meetings facilitate the exchange of information, methodologies and ideas among researchers in the field. The actual research itself, however, is funded by national bodies.[36] As Altenstetter points out, while EU support for such meetings enabled the formation of cross-border contacts which would not otherwise have been forged, in the final analysis, the EU's contribution remains relatively limited. Overall, national AIDS control programmes remain dominant.[37]

Nevertheless, the availability of EU-level research funding for various types of health-related research may have a number of indirect effects at national and EU level. As noted above, what may be quite significant amounts of funding from a supranational source may encourage national research institutions (both public

32 Annex I.
33 € 200 million to be contributed directly from EU funds; € 200 million from participating countries' research programmes; € 200 million from industry.
34 See Commission Press Release IP/02/586 "EU launches € 200m international research programme to fight AIDS, malaria and tuberculosis" Brussels, 18 April 2002; Commission Press Release IP/02/1249 "EU teams up with developing countries to combat AIDS, malaria and tuberculosis" Brussels, 29 August 2002.
35 Article 5 EC.
36 Altenstetter, above n 28, at 421. Although if the proposed European Research Council becomes a reality, this will change, see above n 21.
37 Altenstetter, above n 28, at 435. For details of national AIDS policies in five Member States, see R. Freeman, *The Politics of Health in Europe* (Manchester: MUP, 2000), pp 123–137.

and private) to design research projects of a particular type (and to avoid other types of projects). The EU institutions may thus give a strong "steer" in terms of what is regarded as "ethically acceptable" (and not acceptable) research, and this may eventually lead to convergence in what might be termed the EU's principles of ethical research. This may have an indirect effect on national policy formation, leading to a gradual convergence in approaches. Convergence may also be prompted by the development of common methodologies in research efforts or other projects. Where research leads to the elaboration of "best practice", this may lead directly to the promulgation of soft law, or even, eventually, hard law adopted either at national or EU level. So, for instance, guidelines for the treatment of HIV-positive pregnant women and infants were published on 28 June 2002.[38] These arose from a research project involving a consortium of 15 research teams from seven European countries, coordinated by Professor Newell of University College London. The guidelines aim to reduce the risk of mother to child HIV transmission, and recommend that mothers should undergo HIV testing, those who are HIV positive should deliver by caesarean section, undergo anti-retroviral therapy and avoid breast-feeding. It is likely that such clinical guidelines will be adopted across the EU, thus promoting convergence of best practice arising from EU-level support for research activity.

Further, the availability of EU funding may be used to promote research that might not be viable on a purely national level. This is illustrated by the development of a strand of EU funding for research into "orphan diseases", that is, rare disorders affecting not more than five in 10,000 persons.[39] This heading may be traced to the Commission Communication on the framework for action in public health of 1993,[40] and the Biomed 2 strand of the Fourth Framework Programme.[41] The Biomed 1 strand under the Second and Third Framework Programmes had concentrated on major diseases in the EU such as cancer and cardiovascular disorders. However, a realisation that EU funding was limited and ran the risk of being spread too thinly to be effective (or credible from the point of view of citizens of the EU) if this policy were pursued to its logical conclusion, coupled with the stronger influence of notions of subsidiarity following the Treaty of Maastricht, led to the stronger articulation of the idea of European "added value" in research funding. Selective funding of research where a significant cross-border element was present would be pursued, with funding available for activities only feasible if addressed at

38 Commission Press Release IP/02/905 "AIDS: EU Supported Research leads to Guidelines for Treatment of HIV-positive pregnant women and infants" Brussels, 28 June 2002.

39 This is based on the definition of "orphan medicinal products" in the EU context: see Regulation 141/2000/EC on orphan medicinal products, OJ 2000 L 18/1, Article 3 (1). In the alternative, the person seeking marketing authorisation for the medicinal product may show that it is intended for treatment of a life-threatening, seriously debilitating or serious and chronic condition, and that it is unlikely to prove economical to market it without incentives. Additionally, to fall within the Directive, there must exist no satisfactory alternative treatment for the condition in question. Other states define orphan diseases according to their own definitions.

40 COM(93) 559 final. See chapter 3.

41 Decision 1110/94/EC, OJ 1994 L 126/1.

the EU level. Research into orphan diseases and "orphan medicines" used to treat those diseases clearly falls within that category, as the numbers of those suffering such rare diseases within one state are likely to be too small to contemplate a meaningful cohort for a clinical trial, and the EU has funded over 150 projects in that area since 1994.[42]

The support of the EU in terms of research funding for orphan diseases may also have influenced legislative developments. In 1995, the Council[43] called for further investigation into proposals with a view to improving access to orphan medicines. The Commission duly proposed a Regulation on Orphan Medicinal Products, which was adopted in 2000. Regulation 141/2000/EC[44] aims to encourage research and development of new medicines to treat orphan diseases, by providing protocol assistance under the centralised procedure for marketing authorisations for new pharmaceuticals;[45] by the possibility of a waiver of the fee payable to the European Medicines Evaluation Authority; and by granting exclusive marketing rights for a 10-year period.[46]

Funding for health-related research has also had implications for other regulatory measures with relevance for health law and health protection. For instance, the list of types of medical research funded under Biomed 1 and Biomed 2 formed the starting point for the EU's action programmes in the field of public health.[47] Rare diseases formed one of the eight EU public health programmes that ran from 1999 until the new public health framework programme began in January 2003.[48] In addition to advising on the framework programmes, and EU research funding, the work of the Commission and its advisory bodies in the context of research funding has fed into policy-making and the development of binding measures of EU law such as the Novel Food Regulation.[49]

A number of EU-level advisory bodies have facilitated such policy development in areas related to clinical research. For instance, the Second Framework Programme included a pilot programme relating to the human genome in the area of "predictive

42 For information on projects funded under the Framework Programmes, see the Cordis database, http://www.cordis.lu/.
43 Council Resolution on orphan drugs, OJ 1995 C 350/3.
44 OJ 2000 L 18/1.
45 See further chapter 8.
46 This is a new intellectual property right created by Regulation 141/2000/EC, Article 8. It gives greater protection than the data exclusivity rights given under Regulation 2309/93/EC, which effectively prevent generics manufacturers from using the dossier to file an application, but less protection than a full patent in the new substance. On the provisions of Regulation 2309/93/EC, see further chapter 8.
47 For further discussion of these, see chapter 3.
48 See further chapter 3.
49 Regulation 258/97/EC, OJ 1997 L 43/1; but now see Regulation 1829/2003/EC on genetically modified food and feed, OJ 2003 L 268/1; and Regulation 1830/2003/EC OJ 2003 L 268/24 concerning the traceability and labelling of genetically modified organisms and the traceability of food and feed products produced from genetically modified organisms and amending Directive 2001/18/EC, OJ 2001 L 106/1.

medicine".[50] This led to the establishment of an *ad hoc* Committee on the Ethical, Legal and Social Aspects of Research. EU-level institutions, such as the European Group of Ethical Advisers,[51] undertook ethical review of research proposals which related to controversial issues such as use of embryonic and foetal tissue. One important advisory body was the Group of Advisors on the Ethical Implications of Biotechnology. This group was established by the Commission in 1991. Its terms of reference were:

> "to identify and define the ethical issues raised by biotechnology;
> to assess from the ethical viewpoint the impact of the Community's activities in the field of biotechnology;
> to advise the Commission, in the exercise of its powers, on the ethical aspects of biotechnology and to ensure that the general public is kept properly informed."

The expanding workload of the group is reflected by its expanding membership and agenda. During its first term (1992–94) it had six members; in its second (1994–1996) it had nine. The operation of the group was reinforced by the Commission White Paper *Growth, Competitiveness, Employment*.[52] The role of the body was purely advisory. It was normally requested to advise on a particular matter, but it could decide to investigate a particular issue on its own initiative, as it did in relation to the Directive on the Legal Protection of Biotechnological Inventions.[53] This group's mandate expired in December 1997, but it was promptly replaced by European Group on Ethics in Science and New Technologies.[54] This is a 12-person group established by the Commission to continue and expand the work of the Advisors.

The interface between the notion of a "single research area" and various ethical considerations is reflected in the development of EU-level advisory committees and groups with an ethical remit. The ethical dimension has also been very evident in the Sixth Framework Programme. Decision 1513/2002/EC, which establishes the Sixth Framework Programme,[55] provides in Recital 17 that:

> "Research activities carried out within the sixth framework programme should respect fundamental ethical principles, including those which are reflected in Article 6 of the Treaty on European Union and in the Charter of fundamental rights of the European Union."

50 http://europa.eu.int/comm/research/science-society/ethics/research-history-en.html.
51 Research and Technological Development Activities of the European Union 1999 Annual Report COM(99) 284.
52 Commission, *Growth, Competitiveness, Employment: The Challenges and Ways Forward into the 21st Century*, Bulletin of the European Communities, Supplement 6/93.
53 Directive 98/44/EC, OJ 1998 L 213/13. For further discussion, see below.
54 http:/europa.eu.int/european-group-ethics/index.en.htm.
55 OJ 2002 L 232/1.

Further elaboration is found in Annex 1, which refers to:

> "... principles reflected in the Charter of fundamental rights of the European Union, protection of human dignity and human life, protection of personal data and privacy as well as the environment in accordance with Community law and, where relevant, international conventions, such as the Declaration of Helsinki, the Council of Europe Convention on Human Rights and Biomedicine signed in Oviedo on 4 April 1997 and the Additional Protocol on the Prohibition of Cloning Human Beings signed in Paris on 12 January 1998, the UN Convention on the Rights of the Child, the Universal Declaration on the Human Genome and Human Rights adopted by UNESCO, and the relevant World Health Organisation (WHO) resolutions, the Amsterdam Protocol on Animal Protection and Welfare; and current legislation, regulations and ethical guidelines in countries where the research will be carried out."

These statements have direct implications for what types of (clinical) research may receive funding under the EU programmes. In Decision 2002/834/EC, which adopted the programme "Integrating and Strengthening the European Research Area" (2002–06),[56] a number of principles were set out including that:

> "The following fields of research shall not be financed under this programme:
> - research activities aiming at human cloning for therapeutic purposes;
> - research activity intended to modify the genetic heritage of human beings which could make such change heritable;
> - research activities intended to create human embryos solely for the purpose of research or for the purpose of stem cell procurement, including by means of somatic cell nuclear transfer (often referred to as therapeutic cloning)."

Statements such as these also imply the development of some kind of consensus around common "European values", which, at least rhetorically, underpin research activity and its regulation and financing within the EU.[57] In this sense, the EU is one of the drivers of what might eventually become a convergence of national policies with respect to ethical considerations surrounding clinical research, although there is also the prospect that individual Member States may decide to "opt-out" of such values in an attempt to obtain some economic advantage through being able to attract researchers to their jurisdiction. We turn now from such "soft law" provisions to measures of hard law promulgated at EU level that regulate clinical research carried out within the EU, beginning with a discussion of the Clinical Trials Directive.

56 OJ 2002 L 294/1.

57 See also M. Aziz, "The Value of Implementation and the Implementation of Values", paper presented to conference, "Values and the Draft Constitutional Treaty", Florence, Italy, December 2003.

III. The Clinical Trials Directive

The Clinical Trials Directive[58] regulates the conditions under which certain health-related research, namely clinical trials of pharmaceutical products, may be conducted within the EU. The background to the Clinical Trials Directive can be found in the drive post-Nuremberg to regulate the conduct of clinical research. Over a number of years, a series of international statements were produced, such as the Declaration of Helsinki 1964,[59] the Council of Europe Convention on Human Rights and Biomedicine 1997[60] and the UNESCO Universal Declaration on the Human Genome and Human Rights 1997, with the aim of facilitating ethical practice in clinical trials.[61] In many respects, these international statements fostered convergence of clinical practice guidelines. But, even in the EU context, harmonisation of such guidelines is problematic, because of the divergence in approach by Member States on particular issues. Such sensitive issues include principles of clinical confidentiality and disclosure of patient information in therapeutic and non-therapeutic contexts; and also the inclusion of vulnerable groups, in particular children and mentally incompetent adults, in therapeutic and non-therapeutic trials.[62] In addition, the structures for approval of clinical trials differ considerably across Member States.[63]

Nonetheless, despite divergent approaches at national level, there has been increasing pressure to regulate clinical research practice at EU level. Directives on the licensing and testing of pharmaceutical products required that researchers complied with "good clinical practice".[64] Guidelines setting out such good clinical practice were first issued by the European Commission in 1991. These were replaced by the International Conference on Harmonisation (ICH) Note for Guidance on Good Clinical Practice. This is an internationally recognised initiative agreed by the

58 Directive 2001/20/EC on the approximation of the laws, regulations and administrative provisions of the Member States relating to the implementation of good clinical practice in the conduct of clinical trials on medicinal products for human use, OJ 2001 L 121/34. See A. Baeyens, "Implementation of the Clinical Trials Directive: Pitfalls and Benefits" 9(1) *European Journal of Health Law* (2002) 31.

59 See above n 3.

60 Convention for the Protection of Human Rights and Dignity of the Human Being with Regard to the Application of Biology and Medicine (Convention on Human Rights and Biomedicine) 1997.

61 See S. Gevers, "Medical Research Involving Human Subjects: Towards an International Legal Framework?" 8 *European Journal of Health Law* (2001) 293.

62 Therapeutic trials are those which have the prospect of some health benefit to the participant personally. Non-therapeutic trials involve participants who would not accrue a health benefit to themselves personally through their participation. Such trials usually involve healthy volunteers.

63 See, for example, C. Megone et al, "The Structure, Composition and Operation of European Research Ethics Committees" in S. Mason and C. Megone, eds, *European Neonatal Research: Consent, Ethics Committees and Law* (Aldershot: Ashgate, 2001); H. Nys, "Ethical Committees in Belgium" 2 *European Journal of Health Law* (1995) 175; T. Garanis Papadatos and P. Dalla Vorgia, "Ethical Review Procedures for Clinical Trials in Greece" 7 *European Journal of Health Law* (2000), 441; J. Glass, ed, *Ethics Committees in Central and Eastern Europe* (Limbova: Institute of Medical Ethics and Bioethics Foundation, 2001).

64 See, for example, Directive 91/507/EEC, OJ 1991 L 270/32, Annex, Part 4.B. See further chapter 8.

EU with the US and Japan under the International Conference on Harmonisation of Technical Requirements of Pharmaceuticals for Human use, and is discussed further in chapter 8 below.[65] Good clinical practice has been defined in the ICH guidance as being:

> "a standard for the design, conduct, performance, monitoring, auditing, recording, analyses and reporting of clinical trials that provides assurance that the data and reported results are credible and accurate and that the rights and confidentiality of trial subjects are respected."

The Industrial Research and Development Advisory Committee of the European Commission proposed that legislation relating to the testing of pharmaceutical products should be standardised. [66] Community competence in this respect is found in the provisions on creating and sustaining the internal market, Article 95 EC.[67] In September 1997, a draft Directive on clinical trials on human subjects, concerning the beneficial aspects of new or established medicines before marketing authorisations, was presented by the European Commission to the Council and to the European Parliament.[68] There are discernible different policy aims here. First, through the incorporation of the ICH Guidance on Good Clinical Practice and its effective adoption as binding law,[69] the Directive can be seen in terms of affording protection to individual research subjects. Second, elements of the Directive include harmonisation of the reporting procedures for safety, monitoring and surveillance procedures by the use of inspections. This resonates with public interests in safe clinical research. Third, the Directive can be seen as being driven by commercial concerns, notably that of ensuring that the approval procedures for trials, which were regarded as lengthy by the pharmaceuticals industry, were speeded up to facilitate the progress of scientific research and make it more efficient.

During the adoption process, a number of concerns regarding the Clinical Trials Directive were expressed at national level, in particular in the UK. The ultimate progress of the Directive through the EU legislative procedure proved difficult due to the fact that individual Member States were somewhat resistant to the prospect of harmonisation of the conduct of clinical trial procedures. Baroness Jay, the then Minister of State at the UK Department of Health, in her Explanatory Memorandum, expressed some reservations with respect to the original draft proposal. She was concerned about the harmonisation of procedures for the approval of

65 CPMP/ICH/135/95. For further discussion, see Sprumont, above n 3.

66 See also generally discussion in House of Commons Select Committee on European Legislation, *Sixth Report* (1997–98).

67 See chapter 3. The Commission has sought to frame its regulatory proposals within this provision, even though the Clinical Trials Directive contains many elements that are only tangentially related to the internal market, in particular its provisions concerning ethical principles.

68 Draft directive on the approximation of law, regulations and administrative provisions of the Member States relating to the implementation of good clinical practice in the conduct of clinical trials on medicinal products for human use, COM(97) 369.

69 Directive 2001/20/EC, Article 1 (4): "All clinical trials . . . shall be designed, conducted and reported in accordance with the principles of good clinical practice."

clinical trials by ethics committees; the extent to which the UK should have to comply where a trial was being undertaken solely within the UK; and the time-scale for the conduct of such trials.[70] Some of these concerns expressed at national level were eventually reflected in provisions of the Directive, such as Article 3 (1), which states that the Directive applies without prejudice to national provisions that give more comprehensive protection than the Directive, provided, however, that they are consistent with the procedures and time-scales specified therein.

The legal basis of the Directive is Article 95 EC, which provides for the co-decision procedure. The European Parliament used its powers under this provision to propose amendments to the draft Directive at both its first and second readings. These concerned, in particular, protection of those incapable of giving informed consent, provisions on written consent, provisions on the timeframes for authorisation, and provisions on notification mechanisms in relation to multi-centre or to multi-state trials. An amended proposal was adopted by the European Commission in May 1999.[71] This included a 30-day notification period with regard to most medicinal products. In addition, a procedure of a 60-day authorisation in writing was to be required for biotechnological products and gene and cell therapy products. The role of ethics committees was to be enhanced with them being involved from the start of the trial. At this stage there were still further reservations expressed by the UK government. Baroness Hayman, Parliamentary Under Secretary of State at the Department of Health, responded on 29 May 1999 by saying that, while the UK government welcomed some of the proposals, it reserved its position on a number of matters. These included the concept of "informed consent"; the role of the EMEA;[72] and the harmonisation of ethics committee approval, particularly the time-scales proposed, which were regarded as unduly short.[73] With regard to the latter objection, the tensions between the Directive's commercial concerns and its elements protecting the rights of research subjects are evident here.

Following discussions, some 24 new amendments were drawn up. These were designed to facilitate bringing the parties together, and to allay concerns such as those expressed by the UK Parliament. Subsequently the new proposals were put before the UK Parliament on 11–14 December 2000, whereupon the House of Commons decided to lift its power of scrutiny reserve, because otherwise there was a risk that a blocking majority could have resulted at the Council, with, as a consequence, the

70 House of Commons Select Committee on European Scrutiny, *24th Report* (1998–99), para 6.2.
71 Amended draft directive on the approximation of law, regulations and administrative provisions of the Member States relating to the implementation of good clinical practice in the conduct of clinical trials on medicinal products for human use, COM(99) 193 final.
72 The European Medicines Evaluation Agency; see further discussion on the composition and roles of the EMEA in chapter 8.
73 House of Commons Select Committee on European Scrutiny, *24th Report* (1998–99), para 6.6.

production of other proposals less acceptable to the UK.[74] The Directive was duly adopted by Council and Parliament on 4 April 2001.[75]

The scope of the Clinical Trials Directive is limited: it applies *only* to trials on medicinal products, as defined in Directive 65/65/EEC.[76] "Medicinal products" are "any substance or combination of substances presented for preventing disease in human beings or animals" and "any substance . . . which may be administered to human beings or animals with a view to making a medical diagnosis or to restoring, correcting or modifying physiological functions in human beings or in animals".[77] This covers trials on pharmaceuticals which are in a developmental stage, but also what are termed "investigational medicinal products". These are defined in the Directive as being:

> "a pharmaceutical form of an active substance or placebo being tested or used as a reference in a clinical trial, including products already with a marketing authorization but used or assembled (formulated or packed) in a way different from the authorized form, or when used for an unauthorized indication or where used to gain further information about the authorized form."[78]

However, experimental *treatment* is excluded from the scope of the Directive. Whilst the boundary between innovative treatment and trials is a fine one, nonetheless this does reflect the distinction made on this issue at national level. The Directive does not apply to other health-related research, such as psychological research, research into medical devices, observational studies, research into tissue, organs or blood, or embryo research. Thus the Clinical Trials Directive constitutes a partial harmonisation of the regulation of medical research in the EU, excluding harmonisation in a number of cutting edge areas.

According to the Directive, trials must be undertaken in accordance with "good clinical practice". The Directive defines good clinical practice in Article 1 (2) as being a:

74 The UK House of Commons has resolved that, in principle, no UK minister shall give agreement in Council to any proposal for EU legislation which is still subject to scrutiny by the House of Commons Select Committee on European Scrutiny, or which is awaiting consideration by the House itself; see discussion in House of Commons Select Committee on European Scrutiny, *First Report* (2001–02); resolution of the House of Commons of 17 November 1998.

75 Directive 2001/20/EC on the approximation of the laws, regulations and administrative provisions of the Member States relating to the implementation of good clinical practice in the conduct of clinical trials on medicinal products for human use, OJ 2001 L 121/34.

76 OJ 1965 P 22/369; OJ Sp Ed 1965–6 p 24. For further discussion of this Directive, see chapter 8.

77 Directive 65/65/EEC, Article 1 (2); now in Directive 2001/83/EC, Article 6 (1). See also the rulings of the Court in Case C-227/82 *Van Bennekom* [1983] ECR 3883; Case C-35/85 *Tissier* [1986] ECR 1207; Case C-369/88 *Delattre* [1991] ECR I-1487; Case C-60/89 *Monteil and Samanni* [1991] ECR I-1547; Case C-112/89 *Upjohn* [1991] ECR I-1703; Case C-290/90 *Commission v Germany* [1992] ECR I-3317; Case C-219/91 *Ter Voort* [1992] ECR I-5485; and Case C-212/91 *Angelopharm* [1994] ECR I-171; and the discussions in R. Thompson, *The Single Market for Pharmaceuticals* (London: Butterworths, 1994), pp 17–34; and L. Hancher, "Creating the Internal Market for Pharmaceutical Medicines: An Echternach Jumping Process?" 28 CMLRev (1991) 821. We are not concerned here with the measures concerning veterinary products.

78 Directive 2001/20/EC, Article 2.

> "set of internationally recognized ethical and scientific quality requirements which must be observed for designing, conducting, recording and reporting clinical trials that involve the participation of human subjects. Compliance with this good practice provides assurance that the rights, safety and well-being of trial subjects are protected and that the results of the clinical trial are credible."

In accordance with its duties under the Directive, some further guidance has been issued by the European Commission as to the interpretation of "good clinical practice".[79] This statement, which is based upon the ICH guidelines, notes that clinical trials should be conducted with reference to ethical principles, such as those contained in the Declaration of Helsinki.[80]

Article 3 is headed "Protection of clinical trial subjects" and is indicative of concern for the respect of the rights of subjects in clinical research. The word "subject" is used rather than that of "participant", a term which is used in some instances at Member State level.[81] The term "subject" implies a more passive role in the clinical trial than that of participant. A clinical trial may not be undertaken unless the rights of the subjects of the trial are protected. The rights of the subject include traditional human rights, such as the right to physical and mental integrity, privacy and data protection, in accordance with the Data Protection Directive.[82] Further, trial subjects must give "informed consent" to the trial.

Article 3 places emphasis upon this commitment to informed consent. Informed consent is defined in Article 3 (2) (j) of the Directive as being a decision which is "taken freely after being duly informed of its nature, significance, implications and risks". The consent of the competent research subject must be given in writing, after an interview with the trial investigator, who explains the objectives of the trial and any consequent risks and inconveniences. While informed consent is a principle that is generally recognised in international and national statements of ethics across the globe, in practice there has been considerable divergence as to its interpretation. As Nys has commented:

> "Informed consent might be a generally accepted principle, but under the influence of what I shall, for simplicity's sake, refer to as a 'culture', this principle is interpreted so differently that one wonders whether it can still be called an 'acquis communautaire'?"[83]

Given this, it is perhaps unsurprising that the Directive refers the determination of the boundaries of informed consent back to individual Member State level. How acceptable this will be, however, over a long period may be questioned. There is a real potential here for difficulties in a situation in which it is proposed to conduct a multi-state trial.

79 European Commission, "Detailed Guidelines on the principles of good clinical practice in the conduct in the EU of clinical trials on medicinal products for human use", Brussels, ENTR/6416/01.

80 Para 4.1.

81 UK Research Governance Framework (2001) makes reference to the term "research participant".

82 Directive 95/46/EC, OJ 1995 L 281/31, discussed in chapter 5.

83 H. Nys, "Comparative Health law and the harmonisation of patients' rights in Europe" 8 *European Journal of Health Law* (2001) 317 at 324.

In recent years, the practice has developed across Member States for proposals for clinical trials to be referred to a research ethics committee. Such committees commonly contain a range of members drawn from medical, scientific and social science backgrounds, along with lay members. Practice varies as to whether referral to such bodies is mandatory, although in fact it has virtually become so, due to the fact that scientific journals will not generally accept articles for publication, unless it can be shown that the research received ethics committee approval. The Clinical Trials Directive places the creation of such committees on a formal basis and makes reference to them mandatory. Article 6 (1) provides that Member States shall take the measures necessary for the establishment and operation of research ethics committees. Article 9 provides that sponsors may not begin clinical trials unless an ethics committee has provided them with a favourable opinion.[84]

Article 6 sets out the basic guidelines for the ethics committee to consider when assessing proposed clinical trials. The Directive provides the ethics committee with a series of criteria which it must take into account.[85] First of these is the relevance of the trial and its design.[86] Second, the committee is required to weigh up any foreseeable risks and inconveniences against any anticipated benefit which may accrue to the subject of the trial.[87] Benefits to be considered here include those not only to the trial subject but also to other present and future patients. The Directive thus implicitly recognises both therapeutic trials (those which may benefit the subject personally) and non-therapeutic trials.[88] Third, the protocol is to be considered,[89] in addition to the suitability of investigator and supporting staff[90] and quality of the facilities.[91] Trial protocols are to comply with existing guidance on Good Clinical Practice.[92] The ethics committee is also to consider the adequacy and completeness of written information to be provided and the procedure for obtaining informed consent.[93] The ethics committee is involved, not only in relation to the initial trial approval, but also where researchers intend to submit major amendments to the clinical trial protocol.[94]

Article 6 also provides that ethics committees must be concerned to examine what is the justification for undertaking research on those persons who are incapable of

84 Directive 2001/20/EC, Article 9 (1) and (2).
85 Directive 2001/20/EC, Article 6 (3).
86 Directive 2001/20/EC, Article 6 (3)(a) and see also European Commission "Detailed Guidance on the application form and documentation to be submitted in an application for an ethics committee opinion on the clinical trials of medicinal products for human use", Brussels, April 2003, ENTR/F2/BL/D 2003.
87 Directive 2001/20/EC, Article 6 (3)(b) and see Article 3 (2)(a).
88 Directive 2001/20/EC, Article 3 (2)(a).
89 Directive 2001/20/EC, Article 6 (3)(c).
90 Directive 2001/20/EC, Article 6 (3)(d).
91 Directive 2001/20/EC, Article 6 (3)(f).
92 GPMP/ICH/35/95.
93 Directive 2001/20/EC, Article 6 (3)(g).
94 Article 10 and see European Commission, "Detailed Guidance for the request for authorization of a clinical trial on a medicinal product for human use to the competent authorities, notification of substantial amendments and declaration of the end of the trial", Brussels, April 2003, ENTR/F2/BL/D 2003.

providing informed consent.[95] Specific provisions relate to trials concerning minors (Article 4) and mentally incapacitated adults (Article 5). In the case of the minor, consent should be obtained from the parents or legal representative; in the case of the adult, consent should be obtained from the "legal representative".[96] While it is commonly the case, at individual Member State level, that consent will be routinely sought from the person with parental responsibility on behalf of their children, the use of a legal representative, in the case of the adult, is an important provision which has led some Member States to reconsider their current legal position regarding decision-making in relation to adults.[97] The Directive is, however, silent on procedures to be used to ascertain who is the "legal representative", leaving it to Member States to formulate policy. This may lead to considerable divergence across Member States as to who may be regarded as a suitable person. It is a provision that will also require sensitivity in interpretation as to the extent to which relatives and close family may be appropriate to act as "legal representative" in such a situation. Considerable concern has also been expressed as to the practicality of the requirement of having to obtain consent from a legal representative in an emergency situation and the fact that this may mean that certain trials are as a result impracticable.[98]

The Directive provides in Articles 4(b) and 5(b) respectively that minors and incapacitated adults should be provided with information which is in accordance with their capacity of understanding in relation to the trial, its risks and benefits. In addition where a subject – whether minor or adult – who is capable of forming an opinion, assesses the information and then wishes to refuse to be involved, then the investigator should take this into account.[99]

The Directive requires in both cases that the design of the trial shall minimise pain, discomfort, fear and any other foreseeable risk.[100] This is reflective of the perceived vulnerability of both these groups of research subjects. While in most respects, Articles 4 and 5 can be regarded as being mirror images of one another, one difference in the approach taken to these groups is contained in Article 5(e), which provides that, in relation to mentally incapacitated subjects, trials can only be undertaken where:

> "the research is essential to validate data obtained in a clinical trial on persons able to give informed consent or by other research methods and relates directly to a life-threatening or debilitating clinical condition from which the incapacitated adult concerned suffers."

This phrasing is broader than that contained in earlier drafts of the Directive. The final drafting seems to suggest that non-therapeutic trials on medicinal products, concerning mentally incompetent adults, will be unlawful when the Directive comes into force on 1 May 2004. In contrast, in relation to the child, the

95 Directive 2001/20/EC, Article 6 (3)(g).
96 Directive 2001/20/EC, Article 4(a) and Article 5(a).
97 See further below pp 258–259.
98 E.A. Singer and M. Mullner, "Implications of the EU directive on clinical trials for emergency medicine" 324 BMJ (2002) 1169.
99 Directive 2001/20/EC, Articles 4(c) and 5(c).
100 Directive 2001/20/EC, Articles 4(g) and 5(f).

Directive only requires some direct expected benefit to the group of patients to be shown.[101]

Interestingly, the Directive prohibits incentives or financial inducements to minors and incapacitated adults, save in relation to compensation.[102] There is, however, no provision in the Directive prohibiting such incentive or inducements in relation to competent adults. It appears that this is a matter which is to be determined on a case by case basis by each ethics committee. While, as Mason and McCall Smith comment:

> "it is probable that, in the conditions of present-day society, few suitable volunteers would come forward in the absence of some inducement; large payments would, however, be clearly unethical and a reasonable balance must be set for no other reason than to satisfy the needs of randomization."[103]

Article 4, in the case of the child, and Article 5, in the case of the adult, also require that there should be reference to an ethics committee specialised in such issues or that appropriate advice on "clinical, ethical and psychosocial" questions in relation to children[104] or mentally incapacitated adults[105] should be obtained. The Directive provides that ultimately "the interests of the patient always prevail over those of science and society".[106]

A further issue which the ethics committee is directed to consider under Article 6 is the provision made for indemnity or compensation where the subject suffers personal injury or death as a consequence of involvement in a clinical trial[107] and any insurance or indemnity which exists in relation to the investigator and sponsor.[108] The figure of the "sponsor" is particularly noteworthy. The sponsor is defined in Article 2(e) as "an individual, company, institution or organisation which takes responsibility for the initiation, management and/or financing of a clinical trial". In effect, it is where "the buck stops". This can be seen as a method of providing enhanced protection for the research subject. However, this provision has been noted as problematic for those trials which are funded through public and charitable sources, where the funders may not be happy to undertake such a role, with its consequent responsibilities and potential liabilities,[109] and may indeed be unable to take out appropriate indemnity insurance.

While ethics committee approval may be seen as validating the clinical trial, protocol referral to such a committee also has the potential to delay the conduct of scientific research. The Directive responds to these concerns by establishing

101 Directive 2001/20/EC, Article 4(e).
102 Directive 2001/20/EC, Article 4(d) and 5(d).
103 Mason, McCall Smith and Laurie, above n 1, p 581.
104 Directive 2001/20/EC, Article 4(h).
105 Directive 2001/20/EC, Article 5(g).
106 Directive 2001/20/EC, Articles 4(i) and 5(h).
107 Directive 2001/20/EC, Article 6(h).
108 Directive 2001/20/EC, Article 6(i).
109 R. Watson, "EU legislation threatens clinical trials" 326 BMJ (2003) 1348; Editorial, "Who's afraid of the European Clinical Trials Directive?" 361 *Lancet* (2003) 9376 at 2167.

explicit time limits as part of the approval process. A time limit of 60 days is set for the authorisation of clinical trials,[110] although there is provision for a further 30-day extension in the case of medicinal products for gene therapy and somatic cell therapy (this includes xenogenic cell therapy). This approach has been criticised. For example, Baeyens comments that:

> "Questionable is also whether admitting a time extension for trials involving products of biotechnology is a good option. If the rationale behind this exception is the concern of the possible lack of expertise of the Ethics Committee, one can ask whether it would not have been advisable to require from an Ethics Committee specific expertise in the field concerned."[111]

The Directive does not prescribe the composition of ethics committees. As we noted above, there is, in fact, considerable diversity across Member States on this issue.[112] In addition, if there is a specific "competent authority" concerned with the regulation of clinical trials at Member State level, researchers are required to contact such a body. An illustration of such a body may be an agency concerned with the licensing of medicines.[113] Generally, if there is no response within 60 days, it is assumed that there is no objection. However, in the case of certain issues, such as gene therapy and somatic cell therapy, the Directive requires that specific written authorisation be given by the relevant competent body.[114] There is also a specific provision that states that germ line gene therapy research is prohibited.[115] This provision addresses concerns which have been expressed across Member States as to the legitimacy of this controversial process, and echoes other provisions of EU (soft and hard) law.

Article 7 requires the establishment of procedures for approval within Member States of multi-centred clinical trials. However, one criticism which has been made of the Directive is that it does not deal with an issue which many regarded as being fundamental, namely the operation of multi-state trials. Baeyens has commented that the Directive does not facilitate these trials, because ultimately authorisation for the conduct of each trial must be obtained from the individual Member State.[116]

Article 11 provides that information concerning trials conducted in Member States is to be entered into a central EU database – the EUDRACT database – which is to be accessible only to competent authorities within Member States, the Agency and the Commission. Detailed guidance on the database has been issued by the European Commission,[117] which notes the purposes of the database include

110 Directive 2001/20/EC, Article 9.
111 Baeyens, above n 58, at 35.
112 See above n 63.
113 For example, in the UK this is the Medicines Control Agency.
114 Directive 2001/20/EC, Article 9 (6).
115 *Ibid.*
116 Baeyens, above n 58, at 44.
117 European Commission, "Detailed Guidance on the European clinical trials database EUDRACT", Brussels, ENTR/F2/BL, April 2003.

providing an overview of all EU clinical trials; facilitating communication between Member States, the EMEA[118] and the Commission on clinical trials; the identification of those trials within the EU which are ongoing, completed and terminated; generation of clinical trial statistics; provision of information concerning good clinical practice; and also of notification to the competent authorities where trials are ended for reasons of safety. Member States are to enter extracts from the request that a trial be authorised,[119] amendments which have been made to the trial protocol,[120] the approval of the ethics committee,[121] inspections which have been undertaken to ensure that the conduct of the trial is in accordance with the principles of good clinical practice[122] and the declaration that the trial has come to an end.[123] In addition there is also to be the identification of trials and medicinal products, in order to enable links between clinical trial information and any reports regarding "suspected unexpected serious adverse reactions" (SUSARs).[124]

Those conducting trials are required to notify serious adverse events or reactions to the sponsor,[125] and also to inform the sponsor in relation to "adverse events and/or any laboratory abnormalities" identified in the protocol as critical to safety evaluation.[126] Detailed records of these events are to be kept by the sponsor, and to be notified to the Member State where the trial is being undertaken,[127] and such information shall also be supplied to competent authorities in Member States and to ethics committees. There is also a requirement for the national government, as well as the ethics committee, to be informed annually of any suspected unexpected serious adverse reactions which are fatal and life-threatening.[128] Such information should be given no later than seven days after the sponsor becomes aware of it, and follow-up information should be provided within a period of eight days later.[129] In the case of any other suspected unexpected serious adverse events, these should be notified within a period of 15 days after these first came to the attention of the sponsor.[130] The sponsor is also required to provide this information to all investigators. This provision is necessary, as trials may be being undertaken across a number of sites.[131] Records of such reactions are also to be provided on

118 For further information, see chapter 8.
119 Directive 2001/20/EC, Article 11 (1) (a).
120 Directive 2001/20/EC, Article 11 (1)(b) and (c).
121 Directive 2001/20/EC, Article 11 (1)(d).
122 Directive 2001/20/EC, Article 11 (1)(f).
123 Directive 2001/20/EC, Article 11 (1)(e).
124 European Commission, "Detailed Guidance on the European Clinical Trials Database" above n 117, para 5. For further information on "pharmacovigilance", see chapter 8.
125 Directive 2001/20/EC, Article 16 (1).
126 Directive 2001/20/EC, Article 16 (2); see further on this European Commission, "Detailed Guidance on the collection, verification and presentation of adverse reaction reports arising from clinical trials on medicinal products for human use", Brussels, ENTR/F2/BLD/2003, April 2003.
127 Directive 2001/20/EC, Article 16 (4).
128 Directive 2001/20/EC, Article 17.
129 Directive 2001/20/EC, Article 17 (1)(a).
130 Directive 2001/20/EC, Article 17 (1)(b).
131 Directive 2001/20/EC, Article 17 (1)(d).

an annual basis to the Member State and the ethics committee.[132] The European Commission has also issued guidance on the establishment of a separate database – Eudravigilance-Clinical Trial Module – concerning suspected unexpected serious adverse reactions,[133] which is provided for under Article 17(3)(a) of the Directive. Its role is comparable with that of the EUDRACT database. As set out in the Guidance, the database will include the provision of an overview of the occurrence of SUSARs; facilitate communication between competent authorities in Member States, the Commission and the EMEA; enable a separate review to be undertaken of SUSARs in individual Member States; review of SUSARs and the generation of statistics; and the links between trials and medicinal products to provide links with SUSARs.

Following the entry into force of the Clinical Trials Directive, Member States are now to be required to undertake inspections to ensure that the conduct of clinical trials on medicinal products is in accordance with good clinical practice. These inspections are to be undertaken on behalf of the EU, but are conducted at the Member State level.[134] The Directive requires that the trial sponsor shall inform a competent authority of the Member State and the ethics committee within 90 days of the trial having come to an end.[135] Where a trial ends early, this must be notified within 15 days. Further provisions concern action to be taken in relation to the manufacture and importation of medicinal products and labelling.[136]

The Directive is currently being implemented at national level, where the controversy continues. The deadline for implementation is 1 May 2004. In the UK, the Directive has led to new guidance on research governance being issued[137] and draft statutory instruments to align common law with the Directive.[138] It has also led the UK government to introduce radical changes to decision-making procedures regarding incompetent adults. Since a decision of the House of Lords in *Re F* in 1990, it has been clear that no one has the power to give consent to clinical procedures on behalf of a mentally incompetent adult.[139] Treatment could only be provided on the basis of necessity and this was subject to a test of "best interests" which was to be determined by the medical staff treating that patient. It was generally believed that the consequence of the decision in *Re F* was to render the inclusion of mentally incompetent adults in non-therapeutic research unlawful in all circumstances.[140] Despite the legal uncertainty, such trials did in practice continue, largely due to a

132 Directive 2001/20/EC, Article 17 (2).
133 European Commission, "Detailed Guidance on the European Database of suspected unexpected serious adverse reactions (Eudravigilance Clinical trial module)" Brussels, ENTR/F2/BLD/2003, April 2003.
134 Directive 2001/20/EC, Article 15.
135 Directive 2001/20/EC, Article 10(c).
136 Directive 2001/20/EC, Articles 13 and 14.
137 UK Department of Health Research Governance Framework (2001) and draft Framework (2003).
138 See the UK Medicines for Human Use (Clinical Trials) Regulations 2004, SI 2004/1031; Medicines Control Agency, *Consultation letter on the Medicines for Human Use (Clinical Trials) Regulations* 2003 MLX 287 (referred to as the "MCA Consultation").
139 *Re F* [1990] 2 AC 1.
140 UK Law Commission, *Mental Incapacity* (London: UK Law Commission, 1995).

difference in perception in the medical and scientific community as to what was "legal" and what was "ethical". Following the adoption of the Clinical Trials Directive, the UK government has issued draft regulations to align the common law position with that of the Directive.[141] This will for the first time enable a third party to make decisions on behalf of the incapacitated adult patient. It will also create an anomaly with the existing common law position in relation to all other forms of health-related research, where currently there is no provision for the appointment of a third-party decision-maker.

The Clinical Trials Directive is thus a provision of binding EU law that has a direct impact on the content of the law regulating clinical trials in the Member States of the EU. Clinical trials falling within the scope of the Directive must be conducted in accordance with its provisions, save where protection of research subjects is more comprehensive at national level than that provided by the Directive. Even so, the time scales and procedures set out in the Directive must be adhered to. It should also be noted that, in many respects, the Clinical Trials Directive is limited in its scope. It covers only certain sorts of health-related research. It does not cover some ethically controversial types of research currently being undertaken or proposed, in particular research relating to gene sequencing or cloning, at least not in the earlier stages of biotechnological research leading to the eventual development of a novel pharmaceutical or medical device. However, the existence of a detailed regulatory EU-level measure covering less controversial types of clinical research may, in time, increase the pressure for further regulation of other types of clinical research, and further harmonisation of EU standards with respect to the protection of individual rights and procedural guarantees in the public interest and the interests of the research industry may be expected to follow. We turn now to the impact of EU law to date on such areas of research, focusing in particular on gene sequencing and cloning.

IV. The regulation of medical research using genetic technology

Genetic research offers the tantalising possibility for the development of treatments for many deadly or disabling diseases arising from mutations in DNA sequences. At the same time, the use of gene technology where the genes concerned are human genes, rather than those of animals or plants, raises various highly controversial ethical and legal issues, broadly speaking, concerning the so-called "commodification" or commercialisation of the human body. This is a matter of concern for regulatory bodies at both national and international level. The institutions of the EU have also concerned themselves with the regulatory framework surrounding such gene technology.

The regulation of gene technology in the EU context has to date taken a particular form. The EU institutions have not attempted to constrain or prohibit the use of

141 UK Department of Health Draft Guidance on Consent by a Legal Representative on Behalf of Persons Not Able to Consent under the Medicines for Human Use (Clinical Trials) Regulations 2003.

gene technology within the EU by proscribing certain activities *per se*. Rather, the EU has used intellectual property law as a regulatory mechanism in this field.[142] Intellectual property rights, in particular patents,[143] are used to encourage or discourage types of research activity and the development of new treatments for diseases and other medical conditions. In reality, the inventor of a new treatment will require a reasonable prospect for commercial exploitation of its invention, or the research investment required will not be commercially viable. A patent is a way of encouraging such research investment into new inventions.[144] A patent grants the inventor a protected period of time, during which others wishing to make, use or sell the invention must obtain a licence from the patent holder. The patent holder thus effectively enjoys a monopoly on the invention, and is therefore able to exploit its exclusive right by charging a higher price to the consumer than the market would normally indicate. The patent holder may also recoup its investment outlay through consideration given for licences to make, use or sell the invention. The implication of this is that the availability of patents is essential in order that research into new technologies is actually pursued. Thus, by making patents available within certain types of gene technology, and not others, regulatory bodies are able, if not to forbid certain types of research activity, at least to provide a strong steer to what actually happens on the ground.

The relevant EU legislative provision in this field is the Directive on the Legal Protection of Biotechnological Inventions (the Biotechnology Directive).[145]

142 On whether the patent system is an appropriate mechanism for regulating biotechnology and genetic engineering, see Prof G. Dworkin's evidence to the UK House of Lords Select Committee on the Biotechnology Directive, HL Paper 28, 1994, cited in D. Curley and A. Sharples, "Patenting Biotechnology in Europe: the ethical debate moves on" 24 *European Intellectual Property Review* (2002) 565 at 570.

143 For an explanation of the operation of patent law in this area, see, for example, S. Sterckx, *Biotechnology, Patents and Morality* (Aldershot: Ashgate,1997); D. Beyleveld and R. Brownsword, *Mice, Morality and Patents* (London: Common Law Institute of Property, 1993); D. Beyleveld and R. Brownsword, *Human Dignity in Bioethics and Biolaw* (Oxford: OUP, 2001); S.J.R. Bostyn, "The Prodigal Son: The Relationship between Patent Law and Health Care" 11 *Medical Law Review* (2003) 67; S.J.R. Bostyn, "One Patent a Day Keeps the Doctor Away?" 7 *European Journal of Health Law* (2000) 229; D. Beyleveld, R. Brownsword and M. Llewelyn, "The morality clauses of the Directive on the Legal Protection of Biotechnological Inventions" in R. Goldberg and J. Lonbay, *Pharmaceutical Medicine, Biotechnology and European Law* (Cambridge: CUP, 2000).

144 Patents are available only for "inventions" and not mere "discoveries" of what already exists in nature. However, the *process* of discovering something occurring in nature may be patentable. Further, "if the substance can be properly characterised either by its structure, by the process by which it is obtained or by other parameters and is 'new' in the absolute sense of having no previously recognized existence, then the substance per se may be patentable": European Patent Office Guidelines for Examination of Patent Applications, V.IV.2.3. See also Directive 98/44/EC, Article 3 (2): "Biological material which is isolated from its natural environment or produced by means of a technical process may be the subject of an invention even if it previously occurred in nature."

145 Directive 98/44/EC on the Legal Protection of Biotechnological Inventions, OJ 1998 L 213/13. See further E.R. Gold and A. Gallochat, "The European Biotech Directive: Past as prologue" 7(3) *European Law Journal* (2001) 331; S.J.R. Bostyn, "The Patentability of Genetic Information Carriers" [1999] *Intellectual Property Quarterly* 1; S. Sterckx, "Some Ethically Problematic Aspects of the Proposal for a Directive on the Legal Protection of Biotechnological Inventions" 20 *European*

The background to the adoption of the Biotechnology Directive is the global development of gene technology and sequencing. As the technology progressed, attempts were made to patent gene technology in the US. Cohen and Boyer of Stanford University filed the first patent in the area in 1972. Concerns over the application of the protection of patents in the area of new technology led to an active global debate. Tensions arose between, on the one hand, the perceived need for biotechnological developments such as pharmaceuticals, against, on the other hand, other ethical considerations regarding commercial exploitation or commodification of the human body and its parts. The debate intensified surrounding the Harvard Onco-mouse, the first higher life form to be patented.[146]

In the European context, much of the drive to develop the Biotechnology Directive can be seen in the context of the perceived need to support the biotechnology sector within the EU. The adoption process of the Directive illustrates the tensions between ethical and social considerations and the commercial interests in furthering the EU's research capacity.[147] The background legal context concerned the considerable controversy surrounding the application of the European Patent Convention (EPC)[148] to gene technology. It should be noted here that the European Patent Convention, administered by the European Patent Office, is not part of the EU's legal order, and does not aim to harmonise national patent laws. The European Patent Office simply grants centralised "European patents" which give the same rights as national patent laws in the contracting states designated on the application. The European Patent Convention provides in Article 53 that patents shall not be granted for "inventions the publication or exploitation of which would be contrary to *ordre public* or morality...". Questions arose therefore over whether the patenting of genes, gene sequences or higher organisms fell within the terms of Article 53 EPC, and were thus unpatentable under the Convention.

A draft Biotechnology Directive was first produced in 1988.[149] One aim of this proposal was to clarify the European Patent Convention with regard to the patenting of genetic materials and to facilitate a uniform application of Article 53 EPC across the Member States of the EU. The proposal can be seen very much in the light of the Commission promoting harmonisation in order to facilitate information transfer and technological development[150] and to foster trade and development in the biotechnological industry. However, other actors in the legislative process found in the proposed Biotechnology Directive a medium for raising a number of ethical or moral interests, and what was presented as a relatively simple "harmonisation"

Intellectual Property Review (1998) 123; P. Drahos, "Biotechnology Patents, Markets and Morality" 20 *European Intellectual Property Review* (1998) 441; Curley and Sharples, above n 142.

146 EPO Case No T19/90 [1990] 1 EPOR 4; [1990] 7 EPOR 501; OJ EPO 10/1992, 590.

147 See in particular Gold and Gallochat, above n 145.

148 Convention on the Grant of European Patents, Munich 1973.

149 COM(88) 496 final, OJ 1989 C 10/3; and see T. Roberts, "The Former Biotech Patents Directive" [1995] *Patent World* 27.

150 D.M. Gitter, "Led Astray by the Moral Compass; Incorporating Morality into European Union Biotechnology Patent Law" 19 *Berkeley Journal of International Law* (2001) 1.

measure soon became the vehicle for a complex regulatory and ethical debate. For instance, the Economic and Social Committee reported in 1989 and stated its concerns on the ethical issues, commenting that the Directive should expressly provide for the non-patentability of human beings.[151] The consequences were an extremely contested and protracted legislative process, followed by (unsuccessful) judicial review of the measure,[152] and a considerably more complex and less clear-cut legislative outcome.

The Directive was discussed in the European Parliament under the cooperation procedure in April and October 1992.[153] At this time there was much controversy regarding ethical issues relating to patenting in biotechnology. One catalyst, as Gold and Gallochat note, was the controversial attempt by Craig Venter to patent "expressed sequence tags" (ESTs), which are the short lengths contained in genes, in the US.[154] The rationale for such developments was because ESTs were small components in DNA sequences which result in the production of proteins. An EST is a genetic marker. The EST may enable the identification of the coding of the gene and DNA sequence, and the structure of the protein. Thus, for example, if a defective protein is identified, then this could lead to therapeutic measures being taken in relation to that genetic disease or disability. Further debate related to the patenting of the Harvard Onco-mouse, an animal created specifically with a susceptibility to cancer. In the light of concerns regarding the morality of patenting higher life forms and human material, the Directive was modified, following attempts by the European Parliament to illustrate the need for the inclusion of some ethical principles, for example the exclusion of the human body from patentability. The modified proposal was announced in December 1992.[155]

The Draft Directive provided that inventions should not be denied the protection of a patent solely because living matter is involved. It stated that "biological material" – defined as being "material containing genetic information and capable of reproducing or being reproduced in a biological system"[156] – was in principle patentable, assuming, of course, that it fell within the definition of invention for the purposes of patent law. While plants and animal parts were patentable, plant and animal varieties were not. Further, those processes for modifying the genetic identity of animals, and animals resulting therefrom, were not patentable where the animal suffers unreasonably or is handicapped. In the debates which followed, much attention was given to the "morality" provisions, questions regarding gene ownership and animal welfare. A particular strand of the debate regarding the draft Directive concerned the patenting of human material. Article 2 (3) of the draft

151 Opinion of the Economic and Social Committee on the proposal for a Council Directive on the legal protection of biotechnological inventions, OJ 1989 C 159/10.

152 Case C-377/98 *Netherlands v Parliament and Council (Biotechnology Directive)* [2001] ECR I-7079.

153 See further the discussion in Gold and Gallochat, above n 145, at 378–389.

154 Gold and Gallochat, above n 145, at 338.

155 Amended proposal for a Council Directive on the legal protection of biotechnological inventions, COM(92) 589, OJ 1993 C 44/36.

156 Articles 21 and 22.

excluded "the human body or parts of the human body per se and processes for modifying the genetic identity of the human body for a non-therapeutic purpose which is contrary to the dignity of man". Put simply, there was a clash of interests between the biotechnology research community and those who characterised the issue as the "patenting of life". One of the difficulties with the Directive was the problem of articulating the various ethical concerns in precise terminology. Where the European Parliament favoured broad, open-textured language, the Council of Ministers opposed such language as introducing unnecessary uncertainty into the text.[157]

One major issue of contention related to ownership of human bodily materials, particularly in the light of the John Moore case in the US.[158] Litigation resulted after it was found that Moore's spleen, which had been removed for therapeutic purposes, had been used to develop a commercially lucrative cell line. Moore brought an action in the tort of conversion, and also on the grounds that informed consent had not been given for the use of the human material. He lost on the first point, but succeeded on the second issue. In the Californian Supreme Court, the majority were unwilling to hold that Moore should be accorded a proprietary interest in his human material.[159] The Supreme Court was concerned as to the wider impact had Moore succeeded in his action. This might have stymied the development of future beneficial scientific research. In the Recital to the Directive, it was stated that while ownership of human beings, as such, was excluded, inventions may be included where these were not directly linked to a specific individual. There was a division between Commission and Parliament on the term "linked to a specific individual", and whether this meant associated with that specific individual. The Parliament was of the view that this should only apply where the invention could not be traced back to the individual in question. The ultimate wording presented a somewhat uneasy compromise, which caused some concern amongst the biotechnology industry.

In 1993, with the entry into force of the Treaty of Maastricht, the relevant decision-making procedure altered from "cooperation" to "co-decision". The significance of this was that, under the co-decision procedure, the European Parliament has a blocking veto.[160] Differences of opinion between Parliament and Council remained and a conciliation committee (comprised of members of Council and Parliament) was established in September 1994. An agreed text of the draft Directive was finally approved by the conciliation committee on 23 January 1995. However, in spite of this, the European Parliament, for the first time under the co-decision

157 L. Bentley and B. Sherman, "The ethics of patenting: Towards a Transgenic Patent System" 3 *Medical Law Review* (1995) 275 at 284.

158 *Moore v University of California* 793 P2d 479 Cal (1990).

159 See further, for example, the discussion in E.R. Gold, *Body Parts; Property Rights and the Ownership of Human Biological Materials* (Washington DC: Georgetown University Press, 1996); B. Dickens, "Living Tissue and Organ Donors and Property Law, More on Moore" *Journal of Contemporary Health Law and Policy* (1992) 73.

160 See chapter 2 for further details on the EU legislative process.

procedure, exercised its power of veto and rejected the draft Directive on 1 March 1995 by 188 votes to 240 with 23 abstentions. This was largely due to concerns regarding the ethical considerations.[161]

The Commission then returned to square one, and a new draft Directive was introduced in December 1995.[162] This new text represented the various ethical concerns raised much more strongly than the original draft. For instance, the new proposed Directive took a stance against human cloning and germ line therapy. Subsequently, in July 1997, following a protracted and heated debate largely focussing on the "patenting of the human body", the Parliament adopted 66 amendments to the text of 1995.[163] The Commission, anxious to see this Directive finally adopted, after almost 10 years of debate, accepted virtually all of Parliament's proposed amendments.[164] The Council accepted the modified proposal of the Commission on 26 February 1998[165] and the Parliament's second reading on 12 May 1998[166] led to the final adoption of the Directive in July 1998.[167]

In this chapter, our focus is upon the health law implications of the Biotechnology Directive, although the Directive itself is considerably broader in its scope. Here, we will consider the application of the Directive to gene sequencing; the concept of *ordre public* or morality; the concept of informed consent; and the application of the Directive to reproductive and therapeutic human cloning.

Broadly, the Directive confirms that the general rules of patent law, that inventions must be new and non-obvious and must have an industrial application, are applicable in relation to biological materials.[168] With regard to human biological material, the Directive also explicitly provides that the inventor must

161 European Parliament decision on the joint text adopted by the Conciliation Committee for a European Parliament and Council Directive on the legal protection of biotechnological inventions, OJ 1995 C 68/26.

162 Proposal for a European Parliament and Council Directive on the Legal Protection of Biotechnological Inventions, COM(95) 661, OJ 1996 C 296/4; and see N. Jones, "The new draft Biotechnology Directive" 18(6) *European Intellectual Property Review* (1996) 363.

163 Parliament opinion on the proposal for a European Parliament and Council Directive on the legal protection of biotechnological inventions (First Reading), PE T4-0380/1997, OJ 1997 C 286/71.

164 Amended Proposal for a European Parliament and Council Directive on the Legal Protection of Biotechnological Inventions, COM(97) 446, OJ 1997 C 311/12.

165 Common Position (EC) No 19/98 adopted by the Council on 26 February 1998 with a view to adopting Directive 98/.../EC of the European Parliament and of the Council on the legal protection of biotechnological inventions, CSL 12882/1/1997, OJ 1998 C 110/17.

166 Decision on the common position adopted by the Council with a view to adopting a European Parliament and Council Directive on the legal protection of biotechnological inventions (C4-0132/98 95/0350(COD) (Co-decision procedure: second reading), PE T4-0251/1998, OJ 1998 C 167/17.

167 Directive 98/44/EC on the Legal Protection of Biotechnological Inventions, OJ 1998 L 213/13.

168 Directive 98/44/EC, Article 2 and Recital 22. The recitals of a measure of EU law do not have any binding impact, and only represent a form of soft law (see, for example, F. Snyder, "The Effectiveness of European Community Law: Institutions, Processes, Tools and Techniques" 56 MLR (1993) 56). However, this does not necessarily mean that recitals do not have any effect. In particular, when the content of a recital is reflected in a binding provision, the recital can be used as the basis for interpretation of the binding provision.

disclose not only the invention, but also its industrial application. Article 5 states that:

> "1. The human body, at the various stages of its formation and development, and the simple discovery of one of its elements including the sequence or partial sequence of a gene, cannot constitute patentable inventions.
> 2. An element isolated from the human body or otherwise produced by means of a technical process including the sequence or partial sequence of a gene, may constitute a patentable invention, even if the structure of that element is identical to that of a natural element.
> 3. The industrial application of a sequence or a partial sequence of a human gene must be disclosed in the patent application."

A huge amount of publicity has resulted from the sequencing of the human genome by Celera Genomics in the US and by the Wellcome Trust. Both teams of researchers released their findings in 2000. There has been controversy regarding partial gene sequencing in the US. The Supreme Court had commented that: "to be patentable, a compound must have 'substantial utility' or 'confer a special benefit in its currently available form'."[169] The Supreme Court made it clear that: "a patent is not a hunting license. It is not a reward for the search, but compensation for its successful conclusion." The EU institutions grappled with the application of patent law to gene sequencing in the Biotechnology Directive.

The Directive provides that, although DNA sequences by themselves are not patentable,[170] in some situations partial gene sequences may be patentable.[171] Nonetheless, the Directive makes some exclusionary provisions. Article 5 (1) provides that partial gene sequences are not patentable if they are merely discovered. However, according to Article 5 (2), when isolated from the human body by means of a technical process, such partial gene sequences may be patentable. Article 5 (2) implies that those sequences which have merely been retrieved from automatic processes do not come within the provision. Some commentators take the view that Article 5 (1) is redundant, as in order to "discover" a gene or gene sequence, it must be separated, replicated and isolated by a technical process.[172] This means that the provision in Article 5 (3), requiring the disclosure of the industrial application of a gene sequence or partial sequence, becomes crucial. So, for instance, a partial gene sequence[173] which is useful for genotyping could have an industrial application in determination of paternity, or, where it is associated with a particular disease, may have an industrial application in diagnosis or treatment of that disease. Such partial

169 *Brenner v Manson* 383 US 519, 86 SCt (1966).
170 Directive 98/44/EC, Recital 23 and Article 5 (1).
171 See discussion in Bostyn, above n 145.
172 See D. Schertenleib, "The Patentability and Protection of DNA based inventions in the EPO and the European Union" 25 *European Intellectual Property Review* (2003) 125 at 127; Bostyn, (2000), above n 143 at 234.
173 A "single nucleotide polymorphism" (SNP).

gene sequences would be patentable under the Directive. What is clear, however, is that patents will not be granted under the Directive for partial gene sequences without any known function.

The Directive requires that "industrial application" must be mentioned in the patent application. This is key to the distinction between invention (patentable) and mere discovery (not patentable) within the Directive.[174] The meaning of the term "industrial application" is unclear – does it apply simply to the fact that an industrial application is a necessary precondition for all patents, or has it been inserted with the intention of limiting the scope of the patent, once granted, to that specific application? Recital 25 of the Directive provides that "when sequences overlap only in parts which are not essential to the invention, each sequence will be considered as an independent sequence in patent law terms". This may be read as suggesting that gene product patents are restricted in scope by reference to their function, as disclosed on the patent application.[175]

In common with internationally recognised exceptions in patent law,[176] Article 6 of the Directive makes reference to considerations of *ordre public* and morality, providing that inventions may be regarded as unpatentable "where their commercial exploitation would be contrary to *ordre public* or morality". However, exploitation shall not be deemed to be so contrary "merely because it is prohibited by law or by regulation". This implies an element of harmonisation with respect to the concepts of *ordre public* and morality, which may ultimately need to be resolved by courts, either in the Member States or the European Court of Justice. Some examples of unpatentable inventions contrary to *ordre public* or morality are given in the Directive, such as production of chimeras from germ cells and reproductive cloning of human beings.[177] The Directive also excludes the use of human embryos for industrial and commercial purposes in Article 6 (2)(c), combined with Recital 42. The provision can be considered alongside the Council of Europe Convention on Human Rights and Biomedicine 1997, which prohibits the creation of human embryos for research purposes, while sanctioning the use of embryonic tissue in cloning techniques and in research. A further difficulty concerns the division between commercial and research uses, because of the overlap between these two categories.

There was much debate regarding the approach taken in the Directive to gene therapy. A distinction needs to be drawn between genetic manipulation aimed at preventing an individual developing a disease or disability (somatic cell gene therapy) and genetic manipulation which, if undertaken, would have an impact not just in relation to that particular patient but also subsequent generations (germ

174 See Directive 98/44/EC, Recitals 20 and 22; see Schertenleib, above n 172, at 127.

175 Schertenleib, above n 172, at 136. Schertenleib is critical of this provision, and argues that European patent law should move towards a position where product patents (as opposed to process patents) are not available for gene sequences. This is because "a widespread patenting of sequences will lead to uncertainties in the scope of the claims, and to litigation, with the inevitable unfairness of the first patentees gaining a stranglehold on this area of technology": at 138.

176 For discussion, see, for example, Gitter, above n 150.

177 Directive 98/44/EC, Recitals 36–42 and Article 6.

line gene therapy). Opposition to germ line gene therapy was one reason why the original draft Directive fell. Under the final Directive, somatic cell line gene therapy inventions are patentable, whereas germ cell line therapy inventions are not. The Directive provides that "processes for modifying the germ line genetic identity of human beings" are not patentable, because it is contrary to *ordre public* or morality.[178] Some forms of gene therapy will also not be patentable because they fall within the criteria of medical treatment. A further question mark surrounds personalised treatments and whether they will fall outside the criteria for patentability.

Although there is some reference to the concept of informed consent in the Directive, this is non-binding. Recital 26 provides that:

> "if an invention is based on biological material of human origin or if it uses such material, where a patent application is filed, the person from whose body the material is taken must have had an opportunity of expressing free and informed consent thereto, in accordance with national law."

This may perhaps be seen as somewhat surprising. The Recital does not make it clear whether the consent is to be given for the taking of the material, or for the filing of the patent application. In any case, there is no binding provision expressly to the effect that lack of consent would render an invention based on the material unpatentable.[179] Beyleveld has argued that failure to obtain consent would violate Article 6, as this would be contrary to *ordre public* or morality.[180] This is because the preservation of human dignity is central to morality, as envisaged in the Directive, and, following for example the Convention on Human Rights and Biomedicine, Article 22, consent to the removal of tissue is clearly required for preservation of human dignity as conceptualised in the European context. Beyleveld argues that failure to obtain consent would also violate the Data Protection Directive.[181]

Given that consent is regarded as such an important principle, why has it been dealt with only in a recital, and not in the body of the Directive itself? One approach is to regard this as being a response to the perceived difficulties arising in the US as a consequence of *Moore v University of California* discussed above. In that case, John Moore challenged the commercial exploitation of cells from his spleen by bringing actions for conversion and for failure to obtain informed consent. While he lost on the conversion ground, he succeeded in his claim on the issue of informed consent. There has been considerable opposition to this Recital from industry and also from patent agents. Concerns expressed centre around the difficulty of obtaining consent. Nonetheless, while this may be practically problematic, it can be argued that consent is critical in such a situation to ensure that respect is afforded to the autonomy of the individual and also to respect for the integrity of the human body.

178 See Directive 98/44/EC, Article 6 (1)(b).

179 See Curley and Sharples, above n 142, at 569.

180 D. Beyleveld, "Why Recital 26 of the EC Directive on the Legal Protection of Biotechnological Inventions should be Implemented in National Law" [2000] *Intellectual Property Quarterly* 1.

181 Directive 95/46/EC, OJ 1995 L 281/31, discussed in chapter 5.

The unauthorised use of human material has prompted major inquiries in both the UK and Ireland when it was discovered that vast stores of human material acquired for clinical and scientific purposes had been obtained without informed consent having been given.[182] There may be room for reconsideration of this issue in the future, in the light of the EU Charter on Fundamental Rights and Freedoms, and its proposed incorporation in the Draft Treaty establishing a Constitution for Europe.[183] One reason why it appears that the provision on consent was ultimately included in the Recital, rather than the Directive itself, is the relationship between the Directive and the WTO's Agreement on Trade Related Aspects of Intellectual Property Rights (TRIPS),[184] which also only excludes patents where the commercial use violates *ordre public* or morality. It appears that the Commission was persuaded that the Directive might violate TRIPS if a provision on informed consent had been incorporated.[185]

Article 7 of the Biotechnology Directive provides that the Commission's European Group on Ethics in Science and New Technologies will have the task of evaluating all ethical aspects of biotechnology. Unlike the national ethics committees mandated by the Clinical Trials Directive,[186] the European Group on Ethics merely provides general advisory guidance, and does not provide specific authorisations on individual patent applications. This may be seen as a weakness in the ethics provisions applying to biotechnological research in the EU.[187] Article 16 of the Directive provides that further review is to be provided in the form of the obligation of the European Commission to submit annual reports to the European Council and Parliament on developments in patent law as these concern biotechnology, a biennial report concerning failure to publish or publishing delays in areas which are subject to patent rights, and finally a report on a five-year basis relating to the relationship between Directive and international statements of human rights.

Even after its adoption, the Directive proved controversial. On 19 October 1998, the Netherlands, following an express request from the Dutch state Parliament, brought proceedings under Article 173 (now 230) EC for the annulment of the Directive.[188] The Court delivered its judgment on 9 October 2001 in which it

182 *Report of the Inquiry into the Royal Liverpool Children's Hospital (Alder Hey)* (2001), http://www.rclinquiry.org.uk; Bristol Inquiry Interim Report, *Removal and Retention of Human Material* (2000), http://www.bristol-inquiry.org.uk. There is also an ongoing inquiry into the retention of human materials in the Republic of Ireland, chaired by Ann Dunne SC: see http://www.parentsforjustice.com; http://www.examiner.ie/pport/web/ireland/Full_Story/did-sg3qiW8snHMv6.asp.

183 See further chapter 10.

184 On the relationship between EU law and WTO law, see G. de Búrca and J. Scott, eds, *The EU and the WTO: Legal and Constitutional Issues* (Oxford: Hart, 2001).

185 See Gold and Gallochat, above n 145, at 350.

186 See discussion above.

187 See T. Sampson, "Achieving Ethically Acceptable Biotechnology Patents: A Lesson from the Clinical Trials Directive" 25 *European Intellectual Property Review* (2003) 419.

188 On 3 May 1999, Italy and Norway were also given leave to support these proceedings.

dismissed the annulment action.[189] Here we concentrate upon those arguments applicable to the health issues raised in the proceedings. First, the Netherlands had argued that the basis on which the Directive was enacted, namely Article 100a (now 95) EC, was inadequate. It was argued that the existing differences at national level on biotechnology had not been established as a hindrance to trade.[190] Moreover, if trade was inhibited, this was in relation to trade in countries where the approach taken to such issues was less restrictively regulated such as the US. It was also argued that the Directive stepped outside harmonisation to develop new rights of property. The Netherlands took the view that these measures should have been dealt with under Article 235 (now 308) EC which would have required unanimity in the Council before proceeding.[191] This argument was rejected by the Court. The Court held that the divergences between national laws on these issues were potentially an inhibitor to the internal market. They also took the approach that there were no new rights created.

It was further argued that the Directive infringed the principle of legal certainty, in particular that the concepts of *ordre public* and morality lacked clarity, which could lead to uncertainty across the EU. On the one hand, the Court stated that Article 6 gives Member States a "wide scope for manoeuvre" in applying the exclusion on grounds of *ordre public* or morality. However, on the other-hand the Court was of the view that these were concepts which were recognised in international jurisprudence and that, moreover, there was guidance in the Directive regarding the scope of Article 6, and therefore the principle of legal certainty was not compromised.

The argument that the Directive was inconsistent with international obligations in Conventions such as TRIPS, the European Patent Convention, the Convention on Biological Diversity and the European Convention for the Protection of Human Rights and Fundamental Freedoms was also rejected. In relation to the ECHR, the Court took the approach that the Directive does not replace other provisions safeguarding compliance with fundamental rights. This may have implications for future interpretations of the Directive in the light of development of jurisprudence under the ECHR or indeed other provisions ensuring human rights, such as perhaps the EU Charter of Fundamental Rights.

Following the adoption of the Directive, the European Commission published its strategy for Life Sciences and Biotechnology.[192] These measures included:

(i) incorporation of the Directive into Member State national laws;
(ii) adoption of EC patent regulation;

189 Case C-377/98 above n 152 *Biotechnology*. For discussion, see T.M. Spranger 39 CMLRev (2002) 1147; C. Barnard, [2002] *All ER Review* 165; S. Moore, 24 *European Intellectual Property Review* (2002) 149; A. Scott, 21 *European Intellectual Property Review* (1999) 212.

190 Contrast the Court's approach in relation to the scope of Article 95 EC in Case C-376/98 *Germany v Parliament and Council (Tobacco Advertising)* [2000] ECR I-8419: see chapter 3.

191 For further discussion on Community competence, see chapter 3.

192 COM(2001) 454 of 4 September 2001, http://europa.eu.int/comm/biotechnology.

(iii) clarification of the rules in relation to the ownership of intellectual property which arose following research which was publicly funded; and

(iv) undertaking steps which would promote both dialogue and cooperation which would facilitate international cooperation regarding patent protection in the area of biotechnological inventions.

The Directive remains controversial.[193] A resolution of the European Parliament was passed on 4 October 2001 regarding the undesirability of a US company, Myriad Genetics, having a monopoly in relation to diagnostic tests for the breast cancer gene.[194] This resolution noted "its dismay at the possible consequences of the granting by the EPO of a patent on a human gene". The European Parliament asked the EPO to reconsider such patents. More broadly it also called upon Council, Commission and Member States to:

> "adopt the measures required to ensure that the human genetic code is freely available for research throughout the world and that medical applications of certain human genes are not impeded by means of monopolies based on patents."

While some Member States are implementing the Directive,[195] a number have been slow to do so. Some have appeared to go against the terms of the Directive. So, for example, in France a Bioethics Bill has been introduced which bans the patenting of gene sequences.[196] In Belgium, rather than directly enacting the Directive, instead legislation was introduced including ethical issues which are not explicit in the Directive.[197] These differences between national laws and the provisions of the Directive may lead to future litigation. The tensions between fostering the research community through encouraging commercial exploitation of inventions and the inherent perceptible drivers towards an ethically coherent and acceptable research strategy across the EU are likely to continue.

Meanwhile, in the broader European context, the suitability of patent law for regulating this new technology has been questioned. In 1994, the Parliamentary Assembly of the Council of Europe, in its Recommendation on the protection and patentability of material of human origin, stated that the European Patent Convention was inadequate to respond to concerns arising from "commercialisation" of the human body. There appears to be a divergence between the EU context, where patenting is seen as an appropriate legal framework for regulating biotechnology, and the Council of Europe context, where there is marked reluctance in this respect.

193 S. Moore, "Challenge to the Biotechnology Directive" 24 *European Intellectual Property Review* (2002) 149; G. Van Overwalle, "Belgium goes its own way on biodiversity and patents" 24 *European Intellectual Property Review* (2002) 233.

194 For further details, see M. Rimmer, "Myriad Genetics: Patent Law and Genetic Testing" 25 *European Intellectual Property Review* (2003) 20; R. Watson, "MEPs add their voice to protest at patent for breast cancer gene" 323 BMJ (2001) 888 (20 October).

195 See, for example, Italy, where on 2 April 2003 the Senate approved a text of the draft law implementing the Directive; for example, UK, D. Curley, "UK Bites Biotech Bullet" [2000] 127 *Patent World*, cited in Curley and Sharples, above n 145.

196 A. Wilson and B. Burrows "French thumb their noses at EC Genomics Patenting Directive", http://www.genomeweb.com/articles/view-article.asp?Article=200331495815.

197 See Gold and Gallochat, above n 145, at 349.

Cloning

One major issue in the biotechnology debate, which has concerned the EU institutions, is the question of cloning. There are two issues. First, should human cloning technology be permitted at all; and second, if it is, should the products of such technology be amenable to commercial exploitation?

The context here is the cloning of Dolly the sheep in 1997 at the Roslin Institute in Edinburgh. Cloning involves various techniques. One such technique is "embryo splitting". This is the replication of the process that occurs naturally leading to the production of twins. Embryonic cells are separated at a very early stage before they have had a chance to differentiate. Another cloning technique is that of "nuclear substitution", which consists in replacing the nucleus of an embryo or unfertilised egg with a nucleus taken from another. Cloning may also involve 'cell nuclear replacement' (the technique used to create Dolly), namely replacing the nucleus of one cell with that of another cell and electrically stimulating development.[198] Cloning may be undertaken for therapeutic purposes, such as tissue and organ replacement; or for reproductive purposes, that is, the creation of a new human being.

There are a number of reasons why there has been opposition to cloning procedures in humans, particularly relating to reproductive cloning. First, it is a costly technology and one that is likely to lead to considerable wastage of eggs and a high degree of risk. Dolly was the only normal lamb born from 276 similar attempts. Of these, there were only 29 implantable embryos, and all of these except Dolly resulted in defective pregnancies and grossly deformed births. Other concerns relate to the life expectancy of the clone, which may be reduced due to the fact that a clone could be born prematurely aged because its genetic material would already be as old as the person from whom the genetic material had been removed, and that also cloning may produce resultant health defects. In 1999, a two-month-old cloned calf died after it developed blood and heart problems; and Dolly herself developed arthritis.[199] Numerous ethical and social issues have also been identified. It has been suggested that cloning, particularly reproductive cloning, may amount to using individuals as a means to an end and as such is wrong.[200] Could cloned children be in effect regarded as commodities? There may be the prospect that human rights and dignity may be infringed by the prospect of two or more persons in existence with identical genetic composition. However, proponents of cloning have argued that nature already provides for monozygotic twins which have such identical composition. It has also been suggested that a clone would not be identical to the individual from which it was cloned, because this does not take into account

198 See Chief Medical Officer's Report, *Stem Cell Research: Medical Progress with Responsibility* (London: DOH. 2000)

199 J. Jones, "Cloning may cause health defects" 318 BMJ (1999) 1230; O. Dyer, "Dolly's arthritis dents faith in cloning" 324 BMJ (2001) 67.

200 See generally S.D. Pattison, "Reproductive Cloning: Can Cloning Harm the Clone?" 10 *Medical Law Review* (2002) 295.

social, cultural and environmental contexts, which play a very important part in an individual's development.[201]

In January 1998, 19 members of the Council of Europe signed an agreement in Paris prohibiting:

> "any intervention seeking to create a human being genetically identical to any other human being, whether living or dead, by whatever means."[202]

Opposition to cloning can also be seen in Article 6 (2) (a) of the Directive on Biotechnological Inventions (Biotechnology Directive), which makes the reproductive cloning of human beings non-patentable. According to Article 6:

> "1. Inventions shall be considered unpatentable where their commercial exploitation would be contrary to *ordre public* or morality; however, exploitation shall not be deemed to be so contrary merely because it is prohibited by law or regulation.
> 2. On the basis of paragraph 1, the following shall be considered unpatentable:
> a. processes for cloning human beings;
> b. processes for modifying the germ line genetic identity of human beings;
> c. uses of human embryos for individual or commercial purposes;
> d. processes for modifying the genetic identity of animals which are likely to cause them suffering without any substantial medical benefit to man or animal, and also animals resulting from such processes."

It should be stressed that the Biotechnology Directive does not prohibit cloning per se. There is no measure of EU law that regulates that matter in that respect. The Biotechnology Directive simply regulates the *patentability* of inventions using cloning technology.

Furthermore, the Directive does not appear to exclude definitively the patentability of all such cloning inventions. The draft Biotechnology Directive made reference to the "reproductive cloning of human beings". In the final text, reference is made to "processes for cloning human beings". However, Recital 41 defines cloning as "any process, including techniques of embryo splitting, designed to create a human being with the same genetic information as another living or deceased human being". What constitutes a human being is not defined, and this may lead to difficulties, given the differences in approach taken across Member States on this matter. The reference to *ordre public* or morality might suggest that "human being" should be defined by reference to other measures of international law that protect fundamental human rights, in particular in the context of the EU, any relevant provisions emanating from

201 For example, see further J. Harris *Clones, Genes and Immortality* (Oxford: OUP, 1998).

202 Council of Europe, Additional Protocol to the Convention for the Protection of Human Rights and Dignity of the Human Being with regard to the Application of Biology and Medicine, on the Prohibition of Cloning Human Beings, Paris, 12 January 1998. This provision also finds reflection in Article 3 (2) (d) EUCFR, now found in Article II-3 (2) (d) of the Draft Constitutional Treaty, which provides that: "In the fields of medicine and biology, the following must be respected in particular: . . . the prohibition of the reproductive cloning of human beings."

the Council of Europe, this being the main organisation charged with the protection of human rights across Europe. However, unfortunately the term "human being" is also left undefined in the relevant Council of Europe measure, the Convention on Human Rights and Biomedicine 1997. An additional protocol to this Convention provides that:

> "any invention seeking to create a human being genetically identical to another human being, whether living or dead, is prohibited. For the purpose of this article, the term human being 'genetically identical' to another human being means a human being sharing with another the same nuclear gene set."[203]

Thus it appears to be unclear as to whether EU law is opposed to cloning in general or whether the Biotechnology Directive constitutes implicit sanctioning of therapeutic cloning, while expressing explicit opposition to reproductive cloning. Furthermore, the ruling of the European Court of Justice on the validity of the Biotechnology Directive may be read as implying a wide margin of discretion to Member States in determining such matters, within the concept of *ordre public* or morality.[204]

Since the adoption of the Biotechnology Directive, the debate over cloning has intensified. Attempts are now being made in some Member States by individual scientists to further reproductive cloning technology.[205] Meanwhile, it appears that contrasting approaches have been and are continuing to be taken at EU level. The European Commission has called for debate on the ethical and medical aspects. However, the European Parliament has been exceedingly critical. In September 2000, MEPs supported a resolution to the effect that therapeutic cloning "irreversibly crosses a boundary in research norms and is contrary to public policy" by 237 votes to 230 (with 43 abstentions).[206] The resolution was supporting legislation in Member States banning research concerning human cloning, subject to criminal penalties. It will be recalled that the EU Charter of Fundamental Rights, Article 3 (1), states that:

> "In the fields of medicine and biology, the following must be respected in particular:
> – the prohibition of the reproductive cloning of human beings."

The MEPs' resolution also stated that EU funding should not be available to research institutions which were involved in human cloning.[207] This issue is explored further in the next section.

203 Additional Protocol for the protection of human rights and dignity of the human being with regard to the application of biology and medicine on the prohibition of cloning. Paris, 12 January 1998.

204 Case C-377/98 [2001] ECR I-7079, para 37.

205 For example, Professor Antorini in Rome.

206 Resolution of the European Parliament on Human Cloning of 7 September 2000, B-0710, 0751, 0753, and 0764/2000, based on A5-0168/2000.

207 See discussion of research funding above. Specific critical comment was directed at the UK approach to stem cell cloning following the Chief Medical Officer's Report.

Stem cell research

A further controversial area with which the EU has become concerned, and which interfaces with the cloning debate discussed above, is that of stem cell research. Stem cells can be isolated in the early embryo (whether created through standard fertilisation or through cell nuclear replacement); the foetus; and also from blood taken from the umbilical cord. Stem cells may also be isolated from tissues in children and adults. Stem cells represent a rich resource for research because of their potential to develop for a long period of time whilst undifferentiated. They may also develop into particular specialist cells such as nerve cells, muscle cells or cells which produce insulin.[208] Embryonic stem cells are a particular rich resource because they are "pluripotent". This means that they can develop into any one of a range of 200 cell types. Stem cell technology is being developed with the aim of creating replacement tissue or cells, and treatment of serious chronic conditions such as chronic heart failure and stroke or spinal cord injuries. Considerable publicity has been given to the interest expressed in this technology by the well-known actor Christopher Reeve, who was paralysed after a riding accident. There are considerable ethical issues that arise consequent upon this technology. Whilst this technology is far more restricted in terms of ethical impact than reproductive cloning, nonetheless use of embryonic stem cell technology will mean the destruction of human embryos, which is regarded as being ethically objectionable by those who are associated with "pro-life" groupings.[209]

Across the EU, there is a divergent approach amongst Member States regarding this technology.[210] For example, some Member States (notably Finland,[211] Greece,[212] the Netherlands,[213] Sweden[214] and the UK[215]) sanction the procurement of stem cells subject to conditions. The UK is also developing what is the first large-scale stem cell bank, which is publicly funded through the Medical Research Council. This came into operation in 2003.[216] Germany in contrast, while prohibiting

208 Commission Staff Working Papers, Report on Human Embryonic Stem Cell Research Brussels 3 April 2003, SEC (2003) 441, p 5.

209 See, for instance, the Papal Encyclical of John Paul II "Evangelium Vitae", 25 March 1995, http://www.vatican.va/edocs/ENG0141/_INDEX.HTM.

210 See discussion in Commission Staff Working Paper, above n 208, p 10; Report prepared for conference on *Ethics and biomedicine – balancing risks and benefits*, Umeå, Sweden, 11–12 June 2001, under the Fifth Framework Programme's Life Quality strand; and S. Halliday, "A comparative approach to the regulation of human stem cell research in Europe"12(1) *Medical Law Review* (2004) 40.

211 Medical Research Act 1999.

212 Law 3089/2002.

213 Embryo Act September 2002.

214 Act of 1991 "Measures for Purposes of Research and Treatment Involving Fertilised Human Ova"; Health and Medical Care Act (18-982; 763).

215 Human Fertilisation and Embryology (Research Purposes) Regulations 2001, SI 2001/188 and see the Chief Medical Officer's Expert Group Report, "Stem Cell Research: Medical Progress with Responsibility" (2000); R. Brownsword "Stem cells, Superman and the Report of the Select Committee" 65 MLR (2002) 568; A. Plomer, "Beyond the HFE Act 1990: The Regulation of Stem Cell Research in the UK" 10 *Medical Law Review* (2002) 132.

216 http://www.nibsc.ac.uk/divisions/cbi/stemcell.html.

procurement of stem cells, allows their import and use subject to conditions, including that they were imported and were in existence prior to 1 January 2002.[217] Procurement of stem cells is prohibited in Austria,[218] Denmark,[219] France,[220] Ireland[221] and Spain. A number of other EU countries (Belgium, Italy, Luxembourg and Portugal) have not legislated on this issue. As we saw above, the Biotechnology Directive provides, in Article 6 (2) (c), that "uses of human embryos for individual or commercial purposes" are unpatentable as contrary to *ordre public* or morality. However, it is not clear from the Directive whether this excludes from patentability the creation of human embryos for research purposes.[222]

A catalyst for consideration of the regulation of stem cell research by the EU institutions was provided by the provision under the Sixth Framework Programme for the funding of research into human embryonic stem cells. In priority 1, "Life Sciences, Genomics and Biotechnology for human health" in section I "Application of knowledge and technologies in the fields of genomics and biotechnology for health", it is provided that "research will focus on ... development and testing of new preventive and therapeutic tools, such as somatic gene and cell therapies (in particular stem cell therapies)".[223] The inclusion of this type of research led to controversy. As a result, in September 2002, the European Council of Science Ministers introduced a one-year moratorium on the use of EU funds to support embryonic stem cell research when they approved the Sixth Framework Programme's funding. However, this was followed by objections expressed by the European Parliament's Committee on Industry, External Trade, Research and Energy. The Committee questioned whether the Council's decision was legal. As a compromise, it was proposed that criteria regarding the research activities which involved embryos and stem cells would be established by the end of 2003. The governments of some Member States are expressly opposed to the use of EU funds in this way. Italy, Austria and Germany expressed their opposition to the EU funding stem cell research under the Sixth Framework Programme in 2003 at an Inter-Institutional Seminar in Brussels on the subject of research involving stem cells. The European Parliament has also registered its opposition.[224]

217 Embryo Protection Law (ESchG) 1990 and for a detailed discussion see Halliday, above n 210. German law on embryo research is currently under reconsideration: see J. Burgermeister, "Germany considers relaxing strict embryo research laws" 327 BMJ (2003) 1128 (15 November).

218 Austrian Reproductive Medicine Act 1992.

219 Medically Assisted Procreation Act 1997.

220 Bioethics Law 1994.

221 Irish Constitution 1937 "the State acknowledges the right to life of the unborn".

222 See Curley, and Sharples, above n 145, at 567–568.

223 OJ 2002 L 294/10.

224 See Cordis database, http://www.cordis.lu/, NEWS 27 October 2003, "MEPs' report seeks tougher restrictions on stem cell research than Commission proposals". In particular, the European Parliament's report proposes that, rather than permitting EU funding for projects that aim to create new stem cells from frozen embryos created for IVF purposes before 27 June 2002, research funding should be limited to projects using existing stem cell lines created before August 2001. Subsequently, the European Parliament's industry, trade, research and energy committee voted

The ethical issues were further considered by the opinion of the European Group on Ethics in Sciences and New Technologies regarding "Ethical aspects of human stem cell research and use" published on 14 November 2000.[225] The Group commented that:

> "the creation of embryos by somatic cell nuclear transfer for research on stem cell therapy would be premature, since there is a wide field of research to be carried out with alternative sources of human stem cells (from spare embryos, foetal tissues and adult stem cells)."

The Group took the approach that specially creating embryos for this purpose was unjustifiable, where spare embryos represented an alternative source. This is in line with Article 18 of the Convention on Human Rights and Biomedicine, which prohibits the creation of embryos for research purposes. Nonetheless, the Group stated that it would be appropriate to fund such research under the Framework Programmes, as long as this complied with their ethical and legal requirements. Interestingly, they went on to suggest that:

> "Stem cell research based on alternative sources (spare embryos, foetal tissues and adult stem cells) requires a specific Community research budget. In particular, EU funding should be devoted to testing the validity of recent discoveries about the potential of differentiation of adult stem cells. The EU should insist that the results of such research be widely disseminated and not hidden for reasons of commercial interest."

A number of principles which the Group felt should inform the development of research in this area were identified. First, that of free and informed consent from donors. The importance of informed consent was stressed.[226] The Group were particularly concerned that women undergoing fertility treatment were not placed under pressure to produce "spare" embryos for research purposes. Second, they emphasised the need for approval of research to be provided by an appropriate authority. They cited as an example the UK's Human Fertilisation and Embryology Authority, which regulates the conduct of embryo research. Third, in line with concerns regarding commercial dealing in human material, the Group stated that there should be no financial gain for donors, and noted, in this regard, the EU Charter of Fundamental Rights which provides in Article 3(2) that:

> "In the field of medicine and biology the following must be respected in particular…
> – the prohibition on making the human body and its parts as such a source of financial gain; … "

to approve the Commission's proposals, see Cordis database, NEWS 5 November 2003, "Parliamentary committee rejects majority of stem cell rapporteur's amendments". A key amendment was the removal of any cut-off date.

225 Opinion No 15 of the European Group on Ethics, "The Ethical aspects of human stem cell research and use", http://europa.eu.int/comm/european-group-ethics/index-en.htm.

226 See further the discussion in chapter 10 on the proposed Tissue Directive, COM(2003) 340 final.

as well as making reference to Article 21 of the European Convention on Human Rights and Biomedicine noted above. The need to respect donor anonymity was emphasised, and this was linked to the safeguards for confidential information of donors, and finally transparency in research findings. They noted that a risk-benefit assessment was needed. A further important consideration was the establishment of safeguards for the health of research subjects. The need to ensure that research was widely disseminated was also regarded as being crucial here.

The Group's recommendations have been reflected in the European Commission's recent proposed guidance in relation to research funding in this area. In October 2003, the European Research Commissioner, Philippe Busquin, submitted to the Competitiveness Council[227] the proposed guidelines governing the future funding of stem cell research under the Sixth Framework Programme where this involved embryos and human embryonic stem cells.[228] The rationale for this approach is that the facilitation of collaborative research undertaken at EU level would have the effect of limiting the destruction of embryos, because it would reduce the prospect of unnecessary replication of research. Furthermore, it is seen as desirable in that it may speed up scientific development through an exchange of expertise and results. Nonetheless, the proposed guidelines emphasise that: "The Commission proposal does not aim to set universal ethical principles. Every Member State must decide for itself on this issue."

The proposed guidelines provide that research is to be eligible for funding only where this relates to "spare" embryos created before 27 June 2002 (when the Parliament and the Council adopted the Sixth Framework Programme) and stem cells derived from those embryos. In addition, the research must be shown to comply with the principle of necessity. All research proposals are to be subject to ethical and scientific review. Researchers must also demonstrate that the research can be shown to increase scientific knowledge through basic research, or that it may increase medical knowledge in relation to diagnostic, preventative or therapeutic methods which may be applied to humans. Furthermore, donation of embryos is to be in accordance with existing national law principles. The guidance also notes the need to obtain voluntary informed consent and the need for safeguards to be in place regarding the use of personal data from donors. In addition, there is a requirement for researchers to make best efforts to ensure that stem cell lines which are derived from the research are made widely available to the scientific community on a non-profit basis.

227 News and Events, "Genetics Legislation: Competitiveness Council hears case for stem cell guidelines", http://europa.eu.int/comm/research/biosociety/ne.../news-genetic-legisl-council-en-html.

228 OJ 2002 C 232/1; Proposal for a Council Decision amending Decision 2002/834/EC on the specific programme for research, technological development and demonstration; "Integrating and strengthening the European Research Area" (2002–2006) 9 July 2003, COM(2003) 390, and see Halliday, above n 210.

Of course, the mere promulgation of guidelines with respect to disbursement of EU research funding in no way amounts to EU-level regulation of stem cell research. However, it is possible that the articulation of such principles in this context may provide impetus for future regulatory harmonisation. EU-level meetings of industry actors have called for regulation that more clearly defines what is permitted and forbidden, whether that is promulgated at national or EU level.[229] Furthermore, the articulation of principles such as these, and the availability of funding for such research from the EU's Sixth Framework Programme, may be expected to play an influential role in informing debate at both national and EU levels.[230] However, finding a legitimate legal basis for any such proposal might prove difficult. As we saw in chapter 3, the ruling in *Tobacco Advertising*,[231] and the proposed Draft Treaty on the Constitution of the European Union (DCT) suggest that Article 95 EC and even Article 308 EC are both likely to prove problematic as a lawful legal basis for such measures.[232]

The Commission is also currently considering the issue of patenting of products and methods which involve human embryonic stem cells and human derivatives and it is anticipated that the Group reviewing this issue will report by the end of 2003. The Commission has published a Staff Working Paper "Report on Human Embryonic Stem Cell Research".[233]

The debate regarding stem cell research led to an attempt to regulate this through the proposed new Directive setting standards regarding quality and safety in the context of donation, procurement, testing, processing, storage and distribution of human tissues and cells (we refer to this as the "Tissue Directive").[234] While the background to this Directive is rooted in concerns regarding the regulation of the safety of the use of tissues and of cells in relation to, for example, transplantation and treatment of diseases, as we shall see, there have also been attempts to extend its scope to cover research. The European Group on Ethics in Science and New Technologies

229 Commission Press Release IP/01/1272 "EU supports and coordinates stem cell research", Brussels, 14 September 2001.

230 See Halliday, above n 210.

231 Case C-376/98 *Tobacco Advertising* above n 190.

232 See chapter 3, pp 92–105; M. Dougan, "The Convention's Draft Constitutional Treaty: A 'Tidying-Up Exercise' that needs some Tidying-Up of its Own", www.fedtrust.co.uk/uploads/constitution/27_03.pdf, p 5: "Could Article I-17 (1) be used as the basis for . . . enacting general legislation governing scientific research on issues such as human cloning and genetic manipulation, which might be considered an affront to human dignity? Clearly not: such legislation can be adopted only within the framework of the policies listed in Part III, not as freestanding objectives appropriate for Union intervention."

233 SEC (2003) 441 Brussels, 3 April 2003; and see also an earlier background document examining many of the scientific and other related issues sponsored by the European Group on Ethics of Science and Technology: G. Overwalle, *Study of Patenting of Inventions Relating to Human Stem Cell Research* E.C. Luxembourg 2002/218.

234 Commission Proposal for a Directive of the European Parliament and of the Council on setting standards of quality and safety for the donation, procurement, testing, processing, storage and distribution of human tissues and cells, COM(2002) 319; Amended proposal for a Directive of the European Parliament and of the Council on setting standards of quality and safety for the donation, procurement, testing, processing, storage and distribution of human tissue and cells, COM(2003) 340. See further chapter 10.

has considered this.[235] The Group stated that there was an "urgent need to regulate the conditions under which human tissues circulate within the European market". It was noted that tissues should undergo advance testing with the aim of ensuring "maximum health guarantees in accordance with 'state of the art'". Second, the Group's report confirms the integrity of the human body as an important principle, whether the use of tissue from live or dead donors is concerned. Third, the Group confirmed the importance of the ethical principle of consent. It stated that consent should be provided in clear and precise terms. Fourth, it emphasised the need to protect the identity of donor and of recipient as appropriate. It also stressed the need for adherence to ethical principles, including that of regarding tissue donation in terms of a voluntary act of solidarity. As the explanatory memorandum to the proposed Directive notes, there is considerable divergence on voluntary donation across the EU as a whole.

The draft Tissue Directive was originally submitted in June 2001, and subsequently revised and resubmitted, following the European Parliament's first reading, in May 2003.[236] The draft Directive was based on Article 152 (4) (a) EC. The proposal covers human tissue and cells where these are used for application to the human body. It excludes tissues and cells used as an autologous graft within the same surgical procedure; blood and blood products;[237] and organs or parts of organs if their function is to be used for the same purpose as the entire organ on or in the human body. While the Commission noted its intention to consider fundamental policy concerns regarding organ shortages, these types of issues themselves were excluded from the scope of the proposed Directive.[238] The Commission is considering the possibility of a separate measure on organs, but notes that questions of competence to enact such a measure on the basis of Article 152 EC remain.[239]

In April 2003, the European Parliament considered the draft Tissue Directive and controversially recommended some 76 amendments. Amongst these was a proposal that the scope of the Directive be extended to cover human cells in tissue used in therapy and research.[240] Second, an amendment prohibited the creation of

235 Opinion of the European Group on Ethics in Science and New Technologies to the European Commission, *Ethical aspects of human tissue banking* No 11, 21 July 1998.

236 COM(2003) 340.

237 These are already regulated under Directive 2002/98/EC, OJ 2003 L 33/30 setting standards of quality and safety for the collection, testing, processing, storage and distribution of human blood and blood components (see further chapter 9); Directive 2001/83/EC on the Community code relating to medicinal products for human use, OJ 2000 L 311/67 (see further chapter 8); Directive 2000/70/EC, amending Directive 93/42/EEC as regards medical devices incorporating stable derivates of human blood or human plasma, OJ 1993 L 169/1; Council Recommendation 98/463/EC, on the suitability of blood and plasma donors and screening of donated blood in the European Community, OJ 1998 L 203/14.

238 COM(2002) 319, Explanatory Memorandum, para 13.

239 COM(2003) 340 final, p 2: "This requirement is difficult to accept, because the shortage of available organs and the urgent nature of their use requires organisational aspects that are difficult to address under Article 152, therefore a Proposal on this field needs to be examined carefully."

240 See European Parliament report on the proposal for a European Parliament and Council directive on setting standards of quality and safety for the donation, procurement, testing, processing, storage and distribution of human tissue and cells, A5-0103/2003; see also European Parliament legislative resolution on the proposal for a European Parliament and Council directive on setting

embryos for research alone or the creation of stem cells.[241] Furthermore, there is a proposed prohibition upon the import of such cells into the EU. Only 35 of the amendments made by the Parliament were accepted by the Commission. The Commission has accepted an increase in the breadth of the Directive to therapies other than transplantation, in particular to therapies such as reproductive medicine. The draft Tissue Directive now makes use of the word "human application", as opposed to "transplantation", where appropriate. However, other proposed amendments widening the scope of the Directive have been rejected. The proposed Directive is to relate only to cells and tissues where these are applied to the human body during a clinical trial.[242] It does not cover research using human tissues and cells when used for purposes other than application to the human body, that is, in vitro research or in animal models. The Commission rejected the proposed amendments on stem cell cloning, stating that such measures would fall outside the scope of Article 152 EC.[243] However Member States are to be able to maintain or introduce measures which are more stringent than those in the Directive. In particular, Member States may continue to prohibit the use, and import, of any particular type of human tissue or cell.[244] A further matter of concern for Parliament was the potential for commercial dealing in cells and tissues. This amendment has been largely accepted by the Commission, although it has been redrafted somewhat.

In June 2003, the Employment, Social Policy, Health and Consumer Affairs Council reached agreement on a common position regarding the directive, which is to be formally adopted at a later Council meeting.[245] This is to be then sent to the European Parliament for second reading under the co-decision procedure. Unless the European Parliament rejects the measure in its entirety, we can expect adoption of the Tissue Directive some time in 2004.[246]

V. Conclusions

The law of the EU is undoubtedly having a considerable effect upon clinical research practice within the Member States. Initiatives such as the Clinical Trials Directive provide a good illustration of the powerful impact of EU-level regulatory measures of harmonisation. National laws on clinical trials of pharmaceuticals will have to be amended so that Member States comply with their obligations under this Directive. The EU has also had an indirect impact on research practice in the Member States through the operation of its financial support for health-related research, in

standards of quality and safety for the donation, procurement, testing, processing, storage and distribution of human tissue and cells, 10 May 2002.

241 "MEPs vote to ban stem cell research", http://news.bbc.co.uk/1/hi/health/2932421.stm.

242 COM(2003) 340, Recital 6.

243 In this respect, the Commission is probably correct in law, and see above n 232, concerning the possible use of Article 308 EC for such a measure.

244 COM(2003) 340, Recital 7.

245 2512th Council meeting Employment, Social Policy, Health and Consumer Affairs, Luxembourg, 2 and 3 June 2003; 9688/1/03/REV 1.

246 The Directive was adopted on 31 March 2004, as Directive 2004/23/EC, OJ 2004 L 102/48. See further chapter 10.

particular through the Framework Programmes. Soft law measures aid what may be a gradual process of convergence of legal measures towards a set of "EU values" with respect to ethical clinical research.

However, what is missing is an attempt fully to coordinate such emergent legal and ethical principles, and follow them through to a logical conclusion. The provisions in the Biotechnology Directive, and some of the measures relating to EU research funding imply that certain sorts of research are, to put it at its mildest, in the view of the EU institutions, "ethically suspect". Yet there has been to date no attempt to prohibit the practice of such research at EU level; this has been left to the Member States. If the EU is competent to adopt the Clinical Trials Directive on the basis of Article 95 EC, it is difficult to see why it would not be legally competent to adopt directives regulating other elements of medical research, at least that leading to the production of new medical products or services. Of course, as the process of adoption of the Biotechnology Directive illustrates, the legislative procedures of the EU are such that it would probably be very difficult in practice to reach sufficient consensus of all the different interests finding a voice in that process, in order to adopt such putative directives.

While the EU legislature continues to tinker at the edges of this debate, for instance, by using patent law rather than administrative or criminal law to regulate medical research, a number of consequences arise. First, as we have seen, there is the possibility of the emergence of "regulatory gaps" or at least regulatory tension between the EU's provision with respect to certain clinical research practices, and that promulgated by other European bodies such as the Council of Europe, or at national level within the Member States. Second, the EU remains vulnerable to criticism for failing to take the ethical elements of the field sufficiently seriously. Third, in spite of the relative transparency of the EU's policy-making procedures, there is no doubt that certain interests find it easier than others to make their views count. This suggests an element of governance taking place without sufficient accountability, and thus credibility. Take, for example, the proposal for a directive setting standards of quality and safety in relation to human tissues and cells (Tissue Directive). As Holm has commented:

> "The major problem with the draft directive in its current form is the way wide ranging regulations of ethically contentious areas are being drafted, discussed and decided without public or scholarly input or discussion."[247]

Furthermore, despite the "raised consciousness" among the EU institutions with respect to the regulatory challenges posed by cutting-edge clinical research, overall the EU legislative institutions are open to the charge that their responses are in many respects piecemeal and *ad hoc*, and that this is wholly inappropriate for matters concerning research ethics and in particular the protection of fundamental human rights.

247 S. Holm "Regulating stem cell research in Europe by the back door" 29 *Journal of Medical Ethics* (2003) 203.

8

Regulating pharmaceuticals: risk, choice and compensation

I. Introduction

The development of modern pharmaceutical products has led to a vast improvement in health care globally. Drugs and vaccines have virtually eradicated some of the major health scourges of years gone by, such as smallpox. Improvements in treatment of what were regarded as fatal conditions, such as HIV/AIDS, have resulted from the development of drugs such as AZT. Nonetheless, whilst such developments have great potential, sadly there have been some instances in which pharmaceuticals have been viewed in a considerably less positive light. The drug Thalidomide, given to pregnant women in the 1960s, was linked to the development of major congenital disabilities.[1] Less than a decade later, it was alleged that the pertussis vaccine resulted in infant brain damage.[2] The controversy regarding the administration of vaccines continues to this day, in the light of claims made linking the administration of the combined MMR (measles, mumps and rubella) vaccine to autism.[3] Thus, much of the legal (and political and ethical) debate regarding pharmaceuticals has focused upon the risks which they pose and the need for appropriate regulation,[4] and the prospect for compensation should harm arise from the use of a pharmaceutical

1 *Distillers v Thompson* [1971] AC 458; and see H. Teff and C. Munro, *Thalidomide: the Legal Aftermath* (London: Saxon House, 1976).

2 See, for example, *Loveday v Renton* 1 Medical Law Reports (1990) 117; *Best v Wellcome* 5 Medical Law Reports (1994) 81 (Irish Supreme Court); and D. Brahams, "Court Award for Pertussis Brain Damage" 341 *Lancet* (1993) 1338.

3 The original study, undertaken at the Royal Free Hospital, London, that prompted the concerns is published as A. J. Wakefield et al, "Ileal-lymphoid-nodular hyperplasia, non-specific colitis and pervasive developmental disorder in children" 351(9103) *Lancet* (1998) 637–641. See also the news report, BBC News, "Child vaccine linked to autism", 27 February 1998, http://www.news.bbc.co.uk/hi/english/health/, accessed March 1998. Subsequent research, both in the UK and elsewhere, has cast doubt on these findings: see the studies cited on the UK Department of Health website, http:www.doh.gov.uk/mmr/. See also the discussion in S. Pywell, R. Martin and L. Johnson, (eds.) *Law and the Public Dimension of Health* (London: Cavendish, 2001); see *Re MMR/MR Litigation: Sayers and others v Smithkline Beecham Plc and others* [2002] EWHC 1280 (UK High Court QBD) which concerned medical conditions which arose shortly after the vaccine was administered.

4 J. Abraham and G. Lewis, *Regulating Medicines in Europe: Competition, expertise and public health* (London and New York: Routledge, 2000).

product.[5] These concerns are also reflected in the developments which have taken place in EU law in this area.

In this chapter, which considers the regulation of pharmaceuticals, in common with our overall approach in this book, the focus is on the effects that legal norms promulgated at EU level with respect to the regulation of pharmaceuticals have on national health law and policy in the Member States. A number of themes arise. First, regulation in this field is concerned with the management of risk. The regulatory patterns seen in this chapter, in interactions between EU and national institutional actors, and also elements of self-regulation, reveal, overall, a cautious or conservative risk assessment strategy. Further, there are clear tensions arising from the locus (EU or national) for strategic decision-making with respect to acceptable levels of risk. There are also tensions arising from the indirect implications of regulatory activities for national health (insurance) systems, in terms of the impact on resources that can arise when a new pharmaceutical product is approved for marketing in the EU, or within a particular Member State. Second, regulatory strategies concerning the management of risk have a direct impact on standards of quality, safety and efficacy of pharmaceuticals available in the EU. The entitlements of patients in the EU to the protection of such standards are increasingly determined by EU-level institutional actors. Third, where such standards are not met, the EU has had a (limited) impact on the determination of liability of the pharmaceuticals industry to patients as consumers. Fourth, there is an interesting interaction between the discourse of the market and that of regulation. Industry actors have attempted to use EU law on free movement of goods and also EU competition law in ways which potentially undermine collective public health strategies and policies determined within each Member State.[6] Broadly, the Court has responded to this opportunistic litigation by protecting national health policies, thus favouring collective health protection over individual "rights" in EU law of pharmaceuticals companies. Finally, EU law regulating pharmaceuticals implicitly does so within a "consumer protection" model. The implications of conceptualising patients as "consumers" are only beginning to emerge at a national level, with the increasing concern among patients to become more than passive recipients of health care services, but to exercise their own choices in that respect.[7] The EU's interventions, for instance in terms of the information that must be provided to patients as consumers of pharmaceuticals, may move health law further in that direction.

In all Member States of the EU, the law regulates the development,[8] production, licensing, importation, distribution, marketing and retail of pharmaceuticals.

5 See, for example, P. Ferguson, *Drug Injuries and the Pursuit of Compensation* (London: Sweet and Maxwell, 1996).

6 See further below.

7 See M. Brazier, *Medicine, Patients and the Law* (London: Penguin, 3rd edn. 2003), p 17; J. Montgomery, *Health Care Law* (Oxford: OUP, 2nd edn. 2002), chapter 9; A. Grubb, ed, *Principles of Medical Law* (Oxford: OUP, 2004 forthcoming).

8 For discussion of the regulation of clinical research, see chapter 7.

However, such regulation is not simply a matter of national law. A significant body of EU-level norms, dating back to the 1960s, concerns pharmaceuticals.[9] Moreover, to the extent that national regulations governing pharmaceuticals may impede the "establishment and functioning of the internal market", they may be subject to EU law on the free movement of goods, and EU competition law. These provisions must also be considered in the context of development of increasingly streamlined and homogenous rules at international level, especially through the International Conference on Harmonisation of Technical Requirements of Pharmaceuticals for Human Use (ICH). Reference has already been made to the ICH in chapter 7.[10] The ICH brings together the regulatory authorities of the EU, Japan and the US,[11] and experts from the pharmaceutical industry in those regions, to discuss scientific and technical aspects of the regulation of pharmaceuticals, and to make recommendations with respect to greater harmonisation of such technical requirements, with a view to promoting greater efficiency through avoiding duplication in the testing needed for new pharmaceuticals, and the consequent delay in bringing new medicinal products to the various markets.[12]

EU-level action concerning regulation of pharmaceuticals includes measures aimed (broadly) at protection of patients as the consumers of pharmaceuticals, covering, for instance, the requirement for national systems granting marketing authorisation for new medicinal products; measures on surveillance of safety of pharmaceuticals during their life on the market ("pharmacovigilance"); measures concerning labelling and packaging of pharmaceuticals; and measures on advertising of pharmaceuticals. The requirement for a marketing authorisation aims to ensure quality controls in the development of new pharmaceutical products. General EU-level measures on liability for defective products also apply to pharmaceuticals. Product liability provisions affect the position of manufacturers and

9 More recent provisions cover medical devices.

10 Chapter 7, pp 248–249.

11 The WHO, the European Free Trade Area, represented by Switzerland, and Canada have observer status in the ICH.

12 For further information see http://www.ich.org/. The establishment of the ICH in April 1990 followed the perceived success of the EU in harmonising regulatory requirements for pharmaceuticals during the 1980s. The specific impetus came from the WHO Conference of Drug Regulatory Authorities, Paris, 1989. The EU parties to the ICH are the European Commission and the European Federation of Pharmaceutical Industries and Associations. These parties are represented on the ICH Steering Committee, which determines policies and procedures, selects topics for harmonisation and monitors the progress of harmonisation initiatives. The Committee for Proprietary Medicinal Products (CPMP) of the European Agency for the Evaluation of Medicinal Products (EMEA) provides technical and scientific support for ICH activities. The ICH's topics are divided into "quality", "safety" and "efficacy" topics, with a fourth category of "multidisciplinary" cross-cutting topics. The work of ICH during the 1990s concentrated on harmonisation of technical requirements where significant obstacles to drug development were identified, through developing international scientific consensus between the pharmaceutical industry and regulators. In 2000, the ICH revised its terms of reference, to continue its existing work, but also to move to a greater focus on implementation and monitoring. In 2000, ICH adopted a "Common Technical Document" providing a harmonised format for new product applications. In the EU, this was implemented by the CPMP, as a new Notice to Applicants, issued in June and September 2001 (CPMP/ICH/2887/99).

suppliers of pharmaceuticals with respect to non-contractual liability for damage arising from those products, and patients may have a legally enforceable right to compensation in the case that harmful pharmaceuticals have been negligently produced or marketed. The provisions on labelling and advertisement may have a more tangential effect on patients as consumers, in particular in relation to consent to treatment. Where patients have increased information, they may be less likely to accept without question the recommendations of medical professionals.

Directive 65/65/EEC[13] is the earliest EU-level measure with the aim of harmonising safety and efficacy standards for medicinal products. Enacted in response to the Thalidomide tragedies of the early 1960s,[14] the Directive required Member States to enact laws to ensure that new medicinal products may not be marketed on their territories without the approval of a competent regulatory body. More detailed harmonisation provisions for the criteria and procedures according to which approval may be given by national regulatory bodies for new medicinal products followed. A large number of detailed provisions of secondary legislation now cover all industrially produced medicines, including vaccines, toxins or serums and allergens;[15] blood products;[16] and radio-pharmaceuticals.[17] Provisions also cover medical devices.[18] Technical requirements governing testing of new pharmaceuticals are regularly updated by the Commission, in accordance with power delegated for this purpose by the Council.[19] In addition to criteria relating to quality, safety and efficacy, rules relating to procedures for marketing authorisation (time limits, giving of reasons, publication),[20] to manufacture (quality control, inspections),[21] to labelling (packaging to include information relating to dose, ingredients, side

13 OJ 1965 P 22/369; OJ Sp Ed 1965–6 p 24. Amended and consolidated by Directive 93/39/EC, OJ 1993 L 214/22; and further consolidated by Directive 2001/83/EC, OJ 2001 L 311/67.

14 A. White, "Whither the Pharmaceutical Trade Mark?" 8 *European Intellectual Property Review* (1996) 441 at 441; J. Gardner, "The European Agency for the Evaluation of Medicines and European Regulation of Pharmaceuticals" 2 ELJ (1996) 48 at 52; E. Kaufer, "The Regulation of New Product Development in the Drug Industry", in G. Majone, ed, *Deregulation or Re-regulation? Regulatory Reform in Europe and the United States* (London and New York: Pinter, 1990), p 157.

15 Directive 89/342/EEC, OJ 1989 L 142/14.

16 Directive 89/381/EEC, OJ 1989 L 189/44.

17 Directive 89/343/EEC, OJ 1989 L 142/16.

18 Directive 90/385/EC on active implantable medical devices, OJ 1990 L 189/17; Directive 93/42/EC on medical devices, OJ 1993 L 169/1.

19 Council Recommendations 83/57/EEC and 87/176/EEC concerning tests relating to the placing on the market of proprietary medicinal products, OJ 1983 L 332/11 and OJ 1987 L 71/1. See R. Watson, "EU Harmonises rules for trials" 322 BMJ (2001) 68. See W. Sauer, "The European Community's Pharmaceutical Policy" in A.F. Casparie, H. Hermans and J. Paelinck, eds, *Health Care in Europe After 1992* (Aldershot: Dartmouth, 1992), p 133. Amendments are made according to the "regulatory committee procedure", under which the committee must support the Commission proposal by a qualified majority in order for the amendment to be adopted, see further chapter 2.

20 Directive 93/39/EC, amending Directive 65/65/EEC and Directives 75/318/EEC, 75/319/EEC, OJ 1975 L 147/1.

21 Directives 75/318/EEC and 75/319/EEC; Directive 87/18/EEC on harmonisation concerning the application of principles of good laboratory practice and the verification of their application for tests on chemical substances, OJ 1987 L 15/29; Directive 88/320/EEC on inspection and verification of good laboratory practice, OJ 1988 L 145/35.

effects)[22] and to advertising of medicinal products (advertisement to the general public of prescription drugs is prohibited)[23] have been harmonised. Many of these provisions were consolidated in Directive 2001/83/EC on the Community code relating to medicinal products for human use.[24]

In addition to these "consumer protection" internal market measures, other provisions appear to be aimed more at the commercial practicalities of creating an "internal market" in pharmaceuticals, for instance rules on the mutual recognition of national authorisations, and EU-level procedures facilitating such mutual recognition. At the end of this chapter, we consider briefly ways in which (deregulatory) Treaty provisions on the free movement of goods and EU competition law may affect trade in pharmaceuticals within the EU, and the implications of this for national health (insurance) systems.

Thus, for these deregulatory, reregulatory and coordinating methods of governance, the law and regulatory policy concerning pharmaceuticals in the EU is formed through the interplay of national and EU-level norms, principles and practices, with some influence of international-level norms also. Within this process, EU law therefore has a significant, and we maintain a potentially increasing, effect on this aspect of national health law and policy. We would argue that it also has a potentially significant indirect effect on the provision of national health services within the Member States, as such national health institutions are the principal purchasers of pharmaceuticals within the EU.

Before considering in detail the body of EU law regulating pharmaceuticals, some special features of the pharmaceutical market should be noted. The nature of the pharmaceutical industry, and the products it produces, are such that the pharmaceuticals market cannot simply be considered to be equivalent to any other product market. Although the European Commission has striven to achieve a "single market in pharmaceuticals", the special nature of the pharmaceuticals market[25] has made this a practical impossibility. As we noted in chapter 7, the pharmaceutical industry is an industry of innovation heavily dependent upon investment in research and development, to discover new pharmaceutical products. These may be either for diseases and disorders for which there is currently no treatment, or for better ways of treating disorders for which there exist treatments that have many side-effects, are very expensive[26] or are intrusive to administer. In order to safeguard

22 Directive 92/27/EEC, OJ 1992 L 113/8.

23 Directive 92/28/EEC, OJ 1992 L 113/13. Officially supported vaccination campaigns are exempted (Article 3 (5)). See also Directives 92/25/EEC, OJ 1992 L 113/1 and 92/26/EEC, OJ 1992 L 113/5.

24 OJ 2001 L 311/67.

25 See Commission, *Communication from Commission to Council and European Parliament outlining an industrial policy for the pharmaceutical sector in the EC* COM(93) 718 final, p 17; E. Mossialos and B. Abel-Smith, "The Regulation of the European Pharmaceutical Industry" in S. Stavridis, E. Mossialos, R. Morgan and H. Machlin, eds, *New Challenges to the EU: Policies and Policy-Making* (Aldershot: Dartmouth, 1997); R. Thompson, *The Single Market for Pharmaceuticals* (London: Butterworths, 1994), p 8; L. Hancher, "The European Pharmaceutical Market: problems of partial harmonisation" 15 ELRev (1990) 9 at 10–11.

26 Or, in some cases, very cheap, where the pharmaceutical industry seeks to increase profits by introducing a new pharmaceutical product.

their investment in research and development of new products, pharmaceuticals companies protect their inventions by patents, which normally provide protection for 20 years. The profitability of the leading pharmaceutical companies is, to a large extent, based on a relatively limited number of innovative products during the period in which they enjoy patent protection from competition.[27] Distribution of pharmaceuticals is also subject to regulatory restrictions, with some states restricting the sale of all medicines to pharmacies, and others imposing such a restriction only on prescription medicines. This, in turn, affects the final selling prices of pharmaceuticals.

Moreover, in addition to these special features of the supply side of the pharmaceuticals market, the demand side also has a number of special features. In an "ordinary" market, demand is determined by consumers choosing from competing products on the basis of quality and price. However, in the pharmaceuticals market in the EU, the ultimate consumer of the product (the patient) pays, at most, only part of the price of the product.[28] The remainder of the cost is met either by the government, from taxation, or, in systems where health protection is paid for by (compulsory) insurance, by the insurer, or by a combination of the two. In those circumstances, states may attempt to regulate the prescribing practices of health care professionals with a view to containment of costs.[29] Pharmaceuticals companies rely heavily on promotional activities with health professionals. Further, in the pharmaceuticals market, competition between companies tends to focus on therapeutic innovation and improvements to existing products, and on costs, finances and sales volumes, rather than on price. Finally, access by patients whose diseases or disorders require treatment, to many of the products produced by the pharmaceuticals industry, is perceived to be a matter of "life and death", or at least of "quality of life". Medicines – like other public goods or services such as energy, water or transport – are seen as essential in ways that most other goods are not.

Thus, in the pharmaceuticals market, the ordinary operation of profit incentives and market competition are not generally viewed as automatically generating a "socially optimum" outcome. Rather, there is a conflict between industrial policy objectives (supporting and encouraging a vigorous pharmaceutical industry) and health policy objectives (encouraging the delivery of new safe, high-quality, necessary and efficacious pharmaceuticals in as cost-effective a manner as possible). For this reason, the power to make decisions concerning matters such as price is often delegated to a public regulatory agent. States intervene in the setting of profit or price controls, and the regulation of overall pharmaceuticals consumption, for instance, by fixing prices for pharmaceuticals. Such cost containment measures have

27 This is from generic pharmaceutical products. Such "generics" may take three forms: "true generics", marketed under the "International Non-Proprietary Name (INN)"; "semi-branded" generics, marketed under the INN plus the name of the manufacturer; and "branded generics" sold under their own brand name. See L. Garattini and F. Tediosi, "A Comparative Analysis of Generics Markets in five European countries" 51 *Health Policy* (2000) 149 at 150.

28 In fact, many consumers are exempt from any co-payment at all: see P.R. Noyce et al, "The cost of prescription medicines to patients" 52 *Health Policy* (2000) 129.

29 See further chapter 6.

an impact on the "internal market in pharmaceuticals", which is discussed in more detail below. We turn first to the EU-level regulatory measures concerned with the protection of patients as consumers of pharmaceuticals.

II. EU-level patient (consumer) protection measures

Introduction

As we noted above, the potential of developments in the pharmaceuticals industry needs to be balanced against the prospect that undetermined risks may lead to consequent harm to the patient. A number of measures of EU law have the dual, and potentially contradictory, aims of completing the internal market in pharmaceuticals and the protection of the health of patients as consumers of pharmaceuticals. The earliest of these, Directive 65/65/EEC, although based on Article 100 (now 94) EC, provides that "the primary purpose of any rules concerning the production and distribution of medicinal products must be to safeguard public health".[30] However, this is modified by the second aim of EU pharmaceuticals law, promoting the free movement of pharmaceuticals as goods, and ensuring a system of free competition for the pharmaceutical industry within the EU.[31] Closely related to this latter aim is the development of the European pharmaceutical industry, to enable it to compete on world markets, in particular with US and Japan-based multi-nationals.[32] As we shall see below, these pressures have given rise to fears that the regulation of pharmaceuticals can be seen not so much in terms of aspirational guidelines in relation to the provision of efficacious, safe and high quality pharmaceuticals, but rather in terms of a (potential) "race to the bottom" driven by industrial concerns.[33]

The institutions of the EU did not have formal competence to enact consumer protection measures until 1992, with the insertion of Article 129a (now 153) EC by the Treaty of Maastricht. Article 129 (now 152) EC explicitly excludes Community competence for harmonising measures in the public health field. However, the institutions of the EU have fallen back on the legal basis provisions for completion of the common (Article 100 (now 94) EC) and single internal (Article 100a (now 95) EC) market in order to adopt measures of EU consumer protection law concerning pharmaceuticals. Until the *Tobacco Advertising* case,[34] no legal challenge had been brought against the use of these legal basis provisions for the adoption of what are harmonisation measures, but are centrally concerned with the protection of consumers and public health within the EU.

30 Recital 1. Now in Directive 2001/83/EC, Recital 2.

31 Some have argued that these two aims of EU pharmaceuticals law are fundamentally incompatible: see, for example, Anonymous, "European drug regulation: anti-protection or consumer protection?" 337 *Lancet* (1991) 1571.

32 Recital 2. Now in Directive 2001/83/EC, Recital 3.

33 See Abraham and Lewis, above n 4; J. Abraham, "Making regulation responsive to commercial interests: streamlining drug industry watchdogs" 325 BMJ (2002) 1164 (16 November).

34 Case C-376/98 *Germany v Parliament and Council (Tobacco Advertising)* [2000] ECR I-8419. See discussion in chapter 3.

Marketing authorisations

As a matter of EU law, it is unlawful to market pharmaceuticals within the EU without appropriate authorisation. This fundamental principle[35] of EU pharmaceuticals law was established by Directive 65/65/EEC, Article 3. EU law defines "medicinal products" as "any substance or combination of substances presented for preventing disease in human beings or animals" and "any substance . . . which may be administered to human beings or animals with a view to making a medical diagnosis or to restoring, correcting or modifying physiological functions in human beings or in animals".[36] "Placing on the market" is defined in Directive 93/42/EEC,[37] Article 1 (2) (h) as "the first making available in return for payment or free of charge . . . with a view to distribution and/or use on the Community market".[38] Thus placing on the market covers passing to a distributor, final retailer or national health purchaser.

As with the decision to sanction a clinical trial concerning medicinal products, the authorisation or approval of new pharmaceuticals is still, in principle, basically a matter for national authorities. However, products resulting from biotechnology and innovation or "high technology", which represent a high proportion of new pharmaceuticals, are now subject to a different regime.[39] Moreover, exercise of national competence with respect to "ordinary" new pharmaceuticals is curtailed to a certain extent by EU-level provisions which set out a "decentralised procedure" for approval of a new medicinal product in other Member States, once it has been approved in one Member State. This procedure is essentially an application of the principle of mutual recognition, according to which Member States must provide a good reason for non-recognition of an approval of a new medicinal product granted by another Member State. The "decentralised procedure" is thus an example of the use of "new approach" harmonisation combined with regulatory coordination of national laws.[40] Moreover, and crucially, in the event of a disagreement between Member States about the quality, safety or efficacy of a medicinal product, the matter is to be resolved by a binding Commission decision, reached under a comitology procedure,[41] following a scientific evaluation of the

35 See the Opinion of AG Lenz in Case C-112/89 *Upjohn* [1991] ECR I-1703, para 14: "the requirement of an authorisation thus forms the hub and linchpin of the whole system of rules."

36 Directive 65/65/EEC, Article 1 (2), now in Directive 2001/83/EC, Article 6 (1). See also the rulings of the Court in Case C-227/82 *Van Bennekom* [1983] ECR 3883; Case C-35/85 *Tissier* [1986] ECR 1207; Case C-369/88 *Delattre* [1991] ECR I-1487; Case C-60/89 *Monteil and Samanni* [1991] ECR I-1547; Case C-112/89 *Upjohn* above n 35; Case C-290/90 *Commission v Germany* [1992] ECR I-3317; Case C-219/91 *Ter Voort* [1992] ECR I-5485; and Case C-212/91 *Angelopharm* [1994] ECR I-171; and the discussions in Thompson, above n 25, pp 17–34 and L. Hancher, "Creating the Internal Market for Pharmaceutical Medicines: An Echternach Jumping Process?" 28 CMLRev (1991) 821. We are not concerned here with the measures concerning veterinary products.

37 OJ 1993 L 169/1.

38 This provision applies to "medical devices", but given the close relationship between "medicinal products" and "medical devices" it seems reasonable to assume that the definition applies to both: see Thompson, above n 25, p 53.

39 See further below.

40 See chapter 2.

41 Directive 2001/83/EC, Article 121, referring to Decision 99/468/EC, OJ 1999 L 184/23, Articles 5 and 7.

issues within a European medicinal product evaluation agency.[42] The Commission decision effectively removes national competence to assess risk in the case of the marketing of a new pharmaceutical, and thus may be seen as an example of "old style" harmonisation, where a measure adopted by an EU-level institution "occupies the field", leaving no further room for national regulation.

The EMEA

The European Medicines Evaluation Agency (EMEA), set up by Regulation 2309/93/EC,[43] began operation in February 1995.[44] The legal basis of Regulation 2309/93/EC is Article 235 (now 308) EC, setting this piece of legislation apart from other measures in the field, which are based on Articles 100 (now 94), or 100a (now 95) EC. This is probably due to the fact that Regulation 2309/93/EC goes further than the earlier harmonisation by mutual recognition measures,[45] in that it established an independent EU-level procedure for the authorisation of certain medicinal products, and set up the EMEA.[46] The EMEA is not an "EU institution" in the sense of the Treaties, but is an "agency" of the EU. EU agencies assist the EU institutions with the scientific and technical side of their activities.[47] The EMEA Management Board is comprised of two representatives from the Commission, Parliament and each Member State respectively. The accession states are also represented on the Management Board. The EMEA Management Board is responsible for establishing the annual budget[48] (including setting the industry fees for authorisations) and setting its annual work programme and overall policy direction.[49] The Management Board also appoints the EMEA Executive Director.[50]

The operational strand of the EMEA is effectively its scientific committees, the Committee for Proprietary Medicinal Products (CPMP), the Committee for Orphan Medicinal Products and the Committee for Veterinary Medicinal Products.[51] The CPMP, composed of national experts and members of the Commission, established by Directive 75/319/EEC, is a key actor in the EU procedures for

42 Directive 2001/83/EC, Articles 32–34.
43 OJ 1993 L 214/1.
44 According to the Commission, the EMEA was set up partly in response to demands from consumers' organisations and the European Parliament: Commission, Pharmaceuticals and Cosmetics Unit, *Pharmaceuticals in the EU* (Brussels: European Commission, 2000), p 7. However, a democratic or citizen-focussed motivation is unlikely to provide the whole explanation. The pharmaceutical industry, no doubt, also played a significant role in the establishment of the EMEA.
45 Thompson, above n 25, p 91.
46 A. Cuvillier, "The Role of the European Medicines Evaluation Agency in the harmonisation of pharmaceutical regulation", in R. Goldberg and J. Lonbay, eds, *Pharmaceutical Medicine, Biotechnology and European Law* (Cambridge: CUP, 2000).
47 See further chapter 2.
48 Which must balance.
49 Regulation 2309/93/EC, Articles 56–58.
50 Regulation 2309/93/EC, Article 55.
51 See http://www.emea.eu.int/ for details of membership. Obviously the activities of the Committee for Veterinary Medicinal Products are outside the scope of this book.

authorisation of pharmaceuticals. The CPMP predates the EMEA, but has now been brought within its remit. According to the Preamble of Regulation 2309/93/EC, the scientific role and independence of the CPMP was to be bolstered by the "relocation" of the CPMP within the EMEA, and in particular the establishment of a permanent technical and administrative secretariat supporting its work.[52] A network of some 3000 European scientific experts underpins the work of the EMEA's committees.

The decentralised procedure

The decentralised procedure has been compulsory for all medicinal products to be marketed in a Member State, other than that in which they were first authorised, since 1 January 1998.[53] The basic administrative and procedural arrangements for implementing the decentralised procedure, provided for in Directive 93/39/EC,[54] were already set up at national level in accordance with Directive 65/65/EEC[55] and Directive 75/319/EEC.[56] Under the decentralised procedure, a producer who has obtained approval in one Member State (the "Reference Member State") may seek approval in another Member State (the "Concerned Member State"),[57] simultaneously submitting their application to the CPMP and the Reference Member State. The Reference Member State is required to provide an assessment report for the relevant product. The Concerned Member State must make a decision on approval within 90 days. Approval may be refused only on grounds of risk to public health, that is to say, on quality, safety or efficacy grounds.[58] If the Concerned Member State is minded to reject, the matter is submitted to the CPMP for arbitration.

The CPMP opinion is then submitted to the Commission, for the decision-making process.[59] The Commission Decision is binding on the Member States, who must then comply, for instance, by granting, withdrawing or modifying their marketing authorisation for the product concerned. Under this "comitology" procedure,

52 Cuvillier stresses that the CPMP's role is altered under the EMEA, and states that it plays a more direct role in decision making than under the previous system. He also claims that the CPMP's composition has been changed to reflect a wider range of scientific expertise. See Cuvillier, above n 46.

53 Commission, Pharmaceuticals and Cosmetics Unit, *Pharmaceuticals in the EU* (Brussels: European Commission, 2000). The decentralised procedure is the successor to the "multi-state procedure", (see Sauer, above n 19, p 135; Gardner, above n 14, at 53–54) according to which a producer of a medicinal product authorised in one Member State could request extension of this authorisation to two or more (originally five or more – see Directive 75/319/EEC, now repealed and replaced by Directive 2001/83/EC) other Member States. A formal opinion on authorisation was to be provided by the CPMP. However, under the multi-state procedure, the CPMP could not impose its view on Member States. In the final analysis, Member States remained free to make their own independent decisions on marketing authorisations.

54 OJ 1993 L 214/22. Now repealed and replaced by Directive 2001/83/EC.

55 OJ 1965 P 22/369. Now repealed and replaced by Directive 2001/83/EC.

56 OJ 1975 L 147/13. Now repealed and replaced by Directive 2001/83/EC.

57 There is no longer any need to apply to at least two further Member States, as under the multi-state procedure.

58 Gardner, above n 14, at 60.

59 The Commission conducts internal consultations, between various Directorates General, and the regulatory standing committees on human medicinal products. The Commission (DG Enterprise) takes the final decision.

if there is a serious disagreement among Member States, the matter is resolved by Council.[60]

Under the decentralised procedure, Member States being asked, in effect, to accept the marketing authorisation granted by another Member State, may still object on grounds of a "risk to public health". This provision appears to be more tightly worded than the previous grounds in Article 5 of Directive 65/65/EEC. However, the interpretation of "risk to public health" includes the criteria set out in that provision: quality, safety and efficacy.[61] What is more significant is that, at least in theory, under the decentralised procedure, the final decision is taken by the Commission, or, in cases of severe disagreement among Member States, by Council, but not by the Member States themselves.

The CPMP provides an institutional forum for coordination of national approval systems within which, according to some commentators, the gradual convergence of national approval systems is likely to be fostered. Differences in approaches of national authorities granting marketing permission for new medicinal products, and consequently in their decisions, may be reduced by cooperation of national experts within the CPMP.[62] This is certainly the aim of the procedure, but whether convergence actually takes place remains to be seen.

The centralised procedure

The competence of national authorities to grant marketing authorisations for medicinal products has been further compromised by the development of a new authorisation procedure, at present limited to certain medicinal products only. In

60 The new decentralised procedure constitutes another step along the way to establishing a single market in pharmaceuticals within the EU. Originally, under the "multi-state procedure" of Directive 75/319/EEC, national authorities were able to "put forward a reasoned objection". The reasoned objection was to be on the basis of one of the grounds set out in Article 5 of Directive 65/65/EEC: "that the product is harmful in the normal conditions of use, or that its therapeutic efficacy is lacking or is insufficiently substantiated . . . or that its qualitative or quantitative composition is not as declared" (quality, safety and efficacy). Although the CPMP was required to reach a "reasoned opinion", provision was also made for divergent opinions of its members. The final decision was to be taken by the Member States, who were merely under a duty to "decide what action to take on the Committee's opinion within 60 days of receipt" of the opinion. As Thompson points out, under Directive 75/319/EEC, the CPMP was in effect impotent. There was no requirement for the CPMP to reach a single opinion, no requirement that the Member States should take any notice of the CPMP's opinion, and no provision for the CPMP to prevent the Member States' response to the opinion, however perverse (see Thompson, above n 25, p 77). In practice, invariably the Member States refused to accept authorisations granted by other Member States, and referred the matter to the CPMP for its opinion, before making their own decisions (see Thompson, above n 25, p 81).

61 Thompson, above n 25, p 131. Directive 65/65/EEC, Article 6 provides that Member States may refuse authorisation of contraceptives where the sale of such products is prohibited under their laws. This exceptional provision allows Member States, such as Ireland, to refuse authorisation on grounds other than public health risk, quality, safety or efficacy. See Thompson, above n 25, p 59. Recital 3 of Regulation 2309/93/EC states that Member States should in exceptional circumstances be allowed to prohibit the use of medicinal products "which infringe objectively defined concepts of public order or public morality". This would appear to allow a further exception to Member States, but there is no legislative provision other than Article 6 of Directive 65/65 based on this Recital. See Thompson, above n 25, p 92.

62 Gardner, above n 14, at 59–60.

addition to the decentralised procedure, a "centralised procedure", according to which EU-level approval may (or in some cases must) be given to certain medicinal products, was set up by Regulation 2309/93/EC.[63]

The centralised procedure applies to a limited category of medicinal products: new biotechnological products and innovative "high-technology" products.[64] In fact, however, a significant proportion of newly developed pharmaceuticals fall into this category. Article 3 (1) provides that "no medicinal product referred to in Part A of the Annex may be placed on the market within the Community unless a marketing authorisation has been granted within the Community in accordance with the provisions of this Regulation". The list in Part A covers: "Medicinal products developed by means of the following biotechnological processes: – recombinant DNA technology, – controlled expression of genes coding for biologically active proteins in prokaryotes and eukaryotes, including transferred mammalian cells, – hybridoma and monoclonal antibody methods."[65] This list provides a detailed definition of new biotechnological products. Such products must be authorised according to the centralised procedure.

Article 3 (2) of the Regulation provides that persons responsible for placing products falling within Part B of the Annex "may request that authorisation to place the medicinal product on the market be granted by the Community in accordance with the provisions of this Regulation". Thus for such "innovative" products, the centralised procedure is optional. Unlike that in Part A, the list in Part B of the Annex to the Regulation leaves an element of discretion to the EU institutions. Article 3 (2) applies to:

> "Medicinal products developed by other biotechnological processes which, in the opinion of the Agency [EMEA], constitute a significant innovation;
> Medicinal products administered by means of new delivery systems which, in the opinion of the Agency, constitute a significant innovation;
> Medicinal products presented for an entirely new indication which, in the opinion of the Agency, is of significant therapeutic interest;
> Medicinal products based on radio-isotopes which, in the opinion of the Agency, are of significant therapeutic interest;
> New medicinal products derived from human blood or plasma;
> Medicinal products the manufacture of which employs processes which, in the opinion of the Agency, demonstrate a significant technical advance . . .
> Medicinal products intended for administration to human beings, containing a new active substance which, on the date of entry into force of this Regulation, was not authorised by any Member State for use in a medicinal product intended for human use . . ."

63 OJ 1993 L 214. See Gardner, above n 14, at 56–57.
64 As defined in the Annex (parts A and B) to Regulation 2309/93/EC.
65 This list is identical to the list in Directive 87/22/EEC, OJ 1987 L 15/38 on the approximation of national measures relating to the placing on the market of high-technology medicinal products, particularly those derived from biotechnology.

This list is inspired by that in Part B of the Annex to Directive 87/22/EEC,[66] but with significant alterations. The determination of whether an innovation is sufficiently "significant" becomes a matter for the EMEA, not national authorities. Products derived from blood or plasma are listed separately. Products containing a new active substance, as yet unauthorised anywhere in the EU, are clearly included. The key elements in the list are the use of "high technology", significant innovation, or significant therapeutic interest. Presumably decisions by the EMEA with respect to whether a product falls within this list, and is thus eligible for the centralised procedure, could be the subject of judicial review before the European Court of Justice on the grounds set out in Article 230 EC. However, given that the list refers explicitly to the "opinion of the Agency", successful review would probably be limited in practice to procedural impropriety, or flagrant substantive misuse of power.

An EMEA authorisation is compulsory for products derived from biotechnology (Part A products), and is optional for other innovative (Part B) products.[67] In general, the number of centralised marketing authorisations (compulsory and optional) has grown steadily since 1995. By 2000, 122 medicinal products had received authorisation through the centralised procedure. The numbers of applications in the year 2000 were 54; in 2001, 58; but in 2002, dropped to 31.[68] This appears to be a reflection of a global downturn in innovation in the pharmaceutical industry, the reasons for which are not entirely clear.

The EMEA is responsible for the centralised procedure for authorisation. The undertaking seeking marketing authorisation for a new product that falls within the scope of Article 3 (1) or (2) makes its application for marketing authorisation directly to the EMEA. The application is assigned to a rapporteur designated by the CPMP. The rapporteur prepares a draft report, which is circulated to the CPMP members. Discussion may take place between the CPMP and the applicant. The CPMP is required to give an opinion within 210 days of receipt of the application.[69] The EMEA must then forward its decision to the Commission within 30 days. The second stage of the procedure culminates in a Commission decision.[70] The Pharmaceutical Unit within the Commission ensures that the authorisation complies with EU law. Consultation takes place with other DGs. The Commission must prepare a draft decision within 30 days. This draft decision is then sent to the Standing Committee

66 OJ 1987 L 15/38.

67 Regulation 2309/93/EC, Article 3 (1) and (2). These provisions supersede the earlier Directive 87/22/EEC under which producers of certain products derived from biotechnology and high-technology were granted a 10-year exclusive entitlement to market the product in the EU, in accordance with a procedure imposing obligations of consultation on national authorities. See Sauer, above n 19, p 135; P. Taylor, "Europe Without Frontiers? Balancing Pharmaceutical Interests" in E.M. Normand and P. Vaughan, eds, *Europe Without Frontiers: The Implications for Health* (London: Wiley, 1993), pp 283–294, at p 285; Gardner, above n 14, at 54; Thompson, above n 25, pp 81–88.

68 See EMEA Annual Report 2002, http://www.emea.eu.int/pdfs/general/direct/emeaar/005502en.pdf.

69 Regulation 2309/93/EC, Article 6 (4).

70 Regulation 2309/93/EC, Article 10.

on Medicinal Products for Human Use for its opinion. If the opinion is favourable, the Commission (DG Enterprise and the Information Society) takes a final decision authorising the marketing of the new product.

A product licence granted under the centralised procedure is valid in all Member States, and the product is entered on the Community Register of Medicinal Products.[71] Authorisations are valid for five years, and are renewable on application and presentation to the EMEA of an up-to-date dossier containing "pharmacovigilance" information.[72] Thompson notes that the path towards the centralised procedure has consisted of extremely tentative steps, but nevertheless has consisted in movement in a consistent direction, towards reallocating competence to grant marketing authorisation for pharmaceuticals to the EU institutions.

The centralised procedure: assessment

The centralised procedure, using the EMEA, for pharmaceuticals marketing authorisation in the EU, represents a significant development in the regulatory structures within the EU. The possibility of gaining a single EU-wide marketing authorisation removes significant bureaucratic pressures from manufacturers. The EU's proprietorial pharmaceutical industry, operating on a global basis, has long argued for speedier marketing authorisation approvals, as a shorter time to approval means a quicker return on (significant) investment in a new pharmaceutical product.[73] Access to several markets at once, made possible under the centralised procedure, speeds up the process and reduces costs. It also, at least potentially, lightens the burden on national administrative structures, thus allowing efficiency savings to be made there. Under the centralised procedure, the detailed information needed to secure a marketing authorisation for a new pharmaceutical product needs to be presented and assessed only once. The EU regulations also place time constraints on the administrative structures, thus speeding up the time it takes to bring new products onto the market. This is seen as being beneficial both to the industry and to patients (consumers).

However, the price to be paid under the centralised system is a loss of control over the process at national level, in terms of both the speed at which assessments of new pharmaceuticals are conducted, and the ultimate rejection of a product if it does not meet a nationally determined risk assessment.[74] Indeed, the very notion of a *nationally determined* risk assessment is a casualty of the centralised system. This may leave the outcome of risk assessments vulnerable to regulatory capture by actors privileged by the EU-level processes. A number of commentators have expressed concerns that the lack of transparency in the EMEA's systems may lead to undue influence on the part of the pharmaceutical industry, at the expense of

71 Regulation 2309/93/EC, Article 12.
72 Regulation 2309/93/EC, Article 13.
73 Abraham and Lewis, above n 4, p 81.
74 Abraham and Lewis, above n 4, p 87.

the interests of consumers/patients and of national health care systems.[75] Although the EMEA operates a relatively user-friendly website,[76] the content of the website, in particular the "Summaries of Product Characteristics" for new pharmaceuticals, and the "European Public Assessment Reports" (detailed assessment of new applications), has been criticised for being opaque.[77] Moreover, no information is currently given on negative authorisation decisions, or on those products where the application is withdrawn before a negative decision has been taken. Thus, patients are unable to compare information on successful and unsuccessful new pharmaceutical products. As we will see below, proposals for reform of the EU's legislation include an obligation to publicise withdrawals, and there is also a proposed obligation to publish information on refusals or negative opinions on applications for marketing authorisations.[78]

A more fundamental criticism is that the system itself, emanating from DG Enterprise and centrally concerned with the single market in pharmaceuticals (a matter of Community regulatory competence), but only peripherally concerned with protection of health (a matter from which Community regulatory competence is expressly excluded by the Treaty), tends to favour the interests of the industry over those of patients or national health services. For instance, it is claimed that the EMEA over-emphasises time-to-market for new pharmaceuticals, at the expense of protecting public health.[79] Manufacturers are given information at early stages of the assessment of their new products, which allows them to withdraw an application,[80] or to prepare an appeal to a preliminary negative decision.

The decentralised procedure: assessment

The decentralised procedure, which has been mandatory in the EU since 1998 for all pharmaceuticals (save those to which the centralised procedure applies, homeopathics, products intended to be marketed only in one Member State (relatively few) and generics), also represents a significant development of the EU regulatory structures. In theory, the major change from the earlier multi-state procedure is that differences of opinion in terms of the appropriate risk assessment (framed as assessment of "quality, safety and efficacy") now *must* be resolved at EU level, in the CPMP. There is a conciliation procedure and an arbitration procedure, whereby concerns raised by a Member State wishing to reject an authorisation granted by the Reference Member State are to be resolved. The other significant difference is the imposition of time-frames for action. Whether the time-frames set out in

75 Mossialos and Abel-Smith, in Stavridis et al, eds, above n 25; Abraham and Lewis, above n 4, chapter 7; Abraham, above n 33.

76 http://www.eudra.org/.

77 See the view of the International Society of Drug Bulletins, cited in E. Mossialos and M. McKee, *EU Law and the Social Character of Health Care* (Brussels: PIE Peter Lang, 2002), p 114.

78 It appears that this element of the proposed reform emanated from the European Parliament: see COM(2002) 735 final.

79 Mossialos and McKee, above n 77, pp 113–114.

80 See further below.

the EU legislation are directly effective or not is probably of less significance than the fact that, as national agencies are now competing for "business" (in the form of industry fees), there is intense pressure on them to meet the requirements of the legislation.[81] Abraham and Lewis point to substantial evidence to suggest that national authorities have reduced their assessment times in order to conform with the EU standards.

There are two problems with decentralised procedures. If they leave a great deal of discretion to the Member States, as did the early "multi-state" procedure, then the aim of creating a single market in pharmaceuticals is effectively compromised, and any benefits of such a single market (to the industry, and ultimately to patients as consumers) may not be reaped. Moreover, a system where mutual recognition of national authorisations is compulsory runs the risk that the least demanding regulatory regime sets the standards. Such a "race to the bottom" is not appropriate for products such as pharmaceuticals, where the risks to human life and health are fundamental if regulatory mechanisms are not properly applied and enforced.

Consideration of how the authorisation processes have operated in practice reveals further problems. The decentralised procedure is criticised for representing the interests of the pharmaceutical industry rather than those of patients (consumers). For instance, a company may withdraw, or partially withdraw, an application at any time during the procedure.[82] A company may withdraw from seeking authorisation in a "Concerned Member State" perceived to be "tough" on a particular application. This has the effect of removing that Member State's agencies from discussion of the product's "summary of product characteristics" and any subsequent CPMP deliberations. Unless the remaining Member States are put on guard by such a partial withdrawal of a request for marketing authorisation, the system allows pharmaceutical companies to "cherry pick" regulatory assessment, with the possible risk that "weaker" Member States may be favoured, in particular as "Reference Member States", with corresponding concerns that a full discussion of the product's risks and benefits will have been avoided, to the detriment of patients.[83] More seriously, Abraham and Lewis suggest that the decentralised procedure has effectively suppressed scientific disputes about the benefits and risks of new pharmaceutical products, and the proper assessment of research findings, in the name of "efficiency" in bringing about speedier, harmonised marketing authorisations applicable across the EU.[84] National agencies, reliant on industry fees, compete to be chosen as the "Reference Member State" under the decentralised procedure. As Abraham has noted, in several EU Member States, such as Germany, Sweden and the UK, the restructuring of the pharmaceuticals authorisation process took place in response to the demands of industry.[85] Faster agencies are more popular with

81 Abraham and Lewis, above n 4, p 89; Abraham, above n 33.
82 Except if it has reached arbitration stage.
83 Abraham and Lewis, above n 4, pp 90–92; Abraham, above n 33.
84 Abraham and Lewis, above n 4, pp 95–97.
85 Abraham, above n 33.

industry;[86] the benefits to patients of slower, more painstaking, product assessment are not factored into the system.[87] There are also concerns that pharmaceuticals regulation is driven from a "trade-orientated" (DG Internal Market), rather than health-orientated (DG Health and Consumer Protection), Directorate General of the Commission.[88]

Finally, it is clear that, in practice, the interests of Member States in terms of the burdens potentially imposed on their national health (insurance) services by the granting of a marketing authorisation to a new pharmaceutical product may also be factored into the process. Under the decentralised procedure, the CPMP opinion is translated into a draft Decision by the Commission, and this is adopted by the Standing Committee of (non-scientific) representatives of the Member States. Failing agreement in the Standing Committee, the matter is referred to the Council of Ministers. Technically speaking, neither the Standing Committee nor the Council is supposed to interfere in "scientific" assessment. However, it is clear that even where the CPMP opinion is favourable, this does not necessarily result in a situation where the new product is available EU-wide on the same terms. For instance, in the case of Schering's multiple sclerosis drug Betaferon (beta-interferon), the UK, wishing to avoid "excessive" prescribing of the new product, not because of any concerns over "quality, safety or efficacy", but because of cost considerations, originally issued guidelines restricting prescriptions to specialists. Other Member States, such as Germany, permitted Betaferon to be advertised to all doctors, not just specialist clinicians.[89]

One possible solution to some of these problems would be a centralised EU-level system of marketing authorisation for all medicinal products. Although this would involve significant reallocation of competence from an area traditionally the responsibility of the governments of the Member States, it would seem reasonable to suppose that the general, if very gradual, trend towards such a system will continue. However, it seems likely that the governments of the Member States will continue to exert control over the EU-level regulation, through comitology procedures and other mechanisms. Thus the regulation of pharmaceuticals in the EU will continue to be characterised by these institutions of "multi-level governance", and interactions between them.

Authorisation of manufacture

As with the marketing of medicinal products, it is also unlawful, as a matter of EU law, to manufacture medicinal products within the EU without appropriate

86 Abraham, above n 33.

87 There are proposed new transparency rules on withdrawal, see below, but these can only go part of the way towards alleviating this problem.

88 S. Garattini and V. Bertele, "Adjusting Europe's drug regulation to public health needs" 358 *Lancet* (2001) 64.

89 See Abraham and Lewis, above n 4, pp 117–118. Abraham and Lewis also cite the example of Rhone-Poulenc Rorer's anti-cancer drug "Taxotese".

authorisation. This principle of EU law was established by Directive 75/319/EEC, Article 16.[90] Member States must take all measures to ensure that the manufacture of medicinal products is subject to the holding of an authorisation. Authorisation is required for all activities involved in the manufacture of pharmaceuticals: for both total and partial manufacture, and for the various processes of dividing up, packaging or presentation.[91] However, preparation of pharmaceuticals by pharmacists in dispensing pharmacies and other persons authorised by national authorities to carry out such processes is not covered. The EU rules apply to industrial processes leading to mass-produced uniform products, not to the performance of medical professionals in the treatment of individual patients.[92] For the EU to regulate such matters would be an unlawful incursion into a matter of national law, and would breach the principle of subsidiarity.[93]

Manufacturing authorisation is to be granted by national authorities. Directive 2001/83/EC, Article 41 sets out the requirements that must be met by an applicant seeking manufacturing authorisation. These are that the medicinal products to be manufactured, and the place in which they are to be manufactured, must be specified. The manufacturer must have at its disposal suitable premises, equipment and control facilities, and a "qualified person" within the meaning of Article 48. The requisite qualifications for such a person are set out in Article 49. They are: at least a university-level course for at least four years in pharmacy, medicine, veterinary medicine, chemistry, pharmaceutical chemistry and technology, or biology; and at least two years of practical experience in a relevant field.[94] The qualified person is responsible for checking each batch of product manufactured to ensure compliance with national laws and the requirements of the marketing authorisation.[95] These provisions are an example of "old style" harmonisation.

The Commission has enacted detailed rules in Directive 91/356/EEC[96] laying down the principles and guidelines of good manufacturing practice for medicinal products for human use, and has produced a "Guide to good manufacturing practice for medicinal products", a provision of "soft law". These measures are intended to provide "a common agreed basis throughout the [EU] for maintaining good manufacturing practices in the pharmaceutical industry". Good manufacturing practices apply in respect of quality management, personnel, premises and equipment, documentation, production, quality control, contracted-out work, complaints and product recall, and self-inspection.[97] The effect of these rules is a complex regulatory

90 Now see Directive 2001/83/EC, Article 40.

91 Directive 75/319/EEC, Article 16 (2); now see Directive 2001/83/EC, Article 40 (2).

92 Thompson, above n 25, p 157.

93 See chapters 2 and 3.

94 Provision is made for university courses lasting three and a half years, followed by at least one year of practical training. The duration of practical experience may be reduced by one year where the university course lasts at least five years, and by 18 months where the university course lasts at least six years.

95 Directive 2001/83/EC, Article 51.

96 OJ 1991 L 193/30.

97 Directive 91/356/EEC, preamble, Recital 6, Articles 6–14.

regime, enforced by national authorities and by self-regulation by the pharmaceuticals manufacturers themselves.

Pharmacovigilance

Pharmacovigilance involves the communication of information by consumers, pharmacists, doctors, and the pharmaceutical industry to regulatory authorities. As we saw in the context of the approval of clinical trials upon medicinal products in chapter 7, it forms part of the supervisory process, under which medicinal products authorised for manufacture and marketing within the EU are kept under surveillance, for any risks coming to light through the use of the relevant products over time.

Member States are required by EU law to establish a pharmacovigilance system, in order to ensure the adoption of appropriate regulatory decisions concerning authorised medicinal products, having regard to information obtained about adverse reactions to medicinal products under normal conditions of use.[98] Member States are obliged to set up a system for the collection and collation of information on matters such as adverse reactions to medicinal products, consumption, and frequently observed misuse and serious abuse of such products. Directive 2001/83/EC defines three types of adverse reaction about which information is to be collected: "adverse reaction", "serious adverse reaction", and "unexpected adverse reaction". An unexpected adverse reaction is defined as one the nature, severity or outcome of which is not consistent with the summary product characteristics,[99] which are a key part of the authorisation process. This illustrates the interrelationship between original authorisation and pharmacovigilance. The regulatory authorities are required to compare the information contained in the summary with the information that has come to light in the observation of the product actually in use.

The EMEA, in cooperation with national competent authorities, is given a significant role in the process of pharmacovigilance.[100] This is a process which, in accordance with the principle of subsidiarity, is better done at EU, rather than national, level.[101] The CPMP is required to give opinions in situations where the marketing of a medicinal product originally authorised in more than one Member State is suspended in one of those Member States, due to information coming to light through pharmacovigilance procedures. The Commission Report on the Operation of the CPMP gives some examples of cases where this has happened.[102] For instance, the UK suspended its authorisation of Halcion (triazolam), followed by a reference

98 Directive 75/319/EEC, Article 29a, added by Directive 93/39/EC, Article 2. Now repealed and replaced by Directive 2001/83/EC, Article 102.

99 Directive 2001/83/EC, Article 1 (13).

100 See Regulation 2309/93/EC, Articles 19–26 which impose obligations on the person responsible for placing authorised medical products on the market to notify the EMEA of any serious adverse reactions to the product. Regulation 540/95/EC, OJ 1995 L 55/5 imposes similar obligations in respect of non-serious adverse reactions.

101 Gardner, above n 14, at 58.

102 Commission, *The Operation of the CPMP* SEC(93) 991, pp 44–47.

to the CPMP by France and the Netherlands. In another case, involving Glafenine, a reference to the CPMP by Belgium led ultimately to the withdrawal of the product or the withdrawal or suspension of authorisation in all those Member States where the product had previously been marketed.[103]

For products authorised under the centralised procedure, the EMEA is required to carry out pharmacovigilance. Information is to be conveyed to the EMEA by pharmaceutical companies ("the person responsible for placing the medicinal product on the market") and competent national authorities.[104] Member States are under a duty to ensure that all suspected serious adverse reactions occurring within their territory, with respect to medicinal products authorised by the centralised procedure, are recorded and reported immediately to the EMEA.[105] The EMEA then informs all the authorities of other national pharmacovigilance systems.

Where the "interests of the Community" are concerned, a Member State, the Commission, or a pharmaceutical company may refer a pharmacovigilance matter to the CPMP. This would be appropriate where, for example, there is a potential serious public health risk from a product, or where there are significant differences in approaches taken by different Member States. The CPMP refers the matter to its Pharmacovigilance Working Party, which provides a regulatory forum for EU-wide discussion and coordination of pharmacovigilance matters. The CPMP then advises the Commission, whose final decision is binding on all Member States in which the product is marketed.[106]

The institutions of the EU utilise electronic communications methods in order to ensure speedy and accurate information exchange on pharmacovigilance matters, and other matters related to the authorisation of medicinal products. This takes place through the "EUDRA" projects, run by the Commission's Pharmaceutical Unit.[107] The "EudraWatch" service for the electronic transmission and management of pharmacovigilance reports aims to ensure that pharmacovigilance data becomes an integral part of the marketing authorisation dossier, which must be updated with any application to renew the authorisation. The EU and WHO, working jointly, have developed a complete computer assisted system for the entire authorisation, renewal, follow-up and inspection process. This system – "SIAMED 2000" – is available, free of charge, to national competent authorities in the Member States, and beyond, in particular in Central and Eastern European accession and candidate states.

Criticisms have been made of the EU's pharmacovigilance system. In particular, the need to resolve pharmacovigilance concerns at EU level may be seen to be slower than desirable from the point of view of patients. For instance, as noted

103 Thompson, above n 25, p 187, n 3.
104 Regulation 2309/93/EC, Article 20.
105 Regulation 2309/93/EC, Article 23.
106 Commission, Pharmaceuticals and Cosmetics Unit, *Pharmaceuticals in the EU* (Brussels: European Commission, 2000) pp 17–18.
107 http://eudravigilance.org.

above, the UK withdrew the sleeping pill Halcion from the British market in 1991, on the grounds that the risk of serious adverse psychiatric reactions outweighed any potential benefits. Shortly thereafter, the chair of the CPMP wrote to all the other relevant national regulatory authorities, requesting them not to withdraw Halcion until the CPMP had deliberated. The CPMP set up a working party to examine the product, but, crucially, did not withdraw the product from the EU market while the investigation was under way. From the point of view of patients, this procedure extended the period during which they were exposed to a potentially dangerous pharmaceutical product.[108]

Labelling and packaging

Incorrect use of pharmaceuticals can have drastic and harmful effects. Concerns to ensure that the correct information is given to ensure safety were behind EU regulation with regard to the information that must be presented on the labelling and packaging material for medicinal products. This was originally covered by Directive 92/27/EEC,[109] a measure of EU internal market law, designed to remove the impediments to free trade within the EU imposed by different national regulations on the labelling and packaging of medicinal products. The provision formed part of the 1992 programme on completing the internal market, and replaced earlier piecemeal provisions in Directive 65/65/EEC and Directive 75/319/EEC. Its aim was to harmonise consumer protection standards within the EU, and to leave no discretion to Member States to impose different standards, even if those would imply greater protection for consumers or for public health. It thus resembles a measure of "old style" harmonisation.

Whilst the labelling of medicinal products can be seen as a risk avoidance measure, safeguarding patients from the risk of side-effects, another approach is to view the labelling process in terms of consumer choice and of patients' rights. With the increasing availability of over-the-counter medicines, the patient is faced with an ever-widening choice of products which may be directly purchased or which may be purchased under the supervision of the pharmacist.[110] On an increasing number of occasions, the information provided to the patient, in the form of leaflets and packaging, will constitute the only information which that patient obtains about that product. Information leaflets can be seen as a method of facilitating patient choice, in that patients themselves are able to weigh up the prospect of risks and side-effects of particular products. But this may only operate as an effective means of disseminating information in a few cases. In the vast majority of cases, individuals are still unlikely to be in a position to undertake an in-depth consideration of the drugs offered to treat a particular illness. It will only realistically be in the case of

108 Abraham and Lewis, above n 4, p 148.

109 Now repealed and replaced by Directive 2001/83/EC.

110 However, in practice, the extent to which the pharmacist does prove to be an effective gatekeeper in the context of over-the-counter medicines has been questioned: see D. Prayle and M. Brazier, "Supply of medicines: paternalism, autonomy and reality" 24 *Journal of Medical Ethics* (1998) 93.

long-standing conditions (such as asthma or arthritis) in which the patient will have a genuine chance to review the range of treatments on offer, and perhaps search more broadly for the information which may be available. In such cases, the information leaflet may be seen as one component in a patient's broader search for relevant information.

Even in the context of medicines prescribed by health professionals, information leaflets may lead patients as consumers to make a more informed choice. As we have noted in chapters 1 and 7, the precise boundaries of consent to treatment remain an issue that is currently left to Member States. However, this is an instance of a situation in which EU involvement may have a powerful indirect effect upon the clinical encounter. Patients may decide to reject the pharmaceuticals provided, if they are unhappy with the potential risks of the drug, according to the information contained in the leaflet. Enhanced consumer information may lead to a diminished willingness to trust in the health care professional's expertise. However, as with over-the-counter and pharmacy medicines, in practice such patient involvement is likely to have only a sporadic effect upon the use of such medicinal products. Currently, EU law requires public access only to the name of the holder of the marketing authorisation and its number. If, instead, public access were given to the detailed marketing authorisation files, including opposing scientific opinions, these might be accessed by individual patients (consumers) and also by campaigning groups, who might put increased information into the public domain about particular pharmaceutical products. In those circumstances, EU law might have a greater impact.[111]

The labelling of medicinal products, their packaging, and the leaflets inserted in such packaging are currently covered by Directive 2001/83/EC. Articles 54 to 57 cover the labelling requirements, by specifying mandatory information that must be included on the packaging, about matters such as the active ingredients, method and route of administration. They also require a warning to keep the product out of the reach of children, an expiry date, any special storage precautions, the name of the holder of the marketing authorisation and the number of the marketing authorisation.[112] Article 63 (1) requires that particulars are to be given in the official language or languages of the Member State where the product is placed on the market. This is, of course, a serious impediment to a true single market in pharmaceuticals. Nothing prevents the indication of the particulars in several languages, but physical space on the packaging would preclude more than one or two languages being used. As Thompson points out, in terms of finished pharmaceutical products, only blister packs placed within outer packaging could, therefore, be marketable in each Member State. Even in that case, the blister packs would have to be placed within outer packaging with information in the official language of each Member State.[113]

111 See above n 75–78.
112 Directive 2001/83/EC, Article 54.
113 Thompson, above n 25, p 217.

Given the consumer safety precautions that must be taken with this information, it is difficult to envisage any other solution.

Package leaflets are covered by Directive 2001/83/EC, Articles 58–60. Package leaflets are to be drawn up in accordance with the summary of product characteristics, which is part of the marketing authorisation application. Again, various categories of information are explicitly required. A list of information necessary before taking the pharmaceutical must be included. This covers contra-indications, precautions for use and interactions with other medicinal products and alcohol, tobacco and foodstuffs. A description of side-effects – defined as "undesirable effects which can occur under normal use of the medicinal product"[114] – must be included. There is, of course, no requirement to carry information on alternative forms of treatment or alternative products.

Leaflets do not carry the same constraints of space that apply to packaging itself. It would be significantly cheaper for the pharmaceutical industry to exploit the economies of scale implied by a single European market by inserting different language version leaflets into identically labelled finished packages. This would suggest that the best regulatory approach would be to provide for a bare minimum of information on the package label itself, but to require a leaflet in the appropriate language or languages before marketing in a particular area of the EU. However, the institutions of the EU have not so far adopted that approach. This is presumably because of concerns that leaflets are not physically attached to the product until the moment of administration, unlike the immediate packaging of the product, and therefore there is scope for producer or consumer error. Further, consumers may pay significantly less attention to the information on a leaflet than that displayed on the packaging itself. Also, even if the leaflet approach were to be adopted, no single national authority would be able to approve a leaflet in all the languages of the EU. It is not simply a question of translation, since national authorities retain discretion as to the summary of product characteristics and the information to be included in a leaflet.[115]

Advertisement

The ability of patients and consumers to access information regarding drugs can be seen as being potentially facilitated through the advertising of such products. Indeed, one survey in the US suggested that as many as one in five Americans called or visited their doctor as a consequence of drug advertisement.[116] Whilst the availability of information regarding pharmaceutical products may facilitate enhanced choice, at the same time there is a risk that advertisements may be misleading or positively harmful, if they lead to inappropriate use of medicinal products. The advertising of

114 Directive 2001/83/EC, Article 59 (1) (e).

115 Thompson, above n 25, p 223.

116 S. Gottlieb, "A fifth of Americans contact their doctor as a result of drug advertising" 325 BMJ (2002) 854.

pharmaceuticals in the EU was originally regulated by Directive 92/28/EEC.[117] As an internal market measure, this was centrally concerned with removing barriers to trade. The Directive fits within broader EU internal market provisions regulating advertising, such as Directive 84/450/EEC[118] on misleading advertising and Directive 89/552/EEC,[119] the "TV without frontiers" directive, which explicitly prohibits television advertising for medicinal products and medical treatment available only on prescription in the Member State within whose jurisdiction the broadcaster falls.[120] Only medicines for which a marketing authorisation has been granted may be advertised within the EU.[121]

Directive 2001/83/EC distinguishes between over-the-counter products, most of which may be advertised to the general public, and prescription-only products, which may be advertised only to health professionals. Article 88 provides that Member States shall prohibit the advertising to the general public of medicinal products available on prescription only, certain psychotropic or narcotic substances, and the mentioning in advertising of certain therapeutic indications, such as sexually transmitted diseases, cancer, diabetes and other metabolic illnesses. It appears that this latter provision is probably to prevent serious personal disadvantages for patients in having it widely known that a particular product is used to treat the conditions specified.[122] Member States are also permitted to prohibit advertising of reimbursable medicinal products to the general public.[123] This allows Member States to pursue cost containment policies within their national health (insurance) systems. A central element of national regulation of advertisement of pharmaceuticals is that of "gatekeeping". Widespread "direct-to-consumer" advertisement of pharmaceuticals is likely to lead to increased pressures on national health (insurance) systems. To some extent, the Directive takes account of this "gatekeeping" role.

At present, however, the Directive does not provide for prohibitions with respect to direct-to-consumer advertising that does not fall within the categories above, but may be regarded as undesirable for other policy reasons. For instance, some Member States, such as the Netherlands, have considered a ban on direct-to-consumer advertisement and sales of genetic testing kits.[124] This is because of the concerns of direct consumer access to such information without the provision of genetic counselling about the revelations which may result from such tests, which may be very damaging to individuals. Presumably such a restriction on the free movement of goods would be justifiable on grounds of public policy.[125]

117 OJ 1992 L 113/13. Now repealed and replaced by Directive 2001/83/EC.
118 OJ 1984 L 250/17.
119 OJ 1989 L 298/23.
120 Directive 89/552/EEC, Article 14.
121 Directive 2001/83/EC, Article 87.
122 See Thompson, above n 25, pp 236, 222–223.
123 Article 88 (3).
124 Human Genetics Commission, *Genes Direct* (London: HGC, 2003).
125 See chapter 2, and below.

Advertising must make it clear that it is for a medicinal product.[126] Certain misleading, or potentially misleading, material is prohibited by Article 90. This includes material which suggests that the effects of taking the medicine are guaranteed, or suggests that the health of the subject could be affected by not taking the medicine,[127] is directed at children, could lead to erroneous self-diagnosis, or suggests that the safety or efficacy of the product is due to the fact that it is "natural".

Although the provisions of Directive 2001/83/EC thus restrict the freedom of the pharmaceuticals industry to advertise directly to consumers, it is unlikely that this is in conflict with the right to freedom of expression, a "general principle" of EU law, now incorporated in the EU Charter of Fundamental Rights and Freedoms 2000 (EUCFR), Article 11. As the Explanations relating to the complete text of the Charter explain, Article 11 EUCFR corresponds to Article 10 ECHR. This latter provision expressly states that the freedom of expression may be subject to "such formalities, conditions, restrictions, or penalties as are prescribed by law and are necessary in a democratic society", in the interests, *inter alia*, of the protection of health. Pursuant to Article 52 (3) EUCFR, the meaning and the scope of Article 11 EUCFR are the same as those guaranteed by Article 10 ECHR.

Directive 2001/83/EC also covers advertising to medical professionals, defined as "persons qualified to prescribe or supply" medicinal products.[128] Specific rules govern matters such as sales promotions,[129] hospitality,[130] and provision of free samples.[131] The general principle governing such inducements to health professionals is that they must be inexpensive and relevant to the practice of medicine or pharmacy.[132] However, Article 94 (4) makes an important exception for "existing measures or trade practices in Member States relating to prices, margins and discounts". The provision in Article 94 (4) protects special measures aimed at pharmacists, in particular, who are both health professionals and retailers. A wide variety of schemes and systems exist within the Member States concerning price control of pharmaceuticals and reimbursement for medicinal products from national social insurance schemes. These schemes reflect the special nature of the pharmaceuticals "market", in which the final consumer rarely, if ever, pays the true cost of the product. Some elements of these schemes concern advertising and, without Article 94 (4), Member States would have been prohibited by the Directive from continuing to use such measures as part of their cost containment policies. Article 94 (4) removes such provisions from the scope of Directive 2001/83/EC.[133] Here, then, the Directive leaves the "gatekeeping" element of regulation of advertisement of pharmaceuticals entirely to the national level, and there is no real attempt at harmonisation at EU level.

126 Article 89 (1).
127 An explicit exemption applies to national vaccination campaigns (Article 88 (4)).
128 Article 91 (1).
129 Article 94.
130 Article 95.
131 Article 96.
132 Article 94 (1).
133 Thompson, above n 25, p 242.

The provisions of Directive 2001/83/EC prohibiting "direct to consumer" advertising of pharmaceuticals may be undermined by the use of the internet to advertise pharmaceuticals. Although the EU lags a long way behind the US in this respect, various websites carry health information and advertise pharmaceuticals available in the EU. There are significant concerns about the quality of information available on such sites.[134] One particular issue is that many sites are sponsored by pharmaceuticals manufacturers, who may use health information sites to promote their products. The EU appears to be responding slowly to the regulatory challenges posed by the advertising of pharmaceuticals and provision of health information on the internet. The e-Europe 2005 Action Plan stated that "it is critical that e-health content and services are developed efficiently, are available for all and health related web sites comply with established quality criteria".[135] The Commission has set out a series of criteria for health related websites which are to be applied in addition to any relevant Community law.[136] These include transparency and honesty, authority, privacy and data protection, the updating of information, accountability and accessibility. The challenge of *implementation* of any EU or national level regulation of the internet is likely to prove significant in the future. We return to the issue of the internet and health care delivery in chapter 10.

Product liability

As noted above, defects in pharmaceuticals can lead to grave injury and death, as illustrated by Thalidomide.[137] While individuals harmed by pharmaceuticals are able to bring actions in their national courts, under the applicable laws relating to civil liability, actually establishing such liability frequently presents major difficulties to the litigant. Whilst across Europe there is a growth in malpractice actions, this has not been accompanied by an equivalent rise in the successful number of claims.[138] This is linked to difficulties in establishing civil law liability. One alternative option for compensation is that of the introduction of no-fault compensation schemes. Although, in some EU Member States, provision has been made for no-fault compensation, for example, the UK's Vaccine Damage Payments Act 1979, such schemes are sporadic.[139] One alternative approach was that of the introduction of strict

134 Mossialos and McKee, above n 77, pp 133–134.

135 E-Europe Action Plan, COM(2002) 263 final, adopted by the Commission on 28 May 2002, supported by the European Council in Sevilla, 21–22 June 2002.

136 Communication from the Commission to the Council, the European Parliament, the Economic and Social Committee and the Committee of the Regions, *eEurope 2002: Quality Criteria for Health Related Websites*, Brussels, 29 November 2002, COM(2002) 667 final.

137 G. Howells and T. Wilhelmsson, *EC Consumer Law* (Aldershot: Ashgate, 1997), p 33.

138 See, for example, the contributions to the special edition (2003) 2 *European Journal of Health Law*; for further extensive consideration of the scope of liability in medical negligence in the UK context, see M. Jones, *Medical Negligence* (London: Sweet and Maxwell, 2003).

139 The rationale for special protection in the context of vaccine damage in the UK, as stated by the Pearson Commission, was that of public policy to compensate for injury in a situation in which the state itself supported vaccination, see Pearson Commission, Report of the Royal Commission on the Civil Liability and Compensation for Personal Injury (Cmnd 7054-1, 1978), chapter 25. Thus Pearson, whilst rejecting a general no-fault scheme for medical compensation, was of the view that this was necessary in relation to vaccine damage. See also Sweden, where there has been

liability. When this was initially broached at EU level, national governments argued that to adopt a strict liability standard would place their companies at a competitive disadvantage in the single market. EU-level harmonisation, setting high consumer protection standards, guards against such a potential "race to the bottom".[140] This may help to explain why a strict liability approach was ultimately followed. The Product Liability Directive 85/374/EEC[141] gives consumers the right to compensation for defective products on a strict liability basis.[142] The Directive is an internal market measure, based on Article 100 (now 94) EC. Its aim is said to be to approximate national laws in the Member States on the liability of producers for damage caused by the defectiveness of their products. Otherwise, divergences in such laws may distort competition and affect the free movement of goods within the EU.[143] The term "product" in Directive 85/374/EEC includes medicinal products.[144]

Directive 85/374/EEC adopts a "strict liability" approach, according to which producers[145] are liable for damage caused by defects in their product, irrespective of negligence or culpability. This approach was chosen on the grounds that it is the only means of solving the problem of a fair apportionment of risks between consumers and producers (and, presumably, their insurers) in an age of increasing technological change.[146] A product is defined as defective when it does not provide the safety which a consumer is entitled to expect, taking into account the presentation of the product, its reasonable uses and the time it was put into circulation.[147]

However, the scope of the strict liability of producers for defects in their products is reduced, potentially significantly, by an optional measure in Directive 85/374/EEC, known as the "development risks defence". This was included after pressure from the UK Conservative government, led by Margaret Thatcher, to safeguard the interests of producers, and it was only when this was included that the UK

a patient insurance scheme, a no-fault scheme based on rules of assessment for tort damages. See generally S. McLean, "Can No-Fault Analysis Ease the Problems of Medical Injury Litigation?" and M. Brazier, "The Case for a No-Fault Scheme for Medical Accidents" in S. McLean, ed, *Compensation for Damage: An International Perspective* (Aldershot: Dartmouth, 1993).

140 See discussion in chapter 2.

141 OJ 1985 L 210/29, legal basis, Article 100 EEC.

142 Directive 85/374/EEC, Article 1.

143 Directive 85/374/EEC, preamble, Recital 5. There is some doubt as to whether such differences in national laws do in fact distort competition in this way, suggesting that the consumer protection motivations form a more realistic rationale for the measure. See Howells and Wilhelmsson, above n 137, p 34.

144 Directive 85/374/EEC, Article 2, as amended by Directive 99/34/EC, Article 1, OJ 1999 L 141/20: " 'Product' means all movables even if incorporated into another movable or into an immovable. 'Product' includes electricity."

145 The term "producer" is broadly defined, to include the manufacturer of a finished product, the producer of any raw material or the manufacturer of a component part and any person who, by putting his name, trademark, or other distinguishing feature on the product, presents himself as the producer. Persons who import products into the Community for sale, hire, leasing or distribution are also deemed to be "producers" for the purposes of the Directive: Article 3 (1) and (2). On the application of the Directive in the context of an organ transplant in a public hospital, see Case C-203/99 *Henning Veedfald v Århus Amtskommune* [2001] ECR I-3569.

146 Directive 85/374/EEC, preamble, Recital 6.

147 Directive 85/374/EEC, Article 6.

was prepared to agree to the Directive in Council.[148] If, at the time of manufacture of the product, the state of scientific and technical knowledge was such that the risk of harm was not foreseeable, the producer will not be liable under the Directive.[149] Member States were given the option to retain the development risks defence in their national law implementing the Directive.[150] Most Member States have kept the defence, with the exception of Luxembourg and Finland. In Germany, the defence is not applicable to pharmaceuticals. This is related to the fact that there is a strict liability scheme under the German Pharmaceuticals Act 1976,[151] which provides for liability in respect of developmental risks. In Spain, the defence does not apply in the case of food and medicinal products,[152] and in France it does not apply to products derived from the human body following the controversy relating to contaminated blood.[153] All of the accession states have also adopted the development risks defence.[154]

The Commission took the view that the development risks defence should be defined according to a narrow test. This was shown by its position in a challenge to the UK legislation implementing the Product Liability Directive, brought under Article 169 (now 226) EC.[155] The UK Consumer Protection Act 1987 provides that it is a defence to show "that the state of scientific and technical knowledge at the relevant time was not such that a producer of products of the same description as the product in question might be expected to have discovered the defect if it had existed in his products while they were under his control".[156] This includes the concept of discoverability of the risk, which, in the opinion of the Commission, was broader than the test required by the Directive, which merely concerned the objective state of knowledge of the risk at the relevant time.

The Court did not agree. Following the opinion of its Advocate General,[157] the Court noted that the concept of the relevant scientific and technical knowledge refers to such knowledge in general, not merely in the particular industry sector.[158]

148 See the discussion in R. Goldberg, "The development risk defence and the ECJ" in R. Goldberg and J. Lonbay, *Pharmaceutical Medicine, Biotechnology and European Law* (Cambridge: CUP, 2000), p 186.
149 Directive 85/374/EEC, Article 7 (e).
150 For general discussion see W.C. Hoffman and S. Hill-Arning, *Guide to Product Liability in Europe* (The Hague: Kluwer, 1994).
151 Goldberg, in Goldberg and Lonbay, eds, above n 148, p 194.
152 Goldberg has speculated that the Spanish approach can be related to a toxic syndrome involving cooking oil and to a number of defective drug incidents including MER 29 (a cholesterol reducing drug) which led to blindness, a child vaccine, "quadrigen", leading to brain inflammation and Thalidomide: Goldberg, in Goldberg and Lonbay, eds, above n 148, p 194.
153 Commission, *Green Paper on Liability for Defective Products* COM(99) 396 final, pp 34–35. On the blood scandal in France and other Member States, see further chapter 9.
154 COM(99) 396 final, p 36.
155 Case C-300/95 *Commission v UK (Product Liability Directive)* [1997] ECR I-2649.
156 Consumer Protection Act 1987, section 4(1)(e); and see C. Newdick, "The Development Risk Defence of the Consumer Protection Act 1987" 47 CLJ (1988) 455; Jones above n 138, chapter 8 "Defective Products", pp 664–682.
157 Case C-300/95 *Product Liability Directive* above n 155, AG Opinion, para 20.
158 Case C-300/95 *Product Liability Directive* above n 155, para 26.

However, the *accessibility* of this knowledge is implicit in the wording of the Directive.[159] Therefore the Court considered that the UK's implementing legislation was not contrary to the requirements of the Directive.[160]

The decision has been subject to considerable critical comment and discussion.[161] It has been suggested that, despite the fact that the test has been cast in terms of objectivity, in fact there is still a subjective element, in that the national court is left to ascertain, in relation to a particular case, whether a reasonable producer might have been expected to have discovered the defect.[162] Further, it has been suggested that the ambiguity of the relevant section of the UK Act[163] protected the UK against claims that it has not implemented the Directive correctly because such a "covert, paraphrased reasonableness standard is potentially misleading in its impact".[164] In practice, the availability of the development risks defence in most Member States of the EU has significantly reduced the relevance of the Product Liability Directive in the field of pharmaceuticals. In the case of medicinal products, risks either manifest themselves during the pre-clinical or clinical trial stage before marketing authorisation is granted or not until some years after, as in the case of side effects with a long latency period. Indeed, it has been suggested that the standard required under the Directive is so high that it may arguably never succeed.[165]

The Directive was considered subsequently by the UK courts in *A and Others v National Blood Authority and Another*, in relation to legislation regarding individuals infected with Hepatitis C, through blood transfusions which had used blood from infected donors.[166] Burton J. interpreted the UK Consumer Protection Act 1987 in the light of the Directive. He considered Article 6 of the Directive, which provides that a product is defective "when it does not provide the safety which a person is entitled to expect, taking all circumstances into account . . . ". Burton J. construed the words, "taking all circumstances into account" as being "all relevant circumstances". However, such circumstances did not include whether the defendant could have avoided the risk (the argument in the case put by the defendant). As Grubb comments:

> "He [the judge] was undoubtedly influenced by the fact that the Directive is intended to impose liability irrespective of fault. Strict liability focuses on the conduct of the product

159 Case C-300/95 *Product Liability Directive* above n 155, para 28.

160 For further comment, see Howells and Wilhelmsson, above n 137, pp 42–43; J. McHale and M. Fox, *Health Care Law: Text and Materials* (London: Sweet and Maxwell, 1997), pp 192–193; Newdick, above n 156; Goldberg, above n 148.

161 Goldberg above n 148; Newdick, above n 156.

162 Goldberg, above n 148, p 192.

163 UK Consumer Protection Act 1987, section 4.

164 Goldberg, above n 148, p 193.

165 See discussion in Goldberg, above n 148; and also J.S. Hodges, "Developmental Risks: Unanswered Questions" 61 MLR (1998) 560.

166 [2001] 3 All ER 289 and see discussion in Brazier, above n 7, pp 210–213; A. Grubb, "Consumer Protection Act 1987; Liability for Defective Products" 10 *Medical Law Review* (2002) 82; R. Goldberg, "Paying for Bad Blood: Strict Product Liability after the Hepatitis C Litigation" 10 *Medical Law Review* (2002) 165.

in question, whereas negligence is concerned with the conduct of the producer. If the conduct of the defendants (i.e. what could or should have been done to make the product safe) was to be regarded as a relevant circumstance then it would defeat the purpose of the Directive by letting fault in through the back door."[167]

Burton J. also drew a distinction between "standard" and "non-standard" products. He stated that:

> "Concluding whether the product is standard or non-standard will be done most easily by comparing the offending product with other products of the same type or series produced by that producer. If the respect in which it differs from the series includes the harmful characteristics then it is, for the purposes of Article 6, non-standard. If it does not differ or if the respect to which it differs does not include the harmful characteristic, but all the other products, albeit different, share the harmful characteristic, then it is to be treated as a standard product."

Where a case related to a standard product, then this would probably be due to a design defect. In this particular case, the blood bags which had been used were classed as being non-standard products. Here, Burton J. found that these were defective, as there was an expectation that blood used would be free from infection, and that this was not offset by any warnings or publicity. This approach has been queried by Goldberg, who comments that there are practical difficulties regarding the prospect of warning patients who are admitted to hospital and given blood in an emergency.[168]

The distinction drawn between standard and non-standard products in relation to Burton J.'s interpretation of Article 6 is relevant when we come to consider the discussion of Article 7 of the Directive in that case. On the issue of the interpretation of the development risk defence in Article 7(e), Burton J. considered whether a producer needed to establish either that the defect was not discoverable in that individual product in question, or whether it was the case that the defect could not be discovered in the "population of products". It was this latter approach which Burton J. followed, and which led to him finding the producers liable. In this case, there was a known risk because the risk of infection by Hepatitis C in blood transfusions was knowledge which had been available since the 1970s and, nonetheless, production had still continued. Burton J.'s consideration of Article 7 (e) has been criticised, on the basis that Article 7(e) concerns discoverability of the defect rather than of risk of the product.[169] Second, as Goldberg has noted, the judgment did not address public policy issues, something which might be regarded as crucial here. The Article 7(e) defence will still be applicable in relation to non-standard products but, it has been argued by Grubb, only if the problem is not known and this will be only in rare cases.[170] Goldberg goes further and comments that:

167 Grubb, above n 166, at 86–87.
168 Goldberg, above n 148, at 185.
169 See Goldberg, above n 148, at 191.
170 Grubb, above n 166, at 88.

> "The decision on Article 7(e) would seem to present grave concerns to the producers of innovative products with foreseeable adverse effects that remain undiscoverable, particularly in the pharmaceutical and health care sectors."[171]

It remains to be seen as to what extent the UK approach to the interpretation of these provisions in the Directive is mirrored across other Member States.

The Commission has considered reform of the Product Liability Directive, to include abolition of the development risk defence provision. In its Green Paper of 1999,[172] the Commission noted that the question was whether this would have very damaging consequences for the manufacturing and/or insurance sectors. The Commission is seeking further information on whether the removal of the defence would discourage producers from innovation, especially in sensitive sectors, in particular pharmaceuticals. The follow-up to the Green Paper[173] concluded that more information on how the Product Liability Directive functions at present was needed before the Commission would propose any amendment. Reform of the Directive seems likely, following the ruling of the Court in actions involving France, Greece and Spain.[174]

III. Proposed reform and wider implications

The above overview gives a flavour of the complex regulatory system that governs the marketing, manufacture, surveillance and advertising of pharmaceuticals within the EU, and liability for harmful defects in such products. This is an area in which EU involvement is having both a direct and indirect effect upon health law norms at national level. The need to safeguard patients (consumers) from risk, but also to create the "internal market", have driven the basic structure of the regulatory regimes. EU law has had a direct impact upon compensation systems at national level in relation to negligence, through the application of the Product Liability Directive. Other measures, such as the labelling of pharmaceuticals, have the prospect of an important indirect effect upon fundamental principles such as consent to treatment. As we have seen, the EU legislature has been active in this field, and this action looks set to continue, with a number of proposals currently under consideration.

Reform proposals

Regulation 2309/93/EC, Article 71 requires the Commission to produce a general report on the experience acquired as a result of the operation of the centralised and

171 Goldberg, above n 166, at 200.

172 Commission, *Green Paper on Liability for Defective Products* COM(99) 396 final.

173 Commission, *Report on the Application of Directive 85/374 on liability for defective products* COM(2000) 893 final.

174 See Council Resolution of 19 December 2002 on amendment of the liability for defective products Directive, OJ 2003 C 26/2. In Case C-52/00 *Commission v France* [2002] ECR I-3827; Case C-154/00 *Commission v Greece* [2002] ECR I-3879; Case C-183/00 *Maria Victoria Gonzales Sanchez v Medicina Asturiana SA* [2002] ECR I-3901, the Court took the approach that individual Member States who imposed provisions on supplier liability, which went beyond the scope of the Directive, and were unduly onerous, could be found in breach of their obligations under the Directive.

decentralised procedures. This report was presented by the Commission in 2001,[175] after DG Enterprise had commissioned a report from a private sector consultancy[176] and held a number of workshops and hearings. After issuing a "discussion document",[177] a proposal to repeal and replace Regulation 2309/93/EC and to amend Directive 2001/83/EC followed,[178] and Council reached political agreement on the amended proposal in June 2003.[179] As there appear to be no major points of contention between the three legislative institutions, the amendments are likely to be adopted along the lines of the agreed Council position of September 2003.[180] It is therefore worth discussing briefly some of the key elements of this proposed reform before turning to a more general discussion and assessment of the pharmaceuticals legislation.

The Commission's 2001 report revealed that both procedures, but in particular the centralised procedure, have contributed to the creation of a harmonised EU market in pharmaceuticals. The report found that about half of the companies using the decentralised procedure would have used the centralised procedure had it been available to them. It is therefore proposed to extend the optional application of the centralised procedure to cover an entirely new active substance (that is, a substance that is not already authorised anywhere in the EU), where this is of significant interest to patients, in particular new substances for treating AIDS, cancer, neurodegenerative disorders or diabetes.[181] An accelerated assessment procedure, applicable to products of major interest from the point of view of public health and therapeutic innovation, is envisaged.[182]

175 COM(2001) 606 final.

176 Commission, Enterprise DG, *Evaluation of the operation of Community procedures for the authorisation of medicinal products* "Cameron McKenna/Andersen Consulting report" (Brussels: European Commission, 2000). The research on which the report was based was carried out between February and August 2000, and consisted of interviews and group discussions with a wide variety of interested parties, including senior personnel in all national regulatory authorities responsible for the authorisation of medicines for human use and for veterinary use, the EMEA, the chairs and members of committees such as the CPMP, trade organisations representing pharmaceuticals companies, and ministries in Member States responsible for health, social affairs, finance and agriculture. A questionnaire was sent to all companies that had used the centralised procedure, and to a sample of 159 companies that had used the decentralised procedure, concerning their experience of using the systems. Follow-up interviews were conducted. Consultation was also extended to parties in candidate countries, with a view to considering the possible impact of enlargement on the system. Professional associations for members of the medical profession and patients' associations were also sent a questionnaire.

177 Commission, Enterprise DG, Brussels, 22 January 2001.

178 COM(2001) 404 final, amended by COM(2002) 735 final.

179 The common position of Council and Parliament was formally adopted in September 2003.

180 See Communication from the Commission to the Council concerning Council's common position SEC (2003) 1082 final. Indeed, the proposal was adopted after completion of the manuscript of this book, and may be found as Regulation 726/2004/EC, OJ 2004 L 136/1; and Directive 2004/27/EC, OJ 2004 L 136/34.

181 See COM(2001) 404 final, Annex I and Article 3; Council Doc 10449/03, Recital 8 and Article 3; Council Doc 10450/03, Recital 8. It is currently unclear whether these are cumulative or alternative tests – compare Council Doc 10449/03, Recital 8 (new active substance "and" treatment of AIDS, cancer etc) and Article 3 (new active substance "or" significant innovation of interest to patients). Regulation 726/2004/EC, above n 180, confirms that the requirements are alternative, see Article 3 (2).

182 Council Doc 10449/03, Article 13 (6) – 150 days rather than 210 days; see Regulation 726/2004/EC, above n 180, Article 6 (3) and Article 14 (9).

In its discussion document, the Commission notes that it will potentially be possible to manufacture generic versions of products authorised under the centralised procedure from 2005. The current proposal provides that applications for marketing authorisations for generics of centrally authorised medicinal products may be authorised by either procedure,[183] with the choice left to the generics firm. Where authorisation is sought under the decentralised procedure, the generic product must be in all relevant respects consistent with the centrally authorised proprietorial product, and the same name must be used in all relevant Member States.[184] There will be no need to show results of pre-clinical tests or clinical trials, if the person seeking authorisation for a generic product can show that it is a generic of a proprietary medicinal product which has been authorised for not less than eight years in a Member State or the EU.[185] However, generics cannot be placed on the market until ten years have elapsed from the initial authorisation of the proprietary product. Under the existing legislation, this is six years, or ten years for "high technology" products, but with an option for Member States to extend the protection period to ten years.[186]

The resource implications of the centralised system were considered as part of the proposed reform, particularly in the context of enlargement of the EU. It appears that the hoped-for cost efficiencies of a centralised system have not been forthcoming. Rather, the desire for every national authority to be involved in every assessment activity that may affect its citizens has increased the administrative burden. At the same time, however, the view was widely expressed that the use of a network of experts across all Member States is a good mechanism to utilise the best scientific knowledge available.[187] The proposed reform envisages the appointment of "working parties" and "scientific advisory groups" to which the committees may delegate their tasks. Although such working parties must include a wide range of appropriate scientific expertise, the implication is that not all Member States need to be represented on each of them. Whether this will make any difference in practice remains to be seen. The successor to the CPMP, the "Committee for Medicinal Products for Human Use", will consist of only one representative appointed by each Member State, so after 1 May 2004 it will consist of at least[188] 25 members.

The other reform that is proposed with respect to resources is that marketing authorisations should be subject to only one review after five years, and then remain

183 Council Doc 10449/03, Article 3 (3); Regulation 726/2004/EC, Article 3 (3).

184 Reference is made to all linguistic versions of the international non-proprietary name, see Council Doc 10449/03, Article 3 (3) (c); Regulation 726/2004/EC, Article 3 (3) (c).

185 Council Doc 10450/03, Article 10; Directive 2004/27/EC, Article 8(1) inserting new Article 10 into Directive 2001/83/EC.

186 Directive 2001/83/EC, Article 10 (1) (a) (iii); Now see Regulation 726/2004/EC, Article 14 (11).

187 One CPMP member expressed the view that the centralised system in the EU was capable of providing the best regulatory assessment in the world because it encouraged networking of experts across 15 Member States, but it was admitted that the system was very expensive to run as a result: Cameron McKenna/Andersen Consulting Report, p 20.

188 There is also provision for up to five co-opted members, plus accompanying experts, see Council Doc 10449/03, Article 54 (1); Regulation 726/2004/EC, Article 61 (2).

valid for an unlimited period thereafter.[189] If a medicinal product is not actually marketed for a period of three consecutive years, then the marketing authorisation will lapse. This will remove some of the burden of revisiting marketing authorisations, and maintaining files on authorisations for products that are not actually being marketed. Whether these resources-related reforms will go far enough remains to be seen. A strong criticism of the EU marketing authorisation procedures came from the generics sector, who take the view that resources have been concentrated in the EU procedures (both centralised and decentralised), to the detriment of generics authorisations, and ultimately national health (insurance) systems and patients who could access cheaper generic forms of proprietorial drugs were the authorisation procedures more favourable for generics.

With respect to the decentralised procedure, the Commission's report recognised that this was not operating as well as was hoped, in terms of contributing towards a single market in pharmaceuticals.[190] There is real concern about the willingness of national regulatory authorities to comply with the central principle of mutual recognition. This is demonstrated by the many national authorities who "continue to exhibit an extreme reluctance to accept the assessment of the Reference Member State".[191] Under the decentralised procedure, in practice, national authorities effectively re-evaluate cases, and the medicinal products authorised by other Member States are not actually "recognised". This concern was taken forward by a number of provisions in the Council's text agreed on 2 June 2003, following the Commission's proposal. First, the proposal provides that, where a marketing authorisation is sought in more than one Member State, the decentralised procedure must be used.[192] If a Member State "notes" that the same product is being examined in another Member State, it is obliged to decline to assess the application, and to advise the applicant to use the decentralised procedure.[193] Where a Member State is informed that another Member State has authorised a product that it is also considering, it must reject the application, unless the decentralised procedure is being used.[194]

Second, the proposal amends the procedure that applies where Member States disagree about marketing authorisations. Some pharmaceuticals companies took the view that, were Member States called upon more regularly and more immediately to explain their objections in detail, the system would be improved. It was

189 Council Doc 10449/03, Article 13, Regulation 726/2004/EC, Article 14. Provision is to be made for an additional five-year renewal period, if pharmacovigilance evidence suggests it is necessary. Council Doc 10450/03, Recital 13, Article 24; Regulation 726/2004/EC, Article 14 (2) and (3).

190 See COM(2001) 404.

191 In the responses received by the researchers, only four statements of product characteristics had been accepted unaltered by Concerned Member States.

192 The previous version of the legislation provided only that the Member State "may decide to suspend" its examination of the application.

193 Council Doc 10450/03, Article 17; Directive 2004/27/EC, Article 1 (16), inserting new Article 17 into Directive 2001/83/EC.

194 Council Doc 10450/03, Article 18; Directive 2004/27/EC, Article 1 (16), inserting new Article 18 into Directive 2001/83/EC.

not felt that a better definition of what constitutes a "public health risk" is what is needed. Rather, many responses focused on the procedural deficiencies around the arbitration process. The Recital to the revised version of Directive 2001/83/EC refers to enhanced "opportunities for cooperation between Member States".[195] In practice, what this appears to mean is an extra stage in the dispute resolution process. A "coordination group"[196] is to be set up to formalise the resolution of disputes between Member States under the decentralised procedure. Disputes must be referred to the coordination group, reasons must be given to that group, and a time limit is given within which Member States must "use their best endeavours" within the group to resolve the matter.[197] Failing that, the comitology procedure described above is triggered.[198] The proposal also provides that, where some Member States have approved the authorisation application, they may authorise the product without waiting for the outcome of the comitology procedure.[199]

Third, the proposal seeks to introduce an element of transparency in the practice of withdrawal of applications for marketing authorisations. In practice, where the national authorisation of the Reference Member State is not recognised by a Concerned Member State, the companies withdraw the requests for authorisation[200] (and move towards the more protracted process of a number of individual national authorisations). Thus, instead of moving into the arbitration phase of the procedure, as envisaged by the legislation, an EU-wide resolution of the dispute is effectively precluded. The proposal seeks to go some small way towards rectifying this problem by requiring that, where an authorisation application is withdrawn, the reasons for this must be communicated to the EMEA, and the EMEA will publish them.[201]

Nevertheless, in spite of the criticisms of each procedure, both pharmaceuticals companies and national regulators wished to continue with the two parallel procedures. It was found that both systems secure a high degree of protection for public health, and are, generally, an efficient mechanism for doing so. The reform proposals maintain the parallel procedures, and do not seek a wholesale reform of the general EU approach.

The reform process does not include assessment of the product liability rules, presumably as these are seen as outside the authorisation system. However, from the point of view of consumer protection and public health, these measures form part of the whole package. The exclusion suggests that the Commission's current preoccupation is very much focussed on "creating the internal market" in

195 Council Doc 10450/03, Recital 9; Directive 2004/27/EC, Recital 11.

196 Consisting of one representative per Member State, Council Doc 10450/03, Article 27; Directive 2004/27/EC, Article 1 (16), replacing Directive 2001/83/EC, Article 27.

197 Council Doc 10450/03, Article 29; Directive 2004/27/EC, Article 1 (16), replacing Directive 2001/83/EC, Article 29 (3).

198 Directive 2001/83/EC, Articles 32–34; Article 121 (2). See above pp 291–292.

199 Council Doc 10450/03, Article 29 (5); Directive 2004/27/EC, Article 1 (16), replacing Directive 2001/83/EC, Article 29 (6).

200 In the period 1995–97, 112 out of 249 (that is, 46%) new applications through the decentralised procedure were finalised with at least one withdrawal. In 1997, there were only two arbitration processes. See COM(2002) 735 final.

201 Council Doc 10449/03, Article 10a; Regulation 726/2004/EC, Article 11.

pharmaceuticals, rather than consumer protection more broadly. This may be explained by the lack of involvement of DG Consumer and Health Protection in the process of review of the legislation. DG Enterprise, and in particular the Pharmaceuticals Unit within that DG, is very much in the driving seat behind the current reform process.

Wider implications and assessment

The EU's regulatory system for marketing authorisation of pharmaceuticals is framed in terms of its "objective scientific basis". This "internationalisation" and "objectification" of risk assessment is said to justify the removal of national regulatory authority and its transfer to the EU level. However, it is clear that the regulation of medicines is not simply a matter of "technical science", if that notion can be said to exist at all. The presentation of regulatory choice as "objectively science based" is well known as a public policy mechanism for allocating power between experts and the lay public, among competing interest groups, and between citizens and the state, and for reducing or resolving conflict between interest groups with different views and preferences.[202] Such a mechanism is likely to prove even more appealing for a regime such as the EU, within which the interests of different groups within *and across* the component Member States, and conflict between national and EU experts, citizens, and politicians, must be accommodated. The invocation of a "scientific" basis for EU-level regulatory harmonisation gives an air of objectivity and purports to be neutral as between Member States.[203] However, on the contrary, the regulation of medicines in the EU (as elsewhere) involves political and social judgements, with respect to national traditions, medical practice, cost containment and so on. Simply stating within the law's regulatory regime that risk assessment is carried out on the "objective criteria" of "quality, safety and efficacy" does not make it so. In fact, by suppressing political debate, and forcing it to be framed in the so-called "neutral" terms of the EU's regulatory system, the EU's regulation of pharmaceuticals may be said to be detrimental to the interests of patients (consumers) and providers of health care within the Member States.[204]

Further, and probably even more seriously, some commentators, notably Abraham and Lewis, are critical of the framing of the EU's regulatory systems in terms of "quality, safety and efficacy", to the exclusion of "comparative therapeutic efficiency".[205] This latter concept factors in the need to balance what may be only marginal benefits of a costly new pharmaceutical, as against existing therapies available for the same health problem. By excluding analysis in these terms of the

202 See D. Nelkin, *Technological Decisions and Democracy* (London: Sage, 1977); S. Jasanoff, *The Fifth Branch: Science Advisers as Policymakers* (Cambridge, Mass: Harvard University Press, 1990); D. Nelkin, ed, *Controversy: Politics of Technical Decisions* (London: Sage, 1992); R. Sclove, *Democracy and Technology* (New York: Guilford Press, 1995).

203 For an illustration of the invocation of the objectivity of science in terms of public health assessments on consumer goods within the internal market, see C. Joerges, *Integrating Scientific Expertise into Regulatory Decision Making* EUI Working Paper RSC No 96/10 (Florence: EUI, 1995).

204 See Abraham and Lewis, above n 4.

205 See Abraham and Lewis, above n 4, especially p 209 ff; Abraham, above, p 288, n 33.

desirability of new pharmaceuticals (so-called "comparative therapeutic efficiency") for the EU market, especially the national health (insurance) markets of the Member States, the EU's regulatory system can be condemned for failing to represent sufficiently the interests of patients as determined collectively, by promoting a supply of new drugs that are genuinely *needed*,[206] in the context of increased pressures on national health (insurance) systems. For example, Abraham and Lewis point to the fact that Norway abolished its therapeutic needs clause in preparation for EU membership (which did not, in the event, take place), and Sweden has had to remove its "second choice" classification of marketing authorisation for new pharmaceuticals which are no more effective than established products already on the market.[207] Another example is the EU's centralised approval for Pfizer's Viagra, which posed a significant problem for Member States such as the UK, if the national health service was to pay for millions of Viagra prescriptions.[208] An initial legal challenge to the resulting NHS circular restricting prescription of Viagra "save in exceptional circumstances" was successful before the English High Court.[209] Although the national court held that the measure could be justified under Article 28 EC, on public health grounds, it stressed that purely economic considerations would not constitute sufficient justification.[210] A further part of the reasoning, based on national, rather than EU law, was that it was not lawful for the British government to undermine doctors' statutory duty to prescribe an authorised drug for which there was a clinical need. This, at least potentially, places in question the entire system of the British National Institute for Clinical Excellence (NICE), which advises British doctors about therapeutically efficient prescribing, and is used by the UK government to manage spiralling costs within its national health care system.[211]

Concerns about the interactions between the authorisation procedures and "comparative therapeutic efficiency" were raised during the reform consultation, but ultimately rejected as a basis for reform. Pricing and reimbursement policies, which remain firmly a matter of national competence,[212] operated outside, or indirectly within, authorisation procedures, are seen by the industry and some patients' groups as posing a threat to patients' access to new products. They also pose a

206 As opposed to simply capable of generating profits for the pharmaceutical industry. There are thousands of pharmaceuticals on the EU market. The WHO estimates that only about 250 products are needed to meet basic health requirements.

207 Abraham and Lewis, above n 4, p 210.

208 Abraham and Lewis, above n 4, pp 149–150.

209 *R v Secretary of State for Health, ex parte Pfizer Ltd* [1999] 3 CMLR 875 (English High Court, QBD); and see H. Biggs and R. Mackenzie, "Viagra is coming! The Rhetoric of Choice and Need" in M. Freeman and A. Lewis, eds, *Current Legal Issues 2000* (Oxford: OUP 2000). The policy was then reviewed, and following a full consultation process, taking into account considerations broader than the simply economic, it was decided to keep the substance of the policy in place. Pfizer again sought judicial review of this decision, but its application was refused. The subsequent appeal was dismissed: see *R (Pfizer Ltd) v Secretary of State for Health, ex parte Pfizer Ltd* [2002] EWCA Civ 1566.

210 Applying Case 238/82 *Duphar* [1984] ECR 523.

211 See generally K. Syrett, "NICE Work: Rationing, Review and the Legitimacy Problem in the new NHS" 10 *Medical Law Review* (2002) 1. For discussion of this case in terms of the Transparency of Pharmaceuticals Pricing Directive 89/105/EC, see below.

212 This is also discussed further below.

threat to an integrated market in pharmaceuticals across the EU. The European Parliament raised the issue of "comparative therapeutic efficiency", seeking in effect to alter the basis of authorisation (currently "quality, safety and efficacy"). Neither the Commission nor the Council was prepared to consider reform on this basis.[213] The principle of comparative therapeutic efficiency is not part of the marketing authorisation evaluation process.[214]

The regulation of pharmaceuticals exhibits many characteristics of a multilevel system of governance, with interactions between the various actors at different levels affecting policy outcomes. EU law has played a significant role in the development of this regulatory order, for instance in determining the competence of the various EU institutions to act, in providing procedures to enable the mutual recognition of national regulatory regimes, in setting up EU-level institutional fora (committees and agencies) in which disputes between national authorities may (and in some cases must) be resolved, and in requiring minimum standards of consumer protection, where pharmaceuticals cause, or potentially cause, harm. Within this system, the EU institutions balance the need to meet health and safety requirements with the interests of the various stakeholders in the process, in particular those of the governments and health care authorities of the Member States, of patients (consumers) and of the pharmaceutical industry.

IV. Internal market law

We conclude this chapter with a brief discussion of the ways in which Treaty provisions on the free movement of goods and EU competition law[215] (EU internal market law) may affect trade in pharmaceuticals within the EU, and the consequent effects this may have on health law and policy in the Member States. The relevant provisions of EU law on free movement of goods are directly effective, and thus can be relied on by litigants in national courts. Thus, we are here concerned with "deregulation", in terms of our typology of modes of governance in chapter 2. Where the internal market in pharmaceuticals does not exist in reality,[216] various litigation strategies may be followed in order to exploit this gap in regulatory provision. Such litigation has proved particularly important in cases where protection of intellectual property in pharmaceuticals (such as patents) or significant differences in prices for a pharmaceutical product between Member States encourage "parallel imports" of the relevant product. Where it interferes with price-setting within a national

213 See COM(2002) 735.

214 Council Doc 10449/03, Recitals 11 and 28a, Article 51.

215 Space precludes a detailed discussion of the impact of EC competition law on the regulation of pharmaceuticals. See, for instance, the *Organon* case, discussed in S. Kon and F. Schaeffer, "Parallel Imports of Pharmaceutical Products: A New Realism or Back to Basics?" 18 ELRev (1997) 123 at 128; Case C-277/87 *Sandoz v Commission* [1990] ECR I-45; Case T-41/96 *Bayer AG v Commission* [2000] ECR II-3383; and, in the UK context, *Napp Pharmaceutical Holdings v Director General of Fair Trading* (2002) 69 BMLR 69 (CCAT).

216 For examples, see M. Mäkinen, J. Forsström and P. Rautava, "Delivery of non-national prescriptions within the EU: how flexible is the common market for pharmaceuticals?" 7(1) *eurohealth* (2001) 23.

health (insurance) system, internal market law may have the effect of altering the allocation of resources within that system. In some circumstances, as we will see, an exemption is available to these internal market rules on grounds related to the protection of public health or an "objective public interest", which includes the financial equilibrium of national health (insurance) services.

As we have already seen in previous chapters, the measures of primary EU law establishing the internal market in goods are found in the EC Treaty, Articles 23–25 (ex 9–16), 28–31 (ex 30–36) EC, and these provisions apply to pharmaceuticals. However, national measures falling foul of these provisions of EU law may be *justified* under Article 30 EC, which provides that the Treaty "shall not preclude prohibitions or restrictions on imports . . . justified on grounds of . . . the protection of health and life of humans . . . ". Generally speaking, the Court has tended to give Member States a reasonable margin of discretion in its application of the public health exception in Article 30 EC.[217] Where mass importation of medicinal products is restricted by national law on public health grounds, this is usually held to be consistent with EU law. However, as we saw in chapter 6, in cases concerning private importation of pharmaceuticals by individual patients, the Court has adopted a more rigorous approach.[218] Overall, the rulings applying EU law on free movement of goods to the movement of pharmaceuticals, in drawing a balance between the interests of Member States in protecting patients' or consumers' health and the interests of a single market in pharmaceuticals, tend to respect the legitimate interests underpinning national regulatory structures protecting human health. As EU secondary law in the field increases, there is a gradual reduction in the discretion of Member States to maintain such protections. But otherwise, subject to the guiding principles of EU law of non-discrimination and proportionality, the potential deregulatory impact of EU internal market law is limited by the Court's approach.

Although this is not articulated in the rulings, one function of the national measures at issue in some of the case law concerning free movement of pharmaceuticals may be to protect the prices of pharmaceuticals, either to maintain relatively high price levels, or to seek to constrain prices. Such measures are concerned with the allocation of finite resources within a national health (insurance) system. The application of internal market law in these circumstances may imply an indirect interference with national health policy measures, either those aimed at maintaining national capacity in the pharmaceutical industry, or those aimed at cost containment in national health care provision through the regulation of pricing of pharmaceuticals.

217 See, for example, Case 104/75 *De Peijper* [1976] ECR 613; Case 32/80 *Kortmann* [1981] ECR 251; Cases 266 & 267/87 *R v Royal Pharmaceutical Society of Great Britain, ex parte Association of Pharmaceutical Importers and others* [1989] ECR 1295; Case C-369/88 *Delattre* [1991] ECR I-1487; Case C-60/89 *Monteil and Samanni* above n 36; Case C-55/99 *Commission v France (Medical Reagents)* [2000] ECR I-11499.

218 Case 215/87 *Schumaker* [1989] ECR 617; see also Case C-62/90 *Commission v Germany* [1992] ECR I-2575.

National governments retain a special position as the main purchasers of pharmaceuticals within a state, and, therefore, justify measures to keep this expenditure low. Within the EU, various different methods are utilised to achieve this end.[219] These fall into three main types: volume controls, indirect price controls and profit controls. Volume controls limit, either by "positive lists" or "negative lists", the type of products which may be reimbursed under the national health system.[220] The market for those pharmaceutical products is, thereby, more or less guaranteed within a particular Member State, and conversely, it is almost impossible for products not on a positive list to be successfully marketed within a particular state. Governments aim to ensure that the products for which reimbursement is available are competitively priced, for instance, by using generic rather than proprietary products where possible. Indirect price controls operate in various ways. The level of reimbursement for all products in a particular class may be fixed in order to encourage the use of cheaper generic products. Use of generics may also be encouraged by permitting pharmacists to keep a proportion of savings on products supplied (the Netherlands) or by making prescribing doctors responsible for the cost in some way (UK). Cost-sharing between patient and provider may also operate as an indirect price control. Profit controls may be laid down by legislation or administrative action, or may be the result of negotiations between the national government and the pharmaceutical industry. These limit the levels of profit which may be made on sales of pharmaceutical products to national health services. Where a state is concerned also to support its internal pharmaceutical industry, and to promote its research and development and export capacity, the former two methods are favoured (for instance, Germany, UK). Where there is less of a concern for the home grown pharmaceutical sector, stricter profit or price controls are more likely to be used (for instance, Belgium, Spain, Portugal, Greece).[221] This division goes some way to explaining the division between "high price" Member States such as Germany, and "lower price" Member States such as Belgium.

All of these measures restrain the application of normal market rules to the sale and supply of pharmaceuticals. Consequently, there is no single internal market in pharmaceuticals in the EU. The Commission has attempted several times to introduce harmonising legislation in this area, but, save the "Transparency Directive" 89/105/EEC,[222] no significant progress has been made to this effect. The question arises, therefore, to what extent primary EU law may affect capacity maintenance or cost containment provisions of national health (insurance) systems. Here we consider primary EU law on free movement of goods, although EU competition law

219 See, for example, Kon and Schaeffer, above n 215, at 126; Hancher, above n 25, at 11; Mossialos and Abel-Smith, in Stavridos et al, above n 25, pp 375–383.

220 See Mossialos and Abel-Smith, in Stavridos et al, above n 25, pp 375.

221 See Hancher, above n 25, at 11.

222 Directive 89/105/EEC on the transparency of measures regulating the pricing of medicinal products for human use and their inclusion in the scope of national health insurance schemes, OJ 1989 L 40/8. See further below.

may also become significant in this respect in the future.[223] In a series of decisions, the Court has moved from a position in which such measures were subject to fairly strict scrutiny,[224] to one in which such measures may be justified by an "objective public interest", including by reference to the financial implications for national health (insurance) systems.[225] In *Decker*,[226] the Court explicitly confirmed that the risk of seriously undermining the financial balance of a national health (insurance) system constitutes an objective public interest justification for measures that have the effect of restricting the free movement of goods, which would include pharmaceutical products. The Court made explicit the conflicts between, on the one hand, the internal market's deregulatory rules and, on the other hand, the public health and financial implications of the intervention of internal market law in national health systems' methods of providing medical goods. Here, the Court appears to be referring to a notion of "social solidarity",[227] as justification for restraints on the freedom of movement of goods within the internal market.

223 In Case C-67/96 *Albany International v Stichting Bedrijfspensioenfonds Textielindustrie* [1999] ECR I-5751, the Court confirmed that EU competition law applies in principle to institutions of national welfare schemes. The Court currently has before it a case (Cases C-264/01, C-306/01, C-354/01 and C-355/01 *AOK Bundesverband and others*) in which German rules fixing the amounts reimbursable for certain pharmaceuticals under the German sickness funds are being scrutinised for their consistency with EU competition law. The Advocate General takes the view that such measures would be justified under Article 86 (2) EC. In his opinion, delivered on 22 May 2003, the Advocate General refers to notions of social solidarity. The case was decided on 16 March 2004. The Court found that the German sickness funds are not "undertakings" in the sense of Article 81 EC. There was therefore no need to consider the justification point.

224 See Case 181/82 *Roussel* [1983] ECR 3849, in which possible justifications of the national measures were not discussed. There was no explicit argument from the Dutch government to the effect that the system at issue, which fixed pharmaceuticals prices so as to have the effect of making the sale of imported pharmaceuticals more difficult than that of domestic products, was necessary to prevent exploitation of the Dutch health system by parallel importers of products from other Member States. See also Case 56/87 *Commission v Italy* [1988] ECR 2919, concerning price-fixing rules designed to ensure that pharmaceuticals would be provided to consumers at reasonable prices, and also to promote the national pharmaceutical industry.

225 However, the Court has held firm to its principle that "mere economic or financial considerations" cannot constitute an objective public interest: see, for example, Case 238/82 *Duphar* [1984] ECR 523.

226 Case C-120/95 *Decker v Caisse de Maladie des Employés* [1998] ECR I-1831, paras 39–40. This is the companion case to Case C-158/96 *Kohll* [1998] ECR I-1931 on the freedom to provide and receive cross-border medical services: see further, chapter 4. See also Case C-322/01 *Deutscher Apothekerverband v 0800 DocMorris and Waterval* [2003] ECR I-(11 December 2003, nyr in ECR), discussed in chapter 10.

227 "Social solidarity" was defined by Advocate General Fennelly, in Case C-70/95 *Sodemare* [1997] ECR I-3395, thus: "... the existence of systems of social provision established by Member States on the basis of the principle of solidarity does not constitute, as such, an economic activity, so that any inherent consequent restriction on the free movement of goods, services or persons does not attract the application of Treaty provisions. Social solidarity envisages the inherently uncommercial act of involuntary subsidisation of one social group by another. Rules closely connected with financing such schemes are more likely to escape the reach of the Treaty provisions on establishment and services. Thus, pursuit of social objectives on the basis of solidarity may lead Member States to withdraw all or part of the operations of social security schemes from access by private economic operators" (para 29). See further T. Hervey, "Social solidarity: a buttress against internal market law" in J. Shaw, ed, *Social Law and Policy in an Evolving European Union* (Oxford: Hart, 2000), pp 31–47.

The Transparency of Pharmaceuticals Pricing Directive

In addition to the litigation based on the Treaty provisions on free movement, the EU institutions have attempted to move towards a genuine single market for pharmaceuticals through adoption of secondary legislation. If such a single market were a reality, this would have profound effects on the administration and financing of national health (insurance) systems, as the primary purchasers of pharmaceuticals within the EU. However, the relevant legislation, the Transparency of Pharmaceuticals Pricing Directive 89/105/EEC,[228] goes only a short way towards establishing such a genuine single market in pharmaceuticals, and its impact on national health services is limited.

The Transparency of Pharmaceuticals Pricing Directive is based on Article 100a (now 95) EC. Its objective is to provide an "overall view" of national pricing arrangements for pharmaceuticals, which includes the manner in which they operate in individual cases and all the criteria on which they are based. This information is to be available to all those involved in the pharmaceuticals market within the EU.[229] Competent national authorities must publish, at least once a year, a list of pharmaceuticals the price of which has been fixed during the relevant period of time,[230] and a list of approved price increases for pharmaceuticals during the relevant period of time.[231] A company holding a marketing authorisation for a pharmaceutical product is entitled to a decision on the price to be charged for that product within a fixed period of time from the date on which it applies for such a decision.[232] If the national authorities decide not to authorise the price proposed by the applicant, they must give a reasoned decision to that effect, based on "objective and verifiable criteria".[233] Where national authorities freeze prices on all pharmaceuticals, or certain categories of pharmaceuticals, such price freezes must be reviewed at least once a year, to ascertain whether the macro-economic conditions justify the freeze being continued.[234] Holders of marketing authorisations may apply, giving reasons, for exceptional derogations from price freezes.[235]

Where a Member State uses a system of direct or indirect profitability controls on the pharmaceuticals sector, Article 5 of the Transparency of Pharmaceuticals Pricing Directive applies. The Member State must publish, and communicate to the Commission, its methods used for determining profitability;[236] the range of target

228 Directive 89/105/EEC on the transparency of measures regulating the pricing of medicinal products for human use and their inclusion in the scope of national health insurance schemes, OJ 1989 L 40/8.

229 Directive 89/105/EC, preamble, Recital 9.

230 Directive 89/105/EC, Article 2 (3).

231 Directive 89/105/EC, Article 3 (3).

232 The period is 90 days, and if no decision is taken within that period of time, then the applicant is deemed permitted to market the pharmaceutical product at the price proposed by it in the application: Directive 89/105/EC, Article 2 (1).

233 Directive 89/105/EC, Article 2 (2).

234 Directive 89/105/EC, Article 4 (1).

235 Directive 89/105/EC, Article 4 (2).

236 Return on sales or return on capital or a combination of both.

profit permitted to the industry; the criteria by which this permitted target profit is applied to individual companies, and the criteria according to which they will be allowed to retain profits above this; and the maximum percentage profit which an individual company will be permitted to retain above the target profit.[237]

Articles 6 and 7 of the Transparency of Pharmaceuticals Pricing Directive apply to positive and negative lists. Again, decisions on whether to include products in a positive list must be communicated to applicants within a set period of time,[238] and must be based on "objective and verifiable criteria".[239] Member States must publish and communicate to the Commission their positive or negative lists.[240] The Directive applies to "positive lists" in the classic sense, but also to a register of medicinal products whose costs will normally be borne by the national health insurance scheme, even though the costs of other products, not on the register, may also be borne by that scheme if a doctor determines that the product is necessary for the patient concerned.[241]

Article 6 (2) of the Transparency of Pharmaceuticals Pricing Directive provides that, in the event of a decision on the part of national authorities to exclude a pharmaceutical product from a national list, a statement of reasons must be given. The provision then continues:

> "In addition, the applicant shall be informed of the remedies available to him under the laws in force and of the time limits allowed for applying for such remedies."

The Court has held, in proceedings brought by the Commission under Article 226 (ex 169) EC against Austria, that this provision implies that the Transparency of Pharmaceuticals Pricing Directive requires the availability of a remedy involving recourse to a judicial body.[242] Member States may not simply provide a remedy before an administrative body. In reaching this conclusion, the Court drew on Articles 6 and 13 ECHR, enshrining a general principle of effective legal protection.[243] This interpretation goes beyond the literal wording of the Transparency of Pharmaceuticals Pricing Directive, and involves an incursion into the arrangements for review of administrative decisions on reimbursability taken within national health (insurance) systems in the Member States.

The Court's ruling in the *Austria* case confirms that the idea behind the Transparency of Pharmaceuticals Pricing Directive is to:

> "enable all concerned to verify that the requirements of Community law are being respected by laying down a series of rules regarding time limits, the reasoning and

237 Directive 89/105/EC, Article 5 (a)–(d).

238 Directive 89/105/EC, Article 6 (1).

239 Directive 89/105/EC, Article 6 (2), (5) and (6), Article 7 (1) and (3).

240 Directive 89/105/EC, Articles 6 (4) and 7 (4).

241 Case C-424/99 *Commission v Austria (Transparency Directive)* [2001] ECR I-9285, paras 29–32.

242 Case C-424/99 *Commission v Austria (Transparency Directive)* above n 242, paras 39–46.

243 The Court drew on its previous decisions such as that in Case 224/84 *Johnson* [1986] ECR 1651.

> publication of decisions and so on, which would be directly effective, so that those concerned may defend their interests in the national courts."[244]

The Transparency Directive is supposed to allow sufficient transparency to ensure that the Treaty provisions on free movement of goods are being respected.[245] However, for the Directive to bite, it must be possible to bring appropriate litigation against national practices with respect to pharmaceuticals pricing. Hancher[246] explains that, in an earlier case brought by the Commission against Belgium,[247] the Court found that the Commission had failed to bring sufficient evidence to show that Belgium's maximum price controls, price freeze and the details of its reimbursement regime breached Article 30 (now 28) EC. It follows that if the Commission is to bring a successful action against a "low price" Member State, such as Belgium, this will require more cooperation from the pharmaceutical industry, in terms of revealing its calculation of costs and setting of prices in different Member States, than has hitherto been available. If this is not forthcoming, then the potential impact of the Transparency of Pharmaceuticals Pricing Directive, limited as it is, is likely to be further diminished.

Moreover, for the Transparency of Pharmaceuticals Pricing Directive to have an effect on pharmaceuticals pricing arrangements in the Member States, national courts must be willing to give a robust interpretation to its provisions. For instance, national courts must be prepared to find that criteria applied by national administrative authorities are not "objective and verifiable". This involves an interference with political or administrative processes, over which there is traditionally considerable judicial reluctance. This point is illustrated by the Viagra litigation before the UK courts.

What constitutes an "objective and verifiable criterion" in the terms of the Transparency of Pharmaceuticals Pricing Directive has been the subject of litigation before the UK courts. Pfizer, the manufacturer of the impotence drug Viagra (sildenafil), challenged the decision of the UK Secretary of State for Health to issue guidance to general practitioners to the effect that Viagra should not be prescribed at the expense of the national health system, unless there were exceptional circumstances.[248] The original guidance simply stated that:

> "As an interim measure, the Standing Medical Advisory Committee [a statutory body that advises the Secretary of State for Health on medical matters] has advised that doctors should not prescribe [Viagra]. Health authorities are also advised not to support the provision of [Viagra] at NHS expense to patients requiring treatment for erectile

244 COM(86) 765, cited in Hancher, above n 36, at 847.

245 A. Earl-Slater, "Regulating the prices of the UK's drugs: second thoughts after the government's first report" 314 BMJ (1997) 365 (1 February) takes the view that the UK's regulatory scheme lacks the requisite transparency to meet the UK's obligations under the Transparency Directive, but this has not yet been tested.

246 Hancher, above n 36, at 848–851.

247 Case C-249/88 *Commission v Belgium* [1991] ECR I-1275.

248 UK Health Circular 1998/158.

> disfunction, other than in exceptional circumstances which they should require be cleared in advance with them."

No further explanation for this advice was given. The English High Court[249] therefore held that there had been a breach of Article 7 of the Transparency of Pharmaceuticals Pricing Directive, in that no reasons based on objective and verifiable criteria had been given for the decision effectively to exclude Viagra from the list of pharmaceuticals that may be prescribed under the UK's national health system. The policy was then reviewed, and following a full consultation process, it was decided to keep the substance of the policy in place. The reasons given for this decision were that, on the basis of the forecast levels of expenditure, were Viagra to be available on NHS prescription, this amount of expenditure on impotence treatment could not be justified, having regard to the resources available to the NHS and the priorities for their expenditure. Pfizer again sought judicial review of this decision, but its application was refused.

On appeal to the English Court of Appeal,[250] Pfizer argued that the reasons given by the UK Secretary of State for Health for its decision not to authorise Viagra as available on NHS prescription were inadequate to comply with the Transparency of Pharmaceuticals Pricing Directive. The UK Secretary of State for Health, according to Pfizer, was required not only to publish his criterion and communicate it to the Commission (which he had eventually done in 1999), but also to conduct an analysis as to whether treatment for impotence should *properly* be regarded as constituting a lower priority than the treatment of other non-life threatening conditions. In effect, Pfizer was arguing that Article 7 of the Transparency of Pharmaceuticals Pricing Directive requires a full analysis and reasoning to be articulated with respect to a decision to exclude a particular pharmaceutical product from a list of products authorised for expenditure under a national health (insurance) system. The question was whether Article 7 requires not only that a criterion as to affordability of a particular pharmaceutical under the priorities for national health expenditure be communicated to the Commission, but also that in every case the judgment on affordability *itself* must be explained. The national court held that this was not the proper interpretation of Article 7 of the Transparency of Pharmaceuticals Pricing Directive, taking into account its objective and scope. The appeal was dismissed (without a reference being made to the European Court of Justice under Article 234 EC). Here, the national court was not prepared to allow the Transparency of Pharmaceuticals Pricing Directive to intervene in questions of resource allocation and financial priorities within the national health system. The potential impact of EU law was thus limited.

The Transparency of Pharmaceuticals Pricing Directive was due to be reviewed and further proposals on bringing the pharmaceutical sector closer in line with other sectors of the internal market were to be put forward by the Commission

249 *Pfizer Ltd* (English High Court, QBD) above n 209.
250 See *Pfizer Ltd* (English Court of Appeal) above n 209.

by the end of 1991.[251] The Commission duly issued a consultation document in 1991, but only six Member States replied, all of which opposed the idea of a more proactive role being given to the Commission in the area of pricing and financing procedures for pharmaceuticals. The Commission then issued a draft recommendation, including guidelines on deregulation and the promotion of competition in the pharmaceuticals marketplace. After discussions in the Committee on Pharmaceutical Price Transparency revealed significant opposition from many Member States, the Commission decided not to submit any definite proposals to Council. Instead, the Commission initiated wider discussions with the pharmaceuticals industry, linking the issue of pricing of pharmaceuticals and a single market for pharmaceuticals with the EU's industrial policy for the pharmaceuticals sector. This culminated in the Commission's *Communication to Council and European Parliament on the Outlines of an Industrial Policy for the Pharmaceutical Sector.*[252] The final version of this measure of soft law did not, however, include the proposals for price deregulation. According to Mossialos and Abel-Smith,[253] this was due to the intervention of DG V (now Social Affairs) and the Social Affairs Commissioner, backed by Commission President Delors.[254]

Thus, the process of a gradual opening up of a true single market in pharmaceuticals, begun by the Transparency of Pharmaceuticals Pricing Directive, appears to have halted, or been side-tracked. This, in turn, implies that national arrangements with respect to the pricing of pharmaceuticals, as part of the overall financing and administration of national health (insurance) services, and the allocation of resources therein, are likely to remain relatively sheltered from the application of the free movement provisions of EU internal market law. It appears that the political will to utilise EU legislative institutions and structures to effect a single market in pharmaceuticals, with the corresponding impact on financing and administration of national health (insurance) services, is not present. In the final analysis, the impact and potential of EU free movement law is, therefore, limited, at least for the time being.[255]

V. Conclusions

This chapter gives an overview of two distinct, but inter-related, areas of EU law that affect the production and marketing of pharmaceuticals. These are:

251 Directive 89/105/EC, Article 9.
252 COM(93) 718.
253 Mossialos and Abel-Smith, in Stavridis et al, above n 25, pp 370–374.
254 See also Anonymous, "Bad Medicine in Europe" *The Wall Street Journal Europe*, 22 April 1994, p 8.
255 For an example of the impact of the single European market on pharmaceuticals in a relatively new Member State, see C. Rehnberg, "A Swedish case study on the impact of the SEM on the pharmaceutical market" in R. Busse, M. Wismar and P.C. Berman, *The European Union and Health Services* (Amsterdam: IOS Press, 2002).

Patient (consumer) protection measures, in the form of secondary EU legislation; and EU internal market law, comprising Treaty provisions on the free movement of goods, as interpreted by the extensive jurisprudence of the European Court of Justice; and relevant secondary EU legislation.

In terms of the former category, the EU legislature appears to take a cautious and conservative overall approach to risk. There appears to be a very gradual movement towards effecting risk assessment, and determining standards of quality, safety and efficacy of pharmaceuticals, at least in the context of marketing authorisations, at EU level. Considerable difficulty remains over whether the appropriate site for risk assessment is national or EU level, and, in this respect, the EU's legal order displays characteristics of a multi-level system of governance. Tensions have arisen and are likely to continue to arise from the indirect implications of regulatory activities within this system for national health (insurance) systems, in terms of the impact on resources that can result when a new pharmaceutical product is approved for marketing in the EU, or within a particular Member State. Through its general consumer protection laws, the EU has had a (limited) impact on the determination of liability of the pharmaceuticals industry to patients, conceptualised here as consumers. There may be indirect implications for national health law in terms of the construction by EU law of patients as "consumers", for instance, in the provisions concerning consumer information on pharmaceutical products, or advertising of pharmaceutical products.

In general, the provisions in the latter category apply to the pharmaceutical industry as to any other industry, and treat pharmaceuticals as essentially the same as any other "goods" or "products". However, as we have seen, there are problems with operating on the assumption that the pharmaceuticals industry is simply an industry like any other, operating in a market like any other. Supposing the single market in pharmaceuticals were to become a reality; this would involve consolidation of the existing nationally based industries, which would inevitably involve relocation and restructuring. Such relocation would presumably be beneficial to the EU's economy speaking in terms of aggregate efficiency, but there would clearly be losers, as well as winners, in such a restructuring. Whether national governments would accept the losses in employment and so on, as well as the loss to capacity implied by losing a "home-grown" pharmaceutical industry, is highly doubtful.

Further, in some senses, the goods that the pharmaceuticals industry produces are "public goods". This is reflected in the government intervention in pricing structures for pharmaceuticals, in place in all Member States of the EU. The special nature of pharmaceuticals, their relation to the health of the citizens of a particular state and others resident within its borders, and the need for special consumer protection with respect to their effects, is reflected in the stringent regulatory structures within which pharmaceuticals may be lawfully produced and distributed. In some cases, these regulatory measures have been adopted at EU level. In others, national regulatory measures take their place within the general EU rules on creating and maintaining the single European market. In the final analysis, EU law appears to negotiate this tension between the special case of the pharmaceutical industry and the drive to integrate the internal market using legal mechanisms relatively successfully.

Although various *potential* implications for national health (insurance) systems have been identified, these are yet to have any widespread disruptive effect. This is, at least in part, because the institutional structures of the EU militate against such widespread disruption. It is also due to the Court's increasing awareness of the potential of internal market law, particularly that on free movement of goods, to undermine national social policy provisions, and the Court's corresponding increasing reluctance to allow such internal market provisions to be taken to their logical, deregulatory, conclusion. This suggests a conceptualisation of the legal structure of the internal market as a system of governance within which various interests, not simply those of the market, must be accommodated. Thus, the interests and values (such as social solidarity) underpinning national health (insurance) systems may eventually be more explicitly articulated through norms of EU internal market law, perhaps not simply by the Court, but also, in time, by the EU legislature.

9

Public health law

I. Introduction

The law's engagement with public health provides one of the earliest illustrations of the interface between health and legal regulation.[1] The scourges of typhoid, cholera and the plague led to nation states introducing explicit legal regulation of such diseases. This took the form in many instances of draconian legislative restrictions upon personal freedom. References to the isolation of lepers are to be found in the Old Testament.[2] Practices of quarantine can be traced back to 1000 and Venetian legislative statutes concerning plague quarantine relate to 1127.[3] By the fourteenth century, overseers in Venice were authorised to spend public money for the purpose of quarantining persons, goods and ships on an island in the lagoon.

While, for centuries, detention was the response to perceived dangers to public health, over time, the law in some European countries began to be used to facilitate a more sophisticated response. Concerns regarding the spread of disease were linked to poor living conditions and inadequate sanitation. The revolution in public health in the UK, for example, was linked to the reforming zeal of Edwin Chadwick, who argued that the root cause of infectious disease could be found in poor sanitation.[4] Through the reports of the Royal Commission on the Health of Towns established in 1843, the momentum developed for legislative amendment. In 1848, the UK passed the Public Health Act which, rather than the "reactive" quarantine practices, can be seen as one of the major steps towards "proactive" public health.[5] A general health board was established and there was provision for the establishment of local health

1 See generally L.O. Gostin, *Public Health Law: Power, Duties and Restraints* (Berkeley and Los Angeles: University of California Press, 2000); L. Johnson, "Defining Public Health" and "Issues of Public Health; Infectious Diseases" in R. Martyn and L. Johnson, eds. *Law and the Public Dimension of Health* (London: Cavendish, 2001).

2 See, for example, Leviticus 13: 45–46; Numbers 5: 1–3. See further discussion in Gostin, above n 1, p 204.

3 Gostin, above n 1, p 205.

4 See also the research undertaken by Dr John Snow on the Broad Street Pump, London, in 1854, discussed in L.J. Donaldson and R.J. Donaldson, *Essential Public Health* (Plymouth: Petroc Press, 2003), pp 104–107.

5 See discussion in C. Hamlin and S. Sheard, "Revolutions in public health 1848 and 1998?" 317 BMJ (1998) 587.

boards with powers to alter the environment as well as to act against nuisances. This proactive approach was, however, not generally followed in other European states and so, for example, at that time in France concerns were focused rather on statistical analysis of morbidity.[6] A twin-track approach of coercion and persuasion or promotion in public health medicine is prevalent today.

Across Member States of the EU, public health restrictions upon personal liberty remain in force.[7] This is also the case, as we shall see below, in relation to cross-border travel and migration, where Member States are able to impose restrictions on the basis of public health. The EU's concern with prevention of the spread of communicable diseases is already reflected in its network on communicable diseases, and a Directive on the comparability of data[8] lays down common case definitions for reporting communicable diseases to the network. There are also proposals for the establishment of an EU communicable disease surveillance agency.[9] While communicable disease control is still a live issue internationally (as the SARS epidemic, BSE/nvCJD, HIV/AIDS, the rise of drug-resistant tuberculosis[10] and bioterrorism have all graphically illustrated), nonetheless it is simply one element of the law's engagement with public health issues. As standards of health within individual states have gradually improved, there has inevitably been a shift in focus from coercion to persuasion. The health of citizens in individual Member States of the EU is fostered increasingly through the use of health promotion measures, and here information and education play a crucial role. In this instance, law's role may be limited to determining what information may or must be given about a product, service or lifestyle that is, or is potentially, hazardous to health, and on whom (private companies, public bodies) such a duty rests.

Public health law, while crucially important in practice, has figured only incidentally in many health law textbooks.[11] Various specific elements of public health law have, however, led to considerable discussion and debate by legal and bioethics

6 See Hamlin and Sheard, above n 5.

7 For example, UK Public Health (Control of Disease) Act 1984 and Public Heath Act (Infectious Diseases) Regulations 1985, SI 1985/434 which enable the testing and compulsory detention of those suspected of HIV/AIDS.

8 Decision 2002/253/EC, OJ 2002 L 86/44.

9 See "Strengthening Europe's Defences against health threats; Commission proposes European Centre for Disease Prevention and Control", IP/03/1091 and MEMO/03/155, and Employment, Social Affairs, Consumer Protection and Health Council meeting of 1–2 December 2003.

10 See generally, for example, R. Coker, "Public Health, civil liberties and tuberculosis" 318 BMJ (1999) 1434.

11 Some indeed emphasised its separateness as a discipline. As Tobey commented, writing in 1926, it "should not be confused with medical jurisprudence which is concerned only in the legal aspects of the application of medical and surgical knowledge to individuals . . . Public health is not a branch of medicine but a science in itself, to which, however, preventative medicine is an important contributor. Public health law is that branch of jurisprudence which treats . . . the application of common law and statutory law to the principles of hygiene and sanitation": J.A. Tobey, *Public Health Law: A Manual of Law for Sanitarians* (Baltimore MD: Williams and Wilkins Co, 1926), pp 6–7, cited in J. Areen et al, *Law, Science and Medicine* (Westbury, New York: Foundation Press, 1996), p 485.

commentators. Such elements include HIV/AIDS,[12] immunisation, confidentiality and disease surveillance, and contagious disease transmission.[13] Public health medicine is also today seen as encompassing broader themes, such as genetics, through developments in epidemiology and screening and delivery of clinical genetics services.[14] These all have legal implications. Gostin sees the distinctive characteristics of public health law as being:

> "The government's responsibility to advance the public health;
> The population-based perspective;
> The relationship between the people and the state;
> The discrete set of services and scientific methodologies;
> The role of co-ercion."[15]

Gostin identifies the key themes of public health law as "the trade-offs between public goods and private rights and the dilemma of whether to use co-ercive or voluntary public health measures".[16] These themes are also identifiable in the EU context in relation to public health issues.

The breadth of the potential concerns of public health medicine reflects the breadth of the concept of "health" characterised in the WHO definition and as discussed further in chapter 1.[17] It is not surprising that public health lawyers may be concerned with a very wide range of regulatory measures, or other coercive activity, undertaken by public authorities within states. As we have seen, the containment and management of infectious diseases impacts directly on public health. However, the determinants of health and ill health also include a number of environmental factors, such as air and water quality, pollution, waste disposal and noise. Along with safe drinking water, an adequate supply of safe and nutritious food plays a major role in determining the health of a population. Accident prevention, for instance, in the home or on the roads, forms part of public health policy. Controls of workplace hazards contribute to the health of both workers and the public at large. There are links between the phenomenon of "social exclusion" (in terms of access to employment, housing, communications, transport and other services) and health. All Member States of the EU utilise various legal mechanisms, including the institutions of the criminal law and other enforcement agencies, to effect controls in these areas in order, *inter alia*, to protect public health. Our focus in this chapter is

12 See, for example, C. Erin and R. Bennett, eds, *HIV and AIDS: Testing screening and confidentiality* (Oxford: OUP, 1999); L.O. Gostin and Z. Lazzarini, *Human Rights and Public Health in the AIDS Pandemic* (Oxford: OUP, 1997); R. Haigh and D. Harris, *AIDS and the Law* (London: Routledge, 1995).

13 M. Brazier and J. Harris "Public Health and Private Lives" 4 *Medical Law Review* (1996) 176.

14 See, for example, M.J. Khoury, W. Burke and E.J. Thompson, *Genetics and Public Health in the 21st Century: Using Genetic Information to Improve Health and Prevent Disease* (Oxford: OUP, 2000).

15 See Gostin, above n 1, Preface.

16 See Gostin, above n 1, p xix.

17 See R. Detels, *The Oxford Textbook of Public Health Medicine* (Oxford: OUP, 2002); Donaldson and Donaldson, above n 4, p 113.

the extent to which, and the ways in which, EU-level regulatory activities, financing of health programmes, and soft law have affected such national provisions. Unlike much of the health law and policy discussed earlier in the book, the EU has a specific Treaty-based competence in the public health field in Article 152 EC.[18]

Much of public health law concerns the management of risks to health.[19] The period spanning the late twentieth and early twenty-first centuries has seen a tremendous increase in public concern about actual or potential health hazards. This has taken place in the context of significant and fast-moving technological development. Widespread media coverage has given a high profile to scientific studies of the risks or potential risks to human health of various technological developments, such as genetically modified crops or mobile telephones, and has also in many cases dramatised these in the form of human interest stories. In this context, regulatory authorities have to walk a tightrope of responding to public concerns, without unjustifiably tampering with technological progress and the significant capital investments reflected in new products or processes. In the EU context, this is even more sensitive, as the EU's system of governance does not reflect a fixed and relatively uncontentious constitutional settlement within which various interests are seen as being fairly represented and reflected in the processes of government and institutional structures.[20] Furthermore, European societies appear to be more cautious and averse to risk than those on the other side of the Atlantic. In the context of the WTO, this has created clashes between the interests of free trade, as articulated strongly by such as the US farming lobby, and at least the self-proclaimed interests of a more risk-averse European public.[21]

The EU is involved, to some extent, in all the elements of public health policy outlined above, although in some cases the involvement is tangential. The scope and application of Article 152 EC are discussed in chapter 3.[22] Obviously, we are unable to cover all possible elements of EU law and policy in our discussion in this chapter. There is a significant body of EU environmental law, dating from the 1970s, that regulates matters such as air and water quality, bathing water, waste disposal and so on.[23] The EU has adopted legislation on health and safety at work since the

18 See chapter 3.

19 Today considerable reference is made in academic literature to the "risk society"; see, for example, U. Beck, *Risk Society: Towards a New Modernity* (London: Sage, 1992); and D. Lupton, *Risk* (London: Routledge, 1999).

20 See further chapter 2.

21 For general discussion and history of the WTO's legal order, see the useful collection of the works of Jackson, in J.H. Jackson, *The Jurisprudence of GATT and the WTO* (Cambridge: CUP, 2000). On the legal relationship between the EU and the WTO, see, in particular, G. de Búrca and J. Scott, eds, *The EU and the WTO* (Oxford: Hart, 2001); J. Weiler, ed, *The EU, the WTO and the NAFTA* (Oxford: OUP, 2000); see also S. Griller, "Judicial Enforceability of WTO Law in the European Union" 4 *Journal of International Economic Law* (2001) 441.

22 See also T. Hervey, "The Legal Basis of European Union Public Health Policy" in M. McKee, E. Mossialos and R. Baeten, eds, *The Impact of EU Law on Health Care Systems* (Brussels: PIE Peter Lang, 2002).

23 See, for instance, Directive 76/160/EEC, concerning the quality of bathing water, OJ 1976 L 31/1, as amended; Directive 98/83/EC on the quality of water intended for human consumptions, OJ

1980s, covering workplace hazards, dangerous agents in the workplace, working time and so on.[24] The EU has financed research into accident prevention.[25] The EU is involved in reducing "social exclusion", through the "open method of co-ordination" on social protection.[26]

In this chapter we focus upon two substantive issues which reflect the historical concerns of public health physicians – communicable diseases and health promotion. Both are areas in which the EU has had considerable involvement. We consider their interface with two themes; namely, regulation and risk. As noted above, the control of communicable diseases is historically a concern of both individual states and the wider international community. Here we focus upon two particular disorders: HIV/AIDS and BSE/nvCJD. Second, we consider the area of health promotion (or health communication, as referred to by Gostin[27]) which we consider primarily in relation to the EU involvement in the area of cancer prevention, and in particular tobacco advertising.

The case studies have been chosen to reflect a range of different types of EU-level regulatory activity, encompassing both "hard" and "soft" law responses. They have also been chosen to reflect areas of significant political and social impact, where the EU's involvement has enjoyed a relatively high profile. As we saw in chapter 3, the EU's formal legal competence in the field of health, as set out in the EC Treaty, was directly affected by the aftermath of the BSE/nvCJD affair. This new competence has been used to regulate quality standards with respect to human blood, a key element of health protection in terms of communicable diseases. Finally, they reflect areas where English language literature on those aspects of EU law is relatively sparse.[28]

1998 L 330/32, as amended; Directive 91/271/EEC concerning urban waste-water treatment, OJ 1991 L 135/40, as amended; Water Framework Directive 2000/60/EC, OJ 2001 L 327/1; Directive 75/442/EEC on waste, OJ 1975 L 194/39, as amended; Directive 91/689/EEC on hazardous waste, OJ 1989 L 377/20, as amended; Directive 89/369/EEC on the prevention of air pollution from new municipal waste incineration plants, OJ 1989 L 163/32, to be repealed by Directive 2000/76/EC on the incineration of waste, OJ 2000 L 332/91, from 28 December 2005.

24 See, for instance, the Framework Health and Safety at Work Directive, Directive 89/391/EEC, OJ 1989 L 183/1, and its various "daughter" directives, on minimum health and safety requirements in the workplace, work equipment, handling dangerous loads, VDUs, exposure to chemical, physical and biological agents in the workplace, and so on; the Working Time Directives, Directives 93/104/EC, OJ 1993 L 307/18 and 2000/34/EC, OJ 2000 L 195/41.

25 Community Action Programme on injury prevention 1999–2003, Decision 372/99/EC, OJ 1999 L 46/1; subsumed into the Community's public health framework programme 2003–2008, Decision 1786/2002/EC, OJ 2002 L 271/1; see further chapter 3.

26 For further discussion of the OMC process, see chapters 2 and 10.

27 See Gostin, above n 1, chapter 6 "Health, Communication and Behaviour".

28 In contrast there are several very good texts on EU environmental law: see, for example, J. Scott, *EC Environmental Law* (London: Longman, 1998); L. Krämer, *Casebook on EU Environmental Law* (Oxford: Hart, 2002); J.H. Jans, *European Environmental Law* (Groningen: Europa Law Publishing, 2002); and on EU employment law, see, for example, J. Kenner, *EU Employment Law: From Rome to Amsterdam and Beyond* (Oxford: Hart, 2003); S. O'Leary, *Employment Law at the European Court of Justice* (Oxford: Hart, 2002); C. Barnard, *EC Employment Law* (Oxford: OUP, 2000); B. Bercusson, *European Labour Law* (London: Butterworths, 2000). Randall discusses the EU's health and safety at work policy explicitly as part of health policy in E. Randall, *The European Union and Health Policy* (Basingstoke: Palgrave, 2001), chapter 2.

II. Communicable diseases

Introduction

A key element of national policies on the protection of public health concerns the control of communicable diseases. Here, states control the activities of individuals, in some cases through restricting their fundamental rights, for instance, to personal liberty, in the interests of (collective) public health. Such national policies include controls on the movements of those individuals suffering from certain diseases, controls on the agents (for instance, humans, animals, food, water) by which communicable diseases may be spread, and immunisation programmes, to prevent the spread of certain diseases, and, ultimately, to eradicate them.[29]

Here we are interested in the impact of EU law on such elements of national public health policies. There are a number of points of contact that EU law might have with such measures. First, in terms of limitations on the movement of humans, Treaty provisions might inhibit national public health policies aimed at controlling infectious diseases. However, as we shall see, public health interests are recognised in the Treaty and in secondary legislation as legitimate justifications for such restrictions on free movement. Second, the EU institutions have taken various measures attempting to tackle some elements of the control of communicable diseases, on the basis that such diseases do not respect national boundaries, and the EU may therefore "add value" to national policy responses, either through coordination of such policies, or through harmonisation. For instance, the European Commission has been involved through the World Health Organisation and its coordination of the European Network of Communicable Diseases[30] in facilitating responses by Member States to SARS.[31] Another illustration is the proposal for the establishment of a new European Centre for Disease Prevention and Control.[32] This type of EU-level action is explored in detail below, with respect to the EU's regulation of the safety and quality of human blood, in part in response to the challenges posed by HIV/AIDS. We also consider the significant body of EU-level food law. In addition to general legislation on communicable diseases, legislation relating to food hygiene and safety is an important element of control for food-borne diseases. Here we focus on the specific, high-profile example of BSE and nvCJD, within the context of EU food law more generally.

Applying our typology of types of regulation in the context of communicable diseases, the potentially disruptive deregulatory impetus of internal market law

29 The most resounding success story in this respect has been the global eradication of smallpox, as announced by the World Health Assembly in 1980. The last known natural case of smallpox occurred in Somalia in October 1977. See J. Montgomery, *Health Care Law* (Oxford: OUP, 2003), p 33; Donaldson and Donaldson, above n 4, p 430.

30 Established by Decision 2119/98/EC OJ 1998 L 268/1.

31 http://europa.eu.int/comm/health/ph-threats/com/sars/sars-en.htm and Commission, "Measures Undertaken by Member States, E.F.T.A. and Accession Countries to control the Outbreak of SARS", Brussels, DG SANCO, G4Unit – Communicable, Rare and Emerging Diseases, 2 June 2003.

32 See Commission, above n 9.

has been considerably softened by reregulation at EU level making explicit public health exemptions to Treaty-based free movement provisions. EU public health programmes have funded research into communicable diseases, to promote cross-border exchange of information and formulation of best practice to be shared across EU Member States. Such programmes may promulgate convergence of national public health policies. In some cases, these programmes have formed a platform for subsequent regulatory measures. As formal Community competence in the field of public health develops, soft law measures are gradually being replaced by hard law, often using the "new approach" to harmonisation, leaving discretion to Member States to make provision for more stringent internally applicable regulation. In the case of food safety law, Community competence to create and maintain the internal market, and to protect consumers within it, forms the relevant legal basis. The Treaty provides, in Article 95 EC, that the Commission must "take as a base a high level of protection", in promulgating proposals for legislation that concern "health, safety, environmental protection and consumer protection", which includes food law provisions.

Before we turn to EU law regulating diseases communicated through the food chain, we first discuss the EU's activities in respect of HIV and AIDS. We consider in some detail the EU's HIV/AIDS programmes, as an example of the EU's public health programmes, based on Article 152 EC. We then briefly note the exceptions made to general EU law on free movement of persons within and into the EU for persons with HIV or AIDS. We conclude this section of our discussion by considering the various EU measures regulating the quality and safety of human blood, as an agent for communication of diseases. These have culminated in the recent Blood Safety Directive 2002/98/EC.[33]

HIV/AIDS

The EU public health programmes

The panic which resulted from the spread of AIDS led to reactive responses across jurisdictions world-wide. However, the nature of the responses differed considerably.[34] In the European context, a number of EU Member States took restrictive approaches, whilst others focused upon a response centred on education and health promotion.[35] In spite of these differences, interest in tackling the problems posed for national governments by HIV and AIDS at EU level began in the mid-1980s.[36]

33 Directive 2002/98/EC, OJ 2003 L 33/30.

34 See Handbook for Legislators UNAIDS 99;4EE, http://www.unaids.org.

35 Restrictive approaches included that taken by Sweden in its Communicable Diseases Act 1988: see R. Danziger, "HIV test and HIV Prevention in Sweden" 316 BMJ 293 (1998); for a more "laissez-faire" approach, see the UK; see, for example, J.A. Harrington, "AIDS, public health and the law: a case of structural coupling" 6 *European Journal of Health Law* (1999) 213. See, for example, R. Bennett, C. Erin and J. Harris, *AIDS, Ethics, Justice and European Policy* (Luxembourg: DG Science Research and Development EUR 17789, 1998).

36 The Council and Ministers of State for Health, meeting within Council, included on their agenda matters concerning AIDS/HIV from the mid-1980s. See, for example, Resolution of Representatives of the Governments of Member States, meeting within the Council of 29 May 1986 on AIDS, OJ 1986 C 184/21; Conclusions of Council and the representatives of the

Thus, for instance, the conclusions of the Council meeting in December 1988[37] included an agreement to "improve and extend the current system for the rapid and periodic exchange of epidemiological data at Community level on cases of AIDS". This required coordination of criteria for assessment of effectiveness of preventive measures taken in the Member States. Links between AIDS/HIV and drug abuse[38] and matters concerning employment relationships[39] were also raised at this early stage, although no concrete action was proposed. These early discussions led to the setting up of an EU-level Ad Hoc Working Party on AIDS for the exchange of information.[40] The Commission was requested by Council to draw up a proposal for a co-ordinated programme on combating AIDS/HIV.[41] Both the Commission and the Working Party were to work closely with WHO (Europe). These activities laid the foundation for subsequent EU-level action in the field.

The EU has subsequently adopted various provisions, utilising EU finance to promote public health with respect to HIV/AIDS, since the 1990s. The earliest EU-level programme specifically directed at AIDS/HIV may be found in Decision 91/317/EEC of Council and Ministers of Health of the Member States adopting a plan of action in the framework of the "Europe against AIDS" programme 1991–93,[42] subsequently extended to December 1995.[43] This action plan encompassed training provision, information exchange on services, research and measures to promote the safety of blood. A second "Europe against AIDS" programme,[44] from 1996 to 2000, had the objective of helping to "contain the spread of AIDS and reduce mortality and morbidity due to communicable diseases".[45] The mechanisms by which this was to be achieved are "promoting co-operation between [national] prevention policies and programmes and supporting the activities of non-governmental organisations".[46] The explicit role for NGOs owes its place in this measure to pressure from the European Parliament.[47] The European Commission was responsible for implementation of the programme.[48] The budget – a matter of contention between

Governments of Member States of 15 May 1987 concerning AIDS, OJ 1987 C 178/1; and of 31 May 1988, OJ 1988 C 197/8.

37 OJ 1989 C 28/1.

38 Elaborated in Council Conclusions of 16 May 1989, OJ 1989 C 185/3.

39 Elaborated in Council Conclusions of 15 December 1988, OJ 1989 C 28/2.

40 OJ 1987 C 178/1.

41 Council Conclusions of 16 May 1989, OJ 1989 C 185/3.

42 OJ 1991 L 175/26.

43 Council Resolution, OJ 1994 C 15/4 and Decision 1729/95/EC, OJ 1995 L 168/1.

44 Decision 647/96/EC of the European Parliament and Council, based on old Article 129 EC, OJ 1996 L 95/16, repealed by Decision 1786/2002/EC of the European Parliament and of the Council of 23 September 2002 adopting a programme of Community action in the field of public health (2003–2008) – Commission Statements, OJ 2002 L 271/1.

45 Decision 647/96/EC, Article 1 (2), as amended: see above n 44.

46 Above n 45.

47 See European Parliament's proposed amendments in COM(94) 413, OJ 1995 C 126/60, adopted by 96/269/ECSC: Decision No 647/96/EC of the European Parliament and of the Council of 29 March 1996 adopting a programme of Community action on the prevention of AIDS and certain other communicable diseases within the framework for action in the field of public health (1996 to 2000), OJ 1996 L 95/16.

48 Decision 647/96/EC, Article 2, as amended: see above n 44.

Council and the European Parliament in the adoption of the Decision[49] – was € 49.6 million.[50] Some of the accession and candidate countries in Central and Eastern Europe participated in the programme from the late 1990s.[51]

The technicalities of the operation of the programme were set out in Article 5 of the Decision. The programme was to be administered by a committee comprising two representatives of each Member State, chaired by the Commission. The committee is responsible for establishing the annual work programme, including priorities for action, the criteria for selecting projects for financial support under the programme, the procedure for evaluating projects, and the arrangements for dissemination of results. The committee acted according to the "management committee" procedure, whereby the Commission submits proposals, and the committee votes according to the Council's qualified majority voting rules. If the committee does not support a Commission proposal, then the matter goes to Council. The Council may then take a different decision, within a time limit specified by the Commission in its proposal, in accordance with the urgency of the measure. The significance of this mechanism of delegated legislation is that it preserves a position in which the influence of the governments of Member States, through the Council, is maintained, even where power to act has been delegated to the Commission.[52]

Decision 647/96/EC, Annex, set out four areas (or "chapters") for action under the programme.[53] These were:

1. Surveillance and monitoring of communicable diseases;
2. Combating transmission;
3. Information, education and training; and
4. Support for persons with HIV/AIDS and combating discrimination.

Actions under chapter 1 aimed to improve understanding and the dissemination of data and information on HIV and AIDS, and other communicable diseases. Actions were also to improve the coordination of monitoring systems for those diseases, and of EU-wide responses, particularly in the event of an epidemic. Further EU-level support for control and surveillance of communicable diseases emanates from the setting up of a European network for such surveillance, according to Decision 2119/98/EC.[54] Chapter 2 measures aimed to prevent transmission of AIDS and other sexually transmitted diseases. There was a particular focus on environments

49 See J. Garman and L. Hilditch, "Behind the scenes: an examination of the importance of the informal processes at work in conciliation" 5 *Journal of European Public Policy* (1998) 271 at 277. The authors describe how the "conciliation procedure" – a mechanism by which Council and the European Parliament resolve differences in amendments to proposed legislation, for further information, see chapter 2 – was used to good effect to resolve this and other differences of opinion, leading to quick adoption of the AIDS programme.

50 Decision 647/96/EC, Article 3, as amended: see above n 44.

51 For example, Romania and Bulgaria from 1998; Slovenia and the Czech Republic from 1999.

52 For further discussion of "comitology" procedures, see, for instance, K. Bradley, "The European Parliament and comitology: on the road to nowhere" 3 ELJ (1997) 230; K. Bradley, "Comitology and the Law: Through a glass, darkly" 29 CMLRev (1992) 691; S. Boyron, "Maastricht and the Codecision Procedure: A success story" 45 ICLQ (1996) 293.

53 European Commission, *Public Health in Europe* (Luxembourg, 1997), pp 66–67.

54 OJ 1998 L 268/1.

and persons at risk, such as travel,[55] prisons, prostitutes, and users of injectable drugs. Best practices were to be identified through the exchange of information and experience on different prevention methods and programmes in different Member States. Information, education and training, under chapter 3, was mainly aimed at raising public awareness and information about HIV and AIDS. There was scope for focusing on education of children and young people in respect of sexually transmitted diseases. A contribution to training of health professionals was envisaged. Chapter 4 focuses on the position of seropositive persons and persons with AIDS. It aimed to support exchange of experience and practice between networks of associations involved at national levels in the psycho-social care of such persons. Finally, chapter 4 was concerned with the combating of discrimination against people with HIV/AIDS and the development of a code of good practice for HIV testing.

Overall, priority under the AIDS programme was given to flagship projects, effected by established, "tried and tested" organisations in the field. The projects funded were required to have an "EU dimension", involve cooperation between several Member States, and represent "real added value" in terms of achievement of the objectives of the programme.[56] The projects funded utilised a mixture of innovative approaches and expansion of pre-existing effective projects. This confirms that the role of the EU is not limited simply to financing pilot projects or new ideas, but that the EU is willing to continue to finance worthwhile projects that have proved to be effective. In this respect, the EU is perhaps taking on some of the public health promotion role of the Member States. The force for convergence between national public policies in the field, enhanced by the Commission support of such programmes as the AIDS programme, was noted in terms of the "high intensity of inter-country exchanges, agreement on methods, achievement of a uniform and enhanced quality, and the production of common documents and statements".[57]

One concern of the AIDS programme was the need for the projects funded to target populations in "high risk" groups, such as sexually active gay men, and intravenous drug users of all ages. This was achieved to a limited extent. Moreover, dissemination of results was felt to be limited to the traditional routes of scientific conferences and publications, which were unlikely to reach such target groups directly. The Commission would like to see the results of the projects it finances reaching wider audiences, although it has made no concrete suggestions in terms of who these audiences might be, or how they might be reached. The Commission

55 The "flying condom" educational programme ran in summer 1994, aimed at young people on holiday to encourage the use of condoms. See European Commission, above n 53, pp 68–69.

56 European Commission, above n 53, p 67.

57 Interim Report from Commission to European Parliament, et al, on the implementation of the programmes of Community action on the prevention of cancer, AIDS and certain other communicable diseases, and drug dependence, within the framework for action in the field of public health (1996–2000), COM(99) 463 final. Article 7 of the Directive required an interim evaluation of the programme, which was carried out by the Commission in 1998. The interim report covers the years 1996 and 1997. Overall, budgetary support for chapters 1–3 was broadly equal in amount, with chapter 4 receiving around half the amount of the other chapters.

also suggest, that there is scope here for future improvement in the tackling of the issue of discrimination.[58]

However, the most significant criticism of the AIDS programme is in respect of the issue of EU-level "added value". This is seen to be the most crucial general objective, and one that was judged to be under-developed, especially in the initial projects. The experts' report[59] noted that "the project reports of the networks quite often fail to give a convincing picture of actual capacity to gather expertise and experience from all Member States and from all the relevant agencies in the Member States, as well as to disseminate information provided by those networks".[60] In particular, the report draws a distinction between the *theoretical* position: "the project results in the majority of cases have significant practical relevance, and theoretically should better inform the HIV/STD policy framework and the design and delivery of programmes within the Member States"; and the *practical* position: "at present, there is only limited evidence that project results are actually being disseminated widely and influencing key policy-makers regarding future direction on HIV/STD issues within the Member States and in the European Union as a whole." The Commission is seeking to overcome this by stressing the "enhanced networking of applicants", although precisely what this means in practice remains rather undefined.

Overall, though, in terms of the effectiveness of the programme, and the achievement of its aims, actual coverage by specific projects was reported to be "generally quite sufficient". In general, the AIDS projects delivered a range of appropriate and effective studies and interventions. Positive results included improved co-ordination of surveillance systems, the production of a weekly electronic bulletin, and the creation and development of various European networks, for instance, for HIV/STD prevention among prostitutes, in prisons, and on European public policy on AIDS. The EU's contribution in the field of HIV/AIDS has been succinctly described as:

> "a mixture of ancillary bankroller, discreet disseminator of good practice and ideas, and an increasingly authoritative repository of unique pan-European data."[61]

HIV/AIDS and free movement of persons

As we saw in chapter 4, the EC Treaty makes provision for the free movement across internal borders within the EU, of "citizens of the European Union", in particular as workers and self-employed persons, but also, in certain circumstances, simply as such "citizens of the European Union".[62] The Treaty also now provides for common measures with respect to the movement of persons across the EU's *external* borders, in the form of a common asylum and immigration policy. Underpinning those

58 COM(99) 463 final.

59 The Commission report was based on a report from a team of external experts and the views of the representatives of the Member States on the relevant management committee.

60 COM(99) 463 final, p 11.

61 R. Watson, "EU makes a difference over AIDS" 314 BMJ (1997) 993 (5 April).

62 See, in particular, Case C-85/96 *Martinez Sala* [1998] ECR I-2691; Case C-184/99 *Grzelczyk* [2001] ECR I-6193; Case C-413/99 *Baumbast* [2002] ECR I-7091.

provisions is the idea of an "area of freedom, security and justice", within which, in principle, persons may move as freely as goods or services. One strand of public health protection measures concerned with communicable diseases, with a long historical pedigree, limits the freedom of movement of persons suffering from those diseases. To what extent may EU internal market law (deregulatory, directly effective) and common immigration and asylum law (reregulatory, also largely directly effective) be employed to undermine such public health protection measures?

The answer is to a very limited extent, if at all. The EC Treaty itself recognises protection of public health as an objective public interest that can justify limitations on the Treaty-based freedom of movement of persons. In the specific instance of infectious diseases, this is also reflected in secondary legislation. For instance, Directive 64/221/EEC provides that a number of listed diseases[63] shall justify refusal of entry into the territory of a Member State, or refusal to issue a first residence permit.[64] However, once a citizen of the EU has been granted entry or residence, the onset of such a listed disease cannot justify their expulsion. Member States cannot therefore use expulsion of non-nationals, who are citizens of the EU, as part of their public health policies with respect to communicable diseases. Otherwise, however, restrictions on free movement of persons are permitted on public health grounds.[65]

In fact, in terms of HIV/AIDS, it appears that it is not so much movements within the EU, but rather movements into the EU, especially from Africa, that concern public health officials in the Member States. To what extent might the EU's emergent common immigration policy affect national public health policy here? It seems that the same principles apply with respect to the entry into the territory of the EU of "third country nationals" from elsewhere in the world and their movement around the EU, as apply to movements of citizens of the EU. The EU's common immigration policy recognises the ability of Member States to restrict the entry and residence of such third country nationals on grounds, *inter alia*, of public health.[66] The proposed Directive on conditions of entry and residence of third country nationals for reasons of employment and self-employment[67] explicitly provides that Member States may restrict entry and residence for reasons of public health, and provides that Member

63 These are "1. Diseases subject to quarantine listed in International Health Regulation No 2 of the WHO of 25 May 1951"; 2. Active tuberculosis; 3. Syphilis; and "4. Other infectious diseases or contagious parasitic diseases if they are the subject of provisions for the protection of nationals of the host country": Directive 64/221/EEC, Annex A.

64 Directive 64/221/EEC, Article 4 (1). For a major comparative overview of Member State law concerning free movement and migration, see further J. Carlier, *The Free Movement of Persons Living with HIV/AIDS* (Luxembourg: Office of Official Publications of the European Community, 1999).

65 The "Common Manual" on the "area of freedom, security and justice", OJ 2002 C 313/97, provides in Part II (Border Checks), 1.3.4, that EU citizens "shall be subject to random thorough checks on entry and exit in certain cases where there is reason to believe that the persons concerned might compromise public policy, national security or health".

66 See, for instance, Directive 2003/86/EC on the right to family reunification, OJ 2003 L 251/12, Article 6; proposed Directive on conditions of entry and residence, COM(2001) 386 final, awaiting final decision of Council.

67 This proposal is based on Title IV of the EC Treaty and so will not apply to the UK or Ireland unless they decide otherwise; likewise it will not apply to Denmark.

States may require a health certificate as part of the documentation necessary for a residence permit.[68] However, expulsion or refusal to renew a residence permit may not be carried out on the basis of an illness that manifests itself *after* the original issue of a residence permit. Again, otherwise, however, restrictions on free movement of persons from outside the EU are permitted. So, for instance, a Member State may restrict entry and residence to a person with an infectious disease, and may impose reasonable tests or evidence of a clean bill of health in that respect.[69]

However, the practical dimension in this context concerns the efficacy of such limitations. In practice, ascertaining HIV/AIDS may be very difficult. Does this mean that Member States could require tests at the borders, which would inevitably involve time delays? Simply relying upon health documents from the migrant's home country would be unsatisfactory in the case of a disorder that takes time to manifest itself such as HIV.[70]

Furthermore, it remains to be seen whether any such policies may be subject to challenge by reference to fundamental human rights. Entry restrictions have come under criticism. Gostin and Lazzarini have commented that:

> "testing and excluding persons based upon HIV infection alone is a form of 'status' discrimination. Unless justified by a compelling reason and based upon reasonable and objective criteria, such policies offend the non-discrimination principles contained in the International Bill of Human Rights and countless other documents."[71]

Non-discrimination has been recognised as a "general principle" of EU law, and the EU Charter on Fundamental Rights and Freedoms, which the Draft Constitutional Treaty proposes should become binding EU Treaty law, contains a general non-discrimination principle. Article 21 EUCFR is a broadly drafted clause which states that:

> "1. Any discrimination based on any ground *such as* sex, race, colour, ethnic or social origin, genetic features, language, religion or belief, political or any other opinion, membership of a national minority, property, birth, disability, age or sexual orientation shall be prohibited."[72]

68 Proposal COM(2001) 386 final, Article 27. The European Parliament Committee on Legal Affairs and the Internal Market has proposed that the explicit reference to public health in this proposed provision is not necessary: see A5-0010/2003, January 2003. Neither of the other two Parliamentary Committees proposed any amendment to Article 27.

69 Certainly some Member States, such as the UK, are at least considering compulsory HIV tests for all immigrants: see O. Wright and A. Browne, "All immigrants to have compulsory HIV tests as cases rise", 13 February 2003, http://www.timesonline.co.uk. This would appear to be lawful in EU law.

70 In interviews with McHale as part of her work on the EU Biomed 2 project, *Communicable Diseases, Lifestyles and Personal Responsibility*, one high-ranking public health physician commented that such test results "would not be worth the paper they were written on", and see J. McHale, "Migration and Communicable Diseases: Some Legal Issues" Final Conference Report, Conference on Communicable Diseases, Lifestyles and Responsibility, Amalfi, Italy, September 1998.

71 Gostin and Lazzarini, above n 12.

72 Emphasis added.

There is the possibility that compulsory HIV/AIDS tests on EU citizens crossing borders within the EU, or on third country nationals entering the EU, may contravene such provisions.[73] HIV/AIDS can be distinguished from the majority of public health limitations on entry to a particular territory, due to the fact that transmission risks are considerably lower than those in relation to contagious diseases such as tuberculosis. The objective public interest in restricting movement, contrary to the principle of non-discrimination, may therefore be insufficient to justify restriction of such fundamental human rights.

Blood safety and HIV

One element of public health policy with respect to communicable diseases concerns the regulatory standards surrounding the use of human blood in a health care setting. In the context of AIDS/HIV, such legislation might include measures such as compulsory HIV testing for blood donors, or even the prohibition of paid blood donation, on the grounds that there is significant evidence that paid donors are more likely to carry the virus undeclared.[74] A number of Member States have experienced major "scandals" with respect to HIV-infected blood transfusions, in particular to haemophiliacs.[75] In France, about 4000 people were given transfusions of HIV-infected blood in the mid-1980s.[76] Many of these people died. Some 1300 people have died in Italy from infected blood transfusions since 1985. More than 100 Portuguese haemophiliacs were infected after receiving transfusions of contaminated plasma. In 1993, it was reported that over 350 haemophiliacs in Germany had been infected with the HIV virus from blood products, as a result of the testing of the blood products by using pooled plasma from three donors, instead of testing each donation separately.[77] Blood and blood products are imported by Member States of the EU, so blood safety cannot be considered simply within national borders. A further issue concerns the prospect of "commercialisation" in relation to dealing in blood. The whole concept of commercial dealing in "human material", which may be regarded as including blood, has been the subject of considerable controversy.[78] So much so, in fact, that the Council of Europe Convention on Human Rights and Biomedicine 1997 contains, in Article 21, a statement to the effect that "the human

73 For further discussion of the EUCFR and the Draft Constitutional Treaty, see chapter 10.

74 See P.J. Hagen, *Blood Transfusion in Europe: a "white paper"* (Strasbourg: Council of Europe Press, 1993).

75 See "Aids Scandals around the world" BBC News Online, 9 August 2001; and D. Giesen "Liability for Transfer of HIV Infected Blood in Comparative Perspective" 10 *Professional Negligence* (1994) 2.

76 A subsequent trial led to the conviction of the former health minister Edmond Hervé; but former French premier, Laurent Fabius, and Georgina Dufoix, former social affairs minister, were acquitted of manslaughter.

77 J. Abraham and G. Lewis, *Regulating Medicines in Europe: Competition, expertise and public health* (London and New York: Routledge, 2000), p 73.

78 See, for example, R. Titmuss, *The Gift Relationship*, edited by A. Oakley and J. Ashton (London, LSE Books, 1997); N. Duxbury "Do Markets Degrade" 59 MLR (1996) 331.

body and its parts shall not, as such, give rise to financial gain". This provision has influenced EU-level measures on blood safety.[79]

As we saw in chapter 3, formal Community competence in health matters was established in Article 129 EC, added to the Treaty of Rome at Maastricht, and amended at Amsterdam in the (renumbered) Article 152 EC on public health. Article 152 (4) requires the Council to contribute to the achievement of the objectives of Article 152 through adopting:

> "(a) measures setting high standards of quality and safety of organs and substances of human origin, blood and blood derivatives . . . "

Article 152 (4) (a) EC creates Community competence to adopt "measures", by implication including harmonising regulations or directives, setting high standards of quality in organs and blood products. Thus new Article 152 EC makes clear the Community's competence (and indeed obligation) to enact what is in effect consumer protection legislation in these fields.

Of course, the position of the *formal legality* of such EU-level action should not be considered in isolation from its *political* context. Given the immense variety in tradition, practice and opinions among the Member States of the EU with respect to the regulation of human blood used in a health care context, it might have been expected that sufficient agreement between governments of Member States to ensure the enactment of such harmonisation measures was unlikely to be present. However, this view must be tempered by two factors. First, action under Article 152 (4) (a) EC is to be taken in accordance with the "co-decision procedure",[80] according to which voting in Council is by qualified majority:[81] thus no one national government enjoys a veto in this field. Second, it may be the case that the EU institutions are more likely to forge agreement between governments of Member States in matters of urgency and crisis, or in areas where national level action is inadequate.[82] Both criteria above are met in the case of blood safety regulation, increasing the likelihood of the adoption of EU-level measures.

Some relevant measures of EU law predate the new competence provision in Article 152 EC.[83] Directive 89/381/EEC on the harmonisation of laws relating to

79 For instance, it is reflected in the EUCFR, and now Draft Constitutional Treaty: see Article II-3 (2) (c) DCT.

80 Article 251 EC.

81 For details, see Article 205 (2) EC. For further details on EU legislative procedures, see chapter 2. See also P. Craig and G. de Búrca, *EU Law: Text, Cases and Materials* (Oxford: OUP, 2003), chapters 2 and 3.

82 See, for instance, Commissioner Flynn's speech at http://europa.eu.int/comm/dg05/speeches/990318bpf.html: "I can always count on a strong interest where there is a crisis or political capital to be made." For further details, see, *inter alia*, H. Wallace and W. Wallace, *Policy-Making in the European Union* (Oxford: OUP, 2000), chapter 1.

83 In addition to the measures discussed below, Directive 93/42/EEC, OJ 1993 L 169/1 on medical devices states in its preamble that "medical devices used for protection against the AIDS virus must afford a high level of protection; . . . [and] the design and manufacture of such products should be verified by a Notified Body". Article 11 of the Directive requires quality assurance procedures for the manufacture of medical devices to be put on the market in the EU. "Notified

medicinal products derived from human blood or plasma[84] extends the application of the EU's pharmaceuticals regime[85] to medicinal products derived from human blood or plasma. The Directive requires Member States to take precautions necessary to prevent the transmission of infectious diseases, such as hepatitis and AIDS, including measures recommended by the Council of Europe and WHO, in particular for selection and testing of blood donors.[86] However, the Directive does not apply to blood itself. The legal basis of measures such as this (ex Article 100a (now 95) EC) in effect acted as a constraint for developing further measures of binding law to regulate the safety of blood itself. To frame such regulation in the terms of the internal market, as would be necessitated by such a legal basis, would be to conceptualise blood as a tradable commodity. The considerable distaste for this within Europe is reflected in the Council of Europe's Convention on Human Rights and Biomedicine, Article 21, and now in Article 3 (2) EUCFR.[87]

A number of measures of soft law concerning blood safety were therefore adopted by the EU institutions in the 1990s.[88] Many of these called for the EU to become "self-sufficient" in blood, as a response to the safety concerns raised by the global AIDS epidemic, and the realisation that European countries that had not been reliant on blood imported from elsewhere in the world, in particular the developing world, had very low transmission rates of HIV to haemophiliac patients.[89] In 1998, Council adopted a Recommendation on the suitability of blood and plasma donors and the screening of donated blood in the EU.[90] This set out (non-binding) principles according to which blood donation should be undertaken in the Member States, including principles with respect to consent, the giving of information to donors and gathering of information from them, and the development of common criteria on donor suitability. The Council recommended that "Member States shall do all they can to encourage the voluntary and unpaid donation of blood or plasma".[91]

Bodies" are independent, impartial, accredited certification bodies within the Member States. Directive 98/79/EC, OJ 1998 L 331/1 applies similar requirements to in vitro diagnostic medical devices. Devices listed in Annex II, A, including those for HIV testing, must be verified by a Notified Body, and special quality assurance procedures apply.

84 OJ 1989 L 181/44.

85 See in particular, Directive 2001/83/EC, OJ 2001 L 311/67; see further chapter 8.

86 Directive 89/381/EEC, Article 3 (1).

87 Which it is proposed will be incorporated into the Draft Constitutional Treaty, Article II-3 (2) (c) DCT.

88 See, for instance, Commission Communication on blood self-sufficiency in the European Community, COM(93) 198 final; Council conclusions on self-sufficiency in blood in the European Community, OJ 1994 C 15/6; Commission Communication on blood safety and self-sufficiency in the European Community, COM(94) 652 final; Council Resolution on blood safety and self-sufficiency in the Community, OJ 1995 C 164/1; Council Resolution on strategy towards blood safety and self-sufficiency in the European Community, OJ 1996 C 374/1.

89 This included countries such as Norway, Belgium and Finland: see J. Leikola, "Achieving self sufficiency in blood across Europe" 316 BMJ (1998) 489.

90 Council Recommendation 98/463/EC on the suitability of blood and plasma donors and the screening of donated blood in the European Community, OJ 1998 L 203/14.

91 Recommendation 98/463/EC, para 14. It remains unclear exactly what constitutes "unpaid" donation; for instance, in a number of Member States, a flat rate to cover travel expenses, food

The Blood Safety Directive

The adoption of the new Article 152 EC removed the legal bar to EU level regulatory measures concerned with blood safety. Blood itself (and not merely products derived from blood) may now be regulated at EU level, without the need to frame such regulation within the terms of Article 95 EC. Directive 2002/98/EC setting standards of quality and safety for the collection, testing, processing, storage and distribution of human blood and blood components (the Blood Safety Directive)[92] was adopted in January 2003. This was the first legislative measure based exclusively on Article 152 (4) EC.

The Blood Safety Directive applies to collection and testing of human blood and blood components, irrespective of intended purpose and to their processing, storage and distribution when intended for transfusion.[93] The Directive provides that only duly accredited, authorised or licensed national blood establishments may collect and test human blood, and sets various inspection requirements and quality control systems with respect to such establishments.[94] Quality control systems must include particular elements of record keeping, and the principle of traceability, meaning that "blood and blood components collected, tested, processed, stored, released and/or distributed ... can be traced from donor to recipient and vice versa".[95] Common criteria for the testing of donations to ensure quality and safety are to be established.[96] The implication is that, had such measures been in place in the 1980s and 1990s, the various scandals noted above could probably have been avoided.

The Directive provides for a system whereby common EU-level criteria for donor eligibility will be determined by the committee process.[97] All future blood donors in the EU will have to provide at least a form of identification, health history and a signature.[98] Potential donors must be interviewed and examined by a qualified health professional before giving blood.[99]

The Member States have until 8 February 2005 to adapt their national laws and practices to comply with the Directive.[100] The Directive is a "new approach" measure setting minimum standards, and explicitly states that it does not prevent Member States from maintaining or introducing more stringent national protective measures, for instance, requirements for voluntary and unpaid blood donations.[101] This was necessitated in part by Article 152 (5) EC, which states explicitly that

tokens, theatre tickets, and time off work are given to blood donors: see C. Politis, "Editorial: Blood Donations systems as an integral part of the health system" 17 *Archives of Hellenic Medicine* (2000) 354.

92 OJ 2002 L 33/30.
93 Directive 2002/98/EC, Article 2 (1).
94 Directive 2002/98/EC, Articles 5–8; 11–13.
95 Directive 2002/98/EC, Article 14 (1). Data must be kept for at least 30 years: Article 14 (3).
96 Directive 2002/98/EC, Articles 21, 23, 29.
97 Directive 2002/98/EC, Articles 18 and 29.
98 Directive 2002/98/EC, Article 17.
99 Directive 2002/98/EC, Article 19.
100 Directive 2002/98/EC, Article 32.
101 Directive 2002/98/EC, Article 4 (2).

provisions adopted under Article 152 (4) may not affect national provisions on blood donation.[102] However, in line with the previous soft law measures noted above, the Directive provides the strongest possible steer towards voluntary and unpaid blood donations, in Article 20. This states that:

> "Member States shall take the necessary measures to encourage voluntary and unpaid blood donations with a view to ensuring that blood and blood components are in so far as possible provided from such donations."

Thus, the principle of voluntary and unpaid blood donations has formed a consistent part of measures articulated at EU level with respect to blood donations. The relationship between unpaid donation and blood safety is most famously articulated by Titmuss, in his seminal work *The Gift Relationship*.[103] Titmuss argued that the provision of human blood through a classical "market" mechanism, in which donors are paid for blood, is inappropriate and inefficient. In a post-AIDS era, such arguments are lent even greater weight by the observation that the blood supplied by unpaid donors is also likely to be safer.[104] Most EU Member States do not pay blood donors, and there is no country in Europe with a totally "for-profit" system of blood collection, but in some Member States, for instance, Germany and Austria, plasma and some whole blood donations to commercial centres are "remunerated",[105] or rather expenses are reimbursed.[106] In many accession and candidate countries in Central and Eastern Europe, the system relies on both paid and unpaid blood donation. Most Member States and accession countries that are currently undergoing review and reform of their health sectors include among the objectives of these reforms a move to voluntary unpaid blood donation.[107] International bodies, such as the Council of Europe, the WHO and the Red Cross/Crescent, take the view that, ideally, blood and plasma donors should not be remunerated.[108] One of the main

102 Directive 2002/98/EC, preamble, Recital 22.

103 See Titmuss, above n 78. For a counter-argument in the context of organ donation, see A. Fagot-Largeault, "Does Non-Commercialisation of the Human Body Increase Graft Security?" in Y. Englert, ed, *Organ and Tissue Transplantation in the European Union* (Dordrecht: Martinus Nijhoff, 1995).

104 There is some debate about this among the scientific literature; for a recent overview of various studies: see C.L. van der Poel, E. Seifried and W.P. Schaasberg, "Paying for Blood Donations: still a risk?" 83 *Vox Sanguinis* (2002) 285; and also the letter responding: R. Offergeld and R. Burger, "Remuneration of blood donors and its impact on transfusion safety" 85 *Vox Sanguinis* (2003) 49.

105 At least this was so in 1993: See Hagen, above n 74, pp 50–65.

106 A reimbursement up to a certain amount is given for direct travel and real time expenses in Germany; see F. Von Auer, "Payment for blood donations in Germany" 310 BMJ (1995) 399 (11 February).

107 Politis, above n 91, citing C. Politis and J. Yfantopoulos, *Blood Transfusion and the Challenge of AIDS in Greece: Medical and Economic Aspects* (Athens: Beta Medical, 1993) and C. Politis, *The Transition from paid to unpaid blood donorship* Seventh International Colloquium on the Recruitment of Voluntary non-remunerated blood donors, International Federation of Red Cross and Red Crescent Societies, Geneva, 1999.

108 Council of Europe, *Guide to the preparation, use and quality assurance of blood components* (Strasbourg: Council of Europe, 1997); International Federation of Red Cross and Red Crescent Societies Blood Programme, *Quality Manual and Development Manual* (1998), cited in Politis, above n 91.

reasons for this is the suggestion that clinical paid donors are more likely to conceal potential hazards of the blood they are donating, including the possibility that a donor is seropositive. Unpaid voluntary blood donation has clear resonance with a notion of "solidarity" between donors and recipients. "Solidarity" has been seen as part of a set of distinctively "European" values. The EU institutions may be seen here to be utilising their legislative competence with respect to regulation of blood safety to express and perhaps shore up this "European" value of solidarity.

The next stage of regulation adopted under Article 152 EC will be regulation of organ donation.[109] In 2003, the Commission proposed a new standards-setting Directive (proposed Tissue Directive)[110] on the quality and safety of human tissue. This is discussed further in chapter 10. Having considered some of the main elements of EU law concerning HIV/AIDS, we now turn to the provisions of EU law relevant for protecting public health in respect of various food-borne diseases.[111]

BSE/nvCJD

Introduction

The regulation of food – its production, processing, distribution and retail – is an established part of European societies. Food is a very densely regulated sector in EU law, with over 80 separate pieces of EU-level legislation on the subject. One key reason[112] for the regulation of food is the protection of public health. As Professor Philip James, the "driving force" behind the establishment of the UK Food Standards Agency, has commented: "The medical establishment finds it hard to believe that food and nutrition have much to do with public health."[113] However, there is a fundamental link between food and public health, and to ignore this link is to adopt an incomplete perspective on public health protection. Hazards to human health passed on through the food chain, such as e-coli, salmonella, listeria, or bovine spongiform encephalopathy (BSE), justify regulatory responses. In the EU context,

109 The Commission stated on its website that it "will need to consider the need to identify, monitor and control the factors influencing the quality and safety of organs used for transplantation at EU level" under Article 152 EC: see http://www.europa.eu.int/comm/health/ph_threats/humans_substance/organs-en.htm.

110 Amended Proposal for a Directive of the European Parliament and of the Council on setting standards of quality and safety for the donation, procurement, testing, processing, storage and distribution of human tissues and cells (presented by the Commission pursuant to Article 250(2) of the EC Treaty, COM(2003) 340 final, considered further in chapter 10 below.

111 For a list and descriptions of such common food-borne diseases, see Donaldson and Donaldson, above n 4, chapter 9.

112 Other reasons include the wish to protect certain lifestyles in the agricultural domain; to guard against unemployment among certain social groups; to promote animal welfare; and ecological or environmental reasons, such as the protection of natural areas or biodiversity. See K.P. Rippe, "Novel Foods and Consumer Rights" 12 *Journal of Agricultural and Environmental Ethics* (2000) 71 at 72.

113 Cited in News: "Food is a Public Health Issue" 316 BMJ (1998) 411. We could also say perhaps that health lawyers find it hard to believe that food law has much to do with public health law!

the internal market requires at least a minimum protective standard emanating from the EU level, as, in principle, foodstuffs lawfully produced and marketed in one Member State must be accepted in all other Member States.[114]

Recently, the regulation of food in the EU has come under scrutiny, and has undergone a period of reform. This is for a number of interrelated reasons, chief amongst which is the fallout from the BSE/nvCJD crisis.[115] The failure of the UK government to control the spread of BSE among its cattle herds in the mid-1980s, and the subsequent discovery of a link between BSE and the human disease new variant CJD (nvCJD) shattered consumer confidence in British beef. The EU responded by placing a ban on the export of British beef, but it appears that this was not implemented before cattle herds in other EU countries, such as France, were affected by the disease. A similar problem arose with the dioxin contamination of animal products from animal feed produced in Belgium.

The broader context within which changes in EU food regulation have taken place includes significant changes in the food industry in Europe. European consumers (particularly those in the north of Europe) have increased their use of convenience foods. Food production has changed as a result of new technology, in particular biotechnology, and the use of genetically modified organisms in foodstuffs.[116] These in turn have raised health questions and consumer concerns about the safety of such foods. Food retailing has also changed, in particular in the concentration of food retail outlets into out-of-town multiplex sites and the increasing use by supermarkets of "own-brand" products. In these circumstances, small and medium sized enterprises (SMEs) may choose either to pursue niche quality markets or to supply supermarket own brands. However, the internal market also gives opportunities for producers and suppliers of all sizes to attempt to break into new markets, by

114 The principle of "mutual recognition": see Case 120/78 *Cassis de Dijon* [1979] ECR 649. See further chapter 2.

115 See, in general, M. Westlake, "'Mad Cows and Englishmen': The Institutional Consequences of the BSE Crisis" in N. Nugent, ed, *European Union 1996: the annual review*, published in association with the JCMS, p 11.

116 There is a separate and detailed EU regulatory scheme for genetically modified foods, which is not discussed in detail in this book: see in particular Regulation 258/97/EC, the "Novel Foods Regulation", OJ 1997 L 43/1. This regime is the subject of intense debate in the context of the WTO, especially as the US has adopted a significantly less risk-averse approach to genetically modified foods. See, for instance, E. Vos, "EU Food Safety Regulation in the aftermath of the BSE Crisis" 23 *Journal of Consumer Policy* (2000) 227; J. Scott and E. Vos, "The Juridification of Uncertainty: Observations on the Ambivalence of the Precautionary Principle within the EU and the WTO" in C. Joerges and R. Dehousse, *Good Governance in Europe's Integrated Market* (Oxford: OUP, 2002); J. Scott, "The Precautionary Principle Before the European Courts" in R. Macrory, *Environmental Principles in the EU and the Member States* (Groningen: Europa Law Publishing, forthcoming 2004). Possible health risks arising from genetically modified organisms might include the transfer of carcinogens ("Who's afraid?" *Economist*, 19 June 1999, pp 15–16; "Genetically Modified Food" *Economist*, 19 June 1999, pp 19–21, cited by C.F. Runge and L.A. Jackson, "Labelling, Trade and Genetically Modified Organisms" 34 *Journal of World Trade* (2000) 111 at 112) or allergens. Most food allergies are associated with proteins, with some common foodstuffs, for instance wheat and milk, containing several allergenic proteins.

cross-border supply of food. Moreover, the food and drink sector is extremely important for the European economy as a whole.[117]

These factors all combine to produce an increasing pressure on the institutions of the EU to provide a stable regulatory regime for food in the EU. In general, food regulation may be effected for reasons of consumer safety and protection, or in order to promote quality in foodstuffs.[118] Types of regulation may tend towards "paternalistic" modes, in which government seeks to protect citizens from themselves and to prevent them from making adverse choices (for instance, in forbidding marketing, regulating access, or controlling production of certain types of food) or "autonomy-centred" modes, in which "consumer sovereignty" is guaranteed by requiring consumer information.[119] Paternalistic modes of regulation seek to reduce transaction costs for consumers, by passing to a government agency the responsibility for becoming expert in chemistry, biotechnology, risk assessment and so on. Such modes of regulation also seek to eradicate any tendency of food producers to aim for short-term economic benefits, at the expense of long-term consequences for human health, against which the protection of insurance alone may be economically inefficient, or politically inappropriate.[120] Regulation may also be "industry centred" self-regulation, or "government or governmental agency centred" regulation. The large number of SMEs involved in the EU food industry may affect what are appropriate regulatory models for the EU, if SMEs are to survive in the face of giant agri-business.[121] As will be seen, the EU's current food law regime is relatively autonomy centred, though cautious with respect to risk, and incorporates elements of both industry and governmental agency regulation.

In terms of our typology set out in chapter 2, in the context of food law, the EU utilises, or has utilised at various times, deregulatory mechanisms based on the free movement of goods, "old style" harmonisation, in which detailed standards for food products were set at EU level, and "new approach" harmonisation, incorporating the principle of mutual recognition of nationally imposed standards, coupled with labelling requirements, seen as a proportionate response to concerns about consumer protection. More recently, there has been a turn back towards something more like "old style" harmonisation, in the sense that general principles of food law are being articulated at EU level, to be enforced by national agencies. Thus, EU food law looks more like "classic" EU law than many other areas of law we consider in this book. However, this turn towards "old style" harmonisation has been coupled with a self-regulatory or partnership approach, relying on industry

117 The food and drink industry employs 2.3 million people in the EU, nearly half of whom work in small or medium-sized enterprises (SMEs). Another 10 million work in primary agricultural production. See R. O'Rourke, *European Food Law* (Bembridge: Palladian Law Publishing, 1999), p 5. The industry will become even more important on the accession of Central and Eastern European states to the EU beginning with the first wave on 1 May 2004.

118 Rippe, above n 112, at 73.

119 Rippe, above n 112, at 74.

120 Ibid.

121 O'Rourke, above n 117, p 5.

to "police" itself, rather than using agencies of government for this purpose. This "partnership" approach has echoes in new methods of governance, which, as we saw in chapter 2, are being applied in other areas of EU law.

BSE/nvCJD: historical context

EU food law has developed piecemeal over a long period of time, beginning in the early 1960s.[122] Until 2002,[123] there was no central unifying text setting out the fundamental principles of EU food law and clearly defining the obligations of those involved at every stage of the food production chain. The Commission's initial approach to food law was, not surprisingly, concerned with free movement of foodstuffs within the common market. Proposals for legislation were based on old Article 100 EEC,[124] which required unanimity in Council, therefore adoption rates were slow.

However up until 1985, the Community did adopt a number of measures of "vertical" – in the sense that each measure applied to one particular foodstuff – legislation on food quality,[125] and a general "horizontal" food labelling Directive.[126] Regarded as an advanced piece of legislation at the time of its adoption, this provision has been used as a model by the international *Codex Alimentarius* Committee on Food Labelling.[127] The Directive prohibited labelling likely to mislead consumers, and set eight compulsory items to be included on all food labelling.[128] Further vertical directives[129] drew on this horizontal directive, in addition to setting out rules on compositional standards of the foodstuffs to which they relate.

122 The first EU food directive, concerning colours in foodstuffs, was adopted in 1962. This provision has no number, as no formal system for numbering of EEC laws was in operation at the relevant time: O'Rourke, above n 117, p 3.

123 But now see Regulation 178/2002/EC, OJ 2002 L 31/1.

124 Now Article 94 EC.

125 Detailed legislation was adopted on compositional standards of various different foodstuffs: certain sugars, honey, (Directive 74/409/EEC, OJ 1974 L 221/10; repealed by Directive 2001/110/EC relating to honey, OJ 2002 L 10/47) fruit juices, some dehydrated and preserved milk, fruit jams, jellies, marmalades and chestnut puree, coffee and chicory extracts, cocoa products and chocolate products, (Directive 73/241/EEC, OJ 1973 L 228/23; repealed by Directive 2000/36/EC of the European Parliament and of the Council of 23 June 2000 relating to cocoa and chocolate products intended for human consumption, OJ 2000 L 197/19). For further details on "vertical legislation", see O'Rourke, above n 117, pp 55–72.

126 Directive 79/112/EEC, OJ 1979 L 33/1, as amended and now consolidated in Directive 2000/13/EC, OJ 2000 L 109/29.

127 O'Rourke, above n 117, p 27.

128 Namely: name, ingredients, net quantity, date of minimum durability ("use by date"), any special storage conditions or conditions of use, name and address of manufacturer or packager or seller established within the EU, particulars of place of origin or provenance where required for consumer information and instructions for use where necessary: Directive 79/112/EEC, Article 3.

129 For example, Directive 80/777/EEC, OJ 1980 L 229/1 on natural mineral waters (see Case C-17/96 *Badische Erfrischungs-Getränke v Land BadenWürttemberg* [1997] ECR I-4617 in which it was held that Member States may not require that water marketed as "natural mineral water" possess properties favourable to health), amended by Directive 96/70/EC, OJ 1996 L 229/26); Regulation 1601/91/EEC on aromatized wines, OJ 1991 L 149/1; Regulation 1898/87/EEC on

The mid-1980s saw a change of approach to EU-level regulation,[130] including that in the food sector. The Commission's new regulatory strategy – the "New Approach" – was underpinned by the Court's ruling in *Cassis de Dijon*,[131] to the effect that goods produced according to the regulatory standards of one Member State may, save for the existence of a legitimate justification, be lawfully marketed in all other Member States. Thus, EU-level regulation was needed only to ensure necessary minimum regulatory standards. In line with this new approach, the 1985 Commission Communication, *Completion of the Internal Market – Community Legislation on Foodstuffs*,[132] stated that, in principle, EU legislation on foodstuffs would in future be restricted to only that justified by protection of public health (Article 30 EC[133]); providing consumers with information and protection in matters other than health and ensuring fair trading; and providing for the adequate and necessary official controls of foodstuffs. This Communication was followed by the adoption of a number of "framework directives" on foods, including the framework directive on additives,[134] labelling foods for particular nutritional needs,[135] hygiene[136] and official controls.[137]

The main thrust behind the "New Approach" was the creation of the internal market, by ensuring the free movement of goods throughout the EU. However, food is a commodity that may be less susceptible to free movement than other, less culturally embedded consumer goods, such as clothing, electrical and electronic goods. In food law, perhaps more than in some other sectors, governments of Member States tend to adopt national standards that covertly discriminate against goods produced in other Member States. One role of the Commission is to guard against such divisions of the internal market, using the enforcement mechanism of Article 226 EC.[138] A large number of these enforcement actions concern food law,[139]

milk and milk products, OJ 1987 L 182/36; Regulation 2991/94/EC on spreadable fats, OJ 1994 L 316/2, implemented by Regulation 577/97 EC of 1 April 1997 laying down certain detailed rules for the application of Regulation 2991/94 EC laying down standards for spreadable fats and of Regulation 1898/87 EEC on the protection of designations used in the marketing of milk and milk products, OJ 1997 L 87/3.

130 See further chapter 2.

131 Case 120/78 *Cassis de Dijon* above n 114. This is in fact a case concerning food law; the alcohol content of cassis liqueur.

132 COM(85) 603 final.

133 Ex Article 36 EC.

134 Directive 89/107/EEC, OJ 1989 L 40/27. See Case C-3/00 *Denmark v Commission (Food Additives)* [2003] ECR I-2643, see chapter 3, p 57.

135 Directive 89/398/EEC, OJ 1989 L 186/27.

136 Directive 93/43/EEC, OJ 1993 L 175/1.

137 Directive 89/397/EEC, OJ 1989 L 186/23; to be repealed and replaced by a new Reputation, see COM (2003), 52 final.

138 Ex Article 169 EC. The Commission is aided in this respect by the Transparency Directive 83/189/EEC, OJ 1983 L 109/8, which requires Member States to notify all new technical standards to the Commission before adoption.

139 In 1999 alone, infringement proceedings were brought against France – rubber products in contact with foodstuffs; Germany – barriers to import of food supplements, authorisation delays for food supplements; Greece – price labelling requirements for soft drinks and bottled water; France – restrictions on sale of pasta products; Belgium – unfair restrictions regarding nutritional labelling; and Italy – restrictions on the sale of chocolate products containing vegetable fats. Such

perhaps most famously the *German Beer Purity* case.[140] This concerned the German *Reinheitsgebot* (Beer Purity law) which provided that beer marketed in Germany under the description "Bier" was to be manufactured from barley, hops, yeast and water only. No other additives[141] were permitted. Germany claimed that this rule, which restricted access to the German market for beer produced in other Member States where less stringent rules applied, was justified on grounds of protection of public health. The Court held that it was indeed the case that Member States enjoy a significant margin of discretion with respect to the protection of the health of their residents, in cases where scientific opinion was uncertain as to the potential health hazards posed by the goods concerned. However, applying the principle of proportionality, restrictions on trade between Member States must be only what is necessary actually to secure a genuine need of health policy. Here, Germany had failed to show such a genuine need.

The Commission responded to *Cassis de Dijon* and *Beer Purity* by clarifying the position with respect to trade names for food and additives in foodstuffs and EU internal market law.[142] Generic trade descriptions (such as "beer") were to be permitted, with labelling to inform consumers of the actual contents of the product. Labelling must also alert consumers to the presence of additives in imported foodstuffs. Additives were to be permitted, so long as they were not dangerous to public health, in the light of findings of international scientific research and the eating habits of those in a particular Member State.

The essential thrust, then, of EU food law in the run up to 31 December 1992 was the completion of the internal market, with the main focus being trade and free movement of goods. The general principle was liberalisation of trade, with consumer protection being limited to labelling[143] (an "autonomy centred" approach) and with paternalistic intervention permitted at national level only in exceptional circumstances. However, the consumer information labelling requirements may also be read as favouring a protectionist precautionary approach to risk, as such rules have been interpreted, for instance by the US food industry in the context of the labelling of genetically modified foodstuffs. The deregulatory thrust of the jurisprudence of the Court was balanced by this role for national regulation, and by reregulation at EU level where judged absolutely necessary, but consumer protection and public health clearly seemed to play second fiddle to free trade. In fact, during this time there were often calls for the relocation of the responsibility for food law in

infringement proceedings point to the fact that, although the free movement of foodstuffs is no longer the major focus of European food law, it still has an important role to play in the EU's evolving food policy: O'Rourke, above n 117, p x.

140 Case 178/84 *Commission v Germany (Beer Purity)* [1987] ECR 1227.

141 With the exception of certain processing aids and enzymes.

142 Commission Communication on the Free Movement of Foodstuffs within the Community, OJ 1989 C 271/3.

143 For a critical perspective on the labelling approach, see H. Von Heyebrand u.d. Lasa, "Free Movement of Foodstuffs, Consumer Protection and Food Standards in the EC: Has the Court of Justice got it Wrong?" 16 ELRev (1991) 391; see also C. MacMaolain, "Free Movement Of Foodstuffs, Quality Requirements And Consumer Protection: Have the Court and the Commission Both Got It Wrong?" 26 ELRev (2001) 413.

its entirety back to Member States. EU food law was criticised for "over-regulation, incoherence, fragmentation, [and] lack of transparency and innovation".[144]

However, it became apparent that the 1980s "New Approach" to food law, based on mutual recognition of equivalent national standards, is not appropriate for all areas of food law. The food industry is highly consumer sensitive. Mutual recognition works only where consumers trust the mechanisms of regulation, and, more importantly, of enforcement, in other Member States. Moreover, given that the internal market in food is increasingly well established, the old cliché that "diseases are no respecters of borders" also applies to food-borne diseases. In these circumstances, where food may pose a hazard to human health, simple reallocation of the responsibility for food regulation to national governments is therefore not appropriate. In some circumstances, perhaps in increasing areas, as the market in food becomes increasingly integrated, with multi-national suppliers providing food across borders, detailed regulation at EU level remains necessary.[145] The circumstances in which such detailed regulation is necessary at EU level are a matter of political judgment. Such judgment was profoundly affected by the BSE/nvCJD crisis.

BSE, or bovine spongiform encephalopathy, is a disease of cattle first recognised in Great Britain during the mid-1980s, and subsequently in other European countries such as France, Portugal and Switzerland. The disease was identified as being caused by an agent which was similar to that which causes the sheep disease scrapie. It appears that there is no evidence that BSE can be transmitted other than through the eating of contaminated animal feed. In 1996, there were indications that a new form of Creutzfeldt Jacob Disease[146] that had emerged could be linked to consumption of BSE-infected meat. Thus the EU had within its borders, on an undetermined scale, a new, and fatal, human disease, the spread of which had not been contained at the appropriate time, and about which consumers had been misinformed.[147] Little wonder, then, that the ensuing consumer concern (indeed panic), raised fundamental questions about the effectiveness of the regime for regulation of food in the EU.

The BSE/nvCJD crisis had the effect of undermining the trust – on which mutual recognition is based – between governments and consumers in different Member States. Various anti-BSE measures and procedures were agreed from the late

144 O'Rourke, above n 117, p 4.

145 An example of such an area may be found in Directive 94/65/EC on minced meat, OJ 1994 L 368/10. According to the preamble, this provision is "necessary to take account of the risk presented by some of these meat products if eaten lightly cooked", thus the need for strict requirements to ensure the highest level of protection for public health across the EU. The Directive introduces public health requirements for meat itself, and also establishes a system of approval for establishments producing minced meat and meat preparations. The Directive sets out considerable detail on the health certification approval requirements, conditions for preparation of the meat products, inspection, labelling, packaging, storage and transport, and compositional and microbiological criteria.

146 A rare neurological disorder, which has occurred world-wide over a number of years and provides similar spongiform changes to the human brain to BSE in cattle.

147 The UK government gave various assertions concerning the safety of British beef. Most famously, the incumbent UK Minister of Agriculture, John Gummer, publicly tried to feed a beef burger to his four-year-old daughter on 16 May 1990. See http://www.news.bbc.co.uk/onthisday/hi/dates/stories/may/16/newsid_2913000/2913807.stm.

1980s,[148] but the UK Ministry of Agriculture Fisheries and Food was unable to enforce them effectively.[149] Moreover, the Report of the European Parliament's Temporary Committee of Inquiry into BSE[150] found a number of serious contraventions or maladministration in the implementation of EU law adopted with respect to BSE, and, more significantly, revealed a number of systemic problems with EU food law. The mismanagement of the crisis arose in part from the difficulty in determining divisions of responsibility between the Commission, Council and the UK government. Each of those three institutions was found to have neglected its responsibilities in significant ways.[151] Significantly, the preponderance of British

148 Commission Decision 89/469/EEC *Restrictions on the Dispatch of Certain Live Cattle from the UK*, OJ 1989 L 225/51, repealed by Decision 94/474/EC, OJ 1994 L 194/96; Commission Decision 90/59/EEC, OJ 1990 L 41/23; Commission Decision 90/200/EEC, OJ 1990 L 105/24, repealed by Decision 94/474/EC, OJ 1994 L 194/96; Commission Decision 90/261/EEC, OJ 1990 L 146/29; Commission Decision 91/89/EEC, OJ 1991 L 49/31; Commission Decision 92/290/EEC, OJ 1992 L 152/37, repealed by Commission Regulation 260/2003/EC, OJ 2003 L 37/7; Commission Decision 92/450/EEC, OJ 1992 L 248/77, repealed by Decision 98/12/EC, OJ 1998 L 4/63; Commission Decision 94/381/EC, OJ 1994 L 172/23, repealed by Commission Regulation 1326/2001/EC, OJ 2001 L 177/60; Commission Decision 94/382/EC, OJ 1994 L 172/25, repealed by Decision 96/449/EC, OJ 1996 L 184/43; Commission Decision 94/474/EC, OJ 1994 L 194/96, repealed by Commission Regulation 1326/2001/EC, OJ 2001 177/60; Decision 95/29/EC, OJ 1995 L 38/17; Decision 95/60/EC, OJ 1995 L 55/43; Decision 95/287/EC, OJ 1995 L 181/40; Commission Decision 96/239/EC, OJ 1996 L 78/47 issuing a complete ban on the dispatch of live cattle and all cattle products from the United Kingdom (challenged unsuccessfully in Case C-180/96 R *United Kingdom of Great Britain and Northern Ireland v Commission of the European Communities* [1996] ECR I-3903 (interim suspension); and Case C-180/96 *United Kingdom of Great Britain and Northern Ireland v Commission of the European Communities* [1998] ECR I-2265), repealed by Council Decision 98/256/EC, OJ 1998 L 113/32; Commission Decision 96/385/EC, OJ 1996 L 151/39 on an eradication programme for the UK; Decision 96/449/EC, OJ 1996 L 184/43 on heat treatment for mammalian waste, repealed by Decision 99/534/EC, OJ 1999 L 204/37; Decision 97/534/EC, OJ 1997 L 216/95 on specified risk material, repealed by Decision 2000/418/EC, OJ 2000 L 158/76. See also Commission Decision 96/381/EC, OJ 1996 L 149/25 on an eradication programme for Portugal; Commission Decision 97/189/EC, OJ 1996 L 80/20 on an eradication programme for France; and Commission Decision 97/312/EC, OJ 1997 L 133/38 on an eradication programme for Ireland. For a complete list, see Community legislation on BSE, http://www.europa.ev.int/comm/food/fs/bse/bse15_en.pdf.

149 See the findings of the European Parliament Temporary Committee of Inquiry, below n 150.

150 "Report on alleged contraventions or maladministration in the implementation of Community law in relation to BSE, without prejudice to the jurisdiction of the Community and national courts", 7 February 1997, A4-0020/97. The temporary committee of inquiry was set up following a decision adopted by the European Parliament at its sitting of 18 July 1996, pursuant to its powers under Rule 136 of its Rules of Procedure. See also "Report on the European Commission's follow-up of the recommendations made by the Committee of Inquiry into BSE", 14 November 1997, A4-0362/97.

151 The main elements demonstrating negligence on the part of the UK fell into the following categories. The UK authorities paid insufficient attention to all risks involved; and had given a partial and biased reading to the advice and warnings of scientists. The UK authorities had failed to ensure an effective ban on the feeding of meat-and-bone meal to ruminants; and had failed to respect the national prohibitive legislation outlawing imports of meal from the UK; had failed to implement the legislation by which bovine animals should have been identified and branded and their movements registered; and had failed to implement the provisions of Directive 89/662/EEC concerning veterinary checks in intra-Community trade with a view to the completion of the internal market. Further, the UK placed pressure on the Commission not to include anything related to BSE in its general inspections of slaughterhouses, as periodically carried out between 1990 and 1994 in the context of the UK's adaptation to the internal market; and had possessed a "blocking attitude" within the Community institutions, with the aim of

experts and Ministry of Agriculture officials on the BSE Subgroup of the Scientific Veterinary Committee had increased the influence of British thinking on the Commission.[152] Problems in Council stemmed from the fact that responsibility for the problem was divided between the relevant authorities in agriculture and animal health, and those concerned with public health protection – a situation which was aggravated by the effects of the subsidiarity principle and by the "fragile state of progress in the exercise of Community powers in the public health field". As we have seen, this led to the amendment of the EC Treaty, to clarify and extend Community competence in the health field in the new Article 152 EC. The Commission's failings were manifold,[153] and included failure to take sufficiently seriously scientific evidence of risk, serious administrative mistakes, and failure to take political responsibility for the crisis, especially on the part of the Agriculture Commissioner, Franz

pressing the Commission and Council to lift or ease the embargo; had failed to display sufficient zeal in monitoring the maintenance of the embargo on meat and by-products. Overall, there was the attitude of successive British governments which, despite the considerable amount of legislation implemented since 1988 covering the various aspects of protection against possible BSE risks, had failed to ensure the proper application of those measures and had not carried out the necessary checks – a failure which the committee interpreted as a "refusal to 'play the game' of the proper and transparent co-operation which must govern relations between the Member States of the European Union, even beyond the terms of the Treaty".

152 The committee of inquiry found that by virtue of the opaqueness, complexity and anti-democratic nature of its workings, the existing system of comitology seemed to be totally exempt from any supervision, thereby enabling national and/or industrial interests to infiltrate the Community decision-making process.

153 The committee of inquiry observed the following in relation to the Commission's actions. The Commission had given priority to the management of the market as opposed to possible human health risks. The Commission had tried to follow a policy of downplaying the problem, despite a wide variety of discussions in scientific bodies. There had been an "arrogation to itself of the BSE issue by DG VI [agriculture] and a lack of cooperation and coordination among all the departments with responsibility for food products"; and DG V [health] failed to act to prevent the risks to human health arising from BSE. Too much weight had been placed on the role of the Scientific Veterinary Committee; criticisms could be made of the workings of the Scientific Veterinary Committee; the Commission had no provision for consulting independent, multidisciplinary advisory committees; and the Commission had not encouraged the expression of the views of those scientists who, on the basis of the most recent research findings available, drew conclusions diverging from the views held by the majority of members of the Scientific Veterinary Committee. The Commission had not made efforts to adapt its staffing policy to the real needs arising from the establishment of the internal market; it did not carry out inspections between June 1990 and May 1994; there had been a lack of co-ordination between the veterinary legislation unit and the inspection unit, and a failure to guarantee the proper functioning of veterinary controls within the internal market. The Commission's endeavours to regulate the problem of meat-and-bone meal came too late and were ineffective and contradictory; the Commission did not adopt additional protection measures following identification of the cases of infected animals born subsequently to the ban on administering mammal proteins to ruminants; the Commission exerted political pressure and gave in to manipulation by the industrial sector in favour of lifting the embargo on semen, tallow and gelatine; and the Commission was presently trying to avoid part of its responsibility by trying to deal with the BSE and scrapie dossiers together, without making clear the distinction between the two subjects. Since 1974 and on the basis of Directives 64/432/EEC, 64/433/EEC, and 72/461/EEC, the Commission had possessed sufficient legal instruments to allow it to adopt the necessary measures for the protection of public health from potential risks arising from animal epidemics. However, the Commission had failed to use the means placed at its disposal by the Treaty in order to take the most stringent precautionary measures required.

Fischler.[154] Overall then, it appears that, in the balance between deregulation and reregulation reached with the internal market/mutual recognition approach to food law, a political vacuum had developed, with national governments and EU officials unsure which actions they should and could take to protect public health at the height of the BSE crisis.[155] In the wake of this, there followed a distinct movement back towards detailed and principled regulatory standards for food being imposed at EU level, to guard against risks to public health arising from the food chain.

Regulation 178/2002/EC: the Food Law Regulation

The latest approach to EU food law arises from a number of areas of dissatisfaction with the existing regime, many of which were brought more sharply into focus by the BSE/nvCJD crisis. One key problem is the lag between regulation and scientific knowledge. The time-span for directives from conception to implementation in Member States is something of the order of seven years. Clearly, this is not appropriate where, as in the case of health scares such as BSE/nvCJD, public health protection necessitates speedy action. As Regulations are "binding in their entirety and directly applicable within the Member States",[156] their implementation process is quicker than that of Directives. Another concern focuses around the role of the Commission, and its various advisory committees. Division of responsibilities for food matters within the Commission, with a number of Directorates General potentially being involved, raised the problem of matters falling between several DGs, none of which considered food safety to be its main area of concern. The fact that there was no one Commissioner whose role it was to champion consumer interests in the safety of European food was also seen as problematic. The role of comitology, and in particular the lack of transparency and democratic control over the various advisory committees, in particular the Standing Committee on Foodstuffs,[157] was criticised.[158]

154 The work of the committee of inquiry had revealed that the Commission was guilty of serious errors and omissions. To all appearances, the Commissioners bore a clear political responsibility. The current Commissioner, Mr Fischler, should also take responsibility for blatant instances of negligence, above all the Commission Decision (96/362/EC) lifting the export ban on gelatine, tallow and semen and the misleading of the committee of inquiry on the issue of the legal basis for a ban on exports of meat-and-bone meal. Parliament could not clear the Commission as an institution from responsibility for the errors committed by Commissioners no longer in office, and thus the current Commission must be called on to assume its political responsibilities and take the requisite structural, political and staff-related decisions and measures arising out of the instances of negligence and errors noted by the Committee.

155 O'Rourke, above n 117, p 99.

156 Article 249 EC.

157 Established 1969 by Decision 69/414/EEC, OJ 1969 L 291/9. This committee consists of representatives of Member States. As part of the policy formation process, the Commission sought the views of the Standing Committee on Foodstuffs on the scientific advice given by the independent Scientific Committee for Food, see n 166 below. For further discussion of the (significant) influences of the Standing Committee on EU food law and policy, see J. Neyer, "The Standing Committee for Foodstuffs: Arguing and Bargaining in Comitology" in M. van Schendelen, *EU Committees as Influential Policy-Makers* (Aldershot: Dartmouth, 1998).

158 See in general on comitology, chapter 2, p 50; and see, for instance, M. Andenas and A. Türk, eds, *Delegated Legislation and the Role of Committees in the EC* (The Hague: Kluwer, 2000),

The EU's new food law may be traced to the European Parliament's motion of censure against the Commission for their handling of the BSE/nvCJD crisis. The reform process culminated in Regulation 178/2002/EC.[159] We trace the development of this measure here, considering the approach adopted to the regulation of potential risks to public health posed by the food chain, in terms of the paternalism/autonomy and government/industry dichotomies outlined above.

Regulation 178/2002/EC was the subject of several years of consultation. The Commission first issued a *Green Paper on Food Law*,[160] which provoked considerable debate about the appropriate model or models for EU-level regulation of food law.[161] The Green Paper set out a number of "fundamental goals" of EU food law,[162] which the Commission regarded as non-negotiable. The Green Paper indicated that the Commission's underlying models tended towards autonomy-centred regulation, with a significant degree of self-regulation for the industry. To this end, the use of international and EU-level standards, in particular the ISO 9000 and EN 29000 Series, was to be promoted.[163] The Commission specifically stated that it was not intending to lay down any new compositional and quality standards for groups of foodstuffs. Thus the Commission did not begin its consultation exercise with a "clean sheet", but brought a number of its pre-conceptions as "embedded" in the very nature of EU food law.

The *Green Paper on Food Law* was complemented by the Commission's 1997 Communication on *Consumer Health and Food Safety*.[164] This document explains in detail the Commission's new approach to food safety and consumer health. This new approach has a particular focus on scientific advice and systems of control and inspection. Its underlying basic principle is the separation of risk assessment and risk management. A three-fold approach is established, covering scientific advice;

especially G. Schäfer, "Linking Member State and European Administrations – The Role of Committees and Comitology", and A.E. Toeller and H.C.H. Hofmann, "Democracy and the Reform of Comitology" therein; C. Joerges and E. Vos, *EU Committees: Social regulation, law and politics* (Oxford: Hart, 1999), especially G. Ciavarini Azzi, "Comitology and the European Commission" therein; E. Vos, "The Rise of Committees" 3 ELJ (1997) 210; Bradley, above n 52 (1997); R. Pedler and G. Schäfer, eds, *Shaping European Law and Policy: The Role of Committees in the Political Process* (Maastricht: European Institute of Public Administration, 1996); Bradley, above n 52 (1992).

159 OJ 2002 L 31/1. For the proposal see COM(2000) 716. Further measures elaborating the detail are proposed, see COM (2003) 52 final.

160 COM(97) 176.

161 O'Rourke, above n 117, p 4.

162 These are: 1. The need to provide a high level of protection of public health, and safety, and consumer protection; 2. The need to ensure free movement of goods within the internal market; 3. The need for legislation to be based primarily on scientific evidence and risk assessment; 4. The need to ensure competitiveness of European food industry; 5. The need to place primary responsibility for safe food with industry, producers and suppliers, through HACCP systems (a method of self-regulation) backed up by official controls and enforcement; 6. The need for legislation to be coherent, rational, consistent, simpler, user-friendly and developed in full consultation with interested parties.

163 O'Rourke, above n 117, p 72.

164 COM(97) 183 final.

risk analysis; and control. Additionally, a rapid alert system to deal with emergency situations was to be set up. These elements were all carried forward into the new EU food regulation, Regulation 178/2002/EC.[165]

Scientific advice is the foundation for EU-level regulatory measures designed to protect consumer health. The institutions of the EU gained their scientific advice with respect to food law from the work of the EU's scientific committees, in particular the Scientific Committee for Food.[166] The Communication stressed that the committees are to be based on the scientific and professional excellence of their members, independence, and transparency.[167] The Communication on *Consumer Health and Food Safety* stated that the existing scientific committees were to be reorganised and their mandates revised on the basis of the new policy orientations laid down in the Communication. The Communication was duly followed by two implementing decisions,[168] setting up a scientific steering committee and eight specialised scientific committees. Moreover, in January 2000, it was announced that the Commission had transferred responsibility for all food safety matters, including all relevant scientific committees, to a new Commission Directorate-General for Consumer Policy and Health Protection (DG SANCO), under Commissioner David Byrne.[169] This dealt with the long-standing problem of division of responsibilities for food matters across various of the Commission's Directorates General. As Vos explains,[170] although the Scientific Committee on Foodstuffs and other relevant scientific committees had gained an outstanding reputation,[171] this was shattered by the BSE/nvCJD crisis. The practicalities of running the committee structure on

165 OJ 2002 L 31/1.

166 See Decision 97/579/EC, OJ 1997 L 237/18, replacing Decision 74/234/EEC, OJ 1974 L 136/1. For discussion of the work and influence of the Committee, see P. Gray, "The Scientific Committee for Food" in M. Van Schendelen, ed, *EU Committees as Influential Policy Makers* (Aldershot: Dartmouth, 1998). In May 2003, the five scientific committees in the field of food and feed safety, and animal health and welfare, were transferred to within the structure of the European Food Safety Authority: see further below.

167 Of course, as we noted in chapter 8, the apparent "objectivity" of science in the policy-making process is illusory. See D. Nelkin, *Technological Decisions and Democracy* (London: Sage, 1977); S. Jasanoff, *The Fifth Branch: Science Advisers as Policymakers* (Cambridge, Mass: Harvard University Press, 1990); D. Nelkin, ed, *Controversy: Politics of Technical Decisions* (London: Sage, 1992); R. Sclove, *Democracy and Technology* (New York: Guilford Press, 1995). In the specific context of the BSE crisis, see J. Neyer, "The Regulation of Risks and the Power of the People: Lessons from the BSE Crisis" 4 *European Integration Online Papers* (2000), http://www.eiop.or.at.eiop/; and E. Vos, "EU Committees: the evolution of unforeseen institutional actors in European Product Regulation" in C. Joerges and E. Vos, *EU Committees: Social Regulation, Law and Politics* (Oxford: Hart, 1999), pp 30–39.

168 Decision 97/579/EC, OJ 1997 L 237/18; Decision 97/404/EC, OJ 1997 L 169/85.

169 DG Enterprise and Info Society will continue to be associated with proposals made in the domain of food safety, in context of enterprise and competitiveness responsibilities.

170 Vos, above n 116.

171 The Court had expressed its confidence in the SCF in several rulings, in which the Court found that a national decision to refuse circulation of a food product on a home market should take the findings of the Scientific Committee for Food into account: see, for example, Case 247/84 *Motte* [1985] ECR 3887; Case 304/84 *Muller* [1986] ECR 1511.

an *ad hoc*, rather than a permanent, basis were also placing a significant burden on the individuals concerned.[172]

Risk analysis is, according to the Communication, a three-stage process, involving assessment, management and communication of risk. Risk assessment is the identification and evaluation of hazards to human health. The aim of risk management is to contain or to reduce the levels of risk to acceptable levels. This is the political stage of the regulatory process.[173] Risk communication involves exchange of information between relevant parties, including the general public.

The new approach for *control and inspection* is to be based on the following elements. To deal with the very wide range of potential hazards, with limited resources, risk assessment procedures are used to establish priorities for control and inspection. Second, the "farm to fork" principle requires that the whole chain of food production is to be covered. Formal audit procedures (already in use in the food control sector) allow assessment of self-regulatory control (hazard analysis and critical control point – HACCP) systems operated by the competent national authorities. The Commission Communication on *Food, Veterinary and Plant Health Control and Inspection*[174] and the proposal for a Regulation on official feed and food controls, COM (2003) 52 final, elaborate this approach of partnership between the food industry, national authorities and the Commission. Within this system, the role of the Commission is essentially to "control the controls", for which the national authorities retain primary responsibility.[175]

The Commission's proposed reform of EU food law was consolidated in the *White Paper on Food Safety*, COM (99) 719 final, adopted on 12 January 2000. Based on the "farm to fork" approach, this document proposed a major programme of legislative reform to achieve high standards of food safety in the EU. The White Paper – like the Delors/Cockfield *White Paper on Completion of the Single European Market*[176] – sets out more than 80 separate actions that are to be taken. Most significantly, a proposal on a general EU Food Law was included, covering general principles of food safety: responsibility of feed manufacturers, farmers and food operators; traceability of feed, food and its ingredients; proper risk analysis through risk assessment, risk management and risk communication; and the application of the precautionary

172 See Vos, above n 116, at 244, quoting M. Gibney, at Joint Conference on the EU and Food Security, Brussels, 30 November and 1 December 1998: "Last Monday I attended a meeting of the human risk exposure group of our BSE committee . . . On Thursday I will have my 26th trip to Brussels. Next week I will have two days which will be my 27th trip to Brussels on BSE. I have a job where I am Professor of Nutrition at the University of Dublin. I have to teach, organise research . . . I have to work on Irish government committees and so on. Professor Pascal asked a question yesterday, can this continue? The answer is no, it cannot continue."

173 The separation of the three elements, especially risk assessment and risk management, may be seen as a "convenient political myth" (Gray, in van Schendelen, ed, above n 166, p 77). So-called "independent" scientific risk assessment has a significant effect on policy formation.

174 COM(98) 32 final.

175 O'Rourke, above n 117, p 91.

176 O'Rourke, above n 117, p. ix.

principle[177] where appropriate. The *White Paper on Food Safety* followed the Communication on *Consumer Health and Food Safety* in its proposal for an EU framework of national systems of control for food regulatory measures. Control systems are the responsibility of national authorities, but are to be coordinated at EU level, through the establishment of common operational criteria, and enhanced administrative cooperation between national and EU levels. The EU's Food and Veterinary Office (Dublin) would play a key role in the development of this new EU framework.

The White Paper also proposed the establishment of a "European Food Authority" (EFA). The EFA was envisaged as the solution to many weaknesses in the existing EU system, such as lack of scientific support for the system of scientific advice, inadequacies in monitoring and surveillance on food safety issues, gaps in the rapid alert system, and lack of coordination of scientific cooperation and analytical support. The EFA proposal was inspired only in part by the US Food and Drugs Administration (FDA). The Commission was impressed by the US FDA's role in promoting consumer confidence, and by its independent, science-based structure. However, the Commission rejected the US FDA model of combining the tasks of risk assessor and legislature within one body, envisaging the separation of risk assessment and risk management. The existing EU structure lacked the capacity to carry out risk assessment effectively, based on principles of scientific excellence, transparency and independence. Risk management, in the sense of adoption of regulatory measures to contain risk or reduce it to acceptable levels, continues to be the responsibility of the EU legislature.

Following the *White Paper on Food Safety*, Regulation 178/2002/EC laying down fundamental principles and requirements of food law, establishing a European Food Safety Authority, and laying down procedures for food safety – the centrepiece of

177 The precautionary principle was adopted in the context of international environmental regulation, within structures such as the WTO. The original approach of international environmental regulation was based on an assumption that science can foresee risks arising, and provide technological solutions before serious damage, for instance to human health, takes place. However, it was soon recognised that what may be needed, in some circumstances, is a preventive policy, that looks beyond the scientific knowledge of any given moment. Such a policy is found in the application of the "precautionary principle", which allows and even obliges governments to adopt measures, even where there is scientific uncertainty, if a reasonable fear for irreversible or serious damage exists. Application of the precautionary principle implies that certain human activities, rather than being assumed safe until proven dangerous, are assumed to be dangerous until proven safe. The precautionary principle operates on the assumption that the establishment of scientific proof might come too late to prevent damage. The EU has adopted its own version of the precautionary principle, which was introduced into the Treaty of Rome at Maastricht: Article 174 (ex 130r) (2) EC. See L. Kramer, *EC Environmental Law* (London: Sweet and Maxwell, 2000), pp 16–17. See also Council Resolution on the Precautionary Principle, Nice Council, 7–9 December 2000. However, following recent jurisprudence of the Court of First Instance (Case T-199/96 *Bergaderm* [1998] ECR II-2805, citing, in para 66, Case C-180/96 *UK and Northern Ireland v Commission (BSE)* [1996] ECR I-3903; Case T-13/99 *Pfizer Animal Health* [2002] ECR II-3305; Case T-141/00 *Artegodan* [2002] ECR II-4945) and the European Court of Justice (Case C-236/01 *Monsanto Agricola Italia* [2003] ECR I-(9 September 2003, nyr in ECR)), it is not entirely clear whether the European Courts will adhere to a more cautious approach in applying the precautionary principle than that applied in the context of the WTO. See further, Scott and Vos, above n 116. Scott, above n 116.

the Commission's strategy for a proactive food policy covering the entire food chain, from the farm to the fork – was adopted.[178] The Regulation is based on Articles 37, 95, 133 and 152 (4) (b) EC. It is thus one of the key legislative instruments based on the revised Article 152 EC. Its primary objective is providing a high level of protection of human health, whilst ensuring effective functioning of the internal market.[179]

The Regulation defines "food" as "any substance or product, whether processed, partially processed or unprocessed, intended to be, or reasonably expected to be, ingested by humans".[180] "Food law" covers all laws, regulations and administrative provisions governing food in general, and food safety in particular, in the EU. It covers all stages of production and distribution of food, and also feed where produced for or fed to food-producing animals.[181] Chapter II of the Regulation covers general food law. The general principles of food law are set out in Articles 5–8. These are to apply when any new measure of food law is enacted. Existing food law is to be adapted to comply with the Regulation from 1 January 2007.[182] The objectives of food law are a high level of protection of human life and health, the protection of consumers' interests, and other objectives, as appropriate, including the protection of the environment, the protection of animal health, life and welfare and the protection of plant health and life.[183] Interestingly, these objectives are placed before the free movement objectives[184] in Article 5 of the Regulation, although not in the preamble.

Food law is to be based on scientific risk analysis,[185] and the precautionary principle applies,[186] although only where, following an assessment of available pertinent

178 OJ 2002 L 31/1. For the proposal see COM(2000) 716.
179 Regulation 178/2002/EC, Article 1 (1). Commissioner David Byrne, in presenting the proposal, stated: "Safety is the most important ingredient in our food . . . This legislative package is designed to overcome the weaknesses of the past and put food safety firmly on top of our agenda. The substantive food law and the creation of the European Food Authority are the building blocks, the very foundations, upon which our new food safety policy will rest."
180 Regulation 178/2002/EC, Article 2. Article 2 goes on to say that food: "includes drink, chewing gum and any substance intentionally incorporated into the food during its manufacture, preparation or treatment. It includes water, without prejudice to the requirements of Directives 80/778/EEC and 98/83/EC on the quality of water intended for human consumption. It does not include: feed; live animals unless they are prepared, packaged and/or served for human consumption; plants prior to harvesting; medicinal products within the meaning of Directive 65/65/EEC and Directive 92/73/EEC; cosmetics within the meaning of Directive 76/768/EEC, tobacco and tobacco products within the meaning of Directive 89/622/EEC, or narcotic or psychotropic substances within the meaning of the United Nations Single Convention on Narcotic Drugs, 1961 and the United Nations Convention on Psychotropic Substances, 1971."
181 Regulation 178/2002/EC, Article 3 (1).
182 Regulation 178/2002/EC, Article 4 (2) and (3).
183 Regulation 178/2002/EC, Article 5 (1).
184 Regulation 178/2002/EC, Article 5 (2): "Food law shall aim to achieve the free movement in the Community of food and feed manufactured or marketed according to the general principles and requirements in this Chapter."
185 Regulation 178/2002/EC, Article 6.
186 Regulation 178/2002/EC, Article 7.

information, a risk to health is identified but scientific uncertainty persists.[187] In such circumstances, provisional risk management measures necessary (according to the principle of proportionality, and no more restrictive of trade than necessary) to ensure the high level of health protection chosen in the EU may be adopted, while awaiting further scientific information for a more comprehensive risk assessment. As noted above, it appears that the EU institutions, or at least the EU legislative institutions, have adopted a more cautious version of the precautionary principle than that applicable in, for instance, the WTO context.[188] This ties in with the more cautious risk-averse approach to regulation seen in European societies, as compared for instance with the US. The consumer protection aim of food law is to be pursued on the basis of the principle of informed choice.[189]

Given the legacy of the BSE/nvCJD crisis, it is not surprising that the Regulation gives priority to principles of transparency. These are made more concrete than in the Green and White Papers, by setting out the requirements to consult[190] and inform[191] the public in matters of food safety.

The requirements of food and feed safety are set out in Articles 14 and 15 of the Regulation, followed by provisions on the responsibilities of food and feed producers.[192] Food safety is to be ensured, *inter alia*, through the traceability of food and feed.[193] The partnership approach to responsibility for food safety, put forward in the Communications on *Consumer Health and Food Safety* and *Food, Veterinary and Plant Health Control and Inspection*, and COM (2003) 52 final, is set out in Article 17. Food and feed business operators at all stages of production and distribution within the businesses under their control are to ensure that foods or feeds satisfy the relevant requirements of food law and, to that effect, must put in place systems and procedures to verify and monitor that such requirements are met. Member States are to enforce food law, and monitor and verify that the relevant requirements of food law are respected by food and feed business operators at all stages of production and distribution. Member States must maintain a system of official controls, including public communication on food and feed safety and risk, food and feed safety surveillance and other monitoring activities covering all stages of production and distribution; and must provide effective, proportionate and dissuasive penalties applicable to infringements of food and feed law. The provisions

187 Although, as Scott and Vos point out, the measure does not make clear which authorities (national or EU) will establish that scientific uncertainty exists; see Scott and Vos, above n 116, p 281.

188 See above n 177. Unfortunately, this is not the place to explore the potential implications of such a difference in approach. On the relationship between the EU and WTO's legal orders generally, see de Búrca and Scott, eds, above n 21; Weiler, ed, above n 21.

189 Regulation 178/2002/EC, Article 8.

190 Regulation 178/2002/EC, Article 19.

191 Regulation 178/2002/EC, Article 20.

192 Regulation 178/2002/EC, Articles 17 and 20.

193 Regulation 178/2002/EC, Article 18.

of Chapter II of the Regulation are to be without prejudice to the Product Liability Directive.[194]

European Food Safety Authority

Chapter III of the Regulation concerns the (renamed) European Food Safety Authority (EFSA). The organisational structure of the EFSA involves a Management Board, appointed by Council in consultation with the European Parliament. One member is a Commission representative. Four of the other 14 members are to have a background in representing "consumers and other interests in the food chain".[195] An Advisory Forum, with 15 representatives from food authorities of the Member States, is to advise the EFSA's Executive Director[196] on all matters relating to the EFSA's mission.[197] The scientific opinions of the EFSA are to be provided by a Scientific Committee and eight permanent Scientific Panels.[198] These replace the previously existing Scientific Steering Committee and five sectoral scientific committees. The Scientific Committee, consisting of the eight chairs of the panels and six independent experts, is to play a coordinating role.[199] The EFSA is to employ up to 250 in-house staff, and has a budget of approximately € 40 million, to be reviewed after three years.[200]

The EFSA's remit is to provide "scientific advice and scientific and technical support for the Community's legislation and policies in all fields which have a direct or indirect impact on food and feed safety".[201] It also includes providing scientific advice on human nutrition, other matters relating to animal and plant health, and non-food products relating to genetically modified organisms. This latter could include medicinal products derived from or made from genetically modified organisms.

The main function of the EFSA is to provide independent scientific opinions. The EFSA takes over the tasks of the various EU scientific committees in this respect.[202] Opinions may be requested by the Commission, governments of the Member States, and the European Parliament, or may be own-initiative opinions.[203] The EFSA will provide impartial advice on technical food issues. Special procedural provisions

194 Directive 85/374/EEC, OJ 1985 L 210/29; for further discussion see chapter 8.
195 Regulation 178/2002/EC, Article 25 (1).
196 Appointed by the Management Board, Article 26. It was announced on 2 October 2002 that the Board had appointed Geoffrey Podger, formerly Chief Executive of the UK Food Standards Agency, as the Executive Director of the EFSA.
197 Regulation 178/2002/EC, Article 27.
198 Regulation 178/2002/EC, Article 28. The Scientific Panels cover (a) food additives, flavourings, processing aids and materials in contact with food; (b) additives and products used in animal feed; (c) plant health, plant protection products and their residues; (d) genetically modified organisms; (e) dietetic products, nutrition and allergies; (f) biological hazards; (g) contaminants in the food chain; and (h) animal health and welfare.
199 Regulation 178/2002/EC, Article 28 (2) and (3).
200 Questions and Answers on the European Food Safety Authority, January 2003.
201 Regulation 178/2002/EC, Article 22 (2).
202 Regulation 178/2002/EC, Article 62 (1).
203 Regulation 178/2002/EC, Article 29 (1).

apply where scientific opinion diverges.[204] The EFSA is to collect and analyse EU-wide data on dietary patterns, exposure, risks, and so on, with respect to various foodstuffs.[205] Not surprisingly, given the context of the BSE/nvCJD crisis, the EFSA is specifically charged with the identification of emerging risks to health,[206] and is also to be responsible for the day to day operation of the rapid alert system.[207] The details on the rapid alert system are set out in Chapter IV of the Regulation. This involves a network comprised of the EFSA, the Commission and the governments of the Member States. National food authorities must notify the Commission of any information relating to the existence of a serious direct or indirect risk to human health deriving from food or feed.[208] Any crisis management necessary would be carried out by the Commission setting up a "crisis unit", which would look to the EFSA for scientific advice.[209]

The rapid alert system, and all the scientific reports issued by the EFSA, are subject to the general principle of transparency,[210] but provision is also made for confidentiality where information "is covered by professional secrecy in duly justified cases".[211] Presumably this would apply for instance to prevent the disclosure of personal details about individual patients suffering ill health as a result of exposure to health risks manifest through the food chain. However, if some such personal information, such as for instance information relating to age, or lifestyle, was relevant to the risks involved, confidentiality with respect to such information might not be "duly justified". The balance in EU law between collective rights to protection of health and individual rights, in this instance to confidentiality, would be subject to interpretation by national authorities applying the Regulation, and ultimately national courts if called up to review decisions taken by such authorities, with a possible reference to the European Court of Justice.

Article 39 of the Regulation provides that where information has been received by the EFSA and the EFSA has been asked, for legitimate reasons, to keep this information confidential, that request must be complied with. However, the provision provides that this does not apply where information must be made public, in order to protect public health. This suggests that the balance between confidentiality and transparency has been drawn at EU level in such a way as to favour transparency over confidentiality. This may not be surprising, given the context of the Regulation's adoption, the aftermath of the BSE/nvCJD crisis. However, it may have implications for the protection of confidentiality within national public health systems. Extrapolating from this, in the longer term, the elaboration of such a principle at EU

204 Regulation 178/2002/EC, Article 30.
205 Regulation 178/2002/EC, Article 33.
206 Regulation 178/2002/EC, Article 34.
207 Regulation 178/2002/EC, Article 35.
208 Regulation 178/2002/EC, Article 50 (2).
209 Regulation 178/2002/EC, Articles 55–57.
210 Regulation 178/2002/EC, Articles 10 and 38.
211 Regulation 178/2002/EC, Article 52 (1).

level may also affect the balance, maintained in all national public health systems, between collective interests in public health and individual interests in privacy.

BSE/nvCJD: conclusion

In the wake of the BSE/nvCJD crisis, there is no doubt that the EU's food law has become more explicitly focused on the protection of public health. Legally speaking, this move was assisted by the inclusion of the new legal basis provision in the Treaty of Rome in Article 152 EC. The regulatory approach chosen tends towards something more like the "old style" harmonisation methods of the 1970s than "new approach" harmonisation, but it also contains strong elements of "new governance", in particular a significant role for industry self-regulation. Although more *general* standards have been articulated at EU level, these are not like the *detailed* compositional quality measures of the 1970s for which the EU institutions attracted so much criticism. The approach thus still tends towards consumer autonomy, rather than paternalism. This is further underpinned by clear measures on transparency and communication of risk or potential risk.

From the point of view of its impact on national public health law, EU food law has "occupied the field", in the sense that national policies may not deviate from the standards and procedures set out at EU level, and national authorities have a duty to implement those EU standards and procedures. EU institutions (albeit with considerable representation of national actors within the system) now determine what are the consequences when health protection measures fail to be adequately implemented, and, further, what exactly constitutes the appropriate balance between regulation and risk in this respect. At least the EU legislative institutions appear to favour a more cautious approach to risk than, for instance, applicable in WTO contexts. The "consumer autonomy" principles underpinning EU food law may also be read, as they are in the US, as an element of a protectionist precautionary approach. This implies that national public health policies could not lawfully choose either a more or a less cautious risk averse strategy to the health risks posed by food than that articulated at EU level. The food law element of public health policy is essentially determined within the framework of multilevel governance of the EU.

III. Health promotion

While the majority of legal interventions into public health issues can be seen as reactive (for example, concerning the threat of disease) or regulatory, through the development of regulatory legislation or of regulatory agencies (for example, in relation to food safety), a third dimension of public health – that of health promotion or, as Gostin terms it, "health communication"[212] – has been relatively downplayed

212 Gostin, above n 1.

in health law literature.[213] One reason for this may be related to the emphasis placed in many Western democracies upon the need to respect the autonomy of the individual. While, as we noted above, in those situations in which individual behaviour has broad direct consequences for public health – such as communicable diseases – degrees of state intervention are generally sanctioned, in terms of life-style choices, individuals are allowed considerable discretion to exercise personal autonomy.[214] Thus, while health agencies may promote particular life-style approaches (more exercise; a better diet and so on), this usually does not extend beyond general encouragement. Respect for principles of autonomy may not be the only reason for a "softly-softly" approach to health promotion, as there are also inevitably fundamental practical difficulties regarding the introduction of any form of legal regulation of lifestyle choices. Even in those areas in which there is particular sensitivity regarding the need for health promotion, such as during pregnancy, it appears to be the case that health promotion will not usually result in overtly coercive measures.[215] (Although there are question marks over whether the utilisation of some health promotion measures such as screening during pregnancy may in practice result in coercion.[216]) Despite this, however, health promotion issues may give rise to legal dilemmas in a number of situations.

Problems may arise where a particular health promotion issue is regarded as being of such importance that this legitimates constraints being imposed on personal choice. This may arise in two ways. First, individuals' access to information regarding particular life-style choices may be constrained where this conflicts with a state-adopted health promotion strategy. Second, health promotion measures themselves may be supported by national governments, not simply through persuasion but also through coercion, whether directly or indirectly, as in the case of water fluoridation to facilitate dental hygiene[217] or in relation to a ban on smoking in public places. In relation to the first of these categories, there has been considerable EU involvement – a notable illustration is that of the Tobacco Advertising Directive discussed below. With regard to the second category, however, the EU

213 One of the few academic commentators to address this, in the UK context, is Montgomery in his Health Care Law textbook. Montgomery, above n 29, and this is in relation to life-styles issues (pp 44–45) and the example of water fluoridation (pp 48–50).

214 For a wide-ranging consideration of issues concerning communicable diseases and life-styles in the EU, see J. Harris, *Communicable Diseases: Lifestyles and Personal Responsibility: Ethics and Rights – Report*, http://www.europa.eu.int/comm/research/biosociety.pdf.

215 In contrast, in the US there have been constraints placed upon women during pregnancy including the criminalisation of behaviour considered to have an adverse effect on the foetus: see, for example, J.A. Robertson, *Children of Choice* (Princeton: Princeton University Press, 1994).

216 See, for example, discussion in the context of pregnancy screening in P. de Zulueta "HIV in pregnancy: ethical issues in screening and therapeutic research" in D. Dickenson, ed, *Ethics in Maternal-Fetal Medicine* (Cambridge: CUP, 2002); and see also, for a critique of modern UK health promotion techniques as "social control", M. Fitzpatrick, *The Tyranny of Health: Doctors and the Regulation of Lifestyle* (London: Routledge, 1999).

217 See Montgomery, above n 29.

has left such matters to individual Member States.[218] However, it is possible that in the future EU law may play an enhanced role here also.[219] The consistency of such measures with the proposed Draft Constitutional Treaty,[220] including provisions on Community competence and the EU Charter of Fundamental Rights and Freedoms,[221] may prove to be a site for future litigation.

Various different types of action taken by the EU institutions may be categorised as concerned with the promotion of good health. This includes "hard" harmonising law, for instance, concerning advertising of products harmful to human health. It also includes soft law measures, for instance, recommendations concerning the content of educational programmes for medical professionals. The EU has used some of its budgetary resources to fund various projects to encourage and promote good health, for instance, in terms of education, both of the public directly and of medical professionals. One notable illustration of this includes HIV/AIDS, discussed earlier in this chapter. An area in which the EU is becoming increasingly involved is mental health.[222] In this part of the chapter, we explore some relevant EU provisions, taking as our example the EU's activities in the field of cancer prevention, and in particular the EU's regulation of the composition, presentation, sale and advertising of tobacco.

Cancer and tobacco[223]

Cancer remains one of the biggest causes of death in the Member States of the EU. The link between tobacco consumption and health problems, in particular between smoking and lung cancer, is well established. The WHO confirms that tobacco is the single greatest cause of preventable disease and death. In the EU, 83% of lung

218 Ireland has become the first European country to impose a ban on smoking in public places under the Irish Tobacco Smoking (Prohibition) Regulations 2003, SI 2003/481, 23 October 2003, adopted under the Irish Public Health (Tobacco) Act 2002. These Regulations, which entered into force on 26 January 2004, ban smoking in all workplaces (other than dwellings), which include restaurants, night clubs and bars. A few regional or local authorities elsewhere in the EU are considering similar prohibitions, for instance in the UK, in Scotland (though the proposed private member's bill received no support from the Scottish Executive), Reading and Sheffield (http:www.forestonline.org/output/page1812.asp). Many towns and cities in the US (including New York) have already imposed similar prohibitions.

219 In September 2003, Commissioner David Byrne stated that he is considering an EU-wide public smoking ban: see http:/www.eupolitix.com/ (18 September 2003); http://www.news.bbc.co.uk/1/hi/jea;tj/3121970.stm (19 September 2003).

220 See further chapter 10.

221 Of particular relevance here are Article 1 EUCFR (the right to dignity), Article 3 EUCFR (the right to personal integrity), Article 7 EUCFR (the right of respect for private and family life) and Article 11 EUCFR (freedom of expression).

222 Council Resolution on the promotion of mental health, 18 November 1999, OJ 2000 C 86/1 and see Conference organised by the Presidency on "Mental Illness and Stigma in Europe: facing up to the challenges of social inclusion and equity", http://www.eu2003.gr/en/articles/2003/3/24/2338 and the Council's adoption of "Conclusions on combating stigma and discrimination in relation to mental health" in 2512th Council Meeting, Employment, Social Policy, Health and Consumer Affairs, Luxembourg, 2 and 3 June 2003, 9688/1/03 REV1(Presse 152), pp 12–14.

223 This section is taken partly from T. Hervey, "Up in Smoke: Community (anti) tobacco law and policy" 26 ELRev (2001) 101.

cancers in men are caused by smoking tobacco. Lung cancer is by far the most common fatal cancer in the EU, with an estimated annual death rate per 1000 in the EU of 447.9.[224]

The EU institutions have taken various types of action towards combating cancer. In the health promotion context, these have focused on the promotion of lifestyles that do not increase the risk of cancer, especially lung cancer. The EU has financed anti-cancer programmes since the 1980s, and has also sought to regulate the composition, presentation and sale of tobacco products and the advertising of tobacco products within the EU.

"Europe Against Cancer"

The EU's involvement in combating cancer predates the specific Treaty competence on public health. The European Council at Milan in June 1985 and Luxembourg in December 1985 called for an EU-level initiative to combat cancer. A Resolution of the Council and the Representatives of the Governments of the Member States, meeting within Council, of 7 July 1986, established the "Europe against Cancer" programme.[225] The original programme had three main elements: cancer prevention; information and public awareness; and training.

In December 1986, the European Council, at the London Summit, decided that 1989 should be designated "European Cancer Information Year". Accordingly, the Commission was charged, in collaboration with the Member States, with developing a "sustained and concerted information campaign" across the EU. This constituted the first action plan under the Europe against Cancer programme. The campaign was to cover prevention, early screening and treatment of cancer. The budget for the campaign was a modest € 10million. The Commission was to coordinate information on the subject, for instance by contributing to production of television information and health education programmes for the general public, coordinating exchange of experience with health education teaching materials, and involvement of health professionals. The "fight against cancer", according to the preamble of Decision 88/351/EEC[226] establishing the information campaign, includes "the fight against tobacco". From the very beginning, the EU's anti-tobacco stance has formed an explicit part of its cancer programmes.

On the training point, the Commission proceeded, *inter alia*, by calling on the Advisory Committees on Medical Training, Training in Nursing and Training of Dental Practitioners[227] to review the ways in which the subject of cancer is taught to their respective professions, and to make recommendations for improvement

224 See Commission Press Release MEMO/01/190 *Cancer and Cancer Research in the European Union*, Brussels, 22 May 2001; see also R. Watson, "Europe agrees complete ban on tobacco advertising by 2006" 315 BMJ (1997) 1559, citing research suggesting over 500,000 deaths per annum in the EU are tobacco-related.

225 OJ 1986 C 184/19.

226 OJ 1988 L 160/52.

227 For further information, see chapter 6.

in such training. This review was carried out in 1987–88. Each Committee then adopted a set of recommendations for cancer training of medical professionals in the Member States. The recommendations included such matters as that each medical and dental school should include an element of oncology in its undergraduate teaching programme; and that basic training of nurses should include the prevention, detection and diagnosis of cancer, and participation in public education about the benefits of prevention of and screening for cancer. The need for continuing education, based on current scientific knowledge, was stressed by all three Committees. These recommendations are set out in the annex to Commission Recommendation 89/601/EEC,[228] a measure of "soft law" concerning the training of health personnel in the matter of cancer. The Commission recommended that the conclusions of the Committees receive the widest possible circulation and discussion within the Member States, although whether this was put into action is unclear.

The second phase of the Europe against Cancer programme (1990–94) took forward the above initiatives. The Commission's action plan was adopted by Council and the Representatives of the Governments of the Member States meeting within Council in Decision 90/238/EEC.[229] This action plan established that EU-level action against cancer was to be an ongoing part of EU activity. The three elements of the cancer programme remained unchanged. However, while the first action plan had concentrated on information and public awareness, the second had a much stronger emphasis on prevention. The first mentioned element of the prevention strand of the action plan was prevention of tobacco consumption. The Commission was to stimulate projects of European interest concerning the prevention of nicotine addiction (especially amongst such target groups as young people, women, teachers and members of the health professions); pilot projects to teach methods of breaking nicotine addiction to members of the health professions and to teachers; and innovative information campaigns to prevent the use of tobacco among the general public and in the workplace. The EU would also finance a study on the possibilities for putting tobacco-growing areas to other uses. The Commission was also to stimulate medical research into matters such as diet and cancer; possible carcinogenic risks posed by certain chemicals; and screening programmes.[230] Exchange of experience and networking was to be promoted, including through the extension and monitoring of the European network of breast cancer screening programmes.

The health information and public awareness/education strands proceeded on the basis that the first action plan had been a success, and suggested a repeat of public EU-wide information campaigns. However, an element of targeting of particularly vulnerable groups was envisaged. The training elements, especially the recommendations of the Medical Training Advisory Committees, were taken forward

228 OJ 1989 L 346/1.

229 OJ 1990 L 137/31. The legal basis of this measure was expressed simply as "The Treaties establishing the European Communities".

230 The competences of the EU institutions to stimulate research are discussed in chapter 7.

by EU-level support for measures to encourage exchange of experience between practitioners in the Member States concerned with training, encouraging the collection and exchange of teaching materials of interest at EU level, and the setting up of pilot European networks of medical, nursing and dentistry schools. Taking forward the Commission's recommendation, the EU was to finance national and regional meetings to promote the 1989 recommendations on the oncology element of medical training.

Significantly, the second phase of the cancer programme also saw its institutionalisation within the EU legislature and administration. Decision 90/238/EEC, Article 1 (2) provided that the Commission was to be assisted in its implementation of the action plan by an advisory committee. The duties of the committee were to assess projects to be co-financed from public funds, and to coordinate projects at national level partly funded by NGOs. Presumably "public funds" refers to both EU and national level sources of funding. The budget was set originally at € 50 million,[231] and this was adjusted to € 55 million in 1993.[232]

The Commission submitted an evaluation of the Europe against Cancer programme from 1987 to 1992 on 23 March 1993. Both the European Parliament[233] and the Council responded, essentially proposing that action taken under the cancer programme be strengthened. The Council invited the Commission to propose a further action plan, taking into account the revised objectives of the programme, based on the Commission's evaluation.[234] The Council's resolution took a different approach in establishing the areas of action, with a much stronger focus on prevention, as opposed to the other two areas. "Primary prevention" was to be given high priority in areas where the EU can continue to provide impetus for national action. Primary prevention was to take the form of information and health education. This is to be effected by dissemination of information on health lifestyles, both general and targeted at specific groups. Promulgation of information on the links between cancer and the use of tobacco products would fall within these "lifestyle" issues.

The Council recommendation envisaged a comprehensive approach to fighting cancer by using several complementary means: legal, financial and cooperative. Council noted that "the legal means adopted by the Council must reinforce public health policy on cancer prevention in each Member State, particularly to promote healthy life-styles and to create an environment conducive to such efforts". It is not clear what Council meant by this statement. Creating such an environment might for instance require the prohibition of advertising of tobacco products, a matter taken up by the Tobacco Advertising Directive 98/43/EC, discussed below. A "horizontal" approach should be taken, according to which account is taken of health aspects in all Community policies, with particular attention to cancer risk factors.

231 Decision 90/238/EEC, Article 2.
232 Decision 93/362/EEC, OJ 1993 L 150/43.
233 OJ 1993 C 329/375.
234 Council Resolution of 13 December 1993 concerning future guidelines for the "Europe against Cancer" programme, OJ 1994 C 15/1.

Financial support should be strengthened, especially in the research element of the budget. Cooperation should be increased, for instance by strengthening existing networks and collaborating with international organisations in the field. Finally, the mechanism and effectiveness of evaluation of the programme was to be tightened up.

The third action plan to combat cancer was established in 1996.[235] It was now possible to base the relevant Decision on the new Article 129 EC, introduced into the Treaty of Rome at Maastricht.[236] In response to the Council and European Parliament's resolutions of 1993, the action plan contained revised – and more ambitious – objectives. However, the budgetary increase was relatively modest – from € 55 million to € 64 million[237] – and that to cover five years.

The general objective of the plan – reflecting the language of the (then) new Article 129 EC (now Article 152 EC) – was to contribute towards ensuring a high level of health protection. The action plan was to comprise actions aimed at preventing premature deaths due to cancer; reducing mortality and morbidity due to cancer; promoting the quality of life by improving the general health situation; and promoting the general well-being of the population, particularly by minimising the economic and social consequences of cancer. These actions were set out in detail in the Annex, under the headings of data collection and research; information and health education; early detection and screening; training and quality control and guarantees.

The anti-tobacco elements of the third action plan against cancer were found in the second of the specific objectives, set out in the Annex to Decision 646/96/EC. This objective concerns "information and health education" and is thus the direct descendant of the first cancer action plan. The objectives of the actions taken under this heading were "to help to improve knowledge of cancer risks and cancer prevention among European citizens and encourage them to adopt healthy lifestyles" and "to promote and assess policies and measures related to cancer causes and risks". Specific actions (8) and (9) covered matters relating to the connection between tobacco consumption and cancer. Actions may include:

- encouraging projects with a European dimension relating to the prevention of tobacco consumption;
- assessment of the implementation of recommendations on tobacco consumption in public places, particularly on public transport and in education establishments;
- promotion of strategies aimed at protecting the most vulnerable groups, in particular pregnant women and children, from the risk of passive smoking;

235 Decision 646/96/EC, OJ 1996 L 95/9, repealed by Decision No 1786/2002/EC of the European Parliament and of the Council of 23 September 2002 adopting a programme of Community action in the field of public health (2003–2008) – Commission Statements, OJ 2002 L 271/1.

236 The cumbersome "representatives of the governments of the Member States meeting in Council" was no longer necessary, as the Community now had formal legal competence to enact measures in the public health field.

237 Decision 646/96/EC, Article 3, as repealed: see above n 237.

- assessment of the effect of measures taken in the Member States to reduce tobacco consumption, for example, the banning or control of direct or indirect advertising, taxation measures and the exclusion of tobacco from the price index, and dissemination of knowledge acquired from the assessment process;
- support and assessment of pilot measures for preventing tobacco consumption as part of the exchange networks between Member States, for example, networks of no-smoking towns, no-smoking hospitals and youth clubs in cooperation with health-care workers and teachers;
- selection at European level and dissemination of the best methods of overcoming addiction to smoking, and evaluation of their impact as part of pilot measures to implement these methods in liaison with opinion formers and healthcare workers in the Member States;
- launching, among the pilot projects in the media, of a project to combat passive smoking; and
- continuing classification of dangerous substances and preparations with the aim of improving packaging and labelling.

These envisage EU-level support for potentially wide-ranging activities, all underpinned by the basic thrust of the EU's anti-tobacco position.[238]

The Europe against Cancer programme has now been subsumed within the new public health framework,[239] which runs from 1 January 2003 to 31 December 2008.[240] Two of the three general objectives of the new framework, set out in Article 2 of Decision 1786/2002/EC, are relevant for action in the field of cancer. One is to "improve information and knowledge for the development of public health". The other is "to promote health and prevent disease through addressing health determinants across all policies and activities". Actions include improving health information and knowledge and promoting health and preventing disease.[241] The latter includes "preparing and implementing strategies and measures, including those related to public awareness, on life-style related health determinants, such as nutrition, physical activity, *tobacco*, alcohol, drugs and other substances and mental health ...".[242] Thus the basic thrust of the EU's anti-tobacco measures under the cancer programmes has been carried forward within the new public health framework.

The EU's anti-tobacco and anti-cancer measures have been underpinned by the principle of "consistency and complementarity" with other areas of EU action. Under the new public health programme, this is expressed in terms of the use of "joint actions". Decision 1786/2002/EC, Article 4 provides that: "the measures of the programme may be implemented as joint actions with related Community

238 For example, the Europe against cancer programme has supported a project of the European Forum of Medical Associations and the WHO to create and manage an online tobacco resource centre for health professionals: see http://www.tobacco-control.org/.

239 Decision 1786/2002/EC adopting the new public health framework, OJ 2002 L271/1.

240 Decision 1786/2002/EC, Article 1 (2).

241 Decision 1786/2002/EC, Annex.

242 Decision 1786/2002/EC, Annex 3.1, emphasis added.

programmes and actions, notably in the areas of consumer protection, social protection, research and technological development, telematic exchange of information between administrations (IDA), statistics, education and environment . . . "

The other enduring principle is that of EU-level "added value". The benefits of examining and dealing with cancer at EU, rather than national, level are constantly stressed in documents emanating from the EU institutions. "Added value" precludes the use of EU funding for purely "national" projects so, for instance, *networks* of no-smoking towns, no-smoking hospitals and youth clubs could be supported, but not individual projects towards the same end. This has an effect on the kind of projects that may be financed by the EU's resources in this area. The use of soft law and financial support may have an indirect impact on national health promotion policies, in that extra finances are available for certain types of projects, which makes it more likely that those types of projects will be implemented. So, for instance, the EU's cancer programmes have contributed to changes in the content of education programmes for health professionals. Finally, the EU's cancer programmes have assisted the EU legislature in preparing regulatory measures, by providing the Commission with independent information on market and health-related developments. This is seen for instance in the inclusion of "oral moist snuff tobaccos" in Directive 92/41/EC, discussed below.[243]

Composition of tobacco products

The regulation of tobacco products has taken place at EU level since the late 1980s, in the context of internal market legislation. As discussed in chapter 3, Article 95 EC (formerly Article 100a EC) provides a legal basis for measures which have as their object the establishment and functioning of the internal market. In putting forward proposals for such measures, the Commission must take as a base a high level of protection in matters such as health and consumer protection.[244] Thus, EU-level measures harmonising the marketing and production of tobacco products have a strong health promotion element. Such legislation concerns three broad areas: consumer protection in the form of health information (and essentially warnings) on tobacco products, especially cigarettes; consumer protection in terms of the lawful composition of tobacco products; and measures concerning the advertising of tobacco products. The first two areas are discussed in this section; the third is discussed in the following section.

The first internal market and consumer protection measure concerning tobacco products was Directive 89/622/EEC[245] on the labelling of tobacco products. This measure was substantially amended by Directive 92/41/EEC,[246] and again by the Tobacco Products Consolidation Directive 2001/37/EC.[247] The aim of Directive

243 See further below.
244 Article 100a (3) EC, now Article 95 (3) EC.
245 OJ 1989 L 359/1.
246 OJ 1992 L 158/30.
247 OJ 2001 L 194/26.

2001/37/EC is to eliminate differences in national regulations concerning manufacture, presentation and sale of tobacco products.[248] Such differences constitute a hindrance to trade, and thus impede the establishment and functioning of the internal market. Unlike earlier Directives,[249] Directive 2001/37/EC makes no explicit reference in its preamble to the Europe against Cancer programmes. The health promotion elements of the Directive are downplayed. This is a direct result of the Court's decision in the *Tobacco Advertising Directive* case,[250] discussed in chapter 3, and briefly below. However, the public health elements of the Tobacco Products Consolidation Directive have been emphasised in other contexts, for instance, in a joint statement issued by David Byrne (Commissioner for Consumer and Health Protection) and Dr Gro Harlem Brundtland, Director General of the WHO, during Dr Brundtland's visit to the Commission in September 2000.[251] The Commission was mandated[252] to negotiate the WHO's Framework Convention on Tobacco Control (FCTC). Agreed by the WHO's member states on 17 March 2003, the FCTC is the latest WHO anti-tobacco initiative.[253] The Commission regards the Consolidation Directive as "complementary" to the FCTC, but it seems likely that the Directive formed part of the basis for the Commission's negotiating position.[254] For instance, the FCTC echoes the Directive in that it prohibits terms such as "light", "mild", or "low tar", that could lead people to think that one particular tobacco product is less harmful than others.[255]

Directive 2001/37/EC applies to "tobacco products" defined as "products for the purpose of smoking, sniffing, sucking or chewing, inasmuch as they are, even partly, made of tobacco".[256] All tobacco products (cigarettes, rolling tobaccos, pipe tobacco, cigars, cigarillos etc, chewing tobacco and traditional snuff) marketed in the EU are thus covered by the Directive. A special category of "tobacco for oral use" is defined as "all products for oral use, except those intended to be smoked or chewed, made wholly or partly of tobacco, in powder or particulate form, or in any combination of these forms – particularly those presented in sachet portions or porous sachets – or in any form resembling a food product".[257] This provision, originally enacted in Directive 92/41/EEC, refers to then new products of oral moist snuff tobaccos.

248 Directive 2001/37/EC, preamble, Recitals 2 and 3.

249 See, for example, Directive 89/622/EEC, preamble, Recitals 4 and 5.

250 Case C-376/98 *Germany v Parliament and Council (Tobacco Advertising)* [2000] ECR I-8419.

251 http://europa.eu.int/comm/dgs/health_consumer/library/press/press75_en.html.

252 Under Article 300 EC, in October 1999: see http://europa.eu.int/comm//health/ph/programmes/tobacco/who_minutes_en.htm.

253 The WHO has been considering smoking and its effects on health since at least the 1970s: see WHO Expert Committee Report, *Smoking and its effects on health* (Geneva: WHO, 1975). Successive World Health Assemblies have adopted resolutions aimed at combating smoking, see S. Fluss, "The Development of National Health Legislation in Europe: The Contribution of International Organizations" 2 *European Journal of Health Law* (1995) 193.

254 Information Meeting on the negotiations on the Framework Convention on Tobacco Control, held by the Commission, 13 November 2000, http://europa.eu.int/comm//health/ph/programmes/tobacco/who_minutes_en.htm.

255 See WHO Press Release, *Agreement on Global Tobacco Control*, 17 March 2003.

256 Directive 2001/37/EC, Article 2 (1).

257 Directive 2001/37/EC, Article 2 (4).

These products had come to the attention of the Commission through the first Europe against Cancer programme. They had been put on the world market by two companies, the Swedish Svenska Tobaks, and a US company – United States Tobacco Company – operating in the UK. Several Member States had either taken steps to ban these new oral moist snuff tobaccos, or planned to do so. In other Member States, the new products were not yet known. In 1988, the first European Conference on Tobacco and Health had recommended banning all new tobacco products containing nicotine.[258] Given this, and the scientific evidence of the carcinogenic nature of these oral moist snuff tobaccos,[259] the EU institutions took a pre-emptive strike and adopted an EU-wide ban on the marketing of these products in Directive 92/41/EC. Simply labelling these products with health warnings was not regarded as a suitable response.[260] "Tobacco for oral use", as defined by Directive 2001/37/EC, may not be marketed in the EU.[261] However, the significance of this development must be seen in the light of the fact that Sweden (the only Member State where oral moist snuff is popular[262]) has been granted a permanent derogation from this provision by its Treaty of Accession to the EU.[263]

The Directive brings together the pre-existing provisions on manufacture, presentation and sale of tobacco products in the EU. It reduces the maximum permitted tar level of cigarettes from 12mg to 10mg per cigarette, and introduces ceilings of 1mg nicotine and 10mg carbon monoxide per cigarette, from 1 January 2004.[264] Rules on labelling make up most of the remainder of the Directive. It sets out the health warnings that must be displayed on packets of tobacco products to be marketed within the EU. Each "unit packet" (for instance, a packet of cigarettes) must carry, on its largest surface, the general health warnings specified,[265] in the official

258 Conclusions of the European Conference on Tobacco and Health, Madrid, 7–11 November 1988, point 8.

259 COM(90) 538 final refers to International Agency for Research on Cancer, *Monographs on the evaluation of the risks of carcinogenic substances to humans*, vol 37 (Lyon: IARC, 1985); International Agency for Research on Cancer, *Evaluation of the carcinogenic risk of chemicals to humans: tobacco habits other than smoking, betel-quid and area-nut chewing and some related nitorsamines* (Lyon: IARC, 1985); and US Department of Health and Human Services, *The Health Consequences of Using Smokeless Tobacco: A Report of the Advisory Committee to the Surgeon General*, (Washington DC: Government Printing Office, 1986).

260 COM(90) 538 final, p 7.

261 Directive 2001/37/EC, Article 8.

262 The consumption of oral moist snuff among young people in Sweden had risen from 10% in 1976 to 37% in 1986. See National Smoking and Health Association, *Tobacco habits in Sweden: a short history* (Stockholm: NSHA, 1986).

263 Act of Accession of Austria, Finland and Sweden, Article 151, OJ 1994 C 241/341. Sweden is under a duty to ensure the products are not placed on the market in other Member States. The Commission is to review the measures adopted by Sweden to achieve this.

264 Directive 2001/37/EC, Article 3 (1). Member States are permitted to derogate from this date for cigarettes exported from the EU, but must comply by 1 January 2007 at the latest (Article 3 (2)). Greece has a special temporary derogation for maximum tar yields for cigarettes manufactured and marketed within its territory, until 1 January 2007 (Article 3 (3)).

265 In the case of tobacco products that are smoked, these are "Smoking kills/Smoking can kill" or "Smoking seriously harms you and others around you": Article 5 (2) (a). In the case of smokeless tobacco products, this is "This tobacco product can damage your health and is addictive": Article 5 (4).

language of the Member State in which the products are to be finally marketed.[266] The original proposal suggested that the size of health warning labels on packaging of tobacco products should be increased from 4% to 10%, with corresponding increases for countries with more than one official language, but the European Parliament amended this to 30% of the relevant surface.[267]

Further provision is made for the labelling of cigarettes – the largest market within that of "tobacco products". On the other large surface of the packet, one of a number of additional health warnings, set out in Annex I to the Directive, must be displayed.[268] Each Member State may draw up its own list of warnings taken from the list established in the Directive, and must ensure that each warning selected appears on an approximately equal quantity of packets. The warnings must cover at least 40% of the other large surface of the packet, and be printed in bold black letters, on a white background.[269] Furthermore they must still be intact when the packet is opened,[270] so may not be printed on any external wrapping. Terms such as "low tar", "light", "ultra light" and "mild", which have the effect of conveying the impression that the product is less harmful than others, are not to be used on the packaging of tobacco products from 30 September 2003.[271]

Article 13 (1) of the Directive provides that Member States may not, for reasons relating to the requirements of the Directive, prohibit or restrict the import, sale or consumption of products which comply with the Directive. Thus the Directive contributes to the establishment of a single market in cigarettes and other tobacco products within the EU. However, Member States remain free to adopt more stringent rules concerning the import, sale and consumption of tobacco products in order to protect public health, provided that such regulation is consistent with EU law.[272] It will be remembered that the Treaty provides a specific ground of exemption for public health protection to the provision on free movement of goods (Article 28 EC). Significant differences between national regulations in this respect (for example, concerning permitted additives in cigarettes[273]) do remain. The Directive invites the Commission to submit a proposal on a common list of authorised ingredients for tobacco products,[274] and this would seem to be the next logical step of EU-level regulation.

A number of tobacco companies brought an application for judicial review of the Directive before the English High Court, and this was referred to the European

266 Directive 2001/37/EC, Article 6 (e). Special provision is made for Member States with more than one official language.
267 Directive 2001/37/EC, Article 5 (5).
268 Directive 2001/37/EC, Article 5 (2) (b).
269 Directive 2001/37/EC, Article 5 (5) and (6) (a).
270 Directive 2001/37/EC, Article 5 (7).
271 Directive 2001/37/EC, Article 7; preamble, Recital 27.
272 Directive 2001/37/EC, Article 12 (2).
273 COM(99) 594 final, p 6.
274 Directive 2001/37/EC, Article 12. The Commission is to do so by 31 December 2004.

Court of Justice under Article 234 EC.[275] The companies argued that the Directive was invalid, for a number of reasons, including the argument that Article 95 EC was an inadequate legal basis; and the argument that the provisions on health warnings and the use of terms such as " mild" infringed intellectual property rights.[276] With regard to the first ground, the companies took the view that the Directive is not intended to ensure the free movement of tobacco products, but rather to ensure the protection of public health. Applying the Court's ruling in the *Tobacco Advertising* case,[277] if this were so, the Directive would not be validly adopted on the basis of Article 95 EC. The Court, essentially disagreeing with this approach, stressed that, where Article 95 EC is a correct legal basis, the measure must genuinely have the object of improving the conditions for establishment and functioning of the internal market, and must actually contribute to the elimination of obstacles to the free movement of goods or services, or the removal of distortions of competition.[278] However, a public health factor in the regulatory choices made to this effect does not render Article 95 EC an improper legal basis.[279] The Court found that differences between national regulatory regimes, and proposed new national measures in the pipeline, with respect to elements of tobacco products not covered by the pre-existing EU-level regime would be likely to increase obstacles to the free movement of these products.[280] Unlike the Tobacco Advertising Directive, the Tobacco Products Consolidation Directive guarantees the free movement of products complying with its provisions.[281] It follows that Article 95 EC is the correct legal basis for the Directive,[282] notwithstanding its health promotion elements.

With regard to the argument concerning intellectual property rights, the companies claimed that the Directive infringed the fundamental right to property[283] and/or Article 20 of the TRIPS Agreement, which provides that use of a trade mark in the course of trade is not to be unjustifiably encumbered by special requirements such as its use in a manner detrimental to its capability to distinguish the goods or services of one undertaking from those of other undertakings. It was argued that the very large size of the new warnings required by the Directive constituted an infringement of these fundamental rights, as the warnings will dominate the overall appearance of tobacco product packaging and thus curtail or even prevent tobacco product manufacturers from using their trade marks. The absolute prohibition of terms such as "mild" will deprive tobacco product manufacturers of a

275 Case C-491/01 *R v Secretary of State for Health, ex parte British American Tobacco and Imperial Tobacco* [2002] ECR I-11453.
276 Japan Tobacco, the exclusive licensee of the trade mark "Mild Seven", intervened in the main proceedings.
277 Case C-376/98 *Tobacco Advertising* above n 252, see further chapter 3.
278 Case C-491/01, para 60.
279 Case C-491/01, para 62.
280 Paras 65–73.
281 Para 74.
282 Para 75.
283 Found in Protocol 1, Article 1 ECHR, and Article 17 EUCFR.

number of their trade marks, as they will no longer be permitted to use them.[284] The Court found that the right to property, although a general principle of EU law, is not an absolute right and must be viewed in relation to its social function.[285] The restrictions to the right to property found in the Directive do not constitute a disproportionate and intolerable interference with that right.[286] The Court found that none of the other grounds on which the Directive was argued to be invalid applied, therefore the Directive was upheld as valid.

Thus, the internal market reregulatory regime with respect to tobacco products is a form of "new approach" harmonisation, setting minimum standards for goods moving freely within the EU, but leaving some discretion to Member States to adopt more stringent standards with respect to their home markets. However, the level of detailed EU-level reregulation suggests that the EU is increasingly occupying this field, and moving towards something more like "old style" detailed harmonised standards. The health promotion elements of the EU's anti-tobacco regulatory approach have been implicitly endorsed by the Court in its ruling on the validity of the Tobacco Products Consolidation Directive.

Advertising of tobacco products

The health promotion rationale is also present in internal market legislation applicable to the advertising of tobacco products. In the case of this EU-level legislation, the product or service being regulated, in order to ensure that the internal market in that product or service is established and functioning, is not the tobacco product itself, but rather the advertising products, and more importantly, services promoting the tobacco products.

In 1989, the EU acted to prohibit advertising of cigarettes and other tobacco products on television. The main objectives of the "Television without Frontiers" Directive 89/552/EEC[287] were to ensure free circulation of television broadcasts in the EU and to encourage development of transnational services. The Directive is based on Articles 57(2) (now 47) and 66 (now 55) EC concerning freedom to supply and receive services. Enactment of the Directive was prompted by the ruling of the Court in *Debauve*,[288] in which the Court held that, in the absence of harmonisation of the law at EU level, a Member State might lawfully prevent the retransmission of television adverts from other Member States on public interest grounds. However, development of satellite broadcasting, in conjunction with cable delivery systems, meant that television broadcasts now have the increasing capacity to spill over national boundaries, with the result that Member States were no longer able effectively to regulate this part of the media. The prospect of EU-level regulation thus became more appealing to most Member States.

284 Para 143.
285 Para 149.
286 Paras 149–153.
287 OJ 1989 L 298/23.
288 Case 52/79 *Procureur du Roi v Debauve* [1980] ECR 833.

The "Television without Frontiers" Directive is based on the principle of free circulation, which implies that Member States may not impede reception or retransmission on their territory of broadcasts emanating from other Member States for reasons falling within the fields coordinated by the Directive. Each broadcaster is to be subject only to the laws of the single Member State in which it is established. Broadcasters must comply with a minimum of common standards in the coordinated fields. These common standards essentially cover television advertising, and set standards on matters such as consumer protection, protection of morals and human dignity, protection of minors, and public order. Among these is the health promotion measure prohibiting all forms of television advertising and teleshopping for cigarettes and other tobacco products.[289] The preamble to the Directive gives no explicit justification for this measure, merely notes that "it is necessary to prohibit all television advertising promoting cigarettes".[290] However, the health promotion motif is obviously present.

From a promotion of health point of view, the natural next step to take after banning television advertising of cigarettes and tobacco products would be to ban other forms of advertising of cigarettes and tobacco products that take place away from the point of sale, such as radio advertisements, posters, billboards, and displays in printed matter such as magazines and newspapers. As a significant element of tobacco advertising takes place through sponsorship (particularly in the sporting world), a ban on such sponsorship would advance the public health objective. These seemed to be the true objectives behind Directive 98/43/EC[291] on tobacco advertising and sponsorship.

The original proposal for the Tobacco Advertising Directive was promulgated by the Commission in 1989,[292] nearly ten years before its final adoption. A number of Member States already imposed restrictions on tobacco advertising, including a total ban,[293] a ban on advertising in publications aimed at young people,[294] and partial restrictions on advertising.[295] The latter category included the requirement that tobacco advertising must incorporate the compulsory warning that must appear on packaging of tobacco products. The Commission proposal adopted a partial restriction approach, described by the Commission as "the most advanced system of governing advertising permitted".

As the original proposal was based on (old) Article 100a EC, the European Parliament was consulted under the "cooperation procedure". Parliament delivered its first opinion on 14 March 1990.[296] The European Parliament's response to the proposal was to introduce some 22 amendments, aimed at a total ban on advertising.

289 Directive 89/552/EEC, OJ 1989 L 298/23, Article 13.
290 Directive 89/552/EEC, preamble, Recital 17.
291 Directive 98/43/EC, OJ 1998 L 213/9.
292 COM(89) 163 final.
293 Italy and Portugal.
294 Belgium, Ireland, Luxembourg.
295 Denmark, Spain, the Netherlands and the UK.
296 OJ 1990 No 3 (Annex) 388/78.

However, the Commission regarded this proposal as "premature", in view of the current state of legislation in the Member States.[297] The Commission submitted a slightly amended version, but the proposal did not attract a qualified majority in the Council meeting of 3 December 1990. Rather, it emerged at that Council meeting, and a previous meeting on 17 May 1990, that a number of Member States were in favour of full, rather than partial, harmonisation of the issue, since restricting the subject of harmonisation to authorised advertising would not resolve all the problems for the internal market caused by divergent national regulation.[298] The Commission thus put forward a modified proposal on 6 June 1991. The modified proposal took into account the fact that, since 1989, a number of Member States (notably, France, Belgium and Greece) had moved towards greater restrictions in their regulation of tobacco advertising. It was this proposal, slightly amended in response to the opinion of the European Parliament,[299] that formed the basis for the Directive finally adopted in 1998.

The original Tobacco Advertising Directive provided that all forms of advertising and sponsorship of tobacco products were to be banned within the EU.[300] The definition of "tobacco products" adopted was the same as that in Directive 89/622/EEC,[301] now consolidated in Directive 2001/37/EC. "Advertising" was defined as "any form of commercial communication with the aim or the direct or indirect effect of promoting a tobacco product". This included advertising which "while not specifically mentioning the tobacco product, tries to circumvent the advertising ban by using brand names, trade marks, emblems or other distinctive features of tobacco products". This would cover advertising campaigns such as that for the "Silk Cut" brand of cigarettes, which simply shows pictures of purple silk. Perhaps ironically, it is the health warning at the bottom that confirms that these advertisements are indeed for cigarettes.

The Tobacco Advertising Directive set only a minimum standard (albeit a very strict one), and Member States remained free to lay down stricter requirements on the advertising and sponsorship of tobacco products as they deemed necessary on the grounds of public health.[302] The Directive was to have been implemented by 30 July 2001. The Directive was hotly contested in both the European Parliament[303] and in Council.[304] Considerable economic interests were involved in its implementation. The Council common position was finally reached by a qualified majority

297 Amended proposal for a Council Directive on the authorised advertising of tobacco products in the press and by means of bills and posters, COM(90) 147 final.

298 COM(91) 111 final.

299 OJ 1992 C 67/35.

300 Directive 98/43/EC, Article 4.

301 Directive 98/43/EC, Article 2.

302 Directive 98/43/EC, Article 5.

303 See, for example, Written Questions Nos 1005/98, OJ 1998 C 323/104; 1020/98, OJ 1998 C 354/52; 1091/98, OJ 1998 C 323/112; E-2072/99, OJ 2000 C 219 E/84.

304 It took no fewer than ten meetings of the Health Council before the Directive was adopted.

of health ministers on 4 December 1997, with Germany and Austria voting against, and Spain and Denmark abstaining.

The Tobacco Advertising Directive thus imposed a wide-ranging prohibition on advertising of tobacco products in the EU. It purported to be an internal market measure. However, it contained significant health promotion elements. It is not surprising, therefore, that legal challenges were mounted to the validity of the Directive. There are significant differences of opinion among the (social) scientific community on the effect of advertising on smoking habits – in particular whether advertisements increase the number of smokers, or merely encourage existing smokers to switch between brands. These differences of opinion, along with the significant economic interests of multi-national tobacco companies,[305] were thus able to assert themselves through the legal discourse of challenge to the validity of the EU-level measures. Although it is not the place for its elaboration here,[306] such discourse goes to the "constitutional" foundations of the EU, and in particular the competence given to the Community under the internal market project, be that conceived as a neo-liberal deregulatory area or a fully-fledged socio-economic regulatory "non-state polity", or anywhere in between.[307]

As the Tobacco Advertising Directive was based on the internal market provisions of Article 57 (now 47) (2), 66 (now 55) and 100a (now 95) EC, in order to be lawfully adopted, the Directive must have had an internal market rationale. Perhaps with a view to showing that this was so, Article 1 of the Directive provided that its objective was "to approximate the law, regulations and administrative provisions of the Member States relating to advertising and the sponsorship of tobacco products". The *content* of the Directive, however, could be construed as suggesting otherwise, and it was this issue that was at the heart of the legal challenges to the validity of the Directive in *Tobacco Advertising* and *Imperial Tobacco.* [308] As we saw in chapter 3, the Court concluded that the Directive was not properly enacted on the basis of Articles 100a, 57 (2) and 66 EC, and annulled the Directive.

The ruling of the Court in *Tobacco Advertising* could be regarded as a significant set-back to the EU's anti-tobacco policy, forming part of its measures concerned with health promotion, in particular the promotion of life-styles that are less likely

305 On the responses of the tobacco industry to the Directive in general, see M. Neuman, A. Bitton and S. Glantz, "Tobacco Industry Subversion of European Community Tobacco Advertising Legislation" 359 *Lancet* (2002) 9314 at 1323–1330 (13 April).

306 See K. Lenaerts, "Bricks for a Constitutional Treaty of the European Union: Values, Objectives and Means" 27 ELRev (2002) 377 at 387; G. de Búrca, *Setting Constitutional Limits to EU Competence?* Francisco Lucas Pires Working Papers Series on European Constitutionalism, Working Paper 2001/02; C. Hillion, "Tobacco Advertising: if you must, you may" 60 CLJ (2001) 486; P. Syrpis, "Smoke without Fire: The Social Policy Agenda and the Internal Market" 30 ILJ (2001) 271; J. Usher, "Annotation of Case C-376/98" 38 CMLRev (2001) 1519; Editorial, "Taking the limits of competences seriously" 37 CMLRev (2000) 1301.

307 For further discussion, and references to relevant literature, see chapter 2.

308 Case C-376/98 *Tobacco Advertising,* above n 252; Case C-74/99 *Imperial Tobacco* above n 277.

to cause cancer. However, as Hervey has argued elsewhere,[309] the ruling is very much out of step with the rest of the EU's law and policy in the field. We have seen that the ruling in *Tobacco Advertising* did not prevent the subsequent adoption of the Tobacco Products Consolidation Directive. Subsequently, the Commission put forward[310] a new Tobacco Advertising Directive,[311] which was adopted on 26 May 2003. The new Tobacco Advertising Directive prohibits tobacco advertising in the press and printed media, and on the internet or by email, save those publications intended exclusively for the tobacco trade.[312] All radio advertising of tobacco products is prohibited, and radio programmes may not be sponsored by tobacco companies.[313] Events taking place in several Member States, or otherwise having cross-border effects, may likewise not be sponsored by tobacco companies.[314] The new Directive explicitly provides that Member States may not prohibit the free movement of products or services complying with the Directive.[315]

Germany[316] and the International Automobile Federation[317] have announced their intention to challenge the validity of the new Tobacco Advertising Directive. The basis of Germany's challenge appears to be that the impact of the Directive on local printed media, such as local newspapers, which rely on revenue from tobacco advertising, is disproportionate. The EU institutions will presumably argue in response that as it was not possible to distinguish between "local", "regional" and "national" press, and that all printed media can move across EU borders, taking as a basis a high level of protection for public health, the total ban on tobacco advertising in printed media within the EU was justified. The IAF's challenge appears to be on the basis that the original compromise date for phasing out of tobacco industry sponsorship for Formula 1 motor racing of 2006 in the old Tobacco Advertising Directive has now been set to mid-2005 in the new Tobacco Advertising Directive, and all the planning that focused on the 2006 date is now redundant. Whether the IAF have a ground for review on the basis of legitimate expectations remains to be seen.

The new Tobacco Advertising Directive has been criticised for failing to go far enough as a public health measure.[318] In particular, the failure to regulate "indirect advertising", the use of non-tobacco products to promote tobacco brands, has been seen as a key weakness of the Directive, as it is easy for tobacco companies to replace direct advertising with indirect advertising. Indeed, this was the experience

309 Hervey, above n 225.
310 COM(2001) 283 final; COM(2002) 699 final.
311 Directive 2003/33/EC OJ 2003 L 152/16.
312 Directive 2003/33/EC, Article 3.
313 Directive 2003/33/EC, Article 4.
314 Directive 2003/33/EC, Article 5.
315 Directive 2003/33/EC, Article 8.
316 Reuters, "Germany to sue over EU tobacco advertising directive", 14 September 2003, www.eubusiness.com/; www.tobacco.org.news/; www.forbes.com/business/newswire.
317 S. Murray, "FIA to contest EC tobacco ruling" 3 April 2003, http://www.rte.ie/sport/2003/0403/motorsport/f1.html.
318 See, for instance, the criticisms made by the UK organisation ASH: see http://www.ash.org.uk/.

of several Member States, such as France, that banned direct tobacco advertising. The ban on sponsorship covers only events and activities with a significant cross-border dimension. This means that controversial tobacco industry support for various activities, for instance for research in the University sector,[319] remains unaffected by EU law. It was also feared that the Directive would compromise the Commission's position in the negotiations for the WHO Framework Convention on Tobacco Control (FCTC). These were concluded in May 2003, and the EU signed the FCTC on 16 June 2003, along with ten of its Member States.[320] The FCTC represents the first time in WHO's history that it has exercised its powers to adopt a treaty under Article 19 of its Constitution.[321] The FCTC is a global public health instrument of minimum harmonisation[322] aiming to protect national (or in the case of the EU, regional) legislation from being circumvented by transnational phenomena, such as cross-border advertising. In the event, the FCTC prohibits tobacco advertising, but includes an exception to the duty to ban tobacco advertising for states who cannot do so in accordance with their constitutional principles, such as those of freedom of commercial speech.[323]

Cancer and tobacco: conclusion

The case of tobacco advertising shows how legal structures and institutions at EU level may open up, but also constrain, possibilities for health promotion. The emergent health promotion policy in terms of tobacco advertising is evolving through interactions of actors at national, EU and also international levels. The role of the EU, and the opportunities for effective health promotion legislation being promulgated at EU level, cannot be discounted in this respect. At the same time, however, such opportunities are constrained by the legal provisions on Community competence. From the perspective of health advocates, EU law may be seen as simply another mechanism whereby powerful actors, such as the tobacco industry, seek to block, or at least to delay, the process of adoption of such measures.

IV. Conclusion

As this chapter has illustrated, EU law has had an impact upon various elements of the public health policies of Member States. The impact of the EU's deregulatory

319 In 2001, Professor Richard Smith, editor of the *British Medical Journal*, resigned from the University of Nottingham, UK, in protest at the acceptance of £3.8 million from British American Tobacco to fund an international centre on corporate social responsibility. See *Guardian* 21 May 2001. His resignation followed an online vote among readers of the journal, an overwhelming majority of whom felt that the University should return the money, and a majority of whom felt Professor Smith should resign if it did not.

320 Ireland signed on 16 September 2003.

321 See D.P. Fidler, "World Health Organization's Framework Convention for Tobacco Control" *American Society of International Law Insights*, 28 March 2003, http://www.asil.org/insights/insigh100.htm.

322 FCTC, Article 2.1.

323 FCTC, Articles 13.2 and 13.3.

internal market law has been limited by the Court's application of the Treaty-based public health justification for restrictions on freedom of movement. The availability of the public health justification has been underpinned by re-regulation through secondary legislation applicable to citizens of the EU moving between Member States, and also the EU's emerging common immigration policy. Financial support for EU-wide networking of health promotion agents may have scope for leading to convergence of national policies, although the HIV/AIDS programme considered here suggests that there is currently not a great deal of evidence that this is happening in practice on the ground, at least at present. Soft law measures have paved the way for harmonising measures of hard law with respect to blood safety, once the legal barrier of lack of appropriate legal basis provision in the Treaty was removed with the adoption of Article 152 EC. The model here has been "new approach" harmonisation, with EU-level measures setting minimum safety standards, leaving national discretion to adopt stricter protective measures applicable to establishments within a particular Member State. The EU institutions have also used both hard and soft law to articulate (and possibly shore up) "European" values and approaches to blood safety, in particular the notions of self-sufficiency in blood and voluntary unpaid blood donation. EU-funded policies have helped to develop cross-border networks of public health specialists, which may eventually feed into determination of best practice and gradual convergence of national policies. The EU has used its internal market competence to regulate the production and advertising of products that are harmful to health, relying on the obligation to take as a base a high level of protection in measures concerning health.

Threats to public health cannot be contained within national boundaries. As we noted in chapter 1, public health protection has long been the concern of the international community.[324] It is thus unsurprising that public health is an area of health policy that fits relatively readily within the scope of EU law. Public health is a matter of Community competence. We might therefore expect future incremental developments in EU public health law, with its "multi-level" interactions with national regulatory institutions and measures, along the lines already seen. A notable characteristic of developments in this area has been their reactive nature, for instance as exemplified in the amendments to EU food law following the BSE/nvCJD crisis, or the support of the EU for HIV/AIDS research. However, the reactive nature of EU involvement in public health regulation may change in the future. There are currently identifiable trends paving the way for pre-emptive public health risk reduction, as seen for instance in the EU's activities with respect to communicable disease surveillance.[325] One major area for EU involvement in the future is in relation to tissue and organs. We turn to these future directions in the next, and final, chapter.

324 See, for example, Y. Arai-Takahashi "The Role of International Health Law and the WHO in the Regulation of Public Health" in R. Martyn and L. Johnson, eds. *Law and the Public Dimension of Health* (London: Cavendish, 2001).

325 See further chapter 10, n 278.

Part Three

10

Conclusions and future prospects

I. Introduction: the roles of the EU in health law

Since Diane Blood sought to use EU law to enable her deceased husband's sperm to be exported, so that she could begin IVF treatment,[1] the influence of EU law on health law and policy in the Member States of the EU has grown apace. Although today there is no single body of "European health law", the EU is having an ever-widening involvement in relation to health, which is, in turn, affecting the manner in which individual Member States regulate their national health policies. Some of this involvement may be regarded as incidental or reactive, and indeed EU health policy, in general, has been described as having progressed very much on a "muddling through" basis.[2] However, it is also the case that, in certain areas at least, there is, currently, an increasingly structured involvement. This is particularly notable in the fields of public health and research, but may extend to further areas in the future. Indeed, as we were finishing this book, the health ministers of the existing and future Member States, the European Parliament and the European Commission announced the conclusion of the "High Level Process of Reflection on Patient Mobility and Healthcare Developments in the EU".[3] The Commission will respond to the recommendations made by the report from that High Level process[4] with a Communication in 2004. It is intended, at least by the Commission, that this will develop into an overall EU health strategy.[5]

We hope the examples elaborated in this book will help to convince health lawyers[6] of the need to be increasingly cognisant of the engagement of the EU with their discipline. Equally, we hope that EU lawyers will not simply assume that health is outside the competence of the EU, and therefore the EU has nothing to do with

1 *R v HFEA, ex parte Blood* [1997] 2 All ER 687. See chapters 1 and 4.

2 The phrase used by Hans Stein, the former head of the EU Health Policy Unit, at the Federal Ministry of Health in Germany: H. Stein, "On the Road from Maastricht to a new Europe" 9(2) *eurohealth* (2003) 17.

3 Commission Press Release IP/03/1678, "Cross-border healthcare: Health ministers and civil society call for closer cooperation", Brussels, 9 December 2003.

4 See further below.

5 Stein, above n 2.

6 Or, rather, those who are not already so convinced!

health law. Both health law and EU law are dynamic disciplines, and this, as we noted in chapter 1, presented us with challenges in casting the parameters of our inquiry. In this book, we made the decision to focus upon a number of selected substantive areas: access to health care services, information privacy and data protection, regulation of health professionals, clinical research, pharmaceuticals and public health. All these are commonly to be found in standard health law textbooks. In all these areas, EU law has had a considerable impact (sometimes indirect or incidental rather than direct) upon the approach taken by individual Member States to the legal regulation of health. However, as we have taken as our research question the involvement of the EU in health law, the boundaries of each of the areas discussed in the book, and the emphasis of our discussion, are delineated by the EU's involvement. It follows that many areas of law traditionally represented in health law texts are not covered here.

In this concluding chapter, we step back and try to distil our overall findings. Although we did not begin this study with the aim of finding these, it now appears that certain thematic concerns underpin the engagement of EU law with health. Further research would be necessary to elaborate these themes, but we present them here as a possible starting point for future research projects.[7] More substantially, we also seek to present our research findings within a conceptual structure. This may prove useful in evaluating the different effects that EU law has had on health law and policy in the Member States. It may also provide a means of suggesting future directions. The conceptual structure consists of a simple "spectrum" of different types of effect of EU law on national health law and policy, within which the substantive subject matter of the book is placed. Finally, we ask: where is this area going in the future?

Four themes of "European health law"?

Although we did not set out with any preconceived ideas in this respect,[8] our findings suggest four distinctively identifiable thematic concerns underpinning the engagement of EU law with health law and policy. These may be summarised as "risk", "rights", "solidarity" and "consumerism". We did suggest, in chapter 1, that if the term "European health law" has any meaning at all, it is through the organising constructs of values such as social solidarity. Maybe this, along with the other thematic concerns we have identified, and probably others,[9] marks out what is distinctively "European" in the regulation of health and health care within the EU. Obviously, the brief discussion here, in our concluding chapter, is not a substitute for a sustained research project specifically based on the identification and analysis

7 Our own, and, we hope, those of others.

8 As was noted in chapter 1, our research question was simply a descriptive analytical one: "How – to what extent and in what ways – does EU law affect health law and policy in the Member States?"

9 The principle of equality of access might be an example.

of the significance of any or all of these thematic concerns. Such projects will have to be for the future.

In many of the examples elaborated in this book, the EU legislature appears to take a cautious and conservative overall approach to *risk*. This may be seen, for instance, in the provisions regulating marketing, manufacture, and advertisement of pharmaceuticals, discussed in chapter 8. As we noted in chapters 1 and 9, there is a long history of regulation on the basis of public health protection at both national and EU level. Public health regulation is now determined at neither EU nor national level alone, but by interactions between EU and national institutions. Again, many of these measures appear to reflect caution and conservatism in the approach to regulation of health risks. Examples include the regulation of food, the provisions on blood safety, and proposals on organs. Another example, found in chapters 2 and 3, is the legitimation of national restrictions upon the free movement principles, where public health justifications are given a generous construction, thus permitting national authorities to adopt highly risk-averse strategies.

In the future, the regulation of risks to health is likely to be driven by the proliferation of new scientific and technological development, which inevitably brings with it new uncertainties and potential new risks. There has been a perceptible breakdown in trust in science across EU Member States.[10] Notable illustrations are the BSE/nvCJD crisis[11] and expressed public concern regarding genetically modified foods. Where, as in these examples, hazardous factors easily cross national borders, the desirability of reaching common standards in risk protection at supranational level increases. The interactions between the regulation of risks to health in the EU context, and the legal order of the WTO, deserve more detailed consideration than we were able to give them within this book.[12]

The second thematic concern emerging from our findings is that of *rights*, or to be more precise, the *language* of rights. As we noted in chapter 1, one approach which can be taken to conceptualisation of the discipline of health law is to view it in terms of human rights, and rights-based approaches are also becoming increasingly prominent in the health law literature.[13] At national level, the provision of health services has been increasingly framed in terms of rights discourse.[14] At the same time, with the "solemn proclamation" of the EU Charter of Fundamental Rights 2000, and its proposed incorporation in the Draft Treaty establishing a Constitution for Europe, rights discourse is becoming increasingly prominent within the EU's

10 See, for example, in the UK context, House of Lords Select Committee on Science and Technology: Science and Society, HL paper 38, 2000; and see N. Pidgeon, "Science, uncertainty and society" 8(1) *eurohealth* (2001–02) 16.
11 See discussion in chapter 9.
12 See, for a starting point, the work of Scott, cited in chapter 9, n 21 and 116.
13 See, for example, I. Kennedy and A. Grubb, *Medical Law: Text with Materials* (London: Butterworths, 1991 and 2000).
14 For instance, in patient bills of rights, such as the Danish Patient Rights Act 1998; through the application of legislative statements of human rights; or through the application of the Council of Europe's European Convention on Human Rights 1950.

legal order.[15] The prospect for such an "EU-specific" rights discourse having an effect on national health law needs to be considered further in the light of a discussion of the EU Charter of Fundamental Rights. We consider this below, in the context of a discussion of possible future directions of EU involvement in health law and policy.

The third thematic concern emerging from our findings is that of *solidarity*. Over the last few years, "solidarity", expressed in various forms, has become increasingly prominent in EU legal discourse.[16] It now finds reflection in the Draft Treaty establishing a Constitution for Europe, in Article I-2 DCT:

> "The Union's values. The Union is founded on the values of respect for human dignity, liberty, democracy, equality, the rule of law and respect for human rights. These values are common to the Member States in a society of pluralism, tolerance, justice, solidarity and non-discrimination."

The meaning of "solidarity" remains under-defined, but its essence appears to include "the inherently uncommercial act of involuntary subsidisation of one social group by another".[17] In the context of health law, this could refer to such matters as the cross-subsidisation that takes place within European national health systems (whether through compulsory insurance or taxation) allowing equality of access to health care and treatment, regardless of an individual patient's means; the interference with the normal operation of the market in setting prices for pharmaceuticals

15 There is a link here to the literature on legitimacy, sovereignty and constitutionalism in the EU, see, for a starting point, the literature in chapter 2, n 166.

16 For instance, Article 16 EC, added to the Treaty at Amsterdam, refers to the "place occupied by services of general economic interest in the shared values of the Union", and their "role in promoting social . . . cohesion."; Advocate General Fennelly, in 1997, took the view that national "systems of social provision established . . . on the basis of the principle of solidarity" do not fall within internal market law: see Case C-70/95 *Sodemare* [1997] ECR I-3395. This was followed by application of the principle of generational solidarity by Advocate General Jacobs in a competition law case: Case C-67/96 *Albany International* [1999] ECR I-5751. In 1999, Commissioner Flynn (then Social Affairs Commissioner) defined the "European social model" as being based on two common and balancing principles, competition and "solidarity between citizens", speech for conference "Visions for European Governance": Harvard University, 2 March 1999. See T. Hervey, "Social Solidarity: A Buttress against Internal Market Law?" in J. Shaw, ed, *Social Law and Policy in an Evolving European Union* (Oxford: Hart, 2000). Bernard considers that the Court's jurisprudence in this respect, although not explicitly framed in rights discourse, can be read as consistent with a concern about the protection of fundamental social rights: see N. Bernard, "A 'New Governance' Approach to Economic, Social and Cultural Rights in the EU" in T. Hervey and J. Kenner, eds, *Economic and Social Rights under the EU Charter of Fundamental Rights* (Oxford: Hart, 2003). A number of commentators, notably Weiler and Maduro, have sought to link the value of "solidarity" with the EU's constitutional core: see, for example, J.H.H. Weiler, "A Constitution for Europe? Some hard choices" 40 JCMS (2002) 563; M. Poiares Maduro, "Europe and the constitution: what if this is as good as it gets?" in J.H.H. Weiler and M. Wind, *European Constitutionalism Beyond the State* (Cambridge: CUP, 2003); M. Poiares Maduro, "The Double Constitutional Life of the Charter of Fundamental Rights of the European Union" in T. Hervey and J. Kenner, eds, *Economic and Social Rights under the EU Charter of Fundamental Rights: A Legal Perspective* (Oxford: Hart, 2003); M. Poiares Maduro, "Striking the Elusive Balance Between Economic Freedom and Social Rights in the EU" in P. Alston, ed, *The European Union and Human Rights* (Oxford: OUP, 1999).

17 Opinion of Advocate General Fennelly, Case C-70/95 *Sodemare* above n 16.

and other medical products; and the voluntary and unpaid donation of blood or organs.

The theme of solidarity appears in various places in the book. The free movement of health care services and patients litigation,[18] discussed mainly in chapter 4, but also in chapters 6 and 8, operates on the basis of the "deregulatory" mode of EU governance. Where the European Court of Justice assesses objective public interest justifications for restrictions on the free movement of factors of production within the internal market, it explicitly considers the potential threats to the financial balance of a national health (insurance) system. The same applies to litigation involving the free movement of goods – be those pharmaceuticals or other "medical goods".[19] An example concerning a pharmacy (DocMorris) operating across borders, through mail order and the internet, is discussed below. The Court makes explicit the conflicts between, on the one hand, the internal market's deregulatory rules and, on the other hand, the public health and financial implications of the intervention of internal market law in the structures and mechanisms of national health systems. It may be that this jurisprudence also extends to the potentially disruptive effects of EU competition law.[20]

The final major theme that emerges from our consideration of the effects of EU law on health law and policy is that of the *patient as consumer*.[21] We noted, in chapter 1, a general trend in health care towards the "consumerisation" of patients. In many of the instances in which EU law engages with patients, it does so through conceptualising the patient as a "consumer". This is particularly so in the cases of the freedom to receive health care services across borders within the EU,[22] free movement of medicinal and other health care goods,[23] and liability for defective medicinal and other health care goods.[24] Much of the legislation discussed in this

18 Case C-158/96 *Kohll* [1998] ECR I-1931; Case C-157/99 *Geraets-Smits and Peerbooms* [2001] ECR I-5473; Case C-368/98 *Vanbraekel* [2001] ECR I-5363; Case C-385/99 *Müller-Fauré* [2003] ECR I-4509; Case C-56/01 *Inizan v Caisse primaire d'assurance maladie des Hauts-de-Seine*; see the discussion in chapter 4.

19 See, for example, Case C-120/95 *Decker v Caisse de Maladie des Employés* [1998] ECR I-1831; Case 104/75 *De Peijper* [1976] ECR 613; Case 32/80 *Kortmann* [1981] ECR 251; Cases 266 & 267/87 *R v Royal Pharmaceutical Society of Great Britain, ex parte Association of Pharmaceutical Importers and others* [1989] ECR 1295; Case C-369/88 *Delattre* [1991] ECR I-1487; Case C-60/89 *Monteil and Samanni* [1991] ECR I-1547; Case C-55/99 *Commission v France (Medical Reagents)* [2000] ECR I-11499; Case 215/87 *Schumaker* [1989] ECR 617; see also Case C-62/90 *Commission v Germany* [1992] ECR I-2575; see the discussion in chapter 8.

20 But see Cases C-264/01, C-306/01, C-354/01 & C-355/01 *AOK Bundesverband and others*, [2004] ECR I-(16 March 2004, nyr in ECR), see chapter 8, n 233.

21 A related theme may be the patient as "trader", in the context of the commercialisation of the human body. As we saw in chapter 7, the EU's engagement with regulation of research utilising human material, including genetic material, has primarily been limited to questions of patentability. Whether the human rights and dignity elements of such regulation are able to circumvent the EU's limited competence and political will in this contentious field remains to be seen.

22 See chapter 4.

23 See chapter 8.

24 See chapter 8.

book is framed as consumer protection legislation, within the context of the creation of a single European market.[25] The EU's conceptualisation of patients as consumers follows directly from the Community competence provisions relating to health. There is very limited Community competence to harmonise national laws in the health field. In contrast, the EU institutions enjoy significant powers and obligations to adopt regulations harmonising measures, including consumer protection measures, that might otherwise impede the establishment and functioning of the internal market. The Commission must take, as a starting point in its proposals in this field, a high level of consumer protection. Thus, the construction of patients as consumers within EU law, in effect, gives the Community competence in the field of health.

In the past, national health systems in the Member States of the EU have operated under a system in which the clinician has operated as "gatekeeper" to the provision of services. However, with the development of private health care services, this has broken down, particularly where services are sought for reasons which some regard as being "non-therapeutic", such as cosmetic surgery. In addition, the ability to access a wider range of services, such as the increasing availability of medicines "over the counter" or through the internet, has facilitated patients' control over their own health care.[26] The patient as consumer is becoming increasingly aware of what is on offer in other Member States. This information transfer may also have an impact upon the care offered in their home state, as states and clinicians come under increasing pressure to provide the range of therapies available elsewhere. There may, of course, be attempts to delimit the availability of such services on public health grounds, and this may lead to observable tension between the rise of consumerism within health care, and that of public health protection. The ways in which the EU's conceptualisation of patients as consumers may interact with the trends in this direction, emanating from privatisation of health care, present an interesting site for future research projects.

II. The "spectrum": how does EU law affect health law and policy in the member states?

As we have outlined in the previous chapters, while some areas of health law are affected directly, and in considerable detail, through the involvement of the EU, in other areas the impact of EU law is much more disparate, incidental or indirect. Nonetheless, when we step back and view the engagement of the EU with the

25 See, for instance, the Data Protection Directive 95/46/EC, OJ 1995 L 281/31, see chapter 5; pharmaceuticals legislation, in particular Directive 2001/83/EC, OJ 2001 L 311/67, see chapter 8; Food Regulation 178/2002/EC, OJ 2002 L 31/1, see chapter 9; Tobacco Advertising Directive 98/43/EC, OJ 1998 L 213/9, see chapter 9; Blood Safety Directive 2002/98/EC, OJ 2003 L 33/30, see chapter 9.

26 See M. Brazier, *Medicine, Patients and the Law* (London: Penguin, 3rd edn. 2003), p 17; J. Montgomery, *Health Care Law* (Oxford: OUP, 2003), chapter 9.

concerns of health law, this can be seen as a continuum. This is inevitable, given both the manner in which the EU has become engaged in health, and the dimensions of those health matters themselves. We set out, in chapter 2, six different modes of governance utilised by the EU institutions, and their differing legal (and practical) effects. These models – deregulation, "old style" harmonisation, "new approach" harmonisation, regulatory coordination, "soft" coordination, and financial incentives – formed our framework for analysis within the substantive chapters of the book. As we noted in chapter 2, some modes of governance, such as "old style" harmonisation by means of Directives and Regulations, will, by definition, have a greater and more direct legal impact than, for example, the use of financial incentives. However, within a particular substantive area under discussion, different modes of governance may be used, either at different times, or contemporaneously. The application or applicability of a particular mode of governance itself, in a particular substantive area, does not tell us the whole story about the effects that EU law has had, or has the potential to have, on those elements of health law and policy within the Member States. What we seek to do here, therefore, is to set out a continuum, or spectrum, of different types of effect, within which the substantive areas chosen for discussion in this book can be situated. This will allow, by extrapolation, a determination of the likely situation for other areas of health law, which we did not have space to discuss.[27] The spectrum ranges from the areas of health law affected most strongly by EU law, through to areas where there is, or at least appears to be, no prospect of convergence or consensus.

Areas of health law affected most strongly

The areas in which the EU appears to have had the most radical effect upon national health law in the Member States are where Regulations and Directives are adopted in relation to what we might call "health law subjects". The key unifying factor here is the identification of a clear Community competence to adopt such measures. Where such competence can be identified, a strong effect of EU law on national health law and policy is to be expected. Because of the indeterminacy of the concept of Community competence, it may not always be possible to predict such an effect, but the key site for regulation here is protection of patients, or EU citizens more generally, conceptualised as "consumer protection". This is either explicitly within the health field under Article 152 (4) EC, or by reference to the more general legal basis provisions of Article 95 EC, or indeed Article 308 EC.[28]

As we noted in chapter 2, a distinction can be made here between "old style" and "new approach" harmonisation. There are a few areas where "old style" harmonisation (total field occupation) applies in relation to health issues. These are primarily in relation to the regulation of marketing and manufacture of pharmaceuticals,

27 The utility or robustness of our spectrum will of course need to be tested by future research projects.
28 See further chapter 3.

discussed in chapter 8, and concern issues of quality, safety and efficacy and the authorisation for marketing of "novel" pharmaceutical and other health care products. Regulatory coordination of national authorisation procedures applies here also.

There is also considerable evidence that the "new" approach to harmonisation, which gives significant discretion to national authorities at the level of detail, is having a major impact across a range of areas. As we saw in chapter 7, the Clinical Trials Directive[29] is leading to a radical reconsideration of the legal principles regarding the regulation of clinical trials concerning medicinal products in Member States. The Directive structures the processes for approval of such trials through the use of research ethics committees, by establishing broad criteria and time limits for the approval of trial protocols, and mechanisms for amendments to the trial, and also measures for pharmacovigilance should things go wrong, in the form of the EUDRACT database. A further illustration, which we considered in chapter 9, is that of Directive 2002/98/EC setting standards of quality and safety for the collection, testing, processing, storage and distribution of human blood and blood components (the Blood Safety Directive).[30] This Directive followed many of the blood contamination scandals, such as HIV-infected blood in France, Germany and Portugal.[31] It sets out standards which will apply across the whole EU, regarding collection, testing, processing, storage and distribution of blood and blood components, and is to be implemented by Member States by 8 February 2005. As we noted in chapter 9, a feature of the Directive is that it sets minimum standards. It expressly states that it does not prevent Member States from maintaining or introducing more stringent national protective measures, for example, relating to requirements regarding voluntary and unpaid blood donations.[32] Here, then, there is a strong effect on national health law, in terms of setting minimum protective standards, but discretion remains with national authorities to adopt more stringent home state controls. As we shall see below, the proposed new Tissue Directive, which relates to quality and safety in relation to donation and storage of tissues, might also be expected to come within this category.

Areas of health law affected by general measures of EU law

There are also a number of instances in which general measures of EU law have had a particular impact upon the legal regulation of health care at Member State level. Predicting such an effect is more difficult than in the case of areas where there is Community competence to adopt harmonisation legislation in a health law field. In order to do so, health lawyers may need to consider EU law in a range of different areas. Those that we have discussed in this book include internal

29 Directive 2001/20/EC on the approximation of the laws, regulations and administrative provisions of the Member States relating to the implementation of good clinical practice in the conduct of clinical trials on medicinal products for human use, OJ 2001 L 121/34.
30 OJ 2002 L 33/30.
31 See chapter 9, p 343.
32 Directive 2002/98/EC, Article 4 (2).

market law and employment law, but a much wider review of EU law, including, for instance, competition law, environmental law and public procurement law, would be necessary to form a complete picture.

For example, at individual Member State level, health information privacy protections have been boosted through the enactment of the Data Protection Directive. This Directive has led to the enactment of wide-ranging data privacy legislation across current and future Member States.[33] In the area of clinical malpractice litigation, while it is the case that the basis of civil litigation and individual causes of action are left to Member States, where indeed the litigation process indicates considerable differences across Member States,[34] the Product Liability Directive has resulted in a new cause of action in relation to defective products through the introduction of strict liability provisions.[35] So, for example, in the UK, the Consumer Protection Act 1987 led to litigation over blood infected with Hepatitis C, while challenges have also been recently brought concerning the transplantation of infected organs.[36] The Working Time Directive 93/104/EC[37] is having an effect upon the structure of professional training, through circumscribing the number of working hours for junior doctors. As we noted in chapter 6, the implementation of this Directive is currently the source of much controversy within certain Member States.[38]

Another major impact in the form of general measures of EU law comes in relation to deregulation: the involvement of EU Treaty law in ensuring the free movement of the factors of production. This can be seen as having quite a strong effect, but perhaps less so than in the case of legislation, as the involvement of EU law arises through the vagaries of individual litigation, rather than from the binding effects of reregulatory measures of EU legislation. A notable illustration of this category is the ability of individual patients to use free movement principles in support of their attempts to seek health care services in other Member States. Whilst the initial effect of such provisions has been sporadic, and largely concerns the ability of individuals to obtain reimbursement for health care services, as we noted in chapter 4, this litigation appears to be expanding.

Deregulatory internal market litigation appears to be operating in three main ways on national health law and policy. First, it has led to the prospect that individual Member States' own approach to health care resource allocation may be circumscribed by judicial perceptions of the applicability of EU law.[39] Attempts by individual Member States to ration health care and contain costs might, potentially, be frustrated through such an approach, although the use of the "solidarity"

33 See discussion in chapter 5.

34 J. Dute, "Medical Malpractice Liability: No Easy Solutions" 10 *European Journal of Health Law* (2003) 85.

35 OJ 1985 L 210/29; see *A and Others v National Blood Authority and Another* [2001] 3 All ER 289.

36 Case C-203/99 *Henning Veedfald v Arhus Regional Authority* [2001] ECR I-3569.

37 OJ 1993 L 307/18.

38 See chapter 6, pp 195–197.

39 See *R (on the application of Yvonne Watts) v Bedford Primary Care Trust and Secretary of State for Health* [2003] EWHC 2228 (Admin), 1 October 2003; see the free movement of patients jurisprudence, above n 18; also see the free movement of pharmaceuticals jurisprudence, above n 19.

principle to justify restrictions on free movement may significantly constrain this potential effect.

Second, the prospect of individual citizens seeking and obtaining treatment in other Member States, with consequent concerns of Member States about the prospect of legal liability should standards in the host Member State be lower than in the home Member State, is one factor in the promotion, by cross-border professional organisations, of common standards in health care provision across the EU.[40] To date, these moves have taken place within non-governmental fora, but, if pressures of cross-border patient mobility increase, there may be an incentive to involve the EU institutions here.[41]

Third, the ability to access services in other Member States may undermine the attempts by individual Member States to restrict the provision of certain health services to individual citizens, on the basis that a particular service is seen as undesirable on ethical grounds. We have discussed some examples of such services – abortion and particular types of modern reproductive technologies – in chapter 4. Another potential future site for such an effect is that of "death tourism", the practice of travelling to another country to seek euthanasia services.[42] Because of the "Easy Jet" or Motorbaan factor – the ability to subvert national law through leaping onto a plane or into a car and seeking services across the border – Member States cannot retain control over the treatments sought and obtained by "their" patients.[43] We return to this issue below.

Whilst there has been increasing interest, by both policy-makers and academics, in the impact of deregulatory principles on health care provision in Member States, there are still considerable limitations on its scope. First, the impact of EU law here is tempered significantly by the possibility of limitations being introduced on public health grounds, and other objective public interest grounds, such as solidarity. Second, while the free movement principles provide a means by which to access services, in practice, of course, application of EU law is filtered through national courts. Litigation here is constrained by the judicial structure of the EU's legal order, and, in particular, the "gatekeeping" role that may be played by national (constitutional) courts in their application of EU law, and their use of the preliminary reference procedure.[44] This means that, in practice, national (constitutional) values may assert themselves, as they have in relation to the regulation of human reproduction,[45] and potentially, in the future, to "death tourism".

40 See chapter 4.

41 See chapter 6.

42 Whilst the notable recent illustrations concerning this practice relate to travel to Switzerland by UK citizens, there is potentially the prospect of more "death tourism" in the future, given the policy shifts within certain EU Member States, namely the Netherlands and Belgium. On the new legal developments on end of life decision-making, see J. De Haan, "The New Dutch Law on Euthanasia" 10 *Medical Law Review* (2002) 57.

43 As we noted in chapter 4, of course this phenomenon is global, rather than specific to the EU.

44 Article 234 EC. See chapter 2.

45 See, for example, *Attorney General v X and others* [1992] ILRM 401 and the discussion of this case in chapter 4, pp 152–153.

Marginal effect

The third category along the spectrum is that in which EU law has had a more marginal effect upon the legal regulation of health care at Member State level. In this third category, either EU law attempts only to coordinate national systems, or harmonisation has not resulted in any significant practical changes.

Take, for example, the coordination and harmonisation of the qualifications of health care professionals (through the sectoral and general directives) discussed in chapter 6. Whilst these measures, in principle, facilitate the movement of health professionals between Member States, in practice they appear to operate very much at the edges. For instance, in the UK, the sectoral directives resulted in the recognition of "specialist medical training", as the UK admitted in the High Court that the procedure for the award of specialist medical accreditation was in breach of the sectoral "doctors directive".[46] Overall, however, the effects of the sectoral directives on professional training appear to have been limited. The degree of movement by health professionals within the EU is marginal, in contrast to migration into the EU by health professionals from outside the EU.

Similarly, as we noted in chapter 4,[47] whilst the provisions of national social security systems have been co-ordinated through Regulation 1408/71/EEC, in particular Title III of this Regulation, which relates to coordination of sickness and invalidity benefits, facilitating movement of persons between Member States, this appears to have had only marginal impact.

It should be noted, however, that, even in those instances where EU involvement is currently of "marginal effect", this position may not be static and there may be a movement towards enhanced EU involvement. This is especially so where there are interactions with other mechanisms, particularly deregulation, as exemplified by the interactions between "freedom to provide services" litigation and Regulation 1408/71/EEC. There may be a movement, over time, from EU-level coordination, or even simply EU financial support, towards the development of harmonised legal provisions. For instance, as we saw in chapter 7, the support of the EU in terms of research funding for orphan diseases may have influenced legislative developments.[48] These interactions may move EU-level activity from the marginal effect category towards a more significant effect.

46 J. Lonbay, "Free Movement of health care professionals" in J. Lonbay and R. Goldberg, eds, *Pharmaceutical Medicine, Biotechnology and European Law* (Cambridge: CUP, 2000), p 79; and see *R v Secretary of State for Health, ex parte Goldstein* [1993] 2 CMLR 589. See also Case C-202/99 *Commission v Italy* [2001] ECR I-9319, see further chapter 6.

47 See chapter 4, pp 152–153.

48 See Commission Communication on the framework for action in public health of 1993, COM(93) 559 final, discussed in chapter 3; the Biomed 2 strand of the Fourth Framework Programme Decision 1110/94/EC, OJ 1994 L 126/1; Council Resolution on orphan drugs, OJ 1995 C 350/3; and Regulation 141/2000/EC, OJ 2000 L 18/1; see further chapter 7.

"Slow convergence" effect

Next along the continuum are those measures which may be seen as having a less immediate effect, but where there is the distinct possibility of a "slow convergence effect". Over a period of time, EU involvement through "soft law", including the open method of coordination, and also instruments such as resolutions, opinions, notices and communications, may increase. This may be illustrated by the EU's increased involvement in HIV/AIDS, elaborated in chapter 9. The influence of the EU may also be brought to bear by financial support, through various action plans and other funding schemes. These "soft" mechanisms may have a persuasive effect on the provisions of national legal systems with respect to health. Furthermore, there is the possibility that initial EU involvement through soft law may, eventually, build up to legislative intervention at EU level, including the possibility of "hard law" harmonisation.

One illustration of this "slow convergence" effect is the EU 's engagement with stem cell research, discussed in chapter 7. Whilst there has been wide-scale condemnation of reproductive cloning, there has been some support for the development of stem cell technology and some consequential cloning developments. Nonetheless, this has led to much debate, and an attempt to stop EU funding of research programmes using stem cell technology. Proposed guidelines were suggested, stating that research is to be eligible for funding only where this relates to "spare" embryos created before 27 June 2002[49] and stem cells derived from those embryos, and the clinical trial protocol must show that the use of these materials is necessary.[50] The controversy continued in relation to the proposed new Directive setting standards of quality and safety for the donation, procurement, testing, processing, storage and distribution of human tissues and cells (the "Tissue Directive").[51] An attempt was made to extend the scope of the Directive to adopt harmonised provisions regulating stem cell research across the EU. Ultimately, in the context of the Tissue Directive, however, the proposals were defeated, and, for the time being at least, such issues remain left to regulation at individual Member State level.

No prospect of convergence or consensus?

There is, finally, a category of concerns of health law where, at least at first sight, there appears to be no real prospect of convergence or consensus at EU level. Indeed,

49 When the Parliament and the Council adopted the Sixth Framework Programme.

50 OJ 2002 C 232/1; Proposal for a Council Decision amending Decision 2002/834/EC on the specific programme for research, technological development and demonstration; "Integrating and strengthening the European Research Area" (2002–2006), 9 September 2003, COM (2003)390, 2003/0151 (CNS); and see S. Halliday, "A comparative approach to the regulation of human stem cell research in Europe" 12(1) *Medical Law Review* (2004) 40.

51 Commission Proposal for a Directive on setting standards of quality and safety for the donation, procurement, testing, processing, storage and distribution of human tissues and cells, COM (2002) 319; Amended proposal for a Directive on setting standards of quality and safety for the donation, procurement, testing, processing, storage and distribution of human tissue and cells, COM(2003) 340.

some may regard the prospect of such convergence or consensus as undesirable. Nys has commented that:

> "There undoubtedly are certain vexed themes in medical law – such as abortion and euthanasia – where the ideas of the various Member States (but also within states) are so far apart due to religious, philosophical, ethical and other reasons that a common European regulation would be simply unthinkable."[52]

As Nys notes, this appears to be the reason for the exclusion of such issues from the Council of Europe's Convention on Human Rights and Biomedicine 1997.[53]

Taking the example of abortion, whilst this is universally regulated across the EU, the extent of that regulation varies extensively.[54] For instance, in the Republic of Ireland, the constitution safeguards the right to life of the foetus.[55] Abortion is sanctioned, but only in limited circumstances.[56] In contrast, countries such as Denmark provide a right to abortion in the first semester. In Germany, abortion has proved particularly controversial, and indeed was left outside the general reunification of East and West Germany.[57] The range of approaches will increase on enlargement of the EU. Most of the accession states and the other Central and Eastern European candidate countries have a fairly liberal perspective on abortion. For instance, in Bulgaria, the Czech Republic, Estonia, Hungary, Latvia, Lithuania, Romania, the Slovak Republic and Slovenia, abortion rates are three times the EU average.[58] Poland is an exception. Here abortions are lawful only in cases of severe risk to the mother's health, high risk of significant foetal abnormality or where the pregnancy is the result of an illegal act such as a rape.[59] Interestingly, in the negotiations over accession to the EU, Poland did not negotiate explicit protection for its constitutional approach to abortion.[60] In contrast, separate negotiations did take place with Malta, which has a restrictive approach to abortion.[61] Protocol No 7, annexed to the Accession Treaty 2003, provides that:

52 H. Nys, "Comparative health law and the harmonisation of patients' rights in Europe" 8 *European Journal of Health Law* (2001) 317 at 325.
53 See also H.D.C. Roscam Abbing, "Human Rights and Medicine; A Council of Europe Convention" 3 *European Journal of Health Law* (1996) 201.
54 See, for example, the discussion in J.K. Mason, R.A. McCall Smith and G. Laurie, *Law and Medical Ethics* (London: Lexis Nexis UK, 6th edn, 2003), pp 151–158.
55 Irish Constitution, Article 40.3.3.
56 *AG v X* [1992] 2 CMLR 277.
57 Treaty on German Unity (31 August 1990).
58 In Romania, induced abortions were legalised in 1990, see WHO and European Commission, *Health Status Overview for Countries of Central and Eastern Europe that are Candidates for Accession to the European Union* (Copenhagen: WHO, 2002), p 20.
59 Polish Act on family planning, human embryo protection and conditions of permissibility of abortion 1993; Ruling of the Polish Constitutional Tribunal, 28 May 1997; see http://www.federa.org.pl/english/abortion.htm and http://www.federa.org.pl/english/constrib.htm.
60 This was probably because of the possibility that the association of a sensitive issue such as abortion with membership of the EU might have made more difficult the process of ratification of the Accession Treaty in Poland. Thanks to Christophe Hillion for elaborating this point.
61 See Maltese Criminal Code, sections 241–243A, http://www.docs.justice.gov.mt/lom/legislation/english/leg/vol_1/chapt9.pdf.

> "Nothing in the Treaty on European Union, or in the Treaties establishing the European Communities, or in the Treaties or Acts modifying or supplementing those Treaties, shall affect the application in the territory of Malta of national legislation relating to abortion."

This wording is virtually identical to that of Protocol No 17 annexed to the Treaty on European Union, applicable to the Irish position on abortion.[62]

The diversity in approach to these ethical issues would suggest that the question of the legal status of the foetus is a matter with which the European Court of Justice is unlikely to engage directly, even if the EU Charter of Fundamental Rights becomes binding on Member States, as is currently proposed under the Draft Treaty establishing a Constitution for Europe. Nor is this likely to be the subject of legislative intervention at EU level. In this respect, a parallel with the European Convention on Human Rights may be instructive. In the jurisprudence under the European Convention on Human Rights, abortion and "rights" of the foetus are matters which have very much been left open.[63] Whether Article 2 applies to the foetus at all, or extends to provide some "weak" form of right, is unresolved.[64] Nonetheless, the ECHR jurisprudence indicates that, in relation to such sensitive ethical issues, a considerable margin of appreciation is likely to be left to individual Member States. We might expect such a pattern to be repeated in the EU context.

Nys' other example is euthanasia. In practice, Member States were, for many years, aligned on this issue, although not through any EU-level intervention. Indeed, across a wide range of jurisdictions, active euthanasia or physician-assisted suicide has been prohibited.[65] Such prohibitions spring from three fundamental reasons. First, they are based on respect for the sanctity of life. The prohibition upon intentional deprivation of life, however ostensibly humane the reason, is common internationally, and respect for sanctity of life is common across faiths. Second, to sanction euthanasia can be seen as in conflict with the role of the physician as "healer". Third, there are practical reasons for such prohibition, which include the boundaries within

62 This reads: "Nothing in the Treaty on European Union, or in the Treaties establishing the European Communities, or in the Treaties or Acts modifying or supplementing those Treaties, shall affect the application in Ireland of Article 40.3.3 of the Constitution of Ireland."

63 See discussion in M. Stauch, "Pregnancy and the Human Rights Act 1998" in J. Tingle, A. Garwood-Gowers and T. Lewis, eds, *Healthcare: the Impact of the Human Rights Act* 1998 (London: Cavendish, 2002). In December 2003, the Strasbourg institutions were seized of a case involving a wrongful abortion. Mrs Thi-Nho Vo is arguing, in the face of what appears to be the position under French law that the doctor involved cannot be prosecuted, that the foetus enjoys a "right to life" under the ECHR. See BBC news online, 10 December 2003.

64 *Paton v UK* (1980) 3 EHRR 408, *H v Norway* (1990) App No 170004/90, *Open Door Counselling and Dublin Well Woman v Ireland* (1992) 15 EHRR 244.

65 See, generally, M. Otlowski, *Voluntary Euthanasia and the Common Law* (Oxford: Clarendon Press, 1997); J. Keown, *Euthanasia, Ethics and Public Policy: An Argument Against Legalisation* (Cambridge: CUP, 2002); J. Keown, ed, *Euthanasia Examined: Ethical, Legal and Clinical Perspectives* (Cambridge: CUP, 1995); J. McHale and M. Fox, *Health Care Law: Text and Materials* (London: Sweet and Maxwell, 1997), chapter 14; I. Kennedy and A. Grubb, *Medical Law* (London: Lexis Nexis UK, 2000), chapter 14; R. Dworkin, *Life's Dominion* (London: Harper Collins, 1993); H. Biggs, *Euthanasia* (Oxford: OUP, 2001).

which any euthanasia law could operate, and the prospect of the "slippery slope" from voluntary to non-voluntary euthanasia.[66]

In the EU context, euthanasia is particularly sensitive, in the light of the abuses of Nazi Germany. Nonetheless, over time, in certain European jurisdictions, the historical position of absolute prohibition has weakened.[67] Initially, in the Netherlands, a policy was adopted of non-prosecution of clinicians involved in euthanasia, where there was compliance with certain notification criteria. The Netherlands[68] and Belgium have recently legalised euthanasia. However, the emphasis placed upon the sanctity of life in other EU Member States has led to continued support for a legal prohibition on euthanasia. So, for example, in 2001, the UK House of Lords affirmed the UK's rejection of active euthanasia and assistance in suicide in the *Pretty* case.[69] The sensitivity of this issue is such that it is unlikely that the EU legislative institutions would ever have any direct involvement.

Nonetheless, even for this category of highly controversial ethical concerns, the prospect of at least a degree of convergence, driven by the EU, cannot be totally ruled out. Take, for example, the application of free movement principles in the health context, through the application of the decision in the *Diane Blood* case discussed in chapter 4 above. It may be the case that the availability of controversial health care services, which citizens can access in other Member States, may lead to pressure within Member States for a change in approach on such controversial issues. Through such indirect processes, deregulatory measures of EU law, such as those relating to free movement, may, in the long run, lead to a fundamental change. The same might be said for the possibility of seeking EU funding for ethically controversial research. One might think that regulation of cloning, and in particular stem cell research, is an area in which convergence or consensus at EU level is highly unlikely. Where such research is banned in a particular Member State, the fact that it is permitted elsewhere in the EU, and the possibility of enhanced public support for research through EU funding mechanisms may contribute, slowly and over time, to a change in approach at national level. Furthermore, as we noted above in the context of the proposed Tissue Directive, it may be that, in the future, the EU is increasingly prepared to become more directly involved in such areas. The regulation of the use of human material is being currently addressed in the EU, largely in the context of safety of product use. As we saw above, some attempt has been made to use this as an opportunity for the EU to take a more radical approach to ethically sensitive issues concerning the regulation of human tissue.[70]

66 D. Lamb, *Down the Slippery Slope* (London: Routledge, 1988), chapter 2: "It started from small beginnings."
67 H. Nys, "Physician involvement in a patient's death: a continental European perspective" 7(2) *Medical Law Review* (1999) 208.
68 See De Haan, above n 42.
69 *R (on the application of Pretty) v DPP* [2002] 1 All ER 1.
70 See European Parliament report on the proposal for a European Parliament and Council directive on setting standards of quality and safety for the donation, procurement, testing, processing, storage and distribution of human tissue and cells, A5-0103/2003; see also European Parliament

However, we can only speculate at the extent to which such changes may take place as a result of the operation of *EU norms*, rather than more general trends in societal change, as a consequence of cultural internationalisation, with increased awareness of different options through media such as books, newspapers, television and the internet. Alternatively, as we noted in chapter 4, the prospect of accessing services such as abortion in other Member States may be seen as a "safety valve". This may mean that the position in individual Member States does not, in fact, alter, because individual citizens have the ability to, in effect, by-pass national law and access services in other Member States. The effect of EU law here is actually to promote and protect *diversity* in regulatory approaches across different Member States, rather than any convergence or consensus.

III. Future directions

Over the last decade, there has been a significant increase in the influences of the EU on health law. But how may the EU become involved here in the future? It may be that the developments which we have charted in this book are indeed only the tip of the iceberg. Health provision itself is still rapidly evolving across the Member States of the EU, fuelled by changing demographics, the influence of the financial disciplines of economic and monetary union on welfare institutions, the reconceptualisation of the boundaries of professional bodies and also by technological developments, such as the new genetics. These developments give rise to new legal and ethical challenges. Any EU regulation here also needs to be viewed in the context of international debates, particularly over ethically controversial matters such as cloning, sex selection and gene therapy. In this final part of our book, we consider some prospects for future EU involvement in health law and policy.

We begin by considering the significant changes that the EU is currently undergoing, in particular the new Draft Constitutional Treaty and the enlargement process. These developments are likely to have a major impact upon EU-level policy developments, in general. We consider their potential specific applications in the field of health. We also consider the potential application of one of the EU's "new" methods of governance, the "open method of coordination" in the health field. We then examine two areas of health law and policy – the use of human material and "e-health"– in which there is the prospect for EU involvement in the future.

The Draft Constitutional Treaty

The "constitutional" framework of the EU[71] is currently under discussion by the Heads of State and Government of the Member States, and accession states, within the IGC process. The "Laeken Declaration" of December 2001 established a

legislative resolution on the proposal for a European Parliament and Council directive on setting standards of quality and safety for the donation, procurement, testing, processing, storage and distribution of human tissue and cells, 10 May 2002, COM(2003) 340, Recital 6.

71 Or, taking a strictly intergovernmentalist view, its Treaty basis.

Constitutional Convention,[72] which produced a Draft Treaty establishing a Constitution for Europe ("Draft Constitutional Treaty" or DCT). This lengthy document[73] was presented to the European Council at its meeting in Thessaloniki in June 2003. The Draft Constitutional Treaty now forms the basis for the IGC negotiations between the Member States. The accession states that are due to join the EU on 1 May 2004 are to participate in the IGC "on an equal footing" with the existing Member States. As we finish our work on this book, the European Council and the Heads of State of the accession states are meeting at the Brussels summit[74] to begin this process.

Although the Draft Constitutional Treaty forms the basis for the current IGC, it is not clear what will survive from the existing text. However, it is worth mentioning here two key elements of direct relevance to our research question: how does EU law affect health law and policy in the Member States? The first of these is the proposals with respect to human rights, and the second concerns Community competence.[75]

Fundamental rights within the DCT

Part II of the DCT brings the Charter of Fundamental Rights of the EU (EUCFR) within the parameters of the Treaty. The Charter is, currently, a measure of "soft law". In the past, the EU, as we noted in chapter 2, has been reluctant to adopt its own explicit binding charter of human rights,[76] but rather has referred to the ECHR, and the common constitutional traditions of the Member States.[77] Under the current legal position, then, the prospect for the articulation of rights *specific to the EU*, or with a specific EU interpretation, in the context of its interactions with national health law therefore remains remote. There may, however, be some change to this position, if the EUCFR takes its place, as proposed, within the DCT.[78]

The legal significance of such an incorporation is that the provisions of the EUCFR would no longer be "soft law" (persuasive, a reference point for interpretation of hard law), but would become "hard" or binding primary EU law. The practical significance of such an incorporation is more difficult to predict, and is

72 For details on the novel "constitutional convention" method, see G. de Búrca, "The Drafting of the European Union Charter of Fundamental Rights" 26 ELRev (2001) 126; K. Lenaerts and M. Desomer, "New Models of Constitution-Making in Europe: The Quest for Legitimacy" 39 CMLRev (2002) 1217.

73 Contrast Napoleon Bonaparte's famous advice: "Une constitution doit être courte et obscure", cited in J. Schwarze, "Constitutional Perspectives of the European Union with Regard to the Next Intergovernmental Conference" 8 *European Public Law* (2002) 241.

74 December 2003.

75 Or Union competence, as it will become if the DCT's proposals are adopted.

76 Proposals for an EU bill of rights date back to the 1950s: see P. Craig and G. de Búrca, *EU Law* (Oxford: OUP, 2003), p 318. The EUCFR is simply a "solemn proclamation", not a measure of Treaty law.

77 See, for example, Case 29/69 *Stauder v City of Ulm* [1969] ECR 419; Case 11/70 *Internationale Handelsgesellschaft* [1970] ECR 1125; Case 4/73 *Nold v Commission* [1974] ECR 491.

78 See discussion in T. Hervey, "The 'Right to Health' in European Union Law" in Hervey and Kenner, eds, above n 16; C. McCrudden, "The Future of the EU Charter of Rights", Jean Monnet Papers, http://www.jeanmonnetprogram.org/papers/01/013001.html.

the subject of differences of opinion among legal commentators.[79] For our purposes, we consider only those provisions that are necessary to provide sufficient context to assess the extent to which the EUCFR may have potential effects on national health law and policy. The starting point for analysis is Article I-7 DCT, which provides first that "the Union shall respect" the "rights, freedoms and principles" of the EUCFR,[80] and, second, that fundamental rights, found in the ECHR and the common constitutional traditions of the Member States, are "general principles" of EU law.[81] This provision appears to suggest that the incorporation of the EUCFR merely codifies the existing position, as developed by the European Court of Justice.[82] In fact, by its reference only to the Union, and not to the Member States, Article I-7 DCT apparently does not go as far as the existing jurisprudence, which places an obligation on Member States to respect fundamental rights as "general principles" of EU law when they are implementing EU law,[83] or when they are derogating from their Treaty obligations.[84] The former of these two obligations is explicitly reflected in Article II-51 (1) DCT.[85] In any case, the point here is that the EUCFR appears to be aimed principally at the "institutions, bodies and agencies" of the EU.[86]

A number of possible effects on national health law and policy, arising from the incorporation of the EUCFR within the DCT, may be considered. We note a few examples here.[87] In the final analysis, however, no *significant* alteration to the current position, according to which fundamental human rights, especially those protected

79 See, for instance, M. Dougan, "The Convention's Draft Constitutional Treaty: A 'Tidying-Up Exercise' that Needs Some Tidying-Up of Its Own", Federal Trust Papers, http://www.fedtrust.co.uk/uploads/constitution/27_03.pdf; P. Craig, "What Constitution Does Europe Need? The House that Giscard Built: Constitutional Rooms with a View", Federal Trust Papers, http://www.fedtrust.co.uk/uploads/constitution/27_03.pdf; P. Eeckhout, "The EU Charter of Fundamental Rights and the Federal Question" 39 CMLRev (2002) 945; J. Schwarze, "Constitutional Perspectives of the European Union with Regard to the Next Intergovernmental Conference" 8 *European Public Law* (2002) 241; B. de Witte, "The Legal Status of the Charter: Vital Question or Non-Issue?" 8 MJ (2001) 81; J. Wouters, "Editorial" 8 MJ (2001) 3 and the other contributions to this special issue of the journal, volume 8 (1); L. Betten, "The EU Charter on Fundamental Rights: a Trojan Horse or a Mouse?" 17 *International Journal of Comparative Labour Law and Industrial Relations* (2001) 151; B. Hepple "The EU Charter of Fundamental Rights" 30 ILJ (2001) 225; K. Lenaerts and P. Foubert, "Social Rights in the Case-Law of the European Court of Justice: the impact of the Charter of Fundamental Rights of the European Union on Standing Case-Law" 28 *Legal Issues of Economic Integration* (2001) 267; Lord Goldsmith, "A Charter of Rights, Freedoms and Principles" 38 CMLRev (2001) 1201.

80 Article I-7 (1) DCT.

81 Article I-7 (2) DCT provides that the EU shall seek accession to the ECHR; this proposal need not concern us here.

82 See further chapter 1.

83 Case 5/88 *Wachauf* [1989] ECR 2609.

84 Case C-260/89 *ERT* [1991] ECR I-2925.

85 It is not clear whether the omission of the latter was deliberate or not, see further Eeckhout, above n 79, at 977–979, and, more generally, de Búrca, above n 72.

86 Article II-51(1) DCT. The word "agencies" has been added from the original EUCFR text, reflecting the proliferation of such agencies with the EU.

87 There is no attempt to be exhaustive. Future research will no doubt elaborate these.

by the ECHR,[88] are protected as general principles of EU law,[89] is expected. First, incorporation of the EUCFR into the DCT implies that the provisions of the EUCFR will become a benchmark for judicial review of legislative and administrative[90] acts of the institutions of the EU.[91] With respect to review of legislation, as Craig has pointed out, we can expect the incorporation of the EUCFR within the DCT to lead to an increased "juridification of political life within the EU".[92] Perhaps we might expect more litigation framed in terms of rights discourse, such as the challenge by the Netherlands to the Biotechnology Directive.[93] Member States, or institutions such as the European Parliament, may seek to express their political disagreements in the form of judicial review of legislation in the health field, on the basis that it breaches fundamental rights protected by the EUCFR. Such litigation is, of course, already possible, by reference to fundamental human rights as "general principles" of EU law. Where might EUCFR provisions, with relevance to health, add to that canon?

If the EU follows the line suggested by the Clinical Trials Directive, the Blood Safety Directive and the proposed Tissue Directive, and continues to legislate in the field of clinical research, one might envisage possible challenges on the basis of Article II-1 DCT on human dignity and Article II-3 DCT on the right to integrity of the person, probably coupled with the right to life.[94] To give a specific example, an EU Directive that permitted stem cell research using foetal material might be subject to such a challenge. However, such a putative judicial review application would have to overcome several hurdles in order to be successful.[95] As we noted

88 The DCT brings the ECHR jurisprudence even more firmly within EU law, see Article II-52 (3) DCT.

89 See chapter 2, nn 63–64.

90 With respect to review of administrative acts, one might imagine challenges within the administrative competencies of the EU institutions examined in this book. For instance, acts of the Commission in disbursing funding for medical research, or even acts of the EMEA or EFSA (agencies are now explicitly included within Article II-51 (1) DCT), could perhaps be challenged for failure to respect EUCFR measures on non-discrimination, if the decision had a disproportionate effect on one of the protected groups (Article II-21 DCT; Article II-24 DCT (rights of the child); Article II-25 DCT (rights of the elderly); Article II-26 (integration of persons with disabilities)). With respect to regulation of research, reference might be made to Article II-13 DCT on the freedom of the arts and sciences. One problem here would be the limited *locus standi* of individuals under Article 230 EC: see Case 25/62 *Plaumann v Commission* [1963] ECR 95; Case C-50/00P *Unión de Pequeños Agricultores (UPA) v Council* [2002] ECR I-6677.

91 Note that the formal legal position is that the EUCFR does not extend Community competence: see Article II-51 (1) and (2) DCT. See also Article II-52 (2), which provides that "Rights recognised by this Charter for which provision is made in other Parts of the Constitution shall be exercised under the conditions and within the limits defined by these relevant Parts". The provisions in the Charter might form a platform for development of soft law or source of inspiration for the EU legislative institutions within the context of existing provisions on Community competence: see T. Hervey, "The 'Right to Health' in EU Law" in Hervey and Kenner, eds, above n 16.

92 Craig, above n 79, p 4.

93 Case C-377/98 *Netherlands v European Parliament and Council (Biotechnology)* [2001] ECR I-7079, see chapter 7.

94 Article II-2 DCT; Article 2 ECHR.

95 In fact, it would probably be more likely to be successful on the ground of lack of competence, see chapter 3, and chapter 7, p 278; Dougan, above n 79.

above, the ECHR jurisprudence is ambivalent about a "right to life" of the foetus, and there is no reason to expect anything different in the EU context. Further, the EUCFR and DCT specifically prohibit "reproductive cloning";[96] silence with respect to "therapeutic cloning" might be taken to imply that this is permissible. Moreover, competing rights to dignity or to life (rights of those who would stand to benefit from the fruits of any research) might be brought into play. A public interest justification might also be suggested.

Another putative example might be an application for judicial review of EU legislation that allows patenting of medicinal products or other medical goods that are made from an individual's genetic material. Article II-3 (2) DCT goes further than the ECHR in providing that "the prohibition on making the human body and its parts as such a source of financial gain" must be respected, in accordance with the right to integrity of the person. Although the Biotechnology Directive itself is now immune from challenge,[97] could it be argued that future EU legislation, for instance, extending the patent protection for an invention based on an individual's genes, breaches this principle? Again, such a challenge would face similarly formidable hurdles in the form of competing rights and public interest arguments. Further, the significance of the words "as such" in Article II-3 (2) DCT might also be relevant, given the nature of biotechnological science.[98]

Second, although the provisions of the EUCFR apply primarily to the EU institutions, Article II-51 (1) DCT confirms that they also apply "to the Member States ... when they are implementing Union law". Where the Member States implement internal market law, for instance, on freedom to provide and receive health care services, they are subject to the rights set out in the EUCFR. For instance, relevant rights that might form the basis for a challenge of national action in the context of human reproduction, could presumably include the right to respect for family life or the right to marry and found a family, which are already part of EU law as emanating from the ECHR.[99] One could envisage a possible challenge to a national implementation of the provisions of the Clinical Trials Directive, regarding consent of mentally incapacitated adults, on the basis that the rights to privacy of such a trial subject were not sufficiently protected. This might arise if the implementing measures adopted too wide a construction of who is the "legal representative" who may give consent.[100] Again, the right to privacy is already recognised as a "general principle of EU law", emanating from the ECHR. Compulsory HIV/AIDS tests on

96 Article II-3 (2) (d) DCT.

97 Article 230 EC provides that an application must be made within two months of the publication of the measure. The Biotechnology Directive was upheld in Case C-377/98 *Biotechnology* above n 93.

98 See chapter 7, pp 265–6, on the synthesis of genetic codes.

99 Again, such a challenge would have to meet various hurdles with respect to competing rights and public interest justifications.

100 See chapter 7.

persons crossing borders within or into the EU[101] might fall foul of the right to non-discrimination in Article II-21 DCT. Freedom of expression,[102] again found in the ECHR, and thus currently a "general principle" of EU law, might form the basis for a challenge to regulation of advertising to protect or promote public health, as is the case for prescription-only pharmaceuticals, or tobacco.[103] One provision that is not part of the ECHR is Article II-8 DCT on the protection of personal data. As we saw in chapter 5, this provision could apply to national measures implementing the Data Protection Directive, and other relevant measures of EU law, in the health care context. The rhetoric of a "right to health care" is now underpinning attempts to use EU law in free movement of patients litigation, as we saw, for instance, in the case of Yvonne Watts.[104] However, there is some doubt as to whether the provisions in the "solidarity chapter" of the EUCFR, which includes Article II-35 DCT on the "right to health care", enjoy the status of "rights", or are merely unenforceable "principles".[105] The DCT appears to confirm the latter, in Article I-7 (1) DCT, which explicitly distinguishes between "rights, freedoms and principles".

Third, it is already the case that the provisions in the EUCFR are a reference point for interpretation of provisions of EU law, and incorporation within the Treaties would make such consistent interpretation an obligation on national and EU courts. In a few circumstances, provisions in the EUCFR might make a significant difference in terms of interpretation of measures of EU law in the health field. The principal example identified in this book is that of rights to information privacy, and data protection. We explored, in chapter 5, various ways in which a rights-based interpretation of the Data Protection Directive might make a difference to its provision on anonymisation and consent. For instance, such an interpretation implies that anonymisation should be subject to an "absolute" test – data cannot be de-anonymised by anyone – rather than a test of proportionality – data cannot be de-anonymised without a significant effort. This may make a significant difference to the conduct of certain research projects.

However, with respect to interpretation of other measures of EU law that are relevant to health, an obligation of consistent interpretation with the EUCFR is unlikely to make a significant difference to outcome. As Hervey has shown elsewhere, where courts interpret the Treaty provisions on freedom to provide and receive services in the context of cross-border health care litigation, the "right to health care" of Article II-35 DCT is unlikely to make a difference, except, perhaps, in the

101 See chapter 9.
102 Article II-11 DCT.
103 See chapters 8 and 9.
104 *Watts* above n 39; and see chapter 4.
105 See Goldsmith, above n 79; Hepple, above n 79; McCrudden, above n 78; compare M. Gijzen, "The Charter: A Milestone for Social Protection in Europe?" 8 MJ (2001) 33.

framing of the discourse.[106] The same can be said for free movement of goods, as applied to medicinal or other medical goods.[107]

Lastly, it is just possible that (some) provisions of the EUCFR, as Part II of the DCT, become directly effective provisions of EU law, enforceable in national courts. This scenario is feasible, though probably unlikely, given the nature of the provisions concerned. [108]

This brief overview suggests that the incorporation of the provisions of the EUCFR within the DCT is unlikely to make a significant alteration to the current position within most of the fields discussed in this book. What we might expect, however, is an increased reference to the *rhetoric* of rights, in both legislative and judicial contexts, and an increased scope for rights discourse to frame the regulation of health within the EU.

Competence within the DCT

The Draft Constitutional Treaty aims to clarify the division of competences between the EU institutions and those of the Member States.[109] It proposes three formal categories of competence: exclusive competence; shared competence; and areas of supporting, coordinating or complementary action, in which Member State competence cannot be superseded.[110] "Common safety concerns in public health matters" are explicitly deemed to be a matter of "shared competence".[111] This was probably

106 See Hervey, in Hervey and Kenner, eds, above n 16, pp 207–210. Article II-35 DCT is based on Article 11 European Social Charter (ESC). The European Committee of Social Rights, that examines compliance reports of the states parties to the ESC, found in 2001 that waiting lists and times for hospital appointments within the British NHS were such that "the organisation of health care in the UK is manifestly not adapted to ensure the right to health for everyone": see Doc c-15-2-en2. Could this require that, in order to be consistent with Article II-35 DCT, the provisions on freedom to provide services in EU law be interpreted to require a British NHS Trust to fund a "cross-border bed"? Even if the court seized of a case in which this was at issue referred to a "right to health", such a right could be found to be respected, by reference to the right to health of other patients, whose health needs would not be met were cross-border beds to be made available, as the resources available are not infinite.

107 See Hervey, in Hervey and Kenner, eds, above n 16, pp 210–211. For instance, must the free movement of goods provisions be interpreted as including a "right to health" in the context of a (putative) restriction on the free movement of single vaccines for measles, mumps and rubella, adopted on the grounds that single vaccines are less effective than the combined MMR vaccine? Again, although the discourse of rights might be involved, the substantive outcome of such a case is unlikely to be affected, as competing interests (the rights of individuals, to choose separate vaccines, as against the good of the community, to be protected by herd immunity) balance one another in such a case.

108 The preconditions for direct effect will be remembered from chapter 2. Such direct effect is really only possible with respect to the more traditional civil and political rights found within the EUCFR. Eeckhout has explored the possibility for such an effect, through an analogy with the jurisprudence of the European Court of Justice on the principle of non-discrimination on grounds of nationality. See Eeckhout, above n 79.

109 The necessity of such a clarification is particularly associated with German legal and political commentators: see J. Schwarze, "Constitutional Perspectives of the European Union with Regard to the Next Intergovernmental Conference" 8 *European Public Law* (2002) 241. See also U. di Fabio, "Some Remarks on the Allocation of Competences between the European Union and its Member States" 39 CMLRev (2002) 1289.

110 Article I-11 DCT.

111 Article I-13 DCT.

seen as desirable, in the light of the Court's apparent constraining of Community competence relating to health under Article 95 EC in the *Tobacco Advertising* ruling.[112] Of more importance, probably, even in the health field, is the fact that the "internal market" and "consumer protection" are also areas of shared competence. The "protection and improvement of human health" is stated to be an area where the EU may take only "supporting, co-ordinating or complementary action".[113] These provisions appear to consolidate the existing position, and therefore, if adopted in the final text, would appear to leave areas for dispute, as is the current situation.[114]

What changes are envisaged for the competence provisions relevant to this book?[115] The internal market provisions remain largely unchanged in Part III of the DCT, which covers the "policies and functioning of the Union". For instance, Article III-65 (3) states that in its proposals for measures to establish the internal market, the Commission must take as a base a high level of protection in proposals concerning health, safety, environmental protection and consumer protection. Protecting human health remains an objective of EU environmental policy[116] and consumer protection policy.[117]

The public health provision (Article III-179 DCT) is in chapter 5 of Part III of the DCT, entitled "Areas where the Union may take coordinating, complementary or supporting action". This provision is very similar to Article 152 EC. "Human health" has become "physical and mental health", which reflects the EU's increasing interest in mental health.[118] Article III-179 (4) DCT now provides that measures of EU law in this field are to be adopted "in order to meet common safety concerns". This may be read as narrowing the scope of the measure, as it imposes an extra hurdle, perhaps by a reference to the subsidiarity principle, for measures to be justifiably based on Article III-179 (4) DCT.[119] The scope of the incentive measures that the EU may adopt has been extended: such measures may be designed to protect and improve human health or to combat the major cross-border health scourges.[120] The provision in Article 152 (2) EC, concerning types of Commission coordination action, has been elaborated, and a duty to inform the European Parliament has been added. In particular, the Commission may take initiatives "aiming at the establishment of guidelines and indicators, the organisation of exchange of best practice, and the preparation of the necessary elements for periodic monitoring and evaluation". This

112 Case C-376/98 *Germany v Parliament and Council (Tobacco Advertising)* [2000] ECR I-8419. See M. Giannakou, member of the Constitutional Convention, "Thoughts on the EC Treaty provisions regarding public health", CONTRIB 229 CONV 536/03, 4 February 2003.

113 Article I-16 DCT.

114 See chapter 3.

115 See chapter 3.

116 Article III-129 DCT.

117 Article III-132 DCT.

118 See below n 282.

119 Belcher, McKee and Rose take the opposite view: see P. Belcher, M. McKee and T. Rose, "Is Health in the European Convention?" 9(2) *eurohealth* (2002) 1.

120 Assuming the correct interpretation of the conjunction "and" in this context is "and/or".

is, presumably, with a view to using the "open method of coordination" within the health field. It is to this that we now turn.

A "health" open method of coordination?

Since the 1990s, the EU has turned towards a number of new methods of governance.[121] This has sparked a significant debate about the place of those new methods in the integration process, and their relationships with the "classic Community method" of harmonisation through binding legal texts.[122] This is not the place for elaboration of that debate. However, one such new method of governance, the "open method of coordination"[123] deserves some discussion here, as there are some indications that it may be applied to the health field in the near future.

What has now come to be called the "open method of coordination" (OMC) was first used after the Treaty of Maastricht for coordinating the Member States' economic and fiscal policies through "broad economic policy guidelines", and subsequently adopted for the EU's employment strategy by the Treaty of Amsterdam. The European Council's Lisbon Summit in March 2000, and subsequent summits, resolved to apply the generic OMC method to a number of other areas, including social protection.[124] It now appears that the OMC on social protection will also eventually encompass an OMC in "health care and long term care for the elderly".[125]

The OMC is a flexible and participatory method of governance, rather than the "top-down", rule-based, Community method of harmonisation. The OMC process uses "mutual learning, benchmarking, best practice and peer pressure"[126] to move

121 See chapter 2.

122 See *European Governance – a White Paper* COM(2001) 428 final. For a starting point in the literature, see the essays collected in the special edition of the *European Law Journal* Vol 8(1) 2002, edited by Scott and Trubek, especially J. Scott and D.M. Trubek, "Mind the Gap: Law and New Approaches to Governance in the European Union" 8 ELJ (2002) 1; see also the online papers from the Jean Monnet Symposium, *Mountain or Molehill: A Critical Appraisal of the Commission White Paper on Governance*, http://www.jeanmonnetprogram.org/papers/01/; C. Joerges and R. Dehousse, eds, *Good Governance in Europe's Integrated Market* (Oxford: OUP, 2002); K. Armstrong, "Tackling Social Exclusion through OMC: Reshaping the Boundaries of EU Governance" in T. Börzel and R. Cichowski, eds, *State of the Union: Law, Politics and Society* (Vol 6) (Oxford: OUP, 2003), pp 170-194; a critical view is found in C. Joerges, "Guest Editorial: The Commission's White Paper on Governance in the EU – A Symptom of Crisis?" 39 CMLRev (2002) 441.

123 For a selection of literature on the OMC, see J. Kenner, "The EU Employment Title and the 'Third Way': Making Soft Law Work?" 15 *International Journal of Comparative Labour Law and Industrial Relations* (1999) 33; C. De La Porte, "Is the Open Method of Coordination Appropriate for Organising Activities at European Level in Sensitive Policy Areas?" 8 ELJ (2002) 38; Armstrong, above n 122; S. Regent, "The Open Method of Coordination: A New Abovenational Form of Governance?" 9 ELJ (2003) 190; F. Scharpf, "The European Social Model: Coping with the Challenges of Diversity" 40 JCMS (2002) 645.

124 An OMC process covering social inclusion and one covering pensions, ensued.

125 See Commission, *Strengthening the social dimension of the Lisbon strategy: Streamlining open coordination in the field of social protection* COM(2003) 261 final. The Council's High Level Group on Patient Mobility and Healthcare, due to report in early 2004, is also considering how or whether health and long-term care should be inserted into the OMC on social protection, see europa.eu.int/com/dgs/health_consumer/library/press/press270_en.pdf and http://europa.eu.int/com/dgs/health_consumer/library/press/press301_en.pdf.

126 Lisbon Summit, March 2000.

national policies towards agreed objectives. Broadly, the process has three stages. First, common objectives are defined, at EU level, to guide national policy. Specific goals or targets may be set, with time-frames. Second, Member States translate these EU guidelines into "national action plans". This process is bolstered by participation of various actors at national and sub-national level, in accordance with the principle of subsidiarity. Finally, the performance of each Member State is evaluated, by the Commission and by a system of peer review, against the EU objectives, using quantitative (or qualitative) indicators. A benchmarking exercise identifies instances of best practices. The OMC process is thus designed to promote deliberation, knowledge creation and mutual learning, as Member States progressively develop their own policies towards agreed common objectives. Although the OMC is a "soft" method of governance, it can produce hard legal effects, for instance, where national action plans include proposals for national law reform. Perhaps more significantly, OMC plays a key role in constructing the policy debate, and thus likely policy outcomes. As Bernard reminds us:

> "Soft instruments . . . provide cognitive maps in which certain topics are constructed as policy issues. While they do not necessarily close the policy space, in the sense that they cannot preclude the emergence of other ideas, one should not underestimate the degree to which they shape that space and provide a worldview in which certain solutions may be regarded as possible and others not and yet others be utterly unthinkable."[127]

Applying the OMC process to health care may open up possibilities for EU-level action in the health field where there is neither Community competence nor political will for EU-level harmonisation.[128] The Member States may seek to use the OMC process to approach common problems with their health care systems (cost containment, changing demographics, and so on). They may also seek to use the OMC to protect a "European social model" of health care from the worst excesses of EU internal market law, or indeed WTO law.[129] OMC thus presents a potential for future developments in health policy at EU level and among deliberations of the governments of the Member States and their relevant sub-national actors.

There are, however, a number of problems with applying an OMC process to health policy.[130] OMC processes in other areas place significant reliance on the identification of "hard" quantitative objectives and indicators, in particular as a basis

127 Bernard, above n 16, p 257.

128 De Búrca and Zeitlin see OMC as a "virtual template" for Community policymaking in areas where there is no possibility for harmonisation, but inaction is politically unacceptable. Health care is one such area: see G. de Búrca and J. Zeitlin, "Constitutionalising the OMC: What should the Convention Propose?", http://www.europa.eu.int/futurum/documents/other/oth010203_en.pdf.

129 Scharpf has argued strongly that the OMC is limited in this respect, as the logic of EU internal market law, as applied by the Court through the doctrine of direct effect, precludes certain welfare policy options: see Scharpf, above n 123. However, as we have seen throughout this book, the Court has protected national welfare choices, often through articulating a 'social solidarity' justification for national welfare policies. See further Armstrong, above n 122; Bernard, above n 16.

130 See R. Busse, "The 'OMC' in European health systems", http://www.tu-berlin.de/fak8/ifg/mig/files/2002/lectures/pdf/Lisbon3105-RB.pdf.

for the evaluation and benchmarking stage of the process. However, it is extremely difficult to compare national health systems of the Member States, given the multi-dimensional aspects of health care. Each national system has grown independently, within a particular historical, cultural and institutional context. Therefore, if OMC is to be effective in this field, extreme caution will have to be exercised in the formulation of indicators and the interpretation of results. The Commission and Council appear to envisage three elements for an OMC in health: equality of access; high quality care; and financial sustainability.[131] Of these, only the financial sustainability of national health (insurance) systems is readily susceptible to quantification. What cannot be so easily quantified is "best practice", in terms of not simply more efficient health care provision, but a more "patient-centred" approach to health care provision. It is here that relationships between an OMC process on health care, and a *right* to access quality health care may come into play.[132] Relations between the OMC process and (fundamental) rights in EU law have been elaborated in a number of contributions to the literature.[133] Bernard has argued that the OMC process may provide an opportunity for the EU to pursue a social rights agenda, by reference to the fundamental social rights contained in the EUCFR.[134] Such social rights would include a "right to health care" (Article 35 EUCFR).

Enlargement

One key context in terms of future developments on the effects of EU law on health law and policy in the Member States is that of enlargement of the EU.[135] Following the "velvet revolution", several Central and Eastern European states embarked on a process that leads towards eventual full membership of the EU for these states.[136]

131 See Commission communication, *The future of health care and care for the elderly: guaranteeing accessibility, quality, and financial viability* COM(2001) 723 final; Joint report by the Commission and the Council, *Supporting national strategies for the future of health care and care for the elderly* Council Doc 7166/03, 10 March 2003.

132 See J. Zeitlin, "Opening the Open Method of Coordination" Committee of the Regions Conference, 30 September–1 October 2002, http:www.cor.eu.int/pdf/omc/zeitlin.pdf.

133 See, in particular, Bernard, above n 16; Armstrong, above n 122; Scharpf, above n 123.

134 Above n 16.

135 Article 49 (ex O) TEU provides that: "Any European state which respects the principles set out in Article 6 (1) [liberty, democracy, respect for human rights and fundamental freedoms, and the rule of law] may apply to become a member of the Union." New Member States must meet the so-called "Copenhagen criteria", laid down at the European Council in Copenhagen in 1993. These are stability of institutions guaranteeing democracy, the rule of law, human rights and respect for minorities; a functioning market economy, capacity to cope with competition and market forces within the EU; adherence to the aims of political, economic and monetary union; and adoption, implementation and enforcement of the *acquis communautaire* – the body of regulations and policies of the EU. Readers should note that the text of this book was completed on 1 December 2003, that is, before 1 May 2004, the date of the EU's enlargement from 15 to 25 Member States. Some minor amendments up to 1 May 2004 have been included in the footnotes.

136 In particular, the EU entered into the so-called "Europe Agreements", which provide a framework for bilateral relations, with ten of these states during the 1990s. These agreements aim progressively to establish a free-trade area between the EU and the candidate states. "Association Councils", consisting of the parties to these treaties, adopted various decisions to this effect. Association Agreements were already in place with respect to Cyprus, Malta and Turkey. The EU also

Cyprus, Malta and Turkey are also seeking membership. A first wave of ten "accession states" (Cyprus, Czech Republic, Estonia, Hungary, Latvia, Lithuania, Malta, Poland, Slovak Republic and Slovenia) signed an Accession Treaty at Athens in April 2003. If ratified by all the accession states, and the current Member States of the EU, this will enter into force on 1 May 2004, at which point the EU will enlarge from the current 15 Member States to 25 Member States. The other "candidate states", Bulgaria and Romania, aim to join the EU in 2007; Turkey still needs to strengthen its human rights protection.

Obviously, the enlargement of the EU has significant constitutional implications, in particular for the functioning of the institutions.[137] The Treaty of Nice,[138] and the Accession Treaty, have attempted to put in place changes that will allow the institutions (European Parliament; Council of Ministers; European Commission; European Court of Justice) to continue to function effectively on enlargement. The new Member States will, of course, also participate fully in the various EU committees and agencies of the EU, thus increasing the number of different national legal backgrounds and traditions represented in such bodies.[139] As de Witte points out, it is hard to imagine how the interactions between national actors, say on an EU committee, will work out with 25 or more delegations sitting around the table.[140] The candidate states have been able to participate in various EU programmes since the late 1990s. For instance, the candidate states participated in the Fifth Framework Programme for research and development, and are participating in the Sixth Framework Programme. They also participated in the public health programmes based on Article 152 EC.[141]

instituted a financial restructuring package, the PHARE programme, to help candidate countries with institution building through "twinning" of civil servants and technical assistance; to provide investment to help candidate countries in their efforts to strengthen their public administrations and institutions; to promote convergence with the EU's extensive legislation; and to promote economic and social cohesion. See http://europa.eu.int/comm/enlargement/faq/. On enlargement as process, see M. Cremona, "Introduction" in M. Cremona, ed, *The Enlargement of the European Union* (Oxford: OUP, 2003). On the pre-accession process in more detail, see M. Maresceau, "Pre-accession" in M. Cremona, ed, *The Enlargement of the European Union* (Oxford: OUP, 2003).

137 See B. de Witte, "The Impact of Enlargement on the Constitution of the EU" in M. Cremona, ed, *The Enlargement of the European Union* (Oxford: OUP, 2003).

138 See Protocol on Enlargement of the EU, added to the TEU and the EC Treaty by the Treaty of Nice, Articles 2, 3 and 4.

139 The candidate states have been participating in the EU's programmes, agencies and committees, on various bases, in particular as observers, as part of the pre-accession process, see Commission, *Participation of Candidate Countries in Community Programmes, Agencies and Committees* COM(1999) 710. This participation has intensified for the accession states. For instance, as at August 2003, five accession states had applied to participate in the European Medicines Evaluation Agency, and preparation was underway for their involvement. This followed from their informal participation as observers in various workshops and certain working parties of the Agency. On the other hand, no formal moves had been made with respect to the European Food Safety Authority. The accession states are being invited to participate in Community committees from April 2003 to 1 May 2004, so as to be involved in the process of adopting new legislation during this "interim period". See http://europa.eu.int/comm/enlargement/pas/ocp/agencies.

140 de Witte, above n 137, pp 225–226.

141 See further chapter 3.

The Central and Eastern European candidate states have adopted wholesale reforms of their national health care systems since 1989. Previously, these states had versions of the Russian "Semashko system", a highly centralised health care system, funded by state budgets, with free access to all.[142] Facilities were state-owned and managed by district and regional authorities, under direct control of the central government. Occupational medical facilities were available for industrial workers. There was an emphasis on hospital care, with under-developed primary care provision. Physicians were salaried, but salaries were low.

Although the new systems are still in flux and, of course, generalisations about their different policy choices are limited in accuracy, welfare restructuring in Central and Eastern European countries has exhibited a number of trends. These include neo-liberalism in the sense of privatisation of former public goods; a turn to the institutions of Church, family and nation; path-dependency in the sense of a return to what was there before the 1940s; and a loss of the power of the state to generate income.[143] Within this broader context, since 1989, Central and Eastern European national health systems have moved back to various versions of "Bismarckian" social insurance,[144] with decentralisation and some partly privatised elements at the fringes. Privatisation and introduction of market competition has been applied only in the fields of dentistry and pharmaceuticals.[145] The candidate states have also sought to adopt the "Beveridge" emphasis on the general practitioner as the gatekeeper, and the foundation of primary health care;[146] and on the notion of universal access. Most of the new health care systems in Central and Eastern European countries are now based on compulsory public or state-owned insurance schemes, mainly financed out of payroll taxes.[147]

The legacy of the Semashko systems remains. There is over-capacity in hospital facilities and an under-provision of primary health care and long-term nursing care.[148] Hospital facilities have been poorly maintained and suffer from lack of investment in new technology.[149] Health care workers suffer from low morale, arising from this and also from low levels of pay (comparable with average skilled blue-collar workers). There is an oversupply of highly specialised physicians. State

142 See J. Marrée and P.P. Groenewegen, *Back to Bismarck: Eastern European Care Systems in Transition* (Aldershot: Avebury, 1997), pp 5–11.

143 Z. Ferge, "Welfare and 'Ill-fare' Systems in Central and Eastern Europe" in R. Sykes, B. Palier and P.M. Prior, eds, *Globalization and European Welfare States: Challenges and Change* (Basingstoke: Palgrave, 2001), p 148.

144 WHO and European Commission, *Health Status Overview for Countries of Central and Eastern Europe that are Candidates for Accession to the European Union* (Copenhagen: WHO, 2002).

145 B. Deacon, "Eastern European welfare states: the impact of the politics of globalisation" 10 *Journal of European Social Policy* (2000) 146 at 155.

146 Marrée and Groenewegen, above n 142, p 20; WHO and European Commission, above n 144.

147 Deacon, above n 145, at 155.

148 Marrée and Groenewegen, above n 142, p 22; WHO and European Commission, above n 144.

149 Marrée and Groenewegen, above n 142, p 17.

health care has been associated with sub-standard health care over a long period of time.[150]

Further, reform of health care systems in the Central and Eastern European candidate states is hampered by lack of political stability, and by the expectations of citizens who are accustomed to a highly subsidised welfare system, necessary as part of indirect incomes.[151] Serious cost-containment problems persist. Central and Eastern European states are spending a falling proportion of their GDP on social policy,[152] of which health care is a significant component. Absolute levels of GDP are lower than those in the existing Member States. In practice, reform has meant a lowering of benefits available, and a curtailing of services accessible through national health insurance systems. Ferge is sceptical about whether these emerging systems will be imbued with any "European values" such as equality of access or social solidarity.[153] Such values were corrupted under socialist dictatorships, which makes it difficult for them to gain political acceptability under current conditions. The criteria for accession to the EU do not focus on such values,[154] but rather concentrate on the internal market and competition law, with only weak elements of social policy in general, and none directly applicable to national health systems. This is, of course, a direct consequence of the EU's lack of competence over national health systems.

On accession, the new Member States will become full Member States of the EU. They have already implemented much of the body of EU legislation (the *acquis communautaire*).[155] In principle, the entire *acquis communautaire* will apply to new Member States on accession. However, for certain sensitive areas, transitional periods, of limited duration, will apply. The *acquis communautaire* includes the principles of freedom to provide and receive services on which the free movement of patients jurisprudence is based. As most accession states have adopted social insurance health systems,[156] the rulings in *Kohll* and its progeny[157] will apply. Given the significantly lower average incomes in the accession states, one might expect movements to be fairly minimal.[158] However, particularly at the borders, there might be exceptions to this principle. Also, at least among the wealthier citizens of the new Member States, the fact that certain treatments may not be available in their

150 Marrée and Groenewegen, above n 142, p 20.

151 It would be easier to introduce some sort of social market welfare system in developing countries that did not have one previously, than to reform a communist welfare system: see A. Inotai, "The 'Eastern Enlargements' of the EU" in M. Cremona, ed, *The Enlargement of the European Union* (Oxford: OUP, 2003).

152 Ferge, above n 143, p 148; Inotai, above n 151.

153 Ferge, above n 143, pp 149–152.

154 For instance, PHARE has not been used to promote a "European social model".

155 See regular progress reports available at http://europa.eu.int/comm/enlargement.

156 Except Cyprus and Malta, which have health care systems financed by general taxation.

157 See chapter 4.

158 No data on likely movements from Central and Eastern European states is currently available: see A.P. den Exter, "Legal Consequences of EU Accession for Central and Eastern European Health Care Systems" 8 ELJ (2002) 556 at 563.

home Member State, and concerns about quality of home health care facilities, may well encourage patients to seek treatments elsewhere in the EU.

Accession states are probably even more concerned about cost containment within their health care systems than the existing Member States. The prospect of many of their patients seeking cross-border health care on the basis of *Kohll*, at the expense of the national health insurance systems, is worrying to the governments of those countries.[159] This may influence the Court's assessment of the justifications with respect to maintaining the balance of a social security system. In terms of authorised movements, under Regulation 1408/71/EEC, these will be open to the new Member States, if they wish to use them, perhaps where their home capacity does not meet the health needs of their populations. This does assume, however, that their health care budgets are able to meet the costs. Most new Member States have taken recent steps to reduce burdens on their health care systems, for instance, by limiting types of treatment available under the national social health insurance systems. One might, therefore, envisage *Peerbooms*-type litigation, where new Member States have refused to authorise types of health care provision that are not available within the home state.

Freedom of movement for workers, including professionals,[160] is of concern to both the new Member States and existing Member States, especially Germany and Austria, who share borders to the east with the new Central and Eastern European Member States. A transitional period will apply, which allows existing Member States to limit movement of workers from the new Member States for a period of up to seven years after accession.[161] However, no measures are envisaged to allow new Member States to limit movements. The Commission cites a series of studies that suggest that movement of persons from the new Member States to the existing Member States is likely to be on a small scale.[162] As we noted in chapter 4, very few citizens of the EU live and work in a Member State other than their home Member State. What about the possibility of movements of health care professionals from the new Member States to the existing Member States? As there is over-capacity, particularly among specialist physicians in the accession countries of Central and Eastern Europe, might we expect numbers of such medical professionals to seek employment or to establish themselves in the existing Member States? Candidate states have been moving towards harmonising standards for professional qualifications with the EU's standards under the Europe Agreements since the early 1990s.[163] The

159 den Exter, above n 158, at 562.

160 See M. Dougan, "A Spectre is Haunting Europe . . . Free Movement of Persons and Eastern Enlargement" in M. Dougan and C. Hillion, eds, *Enlargement of the EU* (Oxford: Hart, 2004).

161 See Accession Treaty, Article 24, and Annexes V-XIV. Special provisions apply to Germany and Austria in particularly sensitive sectors of the economy in this respect, such as construction. The only one of those with possible relevance for health is that of home nursing care, applicable only with respect to Austria.

162 See http://www.europa.eu.int/comm/enlargement/faq/.

163 For further details, see M. Cremona, "Movement of Persons, Establishment and Services" in M. Maresceau, *Enlarging the European Union: Relations between the EU and Central and Eastern Europe* (London: Longman, 1997).

Europe Agreements made provision for the Association Councils to take measures for the mutual recognition of qualifications of the professions covered by the EU's sectoral and general directives on the subject[164] and the Commission's White Paper, *Preparation of the Associated Countries of Central and Eastern Europe for Integration into the Internal Market of the Union*,[165] envisaged an incremental process to this end. Where professionals qualified before these changes were effected, candidate states are supposed to take steps to ensure that such professionals can meet the requirements of EU law, presumably through continuous education. The details of the accession package provide that, in principle, qualifications should be mutually recognised, either under the sectoral directives or the general mutual recognition directives. However, special arrangements apply to qualifications gained, for instance, when the Baltic states were part of the Soviet Union, or when Slovenia was part of Yugoslavia.[166] Moreover, equivalence of qualifications, for instance of medical professionals, is even more difficult to ascertain than it is in the current EU of 15 Member States. The Commission states that "tough monitoring provisions" are envisaged for the sectoral directives.[167] Whether this is sufficient to ensure quality standards and patient protection remain guaranteed remains to be seen.

As we have seen, the accession states have over-capacity of some health care professionals and under-capacity in other areas, in particular primary health care. For instance, accession states are seriously concerned about migration of nurses to existing Member States on accession.[168] In terms of the law, new Member States will be obliged to recognise health care qualifications obtained in the existing Member States, either under the sectoral directives or the general directives on mutual recognition of qualifications. Whether the new Member States will be able to attract health care professionals from the old Member States to fill their capacity gaps seems rather unlikely, given the significant disparities in incomes.

With respect to marketing of pharmaceuticals, the general principle is that full implementation of the relevant EU law is expected by the date of accession. Accession states have moved towards centralised state responsibility for licensing of pharmaceuticals and medical devices. However, transitional arrangements concerning the renewal of marketing authorisations for pharmaceuticals apply to five new Member States: Cyprus, Lithuania, Malta, Poland and Slovenia.[169] Also, the current Polish legislation concerning licences for medical devices will remain valid

164 See, for example, Europe Agreement Hungary, Article 46.

165 COM(95) 163.

166 The new Member State must declare that the qualification in question is equivalent to their own qualifications (which would, on accession, be recognised within the EU), *and* attest that the individual professional concerned has recently been engaged in the activities in question. See http://europa.eu.int/comm/enlargement/negotiations/chapters/chap2/index.htm.

167 See http://europa.eu.int/comm/enlargement/negotiations/chapters/chap2/index.htm.

168 See J. Irwin, "Migration patterns of nurses in the EU" 7 *eurohealth* (2001) 13; S. Nicholas, "Movement of Health Professionals: Trends and enlargement" 8(4) *eurohealth* (2002) 11; M. Zajac, "EU Accession: Implications for Poland's healthcare personnel" 8(4) *eurohealth* (2002) 13.

169 See Act of Accession, Annexes VII, IX, XI, XII and XIII.

until the end of 2005.[170] All accession states have transposed the product liability directive, and no transition period is envisaged.[171] Indeed, several accession states adopted this directive as the model for their revised national product liability legislation.[172]

Public health concerns may be affected by enlargement. In general, "public health", as understood in the EU, is little understood in the accession states, as it is so different to the idea of hygienic control, predominant under communism.[173] Health promotion, through lifestyle information, is particularly important for the candidate states, which have higher prevalence of risk factors such as smoking, alcoholism and unhealthy diets, and corresponding higher levels of cardiovascular disease and lung cancer.[174] Some communicable diseases, such as tuberculosis, are common in the candidate states, and HIV/AIDS[175] may be growing.[176] This may increase pressures to adopt meaningful border checks on the movement of persons who may be carriers of such diseases,[177] although, probably, the general pressure to liberalise movement will prove more significant in the longer term.

The new public health programme, based on Article 152 EC, is open to participation by the candidate states of Central and Eastern Europe, Cyprus, Malta and Turkey. The countries of Central and Eastern Europe are permitted to complement their own financial contributions to the programmes with PHARE funding, some 10% of which is reserved for community action programmes, including public health. Originally set up in 1989, PHARE is the main pre-accession financial instrument for assisting the 10 candidate states in Central and Eastern Europe to prepare for membership of the EU.[178] Participation in the previous public health programmes was supposed to assist candidate states in becoming familiar with EU procedures and the EU's approach to risk management in respect of public health, and to provide support to these countries in tackling the major health problems they face.[179] However, given that disease does not respect borders, a large element of self-interest on the part of the existing Member States must surely be present here. For instance, there is evidence that some of the candidate states concentrated on systemic reforms to their health care systems, at the expense of allowing vaccination

170 Act of Accession, Annex XII.

171 See http://www.europa.eu.int/comm/enlargement/negotiations/chapters/chap23/index.htm.

172 den Exter, above n 158, at 560.

173 European Observatory on Health Care Systems, *Health Policy and European Union Enlargement*, http://www.euro.who.int/eprise/main/WHO/Progs/OBS/Studies/.

174 WHO and European Commission, above n 144.

175 Rare in the candidate countries, save Romania, until recently.

176 See WHO and European Commission, above n 144, p 18.

177 Border checks on persons moving within the enlarged EU will continue after accession. The new Member States will become part of the Schengen arrangements in due course, once the future external borders of the EU are monitored as closely as the Schengen borders are at present. See http://www.europa.eu.int/comm/enlargement//faq/faq2.htm.

178 See http://europa.eu.int/comm/enlargement//faq/; M. Rosenmöller, "Health and Support for EU accession: Phare and other initiatives" 8(4) *eurohealth* (2002) 36.

179 den Exter, above n 158, at 558.

rates to drop,[180] thus seeing a rise in communicable diseases such as tuberculosis. This trend does now appear to be reversing. [181] Participation of candidate states in the public health programmes is aimed at promoting a convergence of approach to public health. So for instance, candidate states are encouraged to set up a framework of epidemiological surveillance and control of communicable diseases, based on common indicators, and to exchange information.[182]

The existing EU Member States have shown concern about threats to public health emanating from the food chain from the new Member States, and these concerns are also shared by the Commission. The public health elements of the *acquis communautaire* were given high priority in the pre-accession activities under the Europe Agreements.[183] On accession, in principle, food produced anywhere in the enlarged EU will circulate freely on the basis of the free movement of goods provisions of EU law. The new Member States have had to adapt their national food safety laws to meet the standards of the Community *acquis* in this respect. However, whether the appropriate control mechanisms and other infrastructure are in place, and adequately functioning, remains a matter of concern. The Commission plays a role in monitoring food safety in the accession states.[184] The EU is also to provide temporary financial assistance – the "Transition Facility" – to new Member States to help strengthen their administrative capacity to implement and enforce EU law, especially in a number of key areas, which include food safety.[185]

Overall, the impact of enlargement on health across the EU is not yet known. A number of studies are currently underway to assess the impact of accession on health in the new Member States.[186]

Having considered the possible effects of three future developments within the EU's legal order (the Draft Constitutional Treaty; the expansion of the open method of coordination; and enlargement) on health law and policy in the Member States, we conclude with a discussion of two substantive sites for future developments. These are regulation of the use of human material and "e-health".

Regulating the use of human material

Developments in tissue and transplant technologies have provided some of the most notable medical "miracles" of the past 50 years. Across the Member States of the EU, there is considerable diversity of approach and, indeed, ethical controversy, over the regulation of the use of human material.[187] Some Member States, such

180 European Observatory on Health Care Systems, *Health Policy and European Union Enlargement*, http://www.euro.who.int/eprise/main/WHO/Progs/OBS/Studies/.

181 WHO and European Commission, above n 144, p 18.

182 den Exter, above n 158, at 571.

183 den Exter, above n 158, at 557.

184 See http://www.europa.eu.int/comm/enlargement//faq/faq2.htm.

185 Article 34, Accession Treaty.

186 See, for instance, the European Observatory on Health Care Systems, above n 180.

187 See, for example, B. New, M. Solomon, R. Dingwall and J. McHale, *A Question of Give and Take: Improving the Supply of Donor Organs for Transplantation* (London: Kings Fund Institute, 1993); D. Price, *Legal and Ethical Issues of Organ Transplantation* (Cambridge: CUP, 2000).

as Belgium, provide for the removal of organs and tissue as a matter of routine, unless the deceased has opted out. Others, for instance the Netherlands,[188] take an "opt-in" approach, permitting removal of human material only with consent from the donor during life, or with consent from next of kin after death. This diversity is likely to continue as the EU enlarges to the east. Poland, for example, does not recognise brain death.[189] Concerns about organ trafficking are reflected in human rights instruments, including the EUCFR.[190] Such a diversity of approach, coupled with the ethical sensitivity of the subject, would appear to make EU-level regulation politically unlikely, even if formal legal competence could be found in the Treaty. Currently, the EU has legislated on the use of human material only in the context of blood safety.[191] However, in spite of the difficulties suggested by the diverse approaches of the Member States, and the political difficulties of achieving agreement on such an ethically sensitive matter, there are a number of indications that the EU may move towards a more active engagement in this area. Chief among these is the Commission's 2003 proposal for a new standards-setting Directive (proposed Tissue Directive)[192] on the quality and safety of human tissue.[193]

The proposed Tissue Directive sets out standards of "quality and safety of tissues and cells for human application" with the aim of ensuring a high standard of protection for human health.[194] It is to extend to "donation, procurement, testing, processing, preservation, storage and distribution of all courses of human tissues[195] and cells[196] which are intended for human application, or those manufactured products which are intended for human application derived from tissue and cells".[197] It includes "haemotopoietic peripheral blood, placenta and bone marrow stem cells; reproductive cells (eggs, sperm); foetal tissues and cells, adult and embryonic stem

188 Netherlands Wet op de Orgaandonatie (Organ Donation Act) 1998. The UK Human Tissue Act 1961 is often discussed as being an opting-in system, but in fact, as commentators such as Price (above n 187) have argued, there are presumed consent dimensions, in that material can, in theory at least, be removed where the deceased has not expressed an opinion and it is not "reasonably practical" to contact the "spouse or surviving relatives".

189 J.K. Mason, R.A. McCall Smith and G. Laurie, *Law and Medical Ethics* (London: Lexis Nexis, 6th edn. 2002), p 349

190 See above. Article 3 (2) EUCFR, inspired by the Council of Europe's Convention on Human Rights and Biomedicine, Article 21, which provides "The human body and its parts, shall not, as such, give rise to financial gain".

191 Directive 2002/98/EC, OJ 2003 L 33/30; see chapter 9.

192 Amended Proposal for a Directive of the European Parliament and of the Council on setting standards of quality and safety for the donation, procurement, testing, processing, storage and distribution of human tissues and cells (presented by the Commission pursuant to Article 250(2) of the EC Treaty, COM(2003) 340 final. Council common position adopted 22 July 2003, OJ 2003 C 240 E/12.

193 As we saw in chapter 7, there has been an unsuccessful attempt to use this Directive as a means of regulating cloning for therapeutic purposes.

194 Article 1.

195 Article 3(b): "all constituent parts of the human body formed by cells."

196 Article 3(a): "individual cells or a collection of cells of human origin when not bound by any form of connective tissue."

197 Article 2.

cells".[198] The Directive specifically excludes from its scope of application those tissues and cells which are used as an autologous[199] graft in the same surgical procedure,[200] blood and blood products[201] (these are already covered by the Blood Safety Directive);[202] and "organs, or parts of organs if their function is to be used for the same person as the entire organ on or in the human body".[203]

The proposed Directive establishes a regulatory framework with the aim of ensuring standards are maintained. Member States will be obliged to ensure that those who undertake tissue and cell procurement have "appropriate training and experience".[204] It requires that establishments which process, preserve, store or distribute human tissues, and cells intended for human application, are accredited, designated, licensed or authorised by a competent body,[205] which will have powers regarding inspection and control.[206] The "competent body" concerned with regulation is also charged with maintaining a register of accredited establishments,[207] and information is to be submitted to them by accredited establishments on an annual basis.[208] Member States will be required to ensure that imports of such materials are undertaken by such establishments.[209] Member States must also introduce measures to ensure that the source of the material may be traced.[210] Procedures for traceability at EU level shall be established by the Commission in accordance with Article 30 (2).[211] Member States are to establish procedures for the notification and recording of serious adverse events and reactions, and the Commission shall also establish the procedure for notifying such reactions at EU level in accordance with Article 30 (2).[212] Member States are to establish mechanisms to ensure the quality and safety of tissues and cells.[213] So, for example, explicit provision is made for the storage conditions for tissues and cells, such as requiring procedures to be established regarding storage times and temperatures.[214]

The proposed Directive emphasises the need to ensure that all national provisions for "mandatory consent" are complied with.[215] However, interestingly, in addition, several more specific provisions are included regarding the consent process. Article

198 Recital, para 3.
199 This is defined as "cells or tissues removed from and applied back to the same person": Article 3(q).
200 Article 2(2)(a).
201 Article 2(2)(c) .
202 See chapter 9.
203 Article 2(2)(d).
204 Article 5.
205 Article 6.
206 Article 8.
207 Article 7(1).
208 Article 7(2).
209 Article 9.
210 Article 10.
211 Article 26.
212 Article 11(3).
213 Article 16.
214 Article 21 and Annex VII.
215 Article 13.

13 (2) provides that "Member States shall take all necessary measures to ensure that the donors, their families or any person granting authorisation on behalf of the donors are provided with the information listed in Annex III". Annex III A provides that, in the case of the living donor:

> "2. The information must be given in an appropriate and clear manner, using terms that are easily understood by the donor.
> 3. The person providing the information must be required and able to answer any questions asked by the donor.
> 4. The information must cover: the purpose and nature of the procurement, its consequences and risks; analytical tests if they are performed; recording and protection of donor data, medical confidentiality and therapeutic purpose.
> 5. For the allogenic[216] living donor (AL) information must be provided to the donor on the evaluation procedure; i.e. the reasons for requiring the donor's medical and personal history, a physical examination and analytical tests.
> 6. Information must be given to donors on the applicable safeguards that are intended to protect them.
> 7. The donor should be informed that he has the right to receive the confirmed result of the analytical tests clearly explained. He shall be free to exercise this right or not.
> 8. Information must be given on the necessity for requiring the applicable mandatory consent, certification and authorisation in order that the tissue and/or cell procurement can be carried out."

Specific provisions exist in relation to the deceased donor. Annex III B provides that:

> "1. All information must be given to the donor's relatives and all necessary consent and authorisations must be obtained prior to the procurement of cells/tissues in accordance with the applicable legislation.
> 2. The confirmed results of the donor's evaluation must be communicated and clearly explained to the donor's relatives when these results have relevance for their health or for public health in accordance with the legislation in member states."

The reference here to the involvement of the deceased's relatives in the consent process is interesting. The appropriateness of consulting relatives, or indeed whether any other person should be consulted, may be questioned. The wording of the Directive presumably means that in a situation in which national legislation does not permit relatives to be provided with information, they will not be informed. Behind these statements are fundamental ethical debates regarding the legal status of the body, and material derived from the body parts, which appear to have been

216 Article 3(q) defines "allogenic" as being "cells or tissues procured from one person and applied to another".

side-stepped in this discussion, in favour of a rather more standard consent-based approach.[217]

The Directive includes provisions concerning donor selection,[218] for example, excluding the deceased where cause of death is unknown or where there is a risk of transmission of diseases such as CJD or HIV. Explicit reference is made to data protection, and the need to ensure that data, including genetic information, is anonymised.[219] This is in line with the approach taken to use of data for research purposes, which was discussed in chapter 5 above, and the argument that it is anonymity which constitutes an effective safeguard of privacy rights. The Directive is a further illustration of the trend, both at EU level and at Member State level, to regulate data and material from which such data may be derived separately, rather than to take a more holistic approach to the regulation of human material.[220]

The proposed Tissue Directive is a measure of "new approach harmonisation", and, therefore, does not preclude the adoption of more stringent measures by individual Member States.[221] The proposed Directive also emphasises the need for voluntary and unpaid donation,[222] anonymity of both donor and recipient, altruism of the donor and solidarity between donor and recipient.[223] Member States are urged to take steps to encourage a strong public and non-profit sector involvement in the provision of tissue and cell application services and related research development.[224] The Commission's approach here is reflected in the European Parliament's recent call for a ban on organ trafficking, and for the introduction of a criminal offence applicable to EU citizens who travel abroad and buy organs.[225]

If the proposed Tissue Directive is adopted, this may mean considerable alteration of the existing positions within Member States. In the UK, there is currently no regulatory body governing the use of human material relating to both live and cadaver material. Interestingly, the new UK Human Tissue Bill 2003 now provides for such a new regulatory body, but this has not, to our knowledge, been influenced by the prospect of EU regulation. Rather, it can be seen in terms of the need for effective legal regulation of the use of human material, following a major scandal

217 There is a vast literature regarding ownership of human material and the human body. For an introduction see, for example, J.W. Harris, "Who Owns My Body?" 16 OJLS (1996) 55; D. Beyleveld and R. Brownsword, *Human Dignity in Bioethics and Biolaw* (Oxford: OUP, 2001), chapter 8; L. Skene, "Arguments Against People Legally 'Owning' Their Own Bodies, Body Parts and Tissue" 2 *MacQuarrie Law Journal* (2002) 165; K. Mason and G. Laurie "Consent or Property? Dealing with the Body and its Parts in the Shadow of Bristol and Alder Hey" 64 MLR (2001) 711; M. Fox and J. McHale *Framing the Clinical Body* (Oxford: Hart Publishing, 2004 forthcoming).

218 Article 5 and Annex IV.

219 Article 14. Data protection and anonymisation is considered further in chapter 5, pp 172–175.

220 See further chapter 7; and J.V. McHale, "Regulating Genetic Databases: Some Legal and Ethical Issues" 12 *Medical Law Review* (2004) 70.

221 Article 4 (2).

222 Article 12.

223 Recital 13.

224 Ibid.

225 See R. Watson, "European Parliament tries to stamp out trafficking in human organs" 327 BMJ (2003) 1003; S. Wheeler, "EU plans organ trade crackdown", BBC news online, 22 October 2003.

involving the unauthorised retention of vast stores of human material in hospitals all over the UK.[226] It may also, however, be seen in terms of the effective alignment of safeguards regarding donors' interests, and also recipients' interests in the safe use of human material.

In addition to the proposed Tissue Directive, there have been further indications of the prospect of further EU involvement in the area of organ transplantation. So, for example, the European Parliament has raised questions about whether the Commission or EU ethics committees have a view on the operations of CRYO-Cell (an American company) which has subsidiaries in many EU Member States, and headquarters, laboratory and storage facilities for all of Europe, in Belgium.[227] CRYO-Cell operates through a website, and asks parents to agree to blood from the foetal umbilical cord or placenta being frozen for 20 years (so as to be potentially on tap in the future), in return for the payment of a fee. Another example is the calls for the establishment of an EU-wide database providing information regarding patients awaiting transplants and regarding legally available organs for transplantation.[228]

"e-Health"

A second site for new technological developments in health care is that of internet medicine, or "e-health",[229] which may take several forms. "Virtual pharmacies" may supply medicinal products by mail order, when ordered through a website. At present, telemedicine (such as consultation with a "virtual" health care professional)[230] and on-line prescribing are in their infancy, but development of such clinical practice is expected.[231] The World Wide Web is a source of a significant amount of health information. The use of remotely accessible databases to track pharmacovigilance information,[232] and public health threats, across boundaries, has been noted in chapters 7, 8 and 9. However, by its very nature, the internet is an uncontrolled source of information, and this can lead to concerns about access to such information. E-health initiatives can also facilitate transference of patient information for health policy purposes, and, through electronic health

226 Bristol Inquiry Interim Report *Removal and Retention of Human Material* (2000), http://www.bristol-inquiry.org.uk; *Report of the Inquiry into the Royal Liverpool Children's Hospital* (Alder Hey) (2001), http://www.rclinquiry.org.uk.

227 Written Question E-1079/01 by R. Oomen-Ruijten, MEP, to the Commission 6 April 2001; and see http://www.parentsguidecordblood.com/html.

228 Watson, above n 225.

229 See, in general, S. Callens, *E-health and the law* (Deventer: Kluwer, 2003), especially S. Callens, "Telemedicine and the E-Commerce Directive" therein, also published in 9 *European Journal of Health Law* (2002) 93.

230 See, for instance, G. Carlsson, "Health care practice by remote expert – a case study from mid-Sweden" in M. Rigby, R. Roberts and M. Thick, eds, *Taking Health Telematics into the 21st Century* (Abingdon: Radcliffe Medical Press, 2000).

231 European Commission High Level Committee on Health Meeting Delphi 8/9 April 2003, *Health Telematics Working Group of the High Level Committee on Health: Final Report* 04/2003.

232 For instance the EUDRACT system, including the "EudraWatch" service, http:/eudravigilance.org; or the joint EU/WHO "SIAMED 2000"; see further chapters 7 and 8.

records, can enable easy access to a life-time health record by a range of health care providers.[233]

Whilst e-health has great potential to facilitate the delivery of health services, there are also very real concerns about the development of on-line health services.[234] Adequate protection of individual patients, through giving of individual information and advice, may be difficult to achieve, if medicines may be ordered remotely, without physical contact with a health care professional, be that doctor or pharmacist. Advice given remotely, by telephone or through the internet, is less likely to be able take into account the patient's physical and psychological state, his or her life-style or current medication, all of which would properly be considered in a face-to-face consultation with a health care professional. In the case of remote prescribing, combined with mail order delivery, there is no means of checking that the packaging, containing patient safety information, such as guidelines for safe use of a medicinal product, reaches the patient intact. Monitoring, follow-up care, and pharmacovigilance measures may be very difficult to maintain.

There are also considerable concerns regarding data protection in the context of on-line medicine.[235] First, it may lead to broader access to health data beyond health professionals to information technologists and support staff, which may lead to greater risks of unauthorised disclosure. Second, dataflow over the internet carries the enhanced risk of interception. Third, as Callens notes, there is the prospect for aggregation of health and other information, and it is more likely that information could be tracked. As he comments: "by clicking on a website and by looking for information on diseases, tele-experts, physicians, hospitals, medicinal products etc., very sensitive information on the website visitor can be tracked, stored, disseminated for totally other purposes."[236] The option to opt in or out of such tracking is thus vital. There are also risks that information may be used by the "tele-specialist" for other purposes, such as research, and therefore controls on use of such data are crucial.

Finally, there may also be concerns about national capacity maintenance in the event that significant numbers of remote health care facilities, such as internet pharmacies, are set up. This would arise if these are able to evade national health system provisions that aim to ensure continuity of supply and equal access to medicinal products for all patients within a particular health system.

233 The Commission has proposed an "electronic health card", to replace the E111 and other forms; see Council Resolution on the European health card, OJ 1996 C 141/104; Commission Action Plan to remove obstacles to EU workers' mobility by 2005, COM(2002) 72 final; Regulation 631/2004/EC, OJ 2004 L 100/1; COM (2004) 356. See further chapter 4.

234 See, for example, S. Mills, "Online Prescribing: Principles, Problems and Policing" 9(1) *Medico-Legal Journal of Ireland* (2003) 36; D. Crolla, "Cyberlaw: A Potent New Medicine for Health on the Internet" in S. Callens, ed, *E-Health and the Law* (London, The Hague and New York: Kluwer Law International, 2003).

235 See Callens, above n 229, pp 40–43; H.D.C. Roscam Abbing, "Editorial: Internet, the Patient and the Right to Care for Health" 7 *European Journal of Health Law* (2000) 221 at 222, 224.

236 Callens, above n 229, p 41.

As "e-health" develops, Member States of the EU are responding to these concerns. For example, the UK General Medical Council has issued guidelines, including the statement that:

> "Consultations and prescribing by phone or e-mail may seriously compromise standards of care where:
> The patient is not previously known to the doctor and
> No examination can be provided, and
> There is little or no provision for inappropriate monitoring of the patient or follow-up care.
> Doctors who wish to provide telephone or on-line services should consider carefully whether such a service will serve their patients' interests, and if necessary, seek advice from their professional association or medical defence society".[237]

In January 2000, a British doctor was found guilty of serious professional misconduct by the UK General Medical Council for selling Viagra and xenical (a "slimming medication") on the "MEDCLINIC" website.[238] In the US, telemedicine is developing accreditation systems, but it appears that this has not yet generally extended itself to the EU.[239] Some states have considered making certain internet services, such as the provision of on-line genetic test kits, subject to criminal penalty.[240] In Germany, the sale by mail order of medicinal products that may only be sold in pharmacies is prohibited.[241] Some of these national responses to the problems surrounding e-health may be subject to challenge on the basis of their compatibility with EU internal market law. This is illustrated by the *DocMorris* case.[242]

In June 2000, a Dutch pharmacy, established in Kerkrade, the Netherlands, began offering non-prescription and prescription medicines for sale on the internet. The internet site operated in several languages, including German. The internet portal was divided into various areas, including "Pharmacy" and "Contact Us". The medicines available from the website were divided into product groups, with a brief introduction for each, about the types of medicine available. Patients accessing the website could contact DocMorris, or the pharmacist, Jacques Waterval, directly, either by a free telephone number or by email or letter. Prescription medicines were supplied by DocMorris only on production of an original prescription.[243]

237 http://www.gmc-uk.org/standards/default.htm.

238 Mills, above n 234, at 38.

239 See discussion in N. Terry, "Regulating health information; a US perspective" 324 BMJ (2002) 602.

240 See chapter 8, p 305.

241 Arzneimittelgesetz (Law on Medicinal Products) BGBl, 1998 I, p 2649.

242 Case C-322/01 *Deutscher Apothekerverband v 0800 DocMorris and Waterval* [2003] ECR I-(11 December 2003, nyr in ECR). See discussion in B.A. Stanberry, "Legal aspects of health on the internet: a European perspective" 324 BMJ (2002) 602.

243 Although there is no specific EU-level legislation regulating delivery of medicines to patients, the logic of the internal market in goods, and the mutual recognition of qualifications doctors directives, implies that a prescription should be recognised in another Member State: see Council Resolution, Doc 395Y1230(04). Within the Nordic countries, delivery of a prescription from another Nordic country is permitted in law. A research project testing whether cross-border prescriptions would be fulfilled found that they were in most Member States, the UK being the main exception:

Delivery of the medicines was either by collection from DocMorris' pharmacy in Landgraaf, a town near the German/Dutch border, or by courier. The activities of DocMorris were challenged by the German Apothekerverband, an association of German pharmacists, on the grounds that they breached provisions of German law prohibiting the sale by mail order of medicinal products that may only be sold in pharmacies.[244] The national court referred to the European Court of Justice on the question whether these provisions of national law were compatible with the Treaty provisions on free movement of goods (Articles 28 and 30 EC). The Treaty provisions applied, as Directive 97/7/EC on distance contracts[245] is a measure of "new approach" harmonisation, allowing Member States to introduce or maintain national measures providing a higher standard of protection for consumers.[246] Such measures must, however, be consistent with primary EU law.[247]

The Court found as follows. Article 28 EC cannot be relied upon to circumvent the system of national marketing authorisations for pharmaceuticals, set up by EU law.[248] Therefore, as regards medicinal products which are subject to, but have not obtained, marketing authorisation in Germany, the national rules were consistent with EU law.[249] For authorised products, the prohibition on sale by mail order of medicines that may only be sold in pharmacies in Germany was a "measure having effect to a quantitative restriction", in the terms of Article 28 EC.[250] The German law requiring that certain medicines be sold only in pharmacies, and prohibiting mail order sales of medicines, is more of an obstacle to pharmacies outside Germany than to those within it.[251] For pharmacies not established in Germany, the internet provides a significant opportunity to gain direct access to the German market. The Court then turned to the question of justification. Two elements of justification were at issue: patient health and the financial integrity of national health systems ("social solidarity").

The Apothekerverband took the view that the purpose of the national measures is to protect the health of patients. Prohibiting sales of medicines by mail order ensures that the patient receives individual information and advice from the pharmacist,

see M. Mäkinen, J. Forsström and R. Rautava, "Delivery of non-national prescriptions within the EU: How flexible is the common market for pharmaceuticals?" 7(1) *eurohealth* (2001) 23.

244 The activities also breached German law prohibiting advertisements for the sale by mail order of medicinal products that may be supplied only by pharmacies, and any advertising for the sale of medicinal products by way of teleshopping. Here the Court found that Directive 2001/83/EC, OJ 2001 L 311/67, Article 88 (1), precludes a national prohibition on advertising the sale by mail order of non-prescription medicinal products which may be supplied only in pharmacies in the Member States concerned. Advertising of prescription products is prohibited in EU law, by Directive 2001/83/EC, Article 88 (1). See further chapter 8.

245 OJ 1997 L 144/19.

246 Directive 97/7/EC, Article 14.

247 Case C-322/01 *DocMorris* above n 242, para 64.

248 For further information on this system, see chapter 8.

249 Paras 53 and 54.

250 Para 76. See Case 8/74 *Dassonville* [1974] ECR 837; Case 120/78 *Cassis de Dijon* [1979] ECR 649; Cases C-267 & 268/91 *Keck* [1993] ECR I-6097; see further chapter 2.

251 Para 74.

when the product is bought. Advice given remotely is not a substitute for face-to-face advice given in a pharmacy, where the pharmacist is able to assess the individual's "physical and psychological state, his bearing, his life-style and his current medication".[252] The argument that prohibiting the sale of prescription medicines over the internet is necessary, to prevent prescription fraud or misuse, was also raised.[253] DocMorris pointed out that expert advice can be given by a pharmacist remotely, by telephone or electronic mail. The quality of advice given in that context may even be superior to that of normal pharmaceutical advice given directly to the patient in the pharmacy. Many patients do not collect their prescriptions in person. On the prevention of fraud point, DocMorris pointed out that it is under an obligation to ensure that prescription medicines are only sent where the pharmacist has received the original prescription, issued by a doctor, and that the person who will receive the medicine is named on the prescription.[254] Overall, DocMorris argued that patient health can be protected equally well in a virtual pharmacy.

The Court found that none of the reasons advanced by the Apothekerverband could justify a ban on sale by mail order of *non-prescription* medicines.[255] As for prescription medicines, the Court found that the arguments relating to the need to provide individual advice to the patient and the need to prevent prescription fraud were persuasive. Such justifications are based on the possible dangers posed by prescription-only medicinal products. These dangers justify the distinction, made at national level, between prescription and non-prescription medicines.[256] The supply of prescription medicines needs to be more strictly controlled than that of non-prescription medicines. Given that there may be risks attached to the use of prescription medicines, the Court held that the need to be able to check that a doctor's prescription is authentic, and that the medicine is given to the person named on the prescription, or someone whom that patient has entrusted with the collection of the medicine, justifies a prohibition on mail order sales.[257]

The Apothekerverband also argued that mail order sales of medicines would jeopardise the continued existence of traditional pharmacies. Traditional pharmacies are subject to a set of obligations in national law, for instance, to maintain a full range of products, stock a minimum quantity of medicines, abide by prices set

252 Para 82.

253 By the Irish government, see para 89.

254 As there is no EU-level harmonisation of which products are prescription only, DocMorris took the most stringent national legislation as its basis, so that national rules concerning the need for a prescription are never evaded: para 97.

255 Paras 112–116.

256 The Court also pointed out that the provision in Article 14 of Directive 97/7/EC on distance selling, which explicitly refers to medicinal products, implies that "the Community legislature did not intend to prevent Member States from prohibiting the sale by mail order of medicinal products merely because the provisions relating to authorisations to market such products within the Community have been harmonised and merely because of the existence of a system of mutual recognition and of provisions intended to coordinate the rules relating to certain activities in the field of pharmacy and the mutual recognition of diplomas in pharmacy": para 110.

257 Para 119.

by national agreements, and provide a duty service out of normal working hours. Such costly obligations do not apply to an internet pharmacy. Therefore, internet pharmacies can "cherry pick" economically profitable sectors of the pharmaceuticals market. Their competitive advantage may place traditional pharmacies, who currently rely on cross-subsidisation of less profitable sectors by more profitable sectors, in jeopardy. Consequently, the prohibition in national law, aimed at ensuring that a reliable and balanced supply of medicines is available to the public at any time, forms an integral part of the national social security system.[258] DocMorris pointed out that, although it is not subject to the regulatory controls on pharmacies in Germany, it is subject to equivalent controls in the state in which it is established, the Netherlands.[259] Since they are bound by national requirements applicable in the Member State of establishment, virtual pharmacies are precluded from confining themselves to selling a range of expensive products.[260] Given that the conditions for access to the profession of pharmacist are harmonised at EU-level, the fact that a pharmaceutical product is bought in a pharmacy in another Member State is not relevant.[261]

The Court found that "the risk of seriously undermining the financial balance of the social security system" may constitute an objective public interest justifying restrictions on freedom to provide services or free movement of goods. Here, the Court referred to its earlier case law on free movement of health care services, such as *Kohll* and its progeny.[262] In this instance, however, no convincing arguments were made in that respect. However, the Court was careful to leave this possible justification open for future litigation.[263] The social solidarity justification is potentially available in these circumstances.

Effective regulation of the provision of health care services at national level within the EU may be thrown into question if significant numbers of health care professionals use the internet to provide e-health. As the *DocMorris* case illustrates, EU deregulatory Treaty provisions on the free movement of goods and freedom to provide services may be engaged. The application of the rules of deregulatory internal market law, in particular home state control, means that services provided remotely are not controlled by professional bodies in the state in which the patients are located. If Member States find this problematic, it may increase the political will to extend EU-level consumer protection legislation into the e-health domain. As we saw in chapter 6, it may also increase the potential for harmonisation of national measures regulating health care professionals, or at least the coordination of national standards, if each Member State loses control over the regulation of the

258 Paras 85–87.
259 The Court agreed with this proposition: see para 105.
260 Para 100.
261 Here DocMorris cited Case 215/87 *Schumaker* [1989] ECR 617: see discussion in chapter 6.
262 See above n 18. See discussion in chapter 4.
263 See Case C-322/01 *DocMorris* above n 242, para 123.

health care professionals to whom "its" patients are turning for health care advice and services.

Some existing EU-level measures may have an effect on developments in e-health. Following the so-called "E-Europe initiative" which was developed at the Lisbon Council of 23–24 March 2000 and the European Council meeting of 19–20 June 2000, the Council endorsed the action plan, *e-Europe – An Information Society for All.*[264] Part of this plan was "Health on-line".[265] This EU action programme "aims to develop an infrastructure of user friendly, validated and interoperable systems for health education, disease prevention and medical care".[266] It is envisaged that the programme will use elements of the OMC process, such as benchmarking, to achieve its aims. The Commission has produced a set of draft guidelines on quality criteria for health-related websites: these focus on transparency and honesty, authority, privacy and confidentiality, currency, accountability and accessibility.[267]

Some of the privacy concerns raised above are regulated by the Data Protection Directive, discussed in chapter 5.[268] The EU has also adopted a directive on "e-commerce", Directive 2000/31/EC.[269] The E-Commerce Directive harmonises national law on "information society services", including commercial communications, electronic contracts, and codes of conduct.[270] Thus, it applies to on-line services such as on-line medicine. Moreover, as Callens notes, the Directive also extends more broadly to "for example, the use of electronic research registers by physicians who pay a fee for accessing the file, the use of a web site by a physician promoting his activities, the sending of medical information among physicians

264 COM(2002) 263 final, Communication From The Commission To The Council, The European Parliament, The Economic And Social Committee And The Committee Of The Regions, eEurope 2005: An information society for all – An Action Plan to be presented in view of the Sevilla European Council, 21–22 June 2002.

265 http://europa.eu.int/comm/information-society/eeurope/documentation/index-en.htm. See further A.J.P. Beurden, "The European Perspective on E-Health" in S. Callens, ed, *E-Health and the Law* (London, The Hague, New York: Kluwer Law International, 2003).

266 Beurden, above n 265, p 101.

267 See http://europa.eu.int/comm/information_society/eeurope/ehealth/quality/draft-guidelines. These are probably inspired by the code of conduct of the Health on the Net Foundation, Geneva, http://www.hon.ch/honcode; see Beurden, above n 265, p 103.

268 The EU Data Protection Working Party has commented that, where data is collected over the internet by hospital or health professionals, then this must:

"state the controller's identity and physical and electronic address;
state the purposes of the processing for which the controller is collecting data via a site;
state the obligatory or optional nature of the information to be provided;
mention the existence of and conditions for exercising the rights to consent or to object to the processing of personal data as well as to access and to rectify and delete data;
list the recipients or categories of recipients of the collected information."

See Data Protection Working Party Recommendation 2/2001 on certain minimum requirements for collecting data online in the European Union, 17 May 2001, 5020/01/EN/Final P6.

269 Directive 2000/31/EC on certain legal aspects of information society services, in particular electronic commerce in the internal market, OJ 2000 L 178/1. See, in general, A.R. Lodder, *eDirectives: Guide to EU Law on E-Commerce* (The Hague: Kluwer, 2002). There is also an "e-Privacy Directive" 2002/58/EC, OJ 2002 L 201/37, Article 13 of which prohibits unsolicited electronic communications ("SPAM") unless prior consent is given.

270 Directive 2000/31/EC, Article 1 (2).

for compensation, etc".[271] The e-commerce Directive provides that, where professionals offer "information society services", Member States must ensure that this is done in compliance with national professional rules regarding, *inter alia*, professional secrecy.[272] Member States and the Commission are to encourage professional associations to adopt EU-level codes of conduct to this effect.[273]

Many examples of "e-health" implicitly treat patients as consumers of health care services or products. This is another example of the move away from the traditional notion of the clinician as the "gatekeeper" to services, towards a system of increased patient choice and control. As we noted above, the patient as consumer is becoming increasingly aware of what is on offer in other Member States. The internet is a key driver in this information transfer. The extent to which the rise of consumerism within health care, and the development of "e-health", may interact with the EU's conceptualisation of patients as consumers, presents an interesting site for future research projects.

Further future developments?

In this book, we have necessarily had to be extremely selective in the substantive topics chosen for discussion. We have not included discussion of medical devices;[274] in-vitro diagnostic devices; health and safety in the workplace;[275] or many areas of public health, such as alcohol regulation,[276] regulation of genetically modified foods and genetically modified pharmaceuticals, immunisation, or bioterrorism. In this concluding chapter, we have been able to include brief discussion of a few further substantive areas in which future developments are likely. Others clamour for attention. For instance, there are now increasing calls for enhanced involvement of the EU legislature in relation to consent to treatment.[277] In areas in which there is already extensive involvement, such as public health, there are clear prospects for a more comprehensive regulatory endeavour. So, for example, the Commission has proposed the creation of a new European Centre for Disease Protection and Control. The existing disease networks are regarded as increasingly inadequate in the light

271 Callens, above n 229, p 31.
272 Directive 2000/31/EC, Article 8 (1).
273 Directive 2000/31/EC, Article 8 (2).
274 Directive 90/385/EC on active implantable medical devices, OJ 1990 L 189/17; Directive 93/42/EC on medical devices, OJ 1993 L 169/1; and Directive 98/79/EC on in vitro devices, OJ 1998 L 331/1. See discussion of the interface between various areas of EU regulation regarding medical devices in C. Hodges, "The Reuse of Medical Devices" 8 *Medical Law Review* (2000) 157; and S. Lierman, "European Product Safety, Liability and Single-Use Devices in a Medical Context" 8 *European Health Law* (2001) 207. In February 2003, the European Parliament called for reclassification of breast implants under the medical devices regime, to protect women from the risks associated with silicone gel implants: see R. Watson, "EU parliament calls for tougher rules on breast implants" 326 BMJ (2003) 414 (22 February).
275 See E. Randall, *The European Union and Health Policy* (Basingstoke: Palgrave, 2001), chapter 2.
276 See P. Kurzer, *Markets and Moral Regulation: Cultural Change in the European Union* (Cambridge: CUP, 2001).
277 See, for example, D. Detmer et al, *The Informed Patient* (Cambridge: Judge Institute of Management Studies, Johnson and Johnson and the Nuffield Foundation, March 2003).

of the "global village", and health threats such as SARS.[278] It is intended that this will be an independent European Agency by 2005, modelled upon bodies such as the European Food Safety Authority, with a small core staff, drawing upon experts across the EU. The new agency is to develop epidemiological surveillance, to provide an "early warning and response" system, with 24-hour availability of disease experts, and to facilitate planning for health emergencies consequent upon epidemics and bioterrorism. There is also the prospect of enhanced EU involvement in promoting screening technologies. For example, a recent proposal has been made for a Council Recommendation in the area of cancer screening.[279] It also remains to be seen whether recent developments in the area of family law and the EU will have an effect on health law and policy. As noted in chapter 1, health law and family law interact closely. Examples are the case of who is able to make decisions regarding health care treatment of children, and, in the case of children born through use of modern reproductive technologies, who exactly is the parent.[280] At present, EU involvement with family law relates to limited proposals, in the context of free movement of persons, relating to stable relationships, marriage and divorce. Nonetheless, this beginning may lead to broader developments. It may be the case that, if Member States are required to amend their domestic family law in these areas, this may have the consequence of a broader national review of status provisions, which would inevitably have a resultant impact in relation to health law.[281]

A further area is that of mental health. In recent years, the EU has shown increasing concern with mental health.[282] In 1999, the EU Social Affairs Commissioner, David Byrne, highlighted particular concerns with mental health of children and adolescents,[283] and, in the following year, statements were made by the EU institutions regarding the need to reduce suicides.[284] In April 1999, the WHO and European Commission held a joint meeting to consider health promotion in the area of mental health. There was a perceived need for a balance between mental health promotion and mental health care. At the meeting, nine key principles for mental health promotion and care were identified. These are personal autonomy;

278 "Strengthening Europe's defences against health threats; Commission proposes European Centre for Disease Prevention and Control" European Press Release Brussels IP/03/1091, 23 July 2003.

279 Commission of the European Communities, *Proposal for a Council Recommendation on Cancer Screening* COM(2003) 230 final 2003/0093 (CNS).

280 Is the mother the gestational mother or the social mother? Is the father the sperm donor or the partner of the mother?

281 For an examination of developments in family law in the EU, see, generally, K. Boele Woelki, ed, *Perspectives for Unification and Harmonisation of Family Law in Europe* (Antwerp: Intensentia, 2003).

282 Council Resolution of 18 November 1999 on the promotion of mental health, OJ 2000 C 86/1; and see Conference organised by the Presidency on "Mental Illness and Stigma in Europe: facing up to the challenges of social inclusion and equity", http://www.eu2003.gr/en/articles/2003/3/24/2338 and the Council's adoption of "Conclusions on combating stigma and discrimination in relation to mental health" in 2512th Council Meeting Employment, Social Policy, Health and Consumer Affairs, Luxembourg, 2 and 3 June 2003, 9688/1/03 REV1(Presse 152), pp 12–14.

283 R. Watson, "EU makes mental illness a top priority" 319 BMJ (1999) 1389b.

284 R. Watson, "EU aims to reduce suicides" 321 BMJ (2000) 825.

sustainability; effectiveness; accessibility; comprehensiveness; equity; accountability; coordination; and efficiency. In addition, ten goals and strategies were pinpointed, namely:

> "Enhancing the visibility and improving recognition of the value of mental health;
> Increasing the interchange of knowledge and experience on mental health;
> Developing innovative and comprehensive explicit mental health policies in consultation with all stakeholders;
> Defining priorities regarding settings, target groups, and target conditions for activities and interventions in mental health promotion, primary, secondary and tertiary prevention, and prevention of mortality;
> Development of primary care and specialised mental health services focusing on quality of care and the development of new, non-stigmatising approaches;
> Tackling inequity in care by giving special attention to the mental health promotion and care needs of marginalised, deprived and socially excluded groups;
> Developing evidence-based guidelines for mental health promotion and for primary and secondary care;
> Developing a human resource strategy and emphasising continuing professional development;
> Highlighting research and development, and establishing mental health information and monitoring systems;
> Development of mental health legislation based on human rights."

Mental health was considered in October 1999 at the European Conference on Promotion of Mental Health and Social Inclusion organised by the Finnish Presidency of the European Union in Tampere, Finland. Further collaboration between WHO and the European Commission has followed through conferences and symposia.[285] In March 2003, a closed conference examining mental illness and stigma was held in Athens under the auspices of the Greek Presidency.[286] The collaboration between the EU, WHO and the Council of Europe is to continue in 2005, when a WHO Ministerial conference is to be held in Helsinki, involving the EU and the Council of Europe, entitled "Mental Health: Facing the Challenges, Building Solutions". Particular concerns have been expressed about mental health abuses in accession states, and the involvement of WHO, along with the EU, in this area is expected to lead to considerable developments in these states.[287] Mental health is likely to be a key area for EU involvement in the future in the light of the Draft Constitutional Treaty, in particular Article III-179 DCT (which replaces Article 152 EC), making explicit reference to EU action directed towards improving public health,

285 Future mental health challenges in Europe: strengthening collaboration between WHO and EU, final report, http://europa.eu.int/comm/health/ph_determinats/life_style/mental/ev_2002211_en.htm; M. Knapp, "Mental Health: Familiar Challenges; unprecedented opportunities" 8(1) *eurohealth* (2001–02) 21.

286 D. McDaid, "Mental Illness and stigma in Europe" 9(1) *eurohealth* (2003) 5.

287 K. Krosnar, "Mentally ill patients in central Europe being kept in padlocked caged cells" 327 BMJ (2003) 249.

including "obviating dangers to physical and mental health". Whilst one obvious area to be involved is that of health promotion, as noted above, mental health has been underpinned by litigation over human rights, and the provisions of the EU Charter of Fundamental Rights may be of particular importance here in the future. For example, this may lead to development of common principles or standards on the treatment of the mentally ill.

Finally it is likely that changing demographic considerations within the EU will give rise to new concerns. Since 1970, life expectancy at birth for women in the EU has risen by 5.5 years, and for men by almost 5 years. A girl born in 1995 can expect to live well over 80 years, a boy to nearly 74 years.[288] As a consequence of increasing life expectancies, more people are suffering from health problems related to old age, such as Alzheimer's Disease and other degenerative disorders. It was estimated that by 2000, 8 million people in the EU would be affected by Alzheimer's Disease.[289] The ageing population is likely to provide new challenges, for health professionals and policy makers alike, across the EU, in relation to mental health, issues of physical disability and transplantation technologies, and to throw into acute relief the allocation of resources within national health (insurance) systems.[290]

IV. Conclusions: health law and the European Union

As we noted in the introductory chapter, at first glance it might appear that the involvement of the EU in matters traditionally within the boundaries of health law may be, at the most, tangential. However, as we have seen in this book, on closer inspection, the practical impact of EU law on health law and policy in the Member States is considerable and wide-ranging. Moreover, this involvement is growing. EU involvement is likely to be highly influenced by the rapid pace of technological development in the area of health. It is also likely to be affected by demographic considerations across the EU as a whole.

In an earlier article, Hervey began to chart the contours of the involvement of the EU in health law.[291] Here, in seeking to describe and to analyse to what extent, and in what ways, EU law affects health law and policy in the Member States, we have gone a stage further. The map is emerging in greater detail. But we do not claim to be comprehensive, or to provide a totally exhaustive guide. Our own journey in this area is only just beginning.

288 COM(98) 230 final, p 1
289 COM(98) 230 final, p 2.
290 For a discussion of some of the legal and ethical issues in the UK context, see Mason, McCall Smith and Laurie, n 54 above, chapter 12 "Treatment of the aged".
291 T. Hervey "Mapping the Contours of European Union Health Law and Policy" 8 *European Public Law* (2002) 69.

Bibliography

Abraham, J. and G. Lewis, *Regulating Medicines in Europe: Competition, expertise and public health* (London: Routledge, 2000).

Abraham, J., "Making regulation responsive to commercial interests: streamlining drug industry watchdogs" 325 BMJ (2002) 1164 (16 November).

Adlung, R., "Health services in a globalising world" 8(3) *eurohealth* (2002) 18.

Agasi, S., "Cross border healthcare in Europe: a perspective from German patients" 8(1) *eurohealth* (2002) 37.

Albrecht, T., "Opportunities and challenges in the provision of cross border care: View from Slovenia" 8(4) *eurohealth* (2002) 8.

Alston, P., ed, *The EU and Human Rights* (Oxford: OUP, 1999).

Alston, P., M. Bustelo and J. Heenan, eds, *Leading by Example: A Human Rights Agenda for the European Union for the Year 2000* (Florence: European University Institute, 1998).

Altenstetter, C., "European Union responses to AIDS/HIV and policy networks in the pre-Maastricht era" 1 *Journal of European Public Policy* (1994) 413 at 418-420.

Alter, K. and S. Meunier-Aitsahalia, "Judicial Politics in the European Community: European Integration and the Path-breaking *Cassis de Dijon* Decision" 26 *Comparative Political Studies* (1994) 535.

Andenas, M. and G. Türk, eds, *Delegated Legislation and the Role of Committees in the EC* (The Hague: Kluwer, 2000).

Anonymous, "European drug regulation: anti-protection or consumer protection?" 337 *Lancet* (1991) 1571 (29 June).

Anonymous, "Bad Medicine in Europe" *The Wall Street Journal Europe*, 22 April 1994, p 8.

Arai-Takahashi, Y., "The role of international health law" in R. Martyn and L. Johnson eds, *Law and the Public Dimension of Health* (London: Cavendish, 2001).

Areen, J. et al, *Law, Science and Medicine* (Westbury, New York: Foundation Press, 1996).

Armstrong, K. and S. Bulmer, *The Governance of the Single European Market* (Manchester: MUP, 1998)

Armstrong, K., "Legal Integration: Theorizing the Legal Dimension of European Integration" 36 JCMS (1998) 155.

Armstrong, K., "The New Institutionalism" in P. Craig and C. Harlow, eds, *Lawmaking in the European Union* (Deventer: Kluwer, 1998).

Armstrong, K., *Regulation, Deregulation, Reregulation* (London: Kogan Page, 2000).

Armstrong, K., "Mutual Recognition" in C. Barnard and J. Scott, eds, *The Law of the Single European Market: Unpacking the Premises* (Oxford: Hart, 2002).

Armstrong, K., "Tackling Social Exclusion through OMC: Reshaping the Boundaries of EU Governance" in T. Börzel and R. Cichowski, eds, *State of the Union: Law, Politics and Society* (Vol 6) (Oxford: OUP, 2003).

Arnull, A. and D. Wincott, eds, *Accountability and Legitimacy in the European Union* (Oxford: OUP, 2002).

Aziz, M., "The Value of Implementation and the Implementation of Values", paper presented to conference *Values and the Draft Constitutional Treaty*, Florence, Italy, December 2003.

Baeten, R., "European Integration and National Healthcare Systems: a challenge for social policy" 8 *info*se (2001) 1 (November).

Baeyens, A., "Implementation of the Clinical Trials Directive: Pitfalls and Benefits" 9(1) *European Journal of Health Law* (2002) 31.

Banta, D., "Quality of healthcare in Europe – an introduction" 6(5) *eurohealth* (2000–01) 18.

Barker, C., *The Health Care Policy Process* (London: Sage, 1996).

Barnard, C., "Social Dumping and the Race to the Bottom: Some Lessons for the EU from Delaware" 25 ELRev (2000) 57.

Barnard, C., *EC Employment Law* (Oxford: OUP, 2000).

Beauchamp, T.L. and J.F. Childress, *Principles of Biomedical Ethics* (Oxford: OUP, 2001).

Beck, U., *Risk Society: Towards a New Modernity* (London: Sage, 1992).

Belcher, P., "Interview with Dr Octavi Quintana: Director of 'Life Sciences: Research for Health' Directorate General for Research, European Commission" 8(3) *eurohealth* (2002) 1.

Belcher, P., M. McKee and T. Rose "Is Health in the European Convention?" 9(2) *eurohealth* (2002) 1.

Bennett, R., C. Erin and J. Harris, *AIDS, Ethics, Justice and European Policy* (Luxembourg: DG Science Research and Development EUR 17789, 1998).

Bentley, L. and B. Sherman, "The ethics of patenting: Towards a Transgenic Patent System" 3 *Medical Law Review* (1995) 275.

Bercusson, B., *European Labour Law* (London: Butterworths, 2000).

Bermann, G.A., "Proportionality and Subsidiarity" in C. Barnard and J. Scott, *The Law of the Single European Market: Unpacking the Premises* (Oxford: Hart, 2002).

Bernard, N., "A 'New Governance' Approach to Economic, Social and Cultural Rights in the EU" in T. Hervey and J. Kenner, eds. *Economic and Social Rights under the EU Charter of Fundamental Rights: A Legal Perspective* (Oxford: Hart, 2003).

Betten, L., "The EU Charter on Fundamental Rights: a Trojan House or a Mouse?"17 *International Journal of Comparative Labour Law and Industrial Relations* (2001) 151.

Beurden, A.J.P., "The European Perspective on E-Health" in S. Callens, ed, *E-Health and the Law* (London, the Hague, New York: Kluwer Law International, 2003).

Beyleveld, D., "Why Recital 26 of the EC Directive on the Legal Protection of

Biotechnological Inventions should be Implemented in National Law" [2000] *Intellectual Property Quarterly* 1.

Beyleveld, D. and R. Brownsword, *Mice, Morality and Patents* (Common Law Institute of Property: London, 1993).

Beyleveld, D. and R. Brownsword, *Human Dignity in Bioethics and Biolaw* (Oxford: OUP, 2001).

Beyleveld, D., R. Brownsword and M. Llewelyn, "The morality clauses of the Directive on the Legal Protection of Biotechnological Inventions" in R. Goldberg and J. Lonbay, *Pharmaceutical Medicine, Biotechnology and European Law* (Cambridge: CUP, 2000).

Beyleveld, D. and E. Histed, "Anonymisation is not Exoneration" 4 *Medical Law International* (1999) 69.

Biggs, H. and R. Mackenzie, "Viagra is coming! The Rhetoric of Choice and Need" in M. Freeman and A. Lewis, eds, *Current Legal Issues 2000* (Oxford: OUP 2000).

Biggs, H., *Euthanasia* (Oxford: OUP, 2001).

Boele Woelki, K., ed, *Perspectives for Unification and Harmonisation of Family Law in Europe* (Antwerp: Intensentia, 2003).

Bossi, J., "European Directive of October 24th 1995 and Protection of Medical Data; The Consequences of the French law Governing Data Processing and Freedoms" 9 *European Journal of Health Law* (2002) 201.

Bostyn, S.J.R., "The Patentability of Genetic Information Carriers" [1999] *Intellectual Property Quarterly* 1.

Bostyn, S.J.R., "One Patent a day keeps the doctor away" 7 *European Journal of Health Law* (2000) 229.

Bostyn, S.J.R., "The Prodigal Son: The Relationship between Patent Law and Health Care" 11 *Medical Law Review* (2003) 67.

Boyron, S., "The Co-Decision Procedure: rethinking the constitutional fundamentals" in P. Craig and C. Harlow, *Law-Making in the European Union* (The Hague: Kluwer, 1998).

Brahams, D., "Court Award for Pertussis Brain Damage" 341 *Lancet* (1993) 1338.

Brazier, M., "Rights and Health Care" in R. Blackburn, ed, *Rights of Citizenship* (London: Mansell, 1993)

Brazier, M., "The Case for a No-Fault Scheme for Medical Accidents" in S. McLean, ed, *Compensation for Damage: An International Perspective* (Aldershot: Dartmouth, 1993).

Brazier, M.,"Can You Buy Children?" 11 CFLQ (1999) 325.

Brazier, M., "Regulating the Reproduction Business" 7 *Medical Law Review* (1999) 166.

Brazier, M., *Medicine Patients and the Law* (London: Penguin, 3rd edn. 2003).

Brazier, M. and N. Glover, "Does Medical Law have a Future?" in D. Hayton, ed, *Law's Futures* (Oxford: Hart, 2000).

Brazier, M. and J. Harris, "Public Health and Private Lives" 4 *Medical Law Review* (1996) 176.

Brearley, S., "Harmonisation of specialist training in Europe: is it a mirage?" 311 BMJ (1995) 297.

Brillon, S., "The European Data Protection Legislation and the Medical Records" in S. Callens, ed, *E-Health and the Law* (London, The Hague, New York: Kluwer Law International, 2003).

Brownsword, R., "Stem cells, Superman and the Report of the Select Committee" 65 MLR (2002) 568.

Buijsen, M.A.J.M., "The Concept of Health Law", paper delivered at the 14th World Health Law Congress, Maastricht, 2002.

Burgermeister, J., "Germany considers relaxing strict embryo research laws" 327 BMJ (2003) 1128 (15 November).

Burley, A.-M. and W. Mattli, "Europe before the Court: a Political Theory of Legal Integration" 47 *International Organization* (1993) 1.

Busquin, P., "Towards a European dialogue between science and society" (2001–02) 8(1) *eurohealth* 5.

Busse, R., "Border-crossing patients in the EU" 8(4) *eurohealth* (2002) 19.

Busse, R., "Consumer choice of healthcare services across borders" in R. Busse, M. Wismar and P.C. Berman, eds, *The European Union and Health Services: The Impact of the Single European Market on Member States* (Amsterdam: IOS Press, 2002).

Busse, R., "The 'OMC' in European health systems" http://www.tuberlin.de/fak8/ifg/mig/files/2002/lectures/pdf/Lisbon3105-RB.pdf.

Cabrai, A., "Cross-border medical care in the European Union-Bringing down a first wall" 24 EL Rev (1999) 387.

Callens, S., "The Privacy Directive and the Use of Medical Data for Research Purposes" 2 *European Journal of Health Law* (1995) 309.

Callens, S., "Telemedicine and the E-Commerce Directive" 9 *European Journal of Health Law* (2002) 93.

Callens, S. *E-health and the law* (London, The Hague, New York: Kluwer Law International, 2003).

Canellopoulou-Bottis, M., "The Implementation of the European Directive 95/46/EC in Greece and Medical/Genetic Data" 9 *European Journal of Health Law* (2002) 207.

Cardwell, M., *The European Model of Agriculture* (Oxford: OUP, 2004).

Carlier, J., *The Free Movement of Persons Living with HIV/AIDS* (Luxembourg: Office of Official Publications of the European Community, 1999).

Carlsson, G., "Health care practice by remote expert – a case study from mid-Sweden" in M. Rigby, R. Roberts and M. Thick, eds, *Taking Health Telematics into the 21st Century* (Abingdon: Radcliffe Medical Press, 2000).

Carmi, A., "Health Law towards the 21st Century" 1 *European Journal of Health Law* (1994) 225.

Case, P., "Confidence Matters: The Rise and Fall of Informational Autonomy in Medical Law" 11(2) *Medical Law Review* (2003) 208.

Cawston, P., "Getting a job in France is difficult" 312 BMJ (1996) 1611.

Cazaban, M. et al, *Santé Publique* (Paris: Masson, 2001).

Chalmers, D., "The Single Market: From Prima Donna to Journeyman" in J. Shaw and G. More, eds, *New Legal Dynamics of European Union* (Oxford: Clarendon, 1995).

Chalmers, D. and E. Szyszczak, *European Union Law Vol II: Towards a European Polity?* (Aldershot: Ashgate, 1998).

Chapman, A., *Exploring a Human Rights Approach to Health Care Reform* (Washington DC: American Association for the Advancement of Science, 1993).

Charlesworth, A. and H. Cullen, "Diplomacy by Other Means: The Use of Legal Basis Litigation as a Political Strategy by the European Parliament and Member States" 36 CMLRev (1999) 1243.

Christiansen, T., K.E. Jorgensen and A. Wiener, "The social construction of Europe" 6 *Journal of European Public Policy* (1999) 528.

Ciavarini Azzi, G., "Comitology and the European Commission" in C. Joerges and E. Vos, *EU Committees: Social regulation, law and politics* (Oxford: Hart, 1999).

Coheur, A., "Integrating care in the border regions" 7(4) *eurohealth* (2001) 10.

Coker, R., "Public Health, civil liberties and tuberculosis" 318 BMJ (1999) 1434.

Cook, R., B.M. Dickens and M.F. Fathalla, *Reproductive Health and Human Rights: Integrating Medicine, Ethics and Law* (Oxford: Clarendon Press, 2003).

Cordess, C. ed, *Confidentiality and Mental Health* (London: Jessica Kingsley Publishers, 2001).

Costello, C., ed, *Fundamental Social Rights: Current European Legal Protection and the Challenge of the EU Charter on Fundamental Rights* (Dublin: Irish Centre for European Law, 2001).

Craig, P., "Once upon a time in the west: Direct Effect and the Federalization of EEC Law" 12 OJLS (1992) 453.

Craig, P., "Directives: Direct Effect, Indirect Effect and the Construction of National Legislation" 22 ELRev (1997) 519.

Craig, P., "Once More unto the Breach: The Community, the State and Damages Liability" 109 LQR (1997) 67.

Craig, P., "The Nature of the Community: Integration, Democracy and Legitimacy" in P. Craig and G. de Búrca, eds, *The Evolution of EU Law* (Oxford: OUP, 1999).

Craig, P., "The Evolution of the Single Market" in C. Barnard and J. Scott, eds, *The Law of the Single European Market: Unpacking the Premises* (Oxford: Hart, 2002).

Craig, P., "What Constitution Does Europe Need? The House that Giscard Built: Constitutional Rooms with a View" Federal Trust Papers, http://www.fedtrust.co.uk/uploads/constitution/26_03.pdf.

Craig, P. and G. de Búrca, *EU Law: Text, Cases and Materials* (Oxford: OUP, 2003).

Cram, L., *Policy-making in the EU: conceptual lenses and the integration process* (London: Routledge, 1997).

Craufurd-Smith, R., "Remedies for Breaches of EC Law in National Courts: Legal Variation and Selection" in P. Craig and G. de Búrca, eds, *The Evolution of EU Law* (Oxford: OUP, 1999).

Cremona, M. "The Doctrine of Exclusivity and the Position of Mixed Agreements in the External Relations of the Community" 2 OJLS (1982) 393.

Cremona, M., "Movement of Persons, Establishment and Services" in M. Maresceau, *Enlarging the European Union: Relations between the EU and Central and Eastern Europe* (London: Longman, 1997).

Cremona, M., "Introduction" in M. Cremona, ed, *The Enlargement of the European Union* (Oxford: OUP, 2003).

Crolla, D., "Cyberlaw: A Potent New Medicine for Health on the Internet" in S. Callens, ed, *E-Health and the Law* (London, The Hague and New York: Kluwer Law International, 2003).

Crosby, S., "The New Tobacco Control Directive: An Illiberal and Illegal Disdain for the Law" 27 ELRev (2002) 177.

Curley, D. and A. Sharples, "Patenting Biotechnology in Europe: the ethical debate moves on" 24 *European Intellectual Property Review* (2002) 565.

Cuvillier, A., "The Role of the European Medicines Evaluation Agency in the harmonisation of pharmaceutical regulation" in R. Goldberg and J. Lonbay, eds, *Pharmaceutical Medicine, Biotechnology and European Law* (Cambridge: CUP, 2000).

Daintith, T., ed, *Implementing EC Law in the UK: Structures for Indirect Rule* (Chichester: Wiley, 1995).

Danziger, R., "HIV test and HIV Prevention in Sweden" 316 BMJ (1998) 293.

Dashwood, A. and C. Hillion, eds, *The General Law of EC External Relations* (London: Sweet and Maxwell, 2000).

Davies, G., "Welfare as a Service" 29 *Legal Issues of Economic Integration* (2002) 27.

de Búrca, G., "Giving Effect to Community Directives" 55 MLR (1992) 215.

de Búrca, G., "The principle of Subsidiarity and the Court of Justice as an Institutional Actor" 36 JCMS (1998) 217.

de Búrca, G., "The Institutional Development of the EU: A Constitutional Analysis" in P. Craig and G. de Búrca, eds, *The Evolution of EU Law* (Oxford: OUP, 1999).

de Búrca, G., "The Drafting of the EU Charter of Fundamental Rights" 26 ELRev (2001) 126.

de Búrca, G., *Setting Constitutional Limits to EU Competence?* Francisco Lucas Pires Working Papers Series on European Constitutionalism, Working Paper 2001/02.

de Búrca, G. and B. de Witte, "The Delimitation of Powers between the EU and its Member States" in A. Arnull and D. Wincott, eds, *Accountability and Legitimacy in the European Union* (Oxford: OUP, 2002).

de Búrca, G. and J. Scott, eds, *The EU and the WTO: Legal and Constitutional Issues* (Oxford: Hart, 2001).

de Búrca, G. and J. Zeitlin, "Constitutionalising the OMC: What should the Convention Propose?" http://www.europa.eu.int/futurum/documents/other/oth010203_en.pdf.

De Haan, J., "The New Dutch Law on Euthanasia" 10 *Medical Law Review* (2002) 57.

De La Porte, C., "Is the Open Method of Coordination Appropriate for Organising Activities at European Level in Sensitive Policy Areas?" 8 ELJ (2002) 38.

de Witte, B., "Direct effect, supremacy and the nature of the Legal Order" in P. Craig and G. de Búrca, eds, *The Evolution of EU Law* (Oxford: OUP, 1999).

de Witte, B., "The Legal Status of the Charter: Vital Question or Non-Issue?" 8 MJ (2001) 81.

de Witte, B., "The Closest Thing to a Constitutional Conversation in Europe: The Semi-Permanent Treaty Revision Process" in P. Beaumont, C. Lyons and N. Walker, *Convergence and Divergence in European Public Law* (Oxford: Hart, 2002).

de Witte, B., "The Impact of Enlargement on the Constitution of the EU" in M. Cremona, ed, *The Enlargement of the European Union* (Oxford: OUP, 2003).

Deacon, B., "Eastern European welfare states: the impact of the politics of globalization" 10 *Journal of European Social Policy* (2000) 146.

Deakin, S., "Labour Law as Market Regulation" in P. Davies et al eds, *European Community Labour Law: Principles and Perspectives* (Oxford: Clarendon, 1996).

Dehousse, R., "Integration v Regulation? On the Dynamics of Regulation in the European Community" 30 JCMS (1992) 383.

Dehousse, R., "Misfits: EU Law and the Transformation of European Governance" in C. Joerges and R. Dehousse, eds, *Good Governance in Europe's Integrated Market* (Oxford: OUP, 2002).

Delcheva, E., "Implementing EU tobacco legislation in Bulgaria: Challenges and opportunities" 8 *eurohealth* (2002) 34.

den Exter, A.P. "Legal Consequences of EU Accession for Central and Eastern European Health Care Systems" 8 *European Law Journal* (2002) 556.

den Exter, A. and H. Hermans, eds, *The Right to Health in Several European Countries* (The Hague: Kluwer, 1999).

Detels, R., *The Oxford Textbook of Public Health Medicine* (Oxford: OUP, 2002).

Detmer, D. et al, *The Informed Patient* (Cambridge: Judge Institute of Management Studies, Johnson and Johnson and the Nuffield Foundation, March 2003).

di Fabio, U., "Some Remarks on the Allocation of Competences between the European Union and its Member States" 39 CMLRev (2002) 1289.

Dickens, B., "Living Tissue and Organ Donors and Property Law, More on Moore" *Journal of Contemporary Health Law and Policy* (1992) 73.

Dickenson, D. ed, *Ethics in Maternal –Fetal Medicine* (Cambridge: CUP, 2002).

Dierks, C., "Data Subject's Consent and Cross-Border Data Processing" in S. Callens, ed, *E-Health and the Law* (London, The Hague and New York: Kluwer Law International, 2003).

Dixon, A. and E. Mossialos, "Funding health care in Europe: recent experiences" in T. Harrison and J. Appleby, eds, *Health care UK* (London: Kings Fund, 2001).

Donaldson, L.J. and R.J. Donaldson, *Essential Public Health* (Plymouth: Petroc Press, 2003).

Donnellan, E., "Medical Fund for treatment abroad is 'a nonsense' says consultant" *Irish Times*, 3 February 2003.

Dorozynski, A., "Mitterand Book Provokes Storm in France" 312 (1996) BMJ 201.

Dougan, M., "The Convention's Draft Constitutional Treaty: A 'Tidying-Up Exercise' that Needs Some Tidying-Up of Its Own" Federal Trust Papers, http://www.fedtrust.co.uk/uploads/constitution/26_03.pdf.

Dougan, M., "A Spectre is Haunting Europe . . . Free Movement of Persons and Eastern Enlargement" in M. Dougan and C. Hillion, eds, *Enlargement of the EU* (Oxford: Hart, 2004).

Drahos, P. "Biotechnology Patents, Markets and Morality" 21 *European Intellectual Property Review* (1999) 441.

Du Pré, F., "Public and Private Harmonisation of Vocational Qualifications in the EU: The Case of the Denturists" 3 *European Journal of Health Law* (1996) 273.

Duncan, B., "Health Policy in the European Union: How it's made and how to influence it" 324 BMJ (2002) 1027.

Dute, J. "Medical Malpractice Liability: No Easy Solutions" 10 *European Journal of Health Law* (2003) 85.

Dutheil de la Rochère, J., "The Attitude of French Courts towards ECJ Case Law" in D. O'Keeffe, ed, *Judicial Review in EC Law* (The Hague: Kluwer, 2000).

Duxbury, N., "Do Markets Degrade?" 59 MLR (1996) 331.

Dworkin, R., *Life's Dominion* (London: Harper Collins, 1993).

Dwyer, P., "Retired EU Migrants, healthcare rights and European social citizenship" 23 *Journal of Social Welfare and Family Law* (2001) 311.

Dyer, C., "Swiss Parliament may ban suicide tourists" 326 BMJ (2003) 242.

Dyer, O., "Dolly's arthritis dents faith in cloning" 324 BMJ (2001) 67.

Earl-Slater, A., "Regulating the prices of the UK's drugs: second thoughts after the government's first report" 314 BMJ (1997) 365 (1 February).

Earnshaw, D. and D. Judge, "From Co-operation to Co-decision: The European Parliament's path to legislative power" in J. Richardson, ed, *European Union: Power and Policy making* (London: Routledge, 1996).

Editorial, "Taking the limits of competences seriously" 37 CMLRev (2000) 1301.

Editorial, "Who's afraid of the European Clinical Trials Directive?" 361 (9376) *Lancet* (2003) 2167.

Edward, D., "Freedom of Movement for the Regulated Professions" in R. White and B. Smythe, eds, *Current Issues in European and International Law* (Festschrift for F. Dowrick) (London: Sweet and Maxwell, 1990).

Eeckhout, P., "The EU Charter of Fundamental Rights and the Federal Question" 39 CMLRev (2002) 945.

Eldridge, P.R.,"Junior Doctors Hours" 308 BMJ (1993) 417.

Elola, J. A. Daponte, and V. Navarro, "Health indicators and the organization of health care systems in Europe" 85 *American Journal of Public Health* (1995) 1397.

Erin, C. and R. Bennett, eds, *HIV and AIDS: Testing screening and confidentiality* (Oxford: OUP, 1999).

Estivenart, G., ed, *Policies and Strategies to Combat Drugs in Europe* (Dordrecht: Martinus Nijhoff, 1995).

Everling, U., "The Maastricht Judgment of the German Federal Constitutional Court" 14 YEL (1994) 1.

Expert Group on Fundamental Rights, *Affirming Fundamental Rights in the European Union: Time to Act* (February 1999).

Eysenbach, G., "Medicine in Europe" in G. Eysenbach, ed, *Medicine and Medical Education in Europe: The Eurodoctor* (Stuttgart: Thieme, 1998).

Fagot-Largeault, A., "Does Non-Commercialisation of the Human Body Increase Graft Security?" in Y. Englert, ed, *Organ and Tissue Transplantation in the European Union* (Dordrecht: Martinus Nijhoff, 1995).

Fallsberg, L., "Patients' Rights in Europe: Where do we stand and where do we go?" 7 *European Journal of Health Law* (2000) 1.

Fallsberg, L., "Patients Rights in the Nordic Countries" 7 *European Journal of Health Law* (2000) 123.

Fallsberg, L., "Consequences of the Amsterdam Declaration: A Rights Revolution in Europe" 10 *European Journal of Health Law* (2003) 5.

Ferge, Z., "Welfare and 'Ill-fare' Systems in Central and Eastern Europe" in R. Sykes, B.

Palier and P. M. Prior, eds, *Globalization and European Welfare States: Challenges and Change* (Basingstoke: Palgrave, 2001).

Ferguson, P., *Drug Injuries and the Pursuit of Compensation* (London: Sweet and Maxwell, 1996).

Fidler, D.P., "World Health Organization's Framework Convention for Tobacco Control" *American Society of International Law Insights* 28 March 2003, http://www.asil.org/insights/insigh100.htm.

Finch, J., "Professional Recognition and Training of Doctors: The 1993 EC Directive" 2 *European Journal of Health Law* (1995) 163.

Fitzpatrick, M., *The Tyranny of Health: Doctors and the Regulation of Lifestyle* (London: Routledge, 1999).

Flear, M., "Case note on *Müller-Fauré*" 41 CMLRev (2004) 209.

Fleming, J.G., "Comparative Law of Torts" 4 OJLS (1984) 235.

Fluss, S., "The Development of National Health Legislation in Europe: The Contribution of International Organizations" 2 *European Journal of Health Law* (1995) 193.

Flynn, R. and G. Williams, *Contracting for Health Quasi Markets and the NHS* (Oxford: OUP, 1997).

Foster, C., *The ethics of medical research on humans* (Cambridge: CUP, 2001).

Fox, M. and J. McHale, *Framing the Clinical Body* (Oxford: Hart Publishing, 2004 forthcoming).

Freddolini, P., "e-health for Europe: The possible and the practical" 8 *eurohealth* (2002) 5.

Freeman, M., "Is Surrogacy Exploitative?" in S. McLean, ed, *Legal Issues in Human Reproduction* (Aldershot: Dartmouth, 1990).

Freeman, M., "Medically Assisted Reproduction" in I. Kennedy and A. Grubb, eds, *Principles of Medical Law* (Oxford: OUP, 1998).

Freeman, M., "Does Surrogacy Have a Future After Brazier?" 7 *Medical Law Review* (1999) 1.

Freeman, R., *The Politics of Health in Europe* (Manchester: MUP, 2000).

Freeman, R. and M. Moran, "Reforming Health Care in Europe" 23 *West European Politics* (2000) 35.

Friedson, E., *Profession of Medicine: A Study of the Sociology of Applied Knowledge* (New York: Dodd Mead, 1988).

Furet, M.D., "The mutual recognition of diplomas in pharmacy within the European Union" 7 *Sciences of Techniques Pharmaceutiques Pharma Pratiques* (1997) 162.

Gaja, G., "New Developments in a Continuing Story: The Relationship between EEC Law and Italian Law" 27 CMLRev (1990) 401.

Garanis Papadatos, T. and P. Dalla Vorgia, "Ethical Review Procedures for Clinical Trials in Greece" 7 *European Journal of Health Law* (2000) 441.

Garattini, L. and F. Tediosi, "A Comparative Analysis of Generics Markets in five European countries" 51 *Health Policy* (2000) 149.

Garattini, S. and V. Bertele, "Adjusting Europe's drug regulation to public health needs" 358 *Lancet* (2001) 64.

Garcia de Cortazar, C., "*Kohll* and *Decker*, or That is Somebody Else's Problem" 6 *European Journal of Health Law* (1999) 397.

Gardner, J., "The European Agency for the Evaluation of Medicines and European Regulation of Pharmaceuticals" 2 ELJ (1996) 48.

Garman, J. and L. Hilditch, "Behind the scenes: an examination of the importance of the informal processes at work in conciliation" 5 *Journal of European Public Policy* (1998) 271.

Garwood-Gowers, A., J.Tingle and T. Lewis, eds, *Healthcare Law; The Impact of the Human Rights Act 1998* (London: Cavendish, 2001).

Gehring, M., "Committees in European Environmental Process Regulation" in C. Joerges and E. Vos, eds, *EU Committees: Social Regulation, Law and Politics* (Oxford: Hart, 1999).

General Medical Council, *Confidentiality* (London: GMC, 2000).

Gevers, S., "Medical Research Involving Human Subjects: Towards an International Legal Framework?" 8 *European Journal of Health Law* (2001) 293.

Gevers, J.K.M., "Medical Research and the Law: A European Perspective" 2 *European Journal of Health Law* (1995) 97.

Geyer, R., *Exploring European Social Policy* (Cambridge: Polity, 2000).

Giesen, D., *International Medical Malpractice Law* (Tubingen: JCB Mohr (Paul Siebeck); Dordrecht, Boston, London: Martinus Nijhoff, 1988).

Giesen, D., "Liability for Transfer of HIV Infected Blood in Comparative Perspective" 10 *Professional Negligence* (1994) 2.

Gijzen, M., "The Charter: A Milestone for Social Protection in Europe?" 8 MJ (2001) 33.

Gillon, R., "Autonomy and Consent" in M. Lockwood, ed, *Moral Dilemmas in Modern Medicine* (Oxford: OUP, 1985).

Gillon, R., *Philosophical Medical Ethics* (Chichester: John Wiley and Sons, 1986).

Gillon, R., "Medical Ethics; Four Principles Plus Attention to Scope" 309 BMJ (1994) 184.

Gilmore, A. and W. Zatonski, "Free trade versus the protection of health: the implications of EU accession for tobacco consumption in Poland?" 8 *eurohealth* (2002) 31.

Gitter, D.M., "Led Astray by the Moral Compass; Incorporating Morality into European Union Biotechnology Patent Law" 19 *Berkeley Journal of International Law* (2001) 1.

Glass, J., ed, *Ethics Committees in Central and Eastern Europe* (Limbova: Institute of Medical Ethics and Bioethics Foundation, 2001).

Glover, J., *Causing Death and Saving Lives* (Harmondsworth: Penguin, 1990).

Lord Goff of Chieveley and G. Jones, *The Law of Restitution* (London: Sweet and Maxwell, 2002).

Gold, E.R. and A. Gallochat, "The European Biotech Directive: Past as prologue" 7(3) *European Law Journal* (2001) 331.

Gold, E.R., *Body Parts; Property Rights and the Ownership of Human Biological Materials* (Washington DC: Georgetown University Press, 1996).

Goldberg, R., "The development risk defence and the ECJ" in R. Goldberg and J. Lonbay, *Pharmaceutical Medicine, Biotechnology and European Law* (Cambridge: CUP, 2000).

Goldberg, R.,"Paying for Bad Blood: Strict Product Liability after the Hepatitis C Litigation" 10 *Medical Law Review* (2002) 165.

Lord Goldsmith, "A Charter of Rights, Freedoms and Principles" 38 CMLRev (2001) 1201.

Gostin, L.O., "Human Rights of Persons With Mental Disabilities" 23 *International Journal of Law and Psychiatry* (2000) 125.

Gostin, L.O., *Public Health Law: Powers, Duties and Restraints* (Berkley and Los Angeles: University of California Press, 2000).

Gostin, L.O. and Z. Lazzarini, *Human Rights and Public Health in the AIDS Pandemic*, (Oxford: OUP, 1997).

Gottlieb, C., O. Lalos and F. Lindblad, "Disclosure of Donor Insemination to the Child: the Impact of Swedish Legislation on Couples' Attitudes" 15 *Human Reproduction* (2000) 2052.

Gottlieb, S., "A fifth of Americans contact their doctor as a result of drug advertising" 325 BMJ (2002) 854.

Gray, P., "The Scientific Committee for Food" in M.P.C.M. Van Schendelen, *EU Committees as Influential Policy-Makers* (Aldershot: Dartmouth, 1998).

Green, N., T. Hartley and J. Usher, *The Legal Foundations of the Single European Market* (Oxford: OUP, 1991).

Griller, S., "Judicial Enforceability of WTO Law in the European Union" 4 *Journal of International Economic Law* (2001) 441.

Grubb, A., *Kennedy and Grubb Medical Law* (Oxford: OUP, 2000).

Grubb, A., "Duties in Contract and Tort" in I. Kennedy and A. Grubb, eds, *Principles of Medical Law* (Oxford: OUP, 1998).

Grubb, A., "Breach of Confidence: Anonymised Information" 8 *Medical Law Review* (2000) 115 at 117.

Grubb, A., "Consumer Protection Act 1987; Liability for Defective Products" 10 *Medical Law Review* (2002) 82.

Grubb, A., ed, *Principles of Medical Law* 2004 forthcoming).

Hagen, P.J., *Blood Transfusion in Europe: a "white paper"* (Strasbourg: Council of Europe Press, 1993).

Haigh, R. and D. Harris, eds. *AIDS and the Law* (London: Routledge, 1995).

Halliday, S., "A comparative approach to the regulation of human stem cell research in Europe" 12 *Medical Law Review* (2004) 40.

Haltern, U.R. and J.H.H. Weiler, "The Autonomy of the Community Legal Order Through the Looking Glass" 37 *Harvard International Law Journal* (1996) 411.

Hamlin, C. and S. Sheard, "Revolutions in Public Health 1848 and 1998?" 317 BMJ (1998) 587.

Hancher, L., "The European Pharmaceutical Market: problems of partial harmonisation" 15 ELRev (1990) 9.

Hancher, L., "Creating the Internal Market for Pharmaceutical Medicines: An Echternach Jumping Process?" 28 CMLRev (1991) 821.

Harding, T.W., "The Application of the European Convention of Human Rights to the Field of Psychiatry" 12 *International Journal of Law and Psychiatry* (1989) 245.

Harlow, C., *Accountability in the European Union* (Oxford: OUP, 2002).

Harrington, J.A., "AIDS, public health and the law: a case of structural coupling" 6 *European Journal of Health Law* (1999) 213.

Harris, J., *The Value of Life* (London: Routledge and Kegan Paul, 1985).

Harris, J., "Who Owns My Body?" 16 OJLS (1996) 55.

Harris, J., *Clones, Genes and Immortality* (Oxford: OUP, 1998).

Harris, J., *Communicable Diseases, Lifestyles and Personal Responsibility: Ethics and Rights Final Report* (Brussels: European Commission, 1999).

Hartley, T., *The Foundations of European Community Law* (Oxford: OUP, 2003).

Hatzopoulos, V., "Killing National Health and Insurance Systems but Healing Patients?" 39 CMLRev (2002) 683 at 696.

Hatzopoulos, V., "Case note on Case C-326/00 *IKA* v *Ioannidis*" 40 CMLRev (2003) 1251.

Havighurst, C., "American Federalism and American Health Care: Lessons for the European Community" in H.E.G.M. Hermans, A.F. Casparie and J.H.P. Paelinck, *Health Care in Europe after 1992* (Aldershot: Dartmouth, 1992).

Helman, C.G., *Culture, Health and Illness* (Oxford: Butterworth-Heinemann, 2000).

Hepple, B., "The EU Charter of Fundamental Rights" 30 ILJ (2001) 225.

Herdegen, M., "Maastricht and the German Constitutional Court: Constitutional Restraints for an Ever Closer Union" 31 CMLRev (1994) 235.

Hermans, H., "Patients' Rights in the European Union" 7(3 Supplement) *European Journal of Public Health* (1997) 11.

Hermesse, J., H. Lewalle and W. Palm, "Patient Mobility Within the European Union" 7 (3 Supplement) *European Journal of Public Health* (1997) 4.

Herr, S.S., "Rights of Disabled Persons: International Principles and American Experiences" 12 *Columbia Human Rights Law Review* (1980) 1.

Herr, S.S., L.O. Gostin and H. Hongju Kerr, eds, *The Human Rights of Persons with Intellectual Disabilities* (Oxford: OUP, 2003).

Hervey, T., "Buy Baby: The European Union and Regulation of Human Reproduction" 18 OJLS (1998) 207.

Hervey, T., "Social solidarity: a buttress against internal market law" in J. Shaw, ed, *Social Law and Policy in an Evolving European Union* (Oxford: Hart, 2000).

Hervey, T., "Community and National Competence in Health after *Tobacco Advertising*" 38 CMLRev (2001) 1421.

Hervey, T., "Regulation of Genetically Modified Products in a Multi-Level System of Governance: Science or Citizens?" 10 *Review of EC and International Environmental Law* (2001) 321.

Hervey, T., "Up in Smoke: Community (anti) tobacco law and policy" 26 ELRev (2001) 101.

Hervey T., "Mapping the Contours of European Union Health Law and Policy" 8 *European Public Law* (2002) 69.

Hervey, T., "The Legal Basis of European Union Public Health Policy" in M. McKee, E. Mossialos and R. Baeten, eds, *The Impact of EU Law on Health Care Systems* (Brussels: PIE Peter Lang, 2002).

Hervey, T., "The right to health in EU law" in T. Hervey and J. Kenner, eds, *Economic and Social Rights under the EU Charter of Fundamental Rights* (Oxford: Hart, 2003).

Hervey, T. and J. Kenner, eds, *Economic and Social Rights under the EU Charter of Fundamental Rights* (Oxford: Hart, 2003).

Hewitt, D., "Mental Health Law" in C. Baker, ed, *Human Rights Act 1998: A Practitioner's Guide* (London: Sweet and Maxwell, 1998).

Hillion, C., "Tobacco Advertising: if you must, you may" 60 CLJ (2001) 486.

Hix, S., "The Study of the European Community: The Challenge to comparative Politics" 17 *West European Politics* (1994) 1.

Hodges, D., "The Reuse of Medical Devices" 8 *Medical Law Review* (2000) 157.

Hodges, J.S., "Developmental Risks: Unanswered Questions" 61 MLR (1998) 560.

Hoffman, W.C. and S. Hill-Arning, *Guide to Product Liability in Europe* (The Hague: Kluwer, 1994).

Holm, S., "Regulating stem cell research in Europe by the back door" 29 *Journal of Medical Ethics* (2003) 203.

Hooghe, L. and G. Marks, *Multilevel Governance and European Integration* (Lanham: Rowman & Littlefield, 2001).

Hooghiemstra, T., "Introduction to the Special Privacy Issue" 9 *European Journal of Health Law* (2002) 181.

Hooghiemstra, T., "The Implementation of Directive 95/46/EC in the Netherlands with Special Regard to Medical Data" 9 *European Journal of Health Law* (2002) 219.

Hoskyns, C., *Integrating Gender* (London: Verso, 1996).

House of Commons Science and Technology Select Committee, *Genetics and Insurance* (Cm 5286, 2001).

Howells, G. and T. Wilhelmsson, *EC Consumer Law* (Aldershot: Ashgate, 1997), p 33.

Hughes, D., "The Reorganisation of the NHS – The Rhetoric and the Reality of the Internal Market" 54 MLR (1991) 88.

Human Genetics Commission, *Inside Information* (London: HGC, 2002).

Human Genetics Commission, *Genes Direct* (London: HGC, 2003).

Ingersent, K.A., A.J. Rayner and R.C. Hine, *The Reform of the Common Agricultural Policy* (Basingstoke: Macmillan, 1998).

Inotai, A., "The 'Eastern Enlargements' of the EU" in M. Cremona, ed, *The Enlargement of the European Union* (Oxford: OUP, 2003).

Irwin, J., "Migration patterns of nurses in the EU" 7 *eurohealth* (2001) 13.

Jackson, E., *Regulating Reproduction: Law, Technology and Autonomy* (Oxford: Hart Publishing, 2001).

Jackson, J.H., *The Jurisprudence of GATT and the WTO* (Cambridge: CUP, 2000).

Jacobs, J., *Doctors and Rules: A Sociology of Professional Values* (New Jersey: Transaction Publishing, 1999).

Jacqueson, C., "Union Citizenship and the Court of Justice: Something New Under the Sun" 27 ELRev (2002) 260.

Jactenfuchs, M., "Theoretical Perspectives on European Governance" 1 ELJ (1995) 115.

Jans, J.H., *European Environmental Law* (Groningen: Europa Law Publishing, 2002).

Jasanoff, S., *The Fifth Branch: Science Advisers as Policymakers* (Cambridge, Mass: Harvard University Press, 1990).

Jinks, C., B.N. Ong and C. Paton, "The mobility of doctors and nurses – a United Kingdom case study" in R. Busse, M. Wismar and P.C. Berman, eds, *The European Union and Health Services* (Amsterdam: IOS Press, 2002).

Joerges, C., "European Economic Law, the Nation State, and the Maastricht Treaty" in R. Dehousse, ed, *Europe after Maastricht: An Ever Closer Union* (Beck, 1994).

Joerges, C., *Integrating Scientific Expertise into Regulatory Decision Making*, EUI Working Paper RSC No 96/10 (Florence: EUI, 1995).

Joerges, C., "Guest Editorial: The Commission's White Paper on Governance in the EU – A Symptom of Crisis?" 39 CMLRev (2002) 441.

Joerges, C. and R. Dehousse, eds, *Good Governance in Europe's Integrated Market* (Oxford: OUP, 2002).

Joerges, C. and J. Neyer, "From Intergovernmental Bargaining to Deliberative Political Processes: The Constitutionalisation of Comitology" 3 ELJ (1997) 273.

Joerges, C. and E. Vos, *EU Committees: Social regulation, law and politics* (Oxford: Hart, 1999).

Johnson, L., "Defining Public Health" and "Issues of Public Health; Infectious Diseases" in R. Martyn and L. Johnson, *Law and the Public Dimension of Health* (London: Cavendish, 2002).

Johnson, T., G. Larkin and M. Saks, eds, *Health Professions and the State in Europe* (London: Routledge, 1995).

Jones, J., "Cloning may cause health defects" 318 BMJ (1999) 1230.

Jones, M., *Medical Negligence* (London: Sweet and Maxwell, 2003).

Jorens, Y., "The Right to Health Care Across Borders" in R. Baeten, M. McKee and E. Mossialos, eds, *The Impact of EU Law on Health Care Systems* (Brussels: PIE Peter Lang, 2003).

Jost T.S., *Readings in Comparative Health Law and Bioethics* (Durham NC: North Carolina Academic Press 2001).

Kalo, I., "Development of quality of health systems in Europe" 6(5) *eurohealth* (2000–01) 20.

Kaufer, E., "The Regulation of New Product Development in the Drug Industry" in G. Majone, ed, *Deregulation or Re-regulation? Regulatory Reform in Europe and the United States* (London and New York: Pinter, 1990).

Kennedy, I., *The Unmasking of Medicine* (London: Allen and Unwin, 1981).

Kennedy, I and A. Grubb, *Medical Law: Text with Materials* (London: Butterworths, 1991 and 2000).

Kenner, J., "The EU Employment Title and the 'Third Way': Making Soft Law Work?" 15 *International Journal of Comparative Labour Law and Industrial Relations* (1999) 33.

Kenner, J., *EU Employment Law: From Rome to Amsterdam and Beyond* (Oxford: Hart, 2003).

Keown, J., ed, *Euthanasia Examined: Ethical, Legal and Clinical Perspectives* (Cambridge: CUP, 1995).

Keown, J., "Restoring Moral and Intellectual Shape to the Law After *Bland*" 113 LQR (1997) 481.

Keown, J., "Review of 'The Principles of Medical Law'" 59 CLJ (2000) 412.

Keown, J., *Euthanasia, Ethics and Public Policy: An Argument Against Legalisation* (Cambridge: CUP, 2002).

Khoury, M.J., W. Burke and E.J. Thompson eds. *Genetics and Public Health in the 21st*

Century: Using Genetic Information to Improve Health and Prevent Disease (Oxford: OUP, 2000).

Kienle, T. "New forms of medical data collection- should be complemented by a new European privacy standard?" 8 *European Journal of Health Law* (2001) 27.

Klemperer, F., "How To Do It: Work in the European Union" 312 (1996) BMJ 567.

Klemperer, F., "Working abroad as a doctor" in G. Eysenbach, ed, *Medicine and Medical Education in Europe: The Eurodoctor* (Stuttgart: Thieme, 1998).

Knapp, M., "Mental Health: Familiar Challenges; unprecedented opportunities" 8(1) *eurohealth* (2001–02) 21.

Knoppers, B.M. and C. Fecteau, "Human Genomic Databases: A Global Public Good?" 10 *European Journal of Health Law* (2003) 27.

Knox, E.G., "Confidential medical records and epidemiological research" 304 BMJ (1992) 727.

Kon, S. and F. Schaeffer, "Parallel Imports of Pharmaceutical Products: A New Realism or Back to Basics?" 18 ELRev (1997) 123.

Krämer, L., *Casebook on EU Environmental Law* (Oxford: Hart, 2002).

Krosnar, K., "Mentally ill patients in central Europe being kept in padlocked caged cells" 327 BMJ (2003) 249.

Kuitenbrouwer, F., "Privacy and Its Fallacies" 9 *European Journal of Health Law* (2002) 173.

Kurzer, P., *Markets and Moral Regulation: Cultural Change in the European Union* (Cambridge: CUP, 2001).

Laffan, B. and M. Shackleton, "The Budget" in H. Wallace and W. Wallace, eds, *Policy-making in the European Union* (Oxford: OUP, 2000).

Lamb, D., *Down the Slippery Slope* (London: Routledge, 1988).

Langdridge, D. and E. Blyth, "Regulation of assisted conception services in Europe: Implications of the new reproductive technologies for the family" 23 *Journal of Social Welfare and Family Law* (2001) 45.

Latham, M., *Regulating Reproduction: A Century of Conflict in Britain and France* (Manchester: MUP, 2002).

Laufs, A., W. Uhlenbruck and H. Genzel, *Handbuch des Artzrechts* (Munich: CH Beck: 2002).

Laurie, G. *Genetic Privacy* (Cambridge: CUP, 2002).

Leary, V., "The Right to Health in International Human Rights Law" 1 *Journal of Health and Human Rights* (1994) 3.

Lee, R. and D. Morgan, *Human Fertilisation and Embryology Regulating the Reproductive Revolution* (Blackstones: London, 2001).

Leenen, H.J.J., "The European Journal of Health Law: A New Publication" 1 *European Journal of Health Law* (1994) 1.

Leibfried, S. and P. Pierson, "European Social Policy" in H. Wallace and W. Wallace, eds, *Policy-Making in the European Union* (Oxford: OUP, 2000).

Leibfried, S. and P. Pierson, "Semi-Sovereign Welfare States: Social Policy in a multitiered Europe" in S. Leibfried and P. Pierson, eds, *European Social Policy: Between Fragmentation and Integration* (Washington: Brookings, 1995).

Leikola, J., "Achieving self sufficiency in blood across Europe" 316 BMJ (1998) 489.

Lenaerts, K., "Bricks for a Constitutional Treaty of the European Union: Values, Objectives and Means" 27 ELRev (2002) 377.

Lenaerts, K., "Regulating the Regulatory Process: Delegation of Powers within the European Community" 18 ELRev (1993) 23.

Lenaerts, K. and M. Desomer, "New Models of Constitution-Making in Europe: The Quest for Legitimacy" 39 CMLRev (2002) 1217.

Lenaerts, K. and P. Foubert, "Social Rights in the Case-Law of the European Court of Justice: the impact of the Charter of Fundamental Rights of the European Union on Standing Case-Law" 28 *Legal Issues of Economic Integration* (2001) 267.

Lenschow, A., "New Regulatory Approaches in 'Greening' EU Policies" 8 ELJ (2002) 19.

Liddell, K., "Did the Watchdog Bark, Bite, Whimper? The UK Report on the Use of Personal Genetic Information" 9 *European Journal of Health Law* (2002) 243.

Lierman, S., "European Product Safety, Liability and Single-Use Devices in a Medical Context" 8 *European Journal of Health Law* (2001) 207.

Lloyd, I., *A Guide to the Data Protection Act 1998* (London: Butterworths, 1998).

Lodder, A.R., *eDirectives: Guide to EU Law on E-Commerce* (The Hague: Kluwer, 2002).

Lonbay, J., "The Mutual Recognition of Professional Qualifications in the EC" in R. Hodgin, ed *Professional Liability: Law and Insurance* (London: LPP Professional Publishing, 1999).

Lonbay, J., "The Free Movement of health care professionals in the European Community" in R. Goldberg and J. Lonbay, eds, *Pharmaceutical Medicine, Biotechnology and European Law* (Cambridge: CUP, 2000).

Lowrance, W., *Learning from Experience: Privacy and the Secondary Use of Data* (Oxford: Nuffield Trust, 2002).

Lowson, K., P. West, S. Chaplin and J. O'Reilly, *York Health Economic Consortium Document; Final Report; Evaluation of Treating Patients Overseas* (York: YHEC, 2002).

Luckhaus, L., "European Social Security Law" in A. Ogus and N. Wikeley, eds, *The Law of Social Security* (London: Butterworths, 1995).

Ludvigsen, C. and K. Roberts, *Health Care Policies and Europe: the implications for practice* (Oxford: Butterworth-Heinemann, 1996).

Lupton, D., *Risk* (London: Routledge, 1999).

Lynge, E., "Misguided Directive on confidential data: a threat to epidemiology" 308 BMJ (1992) 490.

MacCormick, N., "The Maastricht-Urteil: Sovereignty Now" 1 ELJ (1995) 259.

MacCormick, N., *Questioning Sovereignty* (Oxford: OUP, 1999).

MacKellar, C., ed, *Reproductive Medicine and Embryological Research: A European Handbook of Bioethical Legislation* (Edinburgh: European Bioethical Research, 1998).

MacMaolain, C., "Free Movement Of Foodstuffs, Quality Requirements And Consumer Protection: Have the court and the Commission Both Got It Wrong?" 26 ELRev (2001) 413.

Madden, D., *Medicine Law and Ethics in Ireland* (Dublin: Butterworths Law Ireland, 2002).

Magarris, E.,"The Principle of Supremacy of Community Law – The Greek Challenge" 23 ELRev (1998) 179.

Majone, G., "A European regulatory state?" in J. Richardson, ed, *European Union: power and policy-making* (London: Routledge, 1996).

Majone, G., *Regulating Europe* (London: Routledge, 1996).

Majone, G., "Which social policy for Europe?" in Y. Mény, P. Muller and J.-L. Quermonne, eds, *Adjusting to Europe: The impact of the European Union on national institutions and policies* (London: Routledge, 1996).

Majone, G., "The Credibility Crisis of Community Regulation" 38 JCMS (2000) 273.

Majone, G., "Functional Interests: European Agencies" in J. Peterson and M. Shackleton, eds, *The Institutions of the European Union* (Oxford: OUP, 2002).

Mäkinen, M.M. and M. Äärimaa, "The challenge of professional freedom" 7 *eurohealth* (2001) 16.

Mäkinen, M., J. Forsström and P. Rautava, "Delivery of non-national prescriptions within the EU: how flexible is the common market for pharmaceuticals?" 7 (1) *eurohealth* (2001) 23.

Mann, J., L. Gostin et al, "Health and Human Rights" 1 *Journal of Health and Human Rights* (1994) 7.

Marenco, G., "The Notion of Restriction on the Freedom of Establishment and Provision of Services in the Case law of the Court" 11 YEL (1991) 111.

Maresceau, M., "Pre-accession" in M. Cremona, ed, *The Enlargement of the European Union* (Oxford: OUP, 2003).

Marks, G., "Structural Policy in the European Community" in A. Sbragia, ed, *Euro-Politics: Institutions and Policy-Making in the "New" European Community* (Washington: Brookings, 1992), pp 191–224.

Marks, G. et al, *Governance in the European Union* (London: Sage, 1996).

Marks, G., L. Hooghe and K. Blank, "European Integration from the 1980s: State-Centric v. Multi-Level Governance" 34 JCMS (1996) 3.

Marrée, J. and P.P. Groenewegen, *Back to Bismarck: Eastern European Care Systems in Transition* (Aldershot: Avebury, 1997).

Martin, J., "The Principles of the Rights of Patients in Europe: A Commentary" 1 *European Journal of Health Law* (1994) 265.

Martin, P. and J. Kaye, *The Use of Biological Sample Collections and Personal Medical Information in Human Genetic Research* (London: Wellcome Trust, 1999).

Martinsen, D.S., "National Impacts of Institutionalising Social Security Rights for Migrants in the European Union" EUI Working Papers, Law No 2003/13, http://www.ive.it/PUB/law 03–13.pdf

Martinsen, D.S., "Who Has the Right to Intra European Social Security? - From Market Citizens to European Citizens and Beyond" *Annual of German and European Law* (2004 forthcoming).

Mason, J.K. and G. Laurie, "Consent or Property? Dealing with the Body and its Parts in the Shadow of Bristol and Alder Hey" 64 MLR (2001) 711.

Mason, J.K., R.A. McCall Smith and G. Laurie, *Law and Medical Ethics* (London: Lexis-Nexis, 6th edn, 2002).

McCarthy, M. and S. Rees, *Health Systems and Public Health Medicine in the EC* (London: Royal College of Physicians, 1992).

McCrudden, C., "The Future of the EU Charter of Rights" Jean Monnet Papers, http://www.jeanmonnetprogram.org/papers/01/013001.html.

McDaid, D., "Mental Illness and stigma in Europe" 9(1) *eurohealth* (2003) 5.

McGoldrick, D., *International Relations Law of the European Union* (London: Longman, 1997),

McHale, J., *Medical Confidentiality and Legal Privilege* (London: Routledge, 1993).

McHale, J., "Migration and Communicable Diseases: Some Legal Issues" Final Conference Report, Conference Communicable Diseases, Lifestyles and Responsibility, Amalfi, Italy, September 1998.

McHale, J., "Enforcing Health Care Rights in the English Courts" in R. Burchill, D. Harris and A. Owers, eds, *Economic, Social and Cultural Rights: Their Implementation in the United Kingdom* (Nottingham: University of Nottingham Human Rights Law Centre, 1999).

McHale, J., "Nurse Prescribing" 4(5) *Mental Health Care* (2001) 170.

McHale, J., "Quality and Safety in Health Care: A role for the Law?" 11 *Quality and Safety in Health Care* (2002) 88.

McHale, J., "A review of the legal framework for nurse prescribing" 1(3) *Nurse Prescribing* (2003) 107.

McHale, J., "Genetic Databases: Some Legal and Ethical Issues" 11(2) *Medical Law Review* (2004) 70.

McHale, J. and M. Bell, "Traveller's checks" *Health Service Journal* 23 May 2002, pp 39–41.

McHale, J. and M. Fox, *Health Care Law: Text and Materials* (London: Sweet and Maxwell, 1997).

McKee, M., E. Mossialos and P. Belcher, "The Influence of European Law on National Health Policy" 6 *Journal of European Social Policy* (1996) 263.

McLean, S., "Can No-Fault Analysis Ease the Problems of Medical Injury Litigation" in S. McLean, ed, *Compensation for Damage: An International Perspective* (Aldershot: Dartmouth, 1993).

McLean, S., *Consent and the Law: Consultation Document and Questionnaire* (London: DOH, 1997).

Megone, C. et al, "The Structure, Composition and Operation of European Research Ethics Committees" in S. Mason and C. Megone, eds, *European Neonatal Research: Consent, Ethics Committees and Law* (Aldershot: Ashgate, 2001).

Michalowski, S., *Medical Confidentiality and Crime* (Aldershot: Ashgate, 2003).

Mills, S., "Online Prescribing: Principles, Problems and Policing" 9(1) *Medico-Legal Journal of Ireland* (2003) 36.

Millns, S., "Reproducing inequalities; assisted conception and the challenge of legal pluralism" 24 *Journal of Social Welfare and Family Law* (2002) 19.

Montgomery, J., "Medical Law in the Shadow of Hippocrates" 52 MLR (1989) 566.

Montgomery, J., "Medicine, Accountability and Professionalism" 16 *Journal of Law and Society* (1989) 319.

Montgomery, J., "Doctor's Handmaidens: The Legal Contribution" in S. Wheeler and S. McVeigh, eds, *Law, Health and Medical Regulation* (Aldershot: Dartmouth, 1992).

Montgomery, J., "Recognising a Right to Health" in R. Beddard and D.M. Hill, eds, *Economic, Social and Cultural Rights: Progress and Achievement* (Basingstoke: Macmillan, 1992).

Montgomery, J., "Time for a Paradigm Shift? Medical Law in Transition" 53 *Current Legal Problems* (2000) 363.

Montgomery, J., *Health Care Law* (Oxford: OUP, 2nd edn. 2002).

Moore, S., "Challenge to the Biotechnology Directive" 24 *European Intellectual Property Review* (2002) 149.

Moran, M. and B. Wood, *States, Regulation and the Medical Profession* (Buckingham: Open University Press, 1993).

Moravcsik, A., "Negotiating the Single European Act: National Interests and Conventional Statecraft in the European Community" 45 *International Organization* (1991) 19.

Moravcsik, A., "Preferences and Power in the European Community: A Liberal Intergovernmental Approach" 31 JCMS (1993) 473.

Morgan, D., "Surrogacy: An Introductory Essay" in R. Lee and D. Morgan, eds, *Birthrights: Law and Ethics at the Beginnings of Life* (London: Routledge, 1989).

Morgan, D., *Issues in Medical Law and Ethics* (London: Cavendish, 2001).

Morgan, D. and R. Lee, "In the Name of the Father? Ex parte Blood: Dealing with Novelty and Anomaly" 60 MLR (1997) 840.

Morgan, D. and L. Nielsen, "Dangerous Liaisons: Reproduction and European Ethics" in S. Wheeler and S. McVeigh, eds, *Law, Health and Medical Regulation* (Aldershot: Dartmouth, 1992).

Mossialos, E. and B. Abel-Smith, "The Regulation of the European Pharmaceutical Industry" in S. Stavridis, E. Mossialos, R. Morgan and H. Machlin, eds, *New Challenges to the EU: Policies and Policy-Making* (Aldershot: Dartmouth, 1997).

Mossialos, E. and M. McKee, *EU Law and the Social Character of Health Care* (Brussels: PIE Peter Lang, 2002).

Mossialos, E. et al, eds, *Funding Health Care: Options for Europe* (Buckingham: Open University Press, 2002).

Mowbray, A.R. and D.J. Harris, *Cases and Materials on the European Convention on Human Rights* (London: Butterworths, 2001).

Murphy, F., "Maastricht: Implementation in Ireland" 19 ELRev (1994) 94.

Murphy, T., "Bursting Binary Bubbles: Law, Literature and the Sexed Body" in J. Morison and C. Bell, eds, *Tall Stories? Reading Law and Literature* (Aldershot: Dartmouth, 1996).

Nelkin, D., *Technological Decisions and Democracy* (London: Sage, 1977).

Nelkin, D., ed, *Controversy: Politics of Technical Decisions* (London: Sage, 1992).

Neuman, M., A. Bitton and S. Glantz, "Tobacco Industry Subversion of European Community Tobacco Advertising Legislation" 359 *Lancet* (2002) 9314 at 1323–1330 (13 April).

New, B., M. Solomon, R. Dingwall and J. McHale, *A Question of Give and Take: Improving the Supply of Donor Organs for Transplantation* (London: Kings Fund Institute, 1993).

Newdick, C., "The Development Risk Defence of the Consumer Protection Act 1987" 47 CLJ (1988) 455.

Neyer, J., "The Standing Committee for Foodstuffs: Arguing and Bargaining in Comitology" in M. van Schendelen, *EU Committees as Influential Policy-Makers* (Aldershot: Dartmouth, 1998).

Neyer, J., "The Comitology Challenge to Analytical Integration Theory" in C. Joerges and E. Vos, eds, *EU Committees: Social Regulation, Law and Politics* (Oxford: Hart, 1999).

Neyer, J. "The Regulation of Risks and the Power of the People: Lessons from the BSE Crisis" 4 *European Integration Online Papers* (2000), http://www.eiop.or.at.eiop/.

Nicholas, S., "Movement of health professionals: Trends and enlargement" 8(2) *eurohealth* (2002) 11.

Nickless, J., "Were the European Court of Justice decisions in *Kohll* and *Decker* right? 7(1) *eurohealth* (2001) 16.

Nickless, J., "*Smits-Peerbooms:* Clarification of *Kohll* and *Decker*?" 7(4) *eurohealth* (2001) 7.

Nickless, J., "The Internal Market and the Social Nature of Health Care" in R. Baeten, M. McKee and E. Mossialos, eds, *The Impact of EU Law on Health Care Systems* (Brussels: PIE Peter Lang, 2003).

Nielsen, L., "Legal Consensus and Divergence in Europe in the Area of Assisted Conception – Room for Harmonisation" in D. Evans and N. Pickering, *Creating the Child: The ethics, law and practice of assisted procreation* (The Hague: Martinus Nijhoff, 1996).

Nielson, L., "Living Organ Donors – Legal Perspectives from Western Europe" in D. Price and H. Akeveld (eds) *Living Donation in the Nineties: European Medico-Legal Perspectives* (Leicester: Eurotold, 1994).

Noyce, P.R. et al, "The cost of prescription medicines to patients" 52 *Health Policy* (2000) 129.

Nuffield Council on Bioethics, *Genetic Screening: Ethical Issues* (1993).

Nys, H. "Ethical Committees in Belgium" 2 *European Journal of Health Law* (1995) 175

Nys, H., *La Medicine et Le Droit* (Diagem: Kluwer Edit Juridiques, Belgique, 1995).

Nys, H., "Physician involvement in a patient's death: a continental European perspective" 7(2) *Medical Law Review* (1999) 208.

Nys, H., "Comparative health law and the harmonisation of patients' rights in Europe" 8 *European Journal of Health Law* (2001) 317.

Nys, H. and F. van Wijmen, "Maastricht 2002: Health Law in an Era of Globalisation" 9 *European Journal of Health Law* (2002) 1.

O'Donovan, K., "What shall we tell the children? Reflections on Children's Perspectives and the Reproduction Revolution" in R. Lee and D. Morgan, eds, *Birthrights; Law and Ethics at the Beginning of Life* (London: Routledge 1989).

O'Keeffe, D. and H. Schermers, eds, *Mixed Agreements* (The Hague: Martinus Nijhoff, 1983).

O'Keeffe, D. and P. Twomey, eds, *Legal Issues of the Maastricht Treaty* (Chichester: Wiley Chancery, 1994).

O'Leary, S., *Employment Law at the European Court of Justice* (Oxford: Hart, 2002).

O'Neill, O., "Insurance and Genetics: The Current State of Play" 61 MLR (1998) 716.

O'Rourke, R., *European Food Law* (Bembridge: Palladian Law Publishing, 1999).

O'Sullivan, D., "The allocation of scarce resources and the right to life under the European Convention on Human Rights [1998] *Public Law* 389.

Offergeld, R. and R. Burger, "Remuneration of blood donors and its impact on transfusion safety" 85 *Vox Sanguinis* (2003) 49.

Oliver, P., "The French Constitution and the Treaty of Maastricht" 43 ICLQ (1994) 1.

Oostermann-Meulenbeld, A.C., "Quality Regulation on Professional Health Care Practice in the European Community" 1 *Legal Issues of European Integration* (1993) 61.

Otlowski, M., *Voluntary Euthanasia and the Common Law* (Oxford: Clarendon Press, 1997).

Overs, C. and R. White, *The European Convention of Human Rights* (Oxford: OUP, 2003).

Overwalle, G., *Study of Patenting of Inventions Relating to Human Stem Cell Research*, E.C. Luxembourg 2002/218.

Palm, W. and J. Nickless, "Access to healthcare in the European Union" 7(1) *eurohealth* (2001) 13.

Palm, W., J. Nickless, H. Lewalle and A. Coheur *Implications of Recent Jurisprudence on the Coordination of Health Care Protection Systems* Summary Report produced for DG Employment and Social Affairs (Brussels: AIM, 2000).

Parsons, J., "Assisted Conception: The State of the Art" in D. Evans and N. Pickering, *Creating the Child: The ethics, law and practice of assisted procreation* (The Hague: Martinus Nijhoff, 1996).

Pattison, S.D., "Reproductive Cloning: Can Cloning Harm the Clone?" 10 *Medical Law Review* (2002) 295.

Poulsen, J., "Junior Doctors Hours and EC draft directive on working hours" 307 BMJ (1993) 1158.

Pearl, D., "Legal issues arising out of medical provision for ethnic groups" in A. Grubb and M.J. Mehlman, eds, *Justice and Health Care: Comparative Perspectives* (Chichester: John Wiley and Sons 1995).

Pedler, R. and G. Schäfer, eds, *Shaping European Law and Policy: The Role of Committees in the Political Process* (Maastricht: European Institute of Public Administration, 1996).

Pennings, G., "Reproductive tourism as moral pluralism in motion" 28 *Journal of Medical Ethics* (2002) 337.

Pertek, J., "Free Movement of Professionals and Recognition of Higher Education Diplomas" 12 YEL (1999) 293.

Pescatore, P., "The Doctrine of Direct Effect: An Infant Disease of Community Law" 8 ELRev (1983) 155.

Peterson, J., "Decision-Making in the European Union: Towards a Framework for Analysis" 2 *Journal of European Public Policy* (1995) 1.

Peterson, J. and M. Shackleton, *The Institutions of the European Union* (Oxford: OUP, 2002).

Petriccione, R., "Italy: Supremacy of Community Law over National Law" 11 ELRev (1986) 320.

Pidgeon, N., "Science, uncertainty and society" 8(1) *eurohealth* (2001–02) 16.

Pierson, P., "The Path to European Integration: a Historical Institutionalist Analysis" 29 *Comparative Political Studies* (1996) 123.

Plomer, A., "Beyond the HFE Act 1990: The Regulation of Stem Cell Research in the UK" 10 *Medical Law Review* (2002) 132.

Poiares Maduro, M., *We The Court: The European Court of Justice and the European Economic Constitution* (Oxford: Hart, 1998).

Poiares Maduro, M., "Striking the Elusive Balance between Economic Freedom and Social Rights in the EU" in P. Alston, ed, *The EU and Human Rights* (Oxford: OUP, 1999).

Poiares Maduro, M., "Europe and the Constitution: What if this is as good as it gets?" in J.H.H. Weiler and M. Wind, *European Constitutionalism Beyond the State* (Cambridge: CUP, 2003).

Politis, C. "Editorial: Blood Donations systems as an integral part of the health system" 17 *Archives of Hellenic Medicine* (2000) 354.

Poulsen, J., "Medical Manpower in Europe" in G. Eysenbach, ed, *Medicine and Medical Education in Europe: The Eurodoctor* (Stuttgart: Thieme, 1998).

Prechal, S., "Does Direct Effect still Matter?" 37 CMLRev (2000) 1047.

Price, D., *Legal and Ethical Issues of Organ Transplantation* (Cambridge: CUP, 2000).

Price, D. and H. Akeveld, eds, *Living Donation in the Nineties: European Medico-Legal Perspectives* (Leicester: Eurotold, 1994).

Pywell, S., R. Martin and L. Johnson, *Law and the Public Dimension of Health* (London: Cavendish, 2001).

Ramsey, J., "Regulating Surrogacy – A Contravention of Human Rights?" 5 *Medical Law International* (2000) 45.

Ranade, W., "Reforming the British National Health Service: all change, no change?" in W. Ranade, ed, *Markets and Health Care: A Comparative Analysis* (Harlow: Longman, 1998).

Randall, E., *The European Union and Health Policy* (Basingstoke: Palgrave, 2001).

Rasmussen, H., "Confrontation or Peaceful Co-existence? On the Danish Supreme Court's Maastricht Ratification Judgment" in D. O'Keeffe, ed, *Judicial Review in EC Law* (The Hague: Kluwer, 2000).

Regent, S., "The Open Method of Coordination: A New Supranational Form of Governance?" 9 ELJ (2003) 190.

Rehnberg, C., "A Swedish case study on the impact of the SEM on the pharmaceutical market" in R. Busse, M. Wismar and P.C. Berman, *The European Union and Health Services* (Amsterdam: IOS Press, 2002).

Richards, T., "Germany turns away UK trained GP" 322 BMJ (2001) 384 (17 February).

Richardson, J., "Policy-making in the EU: Interests, Ideas and Garbage Cans of Primeval Soup" in J. Richardson, ed, *European Union: power and policy-making* (London: Routledge, 1996).

Rieger, E., "The CAP" in W. Wallace and H. Wallace, eds, *Policy-Making in the European Union* (Oxford: OUP, 2000).

Rimmer, M., "Myriad Genetics: Patent Law and Genetic Testing" 25 *European Intellectual Property Review* (2003) 20.

Rippe, K.P., "Novel Foods and Consumer Rights" 12 *Journal of Agricultural and Environmental Ethics* (2000) 71.

Roberts, T., "The Former Biotech Patents Directive" [1995] *Patent World* 27.

Robertson, J.A. *Children of Choice* (Princeton: Princeton University Press, 1994).

Robinson, R., "Managed competition: health care reform in the Netherlands" in W. Ranade, ed, *Markets and Health Care: A Comparative Analysis* (Harlow: Longman, 1998).

Rosamund, B., *Theories of European Integration* (Basingstoke: Macmillan, 2000).

Roscam Abbing, H.D.C., "European Community and the Right to Health Care" in A.F. Casparie, H. Hermans and J.H.P. Paelinck, eds, *Health Care in Europe After 1992* (Aldershot: Dartmouth, 1992).

Roscam Abbing, H.D.C., "Main Issues and Findings of the Symposium" in *Quality of*

Medical Practice and Professional Misconduct in the European Union (Symposium, Amsterdam, 1997) 4 *European Journal of Health Law* (1997) 273.

Roscam Abbing, H.D.C., "The Right of the Patient to Quality of Medical Practice and the Position of Doctors in the EU" 4 *European Journal of Health Law* (1997) 347.

Roscam Abbing, H.D.C., "Public Health in the Treaty of Amsterdam" 5 *European Journal of Health Law* (1998) 171.

Roscam Abbing, H.D.C., "Editorial: Internet, the Patient and the Right to Care for Health" 7 *European Journal of Health Law* (2000) 221.

Rosenmöller, M., "Health and Support for EU accession: Phare and other initiatives" 8(4) *eurohealth* (2002) 36.

Rosenthal, E. and C.J. Sundram, "The Role of International Human Rights in Domestic Mental Health Legislation" 21 *New York Law School Journal of International and Comparative Law* (2002) **.

Roseren, P., "The Application of Community Law by French Courts from 1982–1993" 31 CMLRev (1994) 315.

Ross, A.P., "The Case Against Showing Patients Their Records" 292 BMJ (1986) 578.

Runge, C.F. and L.A. Jackson, "Labelling, Trade and Genetically Modified Organisms" 34 *Journal of World Trade* (2000) 111.

Salmon, T., "The Structures, Institutions, and Powers of the EU" in J. Gower, ed, *The European Union Handbook* (London and Chicago: Fitzroy Dearborn, 2002).

Saltman, R.B., "A conceptual overview of recent health care reforms" 4 *European Journal of Public Health* (1994) 287.

Saltman, R.B., "Health reform in Sweden: the road beyond cost containment" in W. Ranade, ed, *Markets and Health Care: A Comparative Analysis* (Harlow: Longman, 1998).

Saltman, R.B., J. Figueras and C. Sakallarides, eds, *Critical Challenges for Health Care Reform in Europe* (Buckingham: Open University Press, 1998).

Sampson, T., "Achieving Ethically Acceptable Biotechnology Patents: A Lesson from the Clinical Trials Directive" 25 *European Intellectual Property Review* (2003) 419.

Sandholtz, W. and J. Zysman, "1992: Recasting the European Bargain" [1989] *World Politics* 95.

Sauer, W., "The European Community's Pharmaceutical Policy" in A.F. Casparie, H. Hermans and J. Paelinck, eds, *Health Care in Europe After 1992* (Aldershot: Dartmouth, 1992).

Schäfer, G., "Linking Member State and European Administrations – The Role of Committees and Comitology" in M. Andenas and G. Türk, eds, *Delegated Legislation and the Role of Committees in the EC* (The Hague: Kluwer, 2000).

Scharpf, F., "Community and Autonomy: Multi-Level Policy-Making in the European Union" 1 *Journal of European Public Policy* (1994) 219.

Scharpf, F., *A New Social Contract? Negative and Positive Integration in the Political Economy of European Welfare States* EUI Working Paper RSC 96/44 (1996).

Scharpf, F., *Governing in Europe: Effective and Democratic?* (Oxford: OUP, 1999).

Scharpf, F., "The European Social Model: Coping with the Challenges of Diversity" 40 JCMS (2002) 645.

Schepers, R. and A.F. Casparie, "Continuity or discontinuity in the self-regulation of the Belgian and Dutch medical professions" 19(5) *Sociology of Health and Illness* (1997) 580.

Schepers, R., H. Nys, P. Mokos and I. Van Bael, "Controlling Medical Doctors in Belgium", paper presented to the 14th World Congress on Medical Law, Maastricht, August 2003.

Schertenleib, D., "The Patentability and Protection of DNA based inventions in the EPO and the European Union" 25 *European Intellectual Property Review* (2003) 125.

Schmitter, P., "Imagining the Future of the Euro-Polity with the Help of New Concepts" in G. Marks et al, eds, *Governance in the Emerging European Union* (London: Sage, 1996).

Schwarze, J., "Constitutional Perspectives of the European Union with Regard to the Next Intergovernmental Conference" 8 *European Public Law* (2002) 241.

Sclove, R., *Democracy and Technology* (New York: Guilford Press, 1995).

Scott, J., *EC Environmental Law* (London: Longman, 1998).

Scott, J., "Mandatory or Imperative Requirements in the EU and the WTO" in C. Barnard and J. Scott, eds, *The Law of the Single European Market: Unpacking the Premises* (Oxford: Hart, 2002).

Scott, J., "The Precautionary Principle Before the European Courts" in R. Macrory, *Environmental Principles in the EU and the Member States* (Groningen: Europa Law Publishing, forthcoming 2004).

Scott, J. and D.M. Trubek, "Mind the Gap: Law and New Approaches to Governance in the European Union" 8 ELJ (2002) 1.

Scott, J. and E. Vos, "The Juridification of Uncertainty: Observations on the Ambivalence of the Precautionary Principle within the EU and the WTO" in C. Joerges and R. Dehousse, *Good Governance in Europe's Integrated Market* (Oxford: OUP, 2002).

Segest, E., "Consumer Protection and the Free Movement of Medical Practitioners in the European Union" 4 *European Journal of Health Law* (1997) 267.

Shaw, J., "From the Margins to the Centre: Education and Training Law and Policy" in P. Craig and G. de Búrca, *The Evolution of EU Law* (Oxford: OUP, 1999).

Shaw, J., "Postnational constitutionalism in the European Union" 6 *Journal of European Public Policy* (1999) 579.

Shaw, J., *Law of the European Union* (Basingstoke: Palgrave, 2000).

Sheldon, S. and M. Thompson, eds. *Feminist Perspectives on Health Care Law* (London: Cavendish, 1998).

Sieghart, P., "Professional Ethics for Whose Benefit?" 8 *Journal of Medical Ethics* (1982) 25.

Siegler, M., "Medical Confidentiality – a decrepit concept" 307 *New England Journal of Medicine* (1982) 1518.

Sieveking, K., "The Significance of the Transborder Utilisation of Health Care Benefits for Migrants" 2 *European Journal of Migration and Law* (2000) 143.

Singer, P., *Rethinking Life and Death; the collapse of our traditional ethics* (Oxford: OUP, 1995).

Skene, L., "Arguments Against People Legally 'Owning' Their Own Bodies, Body Parts and Tissue" 2 *MacQuarrie Law Journal* (2002) 165.

Snyder, F., "The Effectiveness of European Community Law: Institutions, Processes, Tools and Techniques" 56 MLR (1993) 19.

Sprangers, F., "The Dutch Experience of implementing the European Working Time Directive" 325 BMJ (2002) 71.

Sprumont, D., "Legal Protection of Human Research Subjects in Europe" 6 *European Journal of Health Law* (1999) 25.

St Clair Bradley, K., "Comitology and the Law: Through a glass, darkly" 29 CMLRev (1992) 691.

St Clair Bradley, K., "The European Parliament and Comitology: On the Road to Nowhere" 3 ELJ (1997) 230.

Stanberry, B.A., "Legal aspects of health on the internet: a European perspective" 324 BMJ (2002) 602.

Stauch, M., "Pregnancy and the Human Rights Act 1998" in J. Tingle, A. Garwood-Gowers and T. Lewis, eds, *Healthcare: the Impact of the Human Rights Act* 1998 (London: Cavendish, 2002).

Stein, E., "Lawyers, Judges and the making of a Transnational Constitution" 75 *American Journal of International Law* (1971) 1.

Stein, H., "On the Road from Maastricht to a new Europe" 9(2) *eurohealth* (2003) 17.

Steiner, J., *Textbook on EEC Law* (London: Blackstones, 1988).

Steiner, J., "Subsidiarity under the Maastricht Treaty" in D. O'Keeffe and P. Twomey, eds, *Legal Issues of the Maastricht Treaty* (London: Chancery, 1994).

Sterckx, S., *Biotechnology, Patents and Morality* (Aldershot: Ashgate, 1997).

Sterckx, S., "Some Ethically Problematic Aspects of the Proposal for a Directive on the Legal Protection of Biotechnological Inventions" 20 *European Intellectual Property Review* (1998) 123.

Steyger, E., "National Health Care Systems Under Fire (but not too heavily)" 29 *Legal Issues of Economic Integration* (2002) 97.

Stone, J., "Infertility Treatment: A Selective Right to Reproduce", in P. Byrne, ed, *Ethics and Law in Health Care and Research* (Chichester: John Wiley, 1990).

Stone Sweet, A., "From free trade to supranational policy: the European court and integration" in W. Sandholtz and A. Stone Sweet, eds, *European Integration and Supranational Governance* (Oxford: OUP, 1998).

Stone Sweet, A., *Governing with Judges: Constitutional Politics in Europe* (Oxford: OUP, 2000).

Streek, W., "Neovoluntarism: A New European Social Policy Regime?" 1 ELJ (1995) 31.

Strobl, J., E. Cave and T. Walley, "Data Protection Legislation: Interpretation and Barriers to Research" 321 BMJ (2000) 890.

Syrett, K., "NICE Work: Rationing, Review and the Legitimacy Problem in the new NHS" 10 *Medical Law Review* (2002) 1.

Syrpis, P., "Smoke without Fire: The Social Policy Agenda and the Internal Market" 30 ILJ (2001) 271.

Szyszczak, E., "The Evolving European Employment Strategy" in J. Shaw, ed, *Social Law and Policy in an Evolving EU* (Oxford: Hart, 2000).

Szyszczak, E., "The New Paradigm for Social Policy: A Virtuous Circle" 38 CMLRev (2001) 1125.

Taylor, P., "Europe Without Frontiers? Balancing Pharmaceutical Interests" in E.M. Normand and P. Vaughan, eds, *Europe Without Frontiers: The Implications for Health* (London: Wiley, 1993).

Teff, H. and C. Munro, *Thalidomide: the Legal Aftermath* (London: Saxon House, 1976).

Tesauro, A.G., "Community Law and National Courts: An Italian Perspective" in D. O'Keeffe, ed, *Judicial Review in EC Law* (The Hague: Kluwer, 2000).

Theodorou, M., "Recent Reforms in the Greek NHS" 8(2) *eurohealth* (2002) 29.

Thompson, I., "The Nature of Confidentiality" 5 *Journal of Medical Ethics* (1979) 57.

Thompson, I.E., "Fundamental ethical principles in health care" 295 BMJ (1987) 1461.

Thompson, R., *The Single Market for Pharmaceuticals* (London: Butterworths, 1994).

Thorold, O., "The Implications of the European Convention on Human Rights for United Kingdom Mental Health Legislation" [1996] EHRLR 619.

Tingle, J. and A. Cribb, eds. *Nursing Law and Ethics* (Oxford: Blackwell Scientific, 2nd edn. 2002).

Titmuss, R., *The Gift Relationship*, edited by A. Oakley and J. Ashton, (London: LSE Books, 1997).

Toebes, B., *The Right to Health as a Human Right in International Law* (Antwerp: Intersentia/ Hart, 1999).

Toebes, B., "The Right to Health" in A. Eide, C. Krause and A. Rosas, eds, *Economic, Cultural and Social Rights* (The Hague: Kluwer, 2001).

Toeller, A.E. and H.C.H. Hofmann, "Democracy and the Reform of Comitology" in A. Andenas and G. Türk, eds, *Delegated Legislation and the Role of Committees in the EC* (The Hague: Kluwer, 2000).

Tomkin, D., and P. Hanafin, *Irish Medical Law* (Dublin: Round Hall Press, 1995).

Toth, A., "A Legal Analysis of Subsidiarity" in D. O'Keeffe and P. Twomey, eds, *Legal Issues of the Maastricht Treaty* (Chichester: Wiley Chancery, 1994).

Tridimas, T., "Fragmentation, Efficiency and Defiance in the Preliminary Reference Procedure" 40 CMLRev (2003) 9.

Turone, F., "Italy to pass new law on assisted reproduction" 328 BMJ (2004) 9.

Usher, J., "Annotation of Case C-376/98" 38 CMLRev (2001) 1519.

Usher, J.A., *Legal Aspects of Agriculture in the EU* (Oxford: Clarendon Press, 1998).

Van der Grinten, T. and M. de Lint, "The impact of Europe on healthcare: The Dutch case" 7(1) *eurohealth* (2001) 19.

Van der Mei, A.P., "Cross-Border Access to Health Care within the European Union: Some Reflections on *Geraets-Smits and Peerbooms* and *Vanbraekel*" 9 MJ (2002) 1.

Van der Mei, A.P., *Free Movement of Persons within the European Community: Cross-Border Access to Public Benefits* (Oxford: Hart, 2003).

Van der Mei, A.P. and L. Waddington, "Public Health and the Treaty of Amsterdam" 5 *European Journal of Health Law* (1998) 129.

van der Poel, C.L., E. Seifried and W.P. Schaasberg, "Paying for Blood Donations: still a risk?" 83 *Vox Sanguinis* (2002) 285.

van Gerven, W., "Bridging the Unbridgeable: Community and National Tort Laws after Francovich and Brasserie" 45 ICLQ (1996) 507.

van Gerven, W., "Of Rights, Remedies and Procedures" 37 CMLRev (2000) 501.

Van Overwalle, G., "Belgium goes its own way on biodiversity and patents" 24 *European Intellectual Property Review* (2002) 233.

Van Schendelen, M.P.C.M. and R.H. Pedler, "Are EU Committees Influential?" in M.P.C.M. Van Schendelen, *EU Committees as Influential Policy-Makers* (Aldershot: Dartmouth, 1998).

Vanchieri, C., "New EC privacy directive worries European epidemiologists" 83 *Journal of the National Cancer Institute* (1993) 1022.

Von Auer, F., "Payment for blood donations in Germany" 310 BMJ (1995) 399 (11 February).

Von Heydebrand u.d. Lasa, H., "Free Movement of Foodstuffs, Consumer Protection and Food Standards in the EC: Has the Court of Justice got it wrong?" 16 ELRev (1991) 391.

Vos, E., "The Rise of Committees" 3 ELJ (1997) 210.

Vos, E., "EU Committees: the evolution of unforeseen institutional actors in European Product Regulation" in C. Joerges and E. Vos, *EU Committees: Social Regulation, Law and Politics* (Oxford: Hart, 1999).

Vos, E., "EU Food Safety Regulation in the aftermath of the BSE Crisis" 23 *Journal of Consumer Policy* (2000) 227.

Vos, E., "Reforming the European Commission: What Role to Play for EU Agencies" 37 CMLRev (2000) 1113.

Wacks, R., *Personal Information Privacy and the Law* (London: Bodley Head, 1979).

Wakefield, A.J. et al, "Ileal-lymphoid-nodular hyperplasia, non-specific colitis and pervasive developmental disorder in children" 351 (9103) *Lancet* (1998) 637.

Walker, N., ed, *Sovereignty in Transition* (Oxford: Hart, 2003).

Wallace, H. and W. Wallace, *Policy-Making in the European Union* (Oxford: OUP, 2000).

Warnock, M., *Making Babies: Is there a right to have children?* (Oxford: OUP, 2002).

Warren, S.D., and L.D. Brandeis, "The Right to Privacy" 4 *Harvard Law Review* (1890–91) 193.

Watson, P. *Social Security Law of the European Communities* (London: Mansell, 1980).

Watson, R., "Focus: Brussels Which 'Europe' should deal with ethical issues?" 308 BMJ (1994) 362.

Watson, R., "EU makes a difference over AIDS" 314 BMJ (1997) 997.

Watson, R., "Europe agrees complete ban on tobacco advertising by 2006" 315 BMJ (1997) 1559.

Watson, R., "EU makes mental illness a top priority" 319 BMJ (1999) 1389b.

Watson, R., "EU aims to reduce suicides" 321 BMJ (2000) 825.

Watson, R., "EU Harmonises rules for trials" 322 BMJ (2001) 68.

Watson, R., "MEPs add their voice to protest at patent for breast cancer gene" 323 BMJ (2001) 888.

Watson, R., "GMC opposes EU proposal to allow greater freedom of movement for doctors" 325 BMJ (2002) 795.

Watson, R., "EU parliament calls for tougher rules on breast implants" 326 BMJ (2003) 414.

Watson, R., "EU legislation threatens clinical trials" 326 BMJ (2003) 1348

Watson, R., "European Parliament tries to stamp out trafficking in human organs" 327 BMJ (2003) 1003.

Weatherill, S., "Beyond Preemption? Shared Competence and Constitutional Change in the European Community" in D. O'Keeffe and P. Twomey, eds, *Legal Issues of the Maastricht Treaty* (London: Chancery, 1994).

Weatherill, S., *Law and Integration in the European Union*, (Oxford: Clarendon, 1995).

Weatherill, S., "Pre-emption, Harmonisation and the Distribution of Competence" in C. Barnard and J. Scott, eds, *The Law of the Single European Market: Unpacking the Premises* (Oxford: Hart, 2002).

Weatherill, S., *Cases and Materials on EU Law* (Oxford: OUP, 2003).

Weiler, J.H.H., "The Community System: The Dual Character of Supranationalism" 1 YEL (1982) 267.

Weiler, J.H.H., "The Transformation of Europe" 100 *Yale Law Journal* (1991) 2403.

Weiler, J.H.H., "Does Europe Need a Constitution? Reflections on Demos, Telos and the German Maastricht Decision" 1 ELJ (1995) 219.

Weiler, J.H.H., *The Constitution of Europe* (Cambridge: CUP, 1999).

Weiler, J.H.H., ed, *The EU, the WTO and the NAFTA* (Oxford: OUP, 2000).

Weiler, J.H.H., "In defence of the status quo: Europe's constitutional *Sonderweg*" in J.H.H. Weiler and M. Wind, eds, *European Constitutionalism Beyond the State* (Cambridge: CUP, 2003).

Weiler, J.H.H. and M. Wind, *European Constitutionalism Beyond the State* (Cambridge: CUP, 2003).

Wellens, K.C. and G.M. Borchardt, "Soft Law in European Community Law" 14 ELRev (1989) 267.

Wessels, W., "Comitology: fusion in action. Politico-administrative trends in the EU system" 5 *Journal of European Public Policy* (1998) 209.

Westerhäll, L. and C. Phillips, eds, *Patients' Rights: Informed Consent, Access and Equality* (Stockholm: Nerenius and Santérus, 1994).

Westerhäll, L., *Medical Law: An Introduction* (Stockholm: Fritzes, 1994).

Westin, A., *Privacy and Freedom* (New York: Atheneum, 1967).

Westlake, M., "'Mad Cows and Englishmen': The Institutional Consequences of the BSE Crisis" in N. Nugent, ed, *European Union 1996: the annual review*, published in association with the JCMS.

Wheeler, S., "EU plans organ trade crackdown" BBC news online, 22 October 2003.

White, A., "Whither the Pharmaceutical Trade Mark?" 8 *European Intellectual Property Review* (1996) 441.

WHO and European Commission, *Health Status Overview for Countries of Central and Eastern Europe that are Candidates for Accession to the European Union* (Copenhagen: WHO, 2002).

WHO Expert Committee Report, *Smoking and its effects on health* (Geneva: WHO, 1975).

Wicks, D., *Nurses and Doctors at Work* (Buckingham: Open University Press, 1998).

Wiener, A., "Editorial: Evolving Norms of Constitutionalism" 9 ELJ (2003) 1.

Wilson, A. and B. Burrows, "French thumb their noses at EC Genomics Patenting Directive" http://www.genomeweb.com/articles/view-article.asp?Article =200331495815.

Wouters, J., "National Constitutions and the EU" in D. O'Keeffe, ed, *Judicial Review in EC Law* (The Hague: Kluwer, 2000).

Wouters, J., "Editorial" 8 MJ (2001) 3.

Wright, O. and A. Browne, "All immigrants to have compulsory HIV tests as cases rise" 13 February 2003, http://www.timesonline.co.uk.

Wyatt, D. and A. Dashwood, *European Union Law* (London: Sweet and Maxwell, 2000).

Zajac, M., "EU Accession: Implications for Poland's Healthcare personnel" 8(4) *eurohealth* (2002) 13.

Zeitlin, J., "Opening the Open Method of Coordination" Committee of the Regions Conference, 30 September-1 October 2002, http://www.cor.eu.int/pdf/omc/zeitlin.pdf.

Zuleeg, M., "The European Constitution under Constitutional Constraints: The German Scenario" 22 ELRev (1997) 19.

Index

abortion 12, 25, 65, 110, 149–150, 152–153, 155, 401–402
administration of health care services 21–23, 110–111, 125–126, 138–144, 156–158, 194; *see also* financing of health care services
Advisory Committee on Medical Training 208–209
Advisory Committee on Pharmaceutical Training 212
agencies 51; *see also* EMEA, European Food Safety Authority
alcohol 55, 56

biotechnology 259–280; *see also* cloning; patents
blood 73, 76–77, 78–80, 87, 279, 309, 310–312, 334, 343–348, 396
  blood donation 347–348
BSE/nvCJD 20–21, 30, 53, 76, 78–79, 86–87, 348–366
budget of the EU 39–40

cancer 368–374; *see also* tobacco
Charter of Fundamental Rights of the European Union 25–27; 64–67, 145, 160, 165, 246–247, 269, 273, 276, 306, 342, 405–410; *see also* human rights
chiropodists, 215, *see also* health care professionals
clinical research 19, 24, 63, 74, 237–281, 396; *see also* biotechnology; cloning
  children 179, 248, 250, 253–255, 274
  clinical trials of medicinal products 248–259
  consent 179, 252, 254–255, 258–259
  data protection 179–181, 188, 252
  ethics committees 250, 253–256
  EU funding 239–247
  good clinical practice 248–249, 251–252
  indemnity insurance 255
  mentally incapacitated adults 179, 248, 250, 253–255, 258–259
  "single European research area" 185, 238–239, 241, 253–254
  sponsor 253, 255, 257–258
  stem cell research 19, 274–280, 400, 403
cloning 145, 247, 264, 266, 271–274; *see also* patents; human rights; medical ethics
  reproductive cloning 271–272
  therapeutic cloning 271–273
comitology 50, 83–84, 208, 215, 221–222, 226–227, 361–362; *see also* Advisory Committee on Medical Training; Advisory Committee on Pharmaceutical Training; Committee for Orphan Medicinal Products; Committee for Proprietary Medicinal Products; Scientific Committee for Food; Standing Committee on Foodstuffs
Committee for Medicinal Products for Human Use 314
Committee for Orphan Medicinal Products 290
Committee for Proprietary Medicinal Products 60, 290–292
Community competence 4, 20, 29, 40–42, 69–106, 222–223, 237–238, 249, 288, 344, 394, 395, 410–412; *see also* legal basis
  "creeping competence" 70, 74
  implied competence 70
  pre-emption 53
  subsidiarity 70, 79, 80, 243
confidentiality 16, 18–19, 160–163, 171–172, 191
consumer protection 18, 47, 94–95, 213–215; *see* also health information privacy; pharmaceuticals
  patients as consumers 18–19, 155, 214, 283, 302–303, 393–394
  product liability 284–285, 307–312
Council of Europe 4, 8, 23, 164–165, 272–273; *see also* human rights
  Convention on Human Rights and Biomedicine 24, 25, 26, 80, 163–164, 237, 248, 273, 276–277, 343–344
  European Convention on Human Rights 23, 64, 145, 154, 163, 269, 306, 402
Council of Ministers 48, 71

data protection, 159–188; *see* also confidentiality; "e-health"; health information privacy
  anonymity 172–175, 180
  consent 169–171, 175–177
  international data transfer 185
  medical records 168–169, 171, 182–184
  personal data 168–172
dentists, *see* health care professionals
direct effect 42, 44, 64, 169
doctors, *see* health care professionals
Draft Constitutional Treaty of the European Union 26, 33, 69, 71, 102, 158, 168, 368, 404–412
drug abuse 33, 74–76, 78, 88–89

"e-health" 18, 426–433
  e-commerce 19, 166, 198–199, 432–433
  electronic health records 164, 165–166, 426–427
  health-related websites 307, 426
  remote prescribing 18, 235
  virtual pharmacies 426, 428–431
employment law 194–197, 397
enlargement of the EU 10, 32, 139–140, 142, 187, 221, 235, 414–421
European Commission 48, 55–56
European Food Safety Authority 51, 361–362, 364–366
European Group on Ethics in Science and New Technologies 246, 268, 276, 278–279
"European health law" 4–6, 27–28, 159, 389, 390
European Medicines Evaluation Authority 257, 290–298
European Parliament 49, 71 *power of veto* 263–264
euthanasia 12, 17, 27, 398, 401–403

fertility tourism, *see* reproductive treatment
financing of health care systems 21–23, 28, 47, 80, 110–111, 125–126, 212, 298, 305–306, 318, 319–322, 427; *see also* administration of health care systems
"flanking policy" 75
food law 21, 30, 46, 51, 55–57, 85, 348–366
free movement of goods 44–47, 56, 90–92, 213–215, 320–322, 352–353
free movement of persons 51–52, 60–61, 340–343; *see also* mutual recognition of qualifications
  free movement of patients 111–138, 397–398
  free movement of workers 112–119, 399
  retired persons 114–115, 117
freedom of establishment 199–203
freedom to provide or receive services 45–47, 119–138, 197–199, 234–235

genetic testing 164; *see also* biotechnology
globalisation/internationalisation 10, 404

health care professionals 11, 13–15, 52, 189–236, 399; *see also* mutual recognition of qualifications
  education and training 141, 143, 190–191, 205–206, 207–211, 217–218, 223–224, 227–228, 370–371
  from outside the EU 230–233
  mobility of health care professionals 219–220
  professional ethical codes 190–193
  professional misconduct 224–225
  regulatory bodies 190–193
health information privacy 18, 21, 159–188, 397; *see also* confidentiality; data protection; "e-health"
  anonymisation of data 172–175
  consent 169–171, 175–177
  international data transfer 185
  medical records 168–169, 171, 182–184
  personal data 168–172
health-specific legislation 17; *see also* specific national legislation listed in the Tables
  patients' rights charters 24
HIV/AIDS 21, 30, 53, 161, 172, 240, 242–244, 336–345, 400
human rights 23–27, 64–67, 391–392; *see also* abortion; confidentiality; Charter of Fundamental Rights of the European Union; Council of Europe; euthanasia
  autonomy 16, 26, 191
  consent to treatment 16, 26, 154, 303
  dignity 5, 16, 24, 26, 27, 109, 145, 191, 240, 247, 263, 267, 271, 380, 392, 407–408
  patients' rights 24–25, 84, 109–110
  privacy 21, 26, 145, 159–188
  right to health 7–9, 27, 156–157
  "right to reproduce" 144–145

internal market 38–39, 44–47, 57–59, 90–105, 123, 165, 166, 181, 202–203

legal basis 40–42, 49, 54–55, 68, 70–106, 269, 278, 288, 308, 333; *see also* Community competence
  choice of legal basis 85–90, 94–100
  general legal basis 73, 105

medical/bio-ethics 11–13, 16, 19, 144, 147–155; *see also* human rights
  professional ethical codes 190–193
medicinal products 18, 251, 289; *see also* pharmaceuticals
mental health 161, 172, 240, 434–436
midwives, *see* health care professionals
multilevel governance 5, 34–37, 156, 319, 366
mutual recognition of qualifications 52, 127, 141, 199–236
  "general directives" 215–218, 227–230
  general practitioners 209–211
  "sectoral directives" 203–215, 218–227

mutual recognition principle 55–59, 208

nurses, *see* health care professionals

open method of coordination 36–37, 62, 143, 157, 235, 412–414
organ transplants 17, 19, 77, 79–80, 87, 110, 279, 348
orphan diseases 39, 240, 244–245, 399; *see also* Committee for Orphan Medicinal Products
orthoptists, *see* health care professionals

parallel imports 45, 319
patents 260–270
  breast cancer gene 270
  European Patent Convention 261
  germ line gene therapy 256, 266–267
  patenting of DNA sequences 262–263, 265–266
  patenting of higher life forms 262, 265
  somatic cell line gene therapy 266–267
  supplementary patent protection certificate 95–96
pharmaceuticals 30, 282–329, 396; *see also* parallel imports
  advertisement 304–307
  clinical trials of pharmaceuticals 248–259
  comparative therapeutic efficacy 297, 317–319
  free movement 213–215
  labelling and packaging 302–304
  manufacture 298–300
  marketing authorisation 49–50, 59–60, 289–298
  "medicinal products" 251, 289
  orphan medicines 39;
  pharmaceutical industry 214–215, 286–288
  pricing 323–327
  product liability 307–312, 397
  quality standards 283
  reform proposals 312–317
pharmacists, *see* health care professionals
public health 11, 19–21, 74, 330–385; *see also* BSE/nvCJD; food law; HIV/AIDS; tobacco
  communicable diseases 20, 331, 433–434
  definition 332
  EU programmes 75, 81–84
  health promotion 331, 366–384
  notifiable diseases 163
  public health monitoring 181–182
  restrictions on mobility 331, 335–336, 340–343

quality of care 110, 111, 126–127, 137, 139, 141, 142, 143, 222–227, 229, 233, 235, 398

reproductive treatment 7, 19, 26–27; *see also* cloning
  embryo screening 145
  IVF 146, 148,–149, 152, 275
  "reproductive tourism" 144–155, 398
  sex selection 145, 148
research, *see* clinical research

Scientific Committee for Food 359, 364
Single European Act 54, 92–93
single market, *see* internal market
soft law 37, 43, 61–62, 141, 143, 239, 244, 281, 299, 345, 400; *see also* Charter of Fundamental Rights of the EU; open method of coordination
solidarity 5–6, 156–158, 322, 329, 392–393
Standing Committee on Foodstuffs 357

tobacco 53
  cancer and tobacco 368–369
  tobacco advertising 53, 96–105, 379–384
  tobacco manufacture, presentation and retail 101–105, 374–379
Treaty on European Union 8, 33, 73–75

waiting lists 116, 140, 142
working time 41, 94, 195–197, 397
World Health Organisation 4, 7, 15, 20, 24, 37, 41, 237, 332